MySQL™ Bible

MySQL™ Bible

Steve Suehring

Wiley Publishing, Inc.

MySQL™ Bible

Published by:
Wiley Publishing, Inc.
909 Third Avenue
New York, NY 10022
www.wiley.com

Library of Congress Control Number: 2002103290

ISBN: 0-7645-4932-4

Printed in the United States of America

10 9 8 7 6 5 4 3 2

1B/RY/QW/QS/IN

Distributed in the United States by Wiley Publishing, Inc.

Distributed by CDG Books Canada Inc. for Canada; by Transworld Publishers Limited in the United Kingdom; by IDG Norge Books for Norway; by IDG Sweden Books for Sweden; by IDG Books Australia Publishing Corporation Pty. Ltd. for Australia and New Zealand; by TransQuest Publishers Pte Ltd. for Singapore, Malaysia, Thailand, Indonesia, and Hong Kong; by Gotop Information Inc. for Taiwan; by ICG Muse, Inc. for Japan; by Intersoft for South Africa; by Eyrolles for France; by International Thomson Publishing for Germany, Austria, and Switzerland; by Distribuidora Cuspide for Argentina; by LR International for Brazil; by Galileo Libros for Chile; by Ediciones ZETA S.C.R. Ltda. for Peru; by WS Computer Publishing Corporation, Inc., for the Philippines; by Contemporanea de Ediciones for Venezuela; by Express Computer Distributors for the Caribbean and West Indies; by Micronesia Media Distributor, Inc. for Micronesia; by Chips Computadoras S.A. de C.V. for Mexico; by Editorial Norma de Panama S.A. for Panama; by American Bookshops for Finland.

For general information on Wiley's products and services please contact our Customer Care department; within the U.S. at 800-762-2974, outside the U.S. at 317-572-3993 or fax 317-572-4002.

For sales inquiries and resellers information, including discounts, premium and bulk quantity sales and foreign language translations please contact our Customer Care department at 800-434-3422, fax 317-572-4002 or write to Wiley Publishing, Inc., Attn: Customer Care department, 10475 Crosspoint Boulevard, Indianapolis, IN 46256.

For information on licensing foreign or domestic rights, please contact our Sub-Rights Customer Care department at 650-653-7098.

For information on using Wiley's products and services in the classroom or for ordering examination copies, please contact our Educational Sales department at 800-434-2086 or fax 317-572-4005.

For press review copies, author interviews, or other publicity information, please contact our Public Relations department at 650-653-7000 or fax 650-653-7500.

For authorization to photocopy items for corporate, personal, or educational use, please contact Copyright Clearance Center, 222 Rosewood Drive, Danvers, MA 01923, or fax 978-750-4470.

About the Author

Steve Suehring is a Senior Systems Engineer for a large Internet provider as well as a consultant for database, security, and Internet projects. Steve has worked with numerous clients to develop and implement database and Internet projects. Through these projects, Steve has worked with MySQL, Oracle, and SQL server for both administration and development. Steve currently holds certifications from Microsoft and Cisco. Steve has also written articles for *Linux Magazine*.

When not in front of a computer screen, Steve enjoys spending time with his wife. Steve also plays guitar, drums, and piano (though seldom simultaneously) and gets into pickup games of basketball and football whenever possible.

Credits

Acquisitions Editor
Terri Varveris

Project Editor
Pat O'Brien

Technical Editor
Scott Hofmann

Copy Editor
Barry Childs-Helton

Proof Editor
TECHBOOKS Production Services

Editorial Manager
Mary Beth Wakefield

Permissions Editor
Laura Moss

Media Development Specialist
Gregory Stephens

Media Development Coordinator
Marisa Pearman

Project Coordinator
Nancee Reeves

Graphics and Production Specialists
Beth Brooks, Sean Decker,
Joyce Haughey, Jackie Nicholas,
Heather Pope, Betty Schulte

Quality Control Technicians
Laura Albert, John Greenough,
Andy Hollandbeck, Carl Pierce

Proofreading and Indexing
TECHBOOKS Production Services

To Rebecca

Preface

Welcome to MySQL Bible. A complete reference for the MySQL database server and environment. Whether you're a database administrator looking to install MySQL, an existing MySQL administrator, a developer looking to use MySQL as a backend, or a combination of all three, this book can help.

Why I Wrote This Book

I wrote this book to give you one place to go for hands-on examples, reference, and best-practices. I've been working with MySQL in real-world situations for years. I believe MySQL to be a robust database solution for just about every type of application. Combine the stability of MySQL with its low of ownership and you quickly come to find it indispensable.

This book looks to provide everything you'll need to know to get MySQL running and expand upon that by examining development and best-practices for MySQL implementations.

What You Need to Know

You don't need to know anything about MySQL. However, you should have at least a little familiarity with the concepts of databases. I've covered those concepts within the pages of the book, but knowing a little about databases can't hurt.

Of course, you need to know how to use a computer.

What You Need to Have

Since MySQL runs on many platforms, you need access to a computer capable of running Windows 95, 98, NT, 2000, XP, or somewhere in between, Linux, or a Mac with OS X. Depending on what you want to do with MySQL, you may need more RAM or a better processor. I have successfully run MySQL in Linux with less than 20 megabytes of RAM and no swap file.

The book is written with version 4 of MySQL in mind. Many of the screenshots were taken using MySQL 3.23.X as version 4 was being stabilized. However, as I wrote it version 4 was being developed. Like many people, I assisted in testing MySQL 4 and so I was able to write this book to include those features.

What the Icons Mean

There are a certain number of icons used throughout the book to highlight various points. This section illustrates what some of those mean.

The Note icon is used to illustrate a point that I thought should be highlighted separately from the main text.

You'll see this icon throughout the book to denote software, scripts, or the like from a particular section.

When you see a Warning icon, pay particular attention. These are typically things that I've done wrong in the past. I highlight them so you don't do the same!

The Cross-Reference icon points you to another section of the book for more information.

How This Book Is Organized

The book is divided into five main parts and a part of appendixes.

Part I: Getting Started

The first section of the book looks at the prerequisites for installing MySQL, the actual installation of MySQL, and the concepts of database design. Installation is examined on Linux, Windows, and Mac. Within the Linux chapter, both binary and source installation of MySQL is examined.

Part II: SQL Essentials

Examination of SQL and some of the tools used with MySQL is the highlight of the second section. The first chapter within the section gives a full look at the MySQL command-line interface program. Alternatives to the CLI are examined including

WInMySQLAdmin, and MySQLGUI. The second chapter examines various SQL statements in MySQL. The final chapter of the section is covers some topics that fit into this section and prepare for other sections.

Part III: Administration

In this part, some server configurations are examined along with variables and options for the MySQL server. MySQL server security is within this section, as well as debugging and repairing MySQL databases and servers.

Part IV: Development

Four popular methods for developing applications with MySQL are examined in section four. This includes Perl, PHP, connecting MySQL to ODBC, and JDBC with Java. Notably, I did not include C or C++ into this section as I strongly feel that many applications for MySQL aren't developed in C or C++. I will grant that there are some, but the widespread languages used that I've seen are Perl, Java, and PHP.

Part V: Advanced Performance

The final group of chapters looks at some topics that don't really fit into another section. These include replication, integration of MySQL with PAM in Linux, and NuSphere MySQL.

Part VI: Appendixes

The Appendixes include standard MySQL reference material, a nifty Glossary, and instructions for the CD-ROM.

About the Companion CD-ROM

Much of the software discussed in the book is included on the CD-ROM with this book. Since software frequently changes versions, you may find a newer version of the software on the respective websites. The MySQL software can be downloaded from the MySQL AB web site.

I've also included software and scripts that I used within the book as examples.

Also on the CD-ROM are links that I use frequently and most likely highlight within the pages of the book as well.

How to Use This Book

If you don't already know about databases in general, or you're getting started with a MySQL system, I recommend reading this book from cover to cover. If you have a challenging task with an existing MySQL system, try the Index and the Table of Contents for your specific problem.

Talk To Me

I'd like to hear feedback on this book. Since the book is my first of this length, I'll be quite happy to know that someone out there actually read it. While I've done my best to make this book accurate, I won't be surprised if you find an error, typographical or otherwise. I'll do what I can to get it fixed, short of going and crossing out each typo with a marker.

I'll be happy to try to answer specific questions about MySQL. However, I can't guarantee that I'll be able to answer questions fully.

You can send email to me at:

`suehring@braingia.com`

I also have a website that contains some fun stuff, as well as other projects that I'm working on:

`http://www.braingia.com`

Acknowledgments

This book wouldn't have been possible without help from many people. First, I need to thank Terri Varveris for her unending patience with a writer on his first book as well as Pat O'Brien. Everyone at Wiley has been a pleasure to work with. Adam Goodman and Jeremy Zawodny from *Linux Magazine* offered some great help to a fledgling writer.

There are many others who should get some credit and are too numerous to mention by name. Inevitably I'm going to leave someone out and I apologize in advance. My wife Rebecca exhibited great understanding, not only with this book, but with me in general. My family, which has always been there to help and offer guidance deserves thanks, as does my friend Chris Tuescher. He wouldn't hesitate to do anything to help a friend in need.

The Nightmare Productions and Capitol Entertainment group of people helped shape who I am. Bob, Mike Feltz, Ernie Taylor, and Chris Tuescher stand out first and foremost. However, Chris Steffen, Ron Mackay, Chad Chasteen, Pat Quimby, and the rest of the gang had their parts too. Just one more time at for Mike at Manawa Middle or Ellen at Mosinee would be nice, wouldn't it?

Of course, Jim Leu, John Hein, Jeremy Guthrie, Andy Berkvam, Brandon, Dan, Erich, Mark, Sarah, Justin, Tara, the CORE Digital gang from Stevens Point. Brian and Jill and Deb Page and Jay Schrank gave me the opportunity and deserve thanks with everyone else. Will you really ever forget the time we had at CORE?

The crew from ExecPC/Voyager/CoreComm needs thanks, too. Michael Mittelstadt for having faith in me. AJ, Aaron, Al, Denise, James, Jerry, Joey Z, Matt, Nic, both Ryans, and the whole gang from #mcp and #jbs. The ExecPC staff and former CORE Digital staff are some of the smartest people to ever walk the face of the earth .

Professors Riley, Miller, and Cates have been a great influence on my life, as have Duff Damos and Gary Wescott. Special thanks to 90fm, Nightmare Squad, Jim Oliva, and John Eckendorf are in order as well for taking the time and effort every year to bring the World's Largest Trivia Contest to life. Yes, it really is the World's Largest.

The book wouldn't have been written without the never ending lunches from Mike Mitchell and JJ at Hilltop. Thanks to Tim at Partner's.

While I was writing the book, Kent Laabs let me borrow one of his drum kits. Quite a few evenings were spent hammering away. Though Kent may find out by the time he reads this, I believe I owe him a new cymbal. Who knows, someday maybe Pat Dunn will let me play with Spicy Tie Band again.

Finally, Eddie Van Halen deserves thanks as well. His music has offered inspiration throughout the writing of the book and beyond. It's almost as if I feel the need to cut him in on the book deal. Almost. If I get that invite to 5150 sometime...

Contents at a Glance

Contents

Part II: SQL Essentials 131

Part V: Advanced Performance 523

Getting Started

PART

I

✦ ✦ ✦ ✦

In This Part

✦ ✦ ✦ ✦

CHAPTER 1

Relational Database Management

In This Chapter

Considering applications for databases

Comparing SQL implementations

Introducing MySQL

Before you sound the depths of MySQL, it would be helpful to look at some applications for databases and at other implementations of SQL servers.

This chapter lays out some groundwork for the rest of the book — in particular, with tables that illustrate MySQL's extensions to the SQL-92 standard and compare some popular functions of database servers.

Applications for Databases

Databases are a part of everyday life, usually without your knowledge. From obvious applications (like customer databases for insurance companies) to not-so-obvious uses (such as storing actual images within a database for recognition), database use is pervasive and increasing.

Customer databases

Not a day goes without telephone calls from people trying to sell products or new long-distance plans. You and I are in more than a few customer databases — and some of the places I've done business with have shared my telephone number with some of their friends, who've then shared it with some of their friends — another fact of life that's traceable to the proliferation of databases.

Taking a look at some information stored in a few "everyday" databases can serve as an example of the different types of information each one collects, tracks, and sometimes stores — about you, me, and probably everyone you know. Whatever your views on issues of politics and privacy, these common examples form a picture of databases in action.

Telephone companies

The telephone company that owns my area stores basic information about me—first and last name, address, city, state, ZIP code, and telephone number—information that's not only basic but also common across almost all customer databases. Beyond the basic information, the local telephone company also requires my social security number (which helps them find me should I attempt to forego payment and leave the area).

Within the telephone company database is a system to keep notes and correspondence. For example, each time I call to talk with a customer service representative, a note goes into my file—indicating what I was calling about, the outcome (if any), as well as the date, time, and representative's name—all of which is recorded automatically when the note is entered.

Beyond the personal information and correspondence notes, the telephone company database also serves as a billing system that generates my phone bill automatically on the fourth day of every month. The database tracks what services I have (such as Call Waiting, Caller ID, and so forth), associates each service with a price, and tallies my bill for the month.

Having customer, billing, and rate information in a database allows the telephone company to produce reports that can pinpoint how many customers have a certain rate group, how many live in a certain area, how many have delinquent payments, and so on.

Beyond customer reports, the telephone company has become much more sophisticated in its use of the data. Previously when I would call for customer service, I would get to talk to a live person after a bit of a wait. They then improved their customer service by allowing me to punch in my 10-digit telephone number and look up my records. From there, I might eventually get to talk to a live person (if I didn't select any of the common tasks on the voice-mail menu). The latest improvement is the use of caller identification to ask me whether I'm calling in regard to the number that I'm calling from. After more menus and prompts, I may be able to reach a live operator.

Behind the scenes during this process is a database that can look up my information when it is fed my 10-digit number. The telephone company database can then give me choices based on the current status of my account. I once had the misfortune of fraudulent charges on my telephone bill—about $650 worth. I immediately put that amount into dispute and was told to pay my normal $45 bill—but I still ended up receiving a disconnection notice. When I called back to inquire into the notice, I was forwarded automatically to the collections department (who, after some discussion, handed me off to the regular customer service department). Moral: Databases can speed up only those aspects of a transaction that don't require the use of common sense.

Online or mail-order stores

Another type of customer database is kept by an online store such as Amazon.com or a mail-order catalog store. The basic information is kept (name, address, and so on); most online and many catalog stores also keep your e-mail address as well. In addition, many stores track payment information so you don't have to give your credit card number every time you want to make a purchase.

As monopolies, most telephone companies can afford to do minimal marketing of their products and services. To survive in a competitive market, however, catalog and online stores keep track of how their customers heard about them. From that information, they can produce a report that helps identify the most effective means of advertising (or look for wiser ways to spend marketing money).

Major catalog and online stores also track your purchases through a database and offer recommendations based upon previous purchase patterns. For example, if you frequently buy books on Linux, Amazon.com might custom-build a page for you of newly released Linux books. All such information is stored in one or more databases.

Catalog and online stores can use the reporting capabilities of an electronic database to watch which items are selling best, discern and track patterns of visitors, and gather data on sales totals for items and departments.

Custom-service Web sites

Another interesting use of customer type databases is to track user preferences. An example of this would be the Web site Slashdot, `http://www.slashdot.org/`. At Slashdot, they don't keep information like credit card number or address, but they do keep track of your e-mail address and what news modules you want to see, among other things. In this manner, you can customize the news you see, as well as other Slashdot features. Some user-preference sites do keep personal information such as name and address.

Though all three examples of customer databases — telephone company, online store, and user-preferences site — track some of the same information, they also track their own, task-specific information. This makes it difficult for an identity thief to gain access to all your personal information in one place. However, personal information security seems to be taking a backseat to the rise of all-in-one tracking services that keep information centrally. Imagine what the telemarketers could do if they had access to all my purchase histories and even my e-mail address!

Internet service providers' databases

Internet service providers (ISPs) use electronic databases more heavily than many other industries. Almost everything an ISP does is in electronic format; being relatively young as an industry, they've grown up with good database tools readily available. In many ways, ISP databases combine the functions of all three types of customer databases I referred to earlier.

The most obvious database use for an ISP is as a customer database—containing the usual (basic) name-and-address information. Like the online or catalog stores, the ISP database also stores information such as credit card or other billing data. Correspondence notes are kept inside a database as well as marketing and referral records to track marketing effectiveness. An ISP database usually has your e-mail address as well.

ISPs also use user-preference databases to remember your settings and make your online experience more productive—they use the same types of database information as a news site.

One area that many people overlook with ISPs what the industry calls *accounting data*—not the dollars-and-cents kind, but rather an accounting of who was using what modem or IP address at a given point in time. This accounting data can then be tracked to find usage patterns of a particular user or group of users. In addition, when an abuse report or subpoena is received, the ISP can quickly locate the user in question and take action or fulfill the subpoena request.

Tip

Many people wrongly believe they are anonymous when online. The reality is quite the contrary. With the use of databases to track accounting information, finding any given user who was online at any given time is almost trivially easy.

Some ISPs use databases as a means to track possible attacks against their equipment. Databases are an efficient way to watch for patterns of attack and keep data from an attack for possible future litigation or action against the attacker.

As you would expect, ISPs also use the reporting features of their databases. Reports can quickly be generated on revenue, high usage customers, or anything else tracked in the database.

Criminology and databases

Law enforcement has been quick to adopt electronic databases as an effective tool for helping to catch criminals. Through identification databases, offender tracking, and face recognition, law enforcement can efficiently assemble varied pieces of information to assist in investigations.

Although fingerprinting technology is not new, the use of electronic databases to store and retrieve fingerprints is a new (and powerful) extension of the technique. Other identification data can also be gathered and tracked for law enforcement—tax records, permits, and driver's-license information can help law enforcement find people. That information can easily be shared with other law enforcement agencies at speeds that weren't imaginable just a generation ago.

The electronic database is an ideal tool for certain other forms of information. For example, when tracking offenders by *modus operandi* (a pattern that emerges in crimes), the investigator can query a database to find suspects who might fit the pattern. Storing actual images of faces (for example, mug shots) in a database can help investigators find matches to faces. However, use of this technology in places other than investigations has led privacy groups to express some concerns.

Advantages of using databases

The speed, accuracy, and thoroughness of electronic databases make them critical to today's 24/7 high-speed exchange of information. Even the handful of examples in this chapter should strongly suggest the advantages — some of which appear in Table 1-1 — of using and developing applications for databases.

Table 1-1
Advantages of Using Databases

Advantage	*Description*
Speed	Format means quick storage and retrieval of information. Users and applications have a quick means for asynchronous reads and writes of data.
Reporting	Information can be gathered, quantified, and custom-analyzed with greater flexibility.
Accuracy	Given careful data input, databases provide accurate and consistent results based on their data.
Thoroughness	Databases can store and report results as complete and detailed as their holdings – at electronic speed.

Comparing SQL Implementations

SQL, or Structured Query Language, is a specialized type of programming language developed to work with relational databases such as MySQL, Oracle, Microsoft SQL Server, PostgreSQL, Informix, and others.

The SQL standard is defined by ANSI, the American National Standards Institute in their ISO/IEC 9075:1992 document. (The standard is commonly referred to as ANSI SQL-92.) Every relational database applies its own version of the SQL standard; many enhance that standard. Standardizing the programming language allows the developer to address the database in much the same way from platform to platform — and every major platform has such products written for it. Table 1-2 compares some popular relational-database products as illustrative examples.

Table 1-2
Comparison of SQL Implementations

RDBMS	***Advantages***	***Drawbacks***
Oracle	Versatile, stable, and secure.	Potentially high TCO.
MS SQL Server	Stable and secure; Microsoft offers excellent support.	Relatively high TCO; proprietary.
PostgreSQL	Up-and-coming database with low TCO.	Has yet to be widely implemented in large-scale business use.
Informix	Stable; has good support available.	Generally higher TCO.
MySQL	Offers a best-case-scenario database in many ways; low TCO, high stability, high security, and excellent support.	Not all available versions can offer the full range of MySQL capabilities.

Oracle

Oracle Corporation, `http://www.oracle.com/`, is arguably the leader in enterprise-level database server software for e-commerce. The Oracle database product is widely used in various types of large applications — including those mentioned in the previous section — and is popular largely because its characteristics apparently have a minimal downside:

✦ **Versatility:** Oracle Corporation offers many e-commerce products that integrate with their databases, which can help streamline the process of designing, building, and using database applications.

✦ **Stability:** Administrators report that Oracle database servers rarely fail — reassuring if your applications require 24/7 uptime.

✦ **Available graphical user interface:** Oracle offers many GUI tools for managing the database server (though whether this feature is a plus or minus depends on which administrator you ask).

✦ **Security:** Versions of Oracle now include a security toolkit that allows encryption of sensitive data *within the database*. Like other RDBMS products, Oracle also provides user-level security within a database to protect the data from malicious users or operator errors.

✦ **Support:** Oracle Corporation has historically been responsive to customer requests for new features in the database product. Oracle moves quickly to seize new opportunities as well — listening to customers, watching market trends, and maintaining thorough online documentation through the Oracle Technology Network (see Figure 1-1).

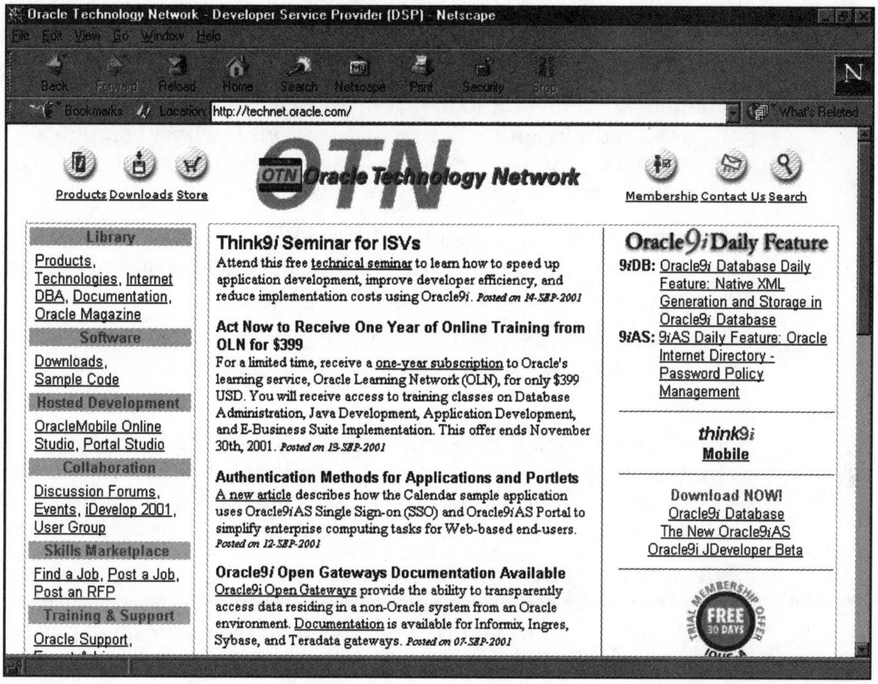

Figure 1-1: The Oracle Technology Network is just one of many support offerings for Oracle.

- ✦ **Cross-platform capability:** Popular versions include Oracle on Microsoft Windows as well as Linux. Oracle also supports ANSI-92 SQL standards with modifications and enhancements.
- ✦ **Potentially high Total Cost of Ownership (TCO):** Oracle's database server requires considerable high-end hardware resources (such as processor speed and RAM capacity) to run at an acceptable level.

Microsoft SQL Server

Like Oracle, Microsoft has been a key player in the database market — though Microsoft has had to play constant catch-up in the realm of the Internet and e-commerce. Although Microsoft is the acknowledged leader in desktop operating systems (thanks to its good sense of the marketplace and emphasis on fulfilling the needs of consumers), that advantage has not translated smoothly to the e-commerce market.

The characteristics of Microsoft SQL Server itself are consistent with its maker's traditional strengths, strategies, and limitations:

- **Fairly high stability:** MS SQL Server offers a degree of stability that is designed to be compatible with Windows OS. However, due to numerous security problems in that underlying operating system, some corporate customers are reluctant to invest in MS SQL Server as a solution for their database needs. In addition, having to reboot the host computer (Windows-style) to update the server or database software is completely unacceptable to potential customers who require maximum server uptime.
- **Ease of use:** MS SQL Server operates via Windows-style GUI, which can help ease the learning curve and add the appeal of familiarity for customers seeking hassle-free transactions.
- **Compliance with ANSI SQL-92:** MS SQL Server not only adheres to the entry-level standard, but also extends it (arguably no less than other relational databases).
- **Accessible support:** SQL Server is available directly from Microsoft, as well as from outside vendors. Microsoft provides a great deal of support information on their SQL Server Web site (and in the Microsoft Knowledge Base)—sometimes too much to find exactly what you are looking for.
- **High Total Cost of Ownership:** Like the operating systems it runs on, SQL Server is extremely resource-intensive of both CPU speed and RAM capacity. This aspect of the product reduces its appeal to many small businesses. Adding to the cost is the licensing—running into thousands of dollars in fees for SQL Server itself—not counting the operating system or other software and hardware to make the database work. However, thorough support and backing for Microsoft products make them worth the cost for some IT professionals (provided their companies can afford the outlay).
- **Proprietary vendor:** Since MS SQL Server is not cross-platform, some potential buyers are afraid to implement it lest they rely too much on one vendor. If the vendor suddenly decides to charge too much for a new feature or patch to the server, the company might have to pay more than it planned.

PostgreSQL

A relative newcomer to the RDBMS field, PostgreSQL, (`http://www.postgresql.org`) has quickly gathered quite a following. PostgreSQL is a work in progress—what software isn't?—but is remarkably stable for such a young a product, as a list of its characteristics shows:

- **Compliance with SQL-92:** PostgreSQL follows most of the SQL-92 standard, and is available for many operating systems—including Windows 2000/NT (through the use of special tools) and MacOS X. An open-source product, PostgreSQL is bundled with many versions of the Linux operating system.
- **Low Total Cost of Ownership:** The PostgreSQL database-server software is available for minimal outlay—the software is free of charge—a potential advantage when compared to Oracle or Microsoft SQL Server.

- **Support:** Like MySQL, PostgreSQL offers commercial support through different independent consulting firms (though its actual documentation is relatively light).
- **Relatively limited adoption:** Although PostgreSQL supports some important functions of larger RDBMS products — in particular, transactions — it can be slower than some of its competitors (including Oracle) when keeping transactional data. Speed may be one reason that not many large-scale businesses have chosen PostgreSQL, despite some advantages over its more expensive database brethren.

Informix

IBM's Informix series of database servers are poised to compete for large-scale database applications. Informix is a popular RDBMS that has the backing of IBM, as is reflected in its characteristics:

- **Diverse product line:** Informix offers a wide array of database servers depending on the needs of the application. From online transactions to parallel processing to high availability and more, Informix produces an optimized server for nearly all uses.
- **Cross-platform capabilities:** Informix runs on a variety of platforms and also offers a range of tools to assist with the development of both back-end and front-end database applications.
- **Potentially high Total Cost of Ownership:** Like its other commercial counterparts, the TCO for Informix can become prohibitive for small business.
- **Documentation and support:** Documentation for Informix is excellent — and much of it is available free from the IBM Web site. As you would expect, IBM provides solid backing of the product and support for Informix customers.

Introducing MySQL

Where does MySQL fit in with all the other RDBMS products available? In many ways, MySQL offers a best-of-all worlds scenario: It runs on many platforms, enjoys a low TCO, and is stable. The documentation for MySQL is excellent. MySQL AB has a thorough Web site containing reference material, as well as a link to mailing-list archives. MySQL AB also offers high-quality support for their products, including a service that allows MySQL developers to log in to your server to correct problems and proactively help with optimization. MySQL is gaining RDBMS market share because it offers stability, support, and low cost.

MySQL versions and features

MySQL is available for many different operating systems on a variety of computer architectures. MySQL currently has versions for Linux, Windows 95/98/NT/2000,

Solaris, FreeBSD, MacOS X, HP-UX, AIX, SCO, SCI Irix, Dec OSF, and BSDi. The Linux version runs on a range of architectures that includes Intel libc6, Alpha, IA64, SPARC, and S/390. The availability of cross-platform versions has enhanced the popularity of MySQL.

In addition to the standard MySQL database server, an enhanced version of MySQL is available — MySQL-Max. MySQL-Max includes the standard MySQL server, plus support for transaction-safe tables such as InnoDB or Berkeley DB (BDB). Table 1-3 shows the platforms and the transactional tables included with MySQL-Max.

Table 1-3
Transaction-Safe Tables in MySQL-Max Versions

Platform of Version	*Berkeley DB Available?*	*InnoDB Available?*
AIX 4.3	No	Yes
HP-UX 11.0	No	Yes
Linux (Alpha)	No	Yes
Linux (Intel)	Yes	Yes
Linux (IA64)	No	Yes
Solaris (Intel)	Yes	Yes
Solaris (SPARC)	Yes	Yes
Windows 2000/NT	Yes	Yes

MySQL is available as either a binary or a source-code download; if you want to add a feature to MySQL for your application, you can download the source code and modify it to your liking.

Tip

Downloading the source code also allows you to include support for transaction-safe tables when you compile the code.

MySQL is covered under the GNU General Public License (GPL) and the GNU Lesser General Public License (LGPL). To that end, most versions of MySQL require no license or purchase.

Cross-Reference

The GNU GPL and LGPL are included for reference in Appendixes B and C, respectively. Additional information on licensing is in Chapter 2.

MySQL also has many Application Programming Interfaces (APIs) to give the developer to access and shape the database via programs in various languages. APIs are available for C, C++, Tcl, Python, PHP, and Perl. Some of the most popular for programming Web interfaces are PHP and Perl. MyODBC makes MySQL ODBC-compliant as well.

Standards and compatibility

MySQL follows nearly the entire SQL-92 standard. As is the case with other RDBMS products, MySQL extends the SQL standard in distinctive ways (though it can be run in an ANSI-only mode). Also, as you would expect, if you use some of the MySQL specific extensions to the standard, your database may no longer be portable to another RDBMS should you choose to change it at a later date.

You can help your MySQL system maintain compatibility with other databases by enclosing any non-standard (MySQL-specific) extensions like this:

```
/*!  (statement) */
```

Other RDBMS systems should ignore the enclosed statement, which saves you from having to recode. MySQL simply ignores the brackets and processes the MySQL-specific statement as normal.

Also, if you add a version number after the exclamation mark, MySQL ignores the statement within the brackets *unless* it follows that version number. For example, consider the following line of code:

```
/*!32343 (statement) */
```

On versions older than 3.23.43, the statement within the brackets would be ignored.

Table 1-4 lists a substantial sample of the numerous MySQL extensions to the SQL-92 standard.

Note

Not all extensions listed in Table 1-4 are unique to MySQL, but their use in the specific context mentioned in the table may be unique to MySQL (or an extension to the standard).

Table 1-4
MySQL Extensions to SQL-92

Extension	***Type/application***	***Description or context***
%	Operator	Used as a substitute for the `mod` command.
\	Operator	Escape character. Used where an operation would include a normally reserved character.
"	Operator	Used to enclose strings.
`andand`	Operator	Logical `AND`.

Continued

Table 1-4 *(continued)*

Extension	***Type/application***	***Description or context***
`||`	Operator	Used as `OR` (not to concatenate).
`:=`	Operator	Used to set variables.
`asc`	Statement extension	Used with `group by` to indicate the order for results.
`analyze table`	Statement	Used to examine a table.
`auto_increment`	Field attribute	Increments a value.
`binary`	Field attribute	Controls case sensitivity.
`bit_and()`	Statement extension	Used with `group by` for `AND`ing of bits.
`bit_count()`	Function	Returns the number of bits.
`bit_or()`	Statement extension	Used with `group by` for `OR`ing of bits.
`blob`	Type	Extensions to `blob` type.
`case`	Function	Flow-control option.
`change <column name>`	Statement extension	Used with `alter table` to modify a column.
`check table`	Statement	Used to examine a table.
`count(distinct)`	Statement extension	Counts multiple items.
`create database`	Statement	Creates a database.
`decode()`	Function	String function.
`delayed`	Statement extension	Used with `INSERT` or `REPLACE`. Causes statements to wait for a free table.
`desc`	Statement extension	Used with `group by` to indicate the order for results.
`drop <column name>`	Statement extension	Used with `alter table` to delete a column from a table.
`drop database`	Statement	Removes a database.
`drop index`	Statement extension	Used with `alter table` to remove an index from a table.
`drop table`	Statement extension	Drops multiple tables.
`elt()`	Function	String function.
`encode()`	Function	String function.
`encrypt()`	Function	Creates acceptable values.
`explain select`	Statement	Describes joined tables.
`flush (option)`	Statement	Clears MySQL caches.

Extension	*Type/application*	*Description or context*
`format()`	Function	Changes the way a value is displayed.
`from_days()`	Function	Returns the number of days.
`if()`	Function	Control function.
`if exists`	Statement extension	Used with `drop table` command to perform the action only if the table exists.
`if not exists`	Statement extension	Used with `create table` that only performs action if table does not exist.
`ignore`	Statement extension	Used with `alter table` to ignore repeat values.
`index`	Statement extension	Used with `create table` to create an index.
`into outfile`	Statement extension	Used with `select` to redirect output to a file.
`key`	Statement extension	Used with `create table` to create a key column.
`last_insert_id()`	Function	Obtains number of last insert.
`like`	Operator	Allowed on numeric values.
`limit`	Statement extension	Used with `delete` to limit the number of rows deleted.
`load data infile`	Statement	Imports data.
`low_priority`	Statement extension	Used with `delete`, `insert`, `replace`, and `update` to indicate that the operation should wait until there are no other threads working with the table.
`md5()`	Function	Used to create an md5 of a value.
`mediumint`	Field type	Indicates a type of column.
`not regexp`	Operator	Extends regular expressions.
`null`	Field attribute	Indicates nothing.
`optimize table`	Statement	Performs optimizations on a table to improve performance.
`password()`	Function	Encrypts a string.
`period_add()`	Function	Performs a date-related function.
`period_diff()`	Function	Performs a date-related function.
`regexp`	Operator	Extends regular expressions.

Continued

Table 1-4 *(continued)*

Extension	***Type/application***	***Description or context***
`rename`	Statement extension	Used with `alter table` to change the name.
`rename table`	Statement	Changes table name.
`repair table`	Statement	Performs repairs on a table.
`replace`	Statement	Instead of deleting, inserts.
`set`	Field type	Sets a value.
`set option`	Statement	Sets an option.
`show`	Statement	Lists objects.
`sql_small_result`	Statement extension	Used with `select`.
`std()`	Statement extension	Used with `group by` to indicate the deviation.
`straight join`	Statement extension	Used with `select` to perform a join of tables.
`temporary`	Statement extension	Used with `create table` to create a temporary table.
`text`	Field type	Extensions to text type.
`to_days()`	Function	Performs a date-related function.
`trim()`	Statement extension	Allows substring trimming.
`unsigned`	Field attribute	Indicates an attribute for a column.
`weekday()`	Function	Performs a date-related function.
`zerofill`	Field attribute	Pads a string.

MySQL-specific properties

In addition to the extensions, field types, and functions listed in Table 1-4, MySQL has the following properties that are not part of the SQL-92 standard:

- ✦ When a database is created, MySQL creates a directory within the MySQL directory structure to hold database files.
- ✦ When the operating system has a case-sensitive file system (as does Linux), MySQL database and table names are case-sensitive.
- ✦ Objects such as the names of databases, tables, indexes, columns, or aliases may begin with — but not completely consist of — digits.

- To move, copy, or delete databases, you can use operating-system functions such as `copy` (`cp`) or `move` (`mv`).
- To access objects in other databases, MySQL uses the following syntax:

  `databasename.tablename`.
- String comparisons are not case-sensitive. This behavior can be changed with the `binary` statement extension.
- MySQL enables you to use more than one `add`, `alter`, `drop`, or `change` statement with an `alter table` statement.
- Comparison operators may be used to the left of the `from` clause within a `SELECT` statement.
- MySQL supports the aliasing of many commands to assist users who are familiar with other SQL implementations.
- The functions `concat` and `char` can be used with more than one argument.
- When using a group by function, you don't need to name all selected columns.

MySQL does offer transactional tables; most other enterprise-level database functionality (such as views, cursors, foreign keys, and the like) is either in testing or planned for a near-future release of MySQL. Table 1-5 illustrates some of these features and their current developmental status with MySQL.

Table 1-5
MySQL Enterprise-Level Database Features

Database feature	***Supported in (extant or expected version)***
Subselects	4.1
Foreign keys	Support (4.0)
Views	4.2
Stored procedures	4.1
Unions	Supported (4.0)
Full join	Supported
Triggers	4.1
Constraints	4.1
Cursors	4.1 or later

What MySQL Does Best

To assist the reader, I've listed some tasks that MySQL does especially well:

- **Web applications:** Web applications typically feature many reads and few writes. MySQL is fast and can meet the demands of Internet speed. In my experience, MySQL has proven time and again that it outperforms other RDBMS products in Web applications.
- **Enterprise-level applications:** MySQL offers support directly through the parent company, MySQL AB. MySQL's feature set includes just about everything that an enterprise-level application would need. Refer back to Table 1-4 for more details.
- **Open-source support:** MySQL AB is responsive to requests for features as well. MySQL is open-source; everyone is welcome to download and extend the code to meet his or her needs.
- **Low overhead**: MySQL runs comfortably for many applications on an Intel Pentium-class computer with 32 MB of RAM or less. I wouldn't *recommend* running an enterprise-level MySQL implementation on such a system, but consider the utter futility of trying to run a Web application on Internet Information Server with Microsoft SQL Server that runs under Windows 2000 on a Pentium-class computer with 32 MB of RAM.
- **Available large table size**: MySQL tables can grow large, though they do sometimes encounter file-size limitations of the host operating system. Some architectures, however, can accommodate up to 8 terabytes (TB) per table using MySQL.
- **Stability:** All software is in development. Some features in MySQL are newer than others, making them possibly less stable than others. Table 1-6 shows some of the features within MySQL and their stability level.

Table 1-6
MySQL Stability

Feature	***Stability level***
Standard table types	Stable
Transactional Tables	Becoming more stable
Basic SQL Functionality	Stable
Client Software	Stable
C API	Stable
Perl and PHP APIs	Stable
Replication	Stable, though always adding features

MySQL compares with — and beats — some of its commercial counterparts in many areas. Particularly in performance, scalability, and stability, MySQL can perform as good or better than its competitors. Table 1-7 compares some popular features in MySQL with other RDBMS. As you can see, MySQL meets or beats the others with two transactional table types to choose from, many development languages, a low Total Cost of Ownership, and other features.

Table 1-7
MySQL Comparison to other RDBMS Products

Feature	*MySQL*	*Oracle*	*MS SQL Server*	*PostgreSQL*
Transactional	Yes	Yes	Yes	Yes
Open-source	Yes	No	No	Yes
TCO	Low	High	High	Low
Development languages	Many	Many	Fewer	Many
Enterprise user base	Yes	Yes	Yes	No
Company support	Yes	Yes	Yes	No?
Cross-platform	Yes	Yes	No	Yes

MySQL has recently added Graphical User Interface (GUI) tools for database management.

What MySQL Can't Do – Quite Yet

MySQL is a stable and extensive RDBMS, but there are simply some things that MySQL cannot do or are unsupported at this time.

- **Foreign keys:** A *foreign key* is a value that relates to (and relies on) the Primary key in another table. This is a popular feature, used frequently in Oracle and other RDBMS products. MySQL started support for foreign keys in version 4.0 and will enhance that support in later versions. In addition, Unions are now supported in MySQL.
- **Views**: This popular method for obtaining data from the database, a planned feature for MySQL, may have been implemented by the time you read this.
- **R-Tree and other extensible index types**: Support for these powerful features will be included in a later version of MySQL.

Note: Inherited tables are not planned for any version of MySQL.

✦ **Subselects**: This type of statement (such as those using the `IN` clause) is not supported in MySQL (though it may be in the near future). For example, the following subselect is not valid MySQL syntax:

```
select * from table where id in (select id from table2);
```

Tip

Though subselects are not yet supported, you can many times get around the missing function by using joins or other commands. If I rewrite the earlier invalid statement as a valid statement in MySQL, it looks like this:

```
select table.* from table,table2 where
table.id=table2.id;
```

In the event that rewriting a subselect doesn't work, I recommend using a front-end application written in Perl (or in your favorite language) to issue multiple statements to the database.

✦ **Stored procedures or triggers:** MySQL doesn't support either one yet, although the MySQL development team is working hard to bring triggers to MySQL for version 4.1.

Note

MySQL current and planned features change rapidly. I recommend checking with MySQL's Web site for the status of any feature necessary for your application.

Should you absolutely need a function not available in MySQL, look into support contracts with MySQL AB. Often the developers are willing to prioritize a major feature—or even customize a version of MySQL just for you!

Summary

Databases are widely used in many applications to track customer information, preferences, and history. Databases offer speed, accuracy, reporting, and thoroughness as advantages.

✦ There are many implementations of Relational Database Management Systems including Oracle, Microsoft SQL Server, PostgreSQL, and Informix.

✦ Each RDBMS offers advantages and disadvantages and shares many common traits.

✦ MySQL is an open source RDBMS that offers many advantages over other RDBMS with few disadvantages.

✦ MySQL supports the SQL-92 standard nearly completely and extends the standard with other features.

✦ ✦ ✦

CHAPTER 2

Preparing for Installation

In This Chapter

Checking system prerequisites for MySQL

Obtaining MySQL

Selecting a MySQL version

Chapter 1 illustrated some basics of a Relational Database Management System (RDBMS), as well as the standards that MySQL follows and extensions to those standards. Before you get your hands dirty installing MySQL, it would be wise to know which version you're going to install. Sounds easy, right? Just download MySQL (or use the CD included with this book) and go. Unfortunately — and fortunately — it's not really that easy.

MySQL includes many variants of the server, each optimized for a different scenario. You can also download the source code and customize MySQL further for your application.

This chapter presents some issues to think about before you install any version of MySQL. In addition, it lists and describes those versions so you can decide which one is right for you.

Prerequisites for MySQL

You should answer some essential questions before installing MySQL. This section reviews some of those questions, along with common requirements for a MySQL installation.

Licensing

Question: Will you be required to purchase a license for MySQL?

MySQL server is covered under the GNU General Public License (GPL). In general, you shouldn't have to purchase a license from MySQL AB for most uses. This includes internal uses as well as commercial Web or other applications. MySQL AB asks that you purchase a support contract or some other level of support to assist them in continuing to develop MySQL.

However, if you should download the source code and make a new application using all or part of the MySQL code base—and you want to market that application or make it proprietary—you would need a commercial license to prevent your code from becoming *GPL'd* (that is, automatically subject to the terms of the GNU General Public License). MySQL AB offers a commercial license that allows you to use all or part of the MySQL code base within your application.

Additionally, if you distribute your own version of MySQL, you must include the source code; if you have an application that works only with MySQL and you choose to distribute MySQL with that application, you would need to purchase a commercial license. Other situations also call for a license, and licensing requirements frequently change. I recommend checking with MySQL's Web site, `http://www.mysql.com/`, for more information.

License fees are very reasonable for MySQL. At the time of writing, a MySQL server license is roughly $200.00, depending on the currency-conversion rate (from Euros to American dollars).

Note: Some older versions of MySQL were covered under a stricter license. This is true for distribution of MySQL with programs or derivations based on the MySQL code for those older versions. In the event that you have an older version of MySQL, make sure you obtain the MySQL Free Public License.

Support

Question: Will you require support directly from MySQL AB for your installation?

MySQL AB offers tiered support, with tiered pricing to match. Because prices change, I won't include costs here. However, I think it would be useful to look at the different levels of support available, though there may be more or fewer options available when you read this.

- **E-mail support:** For a flat fee per year, you can obtain support via e-mail for MySQL. Much of the support can be obtained on MySQL mailing lists, but this option does give you the ability to report problems and ask questions via a special support e-mail address.
- **Priority e-mail support:** A level above the basic e-mail support, this option gives your e-mail priority over others. Additionally, requests for features and additions to MySQL are given more consideration.
- **Login support:** This option gives you the benefits of the extended e-mail support along with the ability to have a MySQL developer attempt to actually connect to your database server to troubleshoot and fix problems. With Login support, your suggestions are given a high level of consideration and many can even be implemented quickly. You can also contact MySQL developers via telephone. MySQL developers will also give you, when possible, suggestions on improving your database implementation and optimization suggestions as well.

✦ **Priority login support:** This option gives you all the benefits of the lower-tiered levels as well as the ability to have your own extensions added to MySQL and custom binary editions of MySQL created for you. In addition, with some other costs, a MySQL developer will visit your site to consult and offer suggestions for improvements.

✦ **Telephone support:** Like the others, this option includes the lower-tiered levels and also gives you access to a Web site that lists current on-call phone numbers for MySQL developers (in the event of an emergency).

Note

If you are using transactional table types such as `BDB` or `InnoDB`, an additional fee is charged, based on the level of support you purchase.

Operating system and architecture

Question: Which one of the many platforms do you run MySQL on?

MySQL runs on different platforms. From AIX to Windows, and many points in between, MySQL is truly cross platform. Table 2-1 shows the operating systems and platforms that MySQL is available for. The architecture and platform you choose could determine how large database objects such as tables can be.

Table 2-1
MySQL Operating Systems and Architecture

OS/Architecture Support	*Available?*
AIX 4.x	Yes
Amiga	Yes
BeOS	Soon
BSDi 2.x-4.x	Yes
DEC UNIX 4.x	Yes
FreeBSD 2.x-4.x	Yes
HP-UX 10.20-11.x	Yes
Linux (Kernel 2.0 or later)	Yes
MacOS X	Yes
NetBSD 1.3-1.4 (Intel)	Yes
NetBSD 1.3 (Alpha)	Yes
OpenBSD	Yes
OS/2 Warp	Yes

Continued

Table 2-1 *(continued)*

OS/Architecture Support	***Available?***
SCO OpenServer	Yes
SCO Unixware 7.0.1	Yes
SGI Irix 6.x	Yes
Solaris 2.5 or higher	Yes
SunOS 4.x	Yes
Tru64 UNIX	Yes
Windows 95, 98, NT, 2000	Yes

Note Some versions of MySQL for some operating systems require additional tools or components. Please consult MySQL's Web site for more information.

MySQL is also more widely supported on certain platforms. MySQL in Linux is a popular application and you have many avenues to pursue for assistance should you need it. MySQL on other operating systems may not be so common and thus it might be more difficult to obtain support.

MySQL runs best on *x*86 Linux platforms simply because that has historically been where the most development and testing has been done. Other UNIX-variant operating systems like Solaris or FreeBSD also have gone through extensive testing. This is not to say that MySQL is unstable on any other platform.

Aside from the operating system itself, another essential choice to make (assuming that cost is no obstacle) is whether to use more than one processor. MySQL can take advantage of Symmetric Multi-Processing (SMP) — a capability that dramatically increases processing speed by using multiple processors — but the version you download may or may not have support for SMP. Check before you install.

Development

Question: What application or applications do you use to develop a MySQL database?

MySQL includes or has available for download many Application Programming Interfaces (APIs). For our purposes, an API defines how a program connects to the database. Once connected, the API defines the operations that can be performed. When you click a search tool at an online store, many times you are using an API on the backend and do not even know it. The API is used in a program, such as a PHP script, to connect to the database and run your search.

Knowing which APIs you'll need could help you determine which platform to use with MySQL. The following APIs are available for MySQL:

- ✦ C
- ✦ C++
- ✦ Eiffel
- ✦ JDBC/Java
- ✦ ODBC
- ✦ Perl
- ✦ PHP
- ✦ Python
- ✦ Tcl

The C API has been developed the most. This is because MySQL is written in C and the developers themselves frequently use the C API. For Web applications and most database-connectivity applications, you use another API (such as Perl, PHP, or ODBC).

Cross-Reference

The Perl, PHP, and ODBC APIs are discussed in Part IV of this book.

Perl is usually included with Linux, so if you expect to be using MySQL and Perl, you should give serious consideration to Linux as your platform. Perl also runs on other platforms as well, including Windows, through the use of additional tools.

For ODBC support to connect MySQL to another application, you will probably want to use MySQL in Windows. MySQL offers the MyODBC API to connect a Windows client to MySQL. MyODBC will also work under UNIX variants with the use of an additional tool. Figure 2-1 shows how an ODBC connection looks when you set it up by using MyODBC in Windows.

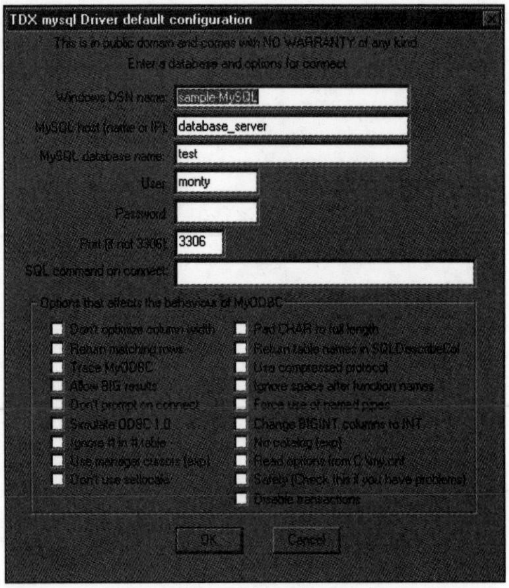

Figure 2-1: The MyODBC connector includes many options (most covered in a later chapter).

Existing data

Question: Will you be importing data from another database?

Though not really a prerequisite to installing MySQL, determining what, if any, data will be imported from other applications or databases is useful to take into account. You can then export that data into a format MySQL can import—or you can download a tool to assist with the export-and-import process.

MySQL supports loading data from delimited text files—for example, those containing comma-separated values (CSV)—and many programs can export data into delimited values, making it easy to load data into MySQL. If you are migrating between versions of MySQL, you have a utility called `mysqldump` that can quickly dump all the contents of an entire database (or even multiple databases) and then load that information back into MySQL—where it automatically creates the table structure as well! Figure 2-2 shows sample output from a `mysqldump` operation.

On the MySQL Web site you have tools for converting from other applications and databases, though MySQL AB does not directly support most of those tools. In fact, most were not written by the main MySQL development team, but by other developers around the world. Such is the beauty of Open Source! Of course, any software—even (and sometimes especially) that produced by the biggest companies—can have bugs, and the MySQL tools are no exception. You should always have extra copies of your data on hand in case something goes wrong (yet another reason to perform regular backups).

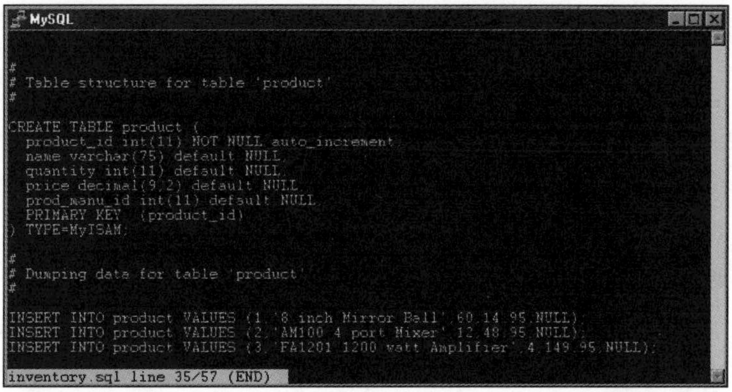

Figure 2-2: The mysqldump utility makes migrating or upgrading MySQL easy.

Table 2-2 shows some popular conversion tools.

Cross-Reference Some conversion and import tools are examined in Chapter 10.

Table 2-2
Conversion Tools for MySQL

Original program	*Tool name*	*Description of conversion*
Microsoft Access	Access to MySQL	From Access to MySQL
	ExportSQL	Improved tool that replaces "Access to MySQL"
	MyAccess	Work with MySQL within Access
Microsoft Excel	`excel2mysql`	From Excel to MySQL
FoxPro	`dbf2mysql`	From .dbf files to MySQL
mSQL	`msql2mysql`	From mSQL to MySQL
Oracle	`oracledump`	From Oracle to MySQL
Microsoft SQL Server	`mssql2mysql`	From SQL Server to MySQL

Note Some tools have similar names, may change names, be unavailable, broken, or otherwise problematic. Check the MySQL Web site for the latest availability.

If you are porting from Oracle to MySQL and have applications currently in Oracle, chances are you'll have to rewrite some of those applications. Although MySQL strives to provide the same functionality as Oracle and at least provide the same syntax, not all queries will work the same between the two RDBMS. A line-by-line examination of application code is the only way to ensure that the rollout of MySQL will go smoothly.

If you want to get data *out* of MySQL, the process is much easier. MySQL exports into common file types that many other RDBMS and applications can recognize. If Microsoft Access is the destination, you have a companion program to the ExportSQL program that allows data to be imported into Access through ODBC.

Cross-Reference Exporting from MySQL is covered in Chapter 10.

Default language and character set

Question: What default language and character set should I choose for my installation of MySQL?

The default language and character set you choose for the MySQL server will determine things like sorting and grouping order for select statements, error message language, and allowable characters. The MySQL binary versions come precompiled with the Latin1 character set by default. This character set is acceptable for sorting and grouping in the United States and Western Europe.

If you require additional character sets, compile MySQL from source code with the `--with-charset` or `--with-extra-charsets` option. In addition, you'll have to start the server with a command-line option of `--default-character-set`.

MySQL can print error messages in many different languages. To make MySQL do so, use the `--language=<languagename>` syntax when you start the server.

Note By default, language names are displayed in lowercase and located in the `<mysqldir>/SHARE/` directory.

Twenty languages are available to MySQL. In alphabetical order, they are Czech, Danish, Dutch, English (default), Estonian, French, German, Greek, Hungarian, Italian, Japanese, Korean, Norwegian, Polish, Portuguese, Romanian, Russian, Slovak, Spanish, and Swedish.

Note With some languages (especially those using non-Western alphabets), you have to load a different default character set.

Management

Question: How do you manage the server and how do clients connect to the database?

Connection and management are two aspects of the same question. MySQL offers a few different methods for management of the server. The most common is via the MySQL Command-Line Interface (CLI). Another common method for management is through a tool called PHPMyAdmin that runs via a Web interface with PHP. MySQL AB also has a Graphical User Interface (GUI) management and client interface called MySQLGUI, see Figure 2-3.

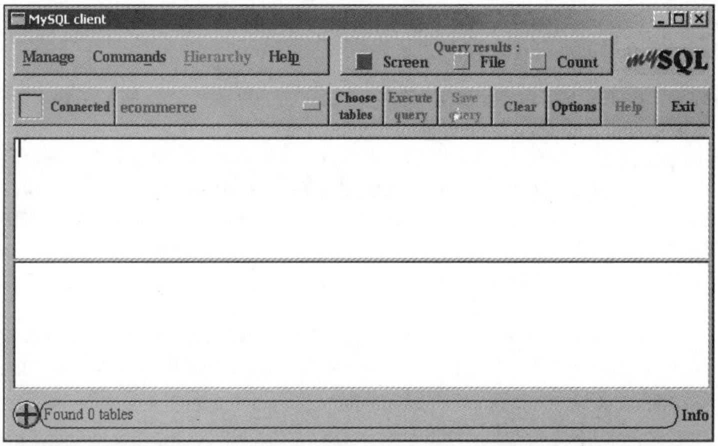

Figure 2-3: MySQLGUI is a new application for working with MySQL.

One of the simplest ways to manage and work with MySQL is via the MySQL CLI. Using the MySQL CLI or the `mysql` command from the command line, you can interact with the server to create and alter tables, run queries, diagnose the server, and much more. See Figure 2-4 for an example of the MySQL CLI in action.

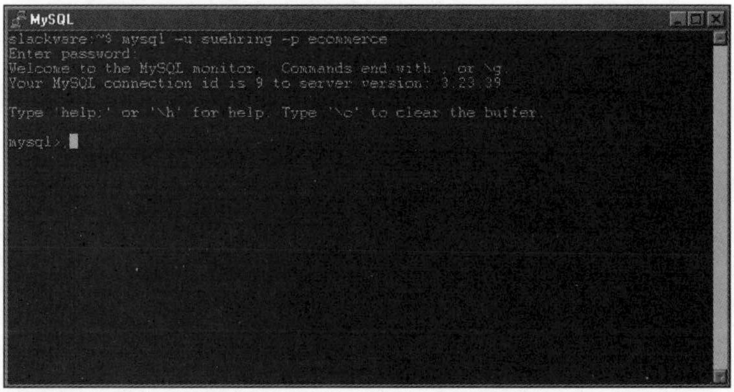

Figure 2-4: The MySQL CLI is the traditional method for working with MySQL.

Cross-Reference

The MySQL CLI is discussed in greater detail throughout the book and in Chapter 8.

If you are having users connect to the MySQL server via the CLI or other tools, you will have to install those tools on the client computers. In addition, you must grant access for those users so they can connect and work with the MySQL server.

Where to Obtain MySQL

Question: Where can I get MySQL, and do particular sources offer advantages?

By far the most popular method for obtaining a copy of MySQL is via the MySQL AB Web site at `http://www.mysql.com/`. From that site, you can get the version of MySQL that you need for your particular installation, as well as obtain other tools related to MySQL. You have geographically dispersed Mirror sites listed so that you can download from the nearest site.

Another way to obtain MySQL is on CD-ROM with various Linux releases. Also, some Linux versions, notably Debian Linux, allow you to download MySQL via their great `apt-get` or `dselect` package tools.

In addition, a company called NuSphere has its own version of MySQL available. That release, obtainable directly from NuSphere, and is covered in more depth in Chapter 20.

Overview of MySQL Versions

Question: Which version of MySQL is appropriate for my database?

Aside from the operating system and platform for MySQL, different versions available for download. Choosing the right version can make the difference between a successful and an unsuccessful installation.

MySQL numbering scheme

MySQL uses a three-digit numbering scheme for versions, for example, 4.00.00. The first number indicates the *file format* used. Therefore, beware if you are attempting to upgrade from a 3.*xx.xx* version to a 4.*xx.xx* version; the file format is different. The second number is known as the *release level*. MySQL usually has two different release-level numbers available at any one time, a *stable* version and a *development* version. If you use a development branch, it may be unstable. The final number is the actual release number and contains bug fixes and usually some improvements over the previous release.

Binary versions of MySQL

In general, it's good practice to download and install the binary version of MySQL. This creates a standard installation that's easier to support in the long run.

For Linux, a binary version of MySQL is available and it works on most versions of the operating system. I hesitate to say that MySQL works on *all* versions of Linux; too many idiosyncratic versions of Linux exist for that to be likely. I feel comfortable saying that the binary versions work on *most* versions of Linux, especially the popular ones.

Linux binary versions come compressed, and are meant to be uncompressed right into the folder where they are to be installed.

If you are working with a version of Linux that supports the Red Hat Package Manager (RPM) format, then you can use a copy of MySQL with the `.rpm` extension. The RPM versions should work on Linux OSs that support RPM and `glibc`. Table 2-3 covers the different RPM-based versions of MySQL.

Table 2-3
MySQL RPM Binary Versions

Version name	*Description*
`mysql-version.i386.rpm`	The main MySQL server installation.
`mysql-client-version.i386.rpm`	The MySQL client only. Used to connect to a MySQL server located on another machine.
`mysql-bench-version.i386.rpm`	A suite of testing and benchmarking tools for MySQL.
`mysql-devel-version.i386.rpm`	The libraries and include files. This is needed if you want to use APIs such as Perl or PHP with MySQL.
`mysql-shared.i386.rpm`	Client libraries.
`mysql-src-version.i386.rpm`	Source code `rpm` that contains everything listed above.

You can install individual packages that have only the portions of MySQL needed for your work. If you need only the MySQL CLI client, for example, you don't have to install a full server on your computer.

Cross-Reference

Installation of MySQL in Linux is covered in Chapter 3.

Aside from the RPM binary versions of MySQL, different binary packages available for the different platforms and operating systems. (Refer to Table 2-1 for a list of supported platforms and operating systems.) For the most part, you have binary packages already available.

Source-code versions of MySQL

If you want to compile MySQL for other platforms (such as Alpha or SPARC), or if no binary package is available for your operating system, you can download the source code for MySQL. The source code is available in an RPM or in `tar/gzip` format (for UNIX variants) or zipped source code for Windows. Table 2-4 shows the different source-code versions of MySQL.

Table 2-4
MySQL Source Versions

Version name	*Description*
`mysql-version.tar.gz`	General UNIX-variant source code to compile MySQL.
`mysql-src-version.i386.rpm`	Source-code RPM that contains everything listed in this section of the book.
`mysql-version-win-src.zip`	Source code to compile under Windows.

Downloading a source-code version will allow you to customize the MySQL server installation much more than you can with a binary version. You can tailor the server software to fit your needs and even edit and change the source code itself. Options like debugging, RAID (Redundant Array of Inexpensive Disks), or including just one of the two transactional table types can be accomplished by compiling the source code. In addition, if you ever have to rewrite a portion of the code or patch a portion of the code, having the source code is the only option.

Cross-Reference

Chapter 3 covers installation from source code and from binary packages.

MySQL for Windows

MySQL with Windows in binary version runs on Windows 95, 98, Me, NT, and 2000. The binary version includes the regular MySQL server as well as the MySQL-MAX server that includes transactional tables. If your work requires the server to support transactional tables, the command line that starts MySQL is different. Therefore, if you don't need transactional-table support, I recommend staying with the normal MySQL server; it uses fewer resources. Table 2-5 shows the MySQL executables for Windows.

Note

Not all executables will run on Windows 9x, Me, or XP.

Table 2-5
MySQL Windows Executables

Name	*Description*
`mysqld-nt`	A binary installation specifically for NT/2000. Includes support for named pipes.
`mysqld-opt`	An optimized binary version with no transactional table support.
`mysqld`	Binary version that includes debugging, memory allocation, transactional table types, and symbolic links.
`mysqld-max`	Binary version that includes transactional tables and symbolic links. Note that no named pipe support is included in this version.
`mysqld-max-nt`	This binary version also includes support for named pipes as well as everything included in the mysqld-max version.

By default, when you install MySQL on Windows 2000, the mysql-nt version will start. If you want to choose a different version, you can set the appropriate value in the `my.ini` file (which resides in the `WINNT` directory). Alternatively, you have a GUI admin tool called WinMySQLAdmin that you can use to change the server executable easily. Figure 2-5 shows WinMySQLAdmin in action.

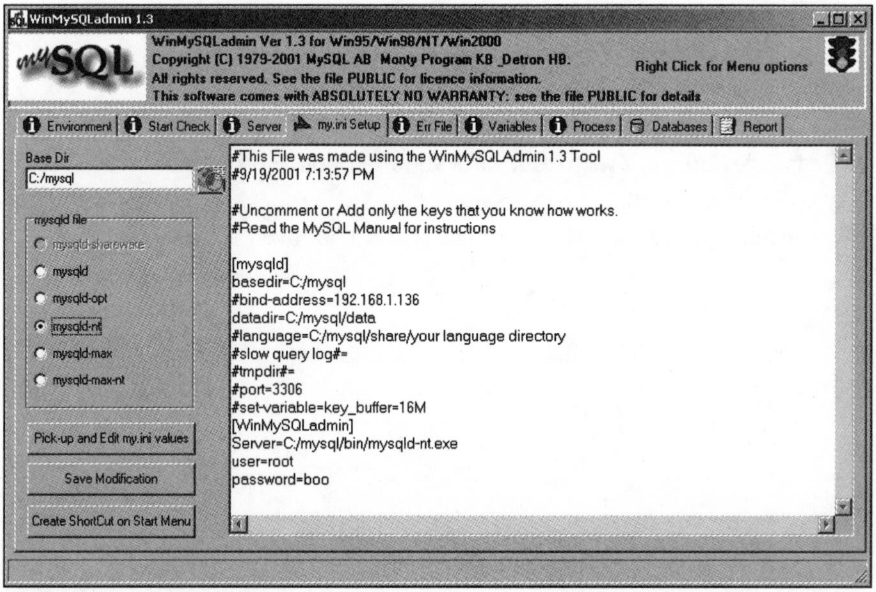

Figure 2-5: WinMySQLAdmin allows changing of the MySQL server executable as well as many other options.

Cross-Reference WinMySQLAdmin is covered in greater detail in Chapter 3.

You have many options, even within a particular operating system, for choosing the version of MySQL you'd like to run. Know what you need before you actually install MySQL—it saves a lot of time and headaches in the future.

MySQL for Mac OS X

MySQL AB also produces a version of the server for Mac OS X. MySQL is included with Mac OS X Server or can be downloaded through the Web site.

MySQL for Mac is available as source code only. At this time no binary versions of MySQL are available for Mac OS X.

Cross-Reference Chapter 5 describes installation of MySQL on a Mac OS X system.

Summary

You have several questions to consider when installing MySQL including licensing, support, and operating system.

- MySQL enables you to use many character sets and default languages.
- MySQL can import many different varieties of existing data; third-party tools are also available to assist with data import.
- MySQL has tools such as the command-line interface and MySQLGUI to manage and work with your data and the database server.
- MySQL has versions available for many operating systems and architectures, the most popular of which are Linux and Windows.

✦ ✦ ✦

CHAPTER 3

Linux Installation

✦ ✦ ✦ ✦

In This Chapter

Listing tasks that binary, RPM, and source-code installation have in common

Installing MySQL (binary)

Installing MySQL (RPM)

Installing MySQL (source)

✦ ✦ ✦ ✦

Many people (including myself) skip the first couple of chapters in a book to get to the heart of the subject matter. If you're one of those people, welcome! I encourage you to review the exquisite prose contained in the first two chapters. Not only did I work hard to bring these chapters to you, they actually contain information you might find useful. At the very least, skim the contents of Chapter 2; it contains information that will help you decide which version of MySQL you should install for your particular needs.

For those of you who have been with me throughout, thank you. I'll now get into some hands-on installation tasks. This chapter concentrates solely on the Linux operating system. If you will be installing MySQL on another operating system, this chapter probably isn't for you.

Common Binary, RPM, and Source MySQL Installation Tasks

Regardless of the method you choose for installation (or the version of Linux you have), some tasks or options are common to all of them. Rather than cover those same options each time, I'll cover them here.

MySQL server startup and shutdown

If you are running a System V–based Linux version such as Red Hat and you want the MySQL server to start whenever the server is rebooted, you should copy the file `/usr/local/mysql/support-files/mysql.server` to the `/etc/rc.d/init.d` directory on your server. Then make the symbolic links to the `rc.d` directories. Alternatively, you can use the `chkconfig` command to add the `mysql.server` script automatically, as shown in Figure 3-1.

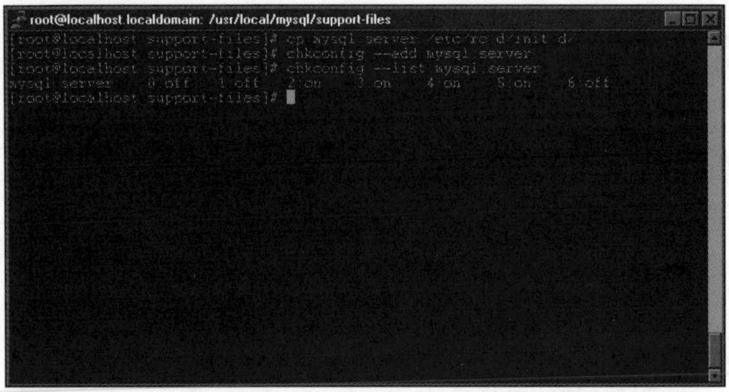

Figure 3-1: The chkconfig command can be used to configure the mysql.server script for automatic startup and shutdown of the MySQL server.

If you are running a BSD-style Linux version such as Slackware, you can still use the `mysql.server` script. However, you'll need to change the permissions on the file to make it executable—and then add it to the `rc.local` script to start the server. Figures 3-2 and 3-3 show the commands and editing of the `/etc/rc.d/rc.local` script on a Slackware Linux system.

Figure 3-2: Copy the file to the /etc/rc.d directory and be sure to make the file executable.

Configuring the MySQL database to stop automatically when the server is rebooted or halted is probably more important than making the database start automatically. If the MySQL database is not shut down properly, you may find broken tables or even loss of data. On SysV systems such as Red Hat and Mandrake, you needn't worry about this step if you've used `chkconfig` to configure the `mysql.server` script. The following configuration steps are necessary for BSD-style systems. Sometimes these configuration steps are not necessary, as the MySQL server will shut down when given a kill command by the system. However, I believe data integrity is too important to leave to chance.

Figure 3-3: Edit the /etc/rc.d/rc.local file to add the command /etc/rc.d/mysql.server start.

If you haven't already copied the `mysql.server` script to `/etc/rc.d` and made the file executable, now is the time to do so. On Slackware, simply edit the `/etc/rc.d/rc.6` file and add `/etc/rc.d/mysql.server stop` to the file near — but not at — the top of the file, as shown in Figure 3-4.

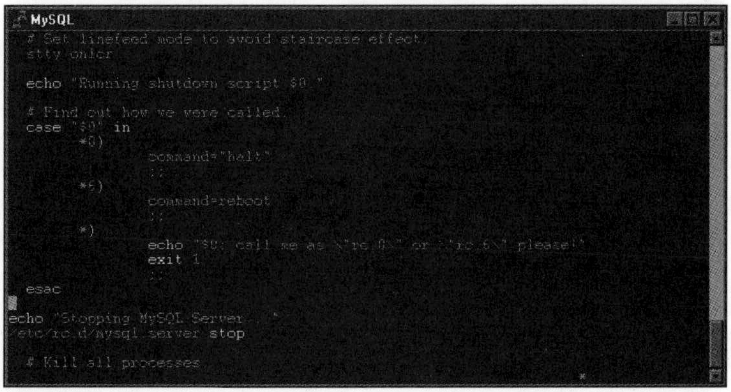

Figure 3-4: Add the mysql.server stop command to your shutdown script.

Tip

Should you need to stop the MySQL server manually, you can do so with the `mysqladmin shutdown` command. For example, the following command would stop the MySQL server on the local machine:

```
mysqladmin -p shutdown
```

Notice the use of the `-p` switch that causes the command to prompt for a password.

Cross-Reference

Command-line switches are frequent topics throughout the book, most notably Chapters 6 and 10 and Appendix A.

Common command-line options for mysqld

The main server executable file for MySQL is called `mysqld`. Here are some important points to keep in mind when you select its command-line options:.

✦ Older versions often run `mysqld` from a *wrapper script* such as `mysqld_safe` or `safe_mysqld`.

Caution

Options that you can set or call when running the wrapper script can change the behavior of the server.

✦ You can set many options from inside the `my.cnf` file (located in the `/etc` directory or sometimes in the `/etc/mysql/` directory).

Tip

As a rule of thumb, use the `my.cnf` file for changing the command-line behavior of MySQL. If you edit the `mysql.server` file, your changes will be lost if the mysql.server script is overwritten by future upgrades of the MySQL software.

The `my.cnf` file is a powerful way to control many aspects of the MySQL software. For Linux installations, the `my.cnf` file is usually located inside the `support-files` directory with the filename my-<*size*>.cnf, where <*size*> indicates the estimated resource amounts of your MySQL server host machine.

Cross-Reference

Chapter 11 examines various configurations that use the `my.cnf` configuration file.

Setting options in the my.cnf file

Within the `my.cnf` file are sections that affect the behavior of the components that make up a MySQL installation. These sections include both the client and server, and they use the following additional commands:

```
mysql

mysqladmin
```

```
mysqld
mysql_safe
mysql.server
mysqldump
myisamchk
mysqlimport
mysqlshow
mysqlcheck
myisampack
```

Using the [mysqld] section

Each section in the `my.cnf` file starts with the bracketed name of the command or area that identifies the section. In Figure 3-5, for example, you can see some options listed under the word `[mysqld]`.

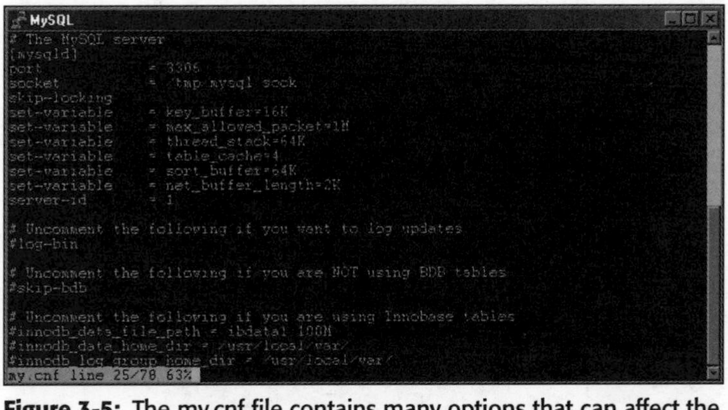

Figure 3-5: The my.cnf file contains many options that can affect the behavior of the MySQL server and client.

If your server is set to run as `root` upon startup, you should add `user = mysql` to the `[mysqld]` section of `my.cnf` and restart the server. To find out what options MySQL will use for startup of the server, use the program `my_print_defaults` contained in the `'bin'` directory of your MySQL installation. Figure 3-6 shows the output for `my_print_defaults` on a sample server; your options may differ slightly.

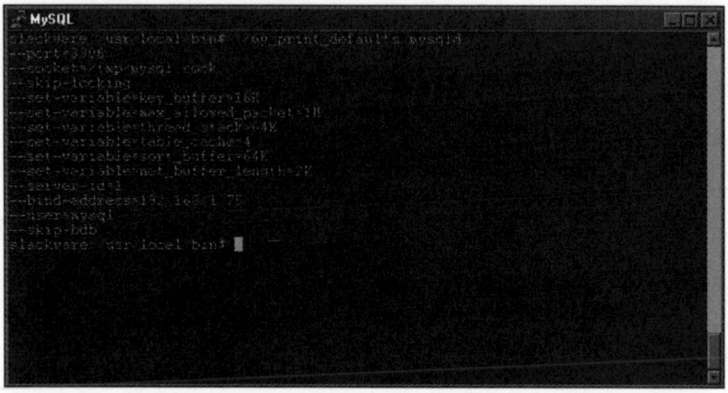

Figure 3-6: The my_print_defaults script shows the default options that MySQL uses for many components.

Some non-default options for the `[mysqld]` section that you may want to consider are `user = mysql` and `bind-address`, which work as follows:

- ✦ The `user = mysql` option causes the server to run as a non-privileged user, which helps enhance security.
- ✦ The `bind-address` may be useful if you have a *multi-homed* host (more than one IP address) and only want to listen for connections on a certain IP address. In Figure 3-7, the address that is bound is the Ethernet IP address for that machine, `192.168.1.75`.

Figure 3-7: Using ifconfig to determine the Ethernet address of the server

Thus, given the correct privileges, I can establish a connection between another machine on the network and the host called `-h <ip` or *`hostname`*`>`, as shown in Figure 3-8.

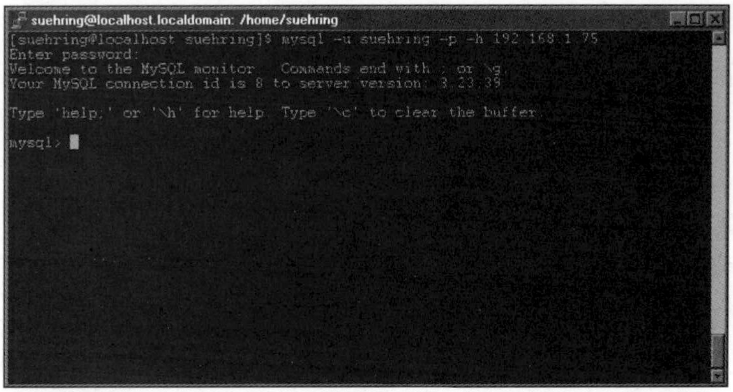
suehring@localhost.localdomain: /home/suehring
[suehring@localhost suehring]$ mysql -u suehring -p -h 192.168.1.75
Enter password:
Welcome to the MySQL monitor. Commands end with ; or \g.
Your MySQL connection id is 8 to server version: 3.23.39
Type 'help;' or '\h' for help. Type '\c' to clear the buffer.
mysql>

Figure 3-8: Connecting from another machine is possible with the MySQL client.

Using the `mysqladmin processlist` command, I can see the current connection to the database from the remote client, as shown in Figure 3-9.

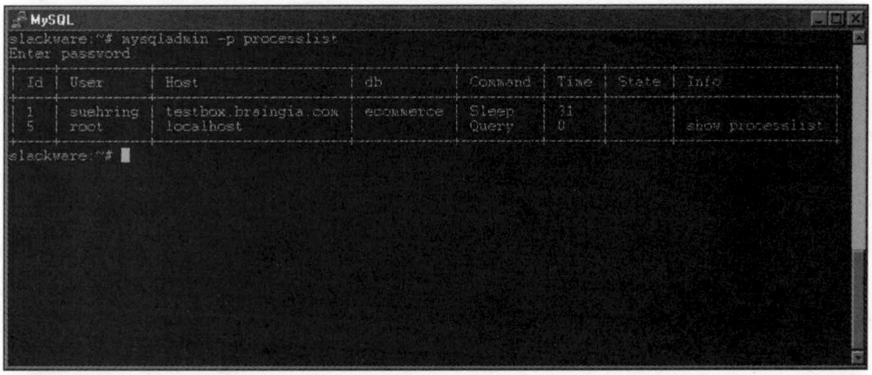
MySQL
slackware:~# mysqladmin -p processlist
Enter password:
Id	User	Host	db	Command	Time	State	Info
1	suehring	testbox.braingia.com	ecommerce	Sleep	31		
5	root	localhost		Query	0		show processlist
slackware:~#

Figure 3-9: Using mysqladmin processlist, the connection from the other machine, "testbox.braingia.com," is shown.

However, if I only needed to connect to the MySQL server from the server itself, I could remove the `bind-address` completely and use the `skip-networking` option. With the `skip-networking` option MySQL uses Unix sockets and no longer listens for connections via TCP/IP. I've edited my.cnf and restarted the server. The output of `my_print_defaults` is now shown in Figure 3-10. Notice that the `bind-address` option has been replaced with the `skip-networking` option.

Figure 3-10: Using bind-address in my.cnf to bind only the loopback address for security purposes

Now when I attempt to connect from the remote computer, I receive an error, as shown in Figure 3-11.

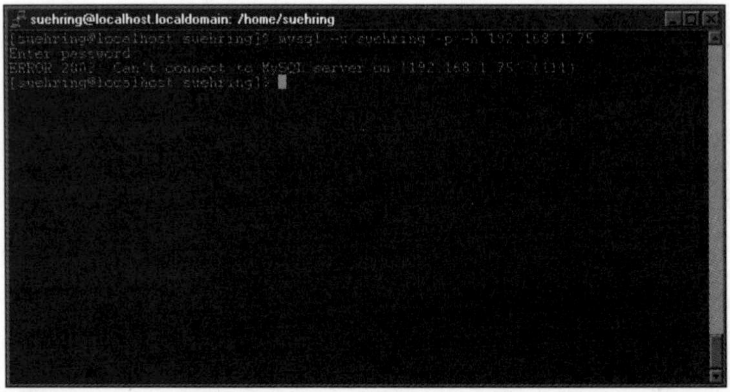

Figure 3-11: A failed attempt to connect to a MySQL server that is no longer listening on its Ethernet address results in an error.

Cross-Reference Other options for `my.cnf` and the MySQL server are discussed in Chapter 11.

Creating default databases and completing installation

The final steps involved in a MySQL installation are common to all Linux versions covered in this book. Please feel free to refer back to this section when you're through the initial install rather than reading this now.

From where you are now, change into the MySQL directory, `cd mysql`. One of the final steps is to run the script to install the default databases. Within the mysql directory, this is accomplished using the `./scripts/mysql_install_db` command. The output will probably scroll past your screen rather quickly, so I've included some of it in Figure 3-12.

> **Caution**
>
> Make sure you type these commands exactly as they appear. Failure to do so could cause problems for your server.

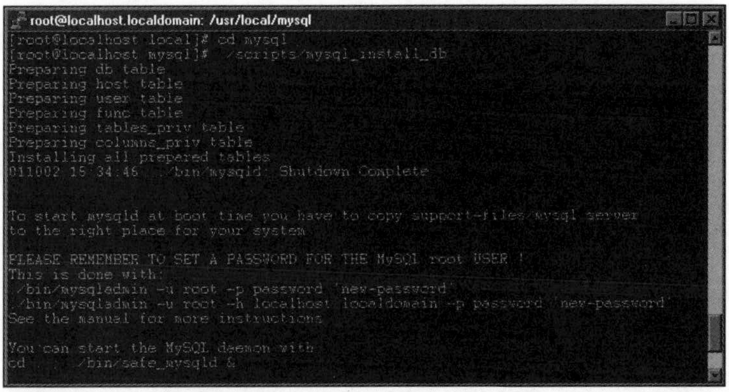

Figure 3-12: The beginning of the output from the mysql_install_db script

The final step before starting the server is to change the permissions for the MySQL files and directories. You can do so with a series of commands, shown in Figure 3-13.

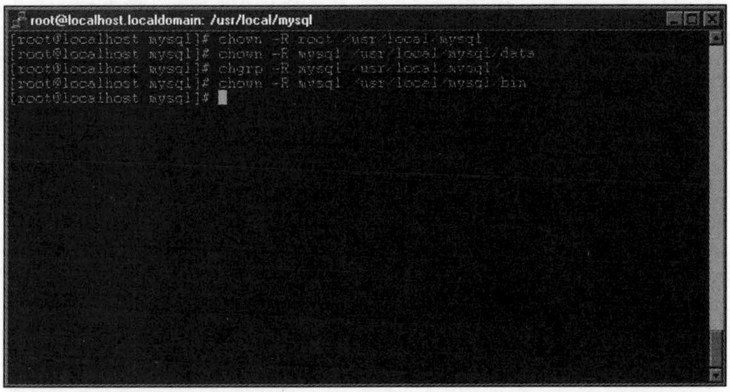

Figure 3-13: Changing ownership on the MySQL files and directories is an important step.

It is now time to start the server. Use the following command:

```
/usr/local/mysql/bin/safe_mysqld --user=mysql &
```

Note: The & character at the end of this command is important because it places the MySQL server in the background.

Alternatively, you can set the user in the my.cnf file. Under the [mysqld] section, place the following line and restart the server:

```
user = mysql
```

Setting an administrator password for MySQL

The first step immediately after starting a MySQL server is to set a password for the server administrator account known as root. This user is different from the root user on your system; setting the password for this user does not affect the password for the root user on your system. (Even so, use care when creating any password, including this one.)

The mysqladmin utility is what you use to set the initial password for the root user. To set the password, the command is run twice—once for the localhost connection and once for connections via the hostname. When the mysqladmin command is run, it will prompt you for the password. If you have not set the password, just press Enter without typing anything and the command will run successfully.

Some versions of MySQL now come with the option skip-networking enabled by default. This causes MySQL to listen only for connections from the localhost and not via the network. The skip-networking option is contained in the [mysqld] section of the MySQL configuration file my.cnf. If this option is enabled, you can't set the password by using the -h hostname. If you remove this option from the configuration file, MySQL listens for connections via the network—in which case, the -h hostname option *will* work.

The syntax for setting the password with mysqladmin is as follows:

```
mysqladmin -u root -p password 'password'
mysqladmin -u root -h hostname -p password 'password'
```

An example of setting the root password is shown in Figure 3-14.

Figure 3-14: Setting the root password with mysqladmin is your first task as a server administrator.

MySQL Linux Binary Installation

MySQL has binary versions available in `.rpm` and gzipped formats. To use the RPM versions, your version of Linux must support RPMs and also have `glibc`. To find out whether your Linux installation procedure supports RPMs, log in as `root` and type `rpm` or `whereis rpm`. If you receive a `Bad Command or File Not Found` message (or a similar error message), you probably don't have support for RPMs and will have to install MySQL as a binary or from source code. (RPM installation is covered later in this chapter.)

When you've obtained the MySQL binary distribution appropriate for your hardware, installation is simply a matter of unpacking the distribution and running some scripts to configure the database. `/usr/local` is the standard place to install MySQL for a binary version. Therefore, prior to going further, you should cd to that directory. Once in `/usr/local`, as shown in Figure 3-15, you can unpack the distribution. Simply type the following command:

```
tar -zxvf [mysql-version-filename]
```

The next step is to add a `mysql` user account and group to your server. I strongly recommend taking this step for security reasons. Should there be a compromise or breach of security through the MySQL server, the attacker would not gain `root` or superuser privileges on your system. Adding the group and user is easy (see Figure 3-16).

Figure 3-15: Unpacking the binary distribution creates a directory containing the MySQL server files.

Figure 3-16: Addition of the mysql user and group is strongly recommended for security.

To further standardize the installation, make a symbolic link between `/usr/local/mysql` and `/usr/local/mysql-version`, which will enable you to move around the file system with ease. Within the `/usr/local` directory, type the following:

```
ln -s [mysql-version] mysql
```

You will now have a directory called `/usr/local/mysql` that is actually a symbolic link to the MySQL server directory, as shown in Figure 3-17.

At this point, refer to the section in this chapter called "Creating default databases and completing installation" for instructions to take you through the rest of this MySQL installation procedure.

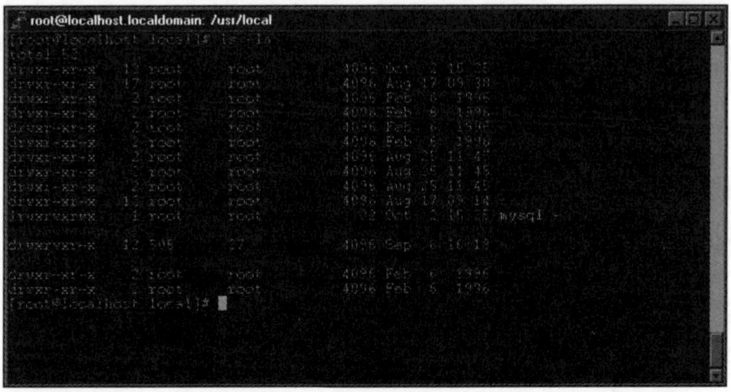

Figure 3-17: Standardization of the MySQL install by making a symbolic link for the MySQL server directory

MySQL Linux RPM Installation

The installation using `rpm` files has five portions, from which you select according to your needs: server, testing suite, client, development libraries, and client libraries. This section illustrates a complete installation that includes all of them. At the most basic level, `rpm` versions are simply binary versions of MySQL rolled into `rpm` files. The locations of files within a binary installation may differ from the `rpm` install.

Each of the files within an `rpm` install simply requires an `rpm -i` command followed by the package name, as in the following example:

```
rpm -i MySQL-client-x.xx.xx-i386.rpm
```

Installing the main `MySQL-x.xx.xx-i386.rpm` file actually installs — and automatically starts — the MySQL server. The RPM even runs the `mysql_install_db` script so you don't have to do it later.

Note You don't need to run `mysql_install_db` (as you're told to do later when you install the main server from RPM).

To install the shared and development libraries and client for MySQL, simply install them via the `rpm -i` command. If you wish to install the benchmarking utilities you will need the Perl MySQL Module available for download from MySQL AB.

Note The Development and Benchmarking RPMs also depend on the MySQL client. Therefore you will need to install the MySQL client RPM prior to installing the Development or Benchmarking RPMs.

RPM installation is quite easy though the file locations may be somewhat different than the other installation methods.

At this point, refer to the section in this chapter called "Creating default databases and completing Installation" for instructions to take you through the rest of this MySQL installation procedure.

MySQL Linux Source Installation

The most configurable and complicated of the install types for MySQL is an installation from source code. This method requires you to compile the server directly and therefore is not for everyone. However, with a source-code install:

- ✦ You have the most control over the components installed.
- ✦ You can edit or modify the source code to fit your installation.

On the CD-ROM

The source code for MySQL for Linux on Intel/x86 systems is contained on the CD included with this book.

The source code will be compressed and tarred, therefore you'll need to untar and uncompress it, then `cd` into the appropriate directory as follows:

```
tar -zxvf mysql-version.tar.gz
cd mysql-version
```

For security reasons, I recommend adding a group and user for MySQL:

```
groupadd myql
useradd -g mysql mysql
```

To enable your installation to closely replicate a binary install, you may want to consider creating a `mysql` directory in `/usr/local`.

```
mkdir /usr/local/mysql
```

Doing so eases administration and future upgrades.

Choosing Options for MySQL

There are a large number of options you can set with a source code install. The options range from simple options about how the configure script will run, to table types to compile, and directories to install components into. The following tables list those options and the defaults are contained in brackets.

Table 3-1
Configure Options for a MySQL Source Installation

Configuration Option	Description
--cache-file=*FILENAME*	The results from testing will be sent to *FILENAME*.
--no-create	Stops creation of output files.
--quiet	Suppresses printing of 'creating' messages.
--silent	Same as the --quiet option.
--srcdir=DIR	Source code is in DIR.

Table 3-2
Directory and File Options for MySQL Source Installation

Configuration option	Description
--*prefix*=DIR	Place architecture-independent files in DIR [/usr/local].
--exec-*prefix*=DIR	Place architecture-dependent files in DIR [*Same as prefix*].
--bindir=DIR	User executables in DIR [*exec-prefix/bin*].
--datadir=DIR	Data files that are read-only and architecture-independent [*prefix*/share].
--includedir=DIR	C header files in DIR [*prefix*/include].
--infodir=DIR	Info style documentation in DIR [*prefix*/info].
--libexecdir=DIR	Program executables in DIR [*exec-prefix*/libexec].
--libdir=DIR	Object code libraries in DIR [*exec-prefix*/lib].
--localstatedir=DIR	Data that is modifiable and single-machine in DIR [prefix/var].
--mandir=DIR	Man documentation in DIR [*prefix*/man].
--oldincludedir=DIR	C header files for non-gcc in DIR [/usr/include].
--program-*prefix*=PREFIX	Prepend *prefix* to installed program names.
--program-*suffix*=SUFFIX	Append *suffix* to installed program names.
--sbindir=DIR	System executables in DIR [exec-*prefix*/sbin].
--sharedstatedir=DIR	Data files that are modifiable and architecture-independent in DIR [*prefix*/com].
--sysconfdir=DIR	Data files that are read-only and single-machine data in DIR [*prefix*/etc].

Table 3-3
Features and Add-ons for MySQL Source Installation

Configuration Option	*Description*
`--disable-largefile`	Omits support for large files.
`--with-berkeley-db[=DIR]`	Includes BerkeleyDB table types and places them in `DIR`.
`--with-berkeley-db-includes=DIR`	MySQL can locate header files for Berkeley DB tables in `DIR`.
`--with-berkeley-db-libs=DIR`	MySQL can locate library files for Berkeley DB tables in `DIR`.
`--with-charset=charset_name`	Includes support for `charset_name`. `[latin1]` (Options are: `big5`, `cp1251`, `cp1257`, `croat`, `czech`, `danish`, `dec8`, `dos`, `estonia`, `euc_kr`, `german1`, `greek`, `hebrew`, `hp8`, `hungarian`, `koi8_ru`, `koi8_ukr`, `latin1`, `latin2`, `latin5`, `swe7`, `usa7`, `win1250`, `win1251ukr`, `ujis`, `sjis`, `tis620`).
`--with-extra-charsets=`*`charset`*`, ...`	Uses additional charsets. Can be specified by group (for example, `none`, `complex`, or `all`), or individually comma-separated from the preceding list.
`--with-gemini[=DIR]`	Includes `Gemini DB` table types and place them in DIR.
`--with-innodb`	Includes support for `Innodb` table types.
`--with-low-memory`	Minimizes use of available memory. Use this option if compiling has a problem because of a shortage of memory.
`--with-mysqld-user=`*`username`*	Specifies a user account as which to run the `mysqld` server (can be set in `my.cnf`).
`--with-raid`	Enables RAID (Redundant Array of Inexpensive Disk) support.
`--with-tcp-port=`*`port-number`*	Specifies port to use for MySQL services (for example, 3306); can be set in `my.cnf`.
`--with-unix-socket-path=`*`socket`*	Absolute location for the UNIX-domain socket.
`--without-debug`	Does not include debugging code.
`--without-server`	Does not build the MySQL server, only the client programs.

Configuration Option	Description
`--without-docs`	Does not build the documentation.
`--without-bench`	Does not build the testing and benchmarking programs.
`--x-includes=DIR`	X include files are in `DIR`.
`--x-libraries=DIR`	X library files are in `DIR`.

The options you choose while compiling are largely up to you — depending on the requirements of your application. For example, if you want to "compile in" the needed support for different character sets, use the `--with-charset` or the `with-extra-charsets` option. To include support for the `BerkeleyDB` transactional table type, use the `--with-berkeleydb` option. The example in the next section gives a common command line for compiling MySQL. Once your options are chosen, installation is straightforward.

Compiling MySQL

To compile with additional options, simply separate them by a space on the configure command line. For the example server, I install into `/usr/local/mysql` and include support for BDB table types, like this:

```
./configure --prefix=/usr/local/mysql --with-berkeley-db
```

The `configure` script runs through each component and prepare it for compilation. Eventually you should see output similar to that in Figure 3-18.

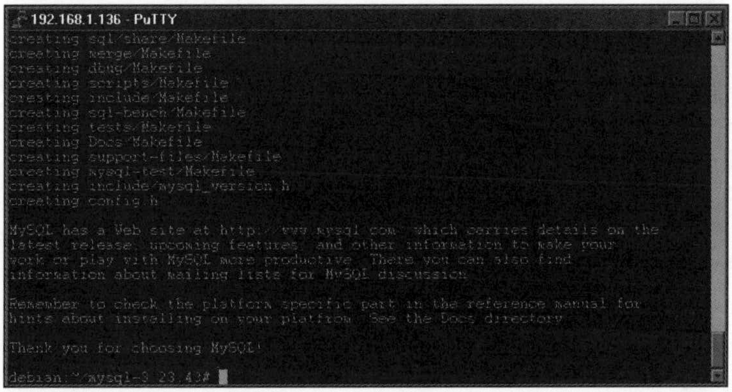

Figure 3-18: The configure script prepares the various components of MySQL to be compiled.

After the `configure` script is complete, compile the software by using the command:

```
make
```

The `make` process will take at least a few minutes depending on the speed of your machine and what else is running on it at the time. Once the software is done compiling, install it with the command:

```
make install
```

In addition, copy the `my.cnf` file appropriate for your implementation to the `/etc/` directory.

Tip **MySQL AB recommends the `my.cnf` file for medium installations be used in most implementations, as follows:**

```
cp support-files/my-medium.cnf /etc/my.cnf
```

At this point, refer to the section in this chapter called "Creating default databases and completing installation" for instructions to take you through the rest of this MySQL installation procedure.

Summary

Always choose secure passwords, for MySQL and all of your computer systems. A good password includes a mix of alphanumeric and non-alphanumeric characters as well as a minimum length and other factors.

- ✦ There are a number of common tasks that you need to perform regardless of installation method. These include creating the default databases, setting options in the `my.cnf` file, configuring MySQL for automatic startup and shutdown, and setting the root administrator password for MySQL.
- ✦ The MySQL binary installation for Linux is the easiest and most recommended method for installation.
- ✦ The MySQL RPM installation is really a binary installation in RPM format. However, file locations are usually different with an RPM installation.
- ✦ The MySQL source code installation is the most configurable; you can set options during compilation and edit the source code directly.

✦ ✦ ✦

CHAPTER 4

Windows Installation

✦ ✦ ✦ ✦

In This Chapter

Choosing effective passwords

Listing the common tasks for binary and source installation of MySQL

Installing MySQL from the binary

✦ ✦ ✦ ✦

This chapter gets down to the nitty-gritty of installing MySQL on a Windows system. (The Linux installation chapter might be of help if you're migrating to Windows from Linux, and want to double-check the differences in procedure.) As groundwork for this chapter, read Chapter 2 (if you haven't already); it gives you some important points to consider before you begin MySQL installation.

MySQL offers two methods for installation under Windows: a binary and a source-code version. The binary version is what most Windows users are familiar with — a setup program that you move through by clicking the Next button. The source-code version is for applications that require additions or changes to MySQL before they can run correctly.

Note Compiling from source code requires a Visual C++ compiler.

Since there are five versions of MySQL included with a binary version, installing from source code is beyond the scope of this book. This chapter begins, however, with some tasks that binary and source-code installation have in common.

Tasks Common to Binary and Source MySQL Installation

Regardless of the method you choose for your MySQL installation, some tasks or options are common to both versions.

MySQL server administration the Windows way

Included with the binary version of MySQL for Windows is an administration tool called WinMySQLAdmin. Using this program, you can configure and change many parameters of the MySQL installation. For Windows administrators who are averse to the command line, this program provides a tool that can perform most administrative tasks from within Windows. To start WinMySQLAdmin, use Windows Explorer and point to the `bin` directory of your MySQL installation (usually `c:\mysql\bin\`). Within the `bin` directory, double-click `winmysqladmin` to start the program. The first time you start WinMySQLAdmin, you're prompted to create a default username and password (see Figure 4-1).

Figure 4-1: Set a default username and password for use with WinMySQLAdmin.

Note

Just a reminder: As an administrator of a MySQL server, you must keep the `root` account secure from unauthorized access. That means (as with all computer systems) choosing secure passwords for MySQL—such passwords have a mix of alphanumeric and non-alphanumeric characters, as well as a minimum length and other attributes that make them hard to guess.

As of this writing, `winmysqladmin` immediately minimizes itself into the taskbar once you've created its default username and password. Therefore, to actually bring up the interface, right-click the stoplight icon in the taskbar and select "Show Me."

Caution

Since WinMySQLAdmin automatically minimizes, you may not think the program has started. Be careful not to start the program more than once.

Once WinMySQLAdmin has started, you see a number of tabs near the top of the program screen (see Figure 4-2).

The tabs near the top of the WinMySQLAdmin screen correspond to actions you can perform or information you can find out about the MySQL server. Some tabs provide their own context menus when you right-click them (as in Figure 4-3).

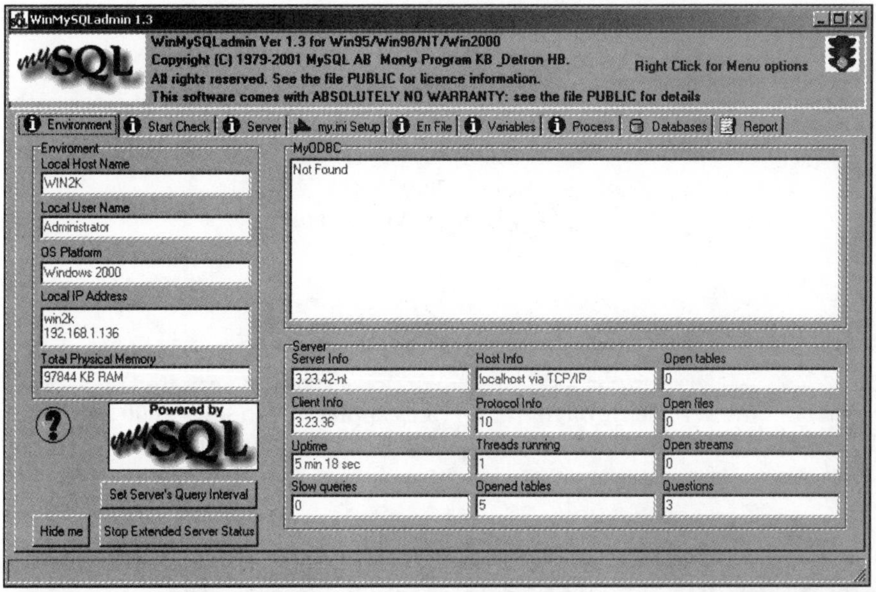

Figure 4-2: WinMySQLAdmin is a powerful, GUI-based program for administering a MySQL server in Windows 2000.

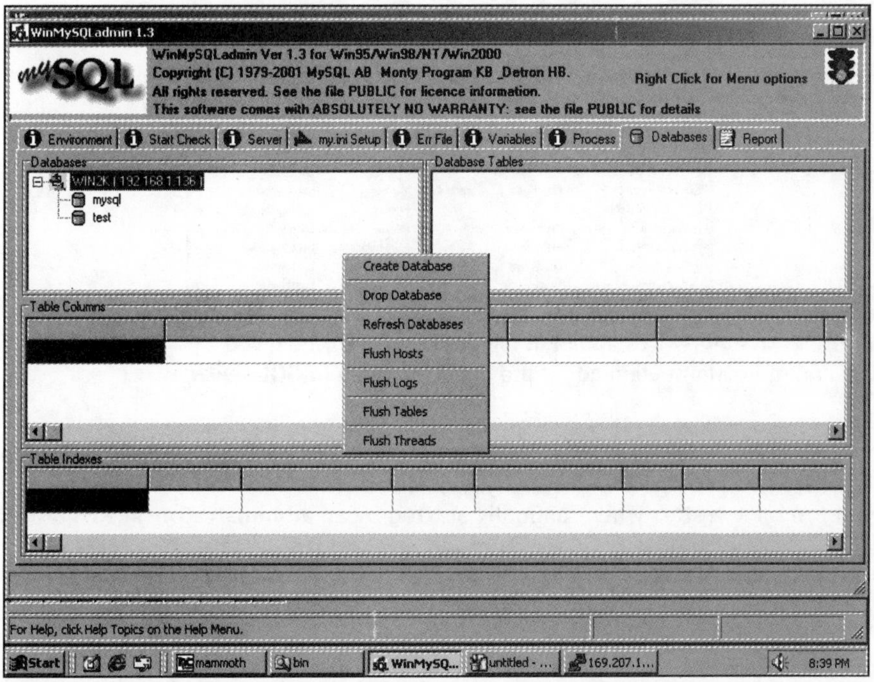

Figure 4-3: Some areas within WinMySQLAdmin have right-click menus that enable you to perform additional functions.

To minimize WinMySQLAdmin, right-click near the top and select "Hide Me."

The other, and more traditional, method for managing a MySQL server is via the command-line utility `mysqladmin`. You can use it to control the behavior of the MySQL server, as well as to create (and drop) databases and gain information about the server.

Cross-Reference Using the `mysqladmin` utility is covered in Chapter 6.

MySQL server startup and shutdown

The MySQL server runs as a service in Windows 2000. You can find more information about the service through the Services applet in Windows 2000 by selecting Start ⇨ Programs ⇨ Administrative Tools ⇨ Services (see Figure 4-4).

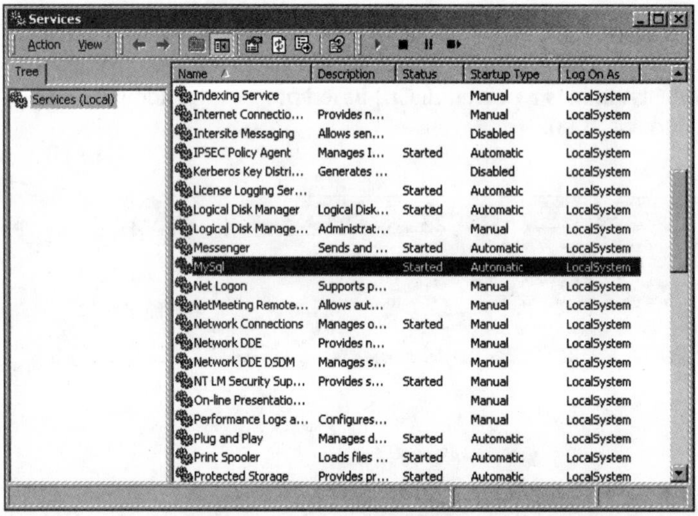

Figure 4-4: The Services applet in Windows 2000 is where you can find more information about the behavior of the MySQL server.

As part of the Services framework in Windows 2000, you can control the behavior of MySQL when starting Windows. MySQL can start automatically with Windows or you can have it start when manually started by an administrator (see Figure 4-5).

There are five different versions of the MySQL server included with the binary distribution, as shown in Table 4-1. Using WinMySQLAdmin (or by editing the `my.ini` file located in `c:\winnt\`), you can choose which server starts by default.

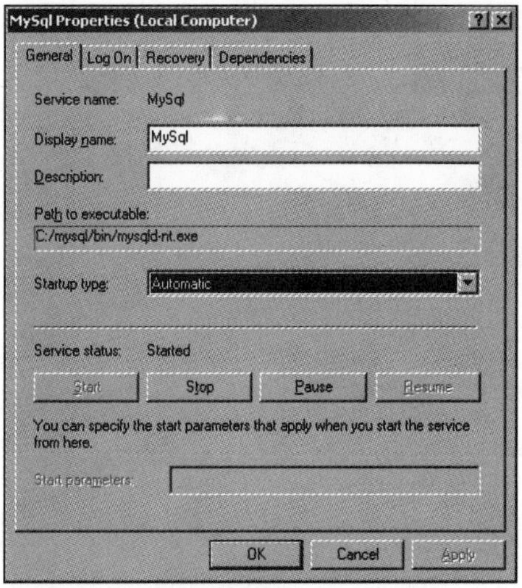

Figure 4-5: The Services applet in Windows 2000 enables you to control the MySQL server startup parameters.

Table 4-1
MySQL Server Versions for Windows 2000

Executable Name	***Description***
`mysqld`	Compiled with full debugging enabled, along with memory-allocation checks. Requires TCP/IP.
`mysqld-max`	Includes support for BDB and `InnoDB` transactional tables.
`mysqld-max-nt`	Includes support for BDB and `InnoDB` tables, as well as for named pipes.
`mysqld-nt`	Contains support for named pipes as a connection method.
`mysqld-opt`	Optimized for Pentium processor, no debugging. Requires TCP/IP.

By normal default, `mysqld-nt` starts when Windows 2000 starts — and this is fine for most installations. Using WinMySQLAdmin (and clicking the `my.ini` tab as shown in Figure 4-6), you can change parameters as needed — including which executable runs for your MySQL server.

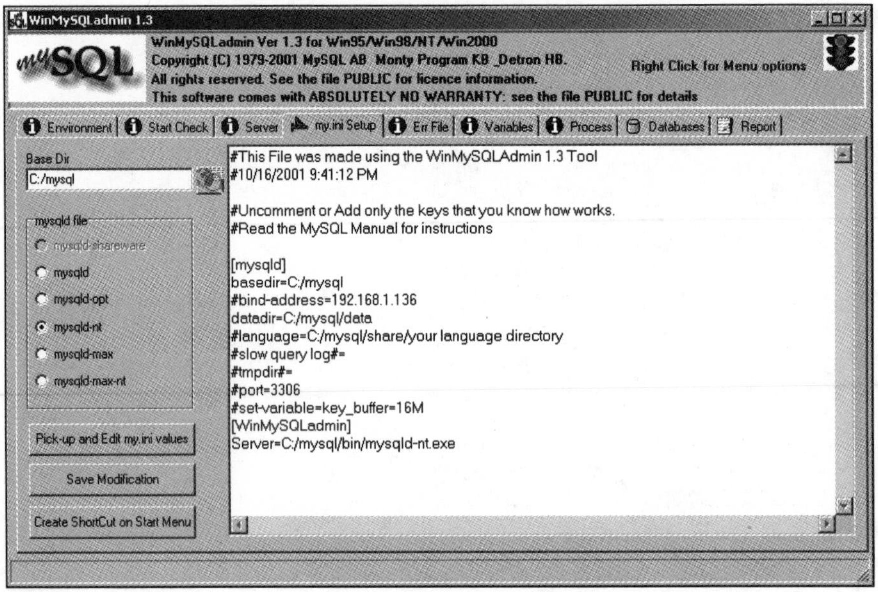

Figure 4-6: Use WinMySQLAdmin to change the server executable to start the MySQL server.

Common command-line options for mysqld

The default server executable file for MySQL in Windows 2000 is called `mysqld-nt`. Some of the options you can set or call when you run `mysqld-nt` actually change the behavior of the server. In addition, many options can be set inside the `my.ini` file (located in the `\WINNT` directory or sometimes in just the root `\` directory).

Note I strongly recommend that you don't make a batch file or script to start MySQL; instead, use the `my.ini` file for changing the command-line behavior of MySQL.

The `my.ini` file is a powerful method for controlling many aspects of the MySQL software. Within the `my.ini` file there are a number of sections that affect the behavior of the various components making up a MySQL installation. These sections include both the client and server, and offer some additional commands:

```
mysql
mysqladmin
mysqld
mysql_safe
mysql.server
mysqldump
```

```
myisamchk
mysqlimport
mysqlshow
mysqlcheck
myisampack
winmysqladmin
```

Each section in the `my.ini` file starts with a name in brackets, which identifies the command or area for that section. To find out which options MySQL uses for starting up the server, use the WinMySQLAdmin tool. Click the `my.ini` tab to see which executable will run, and to check the other parameters for MySQL installation. (Refer to Figure 4-6 for an example: options contained under the `server` section, or the section underneath the word `[mysqld]`.)

Note **If you make changes to the `[mysqld]` section of the `my.ini` file, you must restart the server. One way to do so is through the Services applet in Windows 2000.**

A non-default option for the `[mysqld]` section that you may want to consider is `bind-address`; it's especially useful if you have a *multi-homed* host (one that has more than one IP address) and want only to listen for connections on a particular IP address. In Figure 4-7, the address bound is the Ethernet IP address for that machine, `192.168.1.136`.

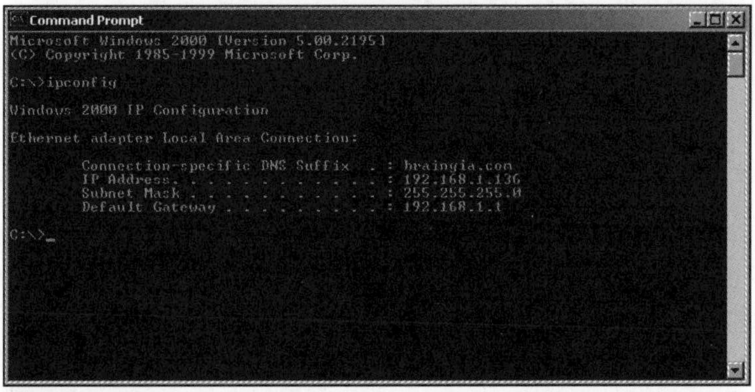

Figure 4-7: Using the ipconfig command to determine the ip address for this host

Having MySQL listen for connections on an Ethernet IP means that, given the correct privileges, I can connect from another machine within the network by using `-h <ip or hostname>`, as shown in Figure 4-8.

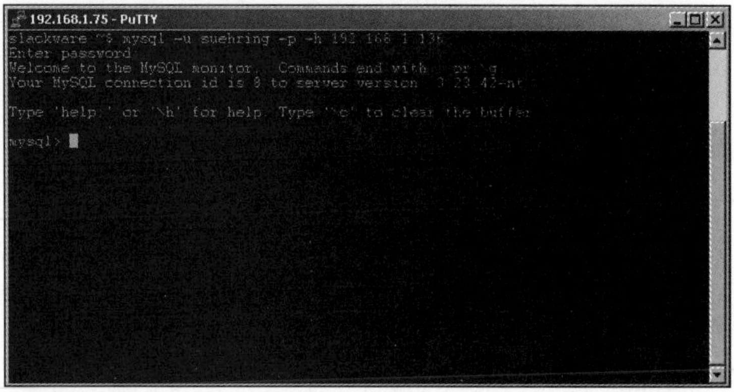

Figure 4-8: Connecting from another machine is possible with the MySQL client

Using WinMySQLAdmin (or the `mysqladmin processlist` command), I can see the current connection to the database from the remote client. An example with WinMySQLAdmin is shown in Figure 4-9.

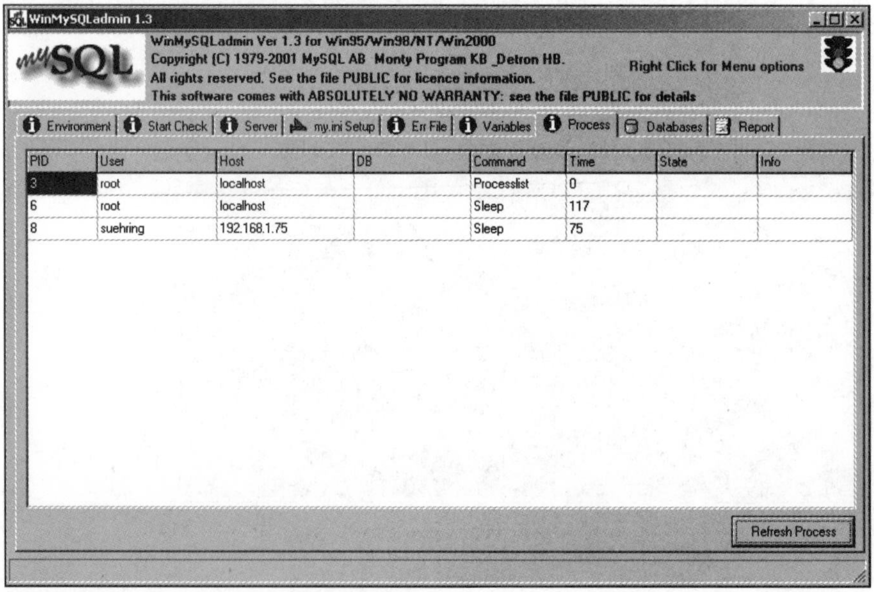

Figure 4-9: Using WinMySQLAdmin displays the connection from the other machine, 192.168.1.75.

However, if I only wanted to connect to the MySQL server from the same server, I could remove the `bind-address` completely and use a different option: The `skip-networking` option uses sockets and no longer listens for connections via TCP/IP. If I choose to follow that route, I edit `my.ini` and restart the server. Then the `my.ini` section of WinMySQLAdmin looks like the one shown in Figure 4-10. Notice that the `bind-address` option has been replaced with the `skip-networking` option.

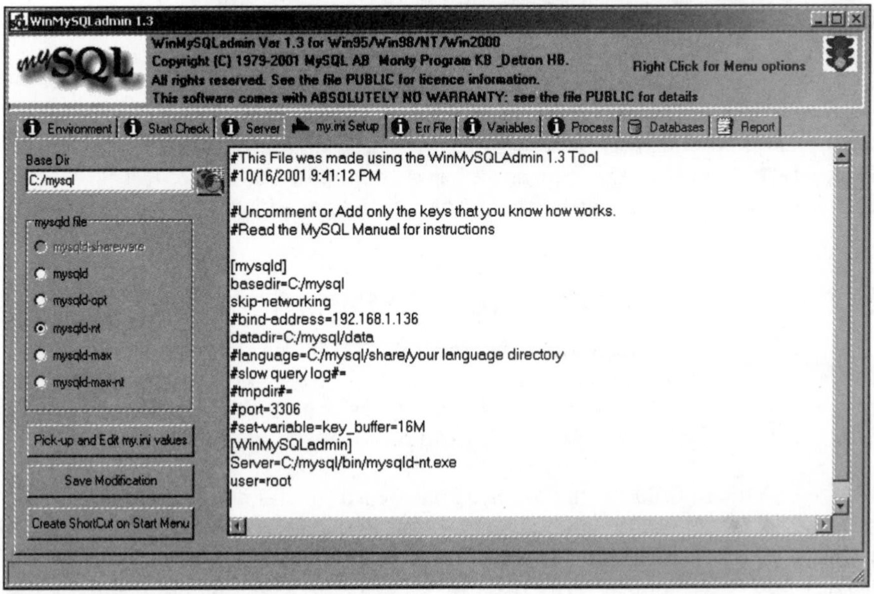

Figure 4-10: Using the skip-networking option in my.ini to stop MySQL from listening for TCP/IP connections

Now, if I attempt to connect from the remote computer, I receive an error message (as shown in Figure 4-11).

Cross-Reference

For more about options for `my.ini` and the MySQL server, see Chapter 11.

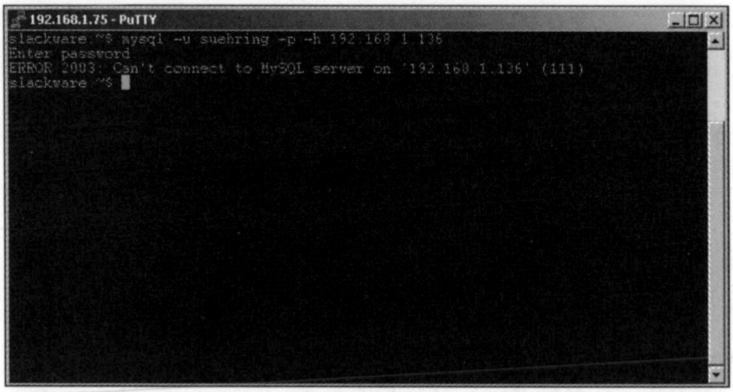

Figure 4-11: Error message following a failed attempt to connect to a MySQL server that's no longer listening on its Ethernet address

Setting an Administrator password for MySQL

The first step immediately after starting a MySQL server is to set a password for the server administrator account known as `root`. This user account is different from the `root` or `administrator` user on your system; setting the password for this user does not affect the password for the root user on your system.

The `mysqladmin` utility sets the initial password for the `root` user. (The WinMySQLAdmin utility can be used as well.) To set the password, you run the command twice—once for the localhost connection and once for connection via the hostname. Then, when you run the `mysqladmin` command, it prompts you for the password. (If you have not set the password, just press Enter without typing anything and the command will run successfully.) The syntax for setting the `mysqladmin` password is as follows:

```
mysqladmin -u root -p password 'password'
mysqladmin -u root -h hostname -p password 'password'
```

Note If you receive an error message that says you can't connect to the server when you try to run the second command, it may be because the MySQL server is not listening for connections via TCP/IP. Make sure the `skip-networking` option is not in the MySQL configuration file. If it is, you will need to remove that line and then restart the MySQL server.

An example of setting the `root` password is shown in Figure 4-12.

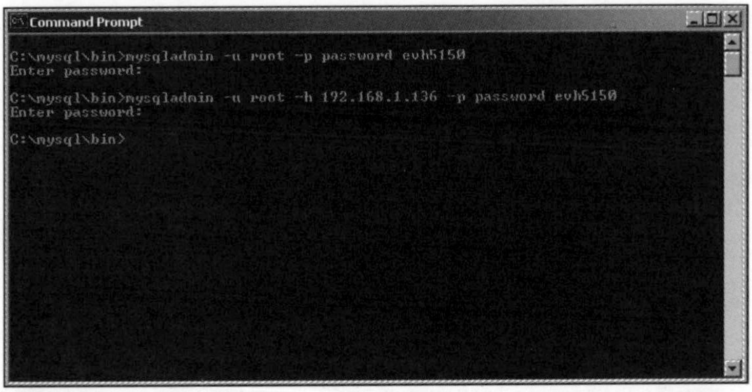

Figure 4-12: Setting the root password with mysqladmin is your first task as a Server Administrator.

Installing MySQL on Windows 2000

Installation of MySQL on Windows 2000 is incredibly simple. MySQL AB has gone to great lengths to ensure a hassle-free installation process.

The first step is to download the installation files or use the ones you can find on the CD-ROM with this book.

On the CD-ROM

The MySQL binary version for Windows is on the CD-ROM that accompanies this book.

Once the files are downloaded or copied, you'll need a program such as WinZip to uncompress the installation files (see Figure 4-13).

Double-click `setup.exe` to start MySQL installation. The installer for MySQL guides you through the procedure, wizard-style. Anyone who has installed a program in Windows should find this installation pretty straightforward.

After an initial Welcome screen, the installer presents you with an Information screen (see Figure 4-14). The information screen is there to remind you that if you change the locations of the directories for your MySQL components, you must create a `my.cnf` file in the root `C:\` directory that contains the location of the MySQL installation and data files.

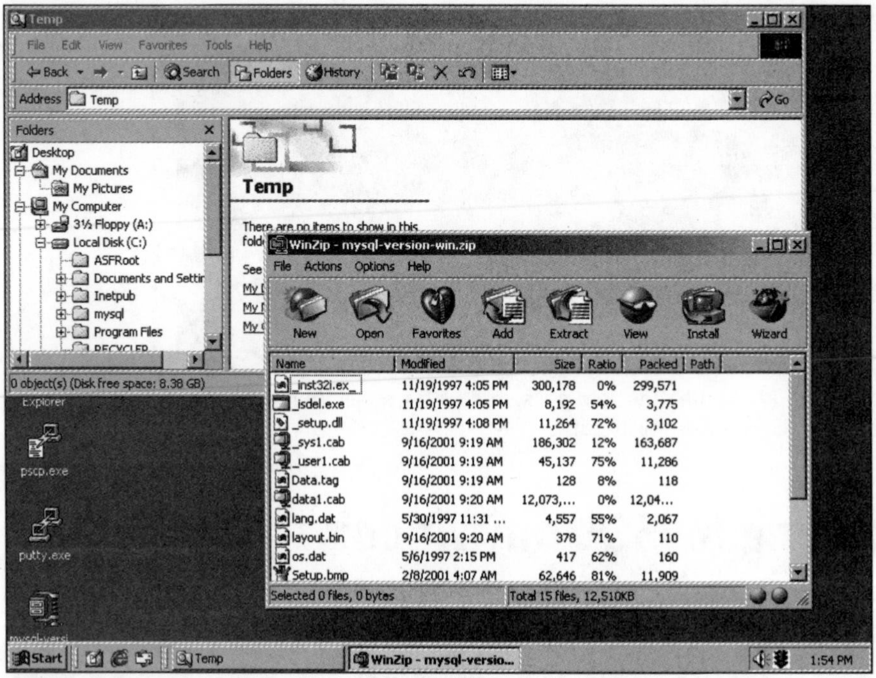

Figure 4-13: Use a program such as WinZip to uncompress the setup and installation files.

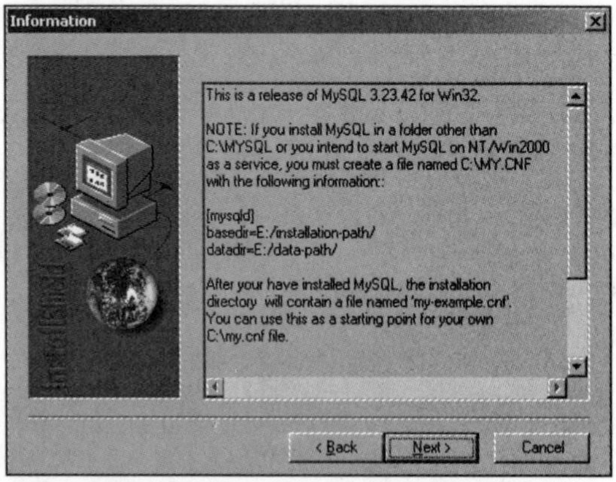

Figure 4-14: Create a my.cnf file if you change the location of the MySQL installation.

The next screen determines where you install the MySQL servers and clients, as shown in Figure 4-15. I recommend leaving it as `c:\mysql` unless you have a specific reason for not wanting to accept the default.

Note This chapter assumes that you use `c:\mysql` as your base directory. Should you choose to install into a different directory, please take that change into account and make the necessary adjustments when you follow the instructions herein.

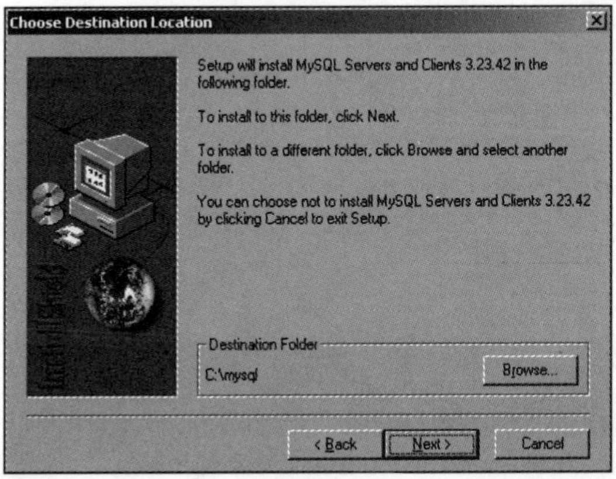

Figure 4-15: Determining where you want to install MySQL

Next is the prompt for installation type, Typical, Compact, or Custom. I recommend leaving the option at Typical (see Figure 4-16). The Typical option installs all components of MySQL. If you don't want to install all components, click the Custom radio button and you get a list of options to unselect (see Figure 4-17).

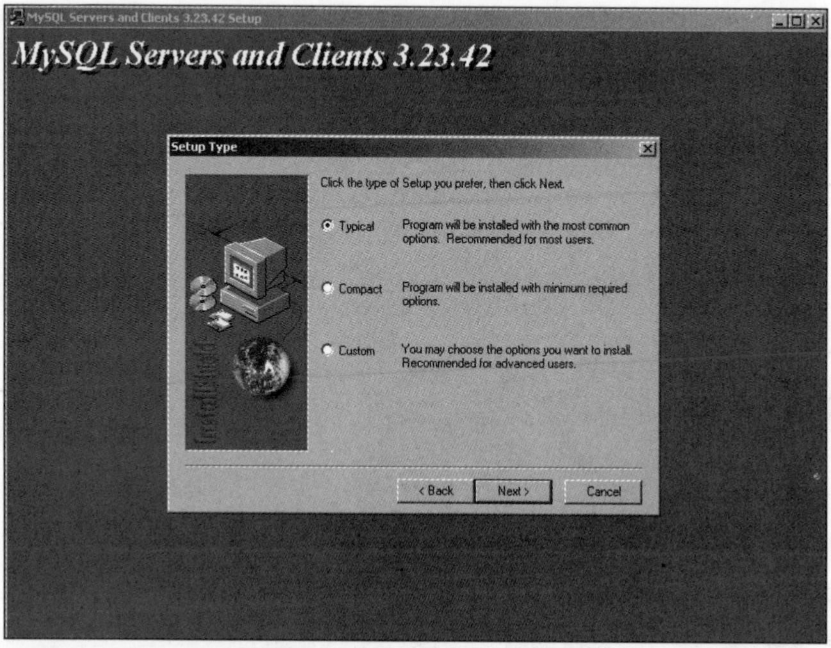

Figure 4-16: The Typical option installs all components and is the default.

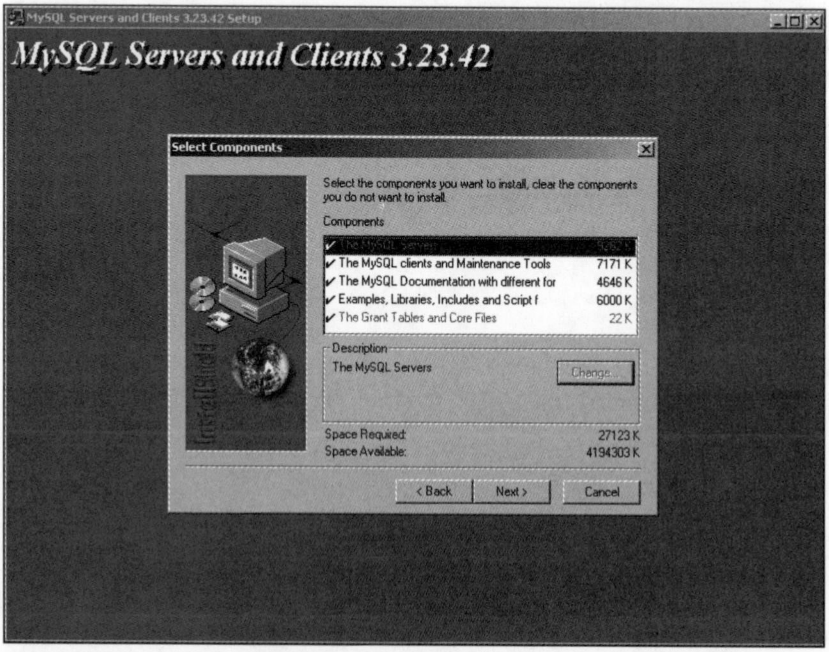

Figure 4-17: By selecting the Custom option, you can unselect components that you don't want to install.

Once you have chosen an installation option (Typical, Compact, or Custom), MySQL begins the installation by copying the appropriate files (see Figure 4-18).

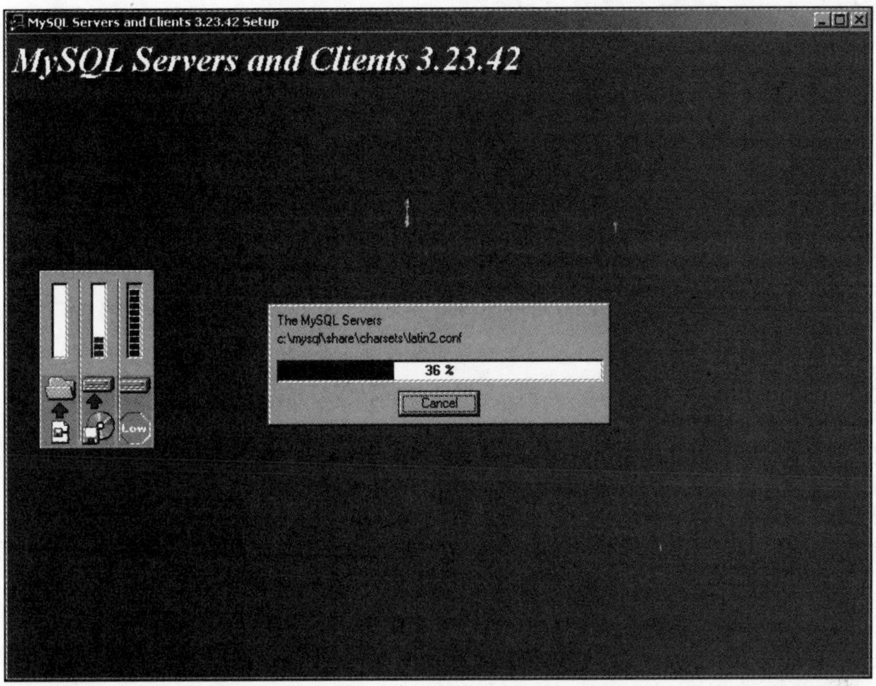

Figure 4-18: MySQL takes over and starts copying files as part of the installation process.

Congratulations! You should see a Finish screen — the step that concludes this stage of the installation (see Figure 4-19).

Note As I usually recommend with Windows, restart the server before going farther.

From here, you should make sure you've done the post-installation tasks (mentioned earlier in the chapter), including setting the `administrator/root` password and determining which binary version of MySQL to run.

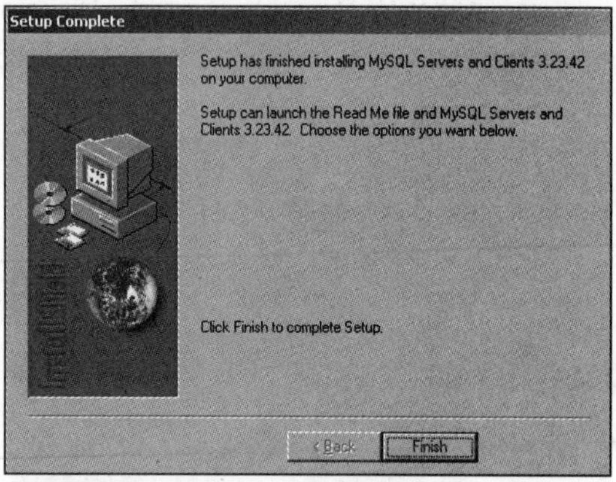

Figure 4-19: Finish up by clicking Finish and restarting the server.

Summary

Before you install MySQL, refer to Chapter 2 for a review of some important groundwork procedures. Then you can use an administrative utility (WinMySQLAdmin for Windows or `mysqladmin`) to install MySQL.

- ✦ With MySQL for Windows, you can use the WinMySQLAdmin program to administer most functions of a MySQL server via a GUI.
- ✦ Five different versions of MySQL are included with a standard binary distribution for Windows. You can choose which server to run by using the WinMySQLAdmin program or by editing the `my.ini` file.
- ✦ A number of options exist for the various components of a MySQL installation; you can set them in the `my.ini` file.
- ✦ Immediately after you start the MySQL server for the first time, you must set a password for the `root` user with the `mysqladmin` command.
- ✦ Should you change the default location of the MySQL installation, you must create a file called `my.cnf` in the `root` directory of the `C:` drive to tell MySQL the where to find the installation.
- ✦ Choosing a Typical installation type installs all components. If you don't actually need all the components, you can choose a Custom installation type and de-select any components you don't need.

✦ ✦ ✦

CHAPTER 5

Macintosh Installation

In This Chapter

Reviewing common tasks for binary and source-code MySQL Installations

Installing MySQL with Mac OS X Server

Installing MySQL binary on Mac OS X

Installing MySQL from source code on Mac OS X

Although traditionally the Macintosh has not been well suited for work as a server, this changed with the release of Mac OS X. Apple's next-generation operating system has a Unix-based foundation, which makes it a good choice for running servers and server applications.

Mac OS X comes in two versions:

- **Mac OS X Server:** This version comes with MySQL already installed.
- **Mac OS X:** No MySQL installed, but it can easily be installed.

This chapter looks at some tasks common to all versions of MySQL, as well as installing MySQL from source code.

Binary and Source-Code MySQL Installation in Mac OS X: Tasks in Common

There are several tasks that you may want to do no matter how you decide to install MySQL. MySQL can be configured to start automatically when Mac OS X is started, it can be manually shut down, and you can change the administrator password.

Setting up MySQL to start automatically

Mac OS X can start applications automatically when the system is booted — but its startup process differs significantly from that of a standard Unix system.

Mac OS X uses a `StartupItems` folder to automatically start applications; although a `/System/Library/StartupItems/` folder exists by default, that is reserved for Apple's use. Personal startup items should be located in the `/Library/StartupItems/` folder.

Creating the /Library/StartupItems folder

Because the `/Library/StartupItems/` folder doesn't exist by default, you must create it if someone else hasn't already.

1. Using the `cd` command, check to see whether this folder exists; if it does not, create it with the `mkdir` command. The code that accomplishes these preparations is as follows (bold indicates the commands to type):

   ```
   [localhost:~] user% cd /Library/StartupItems
   /Library/StartupItems: No such file or directory.
   [localhost:~] user% mkdir /Library/StartupItems/
   ```

2. Prepare to add a startup item to the folder by creating three things:
   - A folder with a descriptive name
   - A command-line script with the same name as the folder (see the steps in the upcoming subsection, "Creating the file for the startup script").
   - A startup parameters file (see the steps in the upcoming subsection, "Creating the `StartupParameters` file").

To create the folder, navigate to the /Library/StartupItems folder and create the new folder with the `mkdir` command.

```
[localhost:~] user% cd /Library/StartupItems/
[localhost:/Library/StartupItems] user% mkdir MySQL
```

You will have to use a text editor to create the files you need: one to contain the startup script and one to contain startup parameters.

Note: This example uses the `pico` text editor, which operates much like any other typical text editor: When you run `pico`, you can type and move around with the arrow keys. When you're done editing the file, simply press Control-X (the Mac equivalent of Ctrl+X) and a prompt asks whether you want to save the file and exit. Press Y to save the file and return to the command line.

Creating the file for the startup script

The first file needed for automatic startup is the *startup script* file. This is the shell script that will actually start MySQL.

1. Create the file and open it for editing in pico with the following command.

   ```
   [localhost:/Library/StartupItems] user% pico MySQL/MySQL
   ```

2. Enter the following script into pico.

```
#!/bin/sh

. /etc/rc.common

if [ "${MYSQL:=-NO-}" = "-YES-" ]; then

    ConsoleMessage "Starting MySQL"
    /usr/local/mysql/share/mysql/mysql.server start

fi
```

3. Use Command-X to exit and save the file.

Creating the StartupParameters file

The second file needed for automatic startup is the *startup parameters* file. This file gives Mac OS X additional information needed for automatically running MySQL.

1. Open the file by typing the following line.

```
[localhost:/Library/StartupItems] user% pico
MySQL/StartupParameters.plist
```

2. Enter the following script into pico.

```
{
  Description     = "MySQL";
  Provides        = ("MySQL");
  Requires        = ("Resolver");
  OrderPreference = "None";
  Messages =
  {
    start = "Starting MySQL";
    stop  = "Stopping MySQL";
  };
}
```

3. Use Command-X to exit and save the file.

4. The ownership and permissions of some files must be changed to securely run the startup item. You must use the sudo command to change ownership. Enter your administrator password when you are prompted for it.

```
[localhost:/Library/StartupItems] user% chmod +x MySQL/MySQL
[localhost:/Library/StartupItems] user% sudo chown -R root
MySQL/
Password:
```

Modifying the hostconfig file

The last thing you have to do is to modify the `hostconfig` file so it tells Mac OS X that you want to run this service. Follow these steps:

1. Enter the following command it will open up an existing file in pico.

```
[localhost:/Library/StartupItems] user% sudo pico
/etc/hostconfig
```

2. Scroll to the bottom of this file and enter MYSQL=-YES- on its own line. This is how it should look.

```
UW PICO(tm) 2.3                    File: /etc/hostconfig
Modified

# Services
AFPSERVER=-NO-
APPLETALK=-NO-
AUTHSERVER=-NO-
AUTOCONFIG=-YES-
AUTODISKMOUNT=-REMOVABLE-
AUTOMOUNT=-YES-
CONFIGSERVER=-NO-
IPFORWARDING=-NO-
MAILSERVER=-NO-
MANAGEMENTSERVER=-NO-
NETBOOTSERVER=-NO-
NISDOMAIN=-NO-
TIMESYNC=-NO-
QTSSERVER=-NO-
SSHSERVER=-NO-
WEBSERVER=-NO-
APPLETALK_HOSTNAME="User's Computer"
MYSQL=-YES-

^G Get Help  ^O WriteOut  ^R Read File ^Y Prev Pg   ^K Cut
Text  ^C Cur Pos
^X Exit      ^J Justify   ^W Where is  ^V Next Pg   ^U UnCut
Text^D Del Char
```

3. Use Command-X to exit and save the file.

When you have all these files in place and properly set up, MySQL is ready to start automatically every time you start up Mac OS X. If you ever want to stop MySQL from starting up automatically, simply edit the `hostconfig` file and change the line that reads `MYSQL=-YES-` to `MYSQL=-NO-`.

Shutting down MySQL Server

If you want to manually shut down the server, you should use the `mysqladmin` command.

Caution: A bug in versions of MySQL prior to 3.23.45 and 4.0.1 prevents the MySQL server from shutting down properly. Make sure you are using these versions or later.

To shut down the server, follow these steps:

1. Log in to the terminal as the `mysql` user.
2. Run the `mysqladmin` command with the `shutdown` parameter, as follows:

```
[localhost:~] mysql% /usr/local/mysql/bin/mysqladmin -u root
shutdown
020304 12:34:56  mysqld ended

[1]  + Done       /usr/local/mysql/bin/safe_mysqld --
user=mysql
[localhost:~] mysql%
```

Setting an administrator password for MySQL

The first step immediately after starting a MySQL server is to set a password for the server administrator account known as `root`.

Note: This user account is different from the `root` user on your system; setting the password for this user doesn't affect the password for the `root` user on your system.

The `mysqladmin` utility is used to set the initial password for the `root` user. To set the password, the command is run twice—once for the `localhost` connection and once for connections via the hostname. When the `mysqladmin` command is run, it will prompt you for the password. If you have not set the password, just press Enter without typing anything and the command will run successfully. The syntax to set the password with `mysqladmin` is as follows:

```
[localhost:local/mysql/sql-bench] mysql%
/usr/local/mysql/bin/mysqladmin \
 -u root password new_password
[localhost:local/mysql/sql-bench] mysql%
```

An example of setting the `root` password is shown in Figure 5-1.

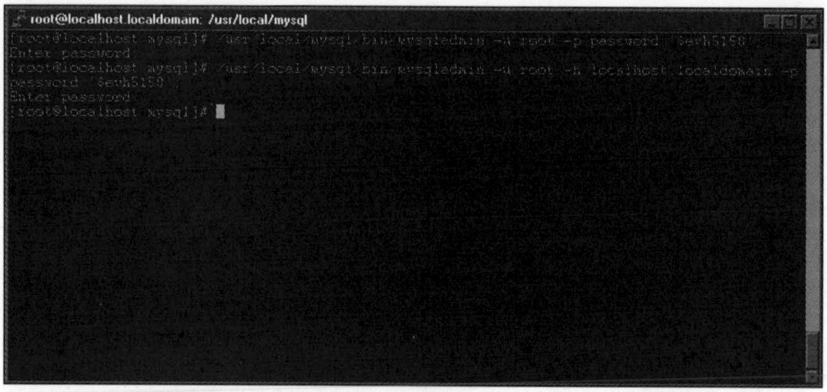

Figure 5-1: Setting the root password with mysqladmin is your first task as a server administrator.

Installing MySQL With Mac OS X Server

Apple includes MySQL with Mac OS X Server 10.0.4 and later. It is installed in the `/usr/local/mysql/` directory but it is neither configured nor set to run by default. Apple has several knowledge-base articles that cover how to install and configure MySQL on a Mac OS X server. To find them, go to Apple's support site at `http://www.apple.com/support/` and search the knowledge base for `"MySQL"`.

Refer to the section called "Binary and Source-Code MySQL Installation in Mac OS X: Tasks in Common" (earlier in this chapter) for more information on starting and stopping MySQL and setting a password for the `root` administrative user.

Installing MySQL Binary on Mac OS X

Compiling and installing your own version of MySQL can be a daunting process. There is an official binary distribution of MySQL for Mac OS X available for download and installation. Many people have created unofficial binary distributions of their own that can be used instead of the official version. Any of these binary versions may be used. They take less time to install and may not require the Apple developer tools to be installed. The drawbacks are that you have less control over the options used and the latest version of the MySQL code may not be available.

The latest official binary version of MySQL for Mac OS X can always be found at `http://www.mysql.com/`. Download the Mac OS X binary appropriate for your Mac OS (Mac OS X or Mac OS X Server).

One of the best independent OS X binary distributions has been created by Marc Liyanage and is available at his Web site (`http://www.entropy.ch/software/macosx/mysql/`).

Installation of each binary distribution is different. Download the installer package and follow the instructions for that distribution.

Installing MySQL Source Code on Mac OS X

The most flexible approach to installing MySQL for Mac OS X is to use the MySQL source code and compile it yourself.

You will need two basics to compile MySQL yourself:

- **The latest version of the MySQL source code.** This can always be found at `http://www.mysql.com/`. Download the "tarball" source package for MySQL.
- **Apple's developer tools.** If you don't already have these installed, they can be found on the Developer Tools CD that is included with every copy of Mac OS X or downloaded from `http://developer.apple.com/tools/`.

Once you have these prerequisites, you can proceed with the installation.

Creating the MySQL User

To run the MySQL server securely, you have to create a user account for the MySQL server itself. Follow these steps:

1. Open System Preferences and select the Users preference panel.
2. If you are not already logged in as an administrator, click the lock icon and enter an administrator name and password in the window shown in Figure 5-2.

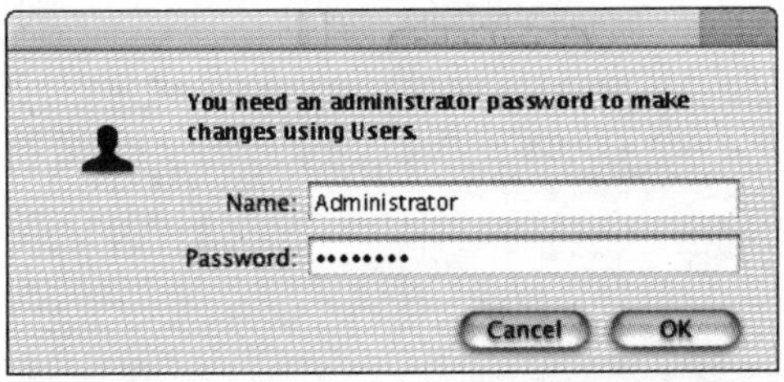

Figure 5-2: Entering the Administrator name and password

3. Click the New User button. Enter **mysql** for the Name and Short Name, as shown in Figure 5-3.

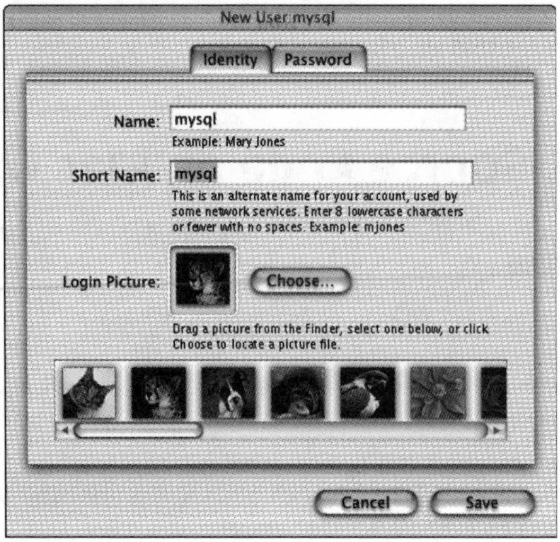

Figure 5-3: Entering the mysql user

4. Select the Password tab and enter a password for the `mysql` user, as shown in Figure 5-4.

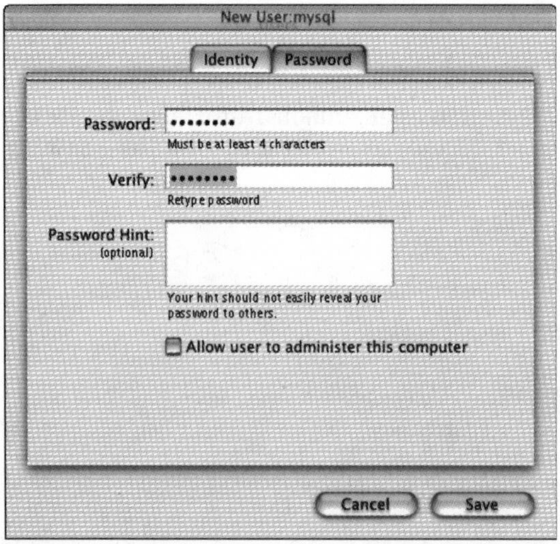

Figure 5-4: Entering the mysql password

5. Click Save and close System Preferences.

Compiling MySQL

The actual MySQL application is installed by unpacking, configuring, and compiling the code you have downloaded. The procedure looks like this:

1. Open the Terminal application and navigate to the location to which you downloaded the MySQL "tarball" source package, much like this:

```
[localhost:~] user% cd Desktop/
[localhost:~/Desktop] user% ls
mysql-VERSION.tar.gz
```

2. Use the `tar` command to expand the source package into its own folder:

```
[localhost:~/Desktop] user% tar zxvf mysql-VERSION.tar.gz
...
mysql-VERSION/support-files/mysql.server.sh
mysql-VERSION/support-files/binary-configure.sh
mysql-VERSION/support-files/magic
[localhost:~/Desktop] user%
```

3. Navigate into the new folder and run the `configure` script, which prepares the package to be compiled on your particular system:

```
[localhost:~/Desktop] user% cd mysql-VERSION/
[localhost:~/Desktop/mysql-VERSION] user% ./configure --
prefix=/usr/local/mysql
...
creating mysql-test/Makefile
creating include/mysql_version.h
creating config.h


[localhost:~/Desktop/mysql-VERSION] user%
```

4. Run the `make` command, which actually compiles the MySQL package.

Note: Compilation normally takes quite some time, even on a fast Macintosh.

The procedure looks like this:

```
[localhost:~/Desktop/mysql-VERSION] user% make
...
-e 's!''PERL_DATA_DUMPER''@!@PERL_DATA_DUMPER@!' \
binary-configure.sh > binary-configure-t
/bin/mv binary-configure-t binary-configure
make[2]: Nothing to be done for `all-am'.
[localhost:~/Desktop/mysql-VERSION] user%
```

5. Install MySQL by running the `make install` command. Since installing MySQL requires administrative privileges you must use the `sudo` command before you use the installation command. When the `sudo` command prompts you for a password, enter your Mac OS X administration password (see the second line of code in this snippet):

```
[localhost:~/Desktop/mysql-VERSION] user% sudo make install
Password:
...
/usr/bin/install -c -m 644 ./binary-configure
/usr/local/mysql/share/mysql/binary-configure
make[2]: Nothing to be done for `install-exec-am'.
make[2]: Nothing to be done for `install-data-am'.
[localhost:~/Desktop/mysql-VERSION] user%
```

Configuring MySQL

MySQL must be configured before it can be run. Run the `mysql_install_db` script with the `sudo` command to configure MySQL. The procedure looks like this:

1. Configure MySQL by running the `mysql_install_db` script with the `sudo` command. The procedure looks like this:

```
[localhost:~/Desktop/mysql-VERSION] user% sudo
scripts/mysql_install_db
Password:

...

To start mysqld at boot time you have to copy
support-files/mysql.server to the right place for your system

PLEASE REMEMBER TO SET A PASSWORD FOR THE MySQL root USER !
This is done with:
/usr/local/mysql/bin/mysqladmin -u root -p password 'new-
password'
/usr/local/mysql/bin/mysqladmin -u root -h localhost -p
password 'new-password'
See the manual for more instructions.

You can start the MySQL daemon with:
cd /usr/local/mysql ; /usr/local/mysql/bin/safe_mysqld &

You can test the MySQL daemon with the benchmarks in the
'sql-bench' directory:
cd sql-bench ; run-all-tests

Please report any problems with the
/usr/local/mysql/bin/mysqlbug script!

The latest information about MySQL is available on the Web at
http://www.mysql.com
Support MySQL by buying support/licenses at
https://order.mysql.com
[localhost:~/Desktop/mysql-VERSION] user%
```

2. You must change the ownership of a file and a folder in order to run MySQL. Use the `chown` command with `sudo` to do so, as follows:

```
[localhost:~/Desktop/mysql-VERSION] user% sudo chown -R root
/usr/local/mysql
[localhost:~/Desktop/mysql-VERSION] user% sudo chown -R mysql
/usr/local/mysql/var
```

Testing MySQL

You should test your installation to make sure everything installed correctly. Do so by starting the MySQL server and having it display its version, as follows:

1. To start the MySQL server, you have to log in as the `mysql` user you created earlier. You can do so with the `su` command. Enter the `mysql` user's password when you are prompted for it, as shown in the second line of the code snippet that follows:

```
[localhost:~] user% su - mysql
Password:
[localhost:~] mysql%
[localhost:~] mysql% /usr/local/mysql/bin/safe_mysqld --
user=mysql &
[1] 14542


[localhost:~] mysql%
[localhost:~] mysql% Starting mysqld daemon with databases
from /usr/local/mysql/var
```

2. Once MySQL is running, check it by using the `mysqladmin` command to check the version of the MySQL server. The procedure looks like this:

```
[localhost:~] mysql% /usr/local/mysql/bin/mysqladmin version
/usr/local/mysql/bin/mysqladmin  Ver 8.23 Distrib 3.23.49,
for apple-darwin5.3
on powerpc
Copyright (C) 2000 MySQL AB & MySQL Finland AB & TCX
DataKonsult AB
This software comes with ABSOLUTELY NO WARRANTY. This is free
software,
and you are welcome to modify and redistribute it under the
GPL license

Server version          3.23.49
Protocol version        10
Connection              Localhost via UNIX socket
UNIX socket             /tmp/mysql.sock
Uptime:                 1 min 30 sec

Threads: 1  Questions: 1  Slow queries: 0  Opens: 5  Flush
tables: 1  Open tables: 0
Queries per second avg: 0.011
```

Summary

A number of installation tasks must be performed regardless of installation method. These include configuring MySQL for automatic startup and shutdown, and setting the `root` administrator password for MySQL.

- ✦ Mac OS X Server includes MySQL preinstalled; not much configuration is necessary.
- ✦ There is an official MySQL binary installation for Mac OS X as well as several unofficial independent binary distributions (the most notable of which is Marc Liyanage's).
- ✦ The advantages of binary distributions (less time, simpler) have to be weighed against the disadvantages (less control, latest versions may not be available).
- ✦ Installing MySQL from source code is the most configurable method; options are available even during compilation, and editing the source code directly is the most efficient way to customize your implementation of MySQL.

✦ ✦ ✦

CHAPTER 6

Starting MySQL

MySQL is a large and often complex collection of client and server software to store and retrieve data. Sometimes a person who is new to MySQL or SQL entirely is overwhelmed by the depth and number of options involved with what seems to be a simple database task. In this chapter I'll cover some of the basic concepts that developers and administrators alike will probably encounter. My goal is to help the reader become comfortable with MySQL and show some of the common day-to-day tasks performed with MySQL.

✦ ✦ ✦ ✦

In This Chapter

Introducing MySQL server administration and security

Trying out frequently used MySQL database functions

✦ ✦ ✦ ✦

MySQL Server Administration and Security

This section shows you some common and useful commands that can get a MySQL server running and to keep it running. The first of these — `mysqladmin` — is critically important, frequently used by administrators, and one you should always run on a newly installed MySQL server to ensure the security of the `root` "superuser" account.

Also, though MySQL is a very stable application (even in large implementations), sooner or later you may face common administrative challenges such as these:

- Preventing, limiting, or undoing the effects of a security breach
- Integrating new components into the system
- Removing (or changing the privileges granted to) specific user accounts
- Dealing with trouble reports from users who encounter problems with the database

The versatile `mysqladmin` command is a good starting point for understanding and implementing good security and sound administrative policy. This section explores some of its major uses.

Using mysqladmin

You can use `mysqladmin` to accomplish various goals, such as

- ✦ Restoring or enhancing the security of the `root` account
- ✦ Determining the status of the MySQL server while it's running
- ✦ Shutting down the server for upgrades or emergency hardware replacements

This section gives you a glimpse of what you can do with this useful command.

A very useful administration program for MySQL is `mysqladmin`. With `mysqladmin`, the operator can perform many administrative functions without having to enter into the MySQL Command Line Interface (CLI). For example, databases can be created and dropped via `mysqladmin`, and the server can be diagnosed or even shut down. Chapter 10 will cover `mysqladmin` in greater detail. For now I'll concentrate on a few useful options to get you started.

Setting the root password

As shown in Chapters 3 through 5, the `mysqladmin` command is what you use to set up the initial password for the `root` user in MySQL, and that is the first thing you should do once you get a MySQL server running. To set the `root` password, issue the following command:

```
mysqladmin -u root password 'newpassword'
```

If the password has already been set for the `root` user, you must add the `-p` switch to the command and provide the existing password when prompted. Doing so looks like this:

```
mysqladmin -u root -p password 'mY$qL53'
Enter password:
```

Note Choose a password carefully. Passwords based on dictionary words (or which are otherwise easily guessable) are not acceptable for most environments. For better data protection, choose a password that is at least 6 characters and includes non-alphanumeric characters.

Most operations with `mysqladmin` require the `-p` switch to be set. If the `-p` switch is not set, you will probably see an error message (as shown in Figure 6-1):

Figure 6-1: Common error message when password (-p) is not specified

Checking MySQL server status

You can use `mysqladmin` to check the status of the MySQL server via the `ping` switch. The command looks like this:

```
mysqladmin -p ping
```

A brief status summary of the MySQL server is available via the `status` switch. An extended version of the `status` switch is `extended-status` (covered in Chapter 10). The output of the `status` statement will look something like Figure 6-2, in which the uptime for this particular server is 1350 seconds (of course, this server isn't very busy—only one thread running and no open tables).

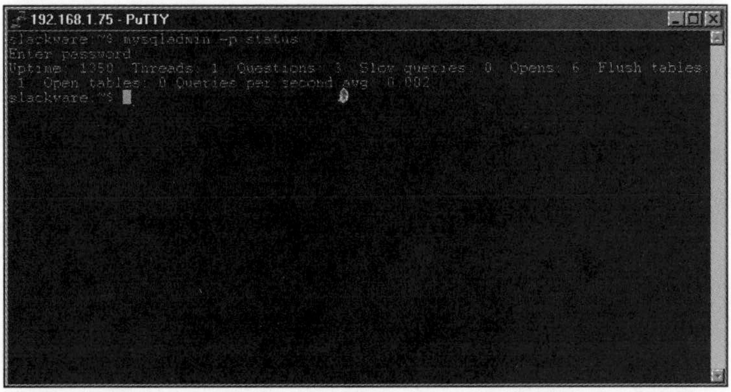

Figure 6-2: Output of the mysqladmin status statement

Note Your `status` output can (and probably will) be substantially different from what's shown here.

Dealing with inactive connections

Sometimes clients connect to the MySQL server but don't disconnect. As a result, the server can quickly exceed its maximum number of connections (especially if it's normally busy) in which case MySQL refuses further client connections till the traffic lets up.

The number of connections allowed in MySQL varies according to the system hardware, but the administrator can also set some variables to limit. I cover different size implementations in another chapter. To find out what connections are active to the MySQL server, use the `processlist` switch as shown in Figure 6-3:

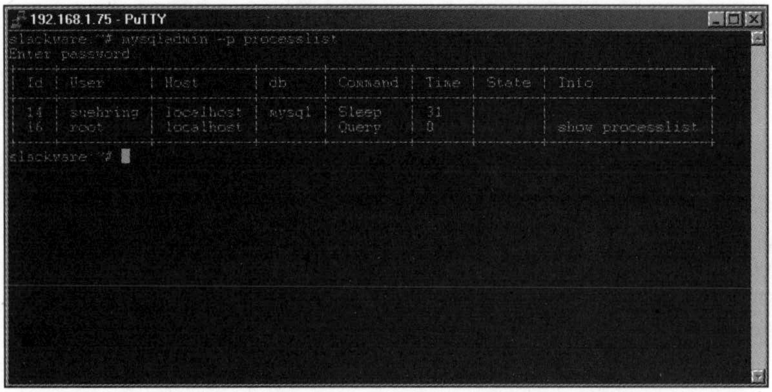
192.168.1.75 - PuTTY
slackware:~# mysqladmin -p processlist
Enter password:
Id	User	Host	db	Command	Time	State	Info
14	suehring	localhost	mysql	Sleep	31		
16	root	localhost		Query	0		show processlist
slackware:~#

Figure 6-3: Output of the mysqladmin processlist statement

From the output in Figure 6-3, you can see a user named `suehring` is connected from `localhost` to the `mysql` database. The user is currently idle, as shown by the word `sleep` under the `Command` column. Also shown is the `root` user running a query to show the `processlist`.

With the `mysqladmin kill` command, you can end a connection to the MySQL database as well. The syntax for killing a connection is a follows:

```
mysqladmin kill <id>
```

For example, to kill `suehring`'s connection to the database, you would issue the following command:

```
mysqladmin -p kill 14
```

Looking at the `processlist` output in Figure 6-4 you can see that the connection by `suehring` no longer exists:

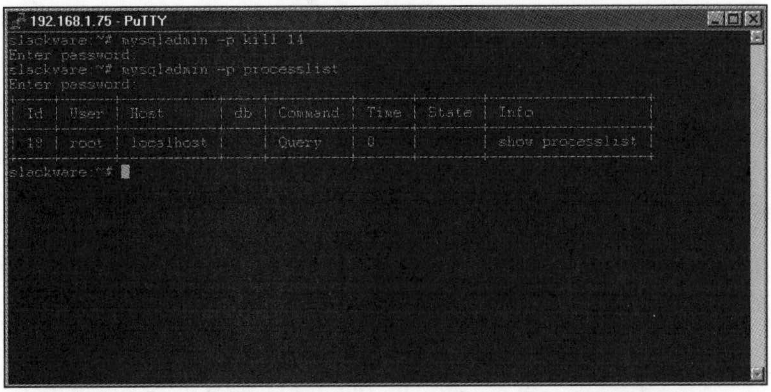
192.168.1.75 - PuTTY
slackware:~# mysqladmin -p kill 14
Enter password:
slackware:~# mysqladmin -p processlist
Enter password:
| Id | User | Host | db | Command | Time | State | Info |
| 18 | root | localhost | | Query | 0 | | show processlist |
slackware:~#

Figure 6-4: A processlist statement after a thread has been killed

If `suehring` was connected via the MySQL CLI, the user will receive the following message when they attempt to perform an operation:

```
ERROR 2006: MySQL server has gone away
No connection. Trying to reconnect...
```

If the connection attempt is successful, the connection is issued a new ID and the operation is executed, as shown by the new `processlist` in Figure 6-5:

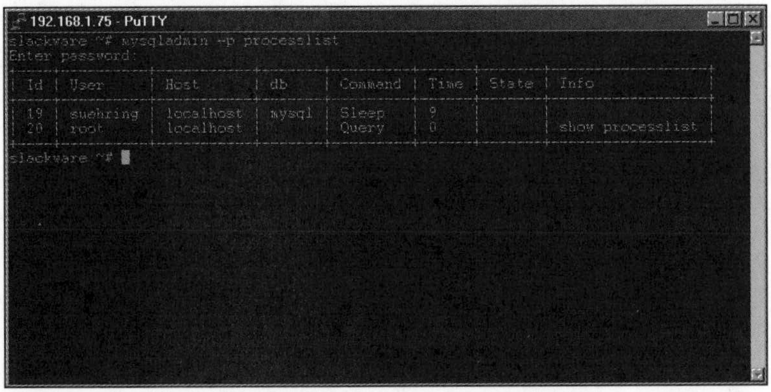
192.168.1.75 - PuTTY
slackware:~# mysqladmin -p processlist
Enter password:
Id	User	Host	db	Command	Time	State	Info
19	suehring	localhost	mysql	Sleep	9		
20	root	localhost		Query	0		show processlist
slackware:~#

Figure 6-5: A new connection was created for the user.

Shut down the server

mysqladmin can also be used to shut down the MySQL server. The syntax is intuitive for this operation:

```
mysqladmin -p shutdown
```

mysqladmin has a wide range of such useful switches, which provide the versatility that an administrative tool must have.

Basic MySQL security

One of the first things you should do as a MySQL database administrator is change the root password. Accomplishing this task with mysqladmin is explained in Chapters 3, 4, and 5 depending on your installation and is covered in this chapter as well. If you have not already done so, now is the time to configure a secure root password for your MySQL server. No amount of database security will help if the root account can connect with a blank password or no password at all!

Another important, but sometimes overlooked, area of security for MySQL is the security of the machine that houses the MySQL server. If that computer, regardless of operating system, is not kept secure by applying the latest patches and rigorously maintaining security, no amount of database security will keep your data safe. If possible, utilize a firewall to prevent outside connections to the MySQL server or restrict connections to the MySQL server machine in another way such as netfilter or ipchains in Linux or via an access list on a router.

Numerous options exist for the way that the MySQL server itself is run. Those options are beyond the scope of this chapter but are covered in another chapter . Some options to consider when starting the server are the --skip-networking option which prevents the server from listen for network connections and the --skip-show-database option which prevents users from showing the names of the databases available on the server.

Adding a user to MySQL

It is neither customary nor wise to give a mechanic the keys to your house so he or she can fix your car; doing so only creates unnecessary risks. The same can be said for granting access to your data: Using MySQL's root user account to perform everyday database operations is a bad idea. It is much more preferable to grant only the necessary access to specific users. Only allow as many privileges as are necessary for each user to complete his or her job.

MySQL access is based on a privilege system. MySQL holds an internal database aptly titled mysql with tables for housing privilege data called user, host, db, tables_priv, and columns_priv. A given user's access to data can be defined down to which columns the user can perform operations on in a particular database table.

For example, a user created for accessing product information for a Web site can be given read access to the product name and price columns in the inventory database's product table. In this manner, if a malicious or even well intentioned user were to gain access to your data through that username and password, they could only read the data and not modify it.

As stated above, access is based upon a privilege system. Privileges are granted and revoked based upon the username, host connecting from, operation requested, database, table, and column. Since MySQL holds the privilege data within tables, normal insert, delete, select, and update operations work as expected.

The basic statement to add a user and allow access to MySQL is the `grant` statement. Recall from my discussion on conventions used in this book that brackets such as <> denote required portions of syntax for the command, square brackets such as `[]` denote additional modifiers and parentheses such as `()` denote optional portions of commands. The syntax for the `grant` statement is as follows:

```
GRANT <privilege [ column(s) ] ( , privilege [ column(s) ] )> to
<user>(@host) (IDENTIFIED BY 'password') [ WITH GRANT OPTION ];
```

MySQL provides a couple of macros for assigning common privileges. These include `all` and `usage`. By using the `all` macro, you grant all possible privileges to a user (as you may imagine, it's best to use this one sparingly). The `usage` macro is for adding a user account to MySQL without granting any privileges (and it's probably best not to leave it that way, since a user without privileges can't do anything on the system, including work).

As an example, I'll show you how to add a more-or-less typical user account to MySQL—after which you can use it throughout the book to try out many database operations. Although you don't grant this sample user account any privileges, you would add privileges in a real network situation (or there would be no reason to create the user). Adding users and granting privileges is covered in more detail in later chapters, including Chapter 12.

Connect to the `mysql` database as the `root` user from the MySQL CLI, as follows:

```
mysql -u root -p mysql

mysql> grant usage on *.* to dbuser@localhost identified by
'evh$5150';
Query OK, 0 rows affected (0.01 sec)
```

Note **It is not necessary to connect to the mysql database in order to grant and revoke access to the database via the `grant` and `revoke` statements.**

Later on in the chapter, a different exercise adds specific privileges for this user account so it can connect to the database that you're about to create.

Frequently Used MySQL Database Functions

Many of the functions that you use often with MySQL are covered in this section. Having worked with databases and MySQL for years, I encounter the same tasks on a frequent basis: Inserting and updating data, as well as simple selecting, are the bread and butter of many database operators and administrators' livelihoods. Even if you don't create databases often, you'll probably create one with MySQL at some point. Therefore this section shows you how to create your first database, offers a few sample tables, and lays out the building blocks for understanding Structured Query Language (SQL).

Creating a database

Although the full syntax of the MySQL client interface can be about as complex as you need it to be (it's covered in Chapter 8), creating a database in MySQL is actually pretty simple.

Note: As a prerequisite for creating a MySQL database, make sure your MySQL software is installed and running already. (If it's not, refer to Chapter 3, 4, or 5 to install the version of MySQL that's appropriate for your platform.)

There are two ways to create a database with MySQL:

- via the 'mysqladmin' command, like this:

```
mysqladmin (-p) create inventory
```

- from within the MySQL CLI, using the following syntax:

```
CREATE DATABASE [ if not exists ] <databasename>
```

Note: The `if not exists` keyword produces an error message if a database already exists with the name given.

Recall that statements can span multiple lines in the MySQL CLI, and that you terminate a statement with a semicolon (;). Therefore, to create an example database from within the MySQL CLI, type the following:

```
mysql> create database inventory;
Query OK, 1 row affected (0.00 sec)
```

The next step is to create tables within the database you just created. To create tables, you'll need to connect to the actual database you want to use. MySQL actually does not require you to be connected to the database in order to create tables. Although you can create tables by using a *<databasename.tablename>* syntax from within the MySQL CLI, it's often less confusing (which saves debugging time) if you connect to the database itself. If you are already within the MySQL CLI, you can type the following:

```
mysql> connect inventory;
Connection id:    10
Current database: inventory
```

If you are at the command prompt, you can get into the MySQL CLI and connect to the database by issuing the following command:

```
mysql -u <username> -p <databasename>
```

For example, here's one that connects the `root` account to the `inventory` database:

```
mysql -u root -p inventory
```

Creating tables

Regardless of the method you choose, working with the database via the MySQL CLI means you can create tables to store information for a Web site. Before you can create the tables, however, you need a design for the database.

Cross-Reference For help with developing a database design, review Chapter 7.

Assessing the needs of your site can suggest a practical direction for database design. For example, the Web site e-commerce database must track a range of different variables — including name of product, type of product, manufacturer, price, and quantity on hand. The initial design calls for three individual tables within the database; Tables 6-1, 6-2, and 6-3 provide examples of how such tables contribute to the design of the example database.

Table 6-1
Product Table

Column Title	*Column Type*	*Constraints*
product_id	int	not-null primary key auto_increment
name	varchar(75)	
quantity	int	
price	decimal(9,2)	

Table 6-2
Manufacturer Table

Column Title	*Column Type*	*Constraints*
`manufacturer_id`	`int`	not-null primary key `auto_increment`
`name`	`varchar(50)`	

Table 6-3
Category Table

Column Title	*Column Type*	*Constraints*
`category_id`	`int`	not-null primary key `auto_increment`
`product_category`	`varchar(50)`	

The basic syntax for table creation in MySQL is as follows:

```
CREATE [ temporary ] TABLE [ if not exists ] <tablename>
[ ( <column definition,> ... ) ] [ <table options> ] [ <select
statement> ]
```

The *temporary* keyword creates a table that exists only for the duration of the connection.

✦ If there is a table of the same name, the existing table is hidden.

✦ Two separate connections can utilize the same temporary table name.

The `if not exists` keyword prevents the table from being created if a table of the same name exists. MySQL only verifies the name of the table and does not attempt to verify if the table structures are the same. When the `if not exists` keyword is used, the operation returns an `OK` regardless of the success or failure of the statement.

As indicated by the brackets (`[ ]`) around the column definition, it is not necessary to add all of the definitions for the columns when creating a table. At least one column definition is required. The column definition can be modified later through the use of the `ALTER TABLE` statement.

table options are used to create different types of tables. The basic table types with MySQL are `ISAM`, `MyISAM` and `heap`. Some table types, including `bdb` (`Berkeley_db`), `Gemini`, and `innodb` may or may not be included with your MySQL distribution, depending on the version of MySQL you have and the options chosen while compiling (if applicable). Table 6-4 illustrates the types of tables in MySQL.

Caution `MyISAM` is the default table type in MySQL. If you try to create a table using a table type that is not supported by your version, MySQL creates it as `MyISAM` instead—with no warning or error message (though future versions of MySQL will produce a warning when the table type is not supported).

Table 6-4
MySQL Table Types

Table Type	*Attribute*
`bdb` or `Berkeley_db`	Transactional, page-locking.
`gemini`	Transactional, row-level locking, not open-source. Available with NuSphere MySQL.
`heap`	Data is only stored in volatile memory.
`isam`	Normal or standard table.
`innodb`	Another type of transactional, row-level locking table.
`merge`	Collection of `MyISAM` tables to be used as a single table.
`myisam`	As the newer version of `isam`, this is the default table type.

You can help ensure the safety of your data by using a transactional table type such as `bdb`, `Gemini`, or `innodb`, and here's why:

- ✦ If a problem occurs within the database or system housing the database, the data within a transactional table can be recovered through the use of a rollback or the backup and update logs.
- ✦ Changes made to data can be rolled back or automatically undone if a portion of the update fails.

Note Transactional tables require more disk space, memory usage, and processor usage than `MyISAM` tables.

The example database will not need enhancements of transactional tables, therefore the default MyISAM table type will be acceptable.

Cross-Reference More information on table types is available in Chapter 10.

For example, to create all three of the example tables, you would type in the following code:

```
CREATE TABLE product (
product_id int not null primary key auto_increment,
name varchar(75),
quantity int,
price decimal(9,2)
);

CREATE TABLE manufacturer (
manufacturer_id int not null primary key auto_increment,
name varchar(50)
);

CREATE TABLE category (
category_id int not null primary key auto_increment,
product_category varchar(50)
);
```

The constraints placed on the `id` columns in the tables create a primary key, which is not tied specifically to any real-world use. Accordingly, it's both safe and desirable to `auto_increment` the value as new records are added to the table.

You now have a working database system that can track inventory for an e-commerce Web site.

Inserting and updating data

A database is only as useful as the data it contains. Therefore, you need to add products to the inventory database. In this section I'll look at how to insert data as well as how to update the data, which is often just as important as the initial insert of the data itself.

Inserting data

You're ready to insert a few records into the database. You'll accomplish this task via the MySQL CLI. You can insert data into a database via a number of methods including importing from a file or inserting through a program or script. Those topics are covered elsewhere in this book. For now, the MySQL CLI will work because you are only going to add a few records. The basic syntax for an insert is as follows:

```
INSERT [ low_priority | delayed ] [ ignore ] [ into ]
<tablename>
[ ( <columnname>, ...) ] VALUES (<insert expression>,)
```

Cross-Reference

Other syntax for the insert statement is discussed in Chapter 9 and in Appendix A.

The low_priority keyword delays the insert until no other clients are reading from the table. Use of the low_priority keyword is not recommended for MyISAM table types because simultaneous inserts are not possible in such usage.

Use the delayed keyword if some clients cannot wait for an insert to complete. This keyword only works with ISAM and MyISAM table types. The client receives an OK for the statement immediately, and the insert is run when the table is not in use by another thread.

Specifying the ignore keyword causes duplicate rows to be ignored and not entered when a value collides with a primary key or unique value. If this keyword is not specified, an error occurs and the insert is aborted. It is important to note that records will be inserted up to the record where the collision occurred. For example, if you import a number of records and a collision occurs at record number 432, all records up to number 432 will be inserted into the database.

The into keyword is not required, though it can be useful for improving readability.

Note If you don't want to insert values into all columns in a table, specify the column names in parentheses, separated by commas, before you type the required VALUE keyword.

You can now insert a few rows of data into the example database; the SQL for the insert is as follows:

```
INSERT into product VALUES (NULL, "8 inch Mirror Ball", 48,
14.95);
INSERT into product VALUES (NULL, "AM100 4 port Mixer", 12,
48.95);
INSERT into product VALUES (NULL, "FA1201 1200 watt Amplifier",
4, 149.95);
```

The sample data just given shows the most common type of insert. Notice that you placed the keyword NULL in the first value. Recall that the first column in the table definition is product_id, which is an auto-incrementing field; therefore, it is not acceptable to enter a value for this field. The NULL keyword is used as a placeholder in this example and will be substituted automatically with the correct value by MySQL.

Selecting data

Because selecting is at least as common as inserting, I'll jump ahead slightly and use a simple SELECT statement. Figure 6-6 shows the three records you just entered.

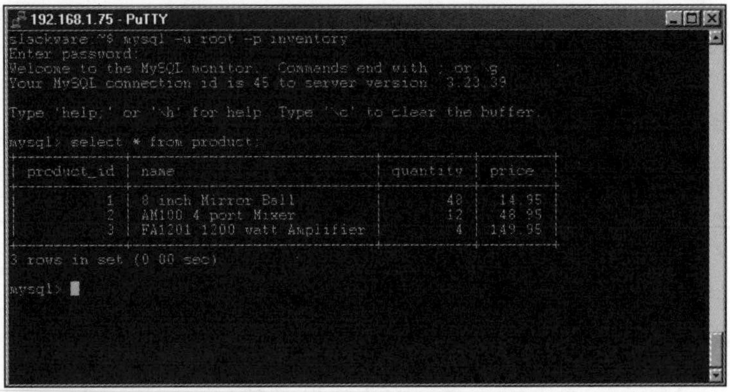
192.168.1.75 - PuTTY
slackware:~$ mysql -u root -p inventory
Enter password:
Welcome to the MySQL monitor. Commands end with ; or \g.
Your MySQL connection id is 45 to server version: 3.23.39
Type 'help;' or '\h' for help. Type '\c' to clear the buffer.
mysql> select * from product;
product_id	name	quantity	price
1	8 inch Mirror Ball	48	14.95
2	AM100 4 port Mixer	12	48.95
3	FA1201 1200 watt Amplifier	4	149.95
3 rows in set (0.00 sec)
mysql>

Figure 6-6: Sample output of a basic SELECT statement

Cross-Reference For the full syntax of the `SELECT` statement, see Chapter 9.

Since I'm looking to jumpstart your usage of MySQL, the basic syntax for the `SELECT` statement is as follows:

```
SELECT <select phrase> [ FROM <table(s)> [ WHERE <where phrase> ]
[ GROUP BY <group-by clause> ] [ORDER BY <order-by clause> ]
[ LIMIT # of rows ] ]
```

The example above selects all columns and rows from the product table.

Use of the `where` clause modifies the select statement to look only for rows that match the *<where phrase>*. For example, if you wanted to look for products that had a price less than $30.00 you could issue the statement in Figure 6-7.

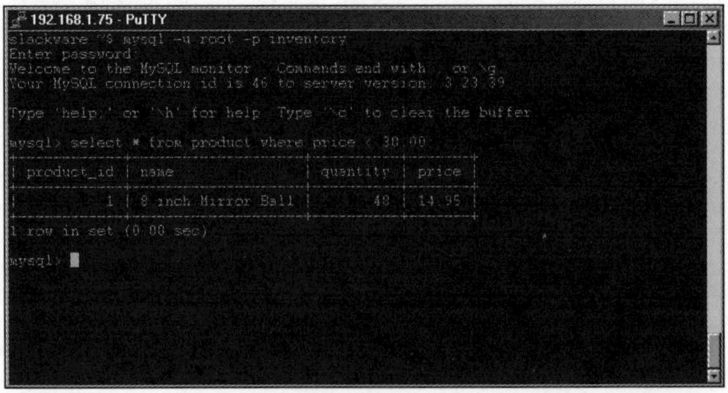
192.168.1.75 - PuTTY
slackware:~$ mysql -u root -p inventory
Enter password:
Welcome to the MySQL monitor. Commands end with ; or \g.
Your MySQL connection id is 46 to server version: 3.23.39
Type 'help;' or '\h' for help. Type '\c' to clear the buffer.
mysql> select * from product where price < 30.00;
| product_id | name | quantity | price |
| 1 | 8 inch Mirror Ball | 48 | 14.95 |
1 row in set (0.00 sec)
mysql>

Figure 6-7: Selecting records that show a price less than $30.00.

The `where` clause is extremely useful (and almost constantly in use) whenever you work with data in a MySQL database.

The `group by` clause modifies the results of the select by ordering the columns by similar data. The `order by` clause arranges the resulting data from a select statement into the order specified by the order-by clause. For example, to select all the products in order by price (from lowest to highest), you issue the statement like the following (its results are shown in Figure 6-8):

```
select * from product order by price;
```

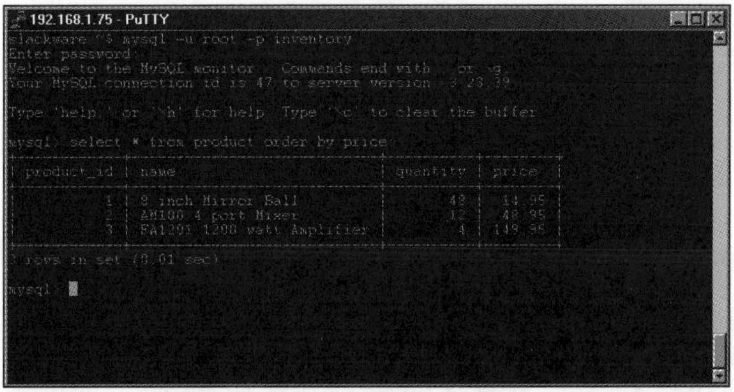
192.168.1.75 - PuTTY
slackware ~$ mysql -u root -p inventory
Enter password:
Welcome to the MySQL monitor. Commands end with ; or \g.
Your MySQL connection id is 47 to server version: 3.23.39
Type 'help;' or '\h' for help. Type '\c' to clear the buffer
mysql> select * from product order by price;
product_id	name	quantity	price
1	8 inch Mirror Ball	48	14.95
2	AM100 4 port Mixer	12	48.95
3	FA1201 1200 watt Amplifier	4	149.95
3 rows in set (0.01 sec)
mysql>

Figure 6-8: Selecting records in a certain order

Note It just happens that the price is in order of product ID for the example database. Such a neat result rarely happens with live data.

If you had a large amount of data in a table and you needed to look at the first *n* rows of data, you could do so by adding the `limit` clause onto the end of the `SELECT` statement. An example is shown in Figure 6-9.

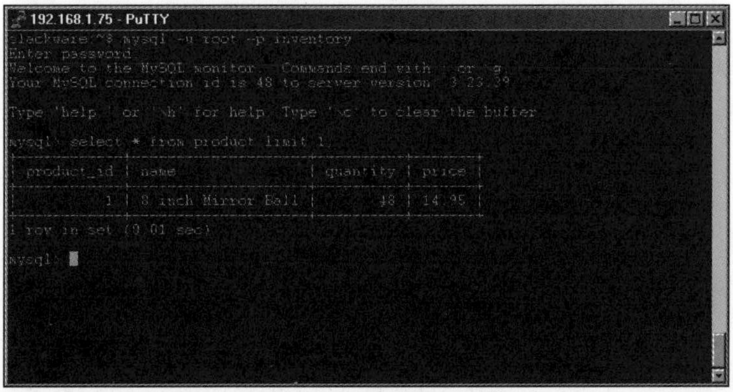
192.168.1.75 - PuTTY
slackware ~$ mysql -u root -p inventory
Enter password:
Welcome to the MySQL monitor. Commands end with ; or \g.
Your MySQL connection id is 48 to server version: 3.23.39
Type 'help;' or '\h' for help. Type '\c' to clear the buffer
mysql> select * from product limit 1;
| product_id | name | quantity | price |
| 1 | 8 inch Mirror Ball | 48 | 14.95 |
1 row in set (0.01 sec)
mysql>

Figure 6-9: Limiting rows of a SELECT statement

Cross-Reference There are many more options for the `SELECT` statement. Those options, along with additional coverage of the `where`, `group_by`, `order_by`, and `limit` clauses, appear in greater detail in Chapter 9 and in Appendix A.

Updating data

Updating your data is just as important as inserting the original data—if not more so. Commonly used syntax for the `UPDATE` statement looks like this:

```
UPDATE <tablename> SET <columnname> = <value> ( , <columnname>
= <value> ) [ WHERE <where phrase> ] [ LIMIT <# of rows> ];
```

For example, to update the price of one of the products you could do the following:

```
update product set price = '15.95' where product_id = '1';
```

Figure 6-10 shows the output of a `SELECT` statement that enables the administrator to look at that product after updating.

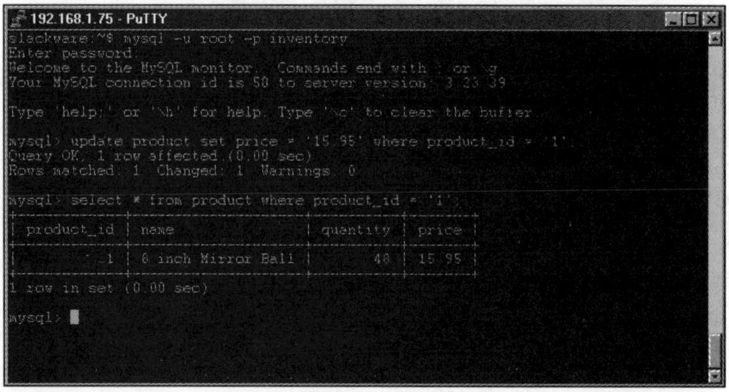

Figure 6-10: The updated product is now shown in the database

If you wanted to update both the price and quantity of a product, you could do so with the following example:

```
update product set price = '14.95',quantity = '60' where
product_id = '1';
```

Figure 6-11 shows the final table. Notice the price for the "`8 inch Mirror Ball`" is once again $14.95 and the quantity is now 60.

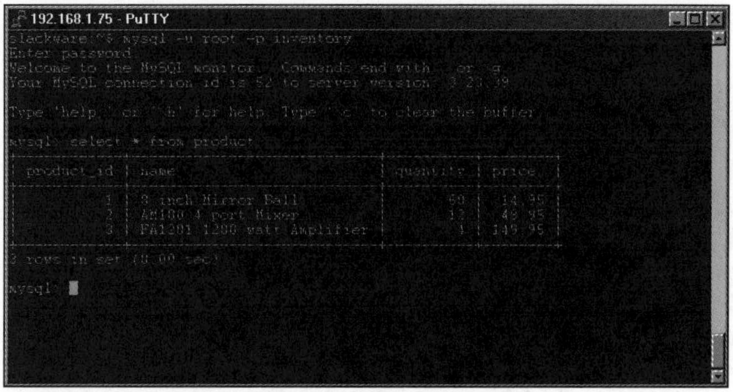

Figure 6-11: The final table layout after updates

Preparing a new user for access to the database

Up until now you've been doing the inserts, selects, and updates in the inventory database as the `root` user. Recall (from a bit earlier in this chapter) that you added a user to the database but you couldn't grant any access rights since you didn't have the database built. It's now time to allow the new user access to the `inventory` database.

Since you've already added the user account, you can utilize the `update` statement to revise the permissions and privileges for that user. If you are still in the MySQL CLI, connect to the database called `mysql` by typing the following:

```
connect mysql;
```

The statement should have similar output to this:

```
Connection id:    X
Current database: mysql
```

You are now connected to the `'mysql'` database, which holds the grant tables for privileges within the server across all databases.

> **Note** You could have remained connected to the `inventory` database and still granted privileges. For simplicity's sake (and to save time in the jumpstart), I had you connect to the `mysql` database instead.

Since you granted the `usage` privilege for the new user in a previous section, the basic framework has already been created for us within the user table. To verify that the user exists, issue the following query:

```
select user,host from user where user = 'dbuser';
```

You should see output similar to the Figure 6-12.

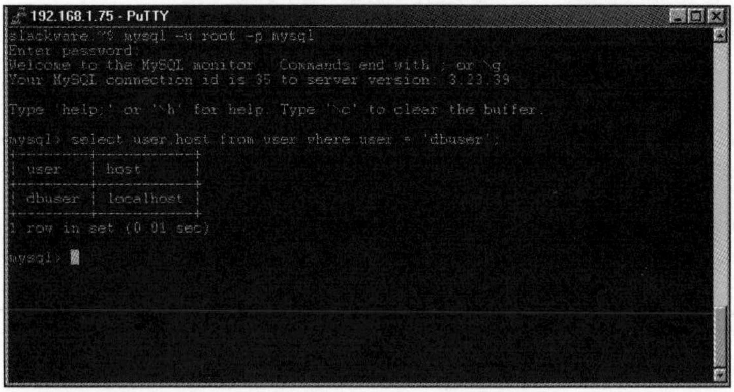

Figure 6-12: The new user in the database server

If you don't see the output shown in Figure 6-12 when the query has finished, you may want to review the "Adding Users to MySQL" section in this chapter and do some troubleshooting.

Assuming that you have the same output as given in Figure 6-12, it's now time to modify the privileges for this user account so you can connect to the `inventory` database and perform the necessary operations safely. The user account must be able to select rows from the database, as well as insert, update, and delete records. The statement that grants these privileges looks like this:

```
grant select,insert,update,delete on inventory.* to
dbuser@localhost;
```

Exit the MySQL CLI by typing `exit` or `quit`. Reconnect as the new user, like this:

```
mysql -u dbuser -p inventory
```

You should now be prompted for the password that you used to create the user. Upon entering the password you will be granted access to the inventory database. Test out your new privileges by issuing a simple `select * from product;` query. Your results should be similar to the example in the previous section.

You now have a simplified version of an electronic-commerce database.

Altering tables

Regardless of how much time, money, and effort is put into database design, inevitably databases need some redesigning or modification now and then. The reason is simple: Business rules change. The way you use data — and the way data is gathered and stored — changes as time goes by. MySQL allows the database administrator to change the layout of tables within a database—adding, removing, or modifying columns—via the `alter table` statement. The basic syntax of this command is as follows:

```
ALTER (IGNORE) TABLE <tablename> <alter phrase> [ , <alter
phrase> ]
```

Common `<alter phrase>` variables to use with the `ALTER TABLE` statement include the following:

```
ADD <columnname> <create specification>
CHANGE (COLUMN) <oldcolumnname> <create specification>
MODIFY (COLUMN) <create specification>
DROP (COLUMN) <columnname>
RENAME (TO) <newtablename>
```

Cross-Reference

For more about `<alter phrase>` variables, see Chapter 9.

The `IGNORE` modifier handles instances where there are duplicate values for a column that is being modified to a type where uniqueness is enforced. With `IGNORE` specified the first row is kept where values collide and all others are discarded. If `IGNORE` is not specified and a collision occurs between two values, the change is aborted and any specified changes are rolled back.

The `inventory` database shows that the `product` table is not tied to the `manufacturer` table in any way; there's no convenient way to link a product with a manufacturer. This was a purposeful flaw in the database design so you could use the `ALTER TABLE` statement to modify the product table and remedy this situation. From the MySQL CLI, enter the following command:

```
alter table product add manufacturer_id int;
```

If you've followed along thus far, you should receive an error message when you perform this operation. That's because you connected to the MySQL `inventory` database as the `dbuser` you created—but you didn't grant that user the privilege to alter tables. The error message you receive should look like this:

```
ERROR 1044: Access denied for user: 'dbuser@localhost' to
database 'inventory'
```

Disconnect from the CLI and reconnect to the `inventory` database as the `root` user:

```
mysql -u root -p inventory
```

When you run the `alter table` statement from above again you should have much better luck and the `inventory` database will now be updated so that you can include a manufacturer ID in the table. However, since you named the `manufacturer_id` column the same in both the product and the `manufacturer` tables, you should probably rename the `manufacturer_id` column in the `product` table so you don't get them mixed up later. Here's the necessary command:

```
alter table product change manufacturer_id prod_manu_id int;
```

After you've run this command, disconnect from the CLI and reconnect as the `dbuser` that you created earlier.

Describing tables

You should now be connected via the MySQL CLI as the `dbuser` username that you created earlier. A description of a column or columns in any table is available when you issue the `DESCRIBE` statement. Its basic syntax is as follows:

```
DESCRIBE <tablename> (columnname  [ wildcard ])
```

Note **The `DESCRIBE` statement may be abbreviated to `desc` and like other statements and commands in MySQL, it is not case-sensitive.**

You can use the optional *`columnname`* and *`wildcard`* arguments to obtain descriptions of the column or columns specified.

The `SHOW` statement (which works much like the `DESCRIBE` statement) shows the columns in a table, though it's quicker to use the `DESCRIBE` statement (or even its `desc` abbreviation) to do so. The command syntax looks like this:

```
SHOW columns FROM <tablename> [ FROM <databasename> ] [ LIKE
<wildcard> ]
```

For example, Figure 6-13 shows the changes you made in the last section, using the `desc` statement.

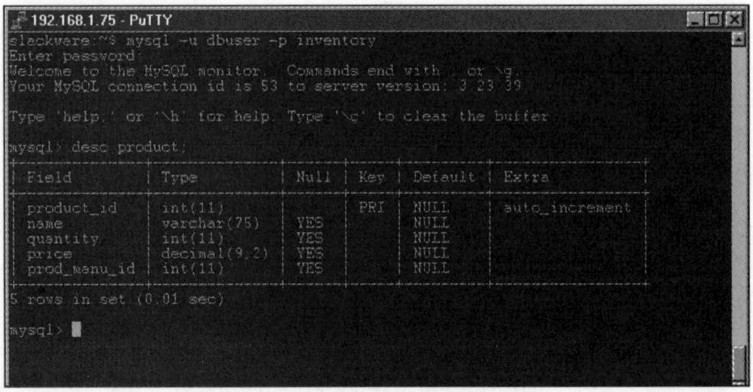
192.168.1.75 - PuTTY
slackware:~$ mysql -u dbuser -p inventory
Enter password:
Welcome to the MySQL monitor. Commands end with ; or \g.
Your MySQL connection id is 53 to server version: 3.23.39
Type 'help;' or '\h' for help. Type '\c' to clear the buffer.
mysql> desc product;
Field	Type	Null	Key	Default	Extra
product_id	int(11)		PRI	NULL	auto_increment
name	varchar(75)	YES		NULL	
quantity	int(11)	YES		NULL	
price	decimal(9,2)	YES		NULL	
prod_manu_id	int(11)	YES		NULL	
5 rows in set (0.01 sec)
mysql>

Figure 6-13: Using desc to describe a table layout

The same command using the `SHOW` statement is as follows:

```
show columns from product;
```

An example of a `wildcard` column search uses the following query to see all columns in the `product` table that start with the letter `"p"` (the output is shown in Figure 6-14):

```
desc product 'p%';
```

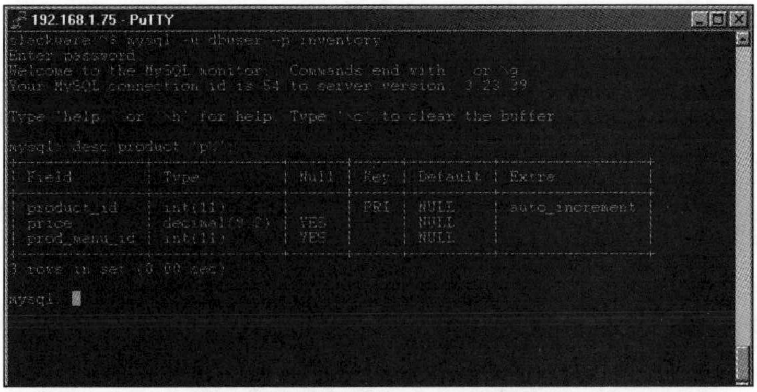

Figure 6-14: Using a wildcard in a DESCRIBE statement

The same statement using the `show` statement looks like this:

```
show columns from product like 'p%';
```

Looking at other database objects

The previous section covered the `DESCRIBE` statement as well as the `SHOW` statement for looking at column information within a table. Using the `SHOW` statement, you can get a list of database objects. This section looks at some typical and useful examples of this statement.

Cross-Reference

Full coverage of the `SHOW` statement is in Chapter 9.

Consider the following command as an initial example:

```
SHOW DATABASES (LIKE <wildcard>);
```

This statement shows all the databases in MySQL. If a wildcard is specified, the statement returns databases matching the wildcard, if any.

Note

The capability of merely looking at the names of the databases does not imply that the current user has permissions to connect or use those databases.

To see the tables in detail, you would issue the following command:

```
SHOW (OPEN) TABLES (FROM <databasename>) (LIKE <wildcard>);
```

The SHOW TABLES statement is very useful to find out names of tables in the current database or any database through the use of the from modifier.

```
SHOW CREATE TABLE <tablename>;
```

Sometimes you may have to dump table structure if you want to recreate the tables later (or on another system) for some different use. For example, as shown in Figure 6-15, some output from the SHOW CREATE TABLE statement from the inventory database looks like this:

```
SHOW CREATE TABLE product;
```

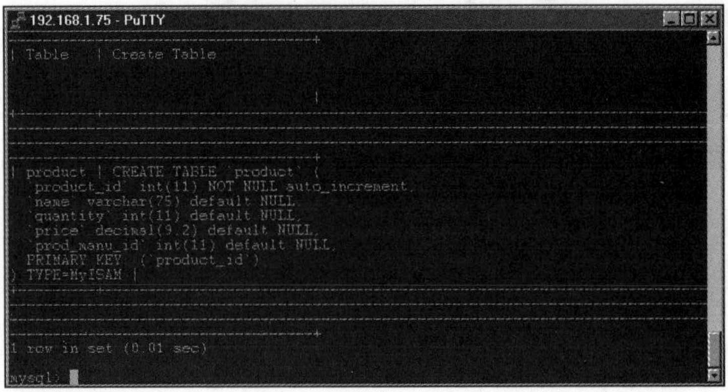

Figure 6-15: Output of the SHOW CREATE TABLE statement for the product table

With the information from the SHOW CREATE TABLE statement, the database administrator could copy the output to create a copy of the table or save the output for later use.

Summary

This chapter gave a brief overview of some of the most common tasks involved in creating and managing a database.

✦ mysqladmin is a useful command for obtaining status information of the server, changing passwords, killing server processes, and shutting down the server itself.

- Basic security includes not only creating strong passwords, but also granting users only those privileges that are necessary to complete their tasks.
- You can create a database creation by using `mysqladmin` or by issuing the appropriate commands from the MySQL Command-Line Interface (CLI).
- Creating and altering tables as well as inserting and updating data is a common task in MySQL.
- The `SELECT` statement is another versatile command, used frequently in the course of administering a MySQL system.

✦ ✦ ✦

CHAPTER 7

Database Concepts and Design

In This Chapter

Comparing concepts of databases

Creating a database design

Analyzing requirements and defining logical design

Approaching physical design and implementation

Though many database books begin with a chapter on database concepts and design, we get our hands dirty with what you should know both with databases and with MySQL in particular. However, the underlying concepts of databases and their design are important.

Concepts of Databases

Databases are many things to many people. It is a mistake to say that all databases are electronic. Some other databases include a library and a recipe card file.

What is data?

Data is just about anything you can imagine *and quantify*. For example, the records and numbers you keep in a checkbook register are data. The stats you write down if you keep score at a baseball game are data.

For our purposes, I ignore checkbook registers and concentrate on the electronic form of data. However, you could enter personal checks or baseball stats into a computer database program. At the basic level, data is data.

What is a database?

Databases are not simply electronic places to store data. As already alluded to, thinking of databases in terms not limited to computers is one of the first steps to understanding the concepts.

Note

MySQL is not a database. It is software for *creating and managing* a database.

Databases keep information in *tables*. A table is a structure consisting of at least one column, but usually many more. A database is then a collection of one or more tables of related information. Sorting, indexing, and queries organize data to help the database user.

The letters SQL stand for Structured Query Language.

Why use a Database?

Someone much wiser than I am said, "Always use the right tool for the job"—and it's no less true in the world of computing. I've seen countless uses of applications such as spreadsheets and word processors (instead of databases) to store data. For an annual holiday card list, this is fine; the time required to set up a database is probably out of proportion to the modest amount of data involved. In the business world, however, a spreadsheet is not an acceptable tool for storing large amounts of data.

For such applications as product catalogs and customer information, a database is by far the best method of storing and retrieving data. Databases offer a way to utilize data efficiently.

Most enterprise-level databases must be created via software designed for the purpose: a Relational Database Management System (RDBMS). Such programs, including MySQL, support *transactional table types*—tables designed to handle the frequent updates and modifications that electronic commerce entails. Each operation performed on data within a database is known as a *transaction*.

Note

A transactional system can recreate its steps in case of data corruption. In the event of a system crash, data could be restored from the last tape backup and then the transaction log could be played against the database to restore the data to its condition just before the system crash.

Caution

Transactional tables are not completely free from the risk of data loss. Even the best RDBMS cannot offer a 100-percent guarantee that no data loss will occur in a catastrophic system failure.

A successful RDBMS meets the *ACID* test for these issues:

✦ **Atomicity:** When a transaction is sent from the user to the database server, the operation is either committed fully or rolled back. In other words, if the hard disk can't hold the whole transaction, the transaction would be rolled back as if it had never happened. In this manner, data can always be kept consistent.

✦ **Consistency:** Operations that violate a rule or a similar mechanism are not committed to the database. If a user doesn't have access permission, attempts to write to the table are rejected.

✦ **Isolation:** An operation on the database is complete before another operation becomes aware of it. If a user is adding records to tables while another user is reading from the same tables, the reader isn't shown results from partial operations. Such partial information could lead to inconsistent and confusing results for the reader.

✦ **Durability:** Once a transaction is committed to the database, it is guaranteed to be there. If a catastrophic event happens to the disk, the database will still hold that transaction (assuming no other hardware failure causes a disk corruption).

How are databases used?

Databases are used in all areas of business. Companies track information about their customers inside of databases. Ever wonder why insurance costs more in some geographical areas than others? Behind the answer is a database. Insurance companies keep general claim information so they may sort and query the data to find patterns that exhibit higher risks — and pass the cost of those risks on to the customer as higher premiums.

Databases have also been there for the explosive growth of the Internet. Online shopping is driven by databases — some of them running on MySQL. When you search for the latest Van Halen CD at your favorite online music store, your search is handed back to a database that then looks up and retrieves the right information, hopefully within a few seconds. Databases can retrieve information lightning-quick and most database server implementations, including MySQL, support *replication* so that the database administrator can add more servers to handle requests.

Databases are becoming more visible in law enforcement. Databases to aid law enforcement are nothing new. (Watching an episode of *Dragnet* from the Sixties, you can see the use of punch cards to search for Social Security records). But databases are more widely used and in ways barely imagined when Jack Webb caught television bandits.

Database Design

Database design is the process of determining and organizing the information to track. Many iterations of a database design occur as you try to achieve an efficient design and maximize your use of resources.

Tip

Many simple database applications don't need a strict database design. The effort isn't warranted for the application. I may be invoking the ire of traditional database administrators and designers by stating this. However, spending three months in design meetings for a database that is used once a month for non-critical functions is a waste of resources. For complicated business processes, I strongly recommend spending time designing the database.

The process of designing a complicated database correctly is not easy. It takes time and effort, but the result is worth it. Data modeling is usually the first step in the process. This includes defining the business processes and building an Entity Relationship Diagram.

One of the first processes to design a database is to meet with the end user of the database or data. If you are that person, hold a meeting with yourself. Offer yourself refreshments, too. If you are meeting with clients (internal or external), prepare to get as much information as possible about the business process or database to be designed. The extra work at this stage goes a long way towards making the database successful. A quality data model easily translates into a database.

The Database Life Cycle

Especially in the business world, a database system behaves much like a living thing. Each stage of its life cycle has distinctive concerns and tasks that fall into a rough sequence much like the following:

1. **Requirements analysis:** This first step is made up of what seemingly endless meetings that analyze what is required for the new database. The owners and users of the database define their business processes and document the entities, attributes, and relationships that will make up the database.

   This analysis is most important to the success of the database project. Without a complete picture of the business process — or full documentation of what the application must have and be — the project will fail. Regardless of how much time goes into the next phases of the project, it's headed for disruption (at best) or disaster (at worst) if you overlook a major item in this step.

   Sometimes the systems analyst (you, as administrator) can get so wrapped up in the project itself that he or she neglects to put much thought into the end user. I've found it most helpful to involve the actual end user of the application during the first phase of the design — through interviews and observation. In most instances, you are designing a replacement or improvement for an existing system. The end users are your best source of ideas for improvements in the next version.

   Involvement of the end user can come in many forms. End users can be in planning meetings where the application functions and needs can be determined. However, a more successful method for learning how an application is used and can be improved is *observation* of the end users doing their jobs.

   Many times those being observed will alter their behavior, either consciously or subconsciously, thus lessening the effectiveness of the information gathered. I recommend a combination of interviews or meetings, and direct observation for a successful analysis.

2. **Logical design of the database:** This step lays out the logical structure of the program in terms of its tables and their relationships. Three tasks predominate:

   - Designing the layout of the database tables (often starting with an Entity-Relationship Diagram)

- Normalizing the candidate tables
- Writing the SQL to produce the database and tables

This second stage can quickly slow a project to a snail's pace. If you get too many cooks in the kitchen during the first phase, the proverbial database soup can spoil. Keeping the second phase organized and on track takes effort. Many times people will want to iterate over a database design not realizing that business rules change and the database will have to change with it.

3. **Physical design of the database:** This step involves actually developing and planning the physical layout of the data within your network and system topology. In a distributed environment, this step includes

   - Planning for data distribution
   - Organizing such physical elements as memory use, table-cache size, and buffer size

Cross-Reference

MySQL server variables are discussed in a later chapter.

4. **Implementation and subsequent modification of the database:** During these last steps in the database life cycle, you enter the SQL or other language into your database, along with other scripts and management tools that you've developed while planning and designing the database.

If all goes well, then by the time you reach this last step, you've found all the objects that should be included in the database. Don't worry if you suddenly implement the database and find that you should add a column to all its tables. MySQL syntax can alter table structure rather painlessly.

Note

Regardless of how much research and planning you do, a long-term application will must change to be useful. Business rules and processes change over time, so the database and applications must change, too. Good planning in the beginning will make those changes easier and less costly.

Logical Design

After you gather information on the business process and items to be documented, you are ready to create the *logical design*. This master plan for the logical entities (and their relationships) that make up the database should be as complete and thorough as possible. A good logical design has many facets and phases, including the analysis of relationships and the setting of constraints.

Entities and attributes

At a basic level of a data model are *entities*—objects that you are interested in as part of the data model you are creating. For example, if you were making an online store, you would want to know the customer's name. *Steve Suehring* is an example of an entity. The specific name, Steve Suehring, is the entity. For a successful online store, you probably want more than one customer. Therefore you should *abstract* the entity into a general *entity type*. For this example, the entity type would be *Customer*.

Entities have identifying qualities—*attributes*. For example, the *Customer* entity of Steve Suehring has such attributes as height, weight, home address, and telephone number. To manage all the attributes of all the entities, you abstract the attributes into *attribute types* that become part of all the entity types.

At the initial meeting(s) for producing a data model, you define the entities—and subsequent entity types—that you are interested in. In addition, you will most likely start determining attributes and attribute types as well. For now, the entity types can be written down as a simple list. For example, suppose you know that both customer information and product information are to be kept in the database. You could create a list somewhat like the one given here—which, though incomplete, works fine for a basic site:

- Customer
- Product
- Manufacturer

That gives you three entity types. At this point in the research process, I usually jump right into listing some attribute types for each entity type, like this:

- Name
- Address
- Supplemental Address
- City
- State
- Zip
- Telephone Number
- E-mail Address
- Credit Card Number
- Credit Card Expiration
- Name on Card
- Product Name
- Product Price
- Quantity on Hand
- Manufacturer
- Product Category

Tip

You can add fun things like Ratings and Reviews for products later. (And if the attribute types in the list are starting to resemble column headings, that's not accidental. More about that later.)

Upon further review, I believe Name should be broken into two separate attributes, First Name and Last Name. I also believe Telephone Number should be broken apart to account for area code and number. (I assume that the online store only ships within the United States, otherwise I would add Country Code as well.) It would also be useful to know the credit card type, even though this information can usually be gleaned from the digits of the card. Having the credit-card type allows some *sanity checking* (the use of a special program to ferret out and report system problems) later in the process. In addition, it would be useful to keep information about the manufacturers such as their address and contact information as well. Here's what the new attribute type list looks like:

- First Name
- Last Name
- Address
- Supplemental Address
- City
- State
- Zip
- Area Code
- Telephone Number
- E-mail Address
- Credit Card Type
- Credit Card Number
- Credit Card Expiration
- Name on Card
- Product Name
- Product Price
- Quantity On Hand
- Manufacturer Name
- Manufacturer Address
- Manufacturer City
- Manufacturer State
- Manufacturer Zip

✦ Manufacturer Contact

✦ Manufacturer Area Code

✦ Manufacturer Telephone Number

✦ Product Category

Now that I have a list of entity types and attribute types for the data model, I can start to analyze how they relate.

Relationships

In my example, it's obvious that some attribute types relate to each other. For example, each First and Last Name pair can have one or more Addresses, Supplemental Addresses, Cities, States, and Zips.

As should be evident, First Name/Last Name (which I will refer to as Customer Name for brevity's sake), Address, Supplemental Address, City, State, Zip (which I will refer to simply as Address), and so on are all items relating to the Customer entity type. It quickly becomes clear that I could go down a slippery slope because one Customer Name could have more than one Address and one Address could have more than one Customer Name.

However, what may appear clear is not necessarily as clear as you may think. While it is true that a Customer Name could have more than one Address, a Customer Record is made up of one and only one Address. What appeared to be a problem in the design is actually a false relationship.

Tip: By adding other entity types, you can add support for more than one address to allow the customer to ship to different addresses.

Each relationship has a degree of *cardinality*. In other words, there can be one and only one Manufacturer of a certain product, but that Manufacturer can have many products. Determining the relationships is an art that takes practice. Thinking through the business process thoroughly will help to work out the true relationships for your data model.

Figure 7-1 shows an example of relationships in an Entity-Relationship Diagram. The example illustrates the relationship between manufacturer and products.

✦ Each manufacturer can have one or more products, represented by the crow's-foot line near the Product box.

✦ Each product can and must have one and only one manufacturer, as represented by the single line near the manufacturer box.

Tip

The O shape near the Product entity type indicates that the existence of a product is not required for a Manufacturer to exist in the database. This O is missing from the Manufacturer side of the relationship because a manufacturer is required if there is a product in the database.

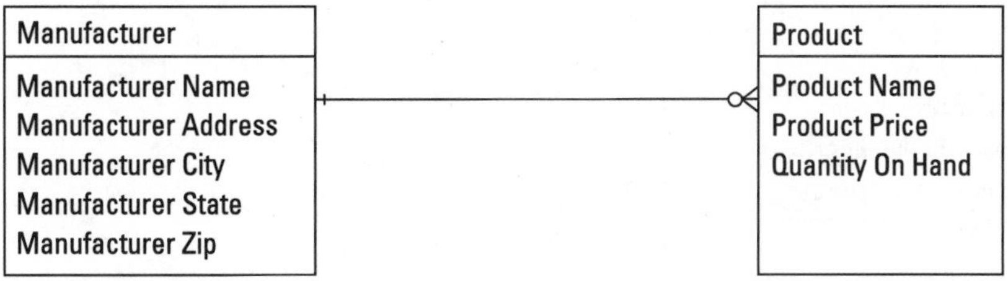

Figure 7-1: Relationships among some example entity types

Entity-relationship diagrams

With a list of entity and attribute types for a data model in place—and a basic understanding of how to relate them to each other—you create a diagram that formally shows the relationships of each entity type. The diagram simply groups together like information. This will help to normalize the data and understand the business processes, and possibly find additional entities, attributes, and relationships that must be included in the data model.

Square or *rectangular* boxes on the diagram represent entities. Relationships can be represented by number of line formats.

In looking again at the list of attribute types in the example, it is evident that certain customer-related information is stored in the database. My initial draft of an Entity-Relationship Diagram (ERD) for the example database is shown in Figure 7-2.

Analysis of diagrams

As I touched on earlier, the manufacturer and product relationships are (mostly) fine. One manufacturer can have many products, but a given product can have only one manufacturer. Examining customer and credit-card relationships in the draft of the ERD in Figure 7-2, you can see that each customer can have more than one credit card stored in the database. However, each credit card can only be associated with one customer. This is not what I would like—I want the entire family to create accounts and use Dad's credit card to buy. To alleviate this problem, I must make both sides of the relationship many-to-many. The second draft of the ERD, in Figure 7-3, shows the new many-to-many relationship.

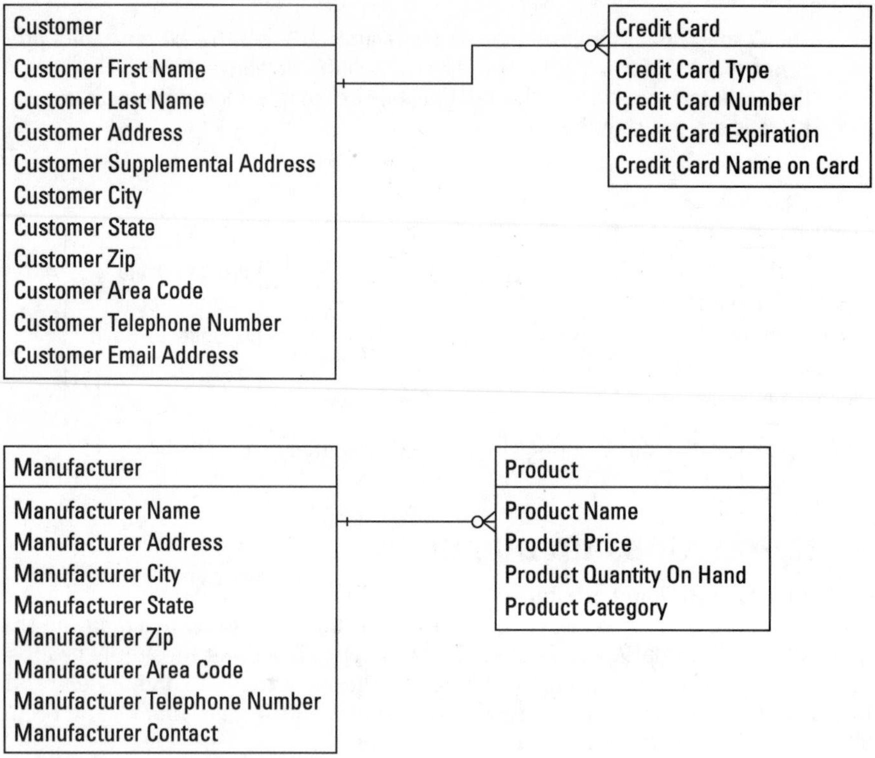

Figure 7-2: First Draft of an ERD for the online store

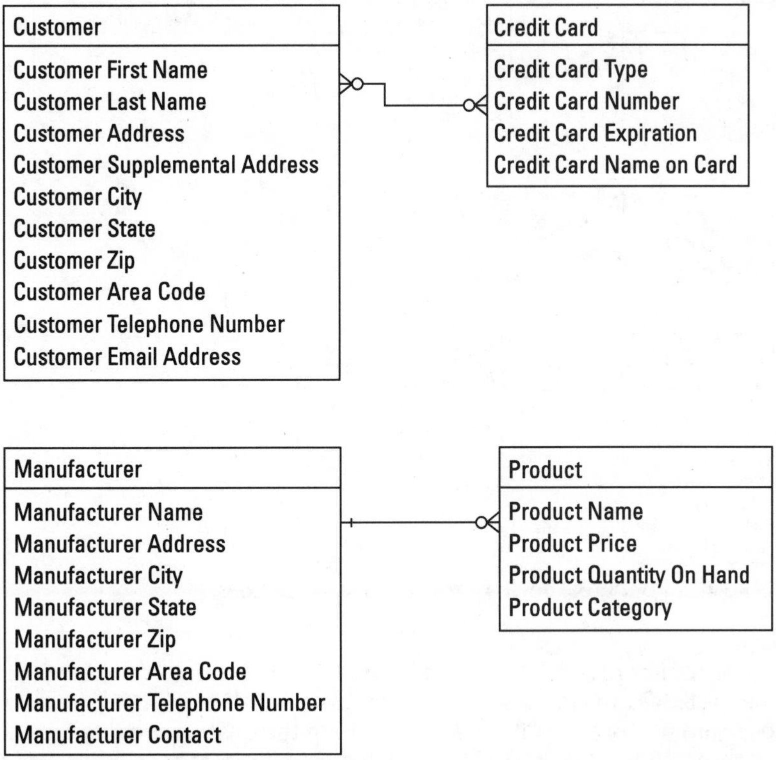

Figure 7-3: Customers can use more than one card, and more than one customer can use the card.

However, a many-to-many relationship should be broken down into two separate one-to-many relationships. Along with breaking the many-to-many relationship apart, I must search for extra attributes that may be disguising themselves as relationships. The result of this analysis is shown in Figure 7-4.

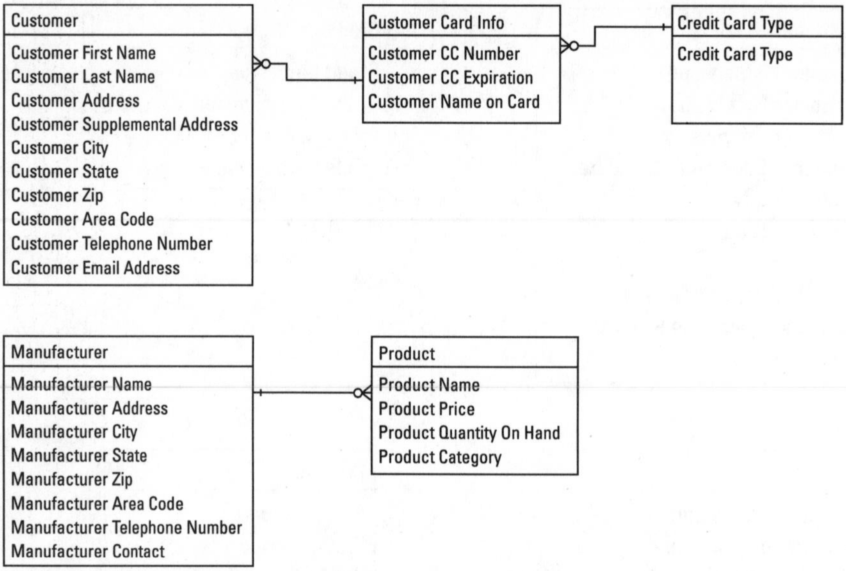

Figure 7-4: Results from breakdown of many-to-many relationship.

One major area for improvement in this data model is in the area of the City, State and Zip storage. Since Zip codes define and are always tied to one city and state, there is no reason to store the City and State in both the Customer entity type and the Manufacturer entity type. It would be much more efficient to make another entity type to house the City and State and relate that entity type to both the Customer and Manufacturer entity types. This draft of the ERD is shown in Figure 7-5.

As you can see from the new draft of the data model shown in Figure 7-5, the Zip attribute type is duplicated in both the Customer/Manufacturer entity types and in the Locale entity type as well. This is so I can join or match the information together. For example, I have a customer with a Zip code of 54481. I can then look up the city and state for the zip code of 54481 in the Locale table. Without the zip code being stored in the Customer table, I would have no way to know where the customer lives or where to ship their goodies!

The Zip Code attribute within the Customer entity is known as a foreign key. A foreign key enables you to relate an attribute in one entity to the attribute of another entity. In this case, the Zip Code attribute in the Customer entity type is related to the Zip Code attribute of the Locale entity type.

Based on information about foreign keys, the astute observer may have already noticed the flaw in the Customer to Credit Card relationship. There is no way to tie customers to their credit card information. Either I charge random cards or don't charge at all. A recipe for disaster no matter how you look at it. I must choose a way to relate a customer with their credit card info. Customer name is out because I hope to have more than one John Smith shop at my store. I must find an attribute type that will always be unique within the Customer entity type.

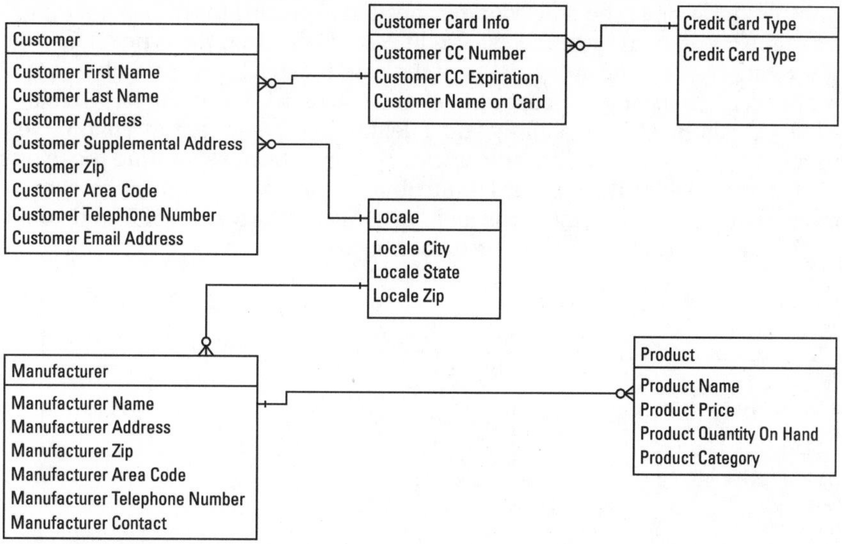

Figure 7-5: Placing City, State, and Zip in another entity type makes the model more efficient.

Many online stores choose E-mail Address as the unique attribute in a customer's information. I believe this is a good idea, so I implement my customers' e-mail addresses to relate their credit card information to them, as shown in Figure 7-6.

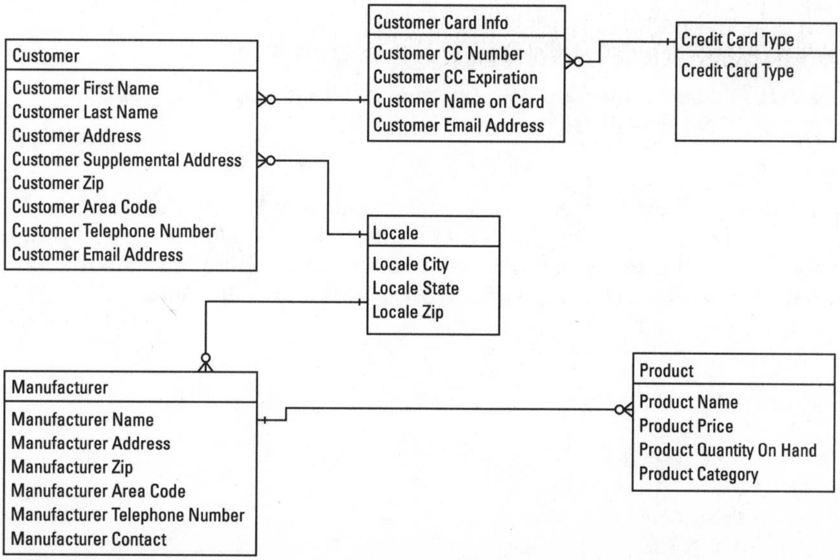

Figure 7-6: Relating customers to their credit cards is rather important.

Yet another iteration of the data model is needed because I must create a relationship between the credit-card type and the credit card. Recall that the type of card could be determined by looking at the digits of the card itself. However, I'd like to do some error checking, so having the customer choose the card type is useful. To relate card type to card number, I could simply add a field to the Customer Card Info table. However, doing so would nullify any efficiency gained from separating those entity types. Therefore I will create a Card ID attribute type that is simply an integer. For example, I will give Visa credit cards an ID of 1, MasterCard an ID of 2, and so on. Figure 7-7 shows the next draft of the data model.

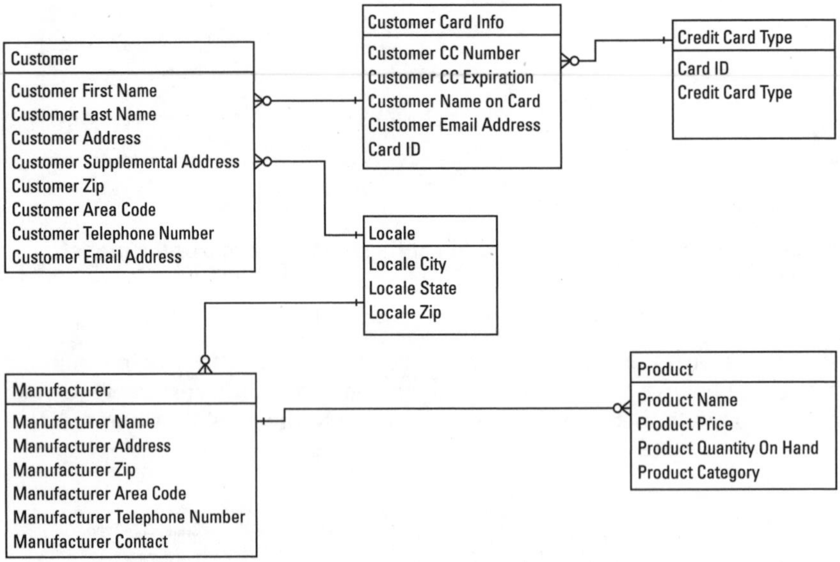

Figure 7-7: Addition of the Card ID entity type enables joining of the Customer Card Info and Card Type tables.

An examination of the Product entity type reveals that the Product Category attribute really doesn't belong with that entity type. Therefore I create a new entity type for Product Types. I can now add a Product ID attribute to relate that entity type back to the Product entity type. The result is shown in Figure 7-8.

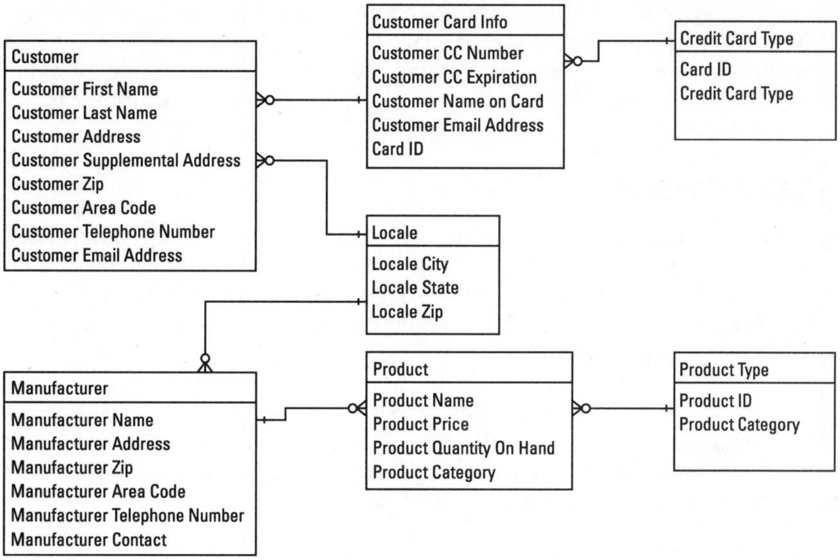

Figure 7-8: Separation of the Product Category from the Product Table

Constraints

Constraints are limitations or controls placed on attributes within an entity. They are used to maintain order and keep the model true to the business process it is describing.

The Uniqueness constraint is one that you encounter frequently. For the online store model to work, the e-mail address of each customer will need to be unique. Additional attributes within other entities also must be guaranteed to be unique, such as the Zip Code attributes in the Locale entity.

Note The Uniqueness constraint is sometimes called a *primary key* within a database table though Uniqueness is only one of the attributes of a primary key.

An *Exclusion constraint* is a logically exclusive `OR` relationship. With such a constraint, one and only one entity may participate in a relationship with a root entity. For example, if you manufactured widgets and could get parts from an internal or external supplier, one and only one supplier would supply the part for a specific order.

Any entity that exists and has a primary key must also ensure that the primary key exists to meet the constraint of *Entity Integrity*. Since e-mail address is the primary key for the customer entity, if you start a customer record for your online store, they must have an e-mail address to exist at all according to this constraint.

Referential integrity means that any foreign key that exists within one table must also have a corresponding row and primary key within the related table. For example, if a Zip Code exists within a customer's record in the example, there must be a corresponding Zip Code record in the `Locale` table for referential integrity.

Normalization

Long the woe of many a college student learning database concepts, normalization is the practice of getting a database design into a format with no duplications or redundancy of data within the database so the database operates as efficiently as possible. This has obvious benefits of efficiency. However, it can also prevent catastrophic inconsistencies.

There are five *forms* that a data model passes through on its way to being normalized. For our purposes, I'll deal with only the first three forms. As a data model is normalized, it is said to be in (and pass through) First Normal Form, Second Normal Form, Third Normal Form, and so on, like this:

✦ **First Normal Form (1NF).** This form is achieved when there are *no repeating attributes.* Table 7-1 shows such a table. For many small projects this type of table is fine. While there is repeated data such as the Team and Location, having the repeats doesn't adversely affect performance on small tables and projects. However, if you had to make a change to the Team for one of the people in the table, the update could take longer. Additionally, if you delete the Steve Suehring record from the table, you would lose all of the Team and Location info, resulting in unforeseen data loss.

Table 7-1
Table in First Normal Form

ID	Name	Location	Loc_ID	Team	Team_ID
3	Don Sutton	Baseball Hall of Fame	355	Braves	95
4	Steve Suehring	Bat Boy	515	Dodgers	78
5	Greg Maddux	Baseball Hall of Fame	355	Braves	95
6	Jerry Rice	NFL Hall of Fame	400	49ers	94
7	Mika Hakkinen	Formula One	411	McLaren	99
8	Steve Young	NFL Hall of Fame	400	49ers	94

✦ **Second Normal Form (2NF):** This form includes the 1NF definition and requires that all attributes of a specific entity depend on the *entire key value.* If the key value is only one value, then attributes that depend on it already depend on the entire value, as shown in Figure 7-9.

Person

Person ID	Person Name
3	Don Sutton
4	Steve Suehring
5	Greg Maddux
6	Jerry Rice
7	Mika Hakkinen
8	Steve Young

Location

Loc_ID	Location
355	Baseball Hall of Fame
515	Bat Boy
355	Baseball Hall of Fame
400	NFL Hall of Fame
411	Formula One
400	NFL Hall of Fame

Team

Team ID	Team Name
95	Braves
78	Dodgers
95	Braves
94	49ers
99	Mclaren
94	49ers

Table4

Person ID	Loc_ID	Team ID
3	355	95
4	515	78
5	355	95
6	400	94
7	411	99
8	400	94

Figure 7-9: Making sure all attributes depend on the key

✦ **Third Normal Form (3NF):** This form includes the 2NF definition and requires that all attributes of a specific entity *depend only on the key,* not on other attributes. In other words, the Team is dependent only on the Team_ID, not on the Name of the person. Figure 7-10 illustrates the final tables for this example.

Note that foreign-key constraints could be used to remove Table4 from the example.

Person	
Person ID	Person Name
3	Don Sutton
4	Steve Suehring
5	Greg Maddux
6	Jerry Rice
7	Mika Hakkinen
8	Steve Young

Location	
Loc_ID	Location
355	Baseball Hall of Fame
515	Bat Boy
400	NFL Hall of Fame
411	FormulaOne

Team	
Team ID	Team Name
95	Braves
78	Dodgers
94	49ers
99	Mclaren

Table4		
Person ID	Loc_ID	Team ID
3	355	95
4	515	78
5	355	95
6	400	94
7	411	99
8	400	94

Figure 7-10: Final example tables, normalized

Data Definition Language and Data Markup Language

Data Definition Language (DDL) and *Data Markup Language (DML)* are common names for the tools and syntax used to create and work with a database.

✦ DDL defines how the data is addressed. DDL examples include `CREATE TABLE`, `CREATE INDEX`, and such privilege options as `GRANT` and `REVOKE`.

Note DDL statements do not work with data directly.

✦ DML statements actually work with real data. Examples of such statements are `INSERT` and `DELETE`.

Producing the SQL

The last step of Logical Design is creation of the SQL for the database. As this point, you must make some important decisions involving column types and constraints for the candidate tables. There are a number of column types supported by MySQL.

Cross-Reference: Refer to Appendix A for a complete listing of column types supported by MySQL.

Recalling Figure 7-10's candidate tables, I recommend using `integer` type for the `ID` columns in all tables. Further, I would recommend column types of `varchar` for the name columns.

For constraints, the `ID` column in all tables should be required and unique. This makes them primary keys.

Note: To create a primary key in MySQL, you must specify the column as `NOT NULL` and `PRIMARY KEY`.

The SQL to create the example tables in MySQL is as follows:

```
CREATE TABLE person (
     person_id int NOT NULL PRIMARY KEY,
     person varchar(50)
);
CREATE TABLE location (
     loc_id int NOT NULL PRIMARY KEY,
     location varchar(50)
);
CREATE TABLE team (
     team_id int NOT NULL PRIMARY KEY,
     team varchar(50)
);
CREATE TABLE table4 (
     tperson_id int NOT NULL PRIMARY KEY,
     tloc_id int,
     tteam_id int
);
```

Going back to my ongoing example of an e-commerce Web site, the candidate tables for the structure are created by the following code:

```
CREATE TABLE customer (
     e-mail_address varchar(75) NOT NULL PRIMARY KEY,
     first_name varchar(50),
     last_name varchar(50),
     address1 varchar(50),
     address2 varchar(50),
     customer_zip varchar(10),
     area_code char(3),
     telephone_number char(7)
);
CREATE TABLE cardinfo (
     card_id int NOT NULL PRIMARY KEY,
     ccnum varchar(16),
     ccexp date,
     name_on_card varchar(100),
     e-mail_address varchar(75)
```

```
);
CREATE TABLE cardtype (
     card_id int NOT NULL PRIMARY KEY,
     card_type varchar(20)
);
CREATE TABLE locale (
     zip varchar(10) NOT NULL PRIMARY KEY,
     city varchar(50),
     state char(2)
);
CREATE TABLE manufacturer (
     id int NOT NULL PRIMARY KEY,
     name varchar(50),
     address varchar(50),
     zip varchar(10),
     area_code char(3),
     telephone_number char(7),
     contact_name varchar(50)
);
CREATE TABLE product (
     id int NOT NULL PRIMARY KEY,
     name varchar(50),
     price decimal(9,2),
     quantity integer,
     manu_id int
);
CREATE TABLE producttype (
     id int NOT NULL PRIMARY KEY,
     category varchar(50)
);
```

The `varchar` column type is chosen because it uses space more efficiently than the `char` type. The `char` column type pads the column with extra spaces to fill the length of the column; the `varchar` type adds only one extra byte to store the length of the column. For example, if `char` the column type for the `city` column, the database would always use 50 bytes, regardless of whether the city was named `Ames` or `Stevens Point`. The `char` type is fine for area-code and telephone-number columns (which are always the same length for U.S. phone numbers). The `decimal` column type is chosen for the `product` table's `price` column because the precision can be specified before and after the decimal point. In the example, I use the (9,2) definition that calls for up to 9 digits before the decimal and 2 digits after the decimal. Therefore I can list prices of up to 999,999,999.99 for products in the database.

Cross-Reference For a summary of MySQL's column types, see Appendix A.

Physical Design and Implementation

Once you have a normalized design, turning that design into the actual database and tables on the server is easy.

The Physical Design phase is the third step in the database life cycle. Now is the time to decide how many servers you are going to use for your database application, where they will be physically located, and so on.

The final step after Physical Design planning is to take the SQL statements and create the database. Since you've already designed the SQL for the normalized tables, it is now a matter of simply executing the code to make the database and tables.

Cross-Reference

There are a number of ways to import data into MySQL, many of which are covered in another chapter.

Indexing

Much like an index entry in a book, an index entry in a database allows the server to quickly locate information. As you create the physical design of your database, you should choose indices that accelerate queries and thus accelerate the operation of your database server and applications.

With MySQL, an index can be created either during the initial DDL to create the table or during later operation. An example of creating the index with the initial DDL is as follows:

```
CREATE TABLE example (
     id int NOT NULL,
     name varchar(50),
     address varchar(50),
     zip varchar(10),
     INDEX (id, name)
);
```

To specify an index after the initial table has been created, the syntax is generally intuitive:

```
CREATE INDEX index_name on table_name (
     column1,
     column2,
     ...
);
```

MySQL has commands that can help you determine what indices to create. The `DESCRIBE` command allows you to describe a `SELECT` statement as well, to see possible keys or indices to create. Another name for the `DESCRIBE` command in this context is the `EXPLAIN` command. Some database operators may be familiar with one or the other of these commands; their functions overlap somewhat.

For the example, I've created a test database called `ecommerce` that uses the same example tables as the rest of the chapter.

Tip

I write table definitions in a text editor such as `vi` in Linux or Notepad in Windows, as shown in Figures 7-11 and 7-12. By using a text editor to create long DDL and DML commands, you can easily copy and paste them into the MySQL CLI or typing them in through the command line. This can be a lifesaver if you run into problems with the database server (or if your syntax or spelling is wrong for a particular command).

On the CD-ROM

The example database tables are on the CD-ROM so you don't have to type them (though it is good practice).

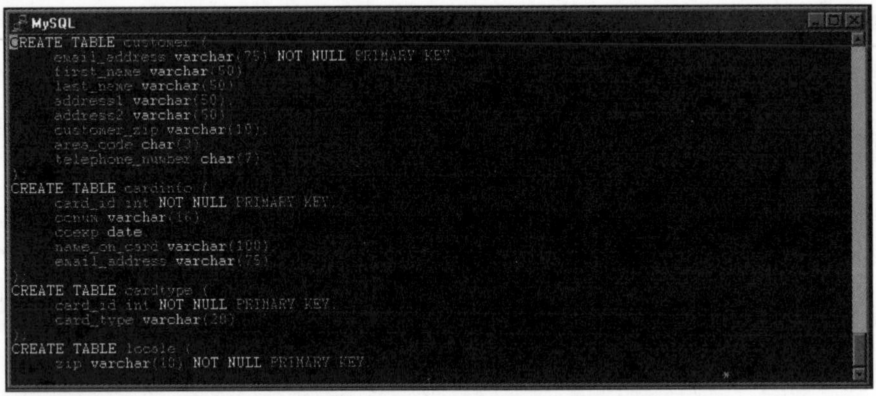

MySQL
CREATE TABLE customer (
email_address varchar(75) NOT NULL PRIMARY KEY,
first_name varchar(50),
last_name varchar(50),
address1 varchar(50),
address2 varchar(50),
customer_zip varchar(10),
area_code char(3),
telephone_number char(7)
);
CREATE TABLE cardinfo (
card_id int NOT NULL PRIMARY KEY,
ccnum varchar(16),
ccexp date,
name_on_card varchar(100),
email_address varchar(75)
);
CREATE TABLE cardtype (
card_id int NOT NULL PRIMARY KEY,
card_type varchar(20)
);
CREATE TABLE locale (
zip varchar(10) NOT NULL PRIMARY KEY,

Figure 7-11: Using vi to write DDL and DML can be a great timesaver.

For the indexing example, I can add a record into the `locale` and `customer` tables.

```
insert into locale values ('54481','Stevens Point','WI');
insert into customer values
('suehring↓ngermen.com','Steve','Suehring','834 Main
St.',NULL,'54481','715','5551212');
```

Indexing will usually not help a simple `SELECT` statement such as `select * from locale`. To confirm this, you can try the `EXPLAIN` command, as shown in Figure 7-13.

In Figure 7-13, you can see information on the select statement and extra information about how MySQL ran the query. For determining possible indices, the important place to look is the `possible_keys` column; it tells you what columns could be created as an index to improve the performance of the query. For the example, MySQL did not need any indices to efficiently handle the query (as evidenced by the `NULL` in the `primary_keys` column).

For a more complicated query (shown in Figure 7-14), MySQL believes that it could use a primary key index in the `locale` table to boost efficiency. Since the `Zip` column is already a primary key, the query can run efficiently.

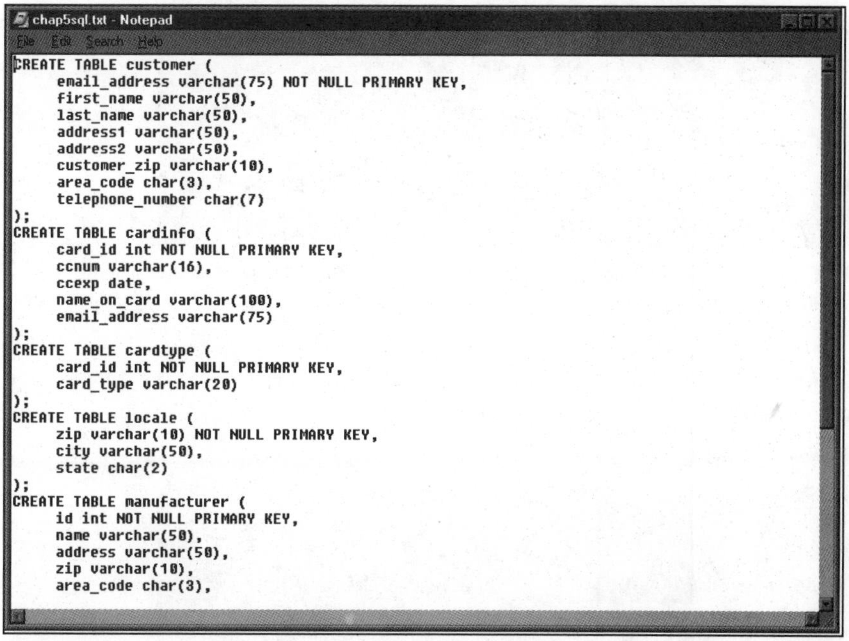
chap5sql.txt - Notepad
File Edit Search Help
CREATE TABLE customer (
email_address varchar(75) NOT NULL PRIMARY KEY,
first_name varchar(50),
last_name varchar(50),
address1 varchar(50),
address2 varchar(50),
customer_zip varchar(10),
area_code char(3),
telephone_number char(7)
);
CREATE TABLE cardinfo (
card_id int NOT NULL PRIMARY KEY,
ccnum varchar(16),
ccexp date,
name_on_card varchar(100),
email_address varchar(75)
);
CREATE TABLE cardtype (
card_id int NOT NULL PRIMARY KEY,
card_type varchar(20)
);
CREATE TABLE locale (
zip varchar(10) NOT NULL PRIMARY KEY,
city varchar(50),
state char(2)
);
CREATE TABLE manufacturer (
id int NOT NULL PRIMARY KEY,
name varchar(50),
address varchar(50),
zip varchar(10),
area_code char(3),

Figure 7-12: Notepad can be used as a source for creating long DDL and DML commands.

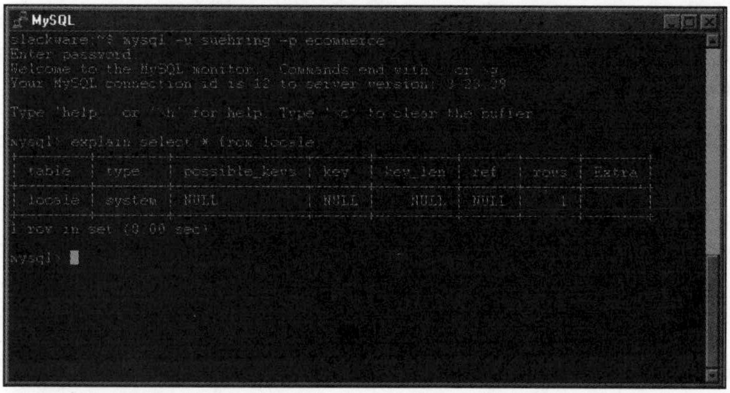
MySQL
slackware:~$ mysql -u suehring -p ecommerce
Enter password:
mysql> explain select * from locale;
table | type | possible_keys | key | key_len | ref | rows | Extra
locale | system | NULL | NULL | NULL | NULL | 1 |
1 row in set (0.00 sec)
mysql>

Figure 7-13: Indexing usually doesn't assist with simple queries.

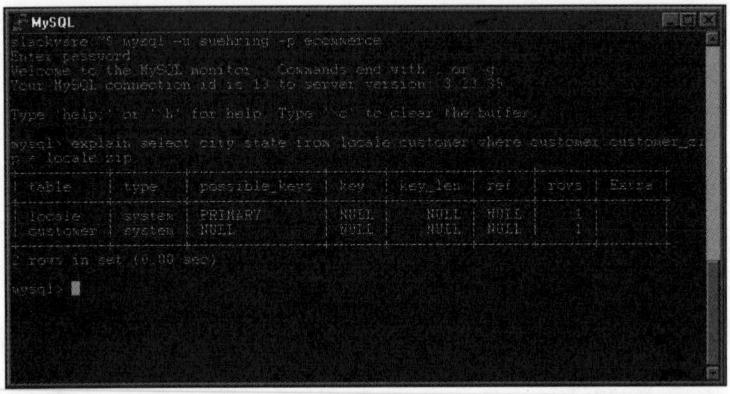

Figure 7-14: The primary key index on the locale table assists MySQL in performing this query.

To confirm the existence of the primary key index on the `locale` table, the `show index` command can be used (see Figure 7-15).

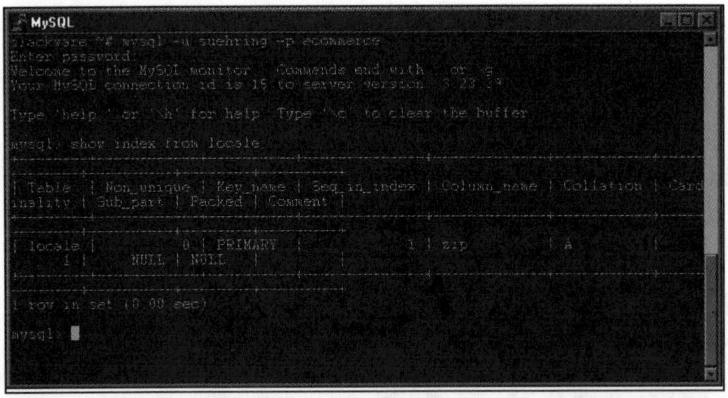

Figure 7-15: The show index command gives useful information about indexes.

MySQL allows you to create indexes in a number of ways (even while creating the table itself), via the `alter table` command or the `create index` command.

> **Cross-Reference**
> Indexing and other optimizations for MySQL are discussed in Chapter 12.

Implementation

The final step in the database life cycle is implementation, which includes:

- ✦ Creation of the physical database and tables on the server
- ✦ Ongoing administration and maintenance of the database

Physically creating the tables for a normalized database design on the database server is simple. The actual writing of the SQL for table creation was done during the Logical Design. Now it is a matter of executing that code on the server.

To create the `ecommerce` example database, I use the `mysqladmin` tool, as shown in Figure 7-16. I'm highlighting this command inside a whole figure to show that it is normal for the command to return no message when it succeeds. If you have an error, `mysqladmin` will let you know.

Cross-Reference

Syntax for mysqladmin is contained in Chapter 8.

Figure 7-16: The mysqladmin command returns no message upon successful completion of a database creation.

Once the database is created, you can create the tables within the database based upon the SQL you wrote during the logical design phase. You're ready to enter the DDL to create the tables into the MySQL CLI to create the tables.

Congratulations, the database is complete! However, the database life cycle isn't over. You now have to maintain the database server by

- ✦ Making sure queries are operating as efficiently as possible
- ✦ Checking table health and repairing tables when needed
- ✦ Actively applying bug fixes and security audits.

Note Since databases are practically living things, changes often are required in the life cycle. Using DDL statements like alter table, you can keep the database useful as business rules and processes change.

Summary

Data is really anything you can imagine and quantify. Though it's not just information in a computer or within a database, Relational Database Management Systems (of which MySQL is an example) make large amounts of data efficiently retrievable and usable.

- A database is a group of organized information, not necessarily on a computer.
- The database life cycle includes analysis, logical design, physical design, and implementation of the database.
- Entities, Attributes, and Relationships are the objects that make up a database design.
- An Entity-Relationship Diagram (ERD) models the layout of the entities, attributes, and relationships. The ERD can be transformed easily into normalized form and then into the physical layout of the database.
- Normalization is the process of reducing redundancy and waste in a database while improving performance and possibly removing errors.
- Indexing helps a database to quickly retrieve information.
- The actual implementation of the database onto the server is the first step in the final phase of the database life cycle. Maintaining and administering the database server is an ongoing process throughout the lifetime of the database.

✦ ✦ ✦

SQL Essentials

PART

II

✦ ✦ ✦ ✦

In This Part

✦ ✦ ✦ ✦

CHAPTER 8

Command Line Interface (CLI)

✦ ✦ ✦ ✦

In This Chapter

Introducing the CLI

Starting the CLI — basics

Using environment variables in MySQL CLI

Choosing when to use the CLI Interactive mode

Configuring a useful MySQL CLI environment

Avoiding common CLI user errors

Listing alternatives to the CLI

✦ ✦ ✦ ✦

The MySQL Command-Line Interface — abbreviated CLI and also known as the *command-line tool* — is the program through which the users handle most of their daily interactions with the database. You access the CLI by issuing the `mysql` command.

This chapter looks at some normal CLI tasks, as well as some that may not be obvious but are still useful. An introduction to the CLI lays the groundwork; before long, you can get your hands dirty with some real functions and try out some uses of the CLI.

Introducing the CLI

Before the advent of GUIs and third-party tools, the MySQL CLI provided the only way to interact with the database. However the CLI offers advantages over some of its newer counterparts insofar as it is tested and stable, it is lightweight, and it comes standard with most installations of MySQL.

The basic syntax for to use the MySQL CLI is as follows:

```
mysql (options) [database]
```

The options for this command help make the MySQL CLI configurable as well as powerful. Should you forget the options and not have this book available, you can get help from the `mysql` command itself by adding the `--help` or -? switches after you type it, as shown in Figure 8-1.

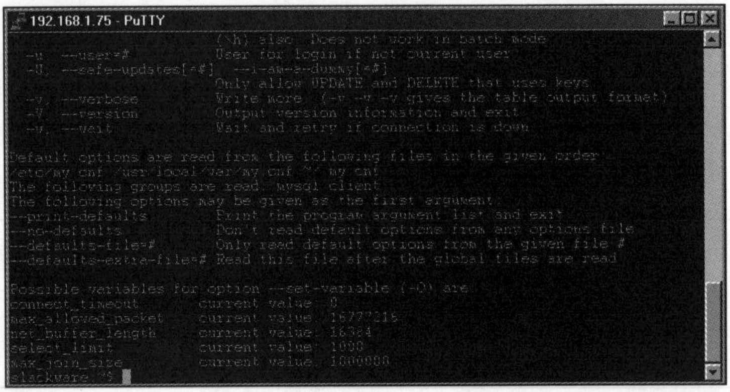

Figure 8-1: Here I use the help switch to remind myself of the correct syntax for the mysql command.

The CLI can be used in interactive mode where you are talking directly with the server and it is talking back to you, in a sense. In interactive mode the commands you type are sent directly to the server and the results are given back to you within the CLI. An example of the CLI in interactive mode is in Figure 8-2. You can obtain help from within in CLI by typing `help;` or `\h`.

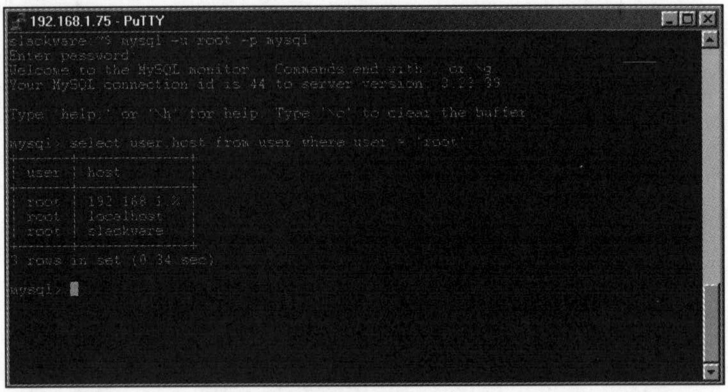

Figure 8-2: The CLI in interactive mode

Interactive-mode CLI is a great tool for troubleshooting database problems. For example, you can use the CLI in interactive mode to make sure queries return the expected results or see why they aren't running correctly. You can use commands to analyze tables and queries with the CLI—and you can alter tables to add indexes, change structure, and more. In addition, when using the CLI in interactive mode a history file is recorded. Not only is this a great way to save keystrokes for frequently (or infrequently) used commands, but it can also provide a means (though insecure) of tracking what a user did to break something. Using the CLI interactively makes a number of database tasks easier, including these:

✦ Troubleshooting queries

✦ Adding users to MySQL

✦ Analyzing tables

✦ Analyzing queries

✦ Altering tables

✦ Checking replication status

✦ Looking at server health

The `mysql` command can also be used in non-interactive mode, directly from the command line or command prompt. The CLI is also useful in non-interactive mode, as shown in Figure 8-3.

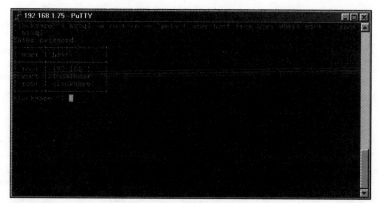

Figure 8-3: The CLI in non-interactive mode in Linux

In non-interactive mode, the CLI provides many of the same functions as in interactive mode. However, in non-interactive mode you don't receive the same feedback from the server (along with the results).

For example, if you perform an `INSERT` operation using the `-e` switch in non-interactive mode, you won't receive a message that tells you the number of rows inserted. When you insert rows in interactive mode, the server gives you feedback that includes the number of rows from the statement.

Some CLI switches are useful only in non-interactive mode, most notably is the `-e` or `--execute` switch. An example of the `-e` switch is shown in Figure 8-4. In the example in Figure 8-4, the `-p` switch specifies that MySQL should prompt for a password and the word `mysql` at the end of the command indicates the database I'd like to connect to—and within which I plan to execute the query that appears in quotes after the `-e` switch. (I provide more information on these switches, and on the syntax of the CLI, later in this chapter.)

Figure 8-4: Using the -e switch to execute a query in non-interactive mode

Although it is possible to execute other commands with the `-e` switch, I don't normally recommend executing DDL (Data Definition Language) commands such as `ALTER TABLE` with the `-e` switch. MySQL still prints error messages back to the command line, but I've found that DDL commands usually require more than one command to be run (for example, a command to describe a table) before alteration can begin.

Command recall—reusing the command or statement you last typed by pressing the up-arrow on the keyboard—is one of the best features of the MySQL CLI. This feature saves countless keystrokes when you make a typographical or spelling error in the middle of a long query and have to run it again. Additionally, command recall makes large and complex queries easier to work with; if you find that the output is not exactly as you want it, simply use the up-arrow and tweak the query when it appears on-screen.

Starting the CLI – the Basics

By now you've probably already been introduced to the CLI through some earlier chapters or the introduction in this chapter. Don't worry if you haven't read those chapters; the CLI itself makes only a brief appearance there.

The command to start the MySQL CLI is contained normally in the bin directory of the MySQL installation. However, it may be located in another directory depending on how you installed MySQL or the operating system you are using. In Linux, I've seen the command located in `/usr/bin`, `/usr/local/bin`, `/usr/local/mysql/bin` and somewhere in the `/var` mount.

How you start the MySQL CLI depends largely on what you want to do. To work with a database interactively, you have to supply credentials to establish a connection. Normally those credentials come in the form of a username and a password — though they can include an optional name of the database you're working with, as well as the hostname (or IP address) of the server. In Figure 8-5, for example, I'm connecting to the local server (`localhost`) as username `suehring` and telling the program to perform two tasks: Ask me for a password and connect me to the `ecommerce` server.

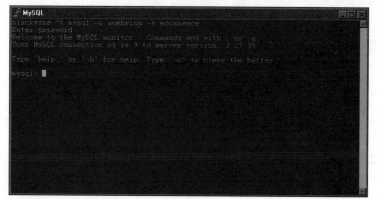

Figure 8-5: Connecting as username suehring to the ecommerce database and specifying a password

Cross-Reference

The examples throughout this chapter assume that the user account you're using has sufficient access privileges to perform the operations. If this is not the case, consult Chapter 12 for a description of how to add a user account with specified privileges.

Specifying the username

When using `mysql` in Linux, normally you need not add the `-u` (username) switch. If the `-u` username switch is not specified, the `mysql` command uses the username from your environment variables. For that authentication to work, the MySQL server must have a user entry with correct privileges in its user table. In Figure 8-6, the `-u` switch is not used, so MySQL grabs the username `suehring` from the environment variables. Because a user `suehring` exists in the MySQL database and has the proper privileges, I can connect to the database server after supplying the correct password.

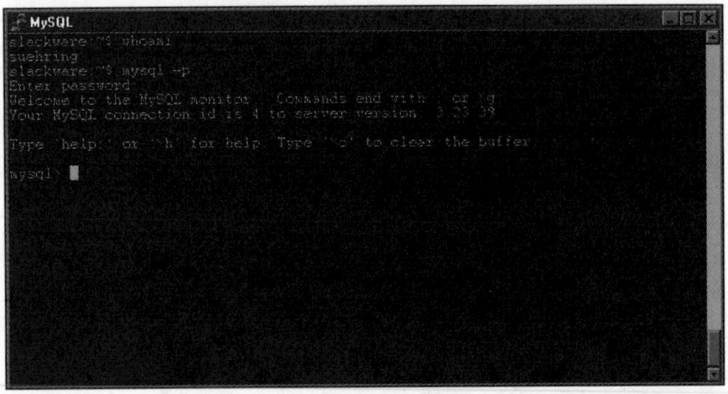

Figure 8-6: MySQL uses the username of the current user if the -u switch is not used.

Accordingly, if you are using the CLI as the `root` user, MySQL attempts to connect as the `root` user if the `-u` switch is not used.

If you want to override the default user and have the MySQL CLI authenticate as a different user every time, you can add the `username=<username>` clause to the MySQL configuration file.

Cross-Reference

For details on how to set and change default variables for the MySQL CLI, see the "MySQL CLI Environment Variables" section later in this chapter.

Specifying the password

One source of confusion for some is the use of the `-p` switch to specify the password. Often people believe that what follows the `-p` is actually the password—but this isn't always the case. The `-p` switch simply tells the `mysql` program to *prompt* for the password if none is given. In the example in Figure 8-5, a space appears after the `-p` switch—it's prompting you for the password. If you want to specify the password on the command line, you can do so by placing the password immediately after the `-p` switch, as shown in Figure 8-7.

Caution

Specifying the password on the command line should be considered a security risk because the password is right in plain sight for a would-be attacker to see.

Additionally, the `--password` switch can be substituted for the `-p` switch and is used much the same way. If you provide just the `--password` switch you are prompted for the password. However, unlike the `-p` switch, the `--password` syntax requires you to specify the password on the command line by using an equals sign (=), as shown in Figure 8-8.

Figure 8-7: Specifying the password immediately following the -p switch prevents the CLI from prompting for a password.

Figure 8-8: The syntax for the --password switch is slightly different from the -p switch.

The `password=<password>` switch can be added into the MySQL configuration file and thus saved between sessions. This is also a security risk. Alternatively, you could simply place the word `password` under the `[mysql]` section of the configuration file and you are prompted for the password just as if you used the `-p` switch. (See this chapter's "MySQL CLI Environment Variables" section for more about working with CLI variables.)

Specifying the host

In much the same way that MySQL uses the current user if the `-u` switch is not used, not using the `-h` switch makes MySQL assume you mean to connect to the server on the *localhost* (the current machine). If you want to connect to a MySQL server on another machine, you can specify the IP address or hostname of the other MySQL server via the `-h` switch, as shown in Figure 8-9.

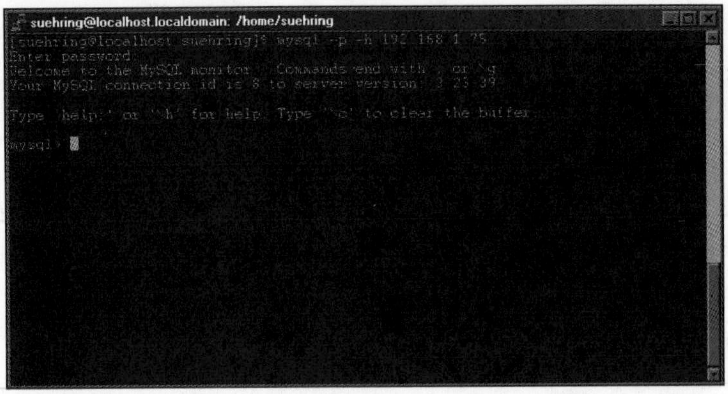
suehring@localhost.localdomain: /home/suehring
[suehring@localhost suehring]$ mysql -p -h 192.168.1.75
Enter password:
Welcome to the MySQL monitor. Commands end with ; or \g.
Your MySQL connection id is 8 to server version: 3.23.39
Type 'help;' or '\h' for help. Type '\c' to clear the buffer.
mysql>

Figure 8-9: Use the -h switch to connect to another MySQL server or leave it blank to connect to the local machine.

If you want to set a default host other than localhost without having to specify the `-h <server>` switch every time you can set the host inside the configuration file, see the discussion of environment variables (later in this chapter) for details on how to set and change default variables for the MySQL CLI. Any host specified in a configuration file is overridden if you specify another `-h <server>` on the command line.

Specifying the database

The MySQL CLI enables you to specify the database to use without the addition of any switches to the command line. The command expects the database to be specified as the last part of the command line. For example, to use a database called `inventory`, simply add it to the command at the end, like this:

```
mysql -p -u suehring inventory
```

If no database is specified on the command line (assuming you have access privileges), you return automatically to the MySQL CLI—in interactive mode but not connected to any database. To connect and use a database, issue the `connect` statement. In Figure 8-10, I connect to the MySQL server without specifying a database. I can then connect to a database by using the `connect` statement.

If you want to specify the database at a location other than the end of the command line, you can use the `-D` or `--database=<databasename>` switches. To set a default database for MySQL to use upon startup, add a `database=<databasename>` to the MySQL configuration file, see the section on Environment Variables in this chapter for details on how to set and change default variables for the MySQL CLI.

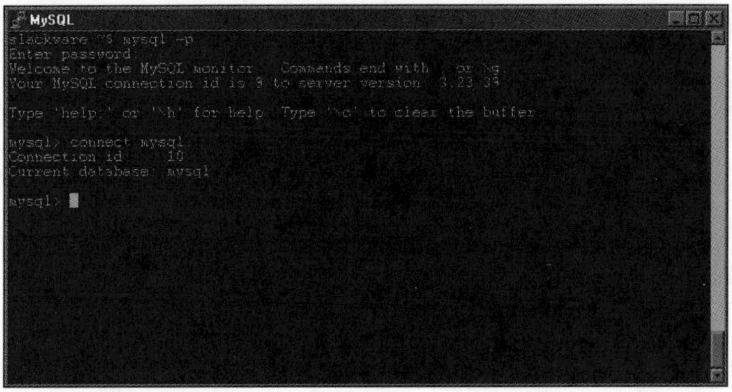

Figure 8-10: Using the CLI and specifying a database from within the CLI

MySQL CLI Environment Variables

Regardless of whether you use the CLI in interactive mode, variables are available to control how the CLI operates. When read from configuration files, those variables can be set globally with the use of configuration files — in particular, `my.cnf` or `my.ini` (usually located in the `/etc` or `/usr/local` Linux directory or the `WINNT` directory in Windows 2000).

Note If you want to set the variables on a per-user basis, a `.my.cnf` file in each user's home directory can provide customized individual use of the MySQL CLI. Make sure that a dot (`.`) immediately precedes each user's `.my.cnf` filename—for example, `.my.cnf`. Since the configuration file can reside in each user's home directory, it is only applied when logged in as that user.

Determining and changing default variables

To determine the variables the MySQL CLI uses for a particular session, use the `--print-defaults` switch, as shown in Figure 8-11.

Changing a default variable is as simple as editing the configuration file. For example, if I want to change the socket that MySQL connects through from the default `/tmp/mysql.sock`, I could make a `.my.cnf` file (as shown in Figure 8-12) and include a section for the MySQL CLI in brackets with the `socket` option underneath.

Figure 8-11: The --print-defaults switch shows you which environment variables MySQL uses for your session.

Figure 8-12: Creating a .my.cnf file in my home directory so I can set defaults for the MySQL CLI

In Figure 8-13, the output of the `--print-defaults` switch, note the new socket name — actually *two* socket defaults. Because local options are read last, the last `socket` option to be read is applied.

Figure 8-13: The --print-defaults switch now shows the new defaults that go into effect the next time you start the MySQL CLI.

In the example in Figure 8-13, I changed the socket to a bogus filename that won't actually connect to the MySQL server. The result is the error message you see in Figure 8-14.

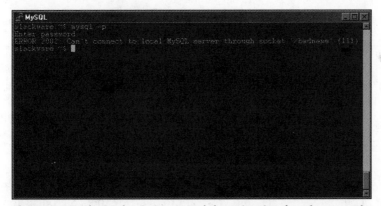

Figure 8-14: The socket name I used doesn't exist; therefore I receive an error message when I try to connect.

Some of the more useful client or CLI variables are shown in Table 8-1.

Table 8-1
Frequently Used MySQL CLI Variables

Variable	*Use*
socket	Changes the socket for local connections.
port	Changes the port for connections via TCP/IP.
password	Sets the password to be used by the CLI. Potential security risk.
pager	Sets the pager such as the more or less commands to control scroll.
host	Sets a default host to connect to with all connections.
database	Sets a default database.
skip-column-names	Suppresses the printing of column names with the `select` statements.
vertical	Prints output from queries vertically.
html	Produces output in HTML format, useful when operating in non-interactive mode.
`tee=`*<filename>*	Appends output from interactive mode into the file named *<filename>*.

When calling the MySQL program, you can set its variables either in the `.my.cnf` file or on the command line.

Tip Variables set on the command line supersede those set in configuration files.

In addition to setting variables, a `--no-defaults` command-line option enables you to override any defaults in configuration files. This is useful if your `.my.cnf` file has a number of default values set, and you want to override them all to use some non-default options. In Figure 8-15, for example, I have set some options that enable me to work more efficiently (since most of the work is done on the local machine).

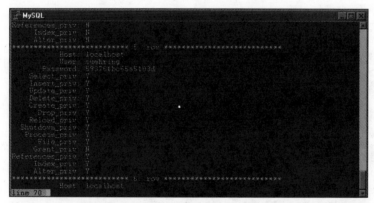

Figure 8-15: Using mysql --print-defaults to see the default options I have for this client

Performing a query with these options yields the results shown in Figure 8-16.

Figure 8-16: Running a query with the default options

However, now I have to connect to another MySQL server—and I don't want the `vertical` or `pager` options but I do need column names printed. To turn off all the defaults at once—and set my own, basing them on the new host—I use the `--no-defaults` option (as shown in Figure 8-17).

Figure 8-17: Using the --no-defaults option on the command line to override all defaults at once

Performing a query shows that the other options (such as `vertical` and `pager`) have been turned off, as shown in Figure 8-18.

Figure 8-18: A query with the defaults turned off yields the expected results.

Using the CLI in Interactive Mode

When you use the CLI in interactive mode, a prompt akin to a shell prompt appears—you get functions, switches, and settings that affect how the CLI operates. Some of these features are better used with the CLI in non-interactive mode; others work more efficiently in interactive mode.

Note: When using the MySQL CLI in interactive mode, all commands must be terminated with a semicolon (;). The only three exceptions to this rule are the `exit` command, the `quit` command, and the `connect` command.

Speeding startup of the CLI

When the CLI starts, it reads in table information to allow for completion, which can sometimes slow the startup. To turn off this default and get a quicker CLI startup, use the `-A` or `--no-auto-rehash` switch. Adding `--no-auto-rehash` to the MySQL configuration file under the `[mysql]` section makes this quicker startup permanent.

Making the CLI quieter

When you start the CLI, a welcoming message prints (along with version and session information). In addition, status messages appear on-screen so you can see the progress of the statements you execute. If you'd like to stop that information from showing up, use the `-s` or `--silent` option. To make this arrangement permanent (except for error messages, which still appear as needed), add the `--silent` option under the `[mysql]` section of your MySQL configuration file.

Using a pager to work with larger amounts of data

Often the results of a `select` statement scroll past the screen when the program has to handle a large (or not even very large) set of data. Through the use of the `pager` option you can set MySQL to return query results split over a number of screens. Using a *pager* command such as the `more` or `less`, you can control the scrolling on a page-by-page basis.

You can set the `pager` option, whether from inside a configuration file or on the command line, by adding the `--pager=`*`<pager>`* option to the `mysql` command, as shown in Figure 8-19.

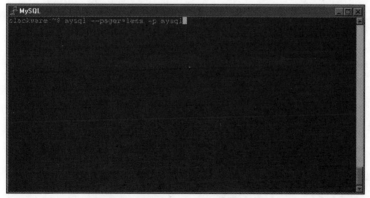

Figure 8-19: Using the --pager option on the command line specifies the program to control scrolling

Note If the `pager` option is set in a MySQL configuration file, you can turn it off by using the `--no-pager` switch on the command line.

Displaying query results vertically

Often the columns in a query result wrap awkwardly around the edges of the screen. Not only is this situation ugly, it's also confusing; the wrapping makes the columns hard to match with their values, as shown in Figure 8-20.

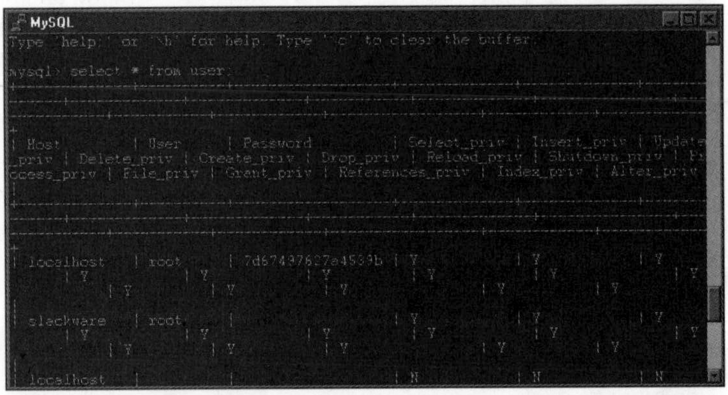

Figure 8-20: Without the vertical option, the output from this query wraps around the screen.

In Figure 8-20, it can be difficult to determine whether a given user actually has the File privilege. However, with the use of the `-E` or `--vertical` switch, the data is displayed with columns following each other vertically. Adding the `vertical` option to the `.my.cnf` file in my home directory—along with the use of a pager command—greatly improved the look and usability of my query's output (as shown in Figure 8-21).

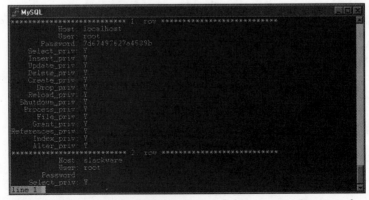

Figure 8-21: Using the vertical option and the pager option to make the output more comprehensible

I added the following lines to the [mysql] section of the .my.cnf configuration file to produce the output in Figure 8-21.

```
[mysql]
host=localhost
vertical
pager=/usr/bin/less
```

Note The use of --pager won't work when using the CLI in non-interactive mode.

Using tee to save output

The tee command takes the entire session—including input and output from a command—and appends it to a file that you specify. This function can be helpful when debugging (for security purposes), or simply as an easy way to get data into a file. The switch to use this function with MySQL is --tee=<*filename*>. Alternately the switch can be set in the MySQL configuration file with the use of tee=<*filename*> For example, Figure 8-22 uses the tee function to append the session onto a file called outputfile.txt.

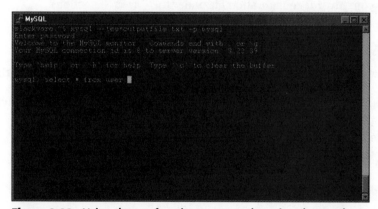

Figure 8-22: Using the tee function to append session data to the content of a file

Figure 8-23 shows session data that has been saved to the outputfile.txt file.

Note If the tee option is set in a MySQL configuration file, it can be turned off by using the --no-tee switch on the command line.

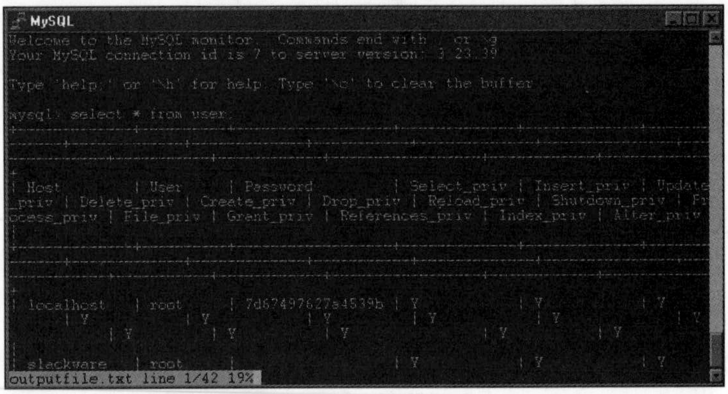

Figure 8-23: Here the Tee function has saved session data in the file.

Printing output in HTML format

Though using the CLI in non-interactive mode is generally the more useful approach, sometimes you may want to run a simple query and then copy and paste its output into a Web page as HTML output. To do so, use the `-H` or `--html` switch (or put the word `html` in your MySQL configuration file under the `[mysql]` section).

Suppressing column names

At times I've found it useful to run a query without having the column names print in the output. From within the CLI, this technique can sometimes prevent some confusion by keeping the output from wrapping around on-screen. As with the switch that produces HTML output, this function may be best used in non-interactive mode—though it's sometimes useful in interactive mode as well.

To suppress column names, start the MySQL CLI with the `-N` or `--skip-column-names` switch. To make this suppression permanent, add `skip-column-names` to your MySQL configuration file in the `[mysql]` section.

Using batch mode to produce tab delimited output

The MySQL CLI also operates in a batch mode that suppresses traditional feedback from the CLI and presents query output in tab-delimited format (see Figure 8-24).

If you enter batch mode and get an error message, the session is immediately terminated. You are sent back to the shell with an echo of the error message (as shown in Figure 8-25).

Figure 8-24: Using the CLI in batch mode to get tab-delimited output while suppressing other information and feedback from the CLI.

Figure 8-25: Errors that occur while you're using batch mode kick you back out to the command shell.

Note

You still have to terminate commands with a semicolon (;) while using batch mode interactively.

If you want to prevent MySQL from terminating your session upon error when in batch mode, use the `-f` or `--force` switch. With the Force option set, the error message is displayed but the session continues, ignoring the error.

Caution

Use the `force` option with care; one error in the beginning of a series of SQL statements can wreak havoc on the rest of the statements—and possibly the data.

Using the CLI in Non-Interactive Mode

The CLI need not be used interactively; sometimes running a simple query or command on the server does the job. For example, you may want to redirect the output of a statement to a file, or use a scheduler (such as `cron`) to schedule the running of a particular command. In such instances, the MySQL CLI can be used in a *non-interactive mode* that makes it operate like any basic, straightforward command.

Executing a statement

When you're operating in non-interactive mode, one of the most frequent and useful operations is to execute a statement. To do so, you use the `-e` or `--execute=command-line` switch. For example, to run a simple query that finds the users and hosts allowed to connect to a particular database, you can use the `-e` switch as illustrated in Figure 8-26.

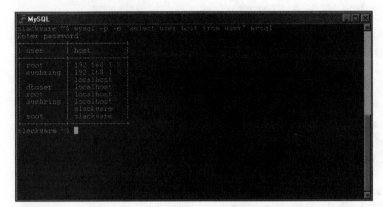

Figure 8-26: Using the -e switch to run a simple query

In Figure 8-26, I specified the `-p` switch to have MySQL prompt for the password. Next comes the `-e` switch, followed by the statement to execute in quotes. Finally comes the name of the database to connect to (in this case, `mysql`, because that's where user data is stored).

Printing HTML output

One especially handy feature of the MySQL CLI is that it can output a query in HTML format — a capability you can use to create a simple Web page from a query without much effort. The switch that produces HTML output is `-H` or `--html`. For example, suppose I want to make a Web page consisting of a simple report of the products in the `ecommerce` database example (yes, all three of them.) In Figure 8-27, I ran the command to produce the output.

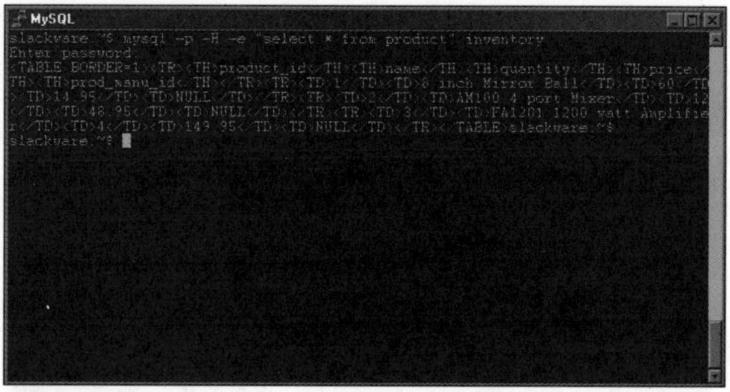

Figure 8-27: The output from a HTML-formatted query that uses the CLI

In Figure 8-27, the switches and the order of the command are what you would expect.

Caution Whenever you add an option or a switch to the `mysql` command, be sure to use the correct case. For example, adding the `-H` option gives MySQL different instructions from those specified by the `-h` switch (lowercase *h*). Adding `-h` instead of `-H` would have made MySQL think you were specifying a host instead of calling for HTML output. As you can see from Figure 8-27, the output isn't pretty.

The greatest usefulness of the HTML switch is redirecting output to a file, as shown in Figure 8-28.

Figure 8-28: Redirecting the output from an HTML-formatted query

In Figure 8-28, the output is redirected by using the greater-than sign (>) and the name of the file that receives the output is `inventory.html`.

Caution

In Linux, the single greater-than sign (>) causes the redirected output to overwrite whatever is in the receiving file. If you want merely to append the output instead of using it to replace what's in the file, use two greater-than signs (>>).

After moving or copying the file (with the newly appended output) to a place where the Web server can get hold of it, I have a Web page consisting of a simple table that shows the products in the inventory. Figure 8-29 shows what it looks like.

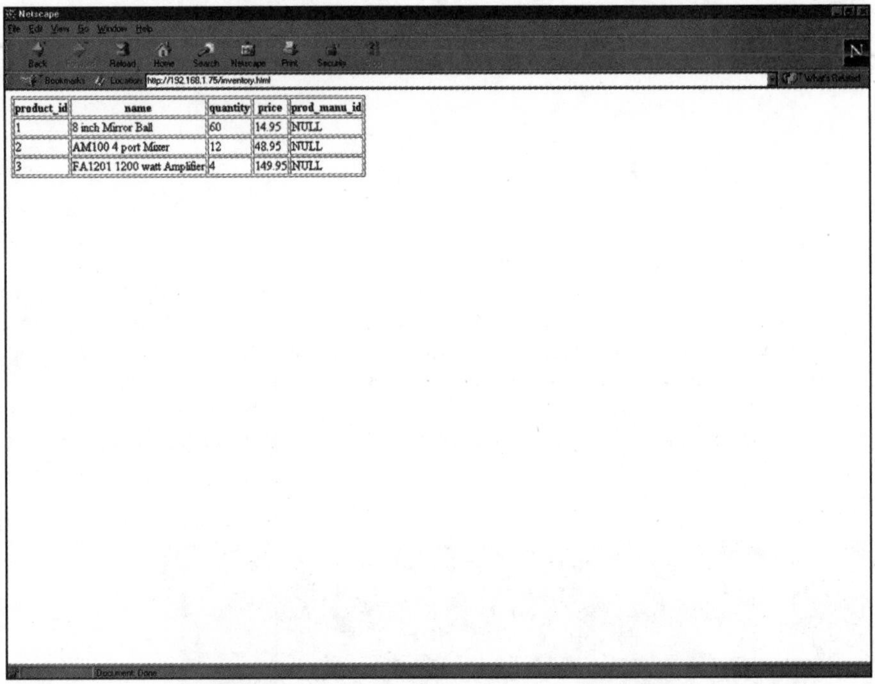

Figure 8-29: A simple Web page produced with the output from the -H switch

Suppressing column names

Every time MySQL runs a query, the output of the query includes column names at the top. If you want to exclude column names (as when you append the output to a different file), you can use an option to suppress them.

To suppress column names, start the MySQL CLI with the `-N` or `--skip-column-names` switch. To make this function permanent, add `skip-column-names` to your MySQL configuration file in the `[mysql]` section.

Printing results vertically

Just as the MySQL CLI can print results vertically when being used interactively to help improve layout, vertical output is sometimes useful in non-interactive mode as well. This is especially true for appending data to a file to be examined later.

The switch to turn on the appropriate option is `-E` or `--vertical`. This format can be made permanent by adding the word `vertical` to your MySQL configuration file under the `[mysql]` section.

Using batch mode to produce tab-delimited output

To produce output that uses tabs as delimiters, you can use MySQL in batch mode. Turn batch mode on with the `-B` or `--batch` switch (or add the word `batch` to your MySQL configuration file under the `[mysql]` section). In batch mode, the output from a `SELECT` statement would show values separated by tabs instead of by columns (useful if you're importing data into another application, because most applications recognize the tab character as a valid field separator).

In Figure 8-30, I issue a simple `SELECT` statement in normal mode, which formats the fields as a table.

Figure 8-30: A query in normal mode produces tabular-formatted output

In Figure 8-31, I issue that same `SELECT` statement, this time in batch mode. Notice that the output no longer has the tabular format. Instead, it shows tabs as delimiters. Using batch mode, I could redirect the output file and import it into another database application.

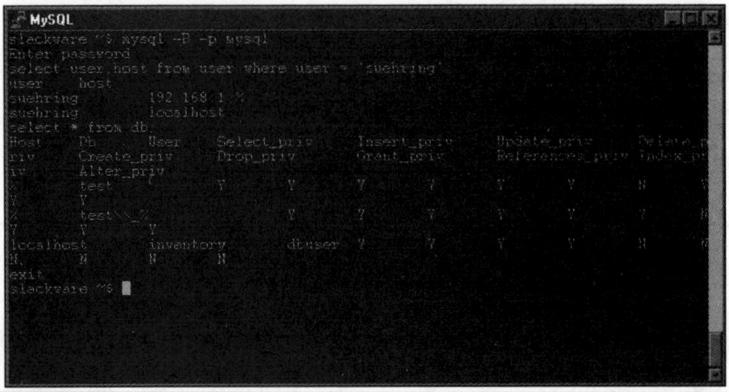

Figure 8-31: Using batch mode to produce output with tab delimiters

Cross-Reference: Some other commands and statements—such as `mysqldump` or `SELECT INTO OUTFILE`—may be better suited to exporting data. Those commands are discussed in Chapter 10.

Creating a Useful MySQL CLI Environment

With all the options covered in this chapter, you may be wondering which ones you should use—and whether to set the options globally (for all users of the CLI), or only for your user account, or only in your home directory. The answers are flexible, determined by what you need your database application to do.

For example, if all users on the computer use the same username to connect to a particular database, you could make that usage a global setting in the MySQL configuration file. Alternatively, if you use a particular username but everyone else uses a different one, you could specify that setting in your local or personal MySQL configuration file.

Tip: Programmers still debate the matter of which pager command is best for displaying results. For practicality's sake, you may want to avoid the debate by specifying that setting only in a local or personal configuration file.

A useful environment for the CLI can be as complicated or as simple as you'd like it to be. Ideally, you could produce a configuration file personalized for your use of the MySQL CLI. With a good configuration, you could save time and increase productivity by not having to specify the same options every time you start the CLI.

A basic MySQL CLI configuration

The following configuration example might be a fine starting point for anyone's use of MySQL. The configuration provides a default pager of less for results that would scroll more than one screen and it will also tell the CLI to automatically prompt for the password on startup. This should be set in your local configuration file such as the `.my.cnf` file in your home directory in Linux.

```
[mysql]
pager=less
password
```

A MySQL administration configuration

The following is an example of what an administrator's configuration might look like for MySQL. You would have to add a username of `admin` with proper privileges to the database. The configuration will connect as the user `'admin'` and prompt for a password. The default database to connect to is the `mysql grants` database that houses user rights and privileges. I've chosen a default pager of `less` to specify fewer results on-screen (less to scroll through). I added the `vertical` option because I've found that displaying the grant tables vertically really helps comprehension since most of the grant tables will wrap around the screen. Finally, all operations within the CLI will be appended to a logfile for tracking

```
[mysql]
user=admin
password
database=mysql
pager=less
vertical
tee=mysqlaudit.log
```

Note The `tee` option does not provide complete security or tracking for operations performed within a database.

A client-only MySQL CLI configuration

If you connect to a remote MySQL server frequently, adding a host=<*hostname*> line to the basic configuration might help. With the host=<*hostname*> configuration, the CLI automatically connects to the remote host without requiring you to specify the `-h` switch on the command line.

```
[mysql]
host=192.168.1.75
pager=less
password
```

Your MySQL CLI configuration

Your MySQL CLI configuration may look somewhat different from the ones I've given as examples. Building and tailoring the configuration to your application and installation is one of many ways you can improve your experience with MySQL.

Common CLI Errors

Using the CLI myself (and working with many people who are new to databases and the CLI), I've seen quite a few error messages. Often the errors crop up simply because I can't seem to type well that day, but just as often they show up for other reasons that call for some simple troubleshooting.

Access Denied errors

The `Access Denied` error has a number of variations, three of which are shown in Figure 8-32.

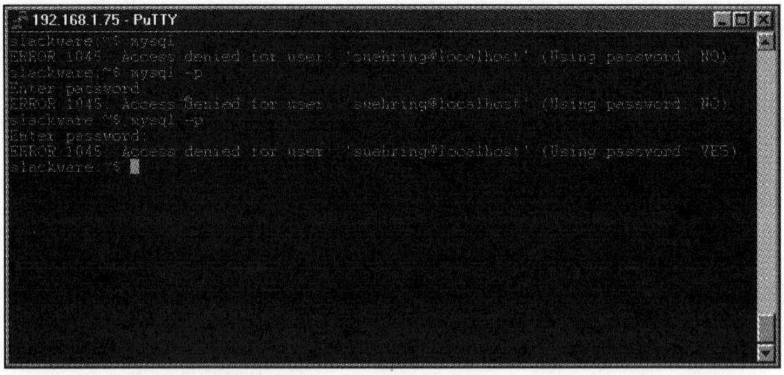

Figure 8-32: Three variations of the Access Denied error with the CLI

Here's what produced the errors shown in Figure 8-32:

- ✦ In the first example I am trying to obtain access to the CLI as the user `suehring` but I am not specifying a password via the `-p` switch. This try fails; the error message hints (not too subtly) why: `Using Password: No`.
- ✦ In the second attempt, I add the `-p` switch but then press Enter instead of typing the password. Notice the similarity of result between the second and first attempts (though I didn't use the `-p` switch in the first one).
- ✦ In the third attempt, I use the `-p` switch but mistype the password. Notice this time that the end of the error message is different: `Using Password: Yes`.

Another variation of the `Access Denied` error is shown in Figure 8-33: I try to connect to a database on which I have no privileges or rights. As you can see, the error number is different, as is the message.

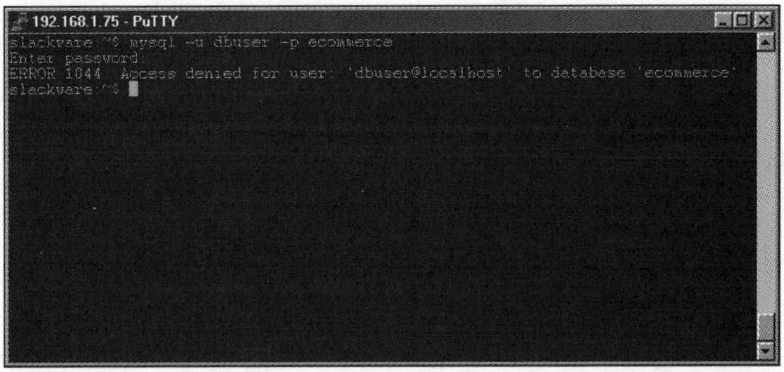

Figure 8-33: Another variation of an Access Denied error occurs when the user doesn't have sufficient privileges to connect to the database.

Figure 8-34 illustrates a common error that can crop up when you try to connect to a MySQL database. There are differing reasons for this error message; the first and foremost is that the MySQL server isn't running. Normally you can solve this problem by starting the MySQL server and attempting to connect again.

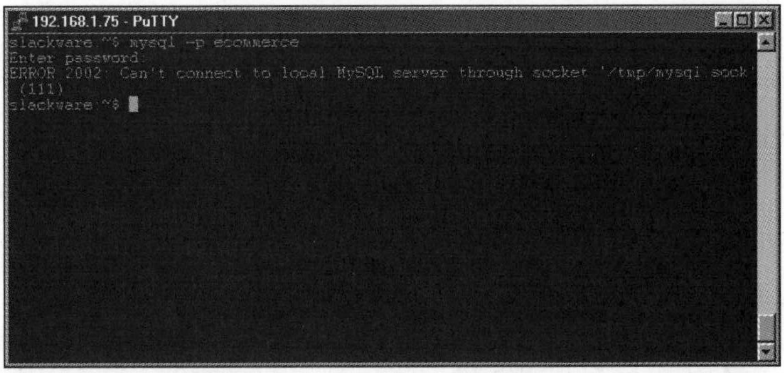

Figure 8-34: A common error can mean one of several different problems may exist.

Another cause of the problem shown in Figure 8-34 is that the CLI is attempting to connect through a socket file that doesn't exist. The remedy for this issue is usually to determine *why* the file doesn't exist — for example, because of permissions problems, a file created in the wrong place, or (again) a MySQL server that isn't running.

Alternatives to the CLI

The CLI is by no means the only method for working with database and data. With the numerous MySQL APIs available, you can write your own method for interacting with the database and data, using many programming languages — or use any of the pre-written programs that were written for working with databases and data. In this section I'm going to discuss two such programs, the MySQLGUI program distributed by MySQL AB as well as the Web-based tool phpMyAdmin.

Of course, since the advent of the Macintosh and Windows graphical user interfaces, the GUI has long been an alternative to the CLI (though some argue that a server operating system shouldn't be required to have a GUI). Although MySQLGUI performs the same functions as the MySQL CLI, it abandons the text-based interface of a traditional CLI and adopts a look that may be more comfortable for longtime Windows and Mac users. You can obtain a copy of the MySQLGUI program directly from MySQL AB.

The MySQLGUI doesn't come with all the bells and whistles that some GUI users expect — in particular, it has no installation or setup program. After you unpack the archive, you have to create your own directories and shortcuts to the program.

The phpMyAdmin suite is a collection of PHP scripts that perform many of the same tasks as the MySQL CLI and its `mysqladmin` command. With phpMyAdmin, you can perform selects, insert, deletes, creation of databases and tables as well as administration tasks such as adding users, showing processes and so forth, all through a Web-based interface.

Installation of phpMyAdmin requires PHP and a Web server such as Apache. You can obtain phpMyAdmin at `http://phpwizard.net`. Because phpMyAdmin runs on a Web server, you can use it to work with your database server and databases from any computer with a Web browser, regardless of platform.

On the CD-ROM

The Apache Web server is included on the CD-ROM with this book, as is PHP.

The basics of MySQLGUI

At first startup, MySQLGUI prompts you for the password (see Figure 8-35). If you enter a password and continue, MySQLGUI attempts to connect as 'root' to the localhost server. If you press the Esc key, however, you get to the MySQLGUI main screen without connecting to the database server.

Figure 8-35: MySQLGUI prompts for the password at startup. Pressing Esc bypasses the Password screen.

Before you can perform any actions on the database server, you must supply credentials such as username and password. MySQLGUI also looks for information in configuration files such as `.my.cnf` and `my.ini`. To set or change these options, click Manage ➪ Options; alternatively, click the Options button on the toolbar. You should see a screen similar to Figure 8-36.

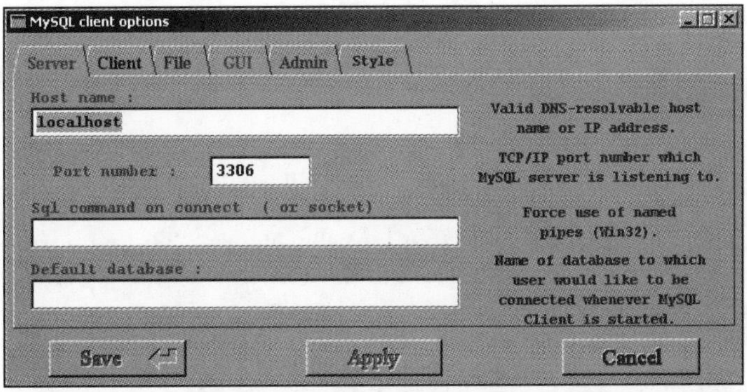

Figure 8-36: The Options screen in MySQLGUI is where you set the credentials for connecting to the database server, as well as other program options.

Note that Figure 8-36 also shows a row of tabs across the top of the dialog box. By default, MySQLGUI attempts a connection to the localhost database server (or the machine on which MySQLGUI is running). You can also supply an IP address or DNS name for another MySQL server. If you want to connect to a specific database such as the default `mysql` database, you can set that on this screen as well.

The Client tab, shown in Figure 8-37, is for establishing some basic settings for the client — for example, username (which is `root` by default) and the timeout interval for the connection. For my example, I connect as the user `suehring` — changing the username.

Caution The `root` username should be reserved for one user only — the administrative "superuser." I strongly recommend that you don't use MySQL's root user to perform day-to-day tasks with MySQL.

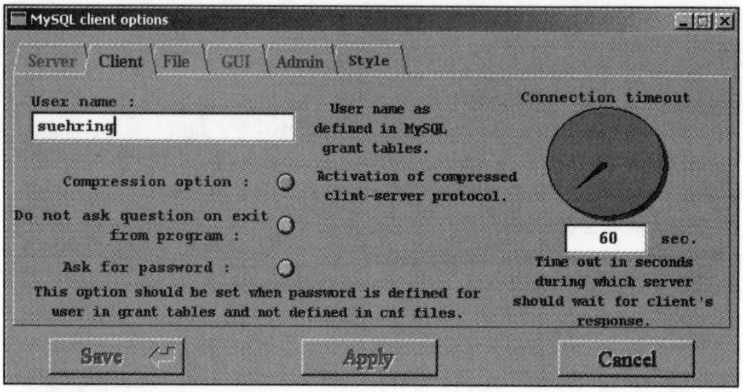

Figure 8-37: The Client tab is where you set options such as username and connection timeout.

When you click the Apply button, the Options dialog box closes. If you want to save your settings for the next time you run the program, you must click the Save button after clicking Apply

Note

Be sure to click the Save button if you want the options to be saved for the next time you run MySQLGUI.

When your options are set, click the Connect button (in the upper-left area of the MyQSLGUI window). A password prompt similar to that in Figure 8-35 appears; mistyping the password produces results that look like Figure 8-38: An informational or error message appears at the bottom of the screen—strikingly similar to the one you'd receive with the MySQL CLI.

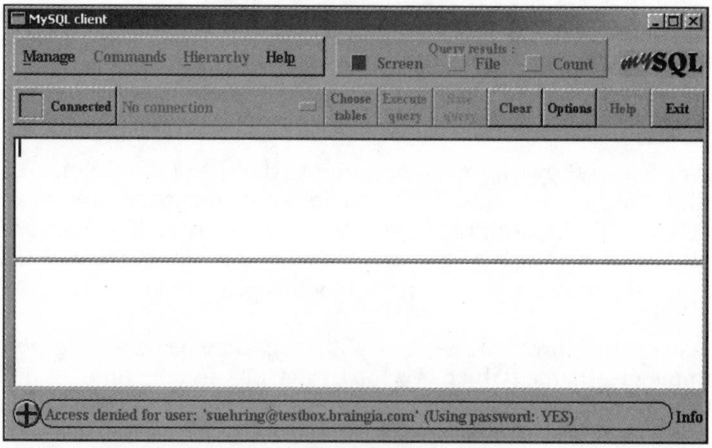

Figure 8-38: I deliberately mistyped my password to show you the error message you get when you do that.

Clicking the Connect button and then typing your password correctly results (logically enough) in a connection to the database server. Notice that if more than one database is available on the server, you can click the drop-down box next to the Connect button and see a complete list (as shown in Figure 8-39). You still see a complete list of databases, even if you don't have any privileges on them. Attempting to connect to a database for which you don't have privileges will result in an error. In addition, when MySQLGUI connects, it places the list of databases in alphabetical order. If you don't have privileges on the first database in that list, you won't be allowed to connect. To correct this problem, set a default database by clicking File ➪ Options.

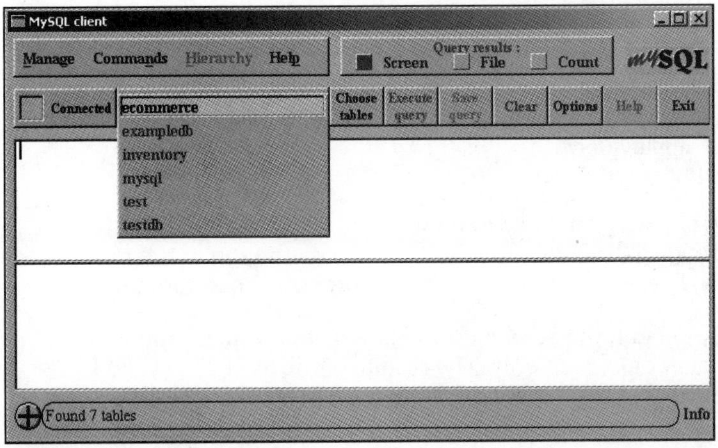

Figure 8-39: Connecting to the database server and looking at the databases available on the server

Running SQL statements with MySQLGUI

Running a query or other SQL statement is really quite simple with MySQLGUI. Simply type the query into the box as shown in Figure 8-40, using a simple query on the `mysql` database such as `SELECT * FROM user`.

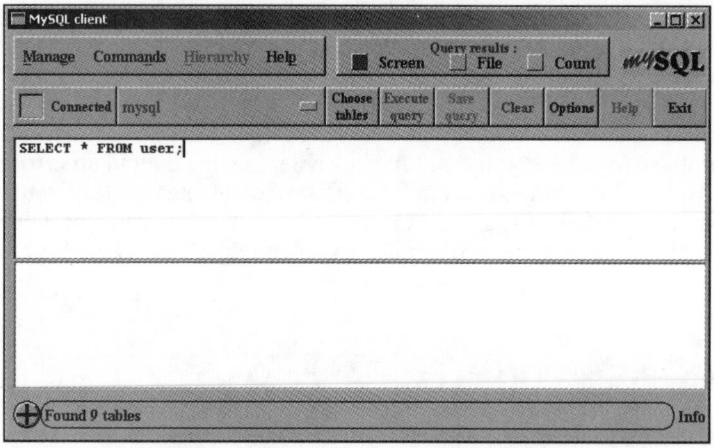

Figure 8-40: Executing SQL statements with MySQLGUI is easy, as shown by this simple query.

You can choose of what you'd like to do with the results from the statement. Figures 8-36 through 8-39 show three buttons across the top of the main MySQLGUI screen — Screen, File, and Count — that also represent those choices:

✦ **Screen:** By default, the Screen option is selected, which prints the results of any statement on-screen only. The results of the `SELECT * FROM user` query open a new dialog box, as shown in Figure 8-41.

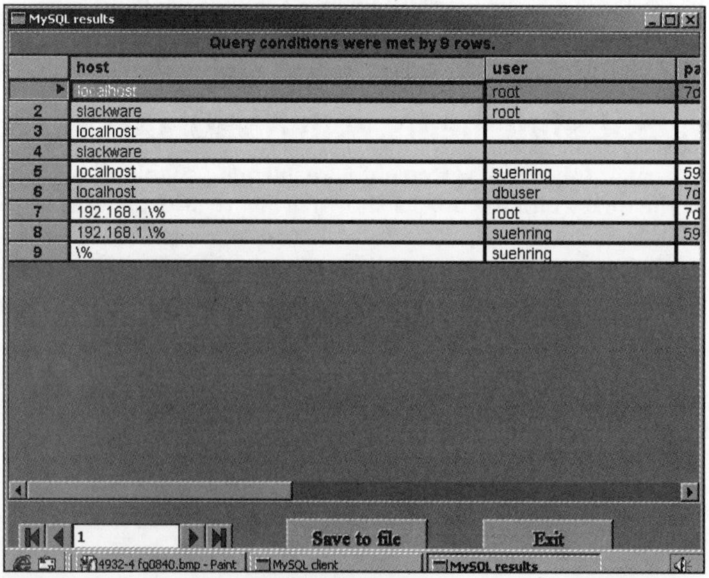

Figure 8-41: When you print the results of a statement to the screen, a new dialog box opens automatically.

The Results box gives you the option to save your results to a file.

✦ **File:** If you want to save the results to a file directly, click the File button. A dialog box similar to the one shown in Figure 8-42 appears, prompting you for the location to which you want to send the results. In response to the prompt for a filename, you can choose to create a new file or append the results to an existing file.

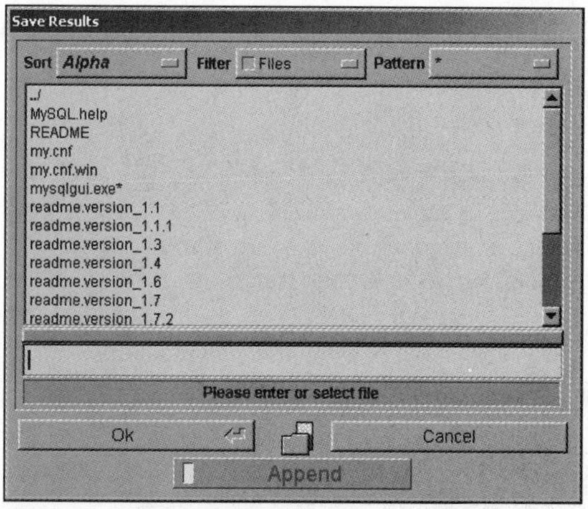

Figure 8-42: To save the results to a file, you must select the location and filename for MySQLGUI to send the results to.

✦ **Count:** Select this button if you want to see a count of the results instead of printing the output to the screen or to a file. The count appears in the Information section at the bottom of the MySQLGUI screen. For example, the `SELECT * FROM user` query returns 9 rows, as shown in Figure 8-43. The count results appear in the Information section at the bottom of the figure.

You can also use MySQLGUI to limit the number of rows returned by a query. Click Commands ➪ Query ➪ With Limit. A slider-bar appears at the bottom of the main MySQLGUI program screen, as shown in Figure 8-44. Simply slide the bar to the left or right, by left-clicking with the mouse and dragging the bar.

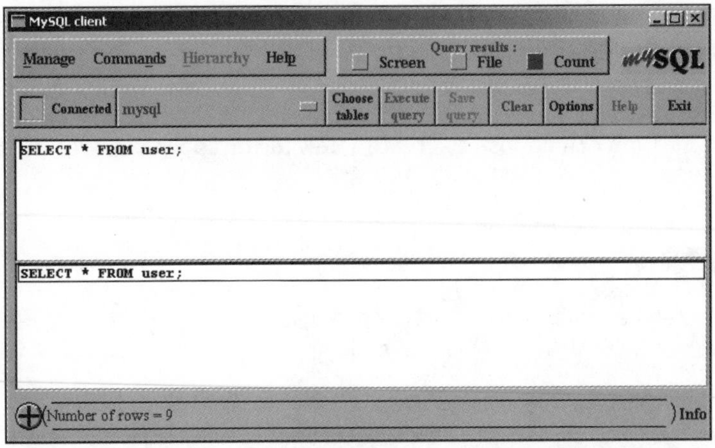

Figure 8-43: Select the Count option displays the number of rows returned by the statement in the Information section of the MySQLGUI screen.

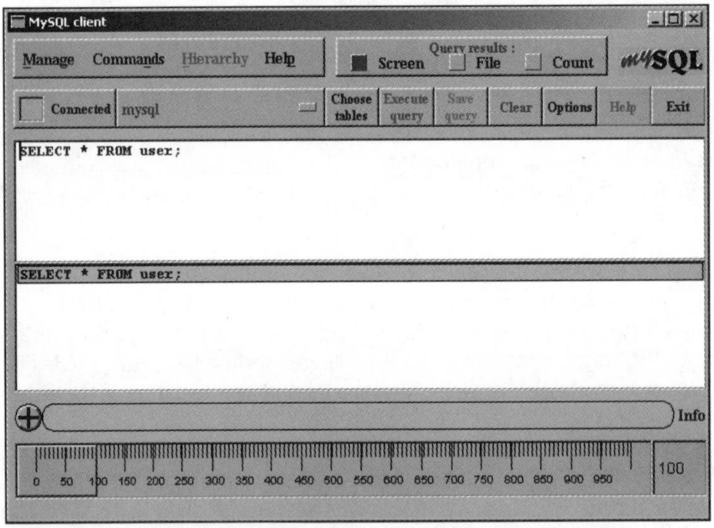

Figure 8-44: You can limit the rows returned by a query by selecting the With Limit option.

Administration with MySQLGUI

In addition to performing standard MySQL CLI duties (such as running SQL statements), you can use MySQLGUI to perform many administrative tasks such as creating and dropping databases, checking the status of the server, and even shutting the server down.

The Administration menu (below the Commands menu bar) is where you can find numerous commands for monitoring and governing the operation of MySQL database server, as shown in Figure 8-45.

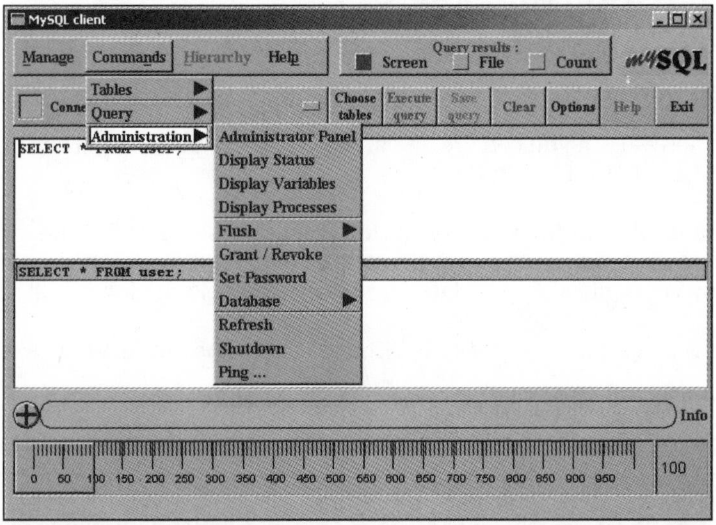

Figure 8-45: The Administration commands available with MySQLGUI

To perform some of these same administrative tasks on the MySQL database server, you can bring up an Administration Panel there as well (as shown in Figure 8-46).

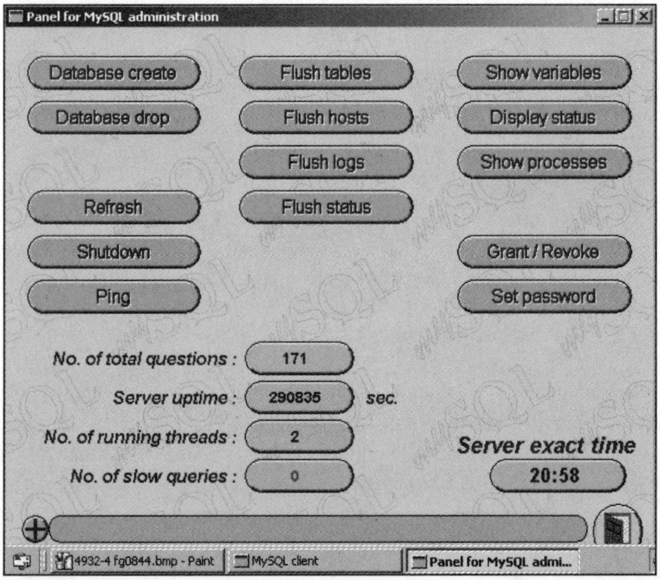

Figure 8-46: The Administration Panel of MySQLGUI

Cross-Reference Administrative commands and tasks are discussed in individual detail throughout this book, most notably in Chapter 9 and Appendix A.

The basics of phpMyAdmin

`phpMyAdmin` is a Web-based interface for working with databases and database servers. `phpMyAdmin` can be used to perform database administration as well as Data Definition Language (DDL) and Data Markup Language (DML) statements. For example, with `phpMyAdmin` you can create databases and tables and perform statements such as `SELECT`, `INSERT`, and `DELETE`.

As an added bonus, `phpMyAdmin` runs on various platforms — provided the machines using them can meet the system requirements. To run `phpMyAdmin`, your system must have not only a MySQL database server, but also the following:

- ✦ A Web server capable of running PHP (for example, Apache Server).
- ✦ PHP version 3 or above.
- ✦ A Web browser such as Netscape Navigator, Microsoft Internet Explorer, or Mozilla.

Though installation of the prerequisites to `phpMyAdmin` is beyond the scope of this book, the actual installation of `phpMyAdmin` is really quite easy. Simply create a directory on your Web server and unpack the `phpMyAdmin` archive to that directory. After unpacking the archive edit the `phpMyAdmin` configuration file to set parameters for your MySQL server, currently this file is called `configuration.inc.php` but that name may change in future versions of phpMyAdmin. There is documentation included with `phpMyAdmin` to assist with steps necessary for installation on your platform.

Caution You must restrict access to the Web server directory into which you install phpMyAdmin. Failure to do so can leave your database server and data open to unauthorized access.

Running SQL statements with phpMyAdmin

As stated previously, `phpMyAdmin` can perform DDL and DML with ease. Many SQL statements can be built through the use of PHP forms or you can type in your own SQL statements to be executed on the server.

In the basic (or Home) screen for `phpMyAdmin`, the frame on the left side lists all the databases that the given user has access to. A plus sign (+) next to the database name indicates the existence of tables within the database; clicking the plus sign expands the list and shows which tables are in the database.

Clicking the actual database name in the left frame changes the right frame to a list of tables. The list also mentions actions you can take to change the table(s).

Scrolling down on the right-hand frame, you can see a number of other actions to perform on the database and tables. These include writing your own SQL statements, viewing the schema, and creating a new table. The default actions for a table include Browse, Select, Insert, Properties, Drop, and Empty. Using these default actions, you can build an SQL statement via PHP forms without having to know the underlying SQL. For example, to issue a `SELECT` statement to show the user and host within the user table of the MySQL database you can click the `mysql` database on the left side, click Select and then build a query.

The results of the query are then printed to the screen in a resulting page. You can also redirect the results to a file by selecting that option from the screen. Using a different set of options, you can Edit or Delete a given row of the result set. Clicking Edit for the user `phpuser` results in another page, with options for editing based on the columns in the table.

Administration with phpMyAdmin

Among the administration tasks that you can perform with `phpMyAdmin` are creation of databases, editing privileges for users, reloading the server, and diagnosing server variables. The main interface page for `phpMyAdmin` in Figure 8-47 shows the actions you can perform. The options are self-explanatory and where you need further assistance, there is a Documentation link that connects you directly to MySQL AB's online documentation.

The administrative tasks you can perform — including the assignment of privileges, creation of databases, and choosing the variables you can see with `phpMyAdmin` — are discussed in greater detail throughout the book.

Summary

The MySQL CLI is a command-line program for working with databases and the database server.

✦ The CLI can be used interactively or non-interactively.

  The basic syntax for using the MySQL CLI is

  `mysql [options] [<databasename>]`

✦ You can set a number of command-line options and variables that affect the behavior of the CLI.

✦ Three important and frequently used command-line options are

  `-u <username>` for specifying the username

  `-p` for telling the CLI to prompt for the password

  `<databasename>` as the last argument to specify the database to connect to with the CLI

✦ You can create a personalized CLI environment through the use of the MySQL configuration files (for example, `~/.my.cnf` in Linux).

✦ Common errors when connecting to the CLI include `Access Denied` errors when you type your password incorrectly or the user doesn't have sufficient privileges on the database, and a `Cannot Connect through Socket` error when the database server isn't running or the socket file doesn't exist.

✦ Two popular alternatives to the text-based CLI are MySQLGUI and `phpMyAdmin`, a cross-platform alternative.

✦ MySQLGUI distributed by MySQL AB as an alternative and addition to the text-based CLI. With MySQLGUI you can perform SQL statements as well as database administration.

✦ `phpMyAdmin` is a cross-platform alternative (and addition) to the text-based CLI. `phpMyAdmin` can help build and perform SQL statements, as well as some administrative tasks.

✦ ✦ ✦

CHAPTER 9

SQL According to MySQL

In This Chapter

Issuing utility and administration commands and statements

Making use of Data Definition Language

Understanding data markup language

Adding examples of SELECT and related functions

MySQL adheres to nearly all ANSI SQL standards. In fact, MySQL frequently extends those standards, offering more functionality and power for database operations and working with data.

This chapter expands upon the `ecommerce` database example that I've been developing throughout the book. As part of the expansion, I examine many SQL statements, their syntax, and their use.

First, I examine some utility and administrative commands in MySQL, which lay the groundwork for later statements. Data Definition Language (DDL) is covered next, along with the steps to take when you create or delete databases and tables. An examination of Data Markup Language (DML) wraps up the chapter.

Utility and Administrative Statements and Commands

Besides Data Definition Language (DDL) or Data Markup Language (DML) statements, other statements and commands in MySQL serve vital purposes. Some of these purposes are administrative; others are basic to the operation of the database and the use of its data.

SHOW statements

As one who works with numerous companies' database systems, I frequently encounter a new database (or revisit one I haven't seen for a year or more) and need a quick update. The `SHOW` statement quickly gets me acquainted with the structure of a database (or that of its individual tables); from there I can troubleshoot problems and look at the state of the server itself.

The syntax for the SHOW statement is as follows:

```
SHOW DATABASES [LIKE <wildcard>]
or SHOW [OPEN] TABLES [FROM <databasename>] [LIKE <wildcard>]
or SHOW [FULL] COLUMNS FROM <tablename> [FROM <databasename>]
[LIKE <wildcard>]
or SHOW INDEX FROM tablename [FROM <databasename>]
or SHOW TABLE STATUS [FROM <databasename>] [LIKE <wildcard>]
or SHOW STATUS [LIKE <wildcard>]
or SHOW VARIABLES [LIKE <wildcard>]
or SHOW LOGS
or SHOW [FULL] PROCESSLIST
or SHOW GRANTS FOR user
or SHOW CREATE TABLE tablename
or SHOW MASTER STATUS
or SHOW MASTER LOGS
or SHOW SLAVE STATUS
```

SHOW DATABASES

In Figure 9-1, I show two examples of the SHOW DATABASES statement: a simple SHOW DATABASES statement, and then using the optional LIKE modifier. The LIKE modifier is useful if you don't know the name of the database you're looking for or if you'd simply like to limit the results to certain databases.

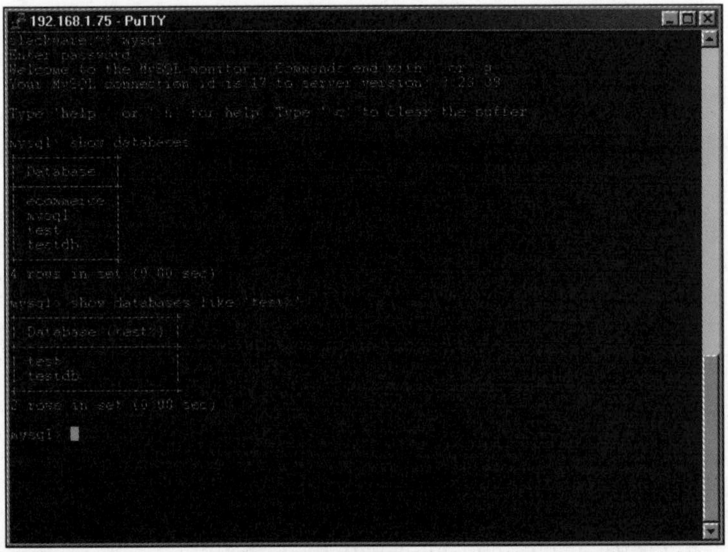

Figure 9-1: Using a SHOW DATABASES statement to learn about the databases on the MySQL server.

SHOW TABLES

The `SHOW TABLES` statement and related modifiers enable you to find out what tables are in a given database. As with the `SHOW DATABASES` statement, the `SHOW TABLES` statement enables listing of tables that match a certain pattern via the `LIKE` modifier. It is also possible to list tables from another database on the same server, even if you're connected to a different database at the time. In Figure 9-2, I am connected to the default `mysql` database but I use the `SHOW TABLES` statement to list tables from the `ecommerce` database.

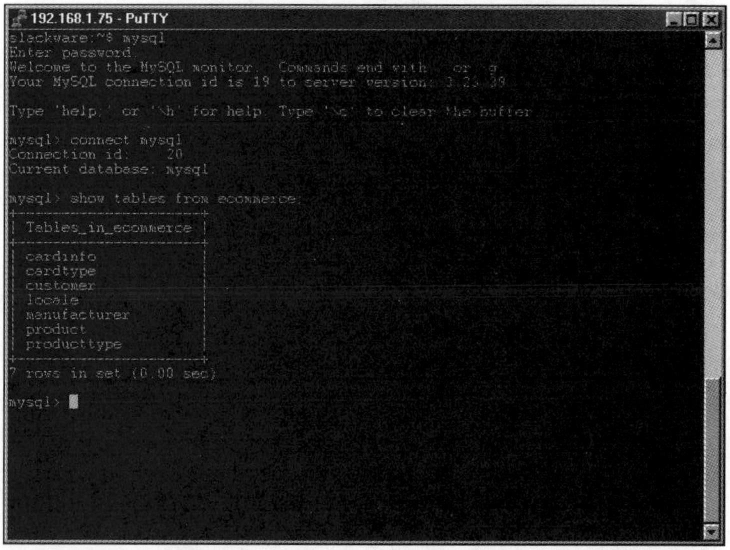

Figure 9-2: The SHOW TABLES statement is flexible enough that you can list tables from another database, even if you're not connected to it at the time.

SHOW OPEN TABLES

The `SHOW OPEN TABLES` statement can assist in troubleshooting and evaluating database performance. The statement gives additional information such as number of cached and in-use copies of the table. In Figure 9-3 I connect to the MySQL server, show tables from the `ecommerce` database, and then connect with another thread to perform a simple selection from the customer table. Looking at the open tables from the `ecommerce` database, you can see that the `Customer` table is open.

SHOW COLUMNS

Using the `SHOW COLUMNS` statement, you can gather information about the columns in a table. For some uses of the `SHOW COLUMNS` statement, the `DESCRIBE` statement can be substituted. As with other `SHOW` statements, the `SHOW COLUMNS` statement supports the use of wildcards. As with the `SHOW TABLES` statement, the optional `FROM` <*databasename*> modifier can be used to look at columns from another database's tables.

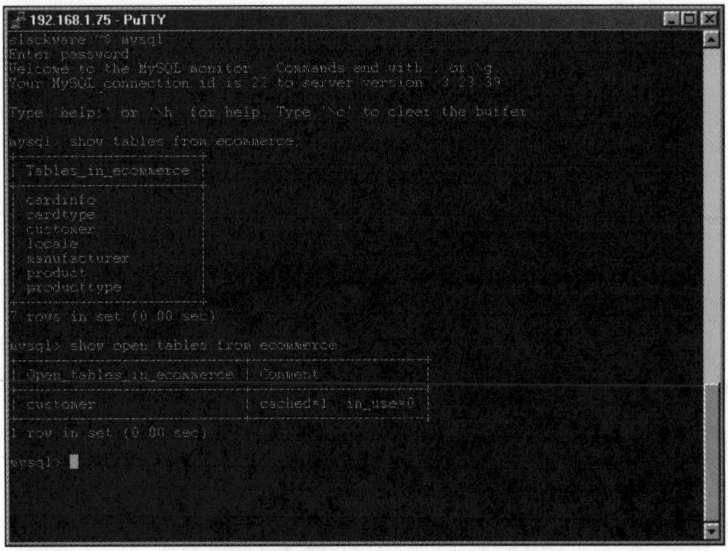

Figure 9-3: Looking at open tables in a database

SHOW FULL COLUMNS

Using the `SHOW FULL COLUMNS` statement, you can determine what privileges you have for the columns in that table. In Figure 9-4, I look at the privileges for my username, `suehring`, in the columns of the `Customer` table.

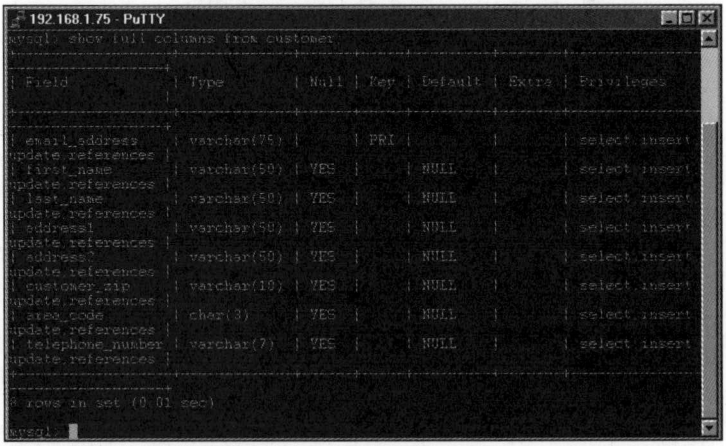

Figure 9-4: Using the SHOW FULL COLUMNS command to look at the privileges the current user has for the table

SHOW INDEX

The `SHOW INDEX` statement also supports the `FROM` *<databasename>* optional argument. The output from the `SHOW INDEX` command is worth some explanation. Figure 9-5 illustrates the output from the `SHOW INDEX` statement run against the `Customer` table from the `ecommerce` database.

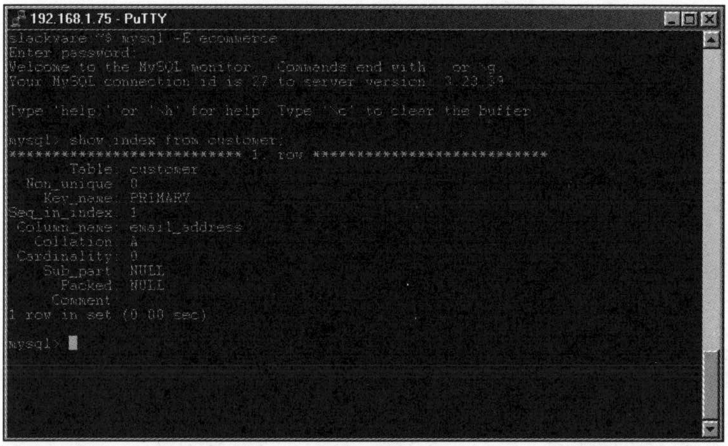

Figure 9-5: Output from the SHOW INDEX statement on the customer table of the ecommerce database

> **Note**
> I am using the `-E` or `vertical` output type for the `SHOW INDEX` statement to produce output that is easier to understand.

From the output in Figure 9-5, you can see the table name is `Customer` and the value of `Non_unique` is 0. A value of 0 in the `Non_unique` field means that the index cannot contain duplicates, which is the case for the `Customer` table. The `Key_name` is `PRIMARY`, which shows that this index is actually the Primary Key index for the table. As no records are in the table yet, the `Seq_in_index` value is 1. The `Seq_in_index` is an abbreviation for Sequence In Index.

The value in the `Column_name` field shows the name of the indexed column (in this case, the `email_addess` column). The collation column indicates the sorting for the index (in this case, A for *ascending*); this value could also be `NULL`, which would indicate no sorting. `Cardinality` indicates the number of unique values in the index. Because no records exist in this table, the value is 0 in the example.

The `Sub_part` field indicates how much of a column is indexed when only a certain number of characters are indexed. This value is `NULL` when the entire key is indexed, as is the case in the example. Finally, the `Comment` field serves to determine whether the index is a `FULLTEXT` index, which it is not for the example shown.

SHOW TABLE STATUS

The `SHOW TABLE STATUS` statement is much like other `SHOW` statements; it will accept wildcards. If no `LIKE` wildcard argument is given, the statement returns the table status for each table in the database. This can be quite a bit of information, so I recommend using a pager to split the output—or using a `LIKE` wildcard to limit the output to the table(s) you want information about.

Cross-Reference

If you're unsure of how to use a pager to divide data, refer to Chapter 8.

Using the `SHOW TABLE STATUS` statement, along with the `LIKE` modifier to limit the output, I can examine the output in greater detail, as in Figure 9-6.

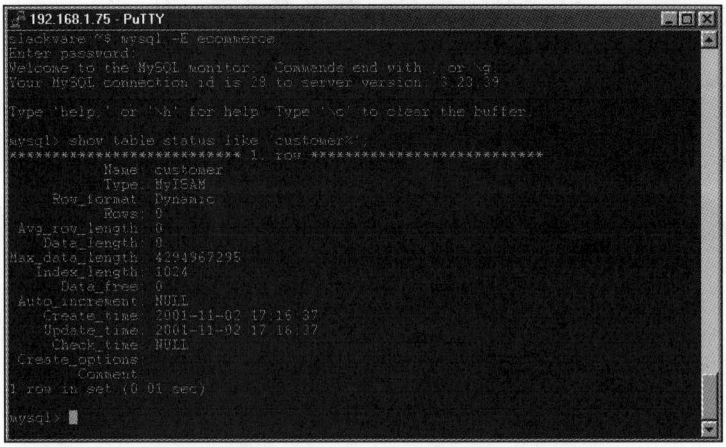

Figure 9-6: Limiting the output of the SHOW TABLE STATUS statement with the LIKE modifier

The name of the table, `Customer`, should be obvious. The `Type` of the table is the default for this database server, `MyISAM`.

Cross-Reference

Other table types are covered in Chapter 10.

The `Row_format` for the table is `Dynamic` but could also be `Fixed` or `Compressed`. Because this table contains no data, the `Rows`, `Avg_row_length`, and `Data_length` all have `0` values. A couple of infrequently used values are the `Max_data_length` value (which indicates the maximum acceptable value for the data file) and the `Index_length` value (which indicates the length of the index). The `Data_free` value would indicate any allocated-but-unused bytes of data in the database.

A sometimes-useful value is the `Auto_increment` field, which in this instance is `NULL` because this table contains no auto-incremented columns. I've been involved in cases where a database operator updates an auto-increment field and thus throw it out of sync. Using the SHOW TABLE STATUS statement I can find out what the next value is and work from there to determine what it needs to be with a SELECT statement.

The Create_time and Update_time show when the table was created and when it was updated, if different. As you can see from the example in Figure 9-6, the table hasn't been updated. The value of the Check_time is NULL for this table, which indicates that it hasn't been checked using a tool such as myisamchk or an OPTIMIZE TABLE statement. The Create_options field is also blank as there were no extra options given to the CREATE statement that produced this table. Finally, the value of the Comment field is blank as well because no comment was given with the CREATE statement for this table.

The SHOW STATUS statement lists the status of many server variables. The output is the same as the mysqladmin extended-status command. Similarly, the SHOW VARIABLES [LIKE <*wild*>] statement also has information that can be obtained through a mysqladmin command. The SHOW VARIABLES statement shows various settings for variables of the MySQL Server. Both statements return quite a bit of information so I recommend using a pager in the CLI to make the output more manageable.

Cross-Reference

For more information on the SHOW STATUS and SHOW VARIABLES statements, see Appendix A or in Chapter 10.

The SHOW PROCESSLIST statement shows the current threads open on the database including the first 100 characters of the query that the thread is running. Given the FULL modifier, the statement shows the entire query.

SHOW GRANTS FOR <*user*>

The SHOW GRANTS FOR <*user*> statement, which I refer to simply as SHOW GRANTS, enables you to find out quickly the privileges that a given user has on a server—and the statements you would have to issue if you were to give that user those same privileges.

For example, one task I am confronted with frequently is giving a user access to a new database system as new servers are implemented. The user almost always needs the same access as they have on the existing system. Using the SHOW GRANTS statement, I can quickly find out their current privilege level and recreate it on the new server. The SHOW GRANTS statement can be a great timesaver (even if some IT pros still tell the user that the change takes at least 48 hours and use the extra time to play video games).

Figure 9-7 shows the grants for a few different users in my test database. As you can see, the dbuser account has privileges only from the localhost—and only on the inventory database. In addition, an error is shown in Figure 9-7 as well. This error occurs because the given user doesn't have privileges to connect from other hosts. To correct the error, I simply specify the host from which the user has privileges.

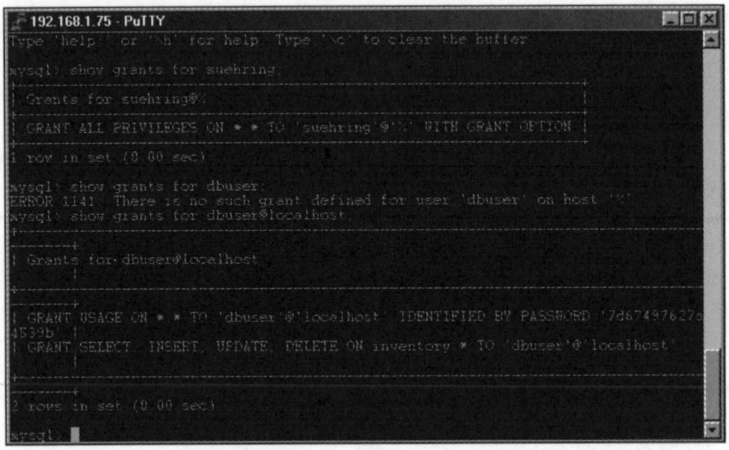

Figure 9-7: The SHOW GRANTS statement is quite useful in determining what privileges a given user has on a database.

SHOW CREATE TABLE

The output from the `SHOW CREATE TABLE <tablename>` statement gives you the SQL required to recreate the table specified by *`<tablename>`*. In Figure 9-8, I execute the `SHOW CREATE TABLE` statement for the `Manufacturer` table of the `ecommerce` example database. Notice that I use the `-E` switch to produce output in vertical mode to make the on-screen display easier to comprehend.

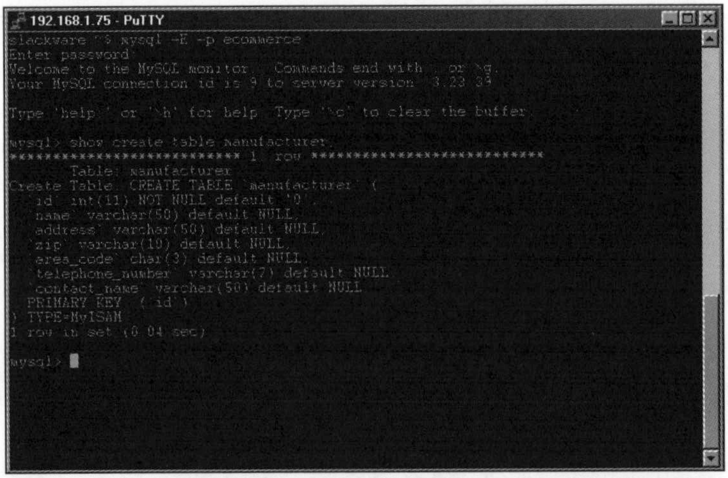

Figure 9-8: The SHOW CREATE TABLE statement executed against the manufacturer table in the ecommerce example database

Using the output from the statement in Figure 9-8, you could copy and paste the SQL into a text editor for archival purposes — or you could paste it into another MySQL CLI and quickly recreate the table.

Cross-Reference For other methods of creating and recreating tables in MySQL, see Chapter 10.

The `SHOW MASTER STATUS`, `SHOW MASTER LOGS`, and `SHOW SLAVE STATUS` statements are used with replication and are thus beyond the scope of this chapter.

Cross-Reference For more information on the `SHOW MASTER STATUS`, `SHOW MASTER LOGS`, and `SHOW SLAVE STATUS` commands, see Chapter 18 or Appendix A.

USE/CONNECT

Though not incredibly difficult to use, I believe it useful to cover the `CONNECT` or matching `USE` statement. I've been using the `CONNECT` statement throughout the examples in the book. Both the USE and CONNECT statements perform the same action; the `USE` statement was added to MySQL for Sybase compatibility. Use the `CONNECT/USE` statement to connect to another database from in the CLI.

The syntax for the `CONNECT` or `USE` statements is

```
CONNECT | USE <databasename>
```

For example, in Figure 9-9, I utilize the `CONNECT` and `USE` statements to perform statements and queries on a few different databases. Notice the difference in feedback from the server between the two statements.

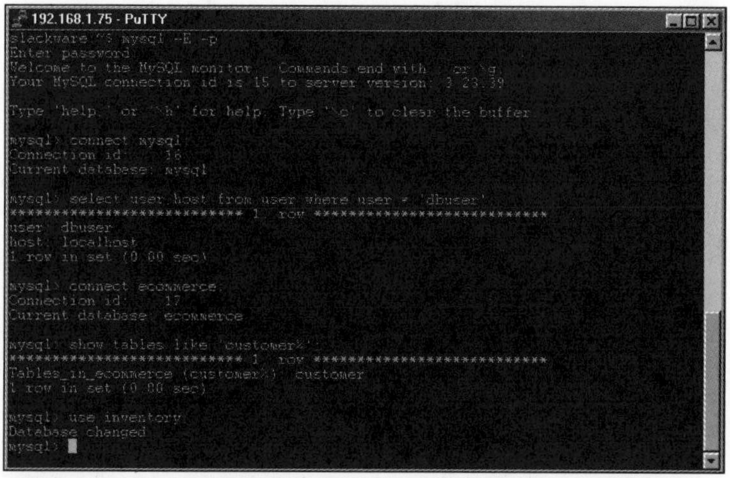

Figure 9-9: Using the CONNECT and USE statements to perform queries on different databases

DESCRIBE

The DESCRIBE statement provides much of the same functionality as the SHOW COLUMNS statement. The DESCRIBE statement, which is provided to for Oracle compatibility, can be abbreviated as DESC and can also be utilized with wildcard characters such as underscore (_) and percent (%). The syntax for the DESCRIBE statement is

```
DESCRIBE | DESC <tablename> (<columnname> | <wildcard>)
```

KILL

The KILL statement destroys a specified thread that is using the MySQL database server. The syntax for the KILL statement is

```
KILL <threadnumber>
```

The value for *<threadnumber>* can be obtained via a SHOW PROCESSLIST statement or with the mysqladmin processlist command. The mysqladmin kill command can also kill threads — a process similar to killing another user's process in Linux (the operation requires superuser status). In MySQL, you must have the PROCESS privilege before you can kill threads owned by other users.

OPTIMIZE TABLE *<tablename>*

The OPTIMIZE TABLE *<tablename>* statement examines a table and makes it more efficient where possible. The statement performs the optimizations by repairing the table and defragmenting the database file. The syntax for the OPTIMIZE TABLE statement is

```
OPTIMIZE TABLE <tablename> (, <tablename>...)
```

For tables that have suffered many deletes or changes to fields such as VARCHAR, BLOB, or TEXT variable length, the OPTIMIZE TABLE statement can make repairs and update indexes to make the table operate more efficiently. Using the OPTIMIZE TABLE statement changes the value of the Check_time field when performing a SHOW TABLE STATUS statement. (The OPTIMIZE TABLE statement is much the same as running a myisamchk on the table, though with only certain options set.)

Caution Although the OPTIMIZE TABLE statement is running, the table is locked.

Data Definition Language

Data Definition Language (DDL) refers to the statements and functions used to create the framework and rules for working with data. Using a DDL statement, you don't work with data directly; rather, you create or alter the database itself (or the tables in the database).

DDL statements can create and delete databases or create, alter, and delete tables. I'll examine many DDL statements in the upcoming pages in the context of the `ecommerce` database example that I've been developing throughout the book.

Cross-Reference In addition to the DDL statements covered here, Appendix A also contains an in-depth walk-through of SQL syntax.

Deleting tables

Eventually I'm going to just delete and re-create the `ecommerce` database example that I've been working with throughout the book. Though it isn't really necessary to delete or drop a database, I thought it would be helpful to show an example of deleting/dropping a table from the `ecommerce` example database that I've been working on.

The syntax for dropping a table is

```
DROP TABLE [IF EXISTS] <tablename> (, <tablename>)
```

The `IF EXISTS` keywords can be given to prevent an error if the table doesn't exist. You can also delete more than one table with the command, as indicated by the `(, <tablename>)` syntax.

In Figure 9-10 I connect to the MySQL server and connect to the `ecommerce` database so I can drop the `product` table, as shown.

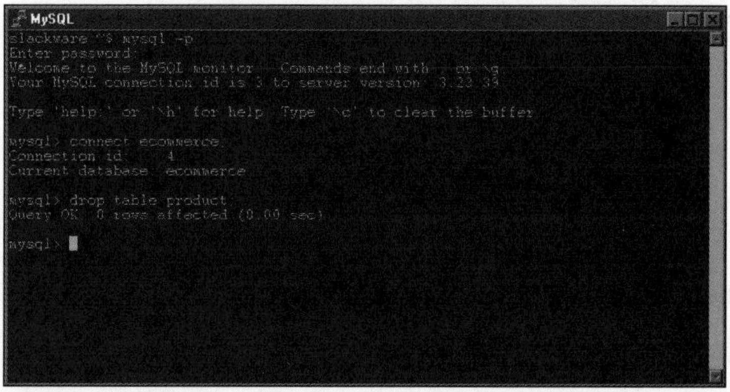

Figure 9-10: Deleting a table from the ecommerce database

Caution Deleting tables is a permanent action with no confirmation. Deleting a table deletes not only the table structure, but also the data contained in the table. In addition, deleting a table is not a transactional process; when a `DROP TABLE` statement is issued, it is immediately committed.

Deleting and creating databases

As the next step in continuing my `ecommerce` database example, I'd like to start fresh so everyone is using the same database design and data. To do so, I use the `DROP DATABASE` statement to delete the existing databases created in previous chapters.

The syntax for the `DROP DATABASE` statement is

```
DROP DATABASE [if exists] <databasename>
```

The syntax for dropping a database with `mysqladmin` is

```
mysqladmin [options] drop <databasename>
```

In previous chapters, I created a couple of different databases, one called `ecommerce` and the other called `inventory`. Databases can be deleted using the MySQL CLI or with the `mysqladmin` command. An example of each is shown in Figure 9-11.

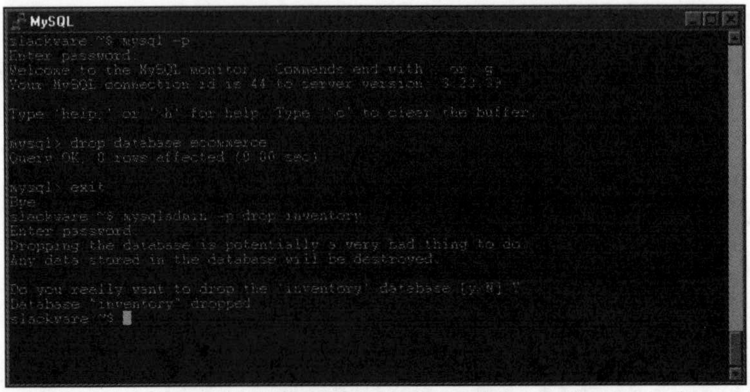

Figure 9-11: Dropping databases via the MySQL CLI and the mysqladmin command

As you can see in Figure 9-11, dropping a database in the MySQL CLI offers no confirmation; thus I recommend using the `mysqladmin` command to drop databases as it offers a confirmation prompt before dropping the database.

Now that the databases have been dropped, I can start a new database—also called `ecommerce` (because I plan to use it with the `ecommerce` site I develop in later chapters). The syntax for creating a database is

```
CREATE DATABASE [IF NOT EXISTS] <databasename>
```

A database can also be created with the `mysqladmin` command:

```
mysqladmin [options] CREATE <databasename>
```

In Figure 9-12 I recreate the `ecommerce` database using the `CREATE DATABASE` statement.

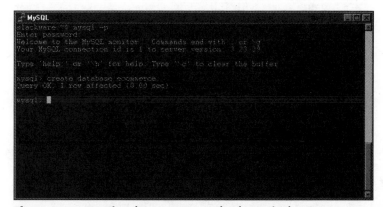

Figure 9-12: Creating the ecommerce database via the CLI

Creating tables

Now that I have a database, it's time to create the tables to actually hold the data. The syntax for the `CREATE TABLE` statement is

```
CREATE [TEMPORARY] TABLE [IF NOT EXISTS] <tablename>
[(<create_statement>,...)]
[table_options] [select_statement]
```

As you can see the statement is quite simple on its face. However numerous options, many of which are beyond the scope of this chapter, make the `CREATE TABLE` statement powerful.

> **Cross-Reference** The `CREATE TABLE` statement and its options are detailed completely in Appendix A.

The *create_statement* portion of the statement is where you include specific information such as column names and types, primary keys, indexes, and constraints. The sample CREATE TABLE statements for the ecommerce database (shown later in the chapter) give you a look at column types and some of their options.

One frequently asked question — and source of confusion — is the AUTO_INCREMENT option. You can add the AUTO_INCREMENT keyword as a column option when creating a table. A table can have only one AUTO_INCREMENT column; that column must be a key as well.

When you insert data into a table with an AUTO_INCREMENT column, the database automatically adds 1 to the last value of the auto-incremented column. By default, the AUTO_INCREMENT value starts with 1. If you want the database to start with a different initial value, you can add this preference as a table option when you create the table.

```
CREATE TABLE example (ID INT AUTO_INCREMENT PRIMARY KEY)
AUTO_INCREMENT = 10;
```

In the previous example, the table would be created and the first value inserted into the table would receive a value of 10 in the ID column.

With the ecommerce database created, I can now create the tables from the data design produced in Chapter 7. The database design is as follows:

```
CREATE TABLE customer (
     e-mail_address varchar(75) NOT NULL PRIMARY KEY,
     first_name varchar(50),
     last_name varchar(50),
     address1 varchar(50),
     address2 varchar(50),
     customer_zip varchar(10),
     area_code char(3),
     telephone_number char(7)
);
CREATE TABLE cardinfo (
     card_ID int,
     ccnum varchar(16),
     ccexp date,
     name_on_card varchar(100),
     e-mail_address varchar(75)
);
CREATE TABLE cardtype (
     card_ID int NOT NULL PRIMARY KEY,
     card_type varchar(20)
);
CREATE TABLE locale (
     zip varchar(10) NOT NULL PRIMARY KEY,
     city varchar(50),
     state char(2)
);
```

```
CREATE TABLE manufacturer (
     ID int NOT NULL PRIMARY KEY,
     name varchar(50),
     address varchar(50),
     zip varchar(10),
     area_code char(3),
     telephone_number char(7),
     contact_name varchar(50)
);
CREATE TABLE product (
     ID int NOT NULL PRIMARY KEY,
     name varchar(50),
     price decimal(9,2),
     quantity integer,
     manu_ID int,
     cate_ID int
);
CREATE TABLE producttype (
     ID int NOT NULL PRIMARY KEY,
     category varchar(50)
);
```

On the CD-ROM

The table layout is available in electronic format on the CD-ROM so you can easily import the design into MySQL.

Using the table layout from the CD-ROM, you can copy and paste tables into the MySQL CLI. Alternatively, you could read the file through the CLI directly (though doing so is beyond the scope of this chapter).

Cross-Reference

In Chapter 10 I'll show examples of importing data and definitions into MySQL.

In Figure 9-13, I take a copy of the table definitions and paste them into the CLI. As you can see the commands complete successfully. By producing statements in another application and saving them, you always have a quick and easy alternative to re-creating or redoing those statements from scratch.

Altering tables

Inevitably there comes in time in all databases' lives when their tables will need to be altered. This can happen for any number of reasons — including a change in business rules, an upgrade to an application, or an oversight during the design of the database. The syntax for the `ALTER TABLE` statement is as follows:

```
ALTER [IGNORE] TABLE tbl_name alter_spec [, alter_spec ...]
alter_specification:
        ADD [COLUMN] create_definition [FIRST | AFTER
column_name ]
  or    ADD [COLUMN] (create_definition, create_definition,...)
  or    ADD INDEX [index_name] (index_col_name,...)
```

```
or     ADD PRIMARY KEY (index_col_name,...)
or     ADD UNIQUE [index_name] (index_col_name,...)
or     ADD FULLTEXT [index_name] (index_col_name,...)
or     ADD [CONSTRAINT symbol] FOREIGN KEY index_name
(index_col_name,...)
           [reference_definition]
or     ALTER [COLUMN] col_name {SET DEFAULT literal | DROP
DEFAULT}
or     CHANGE [COLUMN] old_col_name create_definition
or     MODIFY [COLUMN] create_definition
or     DROP [COLUMN] col_name
or     DROP PRIMARY KEY
or     DROP INDEX index_name
or     DISABLE KEYS
or     ENABLE KEYS
or     RENAME [TO] new_tbl_name
or     ORDER BY col
or     table_options
```

As you can see, this is quite a complex statement with many options (some of which are beyond the scope of this chapter).

Cross-Reference

In Appendix A you'll find more information on the `ALTER TABLE` statement.

Behind the scenes, the `ALTER TABLE` statement makes a temporary copy of the table and then performs the change on the new table before deleting the old table. The only exception to this behavior is the `RENAME` function, which does not create a temporary copy of the table. Any updates made while an `ALTER TABLE` statement is being performed will be made on the temporary copy and thus not lost.

Figure 9-13: Pasting statements into the CLI is a good way to increase productivity.

MySQL offers some extensions to the ANSI92 SQL standard with the ALTER TABLE statement. Specifically, this includes the IGNORE keyword, which causes MySQL to ignore any duplicate values in a primary key or in a unique column type. When a duplicate value is found, MySQL only uses the first instance of that value. MySQL also enables multiple alterations to be performed in the same ALTER TABLE statement.

Many table alterations involve changing a column type or adding a column. Just as common for the database administrator, however, are tasks such as renaming a table and adding indexes.

For example, Figure 9-14 alters the Customer table to add a column. The figure shows the table structure before and after this process, via a DESCRIBE statement (explained earlier in this chapter).

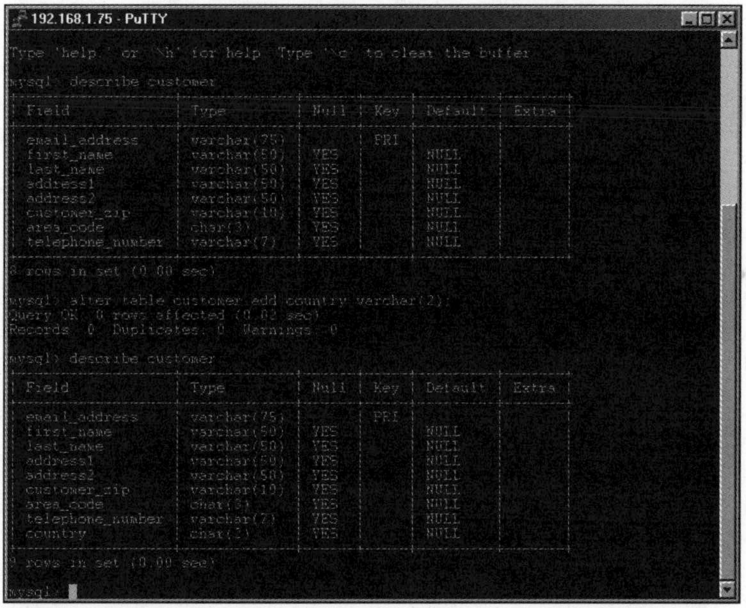

Figure 9-14: The Customer table layout before an ALTER TABLE statement, the ALTER TABLE statement, and the table structure after the ALTER TABLE statement

Because I don't want the Country column to be added to the Customer table, I have a good opportunity to demonstrate how to delete or drop a column from a table. Figure 9-15 describes the table structure both before and after the ALTER TABLE statement drops a column.

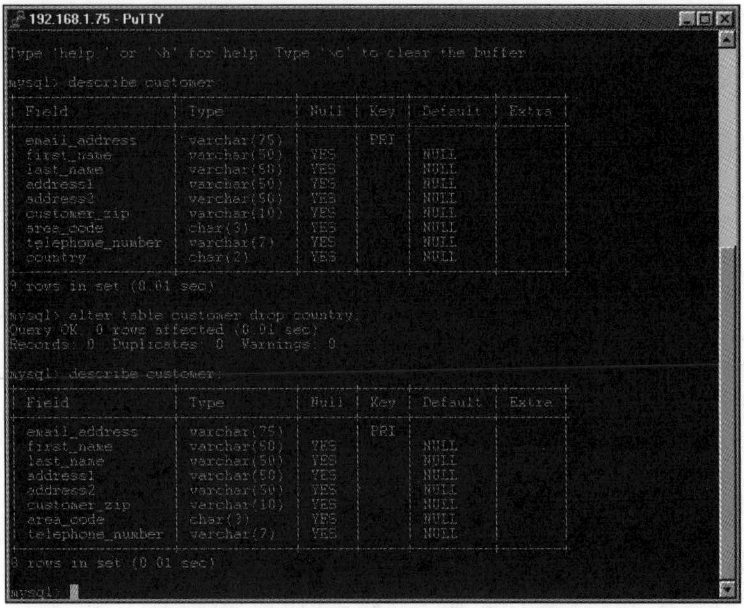

Figure 9-15: The Customer table layout with the extra column both before and after the column is dropped

As you can see by Figure 9-15, the new column, `Country`, was added to the end of the table definition. If I wanted to add the new column to the beginning of the table, or put it in a location where it might be more intuitive—say, near the address or ZIP code—I could use the `FIRST` or `AFTER` keywords on the statement to do so. Figures 9-16 and 9-17 describe the current table layout, run the `ALTER TABLE` statement with the `FIRST` and `AFTER` keywords, and then describe the table layout after the process is complete.

Note Behind the scenes, I dropped the column between examples to assist with this demonstration.

Note Don't forget to drop the extra `Country` column from the `Customer` table before continuing.

You can change column names and definitions at the same time with the `CHANGE` keyword. For example, I'd like to change the `customer_zip` column to `cust_zip` simply because I'm an inherently lazy typist and that's four letters shorter. In Figure 9-18, I used the `CHANGE` keyword to rename the column; note that both columns share the same column definition.

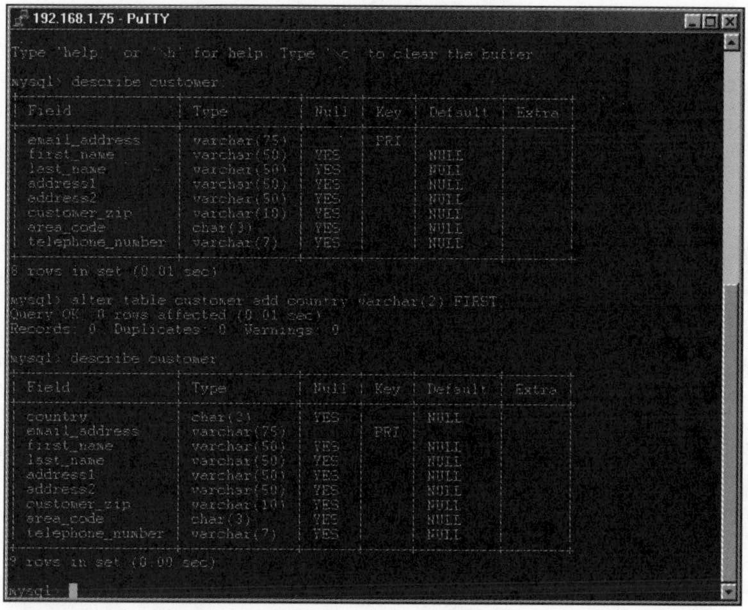

Figure 9-16: Altering the Customer table to add the new column at the top of the table, using the FIRST keyword

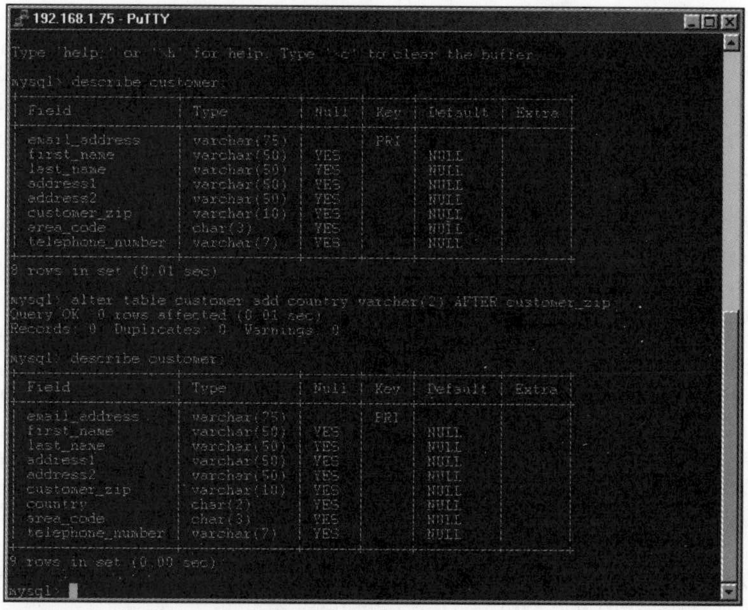

Figure 9-17: Altering the Customer table to add a new column at a specific location in the table definition

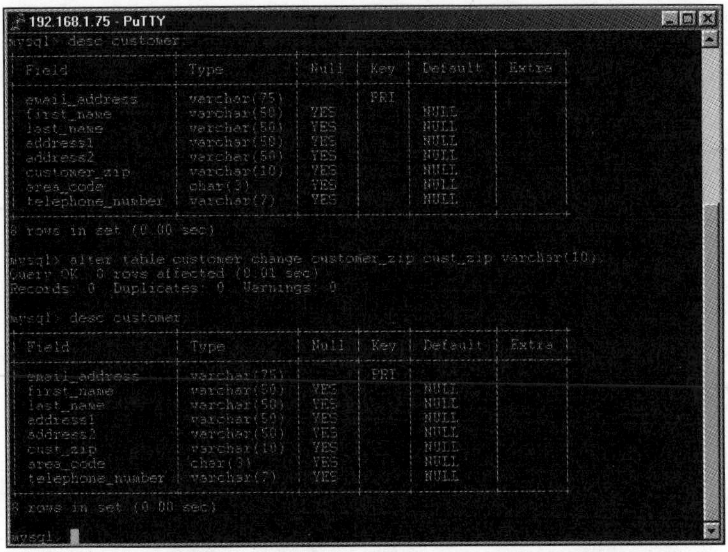

Figure 9-18: Using the CHANGE keyword to rename a column

I could use a different `CREATE` definition when changing the column as well. Since Figure 9-18 was a relatively simple example of renaming a column, I didn't need to change the column definition. To maintain consistency with the table definitions used throughout the book, I changed the column name `cust_zip` back to `customer_zip`; please do so in your database as well.

You can also modify the column definition through the use of the `MODIFY` keyword. In Figure 9-19, I modify the `contact_name` column in the `Manufacturer` table to allow name lengths of up to 75 characters.

> **Note** Be sure to change the length of the `contact_name` column back to 50 to maintain consistency with later examples.

Although I don't need to add any primary keys to the example tables, it is useful for you to know that this can be done with the `ALTER TABLE` statement. You may have to add a primary key when you're improving a table design.

Another method for improvement — after the table has been created — is to add a non-primary key index. You can use the `ALTER TABLE` statement to add an index to the table at any time after the table is created. In effect, the `CREATE INDEX` statement is an alias for an `ALTER TABLE` statement.

You may have to rename a table at some point; the `ALTER TABLE` statement can perform this task as well. The syntax for renaming a table is

```
ALTER TABLE <tablename> RENAME [TO] <newtablename>
```

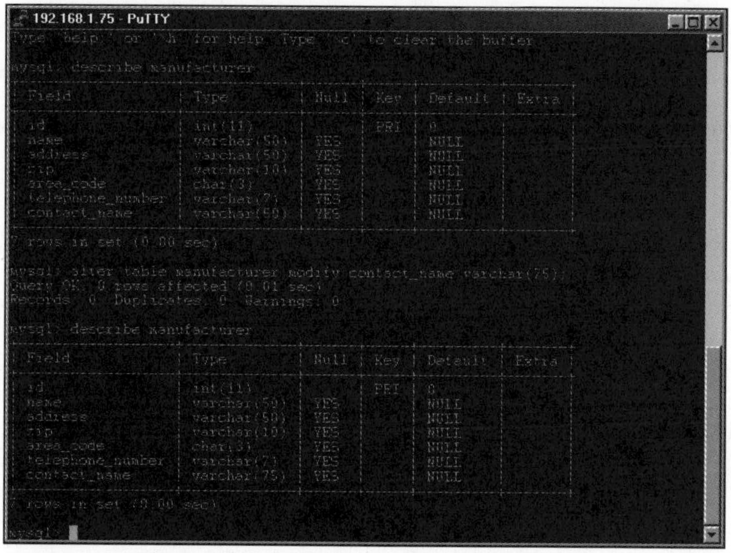

Figure 9-19: Using the MODIFY keyword to lengthen the contact_name column

Tip The word `TO` in brackets, though it's optional, can help make the statement more easily understandable.

Data Markup Language

Data Markup Language (DML for short) refers to SQL statements that work with and manipulate data in a database. Recall that Data Definition Language or DDL statements work with the actual structure of objects in a database such as the database itself, or tables and columns in a database.

DML includes such statements as `SELECT`, `INSERT`, `DELETE`, and `UPDATE`. I will examine each in the context of the `ecommerce` database example where possible.

Cross-Reference In addition to the DML statements covered here, Appendix A also contains an in-depth walk-through of SQL syntax.

Inserting data into the database with INSERT

Any consideration of DML brings up the question of which DML statement to cover first — `SELECT` or `INSERT`. It is another version of the chicken-and-egg question. Although you can't select data without first inserting it, the `INSERT` statement is not the only way to insert data (see Chapter 10 for more information). Because the `INSERT` statement is (perhaps) the most obvious method, I examine it first.

The syntax for the `INSERT` statement is

```
INSERT [LOW_PRIORITY | DELAYED] [IGNORE]
        [INTO] <tablename> [(<columnname>,...)]
        VALUES (expression,...),(...),...
or  INSERT [LOW_PRIORITY | DELAYED] [IGNORE]
        [INTO] <tablename>
        SET <columnname>=expression, <columnname>=expression,
...
or  INSERT [LOW_PRIORITY | DELAYED] [IGNORE]
        [INTO] <tablename> [(<columnname>,...)]
        SELECT ...
```

Three variations of the `INSERT` statement exist. The syntax is really straightforward for all three variations, with the possible exception of the keywords `LOW_PRIORITY`, `DELAYED`, and `IGNORE`. The optional keyword `INTO` is provided to improve readability of the `INSERT` statement. Though it may come as a surprise (since I'm historically a lazy typist), I use the `INTO` statement in most, if not all, of my `INSERT` statements.

Commas separate values for columns in an `INSERT` statement. If you don't specify column names, MySQL expects that you will provide values for each column in the table. If no value is provided for a given column, the insert fails and returns an error. You can use `NULL` as a placeholder for columns that you don't want to provide values for with the insert. Additionally, you can use two single or double quotes to leave those fields blank. However, using single or double quotes instead of `NULL` in a column puts different values in those columns than would be there if they were specified as `NULL`.

If you want to only set values for certain columns you must enumerate those columns in the `INSERT` statement. For example, in the `ecommerce` database example I have a small manufacturer for one of the products. The manufacturer does not require a separate contact name. By enumerating the columns that I want to insert into, I can forego placing any value in the `contact_name` column for this entry, as in Figure 9-20.

You should execute the `INSERT` statement in Figure 9-20 to prepare for other examples (later in this chapter) that use it. The command looks like this:

```
insert into manufacturer
(ID,name,address,zip,area_code,telephone_number) values
(1,'Small Widget Manufacturer','4 Warner
Blvd','91120','818','5551212');
```

If you attempt to insert a value longer than the column for column types such as `VARCHAR`, `CHAR`, and `BLOB`, the portion of the value that exceeds the column length will be lost. In Figure 9-21, I look at the example table called `nametable`, which has one column called `name`. The `name` column allows a maximum length of

10 characters for data. I attempt to insert the 14-character name `Steve Suehring` into the `name` column. As you can see by the `SELECT` statement following the `INSERT`, the value was truncated to ten characters.

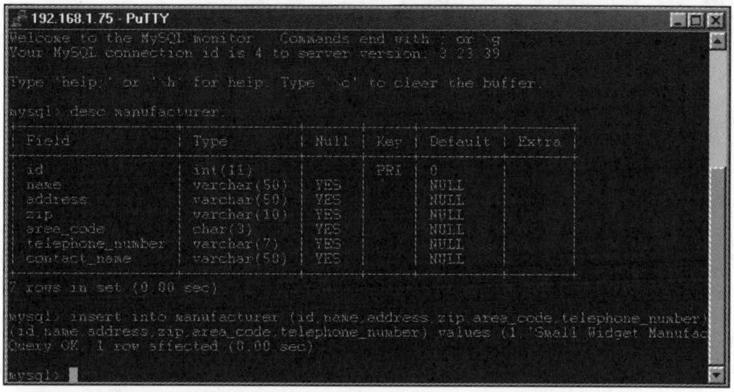

Figure 9-20: Inserting values into some columns of a table is possible by specifying the column names.

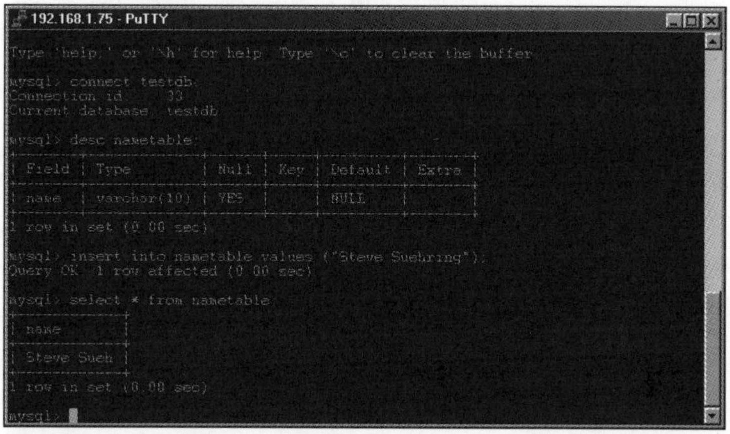

Figure 9-21: Inserting a value longer than the designated length truncates the data.

When inserting a value, an expression can be used on a previously inserted value. An example is Figure 9-22, in which I connect to a test database and show a description of the example table called `exptable`. Two columns refer to quantity in this table — `quantity` and `quantity_needed`. I insert a value of 10 for `quantity`, and would like to have a total of `quantity` + 20 of these widgets on hand. Therefore I use an expression to add 20 to whatever the value of `quantity` is for the `INSERT` statement.

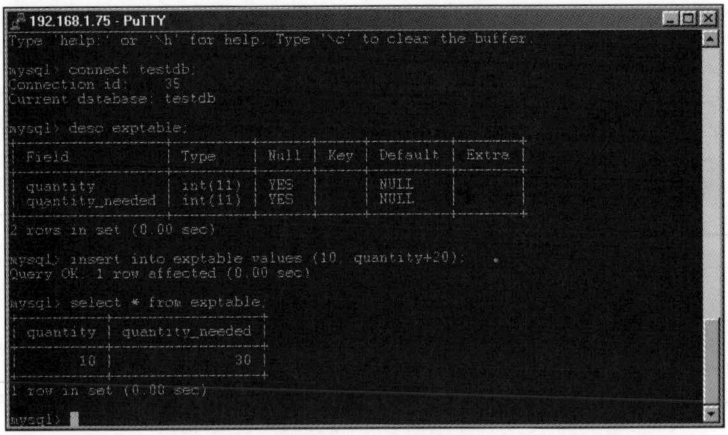

Figure 9-22: Using an expression with an INSERT statement to insert a value that's based on a previously inserted value.

The LOW_PRIORITY and DELAYED keywords modify how, or more appropriately, when the insert is done. With the LOW_PRIORITY keyword the insert is held until no other clients are reading from the table. For many tables, this can take quite a long time—and the client thread can't continue until the INSERT operation is completed. If you use the LOW_PRIORITY keyword with a MyISAM table type, you can't run more than one INSERT statement at a time; I don't recommend using the LOW_PRIORITY keyword with a MyISAM table type unless you have specific needs.

The DELAYED keyword, a MySQL extension to the ANSI SQL standard, returns an OK to the inserting client immediately. This can greatly improve performance of applications where a table may be under heavy use and where the application or client cannot wait for the INSERT to complete. For example, if you run a SELECT statement on a table and that statement takes a long time to complete, the application attempting to perform an insert on the table may appear to be locked up or frozen. Using the INSERT DELAYED statement for such an application may prove beneficial. However, since MyISAM tables support simultaneous selects and inserts, using the INSERT DELAYED statement might not provide any performance improvement.

The actual INSERT statement is placed in a volatile-memory-based queue to be executed when no other threads are using the table. Should the MySQL server crash, be killed, or otherwise stop for any reason, the contents of the INSERT DELAYED queue that haven't been executed are lost. For example, if you have four inserts that all use the INSERT DELAYED statement, two of them get executed and then the MySQL server dies, the remaining two INSERT statements are lost.

Note The INSERT DELAYED statement only works with the ISAM and MyISAM table types.

The IGNORE keyword tells MySQL to ignore any duplicate values for a primary key or unique column. If the IGNORE keyword is not specified and a duplicate value is encountered, MySQL stops the insert process and returns an error. If a duplicate value is encountered and the IGNORE keyword is used, that row of data is not inserted into the table.

The upcoming sections examine each of the three INSERT variations in turn.

The INSERT ... VALUES ... variation

The syntax for such an INSERT statement is

```
INSERT [LOW_PRIORITY | DELAYED] [IGNORE]
       [INTO] tbl_name [(col_name,...)]
       VALUES (expression,...),(...),...
```

I've already given a couple examples using this syntax. At the most basic level, the syntax for this variation of the INSERT statement is

```
INSERT INTO <tablename> VALUES (<expression> (, ...)
```

To facilitate examples that appear later in this chapter, I insert some sample data for two of the tables in the ecommerce database—and into additional tables by using the other variations of the INSERT statement. The operation looks like this:

```
insert into cardtype values (1,'Visa');
insert into cardtype values (2,'Mastercard');

insert into cardinfo values (1, '0123012345678910', '01/02',
'Steve Suehring', 'suehring↓ngermen.com');
insert into cardinfo values (1, '1234567891011121', '07/01',
'Steve Suehring', 'vanhalen@coredcs.com');
insert into cardinfo values (2, '0123456789012345', '04/04',
'Fake Name', 'none@braingia.net');
```

Figure 9-23 shows the results of the statements just given, as they appear when you use the CLI in interactive mode.

Another method for inserting values into a table is to separate them with a comma in the same INSERT statement.

```
INSERT INTO product VALUES (1,'Balance',12.99,5,1,2), (2,'Van
Halen - Best of Volume 1',14.99,5,1,2);
```

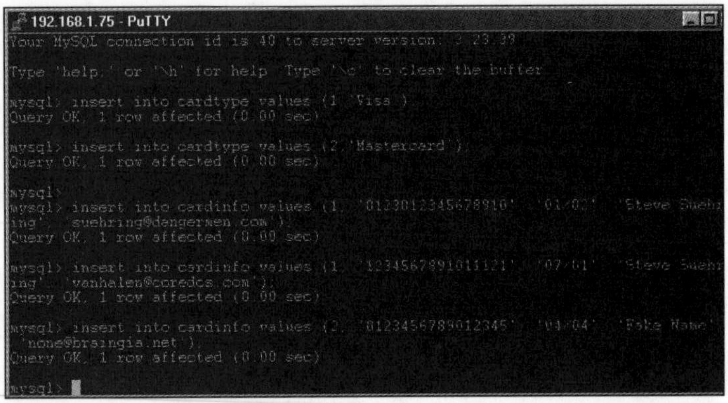

Figure 9-23: Running an INSERT statement to insert sample data into the ecommerce database

The INSERT ... SET ... variation

Another method for inserting data into a table with the `INSERT` statement is via the `SET` syntax. Using the `INSERT ... SET ...` variation you can set values for columns individually. This is particularly useful when you only need to set a small number of columns in a large table. The basic syntax of this variation is as follows:

```
INSERT [LOW_PRIORITY | DELAYED] [IGNORE] [INTO] tbl_name SET
col_name=expression, col_name=expression, ...
```

In addition, the `SET` syntax can also help readability. I'll go back to the `ecommerce` example and insert some cities into the `locale` table by using the `SET` syntax:

```
insert into locale set zip = '54481', city = 'Stevens Point',
state = 'WI';
insert into locale set zip = '54443', city = 'Junction City',
state = 'WI';
insert into locale set zip = '53211', city = 'Shorewood', state
= 'WI';
insert into locale set zip = '54409', city = 'Antigo', state =
'WI';
insert into locale set zip = '54948', city = 'Leopolis', state
= 'WI';
insert into locale set zip = '54949', city = 'Manawa', state =
'WI';
```

The INSERT ... SELECT ... variation

The third variation of the `INSERT` statement is the `INSERT ... SELECT` variation. Using this method you can base the values for the `INSERT` on the results from a `SELECT` statement. The syntax for such an insert is

```
INSERT [LOW_PRIORITY | DELAYED] [IGNORE] [INTO] tbl_name
[(col_name,...)] SELECT ...
```

To quickly populate the customer table with the e-mail addresses that I put in the cardinfo table earlier, I can use an INSERT ... SELECT ... statement. I can then update the rows of data later to fill in the rest of the data:

```
insert into customer (e-mail_address) select e-mail_address
from cardinfo;
```

The previous statement and the results are shown in Figure 9-24.

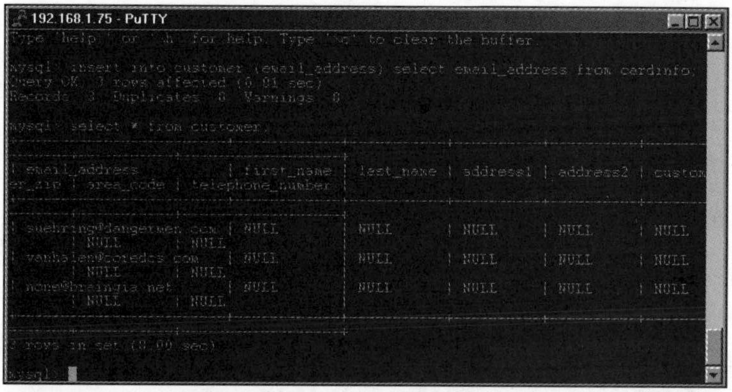

Figure 9-24: Using the INSERT ... SELECT ... statement to populate the customer table of the ecommerce example, using data contained in the locale table

Gathering data with SELECT

By and large, the SELECT statement is used more frequently than the INSERT statement. Normally you would use the INSERT statement to put data into the database only once; a query for looking for data uses the SELECT statement more than once. The actual ratio of queries to inserts is largely determined by the application.

The syntax for the SELECT statement is as follows:

```
SELECT [STRAIGHT_JOIN] [SQL_SMALL_RESULT] [SQL_BIG_RESULT]
[SQL_BUFFER_RESULT]
       [HIGH_PRIORITY]
       [DISTINCT | DISTINCTROW | ALL]
    select_expression,...
    [INTO {OUTFILE | DUMPFILE} 'file_name' export_options]
    [FROM table_references
        [WHERE where_definition]
        [GROUP BY {unsigned_integer | col_name | formula} [ASC
| DESC], ...]
        [HAVING where_definition]
```

```
        [ORDER BY {unsigned_integer | col_name | formula} [ASC
  | DESC] ,...]
        [LIMIT [offset,] rows]
        [PROCEDURE procedure_name]
        [FOR UPDATE | LOCK IN SHARE MODE]]
```

As you can see the `SELECT` statement has many options, some of which are beyond the scope of this chapter. Numerous operators and functions can be used in a `SELECT` statement; I'll look at some of them through examples.

Cross-Reference

In Appendix A the `SELECT` statement's syntax is examined along with a complete list of operators and functions to be used with the `SELECT` statement.

Probably the most basic of `SELECT` statements is a simple:

```
SELECT * FROM <tablename>;
```

The `SELECT` expression in this example uses the asterisk wildcard to ask MySQL for all data in all columns in the table called *<tablename>*. For example, in Figure 9-25 I perform a query for all data in the `user` table of the MySQL database.

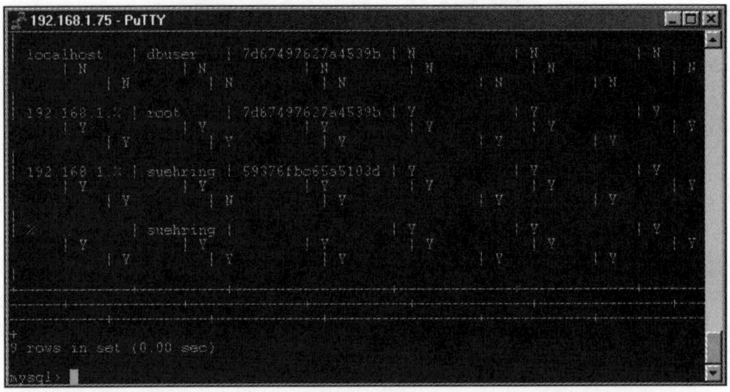

Figure 9-25: One of the most basic queries is a SELECT * from *<tablename>*. In this case, the query calls for all data in the user table of the database that contains MySQL privileges and grants.

In a select expression you can use aliasing through the use of the `AS` keyword. This can be useful when using a complicated `SELECT` expression and you want to make the results return as a more user-friendly or readable column name. An alias can also assist if you want to recall a portion of the `SELECT` expression in another portion of the statement.

Clearly, the power of the `SELECT` statement lies in the `WHERE` modifier; you use that modifier to specify the results that you would like to see from the query. For example, using the `WHERE` modifier with the previous `SELECT * FROM` *`user`* statement I can determine information about only a certain user. Adding a `WHERE` modifier to the look for information on the user `'suehring'` makes the results more useful:

```
SELECT * FROM user WHERE user = 'suehring';
```

The results of the query are in Figure 9-26.

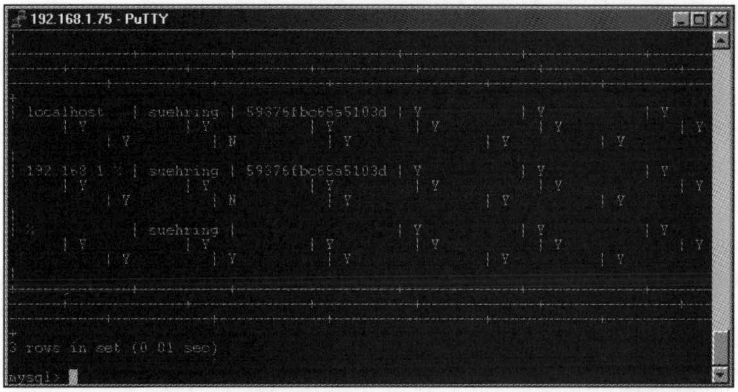
192.168.1.75 - PuTTY
3 rows in set (0.01 sec)
mysql>

Figure 9-26: Adding a WHERE modifier to the SELECT statement to make the results more useful

As you can see from the simple examples I've provided, the `SELECT` statement accepts wildcard characters. You can also place wildcard characters in the `WHERE` portion of the statement as well. To enable the wildcard characters to work, you slightly modify the `WHERE` portion by substituting the word `LIKE` for the equals sign (=). The asterisk (*) is frequently the wildcard to match `none-` or `-any` characters —but the asterisk does not work in the `WHERE` portion of a `SELECT` statement. The percent sign (%) is a substitute for `none-or -any characters` wildcard. For example, people frequently forget how to spell my last name, *Suehring*. Using the `LIKE` function in the `SELECT` statement, I could put a portion of my name in and still come up with valid results, as shown in Figure 9-27.

Now the statement looks like this:

```
SELECT * FROM user WHERE user LIKE 'sue%';
```

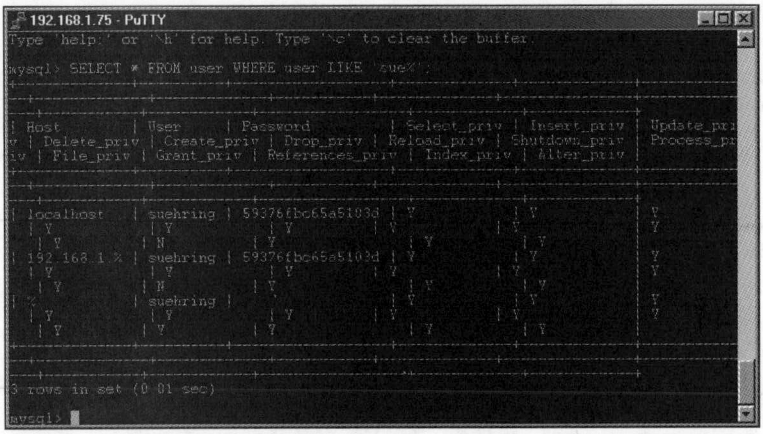

Figure 9-27: Using the LIKE function instead of the equals sign for finding information with a wildcard

Another wildcard, the underscore (_), can be used to substitute one character. Going back to the spelling of my name as an example, people frequently transpose the *h* and the *r*, misspelling the name as *Suerhing*. To find such instances, I could use two underscores together, like this:

```
SELECT * FROM user WHERE user LIKE 'sue__ing';
```

As you can see from Figure 9-28, the results end up the same.

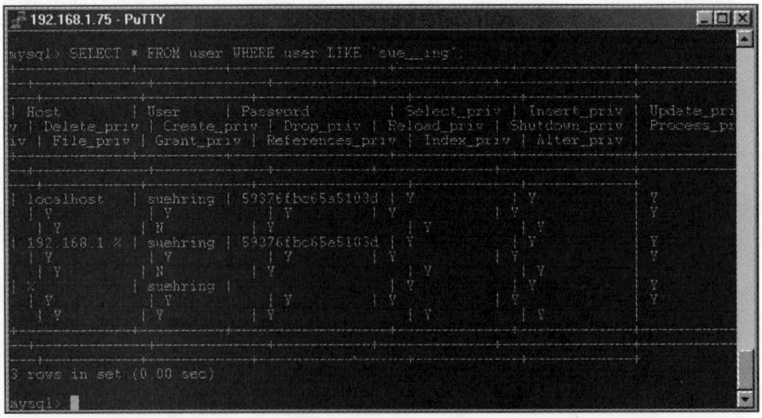

Figure 9-28: Using the underscore as a wildcard to match one character inside a SELECT statement

I'll come back to the WHERE modifier. For now, I need to jump back to the actual select portion of the SELECT statement. Up until this point I've been using the asterisk to select all columns. You can also select many other items with the SELECT statement including specific columns and the results of functions on columns. For example, if I wanted to only determine which hosts the user 'suehring' is allowed to connect from, I could perform the following query (the results of which are shown in Figure 9-29):

```
SELECT user,host FROM user where user = 'suehring';
```

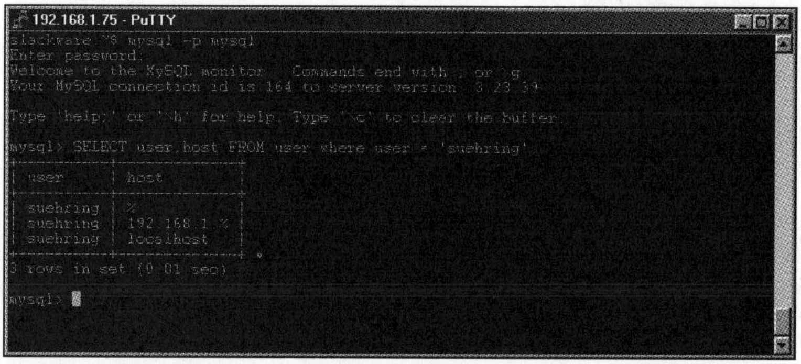
192.168.1.75 - PuTTY
slackware:~$ mysql -p mysql
Enter password:
Welcome to the MySQL monitor. Commands end with ; or \g.
Your MySQL connection id is 164 to server version: 3.23.39
Type 'help;' or '\h' for help. Type '\c' to clear the buffer.
mysql> SELECT user,host FROM user where user = 'suehring';
user | host
suehring | %
suehring | 192.168.1.%
suehring | localhost
3 rows in set (0.01 sec)
mysql>

Figure 9-29: Selecting certain columns with the SELECT statement

SELECT functions

Numerous functions can be used in SELECT statements — some are useful to know (and have around for reference), regardless of whether you use them with a database. This section, however, highlights some functions that illustrate how powerful MySQL can be.

Cross-Reference

In Appendix A all functions and operators for the SELECT statement are covered in detail.

As with many other portions of SELECT statements, functions can be nested inside each other. For example, the following statement uses two functions, the DATE_ADD and the NOW functions. The statement results in two days being added to the current date, as determined by the MySQL server:

```
SELECT DATE_ADD(NOW(), INTERVAL 2 day);
```

MySQL also uses functions such as greater than (>), less than (<), equals (=), and the like. Further, the use of logical AND, OR, and NOT is also supported by MySQL SELECT and WHERE clauses. Usage of these functions is pretty intuitive; I provide examples throughout this section and the rest of the book.

MySQL can join tables together in a number of ways so you can select records from multiple tables — or search them for matching records. Selecting from multiple tables is quite simple, just include the table names in the `SELECT` statement and include a method for finding matching rows. More complicated joins and unions can also be accomplished with MySQL so you can perform cross-joins on different columns in a table.

Cross-Reference In Appendix A you can see examples of `JOIN` and `UNION`.

Dates and times with SELECT

MySQL includes many functions to work with dates and times. These include functions for conversion of dates and times and functions to determine where a given date falls in a year. In Table 9-1, I list some date and time functions for use with the `SELECT` statement. I'll give examples of usage for them following the table.

Table 9-1
Date and time functions with the SELECT statement

Function Name	*Purpose*
`CURDATE()`	Returns the current date.
`CURTIME()`	As with `CURDATE`, this returns the current time.
`DATE_ADD(D, `*`interval`*`)`	Adds <*interval*> onto date, D.
`DATE_FORMAT(D, `*`format`*`)`	Returns the date in the format specified, see example later in the chapter.
`DATE_SUB(D, `*`interval`*`)`	Subtracts <*interval*> from date, D.
`DAYNAME(D)`	Returns the day of the week for a given date in time.
`DAYOFMONTH(D)`	Returns the day of month for a given date, D.
`DAYOFWEEK(D)`	Returns the day of the week that a given date falls upon.
`DAYOFYEAR(D)`	Returns the day of the year for a given date.
`FROM_DAYS(D)`	Returns the actual date that is a number of days, D, away.
`FROM_UNIXTIME(S)`	Converts a Unix/Linux timestamp from native seconds to a date.
`HOUR(T)`	Return the hour from a given time value, T.
`MINUTE(T)`	Returns the minute value from a given time, T.
`MONTH(D)`	Returns the month value from a given date, D.
`MONTHNAME(D)`	Returns the name of the month from a given date, D.
`NOW()`	Returns the current date and timestamp.

Function Name	Purpose
PERIOD_ADD(D,M)	Adds the number of months, M, to the given date, D.
PERIOD_DIFF(D1, D2)	Subtracts the two dates, D1 and D2.
QUARTER(D)	Returns the quarter of the year for the given date, D.
SECOND(T)	Returns the second value from a given time, T.
SEC_TO_TIME(S)	Converts seconds, S, to a time value.
TIME_TO_SEC(T)	Converts a given time, T, to seconds.
TO_DAYS(D)	Returns a value for the number of days from now until date, D.
UNIX_TIMESTAMP((D))	Converts date, D, to Unix time or returns current Unix timestamp.
WEEK(D)	Returns the week of the year for a given date, D.
WEEKDAY(D)	Returns the day of the week beginning with Monday for a given date, D.
YEAR(D)	Returns the year value for a given date, D.

As you can see, MySQL includes quite a few functions for working with dates and times. Some functions convert dates and times, some add or subtract dates and time, and some functions simply provide information.

Among those statements that provide information are CURDATE(), NOW(), and CURTIME(). To use these statements simply call them with a SELECT, as shown in Figure 9-30.

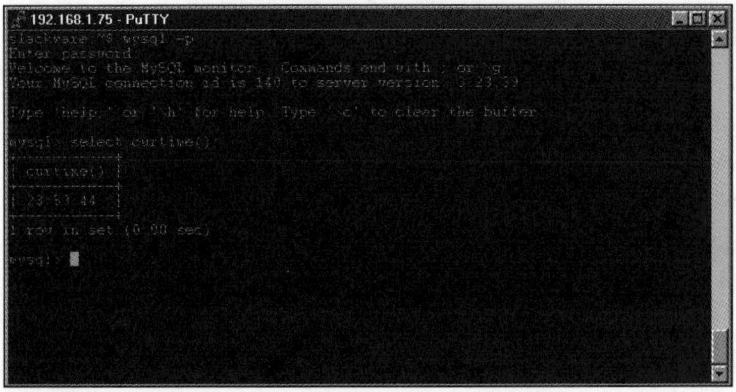

Figure 9-30: Using the CURTIME() function with select to determine the current time

Other informational functions include those that determine a portion of a date or what day of the week a given date falls on and the like. These include DAYNAME, DAYOFWEEK, DAYOFMONTH, DAYOFYEAR, MONTH, MONTHNAME, QUARTER, WEEK, WEEKDAY, and YEAR. Usage of all these is quite similar; however you may be curious what the difference is between DAYOFWEEK and WEEKDAY. Each of the two functions returns a number value representing a day of the week. However, DAYOFWEEK returns 1 as Sunday, 2 as Monday and so forth while WEEKDAY returns 0 as Monday, 1 as Tuesday, and so forth. Syntax examples follow; results are shown in Figures 9-31 and 9-32.

```
SELECT DAYNAME('1961-06-20');
SELECT DAYOFMONTH('1986-10-25');
SELECT DAYOFYEAR('2001-06-16');
SELECT DAYOFWEEK(NOW());
SELECT MONTH('1973-11-25');
SELECT MONTHNAME('1965-01-29');
SELECT QUARTER('1936-04-01');
SELECT WEEK('1979-04-16');
SELECT WEEKDAY(NOW());
SELECT YEAR('1988-08-08');
```

Figure 9-31: Various date determination functions. Note the difference in determining the DAYOFWEEK versus WEEKDAY for today (Friday)

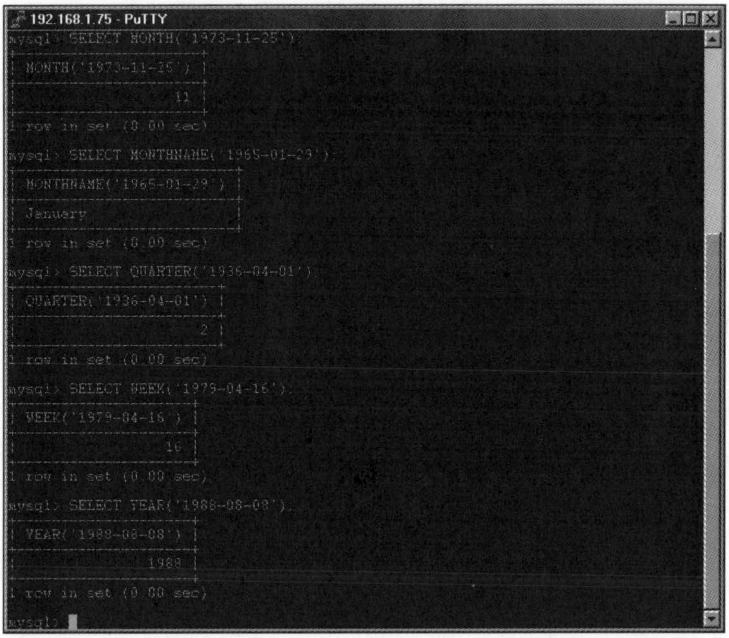

Figure 9-32: Other MySQL date determination functions for week, month, quarter, and year

As with the functions that parse a date and return information, other functions parse a given time and return information. These include `HOUR`, `MINUTE`, and `SECOND`. As with the functions for working with days and weeks, the time-based functions also accept a given date/time argument and return information based on that argument.

Some MySQL date and time functions add or subtract dates and time. For example, `DATE_ADD` and `DATE_SUB` perform addition and subtraction of dates, respectively. Both functions require two arguments, a date and an interval to add or subtract. As stated previously, you can nest functions in statements; this might be a place where you would nest the `NOW()` function in the `DATE_ADD` function to quickly determine the current date.

Both the `DATE_ADD` and `DATE_SUB` functions have synonyms: `ADDDATE` and `SUBDATE`, respectively. In addition, you can also use a plus sign (+) and minus sign (–) as substitutes for the `DATE_ADD` and `DATE_SUB` functions. The functions accept any valid time interval such as year, month, day, hour, and even second. Results from the following examples are shown in Figure 9-33.

```
SELECT DATE_ADD(NOW(), INTERVAL 745 day);
SELECT DATE_ADD('1971-03-12', INTERVAL 3 second);
SELECT '1991-03-16' + 10 year;
SELECT DATE_SUB('1997-01-01', INTERVAL 431 month);
```

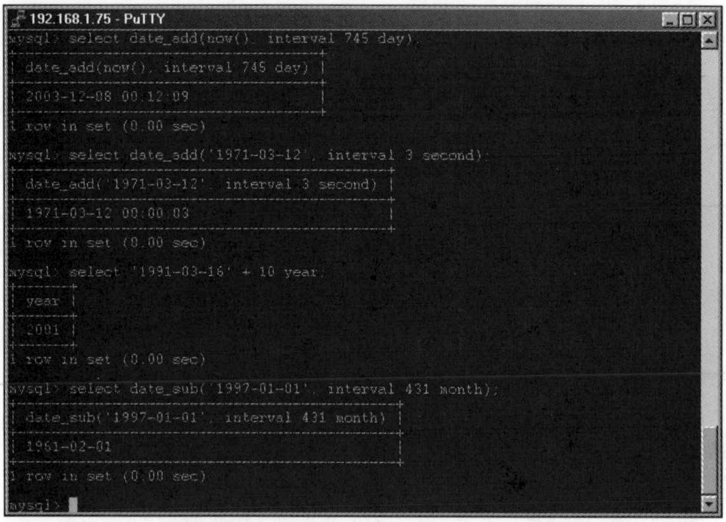

Figure 9-33: Examples of various date addition and subtraction functions with MySQL

The functions `PERIOD_ADD` and `PERIOD_DIFF` also add and subtract dates, though each works with months only. With `PERIOD_ADD`, you add a number of months to a give date. With `PERIOD_DIFF` you can determine the number of months between two pseudo-date values. The syntax looks like these examples (results appear in Figure 9-34):

```
SELECT PERIOD_ADD(200205, 3);
SELECT PERIOD_DIFF(200208,200206);
```

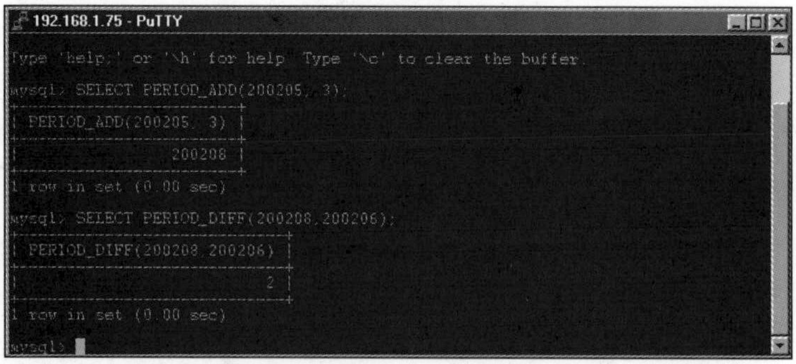

Figure 9-34: Using MySQL's PERIOD_ADD and PERIOD_DIFF functions to work with months

The FROM_DAYS and TO_DAYS functions are similar insofar as they tell you the number of days to or from a certain date (see Figure 9-35). For example, to determine the date in a certain number of days, use the FROM_DAYS with the number as the argument. To determine the number of days from year 0 to a certain date, use the TO_DAYS function like this:

```
SELECT FROM_DAYS('732000');
SELECT TO_DAYS('2003-01-26');
```

Note The functions work with numbers of days since year zero; therefore the values you use will be quite large.

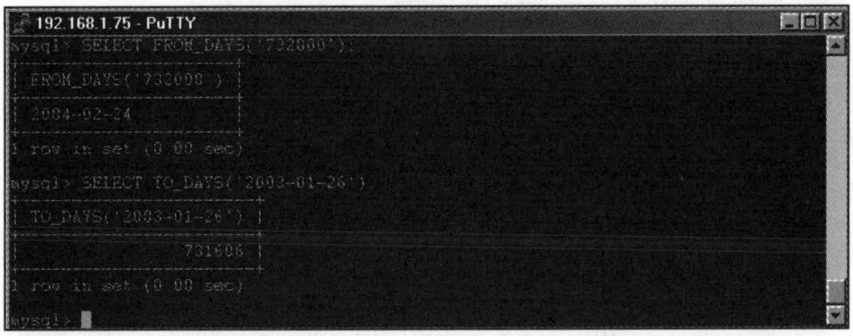

Figure 9-35: The FROM_DAYS and TO_DAYS functions in action. Note the large values used as both of the functions work with the number of days since year 0.

Some date and time functions convert dates and times from one format to another. These functions include FROM_UNIXTIME, SEC_TO_TIME, TIME_TO_SEC, and UNIX_TIMESTAMP. Using these functions in conjunction with other time and date functions, you can transform the dates and times so they are easier to understand. In Unix/Linux, many are based upon the number of seconds. If you have a Unix timestamp and need to convert that to a more easily readable date, use the FROM_UNIXTIME function. The UNIX_TIMESTAMP function gives you the value of the Unix time in seconds. You could nest the two functions to retrieve the current date, but why not just use the CURDATE function? The SEC_TO_TIME and TIME_TO_SEC functions work with times though not necessarily related to times you'd see on a clock. Thus you can use the SEC_TO_TIME function to determine how many hours a session was active. Syntax examples follow (with results in Figure 9-36):

```
SELECT UNIX_TIMESTAMP();
SELECT FROM_UNIXTIME('1000010234');
SELECT SEC_TO_TIME('124024');
SELECT TIME_TO_SEC('51:50:00');
```

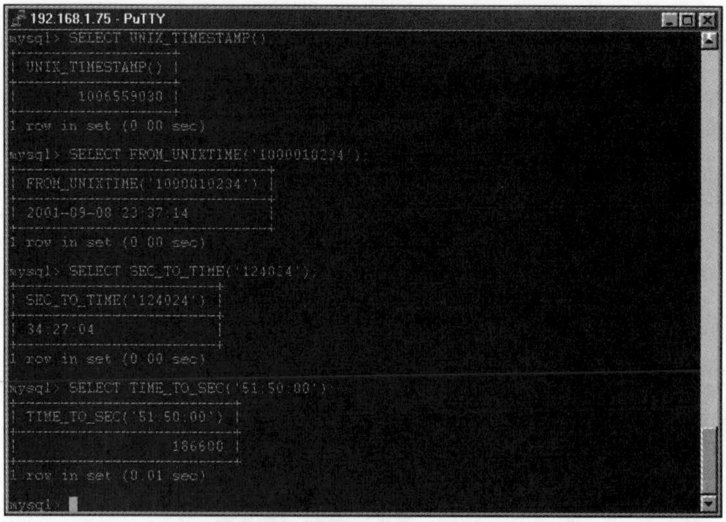

Figure 9-36: Time and second based conversion functions in MySQL

Out of the functions, the DATE_FORMAT statement stands out as unique. This function takes a date and then determines how you would like the date result formatted. Quite a few options exist. Table 9-2 lists the various formatting arguments that you can provide to the DATE_FORMAT function.

Table 9-2
Arguments for use with the DATE_FORMAT function

Argument	*Definition*
%%	A literal percent sign.
%a	Abbreviated weekday names such as Sun, Mon, and so on.
%b	Abbreviated month names, Jan, Feb, and so on.
%c	The month number, where 1 is January.
%D	Numeric day of month with suffix such as 1st, 2nd, and so on.
%d	Two-digit numeric day of month starting with 00, 01, and so on.
%e	One-digit numeric day of month starting with 0.
%H	Two-digit numeric hour starting with 00 in 24-hour format.

Argument	Definition
%h	One-digit numeric hour starting with 0 in 12-hour format.
%I	Two-digit numeric hour starting with 01 in 12-hour format.
%I	Two-digit numeric minute starting with 00.
%j	Three-digit day of year starting with 001.
%k	One-digit numeric hour starting with 0 in 24-hour format.
%l	One-digit numeric hour starting with 1 in 12-hour format.
%M	Long format month name, January, February, and so on.
%m	Two-digit numeric month starting with 01.
%p	AM or PM designation based on the time.
%r	Time in 12-hour format including AM or PM.
%S	Two-digit numeric seconds.
%s	Two-digit numeric seconds, same as %S.
%T	Time in 24-hour format.
%U	One-digit numeric week where Sunday is first day of week.
%u	One-digit numeric week where Monday is first day of week.
%W	Long format weekday name such as Monday, Tuesday.
%w	Numeric day of week where 0 is Sunday.
%Y	Four-digit numeric year.
%y	Two-digit numeric year.

Don't let the options for the DATE_FORMAT function overwhelm you. Some syntax examples for the DATE_FORMAT function are as follows:

```
SELECT DATE_FORMAT(NOW(), '%T');
SELECT DATE_FORMAT('1998-03-16', '%W, %M %D, %Y');
```

The results from the syntax examples for the DATE_FORMAT function are shown in Figure 9-37.

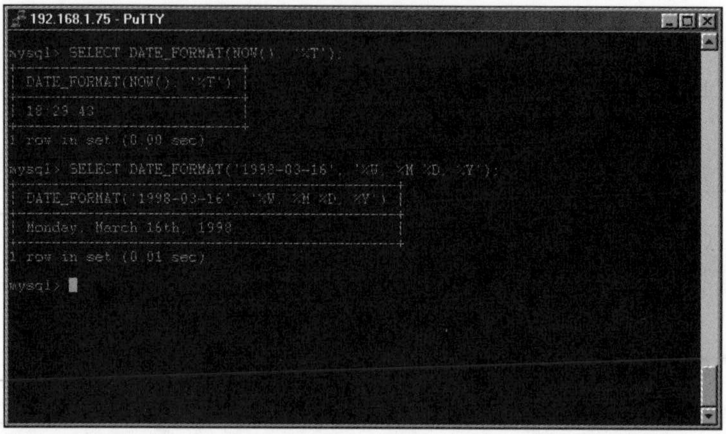

Figure 9-37: The DATE_FORMAT function allows customizing of date and time output to fit your application.

Numerical functions with SELECT

As is the case with dates and times, MySQL also includes a rich feature set of numerical functions. Table 9-3 lists some of those functions.

Table 9-3
Numerical functions with the SELECT statement

`ABS(N)`	Returns the absolute value of a number, N.
`xBIN(N)`	Returns the binary value for the given number, N.
`xFORMAT(N,D)`	Formats the number, N, to the given decimal place, D.
`xGREATEST(N1,N2, ...)`	Provides the highest or greatest number in the given set, N1, N2, and so on.
`xHEX(D)`	Gives the hexadecimal value for a given decimal number, D.
`xLEAST(N1, N2, ...)`	Returns the smallest or least number in the list N1, N2, and so on.
`xMOD(N1, N2)`	Returns the modulo value of the two numbers, N1 and N2.
`xPI()`	Returns the value of Pi.
`POW(N1, N2)`	Raises a number, N1 to the power of another number, N2.
`xROUND(N,(D))`	Rounds a number, N, to the optional decimal places, D.
`SIGN(N)`	Determines whether a value is negative, positive, or zero.

MySQL's numerical functions also include addition, subtraction, multiplication, and division. Addition and subtraction functions can be called through the use of the plus and minus signs, multiplication uses the asterisk, and division uses the front-slash (/). For example, the statement `SELECT 4 + 4` would render a result of 8. The `MOD` function returns the modulo or remainder from a division of numbers. This function can also be called with the percent sign (%).

Beyond the functions listed above, MySQL also includes functions for cosine, tangent, arc cosine, cotangent, random, and more. Many of these functions are used only in specialized applications.

Cross-Reference The additional numerical functions for use with MySQL are detailed in Appendix A.

The numerical functions are really straightforward in their use. Most accept a number as an argument. Some interesting functions include the `BIN`, `HEX`, and `FORMAT` functions. The `BIN` and `HEX` functions convert a number between formats binary and hexadecimal respectively. The format function is useful when you have extra decimal places and want only to use a certain number of decimal places in your application. Syntax examples and results follow (see Figure 9-38). Notice that I sneaked in a nested function, `PI`, in the `FORMAT` function call.

```
SELECT BIN(5);
SELECT BIN(256);
SELECT HEX(134);
SELECT FORMAT(PI(), 2);
```

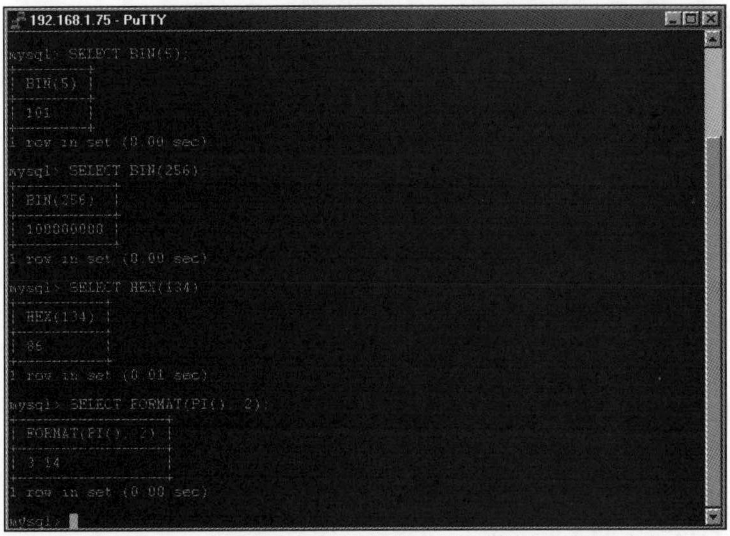

Figure 9-38: Some of MySQL's numerical functions in action

The GREATEST and LEAST functions are similar insofar as they find the maximum or minimum value given a list of numbers, as shown in Figure 9-39.

```
SELECT GREATEST(2,1984,5150,3);
SELECT LEAST(4,87,44,62,41,.21);
```

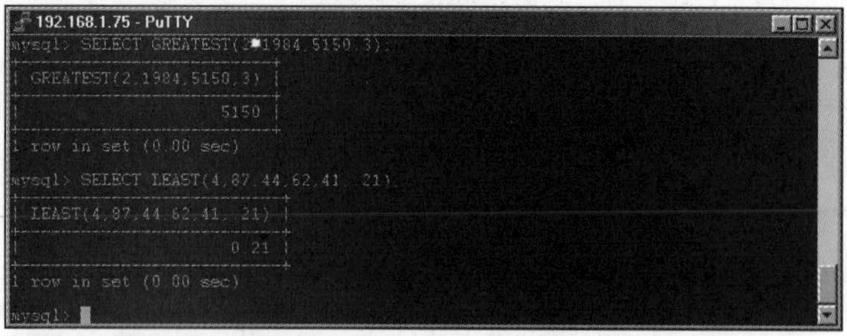

Figure 9-39: The GREATEST and LEAST functions in action

The ROUND function can be called with or without an extra argument specifying the number of digits to include after the decimal (see Figure 9-40). If no extra argument is given, the ROUND function will round to the nearest whole number.

```
SELECT ROUND(6.79);
SELECT ROUND(6.79, 1);
```

Figure 9-40: The ROUND function can be called with or without an argument depending on the precision of rounding that you need.

String functions with the SELECT statement

Functions for working with strings and characters are an important part of MySQL's SELECT and WHERE statements. As with the date and time functions and numerical functions, many string functions are used in specialized cases and applications. Table 9-4 lists many string functions used in MySQL.

Table 9-4
String functions with the SELECT statement

`ASCII(C)`	Returns the ASCII value of the given character, C.
`CHAR(N,N)`	Returns the actual character when given an ASCII number(s), N.
`CONCAT(S1,S2...)`	Concatenates (joins) the strings, S1, S2 and so on.
`CONCAT_WS(S,S1,S2 ..)`	Concatenates the strings S1, S2 and so on using separator, S.
`FIELD(S,S1,S2,...)`	Returns the number indicating the position of a string, S, as located in the field list, S1, S2, and so on.
`LCASE(S)`	Converts string, S, into lowercase.
`LENGTH(S)`	Returns the character length of string, S.
`LIKE`	Compares strings via pattern matching.
`LOAD_FILE(F)`	Loads the contents of file, F, as a string.
`LPAD(S,N,C)`	Left-pads the string, S, with the number, N, of characters, C.
`LTRIM(S)`	Trims whitespace from the left of string, S.
`POSITION(S in S1)`	Determines the first position of substring, S, in string, S1.
`REGEXP`	Compares strings with regular expression pattern matching.
`REPLACE(S,O,N)`	Replaces old string, O, with new string, N, in a given string, S.
`REVERSE(S)`	Reverses string, S.
`RPAD(S,N,C)`	Right-pads the string, S, with the number, N, of characters, C.
`RTRIM(S)`	Trims whitespace from the right of string, S.
`SPACE(N)`	Returns a string consisting of N spaces.
`STRCMP(S1,S2)`	Compares the two strings, S1 and S2.
`TRIM((RS) from S)`	Remove string, RS, from string, S (see example following this list)
`UCASE(S)`	Converts string, S, into uppercase.

Out of the string functions, the ASCII and `CHAR` functions stand out as unique. These two functions work with strings to determine or return their ASCII value. (See Figure 9-41.) The `CHAR` function can accept more than one ASCII number in the argument list.

```
SELECT ASCII('W');
SELECT CHAR(51,65);
```

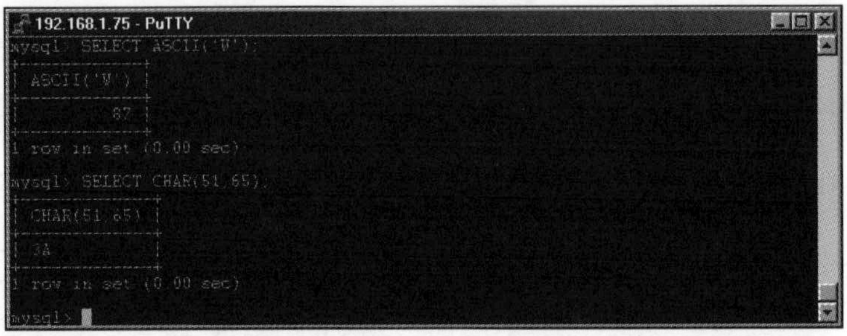

Figure 9-41: The ASCII and CHAR functions. Notice that when given more than one argument, the CHAR value returns the corresponding values without any separation.

The `LTRIM` and `RTRIM` functions along with the `LPAD` and `RPAD` functions both perform similar duties. The `LTRIM` and `LPAD` functions operate on the left side of a string while the `RTRIM` and `RPAD` functions operate on, you guessed it, the right side of a string. The `LTRIM` and `RTRIM` functions remove whitespace from a string while the `LPAD` and `RPAD` functions add a specified number of characters to a string to make it a certain length. The characters to be added with `LPAD` and `RPAD` can be whitespace or other characters. The total length of the string will be the length specified; any initial string longer than that length gets trimmed. (See Figure 9-42.)

```
SELECT LTRIM('      Hello World');
SELECT RTRIM('Goodbye World     ');
SELECT LPAD('Internet',5,' ');
SELECT LPAD('Internet',10,'-');
SELECT RPAD('Another string',16,':');
```

A somewhat different function for removing characters from a string is `TRIM`. Both the `LTRIM` and `RTRIM` functions only remove whitespace characters. However, with `TRIM` you can specify the character or string to remove. With `TRIM` you can also specify whether to remove the characters from the left side, right side, or both sides of the string. The syntax is somewhat specific for the `TRIM` function. If you include options such as `BOTH`, `LEADING`, or TRAILING, you must include the word `FROM` in the statement. The `TRIM` function will remove whitespace if you don't include any options such as `BOTH`, `LEADING`, `TRAILING`, or the string to remove. The command looks like this:

```
TRIM ((BOTH | LEADING | TRAILING) (<stringtoremove>) FROM)
<string>;
```

Syntax examples follow (as well as results in Figure 9-43):

```
SELECT TRIM('     Hello Rebecca');
SELECT TRIM(BOTH '$' FROM '$$$$Survey Says$$$$');
SELECT TRIM(LEADING 'S' FROM 'Steve Suehring');
```

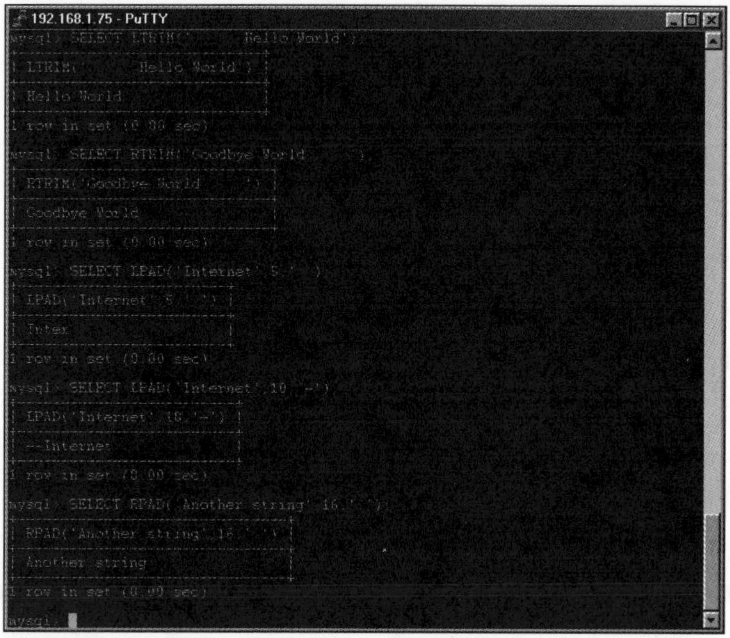

Figure 9-42: Some MySQL string functions in action

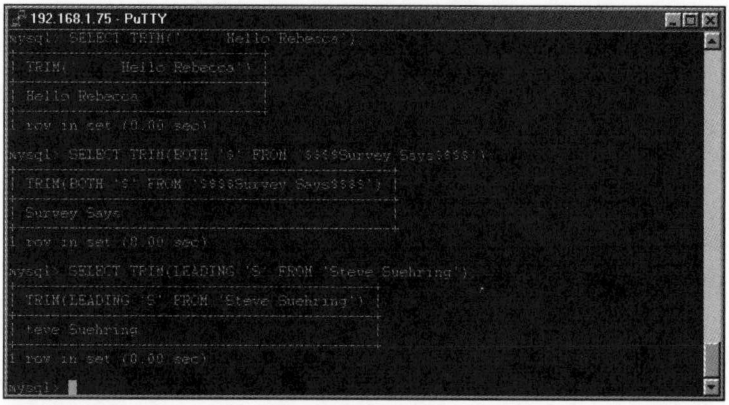

Figure 9-43: Examples of the MySQL TRIM function

The `LCASE` and `UCASE` functions are also related. `LCASE` converts a string to all lowercase characters while `UCASE` converts the string to all uppercase characters. The syntax for their use is the same and is quite simple. The results are shown in Figure 9-44.

```
SELECT LCASE('A Cow Says Moo');
SELECT LCASE('I DON\'T LIKE PEOPLE WHO SHOUT IN E-MAIL');
SELECT UCASE('Change all 7 of these words to uppercase');
```

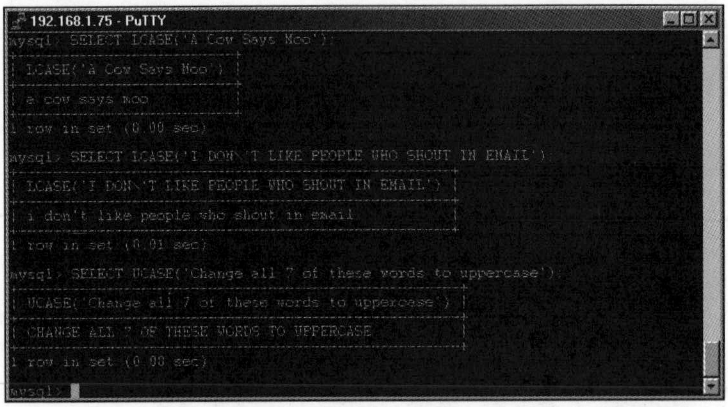

Figure 9-44: The UCASE and LCASE functions for converting strings to upper and lowercase.

Sometimes you just need some space. The good news is that MySQL includes a function to provide you with as many spaces as you'd like. The function is aptly titled `SPACE` and expects the number of spaces as an argument. I'll use the SPACE function in an example with the `CONCAT` function.

Both `CONCAT` and `CONCAT_WS` perform similar functions. Both functions take strings and concatenate or join them together. The `CONCAT_WS` function enables you to specify a separator between the strings, such as a space. One way to use the `CONCAT_WS` function is to join a first name and last name separated by a space:

```
SELECT CONCAT('Firststring','Secondstring');
SELECT CONCAT('Firststring','Secondstring','Thirdstring');
SELECT CONCAT_WS(' ','Firstname','Lastname');
SELECT CONCAT_WS(' ','Ms.','Firstname','Lastname');
```

As an alternative to the `CONCAT_WS` function, you could use the `SPACE` function in the argument list with `CONCAT`, like this:

```
SELECT CONCAT('Firstname',SPACE(1),'Lastname');
```

The results from the syntax examples given here appear in Figure 9-45.

Figure 9-45: The CONCAT and CONCAT_WS functions as well as an example of the SPACE function

The STRCMP function takes two strings as arguments and determines whether they are the same. For example, consider the following instances:

```
SELECT STRCMP('big','bigger');
SELECT STRCMP('larger','bigger');
SELECT STRCMP('same','same');
SELECT STRCMP('this is the same string','this is the same
string');
```

If the strings are the same, the STRCMP function will return 0. If the first string is smaller than the second according to the current ordering, the function returns –1. The STRCMP function returns 1 in all other cases. (See Figure 9-46.)

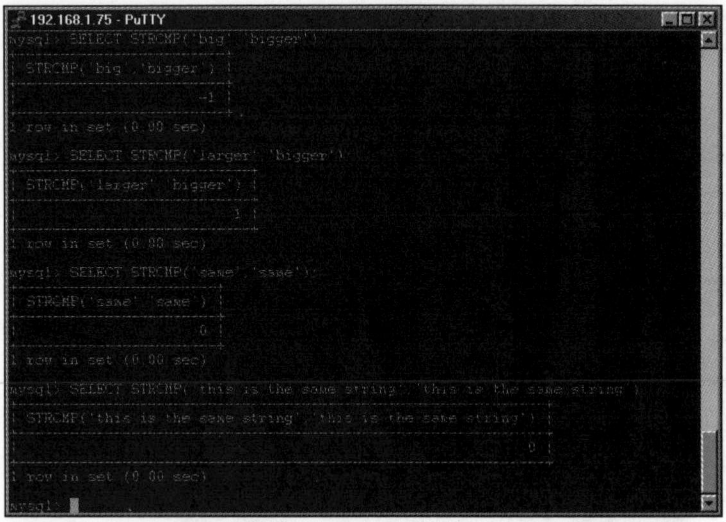

Figure 9-46: The STRCMP function compares strings and returns an integer value based upon the results.

Other methods exist for comparing strings in MySQL. Most notable is the `LIKE` function. The syntax for the `LIKE` function is different from the others that I've been covering in the sections on `SELECT` and `WHERE` functions. As with the other functions that utilize parentheses for their arguments, the `LIKE` function compares the strings much like an equals sign (=) would. However, the `LIKE` function matches a pattern instead of a just a literal string.

```
SELECT 'string1' LIKE 'string1';
SELECT 'string1' LIKE 'string_';
```

The `LIKE` function returns 1 if the comparison matches or 0 otherwise. The power of `LIKE` really emerges with the use of wildcards such as the underscore and the percent sign, as shown in Figure 9-47. Further, the `LIKE` function is most used in the `WHERE` portion of a `SELECT` statement for non-exact matches.

```
SELECT user,host FROM user WHERE user LIKE 'sueh%';
```

If you want to match a literal percent sign or underscore in a pattern, be sure to escape the percent with a backslash. For example, if I wanted to find a value that contained a percent sign, I can query for that by adding a backslash before the percent sign, like this:

```
SELECT user,host FROM user WHERE host LIKE '192.168.1.\%';
```

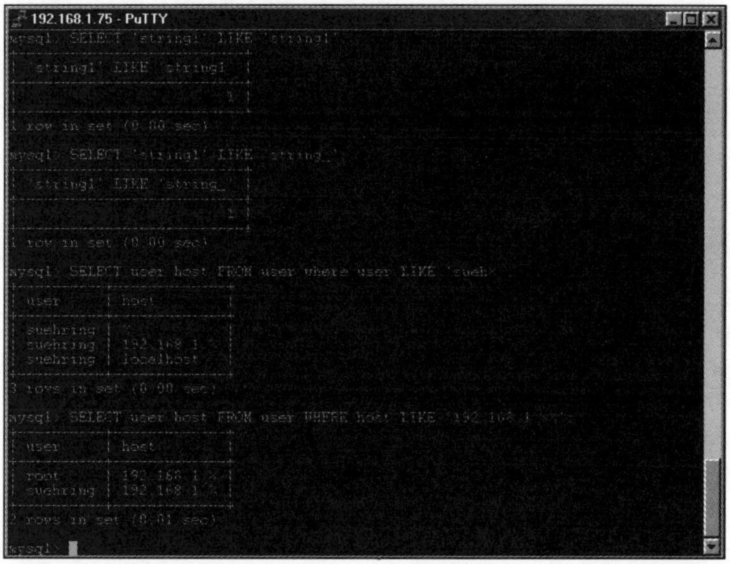

Figure 9-47: Some basic examples with the LIKE function to match patterns, some with wildcards

The LIKE function has two useful modifiers: the ESCAPE and BINARY keywords. (See Figure 9-48.) The ESCAPE modifier changes the character used to escape a literal percent sign or underscore in a pattern. The BINARY keyword changes the case-sensitivity of the pattern match. However, if a column is a binary column already (such as the user column of the MySQL GRANTS database), the BINARY keyword does not change the behavior.

```
SELECT user,host FROM user WHERE user LIKE 'steve|_%' ESCAPE
'|';
SELECT 'suehring' LIKE 'SUEHRING';
SELECT 'suehring' LIKE BINARY 'SUEHRING';
```

MySQL also includes regular expression type matching via the REGEXP or RLIKE function. Using the REGEXP function, of which the RLIKE function is synonym for REGEXP, you can utilize more complicated pattern matching inside the SELECT and WHERE statement.

The LIKE and REGEXP functions can be negated with the use of the NOT keyword, in effect, using NOT LIKE will match those records unlike the pattern.

The FIELD and POSITION functions are somewhat similar and at the same time different. The similarity between the two functions is that they both look for a string position. Consider the following examples:

```
SELECT FIELD('Suehring','Spencer','Tuescher','Guthrie',
'Suehring','Leu','Hein');
SELECT POSITION('Sue' IN 'Steve Suehring');
```

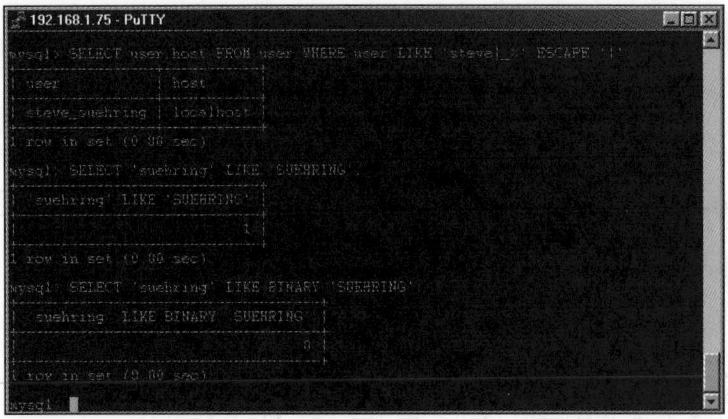

Figure 9-48: Pattern matching with LIKE and the ESCAPE and BINARY modifiers

The difference is that the `FIELD` function returns the number of the argument in the argument list that matches a given string. The `POSITION` function returns the position of a substring in one string. The `FIELD` function looks for the first instance of the string the first argument in the list. In the following example, the `FIELD` function serves to determine the location of the string `'Suehring'` in the list of names. The `POSITION` function looks for a substring in the instance of the given string. (See Figure 9-49.) Note the difference in syntax between the two statements. If the string or substring is not found, both functions return a value of 0.

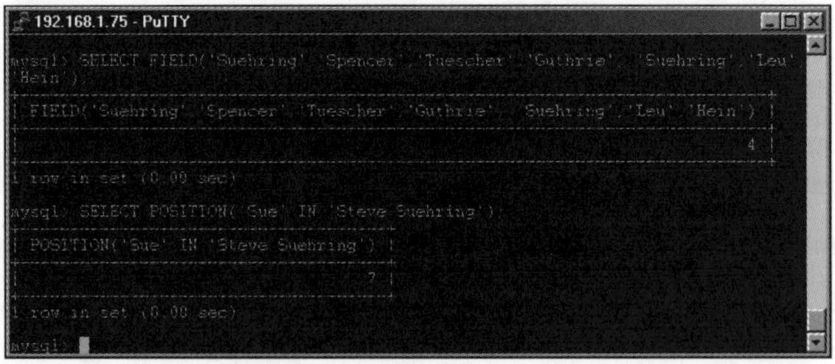

Figure 9-49: The FIELD and POSITION functions in action. Note the difference in syntax between the two statements.

The `REPLACE` function can be useful when preparing for large-scale changes to records. The syntax for the replace function calls for three arguments. The first argument is the string you're looking to search in. The second argument is the old string or the one you want to search for and replace. The third and final argument for the REPLACE function is the new string, or the one that you would like to use as a replacement. See Figure 9-50 for the results from the following syntax example:

```
SELECT REPLACE('I want to work with Old string','Old
string','New string');
```

The LENGTH function can also be quite helpful. The LENGTH function determines the length of a given string. A couple examples follow including a nesting of the REPLACE function. The results from the following examples are shown in Figure 9-50:

```
SELECT LENGTH('What is the length of this string?');
SELECT LENGTH(REPLACE('I want to work with Old string','Old
string','a New string'));
```

One final example to include in Figure 9-50 is the REVERSE function. As you may have guessed, the REVERSE function reverses a string:

```
SELECT REVERSE('Reverse this string');
SELECT REVERSE('abba');
```

I'm not sure how useful this capability would be in the context I'm using it, but when combined or nested with other functions, the REVERSE function can provide a meaningful purpose.

Figure 9-50: The REPLACE, LENGTH, and REVERSE functions. Note the use of nesting with the LENGTH function.

The final string-related SELECT/WHERE function that I cover in this chapter is the LOAD_FILE function. You can use this function to tell MySQL to "read in" the contents of a given file as a string. Note that the contents of the file must be smaller than the MySQL variable max_allowed_packet. The syntax for the LOAD_FILE function calls for you to provide the full path and filename. The function will return NULL if you don't have permission to read the file from the operating system. Examples of successful and failed usage of the LOAD_FILE function look like this:

```
SELECT LOAD_FILE('/home/suehring/testfile.txt');
SELECT LOAD_FILE('/etc/shadow');
```

The results of these examples appear in Figure 9-51.

Note You must have the FILE privilege before you can use the LOAD_FILE function. In addition, you must have appropriate permissions to work with the file itself.

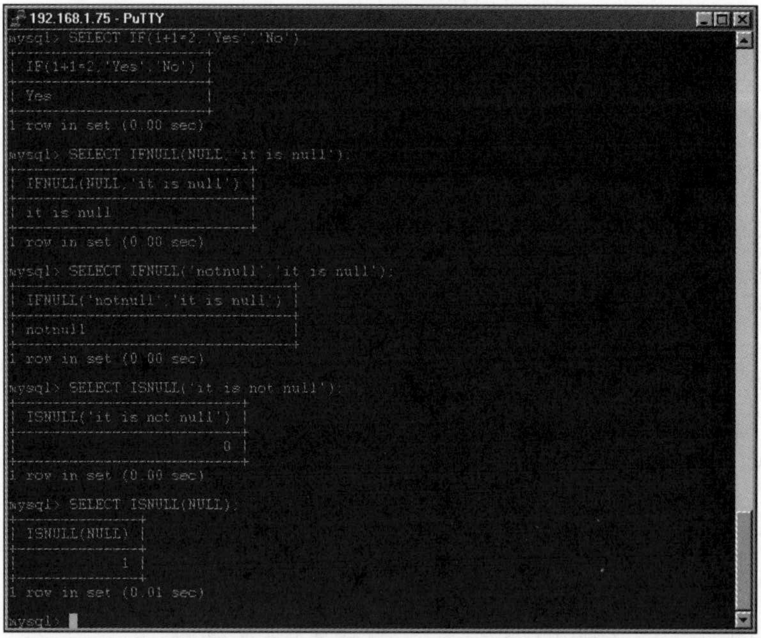

Figure 9-51: A successful and failed use of the LOAD_FILE function

Other functions with the SELECT statement

Some functions in MySQL don't fall into any specific category (such as a string or numerical). Table 9-5 lists some of those functions.

Table 9-5
Other functions with the SELECT statement

Function	*Description*
`DATABASE()`	Returns the name of the current database.
`ENCRYPT(S, salt)`	Encrypt string, S, using optional `salt`.
`IF(T, R1, R2)`	Just like a normal `IF` statement, runs a test, T and returns value R1 if true or value R2 if false.
`IFNULL(R1, R2)`	If R1 is not `NULL`, return R1, else return R2.
`ISNULL(E)`	Returns 1 if expression, E, is `NULL`.
`LAST_INSERT_ID()`	Returns the value of the last ID inserted, useful with `auto_increment` columns.
`MD5(S)`	Returns an MD5 sum for string, S.
`PASSWORD(S)`	Returns an encrypted string, S. Similar to the `passwd` command.
`VERSION()`	Returns the current version of the MySQL server.

As you can see from Table 9-5, these functions are really simple in their use. Most are specialized for use with a particular application or task. Here are examples for some of these functions (with results shown in Figure 9-52):

```
SELECT DATABASE();
SELECT ENCRYPT('newp@$$!');
SELECT PASSWORD('newp@$$!');
SELECT MD5('giveanmd5sum');
SELECT VERSION();
```

Notice the difference between the `ENCRYPT` and `PASSWORD` functions. Use the `PASSWORD` function to encrypt a password for use in the MySQL grant tables.

Note

Use the PASSWORD function to create a password entry for the user table of the MySQL grant tables.

A frequently asked question among MySQL users is how to determine the number of the last ID used on an auto_increment column. The LAST_INSERT_ID function is for this purpose. Simply call SELECT LAST_INSERT_ID() as a statement and you will receive the ID of the last insert. The ID is valid only on a per-connection basis, so you will need to call this after the inserts in the same session.

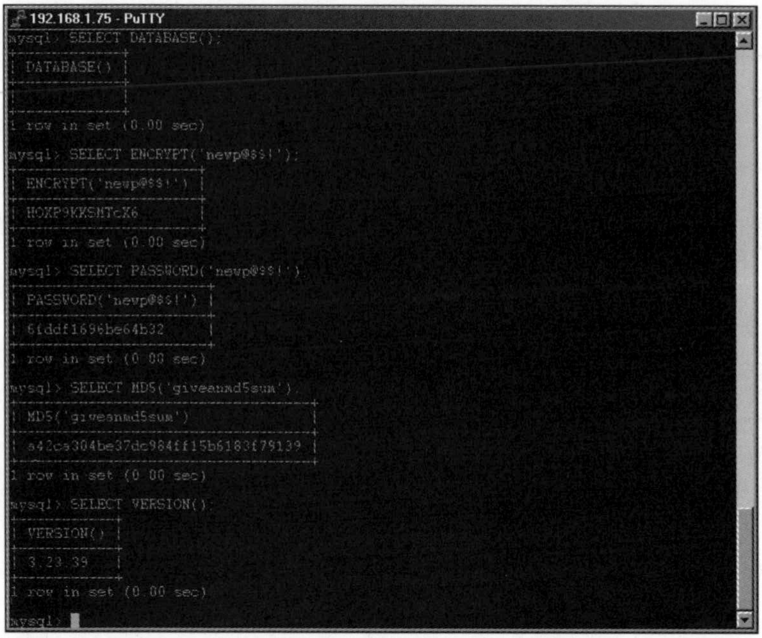

Figure 9-52: Examples of various other functions in MySQL.

The IF, ISNULL, and IFNULL functions all perform tests and return a value based on the results of the test. The IF function runs a test on the first argument and returns the second value if the first expression is true; the function returns the final argument if the expression is false. The IFNULL function returns the second argument if the first argument is NULL, otherwise it returns the first argument. Finally, the ISNULL function returns 1 if the argument is NULL (otherwise the function returns 0). Here are some examples, with results shown in Figure 9-53:

```
SELECT IF(1+1=2,'Yes','No');
SELECT IFNULL(NULL,'it is null');
SELECT IFNULL('notnull','it is null');
SELECT ISNULL('it is not null');
SELECT ISNULL(NULL);
```

Figure 9-53: Functions to test an expression or whether a value is NULL

Grouping, ordering, and limiting with SELECT

The SELECT statement enables powerful grouping and ordering functions that help to sort the results of the statements and thus make them more useful. Table 9-6 lists some grouping functions.

Table 9-6
Grouping functions with SELECT

Function	***Definition***
`COUNT(X)`	Returns a count of the results from expression, X.
`COUNT(DISTINCT X)`	Returns the unique non-null results from expression, X.
`AVG(X)`	Returns the average of expression, X.
`MIN(X)`	Returns the minimum value of expression, X.
`MAX(X)`	Returns the maximum value of expression, X.
`SUM(X)`	Returns the sum of expression, X.

I can show these functions best in the following examples; results are in Figure 9-54:

```
SELECT COUNT(*) FROM user;
SELECT COUNT(user) FROM user where host = 'localhost';
SELECT user,COUNT(DISTINCT user) FROM user GROUP BY user;
SELECT user,COUNT(user) FROM user GROUP BY user;
```

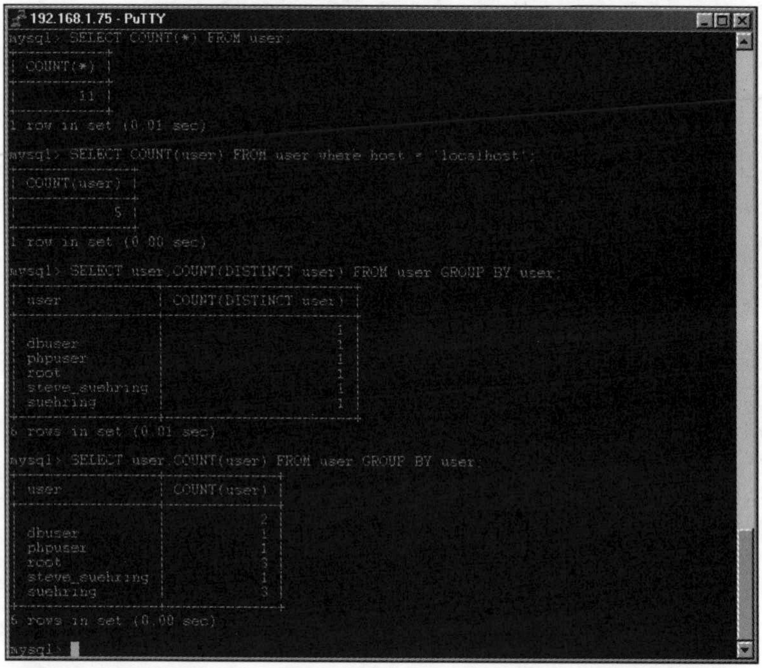

Figure 9-54: Examples of the COUNT function for grouping the results from a query

The next set of examples comes from the `ecommerce` sample database that I've been working with in this chapter and throughout the book (results in Figure 9-55):

```
SELECT AVG(price) FROM product;
SELECT MIN(price) FROM product;
SELECT MAX(ID) FROM manufacturer;
SELECT SUM(price) FROM product;
```

Frequently I have to test a `SELECT` statement. For example, I might have the `WHERE` portion of the statement wrong, or a typo may crop up elsewhere in the statement. I also frequently work with fairly large tables that hold millions of records. Thus the `LIMIT` keyword has helped me countless times. Using `LIMIT`, I can set the `SELECT` statement to only return a subset of the results, thus potentially saving me from running a large and long query on a huge table.

Figure 9-55: The results from some mathematical grouping functions

Looking at one of the previous `COUNT` examples, if you wanted to order the results you could use the `ORDER BY` function. The `ORDER BY` function can sort the results in either ascending or descending order through the use of the `ASC` or `DESC` keywords. In addition, you can use the `HAVING` keyword for even further parsing of results from a `GROUP BY` clause. I'll expand on some earlier examples here (and show the results in Figure 9-56):

```
SELECT user,COUNT(user) FROM user GROUP BY user ORDER BY
'COUNT(user)' DESC;
SELECT user,COUNT(user) FROM user GROUP BY user ORDER BY user
ASC LIMIT 3;
SELECT user,COUNT(user) FROM user GROUP BY user HAVING user =
'suehring';
```

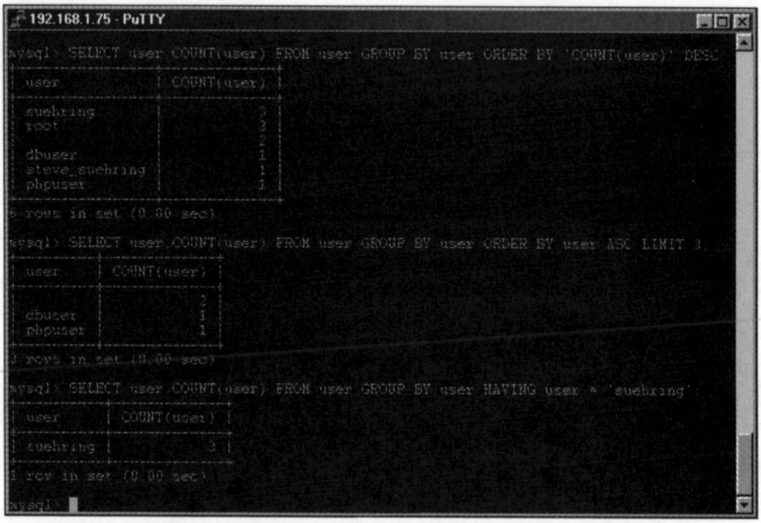

Figure 9-56: Using ORDER BY and HAVING to sort the results from queries

Updating data with the UPDATE statement

I've been attempting to come up with a witty anecdote to begin this section and I cannot. It's certainly not that I don't like the `UPDATE` statement or that I don't believe it is useful. The `UPDATE` statement is really simple and intuitive, with only a few options. The equally simple truth is that the `UPDATE` statement is for making changes to existing records in the database. Its syntax looks like this:

```
UPDATE [LOW_PRIORITY] [IGNORE] tbl_name
    SET col_name1=expr1, [col_name2=expr2, ...]
    [WHERE where_definition]
    [LIMIT #]
```

As does `INSERT`, the `UPDATE` statement includes the `LOW_PRIORITY` and `IGNORE` keywords — and using these keywords has the exact same effects. The `LOW_PRIORITY` keyword tells the `UPDATE` statement to wait until no other clients are reading from the table. The `IGNORE` statement causes any collisions in non-unique columns to be ignored (another similarity to the `INSERT` statement).

As with the `SELECT` statement, you can use a `WHERE` clause in the `UPDATE` statement to modify or drill down to the records you want to update. If you don't include a `WHERE` clause, you update all the records in the table. Another important similarity to `SELECT` is that you can use the `LIMIT` modifier to limit the number of records affected by the statement. Syntax examples follow (with results in Figure 9-57):

```
UPDATE product SET name = 'Van Halen - Balance' WHERE ID = 1;
UPDATE product SET cate_ID = 1 WHERE cate_ID = 2 LIMIT 1;
UPDATE product SET price = '19.99', cate_ID = 2 WHERE ID = 2;
```

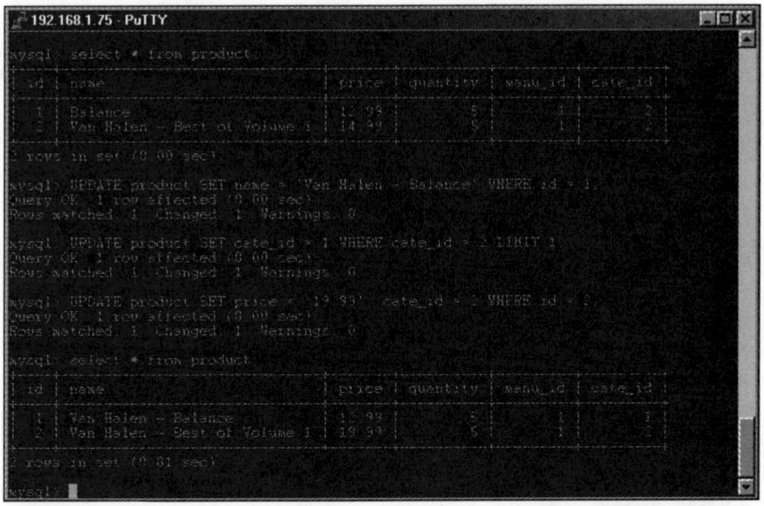

Figure 9-57: A look at the product table prior to the UPDATE statements, the three UPDATE statements, and a look at the product table after the updates

Delete

The `DELETE` statement can be used to delete specific records or the entire contents of tables; its syntax is as follows:

```
DELETE [LOW_PRIORITY | QUICK] FROM <tablename>
    [WHERE where_clause]
    [ORDER BY ...]
    [LIMIT #]
```

or

```
DELETE [LOW_PRIORITY | QUICK] <tablename>[.*] [<tablename>[.*]
...] FROM
tablereferences [WHERE where_clause]
```

I'll dispense with some syntactical commonalities among many of the DML statements. The `LOW_PRIORITY` keyword causes the `DELETE` to wait until no other clients are using the table. The `WHERE` clause tells the `DELETE` statement which records to delete. The `ORDER BY` clause determines the order by which the `DELETE` will occur. The `LIMIT` modifier causes the `DELETE` to only delete the specified number of rows. Though not common to other DML statements, the `QUICK` modifier can assist to speed up certain `DELETE` statements.

The DELETE statement has two versions. The first version of the DELETE statement simply deletes from one table. The second version of the DELETE statement enables deletion from multiple tables. I'll show a syntax example or two for each type of DELETE.

```
DELETE FROM example1 WHERE ID = 1;

DELETE FROM example1 ORDER by ID LIMIT 1;

DELETE example1,example2 FROM example1,example2,example3 WHERE
example1.ID = example2.ID AND example2.ID = example3.ID;
```

In the last of these examples, any matching rows are deleted from the *example1* and *example2* tables only.

Showing my true System Administrator colors, I admit that my favorite action is performing deletes. Few ways of starting a day are more rewarding than removing a few hundred thousand records.

Summary

MySQL includes a large number of commands and statements used for administration as well as performance tuning and informational purposes. These statements include the SHOW, DESCRIBE, and KILL.

- MySQL also includes most ANSI92 compatibility in the Data Definition Language (DDL) statements.
- MySQL extends the ANSI92 standard in some DDL statements.
- As with DDL, MySQL features compatibility with most ANSI92 Data Markup Language (DML) statements.
- Like DDL, MySQL extends the ANSI92 standard in the area of DML.

✦ ✦ ✦

CHAPTER 10

Databases and Data

In This Chapter

Introducing the MySQL table types

Fine-tuning the syntax when using the `mysqladmin` command

Exporting data from MySQL databases

Importing data into MySQL databases

A database is primarily a tool for organizing data into an accessible and usable form. That may seem obvious, but some of questions I'm asked most frequently about are the brass-tacks of organizing data in MySQL database — choosing the right table type, importing and exporting data, and using the `mysqladmin` command to diagnose database problems correctly.

Choosing the right table type is important; different applications may benefit from particular table types. Importing data into MySQL from other applications (such as Microsoft Access or Oracle) is a frequent task facing administrators migrating to MySQL. Finally, using the `mysqladmin` command successfully is an important part of working with a MySQL server. This chapter examines all these subjects in detail.

Choosing the Right MySQL Table Type

A *table type* is one of various sets of characteristics that you can apply to a database table in MySQL — usually for a specialized purpose, even though the appearance of MySQL tables may be similar from type to type. Just as you could use a kitchen table to perform surgery, or a picnic table as a desk, you could use a MySQL table for a purpose other than that for which it's designed — but why?

Tip: All MySQL table types store data — but there's usually a *best* type for any application.

This section examines the table types supported in MySQL. With a solid understanding of the available table types, you're better equipped to choose the correct table type for your application.

MySQL table types

The six types of MySQL tables are best considered as three groups for the sake of compatibility:

✦ **Non-transactional tables.** For many applications, non-transactional table types will be sufficient and will use fewer resources than transactional tables. For example, an online catalog, customer database, application database, and many other applications can utilize non-transactional tables successfully. The default table type in MySQL is the non-transactional MyISAM type. MyISAM is the table type of choice for nearly all applications. The three non-transactional table types are

- `ISAM`
- `HEAP`

  The `HEAP` type is stored in volatile memory. If you are using a `HEAP` table type and MySQL crashes or is shut down, all data in the table is lost! However, the `HEAP` table type is fast, making it a good choice for temporary tables.

- `MyISAM`

  Based on the `ISAM` table type, `MyISAM` is the default for MySQL.

✦ `MERGE` **tables.**

The `MERGE` table type is a special extension of the `MyISAM` table.

✦ **Transaction-safe (transactional) tables.** Transactional tables can combine statements and then commit or roll them back if some fail. Transactional tables are much safer in the event of MySQL or system crashes. These two table types are

- `InnoDB`
- `BerkeleyDB`

The table types you can use depend on the version of MySQL installed on your server. Some table types weren't available in earlier versions of MySQL. Further, the tables available follow these general rules:

✦ If you compiled MySQL from source code, you had the option to choose table types during the compilation process.

✦ If you installed MySQL from a binary version, you may or may not have transactional tables included. The MySQL-MAX version includes both InnoDB and BerkeleyDB. Some MySQL versions specific to flavors of Linux such as Debian include BerkeleyDB.

Cross-Reference **Chapter 2 reviews the advantages of transactional and non-transactional tables.**

To determine which table types your server supports, you can use the `mysqladmin variables` command.

Tip **Running the `mysqladmin variables` command outputs quite a bit of information so you may need to pipe the output to a pager such as *more* or *less*.**

Figure 10-1 shows the output for the command mysqladmin -p variables. I check for the lines that indicate whether BerkeleyDB and InnoDB tables are enabled. Figure 10-1 shows that only BerkeleyDB is available on this server. Therefore, I must use one of two approaches to choosing a table type:

✦ I can choose BerkeleyDB.

✦ Since non-transactional tables are available by default I can choose non-transactional tables, such as

- `ISAM`
- `MyISAM`
- `HEAP`

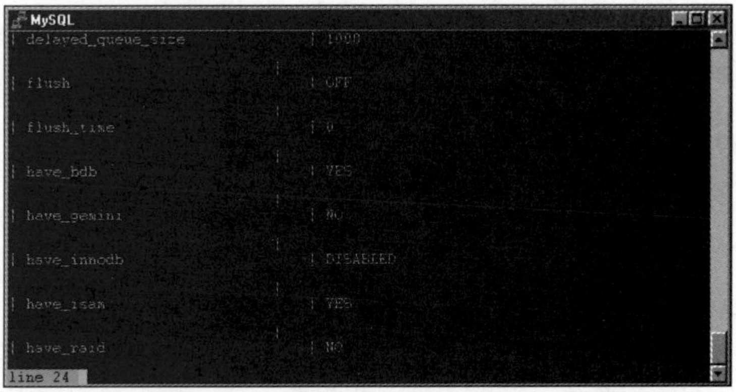

Figure 10-1: Using the mysqladmin -p variables command to determine whether InnoDB or BerkeleyDB tables are supported

Figure 10-2 shows the output of the mysqladmin variables command on a server where both the BerkeleyDB and InnoDB tables enabled.

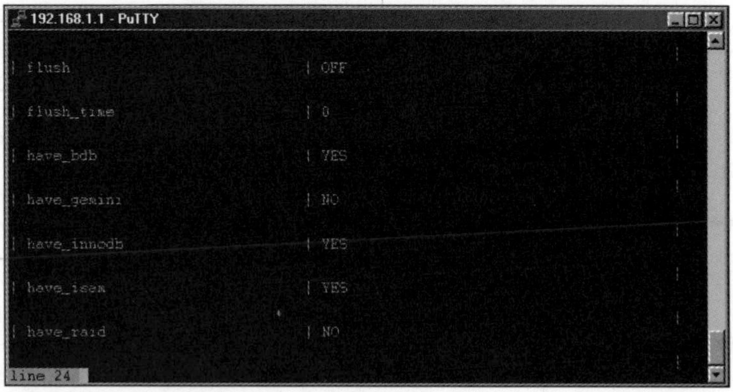

Figure 10-2: The mysqladmin variables command on a server with both BerkeleyDB and InnoDB tables enabled

MyISAM

The default table type for tables created in MySQL is MyISAM. The MyISAM table type is an extension of the ISAM table type.

Note: The MyISAM table type will eventually replace the ISAM table type. In a future version of MySQL, the ISAM table type will no longer be offered.

MyISAM uses a B-tree index type and compresses indexes whenever possible. For string-based indexes such as those on CHAR and VARCHAR columns, MyISAM tables space-compress the index. To use compressed numeric-based indexes add PACK_KEYS=1 in the process of creating the table.

Tables can be damaged by a system crash, a crash of the MySQL server, or any number of unforeseen events. If queries fail to return complete results or other unexplained errors occur, the table may need repair. Corrupt or broken MyISAM tables can be repaired with the myisamchk command.

Cross-Reference: Chapter 13 shows how to repair broken tables and solve other MySQL problems.

There are three table formats for MyISAM tables:

- Static
- Dynamic
- Compressed

MySQL chooses `Static` or `Dynamic` table formats automatically when you create the table. The `Compressed` table format must be created manually through the use of the `myisampack` utility.

Static format

The `Static` table format is the default and is used when there are no variable-length column types in the table such as `VARCHAR` or `BLOB`. If variable-length columns are used, MySQL will choose the `Dynamic` format for the table.

An example of a table definition looks like this as follows:

```
CREATE TABLE example (id int(5) NOT NULL PRIMARY KEY,
     name char(25),
     title char(20)
);
```

In the preceding example table, all columns are fixed length as shown by the `SHOW TABLE STATUS` statement in Figure 10-3.

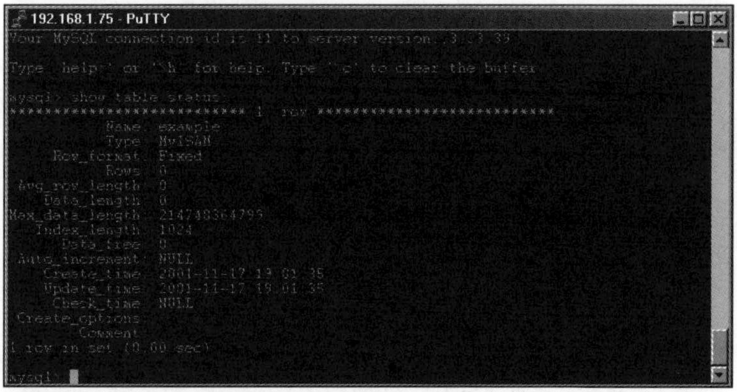

Figure 10-3: The SHOW TABLE STATUS command reveals that the table is in Fixed row format.

Static tables have two advantages:

- ✦ With the exception of volatile-memory table types such as HEAP, the `Static` table format is the fastest of the three `MyISAM` options because its columns are a uniform size. For example, a `CHAR` column is padded with extra whitespace characters to bring the column up to the defined size; a `VARCHAR` column is not padded with extra characters. Since the column is always the same size, MySQL can sort through the data quicker as it knows that the column is a constant length regardless of the size of the data held within the column.
- ✦ Padding of fields to the same size makes `Static` tables safer. The repair utility `myisamchk` can easily predict the boundaries of columns in a row.

Caution

The trade-off for `Static` table speed is *disk space.* Because each record must be padded with characters to bring it to the defined length, each row consumes the maximum defined disk space, even if the actual data is short. Of course, if each record is exactly same fixed length as the definition there is no additional disk space consumption with a `Static` table.

Dynamic format

Dynamic tables minimize disk-space usage because the size of the table depends on the actual size of the data.

Note

Bytes are stored for each column in a `Dynamic` table to keep track of the length of the data.

If you perform an `UPDATE` on a data record, the updated data may actually be stored in a different location in the datafile. For example, if you insert a value into a column such as an address and then update that address to a much longer address, the updated column may actually be stored in a different location or fragmented away from the rest of the record. This fragmentation can be repaired with the `myisamchk` utility.

Moving fixed-length or static data columns into another table may accelerate those tables, if it is possible and reasonable to organize your data this way. You should determine whether fragmentation or variable-length columns adversely affects performance enough to warrant dividing the tables. To accomplish this, compare the number of variable-length columns in the table to the number of static length columns. If an index relies on static columns, it may be beneficial to move the variable-length column to another table. However, moving the variable-length column to another table can add overhead as that table is joined with the original table.

Caution

`Dynamic` tables can be more difficult for MySQL to repair after a crash. Because updates to the data can cause fragmentation, some pieces of a record may be lost when repairing the table. `Static` table repairs are easier because all columns are of the same defined length.

Using the following `ALTER TABLE` statement, I have altered the example table definition shown previously in this section.

```
ALTER TABLE example MODIFY name varchar(10);
```

Note

Changing one column from `CHAR` to `VARCHAR` changes all `CHAR` columns to the variable-length `VARCHAR` format.

Running the `SHOW TABLE STATUS` statement again as shown in Figure 10-4 shows the row format is now `Dynamic` (one or more columns in the table is now a variable-length type).

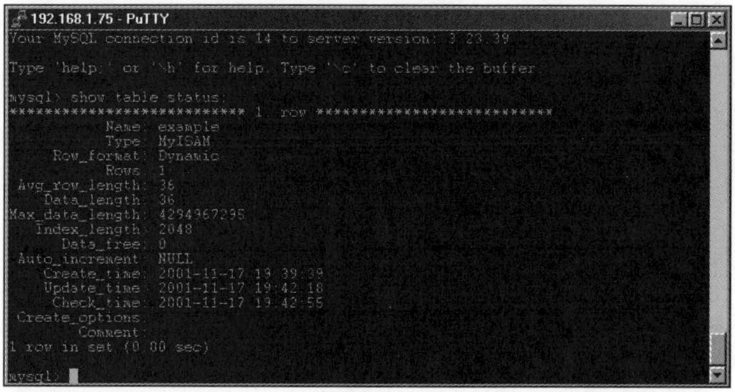

Figure 10-4: The SHOW TABLE STATUS statement now shows the row format has changed due to the alteration of the table definition.

Compressed format

`Compressed` tables are read-only. Because they are read-only, `Compressed` tables are good for rarely changed data — and they take up little disk space. For example, a library may have reference material sorted in a database. The book titles, authors, and other information are static. Taking such information and storing it in a compressed table in a database saves disk space thus enabling the library to store a huge amount of data at a lower cost.

`Compressed` tables are compressed with the *myisampack* utility. `Compressed` tables can be either `Static` or `Dynamic` and can be unpacked with the `myisamchk` command.

Note: Compressed tables cannot have `BLOB` or `TEXT` column types.

MyISAM variables

There are a number of variables and parameters that can change the behavior of `MyISAM` tables. The variables and parameters control things like

- ✦ Automatic recovery of crashed tables
- ✦ Size of buffers and caches
- ✦ How indexes are created

Tip: To determine the current values for the variables and parameters, use the `mysqladmin variables` command, as shown in Figure 10-5.

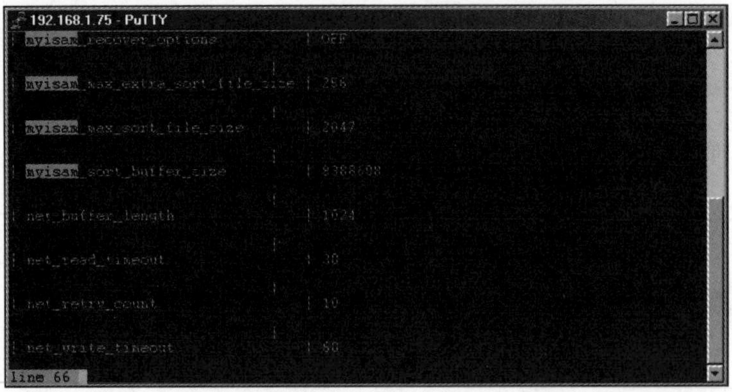

Figure 10-5: The default values for four of the MyISAM table variables and parameters

Note: You may see a slightly different value for the options shown in Figure 10-5 depending on the version of MySQL you're using and the architecture the server is running on.

The variables and parameters can be set two ways:

- ✦ On the command line when starting the MySQL server process
- ✦ Inside a configuration file (such `as /etc/my.cnf` in Linux)

MySQL can be configured to repair MyISAM tables automatically at startup. When a table is closed, MySQL sets a value in the header of the .MYI database file. If this value indicates that the table was not closed properly, a table repair is necessary. Using the `myisam-recover` variable, you can control if and how an automatic repair is performed. The `myisam-recover` variable accepts any combination of four parameters:

`DEFAULT` Setting the option value to `DEFAULT` is the same as simply using `myisam-recover` with no option.

`BACKUP` Using `BACKUP` creates a backup of the datafile (identified with the `.BAK` extension) to prevent loss of data during recovery.

`FORCE` The `FORCE` option repairs the table, regardless of how many rows are lost.

`QUICK` This option attempts only to repair the index. The `QUICK` option can only be used in conjunction with the `skip-locking server` parameter.

Caution: If you are going to use the `FORCE` option it is a good idea to use the `BACKUP` option to prevent unforeseen data loss.

In Figure 10-5, the value of `myisam-recover-options` indicates that there are no options set for recovery in the example. When a table is opened with the `myisam-recover variable` set, MySQL checks the table to make sure it was closed properly.

You can set options either with `myisam-recover` on the command line (as the server is started), or in a configuration file. For example, to use the `BACKUP` and `FORCE` options with `myisam-recover` I add the following line to the `[mysqld]` section of the `/etc/my.cnf` file in Linux.

```
myisam-recover = BACKUP,FORCE
```

After adding the preceding line to the my.cnf configuration file and restarting the server the `mysqladmin variables` command reflects the change, as shown in Figure 10-6.

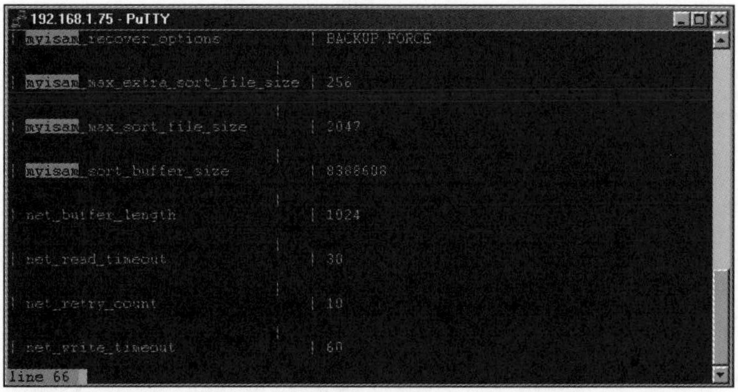

Figure 10-6: Using the BACKUP and FORCE automatic recovery options as shown by the mysqladmin variables command

Note

Some versions of MySQL may show different values for the variables shown in Figure 10-6.

Note

MySQL makes a backup file when using the `BACKUP` option. This `BACKUP` file can be the same size as the table file.

Another option used when recovering tables is `myisam_sort_buffer_size`. This option controls how large the buffers should be for recovery. Set this variable either on the command line using `-O myisam_sort_buffer_size=` or inside a configuration file, using a `set-variable` line in the `[mysqld]` section.

A couple of options deal with indexes and MyISAM tables. These options include myisam_max_extra_sort_file_size and myisam_max_sort_file_size. The options control how to create indexes and when to use other methods to create them. Both options are set on the command line or in the configuration file with a set-variable option.

MERGE

The MERGE table type is a relative newcomer to MySQL. A MERGE table is a collection of identical MyISAM tables grouped together as if they were one table. Only certain operations are allowed with MERGE tables, such as

- SELECT
- INSERT
- DELETE
- UPDATE

Caution **The MyISAM tables must contain the same column definitions and layout. If the tables are not defined exactly the same, you cannot create a MERGE table.**

MERGE tables speed up operations when identical tables need to be joined. However, creating a MERGE table also increases the number of File Descriptors needed. If you have multiple tables with the same layout where you would normally be performing a JOIN on the tables, a MERGE table can be beneficial.

Caution **As of this writing, performing a DROP TABLE or a DELETE FROM with no WHERE specification on a MERGE table only drops or deletes the MERGE table specification, *not* the data contained in the merged tables.**

To create a MERGE table, use the following syntax:

```
CREATE TABLE <tablename> (<column definitions>) TYPE=MERGE
UNION=(<tablename>,<tablename>...) INSERT_METHOD=<LAST|NO>
```

If you do not specify an INSERT_METHOD or set the INSERT_METHOD to NO, you can't perform an INSERT on the newly created table.

ISAM

Though ISAM tables will be disappearing from MySQL, some older or legacy databases still use them.

Tip **Use MyISAM for new databases.**

As with MyISAM tables, ISAM tables use a B-tree index and can compress keys to save on space. ISAM tables can be repaired with the isamchk utility.

Caution ISAM tables are dependent upon the architecture or OS in which they are created. For example, datafiles of an ISAM table running on an Alpha processor can't be moved or copied to a computer running an *x*86-type processor.

HEAP

HEAP-type tables exist only in *volatile memory*. When the MySQL server dies for any reason, all existing HEAP tables die—along with any data they contained. Because they reside in memory only, HEAP tables are useful for temporary tables and are fast.

Tip Think of a HEAP table much like a RAM drive. The RAM drive exists only in memory and is therefore fast–but the contents of the drive go away as soon as the machine is turned off.

Caution Don't store any permanent data in a HEAP table!

HEAP tables are different enough from other tables that knowing their characteristics may help you avoid misusing them. For instance, HEAP tables do not support auto_increment columns, nor do HEAP tables support BLOB or TEXT column types.

Caution Because a HEAP table stores data in RAM, one HEAP table can potentially use all the available memory in your system! To prevent such excess, you can create the table with the MAX_ROWS modifier or you can control the maximum size for the table through the max_heap_table_size server variable.

Using the mysqladmin variables command, I note the default max_heap_table_size value of 16777216 for the MySQL server, as shown in Figure 10-7.

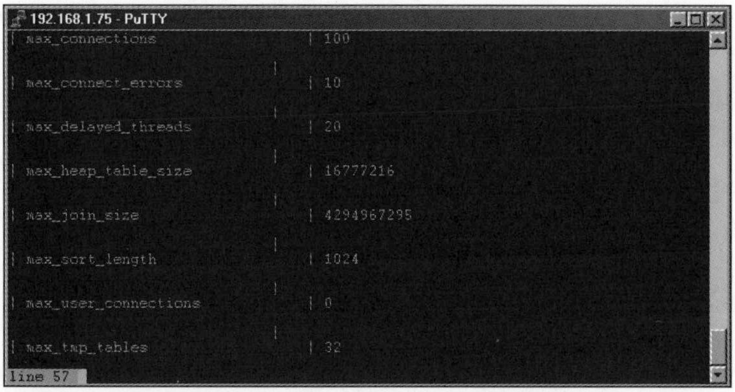
192.168.1.75 - PuTTY
| max_connections | 100
| max_connect_errors | 10
| max_delayed_threads | 20
| max_heap_table_size | 16777216
| max_join_size | 4294967295
| max_sort_length | 1024
| max_user_connections | 0
| max_tmp_tables | 32
line 57

Figure 10-7: The default value for the max_heap_table_size determines how much memory a HEAP table can use.

To change the value, edit the [mysqld] section of your MySQL server configuration file, /etc/my.cnf on some Linux flavors, and add the following (where X is the new value):

```
set-variable = max_heap_table_size=X
```

For example, I want to set the maximum memory usage for a HEAP table on my server to 8MB of RAM. I add the following to the /etc/my.cnf file:

```
set-variable = max_heap_table_size=8M
```

After restarting the MySQL server, I re-run the mysqladmin variables command, as shown in Figure 10-8.

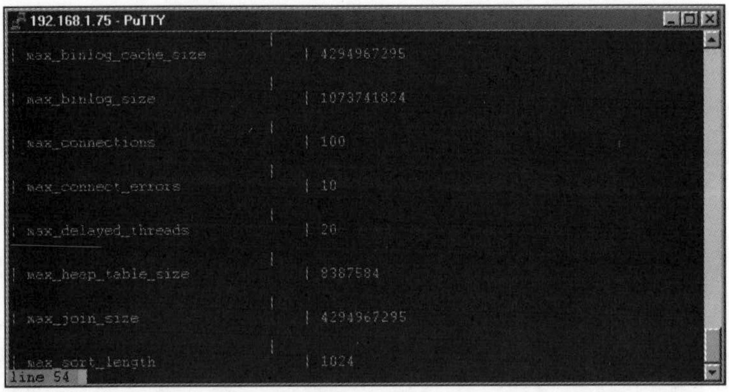
192.168.1.75 - PuTTY
max_binlog_cache_size | 4294967295
max_binlog_size | 1073741824
max_connections | 100
max_connect_errors | 10
max_delayed_threads | 20
max_heap_table_size | 8387584
max_join_size | 4294967295
max_sort_length | 1024
line 54

Figure 10-8: Changing the default value for max_heap_table_size in the MySQL server configuration file

InnoDB

InnoDB is one of two native transactional tables included with MySQL (the other is Gemini, distributed with NuSphere Enhanced MySQL). InnoDB is not included with a normal MySQL binary distribution. To enable InnoDB, you must compile it in or use a MySQL-Max version of MySQL. Further, you must set at least one variable in the my.cnf file, the innodb_data_file_path variable. The variable should be set under the [mysqld] section. Additional variables and parameters can be set to assist with performance of InnoDB tables.

Cross-Reference NuSphere Enhanced MySQL is discussed in greater depth in Chapter 20.

InnoDB tables offer row-level locking and transactional features such as COMMIT and ROLLBACK. The advantage of such a table type is that you can prevent incomplete updates from writing or changing data in the event of a system crash or other event. Additionally, InnoDB supports the use of Foreign Keys to protect referential integrity.

To create an InnoDB table you must specify `Type = InnoDB` with your `CREATE TABLE` statement. A syntax example follows:

```
CREATE TABLE example (
     id int,
     name varchar(30)
)
Type = InnoDB;
```

Tip **If you currently have `MyISAM` tables and want to convert them to `InnoDB`, the easiest method for doing so is simply to create an identical `InnoDB` table and then import or re-insert the data from the existing `MyISAM` table.**

InnoDB tables have a number of limitations.

- ✦ You cannot have a BLOB or TEXT column type in an `InnoDB` table.
- ✦ Tables cannot have more than 1,000 columns.
- ✦ Unique indexes cannot be created on a prefix.

InnoDB variables and parameters

A number of options can be set to boost the performance of `InnoDB` tables. All of these options should be set under the `[mysqld]` section of the configuration file. The `innodb_data_file_path` must be set to `InnoDB` to be enabled. The syntax for this parameter is as follows:

```
innodb_data_file_path=<filename>:<size>
```

The *<filename>* parameter specifies the name of the `InnoDB` database. The <size> parameter is usually given with an M for Megabytes and must be at least ten megabytes (10M). Upon startup, MySQL creates a *<filename>* in the `DATADIR` of the MySQL installation in the size of *<size>* as specified in the configuration file. Additionally, logfiles are created in the `DATADIR`. The parameters can also be separated by semicolons to add more databases and can also be given relative paths. For example, to use two `InnoDB` databases located in a directory — `innodb1` and `innodb2`, each 250 megabytes in size — use the following syntax:

```
innodb_data_file_path =
innodb1/database1:250M;innodb2/database2:250M
```

You can change the location of the data file and the logfiles with the parameters `innodb_data_home_dir` and `innodb_log_group_home_dir` respectively. These options are also set in the `[mysqld]` section of the MySQL configuration file. The options expect paths as values. Any directories specified with the `innodb_data_file_path` are relative from the standpoint of `innodb_data_home_dir`. For example, to set /usr/local/data/innodb as the path for the data, the syntax would be as follows:

```
innodb_data_home_dir = /usr/local/data/innodb
```

In the innodb_data_file_path example earlier, the data files for the two databases would be /usr/local/data/innodb/innodb1 and /usr/local/data/innodb/innodb2 respectively.

Note Check to make sure that the directories you specify actually exist — and that MySQL has permission to access them.

InnoDB logfiles are rotated in a circular pattern. You can set the number of logfiles kept using the innodb_log_files_in_group variable. The default value is 2. Set this variable via the set-variable parameter in the MySQL configuration file or using the -O switch on the mysqld command line.

Another option affecting the logfiles of InnoDB tables is innodb_log_file_size. The innodb_log_file_size variable determines how large to make the logfiles. The bigger the value, the less disk activity is needed due to flushing. However, setting the value of innodb_log_file_size too large can cause recovery time to lengthen. The innodb_log_file_size value can be a maximum of 4 gigabytes for all logfiles combined.

The innodb_log_buffer_size variable controls how large the buffer should be prior to writing to the log. As with the innodb_log_file_size, a larger innodb_log_buffer_size value results in fewer disk operations. The maximum value for this variable is half the innodb_log_file_size.

Another variable that affects disk writes — and thus speed and performance — is innodb_flush_log_at_trx_commit. The default value for innodb_flush_log_at_trx_commit is 1. The value of 1 for this variable indicates that after every COMMIT, the transaction will be written to the logfile and thus made permanent. If you want to compromise this safety for speed, you can set the value for innodb_flush_log_at_trx_commit to 0.

Yet another variable to affect disk performance is the innodb_buffer_pool_size variable. Though it does not affect logging like the preceding variables, the innodb_buffer_pool_size affects how memory is used. With the innodb_buffer_pool_size variable, you tell the MySQL server how much memory to use when it caches table and index data. The larger you set this value, the more data and indexes can be cached in memory, which cuts down on disk operations. Be careful, however, not to set this value too large — if you do, the server may do so many paging or swap-to-disk operations that not enough physical memory is left for normal server processes. Windows-based servers, or other servers that "waste" resources to support a GUI, are especially prone to such memory shortages.

The innodb_additional_mem_pool_size defines the amount of memory that MySQL should use to store data dictionary information. MySQL AB recommends this value be two megabytes (2M). However, if you have a large number of tables, you may want to consider increasing this value.

An important variable to know about even though you may never need to change the default is innodb_lock_wait_timeout. In the event of a lock that the InnoDB handler cannot detect or clear, this variable automatically starts the process to roll the transaction back and release the lock.

BerkeleyDB

BerkeleyDB (which you may see abbreviated as BDB) is another type of transactional table available in the AB version of MySQL. As with InnoDB, BerkeleyDB tables require additional support, which you can get in one of two ways:

- The MySQL MAX version of MySQL offers built-in support.
- You can compile support for BerkeleyDB tables into your version of MySQL if you are installing from source code.

Also as with InnoDB, BerkeleyDB also offers COMMIT and ROLLBACK for transactions. BerkeleyDB is, however, available on only a limited range of architectures:

- Linux on Intel
- Solaris on Sparc
- SCO OpenServer
- SCO UnixWare

Unlike InnoDB, BerkeleyDB requires no particular options be set to enable it.

BerkeleyDB variables and parameters

As with InnoDB, some variables and parameters can be set for BerkeleyDB to affect the behavior of the tables.

- If you want to start the server without BerkeleyDB support, use the --skip-bdb parameter.
- To set the home directory for BerkeleyDB files use the --bdb-home=<*directory*> variable.
- The logfile directory for BerkeleyDB tables is set with the --bdb-logdir=<*directory*> variable.
- The temporary directory is set with the --bdb-tempdir=<*directory*>.

✦ Other options to change the behavior are the `--bdb-nosync` and `--bdb-no-recover` parameters. These options affect the recovery of BerkeleyDB tables.

✦ To change the locking behavior, the `set-variable` (or `-O` if on the command line) `bdb_max_lock=N` should be set. This variable controls the maximum number of locks available for `BerkeleyDB` tables. For example, within the `[mysqld]` section of the MySQL configuration file you would place:

```
set-variable = bdb_max_lock=N
```

✦ The `--bdb-lock-detect=X` parameter sets how MySQL works with locks on tables. Valid values for X are

- `DEFAULT`
- `OLDEST`
- `YOUNGEST`
- `RANDOM`

Note: The variables and parameters can be set on the `mysqld` command line or in the MySQL configuration file.

Administering Your Database with mysqladmin

The `mysqladmin` command serves to perform administration tasks on MySQL databases and database servers. With the `mysqladmin` command you can create and delete databases, stop the server, kill threads, perform server maintenance, and examine server variables. Should you forget the syntax or usage of the `mysqladmin` command, you can always type `mysqladmin` with no arguments or with the `--help` or the `-?` switches and get a summary of the commands and syntax of the `mysqladmin` command. Part of the output from this help is shown in Figure 10-9.

Common switches

Running the `mysqladmin` command with no arguments, you see a number of switches exactly like those used for the MySQL CLI command `mysql`. These options include the `-u` or `--user` switch, the `--password` or `-p` switch, the `--host` or `-h` switch, the `--port` switch, and the `-E` or `--vertical` switch.

Cross-Reference: Chapter 8 covers switches the same as the MySQL CLI.

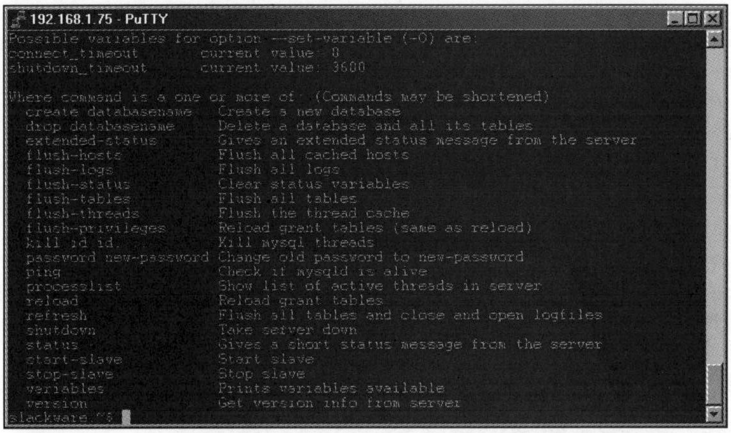

Figure 10-9: Should you forget the commands or syntax of the mysqladmin command, you can simply type **mysqladmin** with no arguments and get a summary.

Special switches

There are also switches specific to the `mysqladmin` command.

A switch that can be useful for monitoring MySQL performance is the `-i` or `–sleep=N` switch. Using this switch, you can set `mysqladmin` to rerun the specified command every *N* seconds. In Figure 10-10, I use the `-i` switch to run the `mysqladmin status` command every 2 seconds. As you can see, the server isn't busy but the example is still useful.

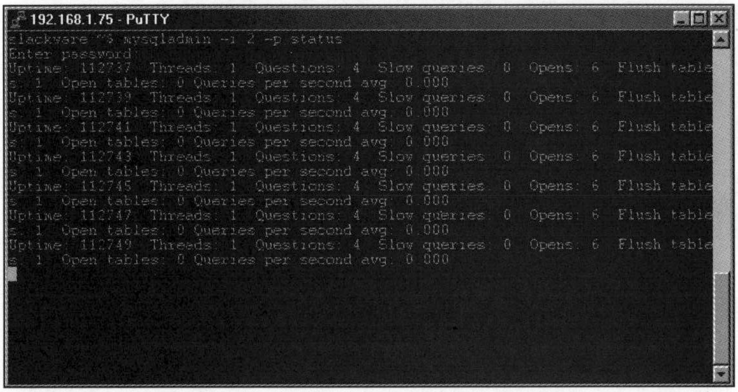

Figure 10-10: Using the -i switch, you can configure mysqladmin to run the specified command at regular intervals.

Another switch to use with the `mysqladmin` command is the `-r` or `--relative` switch. Using the `-r` switch together with the `extended-status` command, you can see the changes in the values provided by the `extended-status` command over the specified time interval. In Figure 10-11 you can see the initial run of the `extended-status` command. In Figure 10-12 you can see the next run after a 10-second interval has elapsed; note the `Uptime` is only 10 because 10 seconds have elapsed.

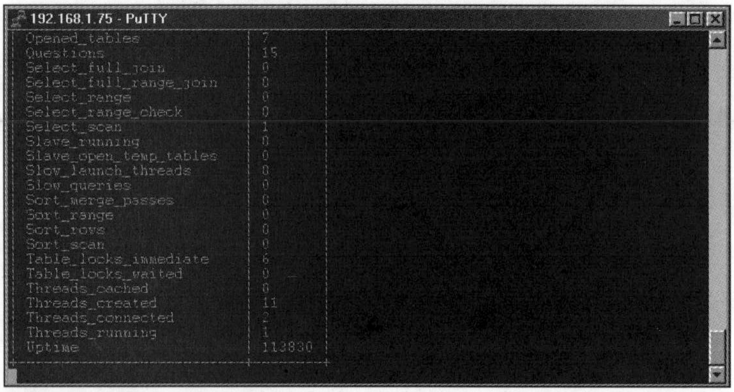

Figure 10-11: First output of the `mysqladmin extended-status` command with the -r switch for keeping track of relative values

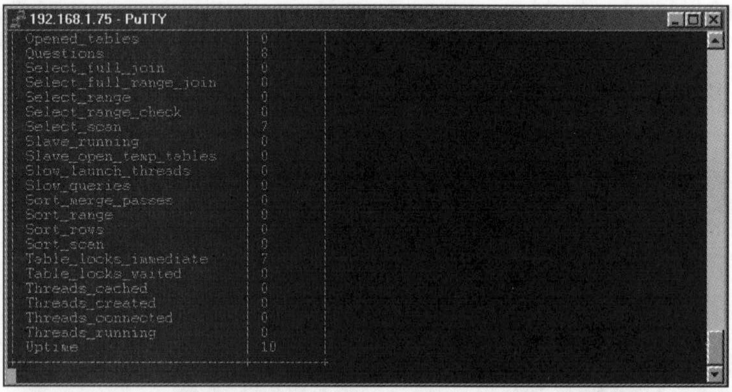

Figure 10-12: The second output of the mysqladmin extended-status command using the -r switch to track relative or changed values

Note

The `-r` or `--relative` switch currently only works with the `mysqladmin extended-status` switch.

Functions with mysqladmin

I've shown quite a few examples of the mysqladmin command throughout the book. It's now time to examine the commands and functions that make the mysqladmin command so useful.

Cross-Reference

Chapter 8 on MySQL CLI explains adding the switches for specifying command line parameters such as user (`-u`) and password (`-p`).

Creating and dropping databases

The `mysqladmin` command serves to create and drop or delete databases. The syntax for creating a database with the `mysqladmin` command is as follows:

```
mysqladmin create <databasename>
```

Similarly, the syntax for dropping a database is much the same:

```
mysqladmin drop <databasename>
```

In Figure 10-13, I create and drop a database. Notice the verification that precedes the actual deletion of the database.

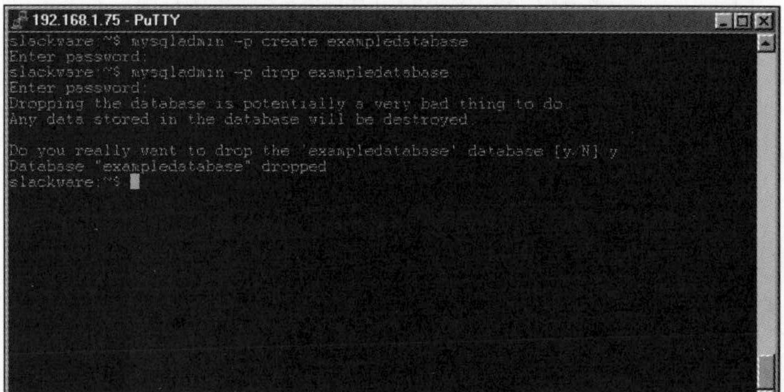

Figure 10-13: Creating and then dropping a database, using the mysqladmin command

Obtaining server status information

An important part of monitoring server performance and diagnosing problems is done by looking at the values of server parameters. A concise overview of many important server values is obtained using the functions in this section.

- **Status.** The `status` function returns a quick overview of some important server parameters:
  - The `Uptime` parameter is the number of seconds the server has been running.
  - The `Threads` column contains the quantity of the number of active clients or threads running or connected at the time.
  - The value of `Questions` is the number of questions or statements that the MySQL server has received since startup.
  - The `Slow queries` value indicates the number of times that a query has taken longer than the value set for a slow query. This value, `long_query_time`, can be set by the administrator and may be helpful in tuning the server.
  - The `Opens` value indicates the total number of tables that MySQL has opened since startup.
  - The `Flush tables` parameter indicates the number of times a `FLUSH`, `RELOAD`, or `REFRESH` statement has been executed.
  - The `Open tables` value indicates the number of tables currently open.
  - `Memory in use` indicates how much memory is currently allocated to mysqld.
  - `Max memory` used indicates the maximum memory amount allocated to `mysqld`.

An example of the output from the `status` function is shown in Figure 10-14.

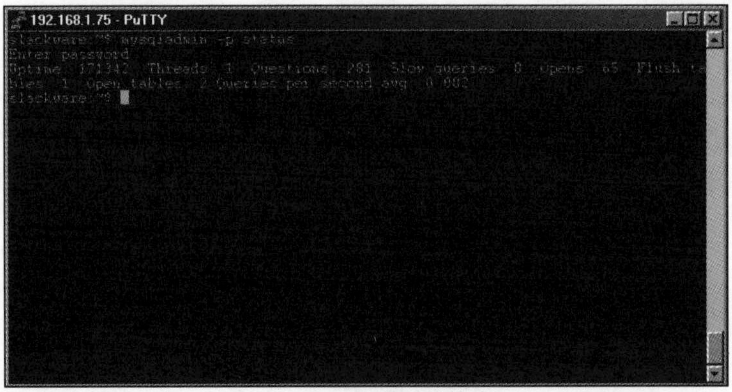

Figure 10-14: Output from the mysqladmin status command

✦ **Extended-status.** As you might expect, the `extended-status` function returns much more information about server parameters and performance than does the `status` function. When you tune server variables to get better performance from the MySQL server, the `extended-status function` is frequently useful.

Cross-Reference Chapter 11 and Chapter 13 cover tuning your server parameters.

Figure 10-15 shows an example of part of the output from the `extended-status` function.

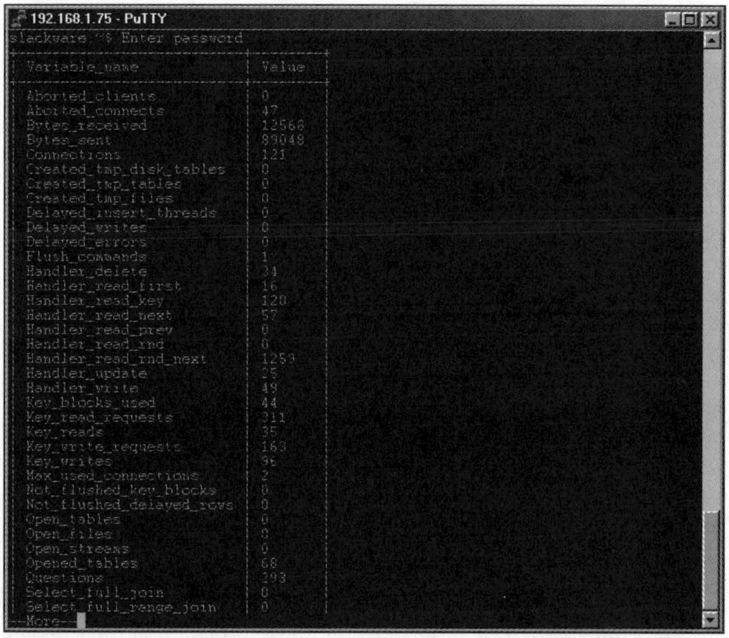

Figure 10-15: Partial output from the mysqladmin extended-status command

✦ **Processlist.** The `processlist` function lists the currently active or open connections to a MySQL server. These can be from applications, the CLI, other MySQL servers, or through any other communication with the MySQL server.

The eight columns in the `processlist` function output provide a snapshot of activity on the database server at the instant the command was run.

- The *`Id`* column is a counter of the connections to the database server and is incremented with each new connection.
- The *`User`* is the user performing the action.
- The *`Host`* is where the user's connection originated.

- A *db* column indicates whether the command or statement involved a database.
- The *Command* column indicates the type of command that was run.
- The *Time* column indicates the time of the connection.
- The *State* column indicates what the process is doing, from waiting, to opening connection, establishing communication, and so forth.
- The *Info* column shows what statement or command the process is running.

An example of the processlist function is shown in Figure 10-16.

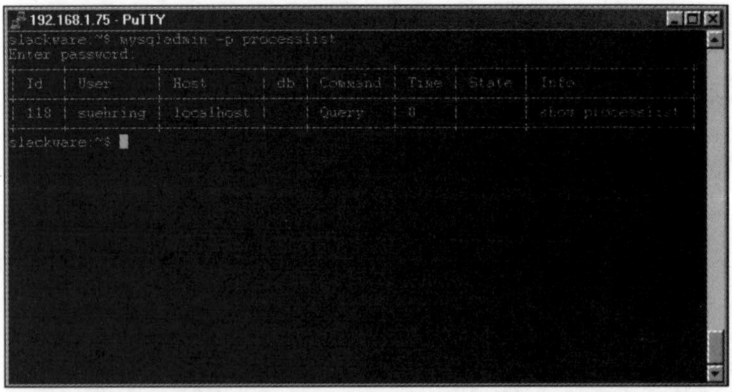
192.168.1.75 - PuTTY
slackware:~$ mysqladmin -p processlist
Enter password:
Id | User | Host | db | Command | Time | State | Info
118 | suehring | localhost | | Query | 0 | | show processlist
slackware:~$

Figure 10-16: The MySQL processlist function for use with the mysqladmin command

Tip

Using the `processlist` function I was able to troubleshoot a problem where a developer was opening multiple connections to the database and closing none of them. The clients would issue a command and then sit idle until they timed out. The server would reach its client connection limit quickly and start refusing legitimate connections. The `processlist` function showed that there were a number of connections from the application user and the connections remained open. By changing the `connection_timeout` value and restarting the server, I was able to solve the problem. Without the processlist command troubleshooting this issue would have been difficult.

✦ **Variables.** The variables function outputs the various options and server parameters that the MySQL server operates with. These include parameters like

- Connection timeouts
- Types of tables included with the server

- Server version
- Sizes of caches and buffers

An example of the output from the `mysqladmin variables` command is shown in Figure 10-17. The command to reproduce this output is `mysqladmin variables`.

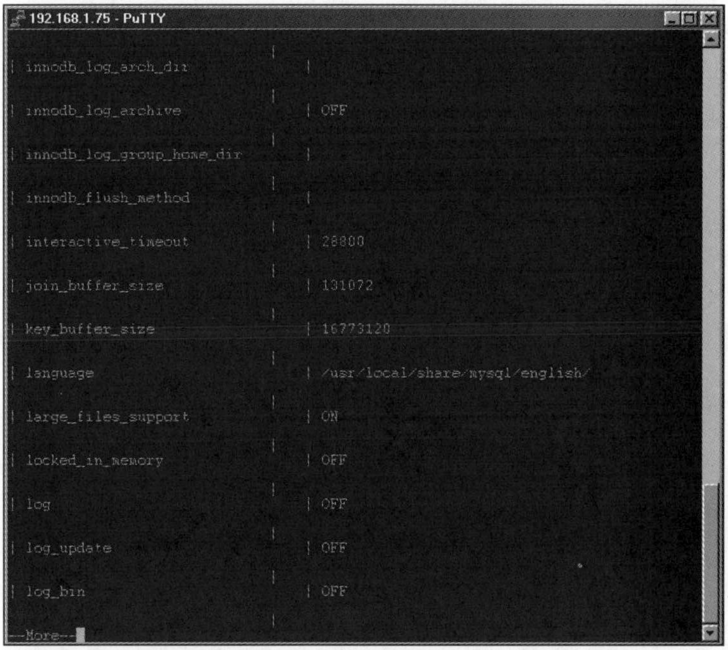

Figure 10-17: The output from the mysqladmin variables command shows the options that the MySQL server uses.

Functions for clearing server parameters

The `mysqladmin` command provides numerous functions for flushing or clearing server parameters. The functions are as follows:

✦ `flush-hosts` This function clears the MySQL DNS host cache. By default MySQL stores the connecting hosts to IP resolution. If you change the host's DNS entry or a number of errors occur during a connection, the host may be blocked by MySQL. Performing a `mysqladmin flush-hosts` operation clears the DNS host cache and solves the problem.

✦ `flush-logs` MySQL also keeps a number of logfiles. These can include update logs and binary update logs. The `flush-logs` function purges logfiles and restarts the logging process. For update logs done with the standard numbering extension, the new logfile has the last logfile's extension incremented by one. The `flush-logs` function does not touch the error log, `<hostname>.err`, typically located in your data directory.

✦ `flush-status` This function takes `status type` variables and resets them to zero — useful for debugging server performance and parameters. Figure 10-18, for example, shows partial output from the `extended-status` function after I run the `flush-status` function. Figure 10-19 shows the results of another run of the `extended-status` function immediately after I run the `flush-status` function. The command to flush the status variables is `mysqladmin flush-status`.

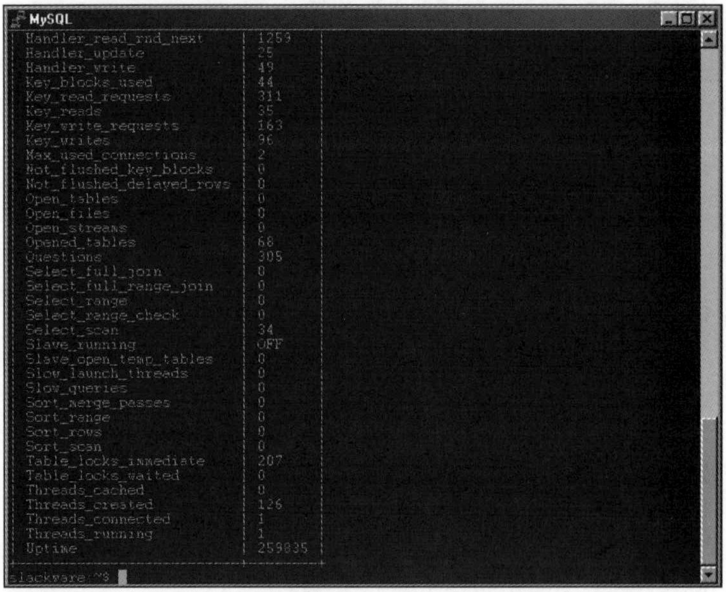

Figure 10-18: A snapshot of server parameters prior to running the mysqladmin flush-status command

✦ `flush-tables` The flush-tables function should be used with care. This function closes any and all open tables. Even if a table is in use, the flush-tables functions closes those as well. This can result in errors to the client. I've found that this function sometimes must be used on extremely busy servers that seem unresponsive to a shutdown command.

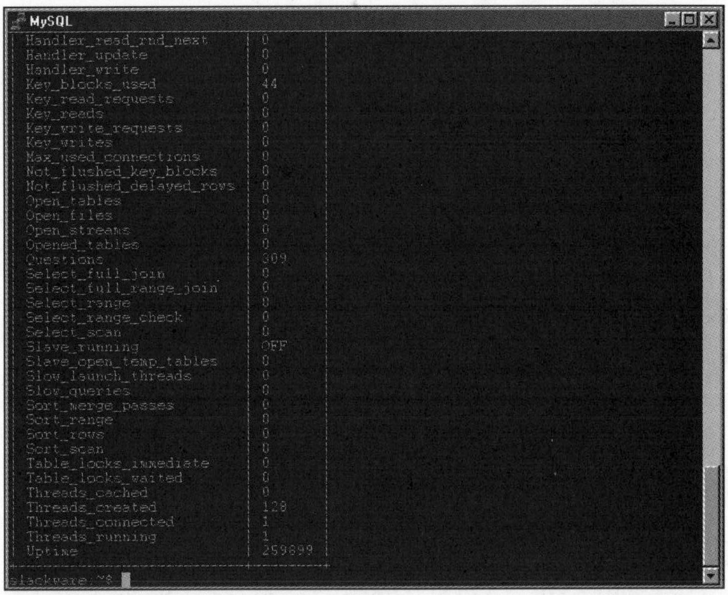

Figure 10-19: Another snapshot of server parameters immediately after the flush-status function

- `refresh` The refresh function is a combination of the flush-tables and flush-logs functions.
- `flush-privileges` A frequently used function, though maybe not via the mysqladmin command, is the `flush-privileges` function. The flush-privileges function causes the `GRANTS` tables to be reloaded, making MySQL aware of any changes to those tables. If statements working with those tables are done with a `GRANT` or `REVOKE` statement, using the `flush-privileges` function in unnecessary. However, if using any other SQL statement on any of the grants tables, you must `flush-privileges` or optionally reload the server.
- `reload` The reload function is a synonym for the flush-privileges function.

Killing MySQL processes

The word *kill* sounds somewhat harsh, but this is the name of the function to terminate a client process or thread in the server. Using the `mysqladmin processlist` command, you can determine the id of a client or process that needs to be terminated. Issuing the `mysqladmin kill` function terminates that process. This does not stop the client from reconnecting; in fact, the CLI reconnects automatically.

Here's a simple example of the `kill` function:

1. Using the MySQL CLI, I connect to the MySQL CLI and issue a simple `SELECT` statement, as shown in Figure 10-20.

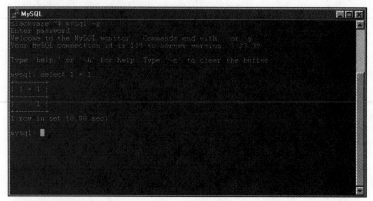

Figure 10-20: Connecting to the MySQL CLI and performing a basic SELECT statement

2. In Figure 10-21 I run the `mysqladmin processlist` command to determine the ID of the other client connection. As you can see it is 139 as shown by the `id` column of the output. Also in Figure 10-21 I issue the `mysqladmin kill` command to terminate the process.

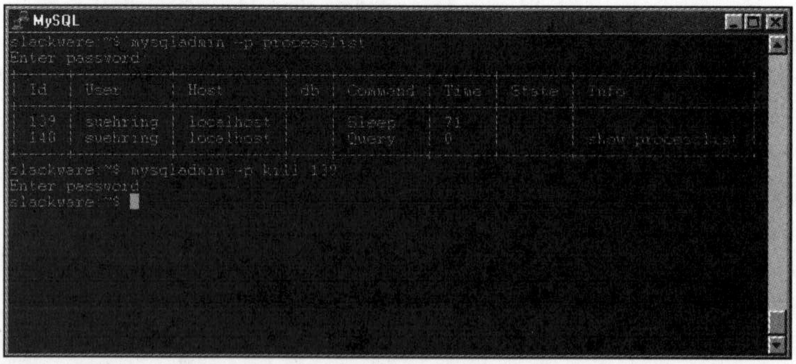

Figure 10-21: Using the mysqladmin processlist and mysqladmin kill commands to terminate a client process

3. Finally, in Figure 10-22 I attempt to run the same `SELECT` statement as in Figure 10-20. Notice the `Error` message produced by the CLI.

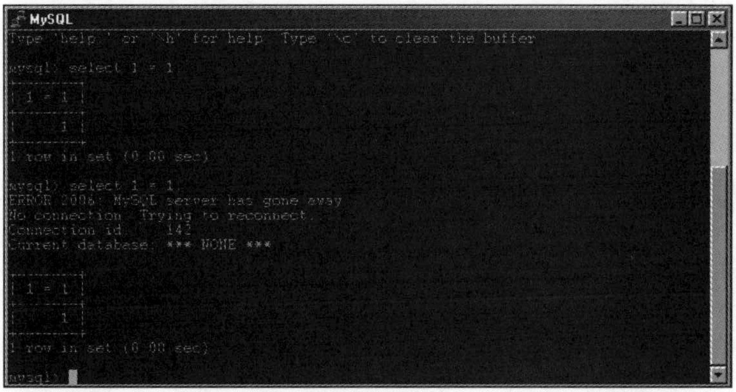

Figure 10-22: Issuing the same SELECT statement as in Figure 10-20 results in an error but the statement runs.

Information functions

✦ The `version` function informs the user what version of the server is running along with some other pertinent information about the server, including status and uptime information. An example is shown in Figure 10-23.

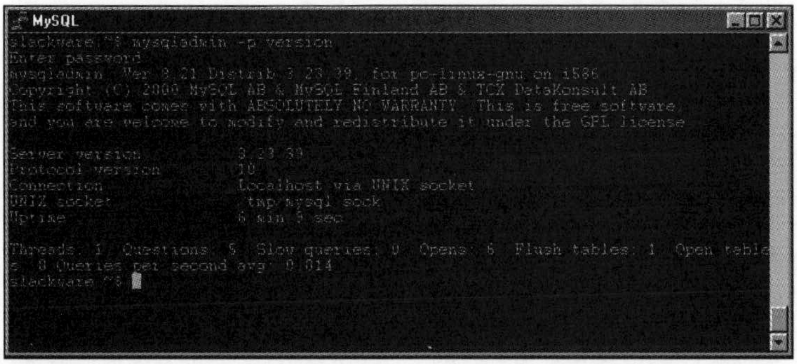

Figure 10-23: Output from the mysqladmin version command shows the server version along with other useful information on server performance.

✦ The `ping` function simply tells the administrator whether the server, `mysqld`, is alive. If the server is not alive, the command returns an error. In Figure 10-24 I run the command on the server while it is running, then secretly stop the server in another window (see **Figure 10-26)** and re-run the `ping` function again.

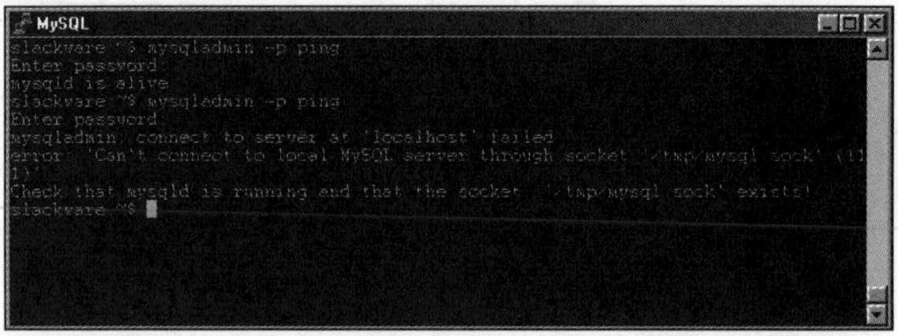

Figure 10-24: The mysqladmin ping command in action. The first attempt is successful; the second fails because I shut the MySQL server down in another window.

Changing passwords through mysqladmin

The `mysqladmin` command can also be used to set or change passwords for users in the MySQL database. In fact, this is how you changed the initial `root` password for the server back when it was installed.

The syntax for the password function can sometimes cause confusion. The syntax is as follows:

```
mysqladmin (-u username) (-p) password 'newpassword'
```

The `-u` *`username`* switch is necessary if you do not want to change the password for the current user. If you need to supply an existing password for the user account specified with the `-u` username switch (or for yourself if you don't use the `-u` *`username`* switch), then you must use the -p switch to have `mysqladmin` prompt for a password. Next the function name, password, is required. Finally, the new password is given as the last argument. The new password must be quoted.

I've prepared a couple of examples, shown in Figure 10-25. The first example changes the password for the current user, which happens to be `suehring`. The second example changes the password for the root user. Both are localhost changes.

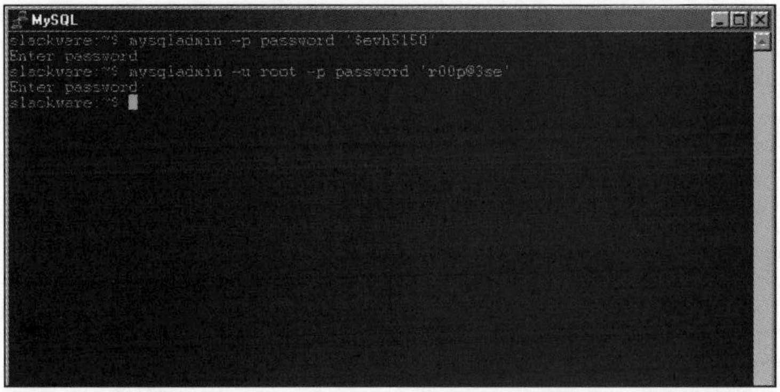

Figure 10-25: Examples of changing passwords with the mysqladmin password command

Stopping the MySQL server with mysqladmin

The `shutdown` function stops the MySQL server through the `mysqladmin` command. As with any shutdown, the command has to wait until threads are through with tables; this requirement protects the integrity of the data. The shutdown function provides no feedback to the user, see Figure 10-26.

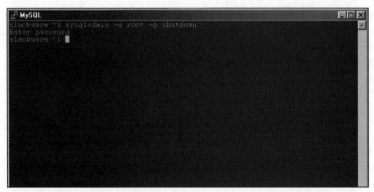

Figure 10-26: The mysqladmin shutdown command provides no feedback to the user upon success.

Replication functions with mysqladmin

There are two main functions of `mysqladmin` for use with replication. These are the `start-slave` and `stop-slave` functions. These functions start and stop a slave replication process.

Cross-Reference

Replication takes updates to data from one server and automatically copies them in real-time to another MySQL server. Chapter 18 covers replication. If you are not using replication, these functions are of no use.

Exporting Data

Two main methods are available for exporting data from a MySQL database:

✦ mysqldump

✦ the SELECT INTO OUTFILE statement.

Whether you're looking to make a simple backup of the server or export certain columns from a table into another program such as Microsoft Access, the exporting utilities and statements included with MySQL will help.

Note

You can also use a program called mysqlhotcopy to make a copy of a database. In addition, through the use of the MySQL CLI in non-interactive mode or with the Tee option, results can be saved or redirected into a file.

mysqldump

The mysqldump utility is a powerful program for extracting database and table structure along with the actual data. The mysqldump utility is sufficiently granular so that you could get the table structure and data from just one table or from all tables of all databases. If you would just like the table structure with no data you can do that as well. If you want just the data with no table structure, mysqldump also provides that functionality. The basic syntax for mysqldump is as follows:

```
mysqldump [OPTIONS] database [tables]
```

Note

When given no arguments, mysqldump simply prints a syntax reference.

Cross-Reference

There are quite a few options with mysqldump. Some of the options and switches such as those for specifying the username and password have been discussed in other chapters. If you are unsure how to specify a username or password with MySQL utilities, please refer to Chapter 8 for more details.

There are two variables that can affect your ability to dump tables with large columns: max_allowed_packet and net_buffer_length. Both can be set using the -O or --set-variable switch on the mysqldump command line or in the MySQL configuration file.

The mysqldump utility uses comments (escaped with /* */) to select options that may only be found in newer versions of MySQL. For example, when creating a database the `IF NOT EXISTS` keywords were introduced in version 3.23.12 of MySQL. The keywords `IF NOT EXISTS` will be enclosed in an escape sequence along with the version number. This allows the functionality of `IF NOT EXISTS` to be used by those versions that can handle it and safely ignored without error on those versions that do not include the function.

Normal usage of `mysqldump` calls for the command along with options such as username and password followed by the name of the database to dump and (optionally) specific tables and columns to dump. In Figure 10-27 the `mysqldump` command is issued to dump just the `db` table of the MySQL `grants` database. The command is as follows:

```
mysqldump -p mysql db
```

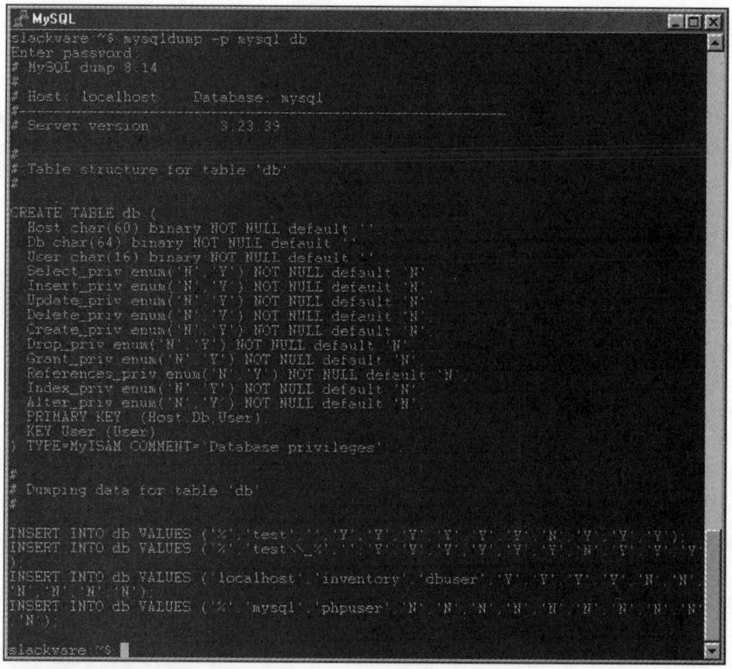

Figure 10-27: Using mysqldump to obtain the DDL and DML for one table of one database

For most of its uses, `mysqldump` redirects the output to a file instead of sending the output to `stdout` or to the screen (which is the default). The characters used to redirect output can vary by OS:

- ✦ In Linux, you perform redirect operations with the greater-than (>) sign.
- ✦ In Windows, use the `-r` or `--result-file=` switch with `mysqldump`, which assists the newline and carriage return.

Figure 10-28 shows examples of both redirect methods.

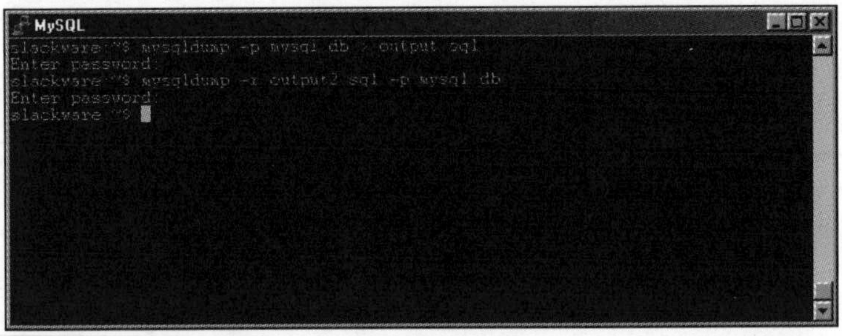

Figure 10-28: Examples of redirecting output via the greater-than sign and the -r switch

Specifying records to be dumped

You can even get more specific than a particular table with `mysqldump`. The use of the `--where=` or `-w` switch enables you to add a `SELECT` statement. For example, to dump only the contents of the user table of the MySQL grants database where the user is `'suehring'`, the command in Figure 10-29 could be issued:

```
mysqldump -p "--where=user='suehring'" mysql user
```

The `where` clause can be longer than one argument. For example, the following command is valid:

```
mysqldump -p "--where=user='suehring' and host = 'localhost'"
mysql user
```

Controlling the INSERT statement

Two options control how any `INSERT` statements are done with `mysqldump`. These options are `-c` (`--complete-insert`), or `-e` (`--extended-insert`). The default is `extended-insert`.

Examples with both types of insert options are shown in Figure 10-30. The commands to reproduce these examples are as follows:

```
mysqldump -t -p -e "--where=user='suehring' and host =
'localhost'" mysql user
mysqldump -t -p -c "--where=user='suehring' and host =
'localhost'" mysql user
```

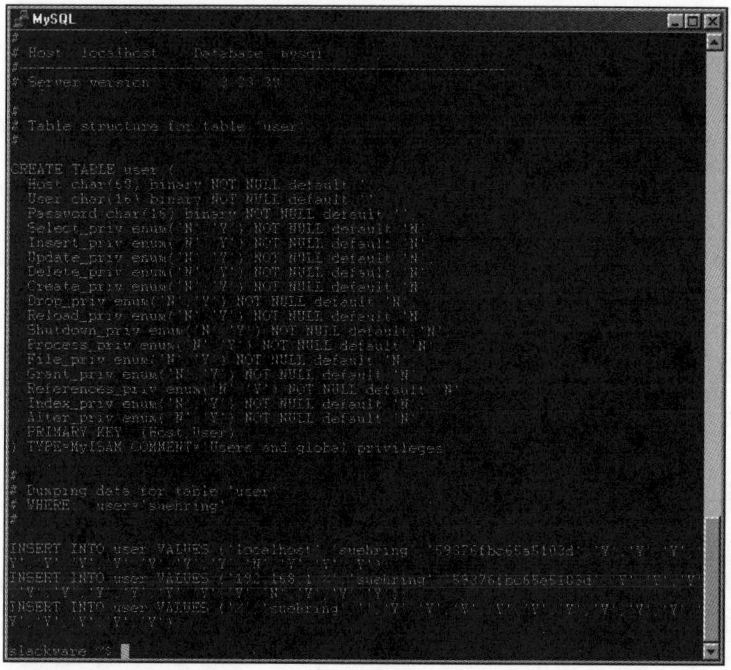

Figure 10-29: Using the --where= switch to specify only certain records to be dumped

Suppressing DDL

In the examples in Figure 10-30, you may have noticed an extra option: `-t` (also known as `--no-create-info`), which suppresses the DDL or the statements that would otherwise create the table.

The `-t` option can be useful for making a quick backup of the data in a table. For example, if you have another server that contains the same table structure and only want to migrate your data to the new server, you could suppress the DDL with the `-t` option. The result is the DML or statements to insert the data into the table or tables.

Suppressing DML and data

Just as you might want to suppress the printing of table creation statements in the output of a `mysqldump`, you might also want to suppress the actual DML or insert statements from the output as well. The switch for this option is `-d` or `--no-data`.

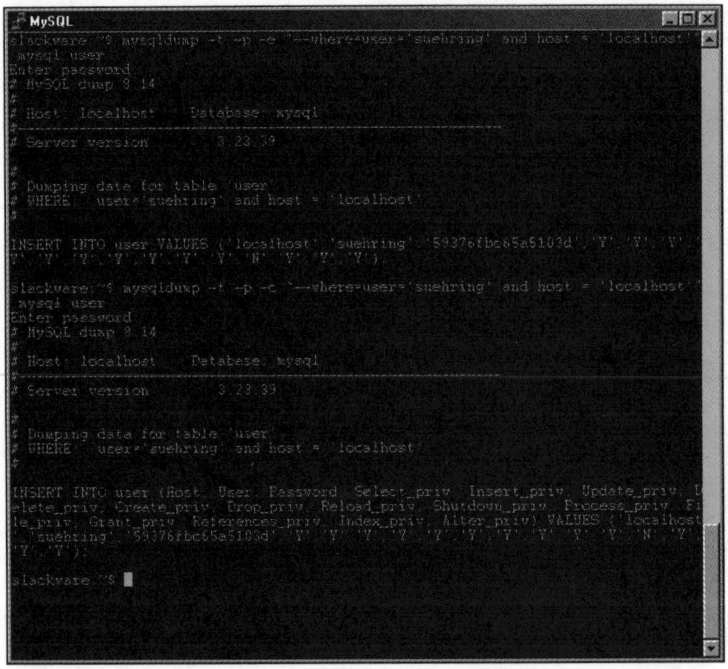

Figure 10-30: Examples of the types of INSERT statements that can be produced by mysqldump

Using the `-d` switch, a `mysqldump` will simply output the table (and possibly database) creation statements. This feature can be useful for making a skeleton copy of the database and table structure on another server. Figure 10-31 is an example of the `-d` switch in action, producing the DDL for the `ecommerce` database. The command for this example is as follows:

```
mysqldump -p -d ecommerce
```

Adding drops and locks

`mysqldump` can be configured to add statements to lock and unlock tables around INSERT statements. Doing so ensures that the `INSERT` will complete without an unexpected change in the data or contention for the table. The switch to enable the locking function is `--add-locks`.

You can also lock the tables around the reads that produce the output of `mysqldump`. The switch `-l` or `--lock-tables` turns this function on.

The `--add-drop-table` switch tells `mysqldump` to add a `DROP TABLE` statement just before creating the table. Adding this switch can be helpful if you already have tables of the same name that do not contain useful data.

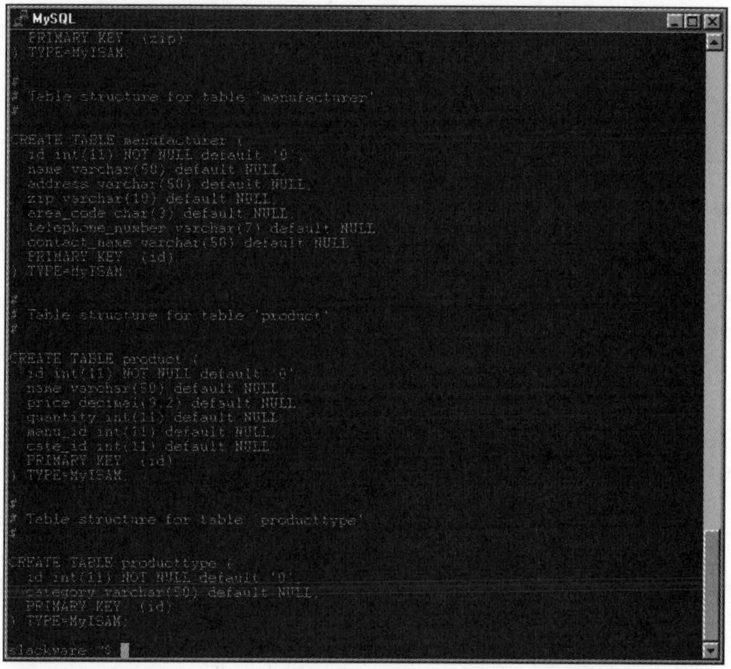

Figure 10-31: The -d or --no-data switch causes mysqldump to exclude the DML or INSERT statements from the output.

Caution

Using the `--add-drop-table` switch will cause all data to be lost in any tables that are removed.

`mysqldump` also includes a switch that can specify a number of the previously discussed options as well as others. The switch is the `--opt` switch and includes the switches `--add`, `--add-drop-tables`, `--add-locks`, `--extended-insert`, `--lock-tables`, and `--quick`.

Tip

If you are going to use the `--add`, `--add-drop-tables`, `--add-locks`, `--extended-insert`, `--lock-tables`, or `--quick` switch, specifying the `--opt` switch is a timesaver.

Special formatting functions with mysqldump

With `mysqldump` you can specify a number of options that determine how the output will look. These include special quotation of fields in the output, escaping or enclosing the fields in a special manner, and terminating lines and fields with the desired character. The switches or options to specify on the `mysqldump` command line are as follows:

```
--quote-names
--tab=
```

```
--fields-terminated-by=
--fields-enclosed-by=
--fields-optionally-enclosed-by=
--fields-escaped-by=
--lines-terminated-by=
```

The first switch, `--quote-names`, places backquotes (`) around the names of tables and databases.

The second switch, `--tab=`, can also be abbreviated as `-T`. The `--tab=` switch causes `mysqldump` to create two files, placing output from each table in the argument list. One file `<tablename>.sql` is the normal output of the DDL that you would expect from `mysqldump`. The second file, `<tablename>.txt`, is a tab-delimited file containing only the data from the table.

Tip: The `--tab=` switch can be useful for importing data into other applications such as Microsoft Access.

The `--tab=` or `-T` switch expects a directory or path as an argument, in effect, using `--tab=outputdir` will cause the results to be placed in a directory called `outputdir`. It is important that MySQL have permission to write into that directory. For this reason, the `--tab=` switch only works when run from the server that `mysqld` runs on. A few examples of the `--tab=` switch are shown in Figure 10-32. The first attempt is unsuccessful because the specified directory does not exist. In the second attempt, the MySQL server does not have permission to write into the directory specified. The final attempt is successful.

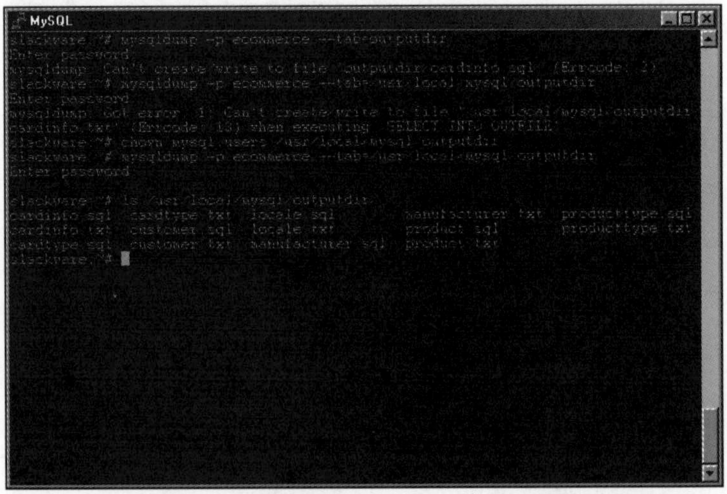

Figure 10-32: Three examples of use of the --tab= switch, two unsuccessful and one successful

The `--line-` and `--fields-` options require the use of the `--tab=` switch. Each option is sufficiently self-explanatory. If you want to terminate or enclose a field of the output with a string you can do so with these functions. Also, things like `\n` for `newline` and `\t` for `tab` are supported, so you can separate fields or lines by those characters as well. The keyword `OPTIONALLY` used with `ENCLOSED` causes only `CHAR` and `VARCHAR` column types to be enclosed in the specified manner. Examples of various `mysqldump` commands that use these switches are shown in Figures 10-33 through 10-36.

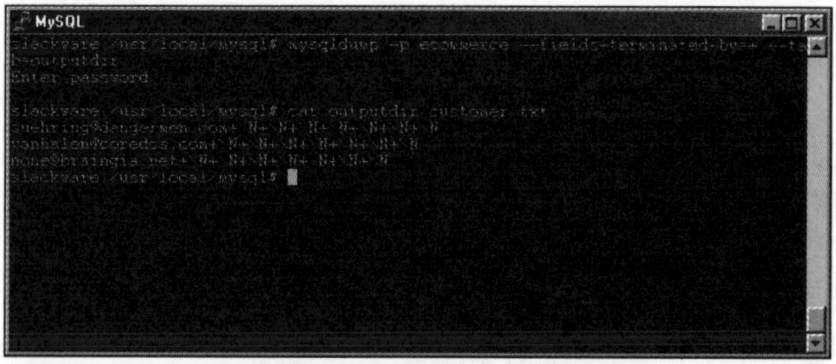

Figure 10-33: Performing the command: mysqldump -p ecommerce --fields-terminated-by=+ --tab=outputdir to produce output with fields terminated by a plus sign (+)

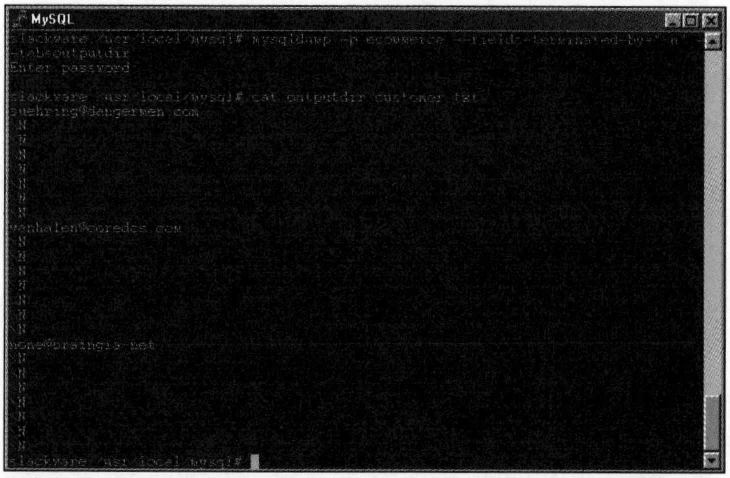

Figure 10-34: Running the command mysqldump -p ecommerce --fields-terminated-by="\n" --tab=outputdir to separate all fields by a newline (\n)

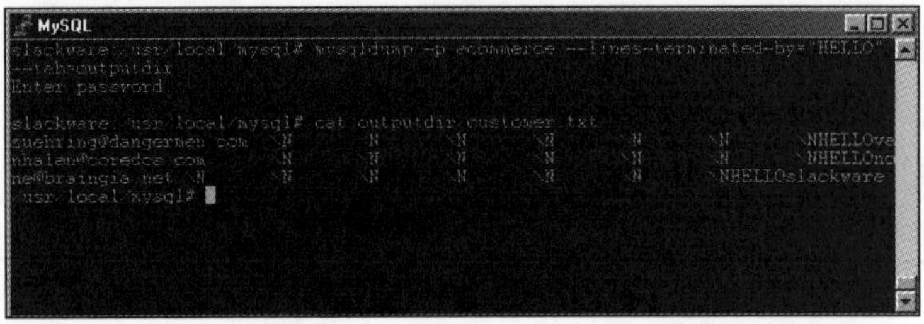

Figure 10-35: The mysqldump -p ecommerce --lines-terminated-by="HELLO" --tab=outputdir command is run to terminate lines by the word HELLO.

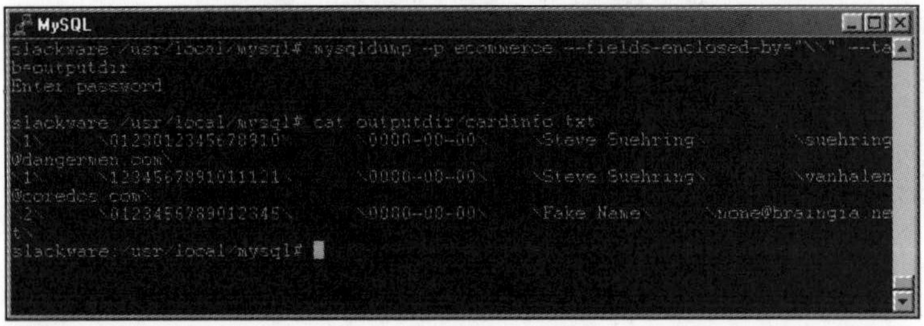

Figure 10-36: The mysqldump -p ecommerce --fields-enclosed-by="\\" --tab=outputdir command to produce output with a backslash around the fields. Note the use of two slashes in the actual command.

The all-databases function

There are two macro-level functions to dump all databases with `mysqldump`. With such functions it is possible to make a backup copy of an entire database server—though MySQL AB recommends that you use the `mysqlhotcopy` utility for this purpose.

Cross-Reference The `mysqlhotcopy` utility for making backups is covered in Chapter 14.

The first option, `--all-databases` or `-A`, dumps all databases, including database structure and data. The `--all-databases` option also creates the actual databases as well.

In Figure 10-37 the `--all-databases` macro serves to dump all databases contained on my example server. The command to run is as follows:

```
mysqldump -A -p
```

Figure 10-37: Using the -A or --all-databases macro to dump the contents of all databases and data on the server.

As you can see by Figure 10-37, all output was sent to the screen. Oops! If there were any large tables on the server, the output could have taken quite some time. Using `mysqldump` avoids tying up the screen by redirecting the output to a file. As stated previously, in Linux you use the greater-than sign (>) to accomplish this redirection. For example, to rerun the `--all-databases` macro from the example in Figure 10-37, the command would be

```
mysqldump -A -p > outfile.txt
```

Performing that command produces a file that could be imported onto another server or servers to create a snapshot of the database server at that point in time. The file could also be used as a backup as well. Figure 10-38 shows another run of the command, followed by a look at the resulting data.

The databases function

The second macro-level function with `mysqldump` is the `--databases` or `-B` function. This option takes databases as arguments, producing the same type of output as the `--all-databases` macro. Specifically, the `--databases` function includes all DDL to create the database(s) and table(s) as well as the `USE` statements to connect to those new databases. The difference between the `--databases` and the `--all-databases` macros is that you can use the `--databases` option to specify only the databases you'd like to use; the `--all-databases` option includes all databases.

Figure 10-38: Taking the mysqldump command and redirecting the output to a file

The `--databases` function expects at least one database name to follow as an argument. If you want to specify more than one database, separate the database names single spaces. In Figure 10-39 the `--databases` function serves to produce a dump of the MySQL grants database and the ecommerce database example. Normally I would redirect the output to a file (as shown in Figure 10-38); the command that produces these results is as follows:

```
mysqldump -p --databases mysql ecommerce
```

Figure 10-39: Using the --databases function to produce a dump of two databases

Another switch, the `--tables` switch, is used with the `--databases` function to specify the tables in the database to include in the output.

Suppressing creation of databases

With the two macro level functions defined previously, the `--all`-databases switch and the `--databases` switch, you can prevent `mysqldump` from issuing the statement to create the database or databases. The switch for this action is `-n` or `--no-create-db`.

For example, if you are migrating from one server to another and already have the databases created there is no reason to include `CREATE DATABASE` statements in the results from `mysqldump`. Using the `-n` switch, no `CREATE DATABASE` statements will be included.

SELECT INTO OUTFILE

Another method for extracting or exporting data from MySQL is with the `SELECT ... INTO OUTFILE` statement. This statement is usually run from inside the MySQL CLI and can produce output much the same as `mysqldump`.

The `SELECT INTO OUTFILE` statement is really a `SELECT` statement at heart, with the `INTO OUTFILE` modifier thrown onto the end to send the output of the query into a file. Therefore, modifiers such as grouping and ordering as well as the `WHERE` clause are available for use with the `INTO OUTFILE` statement.

Cross-Reference

Chapter 9 and Appendix B provide more information on the `SELECT` statement. Chapter 9 shows examples of the SELECT statement in action while Appendix B provides the syntax of the SELECT statement in MySQL.

The output file when using the `INTO OUTFILE` modifier is located in the database's directory on the server. For example, if your "*datadir*" for MySQL is `/usr/local/var` underneath which appear the directories for the various databases, the `OUTFILE` will appear inside the actual database's directory unless specified otherwise.

As with the `mysqldump --tab` utility, the `SELECT INTO OUTFILE` statement produces the data in a tab-delimited format. This makes it easy to import into a program such as Microsoft Access.

Tip

Unlike the `mysqldump` utility, the `SELECT INTO OUTFILE` statement does not support the selection of all tables from multiple databases. If you want to export the data to another MySQL server, `mysqldump` is the better choice.

Much the same as `mysqldump`, `SELECT INTO OUTFILE` supports a number of options that control how the data is exported. These options include `FIELDS TERMINATED BY`, `LINES TERMINATED BY`, `FIELDS ENCLOSED BY`, and `FIELDS ESCAPED BY`. These options work the same as with `mysqldump`.

The file specified in the `SELECT ... INTO OUTFILE` statement cannot already exist. If the file exists, the statement will fail.

Most of the battle with the `SELECT ... INTO OUTFILE` statement is getting the `SELECT` statement correct. Syntax examples for the `SELECT ... INTO OUTFILE` statement follow, as shown in Figures 10-40 and 10-41.

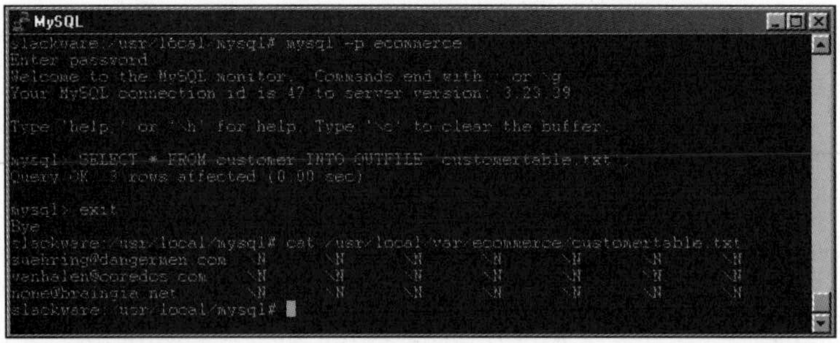

Figure 10-40: An example of a basic SELECT statement coupled with the INTO OUTFILE modifier and then a look at the results in the file

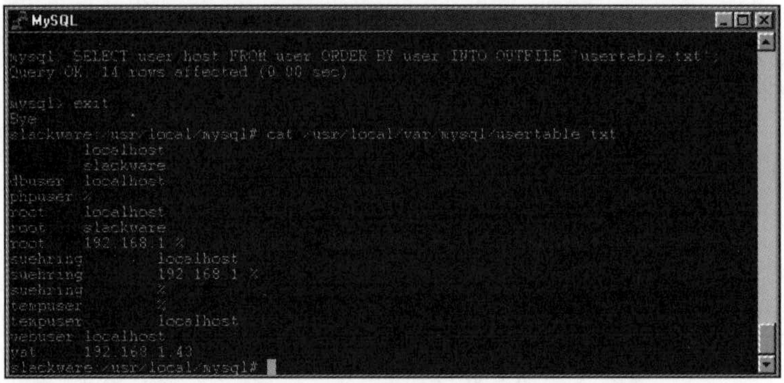

Figure 10-41: Another SELECT statement using an ORDER BY coupled with the INTO OUTFILE modifier and then a look at the results in the file

The output from the statement in Figure 10-40 (and many others exported through MySQL) can be imported into other programs such as Microsoft Access. Most programs can recognize the Tab character as a delimiter. An example of importing the output from Figure 10-41 is shown in Figure 10-42.

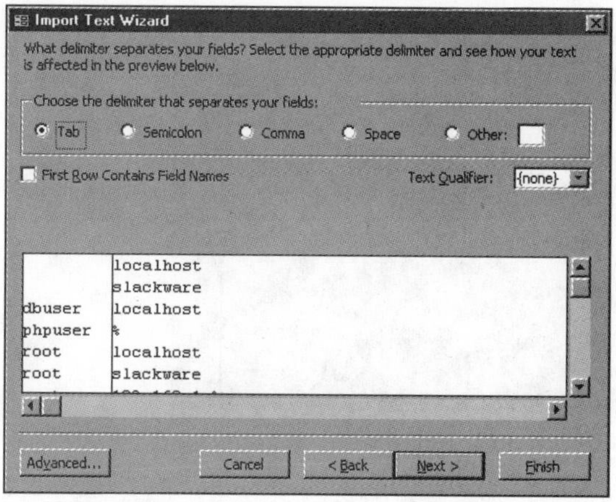

Figure 10-42: Importing the data into Microsoft Access, produced from a SELECT INTO OUTFILE statement

Importing Data

Showing an example of the import process at the end of the preceding section leads directly into this section, Importing Data Into MySQL Databases. This section examines three methods for importing data into MySQL: From the CLI, with the `LOAD DATA INFILE` statement, and with the `mysqlimport` utility.

CLI

The MySQL CLI includes the ability to import data. In reality, the CLI allows any SQL statements in a file to be read in via the command line. The syntax for this feature is as follows:

```
mysql [OPTIONS] database < filename
```

The options would include things like the user, host, and password for the MySQL CLI to authenticate just as with any other use of the CLI. The file is expected to contain valid SQL statements, many times `INSERT` or `UPDATE` statements produced with `mysqldump`.

For example, Figure 10-43 shows the contents of a file to import into the `ecommerce` database. The contents of the file were produced with `mysqldump`. Figure 10-43 also shows the command that will insert these into the database. It really is that simple.

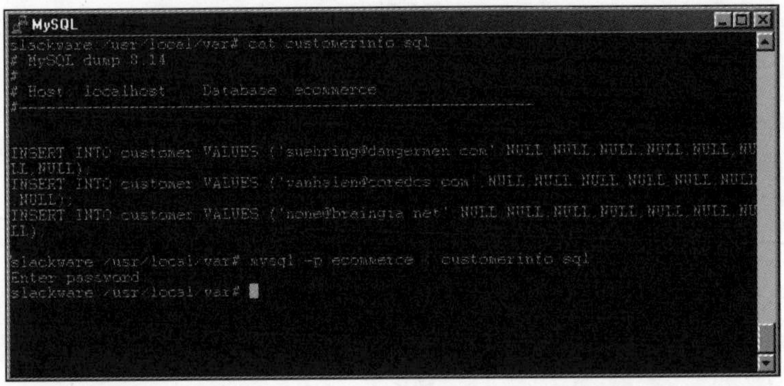

Figure 10-43: Importing the contents of a file into a database through the MySQL CLI

LOAD DATA INFILE

The complement to the `SELECT ... INTO OUTFILE` statement is the `LOAD DATA INFILE` statement. This statement is normally run from the MySQL CLI to import data into a table. The syntax for this statement is as follows:

```
LOAD DATA [LOW_PRIORITY | CONCURRENT] [LOCAL] INFILE
'filename.txt'
    [REPLACE | IGNORE]
    INTO TABLE <tablename>
    [FIELDS
        [TERMINATED BY '\t']
        [[OPTIONALLY] ENCLOSED BY '']
        [ESCAPED BY '\\' ]
    ]
    [LINES TERMINATED BY '\n']
    [IGNORE <N> LINES]
    [(<columnname>,...)]
```

The `LOW_PRIORITY` keyword causes the `LOAD DATA` statement to wait until no other clients are reading from the table. The `CONCURRENT` keyword allows other clients to read from the table while the `LOAD DATA` statement is executing.

Files are normally assumed to be on the server machine. With the `LOCAL` keyword, however, the file is read from the client host that executes the command. The filename specified must be an absolute path, whether in the data directory of MySQL or in the actual database's directory on the server.

Caution Using the `LOCAL` keyword blocks you from stopping the import process once begins.

The `LOAD DATA INFILE` statement enables you to determine the action when a collision occurs for records being imported to a unique column. The statement can either replace the existing record with the new one or ignore the new record entirely. The keywords to specify this behavior are `REPLACE` and `IGNORE`, respectively.

> **Cross-Reference**
> **Other `LOAD DATA INFILE` options (such as the `FIELDS TERMINATED BY`, and `LINES TERMINATED BY`) work the same as in the `SELECT ... INTO OUTFILE` statement and `mysqldump`. This chapter includes descriptions and syntax examples for these options.**

One additional behavior not found in the `SELECT ... INTO OUTFILE` statement or `mysqldump` utility is `IGNORE <N> LINES`. This modifier appears in the `LINES TERMINATED BY` clause. Using the `IGNORE <N> LINES` modifier you can tell the `LOAD DATA INFILE` statement to ignore or skip over a certain number of lines at the beginning of the file to be imported. For example, if you have the column names as the first line of the file you can have the `LOAD DATA INFILE` statement ignore that first line with the addition of `IGNORE 1 LINES` to the `LOAD DATA INFILE STATEMENT`.

You can also specify only certain columns to import into. The column or column list comes at the end of the statement; if specifying more than one column, separate them with a comma. For example, to import one of the files from a previous example and only import the `email_address` column, the following statement is issued:

```
LOAD DATA INFILE 'ecommercecustomer.txt' INTO TABLE customer (email_address);
```

The results from the preceding statement are shown in Figure 10-44.

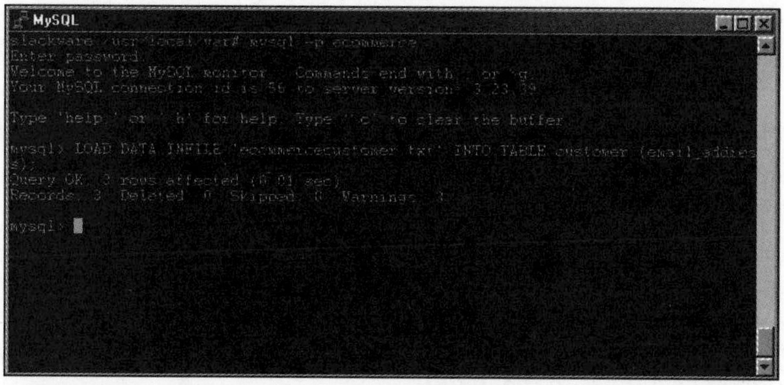

Figure 10-44: An example of using the LOAD DATA INFILE statement to import only one column

mysqlimport

The mysqlimport utility is a command-line program for importing data into a MySQL database. The mysqlimport utility is similar in usage to the LOAD DATA INFILE statement. The basic syntax for the mysqlimport utility is as follows:

```
mysqlimport [OPTIONS] database textfile
```

Tip

As with most MySQL programs, you can obtain a syntax listing for mysqlimport by typing the command with no switches or arguments, or by using the -? or --help switch.

Much like the MySQL CLI, mysqlimport uses the same switches for specifying the user, host, port, password, and so on.

Cross-Reference

Chapter 8 covers the basic switches.

As mysqlimport is really a command-line version of LOAD DATA INFILE, the functionality is nearly the same. One exception not located in another statement or command is the -d or --delete switch. Using --delete, mysqlimport will delete the contents of the table prior to importing.

With LOAD DATA INFILE, if you specify a column or columns to import into you do so by adding them onto the end of the statement. With mysqlimport, this is added with the -c or --columns= switch. The REPLACE and IGNORE functionality is called with the -r or --replace and -I -r --ignore, respectively.

Much like the LOAD DATA INFILE, SELECT ... INTO OUTFILE, and mysqldump utilities the use of switches for formatting is supported by mysqlimport. These are as follows:

```
--fields-terminated-by=
--fields-enclosed-by=
--fields-optionally-enclosed-by=
--fields-escaped-by=
--lines-terminated-by=
```

The --local or -L switch tells mysqlimport to look on the local client for the file to import. This is as opposed to the normal behavior where MySQL will search for the file on the server running mysqld. Notice that the switch is an uppercase *L*. The lowercase L (-l) switch is a synonym for the --lock-tables function that locks all tables before proceeding with the import.

Summary

✦ MySQL includes six table types. Three are non-transactional, two are transactional, and one resides only in volatile memory.

✦ The main table type in MySQL is `MyISAM`. `MyISAM` descends from the `ISAM` table type that includes fewer features. The `MERGE` table type is a collection of MySQL tables for quicker operation.

✦ The two transactional table types in MySQL are `BerkeleyDB` and `InnoDB`. These table types use more resources than regular non-transactional tables but are safer in the event of error.

✦ The `HEAP` table type is a temporary table that resides only in volatile memory.

✦ The `mysqladmin` command is a powerful command for management and administration of a MySQL server.

✦ With `mysqladmin` you can stop the server, troubleshoot performance problems, and create or delete databases.

✦ There are two main methods for exporting data from MySQL, `mysqldump` and the `SELECT ... INTO OUTFILE` statement.

✦ The `mysqldump` utility includes the ability to export both DDL and DML. Therefore, with `mysqldump` you can create a complete snapshot of a server including databases, tables, and the actual data.

✦ The `SELECT ... INTO OUTFILE` statement is normally run from the MySQL CLI. With `SELECT ... INTO OUTFILE` you have the power of a regular `SELECT` statement while exporting data with many powerful options.

✦ There are three main methods for importing data into MySQL. Data can be imported through the MySQL CLI, with the `LOAD DATA INFILE` statement, or with `mysqlimport`.

✦ The MySQL CLI enables you to execute SQL statements by reading the contents of a file from the command line.

✦ With the `LOAD DATA INFILE` statement you can import through the CLI with a number of options such as how to handle duplicate values.

✦ The `mysqlimport` utility is a command-line version of `LOAD DATA INFILE` and includes the same options. The `mysqlimport` utility also includes an option to delete the data from the table prior to import.

✦ ✦ ✦

Administration

PART III

In This Part

CHAPTER 11

Server Configurations

✦ ✦ ✦ ✦

In This Chapter

Classifying MySQL server variables

Benchmarking and testing MySQL

Examining sample configuration files

Developing your own configuration file

Running more than one MySQL Server on the same machine

✦ ✦ ✦ ✦

As evidenced nearly everywhere in this book, MySQL is highly customizable. From customizations during the installation process detailed in Chapters 3, 4, and 5 to configurations for the CLI that I wrote about in Chapter 8, MySQL is the most customizable major database server available. Of course you would expect so since you can download the source code for MySQL and write it to your exact specifications.

In this chapter I'm going to examine server configurations and customizations through the use of the my.cnf or my.ini configuration files. These configurations will mainly work with server variables and switches for the mysqld server process. I'll begin with a look at the variables and switches themselves and then use some samples that come with the MySQL software for small, medium, and large installations.

MySQL Server Variables

MySQL can and should be tuned to the physical server hardware that it is running on and for the main application or applications that it will be serving. A great many variables can be changed that alter the way a server operates. When set correctly these variables can improve the performance of the server and thus the applications using the database. As you would expect, when set incorrectly these variables can degrade the performance of the server as well. In this section I'll examine the variables themselves.

Viewing current server variables

You can look at all the variables and settings for the server through the `SHOW VARIABLES` statement from in the MySQL CLI or with the mysqladmin variables command. The statement and command yield the same results, as shown in Figure 11-1. The command to reproduce the output shown in Figure 11-1 is `mysqladmin variables`; the full output follows.

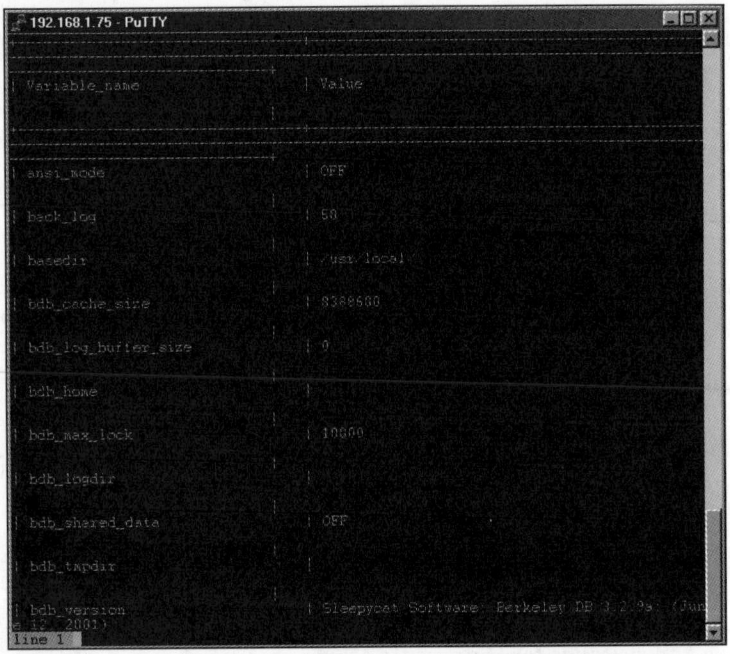

Figure 11-1: Partial output from the mysqladmin variables statement

Table 11-1 shows some MySQL server variables command, along with brief descriptions of their purposes. The additional variables presented in the output of the `mysqladmin` variables do not affect server performance. Most of those variables and settings are discussed in other chapters throughout the book.

Table 11-1
MySQL server variables

Variable	*What it does*
`bdb_cache_size`	Sets size of buffer for caching rows and indexes of BDB tables.
`bdb_log_buffer_size`	Sets size of buffer for the BDB logs.
`bdb_max_lock`	Sets maximum number of locks you can have on a BDB table.
`binlog_cache_size`	Sets size of cache for statements to be put into the binary log.

Variable	*What it does*
connect_timeout	Determines the length of time mysqld will wait for a connection.
delay_key_write	Determines when the key can be flushed (tables with this option active cannot have the key flushed until the table is closed).
delayed_insert_limit	Sets number of rows to be inserted before the delay is released.
delayed_insert_timeout	Sets amount of time to wait for INSERT DELAYED statements.
delayed_queue_size	Sets size of the queue for INSERT DELAYED statements in rows.
flush_time	Sets time (in seconds) to free up resources by closing all tables.
have_bdb	Enabled if BerkeleyDB (BDB) tables are available.
have_gemini	Enabled if Gemini tables are available.
have_innodb	Enabled if InnoDB tables are available.
have_isam	Indicates whether ISAM tables are available.
have_raid	Indicates whether RAID will be used.
have_ssl	Indicates whether SSL is available.
interactive_timeout	Sets amount of time mysqld waits for activity on interactive clients.
join_buffer_size	Sets size of buffer used for full JOIN operations.
key_buffer_size	Sets size of buffer used for indexes shared among threads.
large_files_support	Indicates whether this version of mysqld supports large files.
log	Indicates whether the logging of all queries is enabled.
log_update	Indicates whether the logging of updates is enabled.
log_bin	Indicates whether a binary log file format is in use.
log_slave_updates	Indicates whether updates from the slave should be logged.
long_query_time	Sets number of seconds before the Slow Queries counter is enabled.
max_allowed_packet	Sets maximum size of any one packet.

Continued

Table 11-1 (continued)

Variable	*What it does*
max_binlog_cache_size	Sets maximum size of the cache for the binary log.
max_binlog_size	Sets maximum size of the binary log.
max_connections	Sets maximum number of simultaneous connections.
max_connect_errors	Sets maximum number of errors from a given host.
max_delayed_threads	Sets maximum number of threads to start for INSERT DELAYED statements.
max_heap_table_size	Sets maximum size for a HEAP table.
max_join_size	Sets maximum size for joins.
max_sort_length	Sets number of bytes to use for sorting BLOB and TEXT columns.
max_user_connections	Sets maximum number of simultaneous user connections.
max_tmp_tables	Sets maximum number of temporary tables to create.
max_write_lock_count	Sets number of write locks that occur before a read lock is enabled.
myisam_max_extra_sort_file_size	Sets maximum size before the key cache is used.
myisam_max_sort_file_size	Sets maximum size of the temporary file used to create an index with myisam table.
myisam_sort_buffer_size	Sets size of buffer for myisam index functions.
net_buffer_length	Sets size of communications buffer.
net_read_timeout	Specifies time to wait between reads before closing a thread.
net_retry_count	Specifies number of times to retry a connection before closing.
net_write_timeout	Specifies time to wait between writes before closing a thread.
open_files_limit	Specifies number of file descriptors to open.
query_buffer_size	Sets initial size of the query buffer.
record_buffer	Specifies buffer to use for threads that do sequential scans.
skip_locking	Indicates whether internal or external locking is in use.

Variable	What it does
slow_launch_time	Increments a counter if a thread takes longer than this interval to launch.
sort_buffer	Allocates buffer for functions that sort.
table_cache	Sets maximum number of open tables across all threads.
thread_cache_size	Sets number of threads to keep in cache for reuse.
thread_stack	Sets size of stack for an individual thread.
tmp_table_size	Sets maximum size for a temp table before being converted to myisam.
wait_timeout	Sets maximum time to wait for a connection until it is timed out.

The server I've been using in many of the examples in this book is a convenient example of setting variables. It's a Pentium 200MMX with 96MB RAM, running Slackware Linux. On this server, I had to change a couple of settings to avoid using up all the memory. The defaults for my server are as follows:

```
*************************** 1. row
Variable_name: ansi_mode
        Value: OFF
*************************** 2. row
Variable_name: back_log
        Value: 50
*************************** 3. row
Variable_name: basedir
        Value: /usr/local/
*************************** 4. row
Variable_name: bdb_cache_size
        Value: 8388600
*************************** 5. row
Variable_name: bdb_log_buffer_size
        Value: 0
*************************** 6. row
Variable_name: bdb_home
        Value:
*************************** 7. row
Variable_name: bdb_max_lock
        Value: 10000
*************************** 8. row
Variable_name: bdb_logdir
        Value:
*************************** 9. row
Variable_name: bdb_shared_data
        Value: OFF
```

```
*************************** 10. row
Variable_name: bdb_tmpdir
        Value:
*************************** 11. row
Variable_name: bdb_version
        Value: Sleepycat Software: Berkeley DB 3.2.9a: (June
12, 2001)
*************************** 12. row
Variable_name: binlog_cache_size
        Value: 32768
*************************** 13. row
Variable_name: character_set
        Value: latin1
*************************** 14. row
Variable_name: character_sets
        Value: latin1 dec8 dos german1 hp8 koi8_ru latin2 swe7
usa7 cp1251 danish hebrew win1251 estonia hungarian koi8_ukr
win1251ukr greek win1250 croat cp1257 latin5
*************************** 15. row
Variable_name: concurrent_insert
        Value: ON
*************************** 16. row
Variable_name: connect_timeout
        Value: 5
*************************** 17. row
Variable_name: datadir
        Value: /usr/local/var/
*************************** 18. row
Variable_name: delay_key_write
        Value: ON
*************************** 19. row
Variable_name: delayed_insert_limit
        Value: 100
*************************** 20. row
Variable_name: delayed_insert_timeout
        Value: 300
*************************** 21. row
Variable_name: delayed_queue_size
        Value: 1000
*************************** 22. row
Variable_name: flush
        Value: OFF
*************************** 23. row
Variable_name: flush_time
        Value: 0
*************************** 24. row
Variable_name: have_bdb
        Value: DISABLED
*************************** 25. row
Variable_name: have_gemini
        Value: NO
```

```
*************************** 26. row
Variable_name: have_innodb
        Value: DISABLED
*************************** 27. row
Variable_name: have_isam
        Value: YES
*************************** 28. row
Variable_name: have_raid
        Value: NO
*************************** 29. row
Variable_name: have_ssl
        Value: NO
*************************** 30. row
Variable_name: init_file
        Value:
*************************** 31. row
Variable_name: innodb_data_file_path
        Value:
*************************** 32. row
Variable_name: innodb_data_home_dir
        Value:
*************************** 33. row
Variable_name: innodb_flush_log_at_trx_commit
        Value: OFF
*************************** 34. row
Variable_name: innodb_log_arch_dir
        Value:
*************************** 35. row
Variable_name: innodb_log_archive
        Value: OFF
*************************** 36. row
Variable_name: innodb_log_group_home_dir
        Value:
*************************** 37. row
Variable_name: innodb_flush_method
        Value:
*************************** 38. row
Variable_name: interactive_timeout
        Value: 28800
*************************** 39. row
Variable_name: join_buffer_size
        Value: 131072
*************************** 40. row
Variable_name: key_buffer_size
        Value: 12288
*************************** 41. row
Variable_name: language
        Value: /usr/local/share/mysql/english/
*************************** 42. row
Variable_name: large_files_support
        Value: ON
```

```
*************************** 43. row
Variable_name: locked_in_memory
        Value: OFF
*************************** 44. row
Variable_name: log
        Value: OFF
*************************** 45. row
Variable_name: log_update
        Value: OFF
*************************** 46. row
Variable_name: log_bin
        Value: OFF
*************************** 47. row
Variable_name: log_slave_updates
        Value: OFF
*************************** 48. row
Variable_name: long_query_time
        Value: 10
*************************** 49. row
Variable_name: low_priority_updates
        Value: OFF
*************************** 50. row
Variable_name: lower_case_table_names
        Value: 0
*************************** 51. row
Variable_name: max_allowed_packet
        Value: 1047552
*************************** 52. row
Variable_name: max_binlog_cache_size
        Value: 4294967295
*************************** 53. row
Variable_name: max_binlog_size
        Value: 1073741824
*************************** 54. row
Variable_name: max_connections
        Value: 100
*************************** 55. row
Variable_name: max_connect_errors
        Value: 10
*************************** 56. row
Variable_name: max_delayed_threads
        Value: 20
*************************** 57. row
Variable_name: max_heap_table_size
        Value: 8387584
*************************** 58. row
Variable_name: max_join_size
        Value: 4294967295
*************************** 59. row
Variable_name: max_sort_length
        Value: 1024
```

```
*************************** 60. row
Variable_name: max_user_connections
        Value: 0
*************************** 61. row
Variable_name: max_tmp_tables
        Value: 32
*************************** 62. row
Variable_name: max_write_lock_count
        Value: 4294967295
*************************** 63. row
Variable_name: myisam_recover_options
        Value: BACKUP,FORCE
*************************** 64. row
Variable_name: myisam_max_extra_sort_file_size
        Value: 256
*************************** 65. row
Variable_name: myisam_max_sort_file_size
        Value: 2047
*************************** 66. row
Variable_name: myisam_sort_buffer_size
        Value: 8388608
*************************** 67. row
Variable_name: net_buffer_length
        Value: 1024
*************************** 68. row
Variable_name: net_read_timeout
        Value: 30
*************************** 69. row
Variable_name: net_retry_count
        Value: 10
*************************** 70. row
Variable_name: net_write_timeout
        Value: 60
*************************** 71. row
Variable_name: open_files_limit
        Value: 0
*************************** 72. row
Variable_name: pid_file
        Value: /usr/local/var/slackware.pid
*************************** 73. row
Variable_name: port
        Value: 3306
*************************** 74. row
Variable_name: protocol_version
        Value: 10
*************************** 75. row
Variable_name: record_buffer
        Value: 131072
*************************** 76. row
Variable_name: query_buffer_size
        Value: 0
```

```
*************************** 77. row
Variable_name: safe_show_database
        Value: OFF
*************************** 78. row
Variable_name: server_id
        Value: 1
*************************** 79. row
Variable_name: skip_locking
        Value: ON
*************************** 80. row
Variable_name: skip_networking
        Value: OFF
*************************** 81. row
Variable_name: skip_show_database
        Value: OFF
*************************** 82. row
Variable_name: slow_launch_time
        Value: 2
*************************** 83. row
Variable_name: socket
        Value: /tmp/mysql.sock
*************************** 84. row
Variable_name: sort_buffer
        Value: 65528
*************************** 85. row
Variable_name: table_cache
        Value: 4
*************************** 86. row
Variable_name: table_type
        Value: MYISAM
*************************** 87. row
Variable_name: thread_cache_size
        Value: 0
*************************** 88. row
Variable_name: thread_stack
        Value: 65536
*************************** 89. row
Variable_name: transaction_isolation
        Value: READ-COMMITTED
*************************** 90. row
Variable_name: timezone
        Value: CST
*************************** 91. row
Variable_name: tmp_table_size
        Value: 33554432
*************************** 92. row
Variable_name: tmpdir
        Value: /tmp/
*************************** 93. row
Variable_name: version
        Value: 3.23.39
*************************** 94. row
Variable_name: wait_timeout
        Value: 28800
```

Although the SHOW VARIABLES output given here does contain even more variables, these are beyond the scope of this chapter.

So many variables, so little time

As you can see from Table 11-1 and the variable printout, I speak the truth about the large number of server variables and settings available for an administrator to work with. When you add capabilities such as replication, even more variables and settings must be considered.

At this point you may be asking, "Which variables and settings do I *really* have to change and which ones can be left at the defaults?" I certainly can't preach that all variables must be set for each server; in my view, that's neither true nor practical. Responding to testing and feedback from users of MySQL, MySQL AB has set defaults for most variables that will work well.

Another reason not to set all the variables is that the MySQL server itself is quite efficient for most uses of the database—anywhere from just a few records to a few hundred thousand or more. I've worked with large databases (*millions* of rows) on what I would consider normal hardware—Pentium-class computers with 128MB RAM—and noticed no performance problems that would make me want to change too many server variables.

However, working with specific applications or databases may require that you set or change variables to improve performance of the MySQL server. Some reasons you may have to set variables include the following:

- A specific application performs operations on the database slow or cause the server to lag.
- The use of lower-end hardware or small amounts of resources.
- Using MySQL on a server that runs many other applications and services.
- Inefficient or poorly written applications that cause problems for the server or database.
- A desire to improve your server's performance.

Coming back to the original question in this section, how do you know which variables to set if you want optimal performance from MySQL? Luckily, MySQL AB has done some of the homework for many implementations; two features of its installation program can help you optimize MySQL:

- **A suite of applications helps you benchmark your server's performance.** MySQL also includes another set of tests known as the *Crash-me* tests. Together with the MySQL Benchmark applications, the Crash-me tests help you give your server a vigorous test. These applications and scripts help determine and test the limits of your server by simulating real-world scenarios. The benchmarking applications are a series of tests contained in the sql-bench directory within your MySQL installation. The Crash-me tests are contained within one program aptly titled `crash-me`, and also in the sql-bench directory. In the next section I'll look at some of the benchmarking applications included with MySQL.

Tip

Even with the tests and benchmarking, you still need a way to simulate a real-world load on a database server. A program called Super-smack does that job; you can use it to try out various values as you set parameters until you get the ones that work best for your configuration. Super-smack is available for free from MySQL AB. To get Super-smack, go to the Contributed Software section of the MySQL Web site `http://www.mysql.com/downloads/contrib.html`.

✦ **Sample configuration files let you try out different-size implementations.** Look for these sample configs in the `support-files` directory of your MySQL installation. Four sample configuration files are included:

- `my-small.cnf`
- `my-medium.cnf`
- `my-large.cnf`
- `my-hugr.cnf`

The sample configuration files are covered in detail later in this chapter.

MySQL Benchmarking and Testing

Included with the MySQL software are applications and scripts for testing the limits and variables of the MySQL server. These tests can help to improve performance by showing obvious bottlenecks on the actual hardware with close to real-world scenarios. Using specific tests you can simulate how your server will be used and see what improvements must be made. I've had times where running the tests saved me from implementing a server on hardware that couldn't stand up to the load for the application to be run.

Requirements for the applications

The Benchmark and Crash-me applications use a number of different types of statements and functions. The applications are included with Binary installations of MySQL and MySQL-Max as well as with the MySQL source code. To use the applications from an RPM-based installation, make sure you install the `mysql-bench` RPM (in addition to the other MySQL RPMs). Additional requirements for the benchmarking and Crash-me applications are as follows:

✦ Perl

✦ Perl-DBI

✦ Msql-Mysql-modules

All the latest copies of the Perl-DBI and the Msql-Mysql-modules can be found on CPAN, `http://www.cpan.org`.

Perl is normally included with Linux, though you may not have installed it when you installed the operating system. Follow the instructions included with the Perl-DBI for installation of the software. The Msql-Mysql-modules ask some relevant questions during the installation, see Figure 11-2.

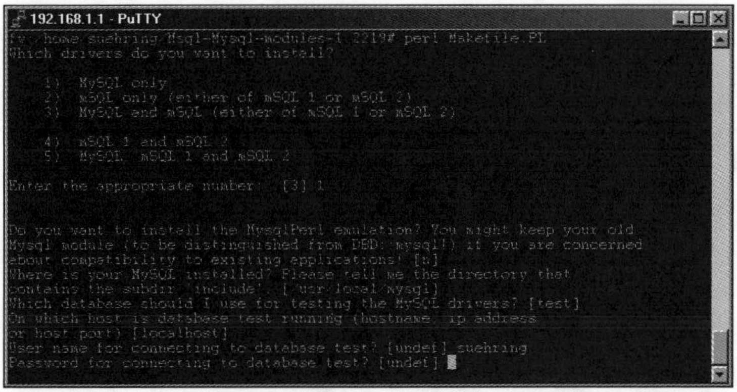

Figure 11-2: Running Makefile.PL for the Msql-Mysql-modules poses some questions about how you would like to configure the modules.

How you answer the questions for installation largely depends on how you intend to use the modules, and whether you have a previous version installed. If you intend to use `mSQL` through a Perl application, you may want to consider installing the module for that in addition to the MySQL module. In Figure 11-2, I simply select MySQL because I don't plan to use `mSQL`, via Perl or otherwise, for the examples.

Running the tests

Once you have the prerequisites installed you can run the Benchmark applications and Crash-me tests. The applications are located in the `sql-bench` directory in your MySQL server directory. The Benchmarking suite includes various tests for different types of applications to look at different aspects of server performance — in particular, how it handles some crucial aspects of database operation:

- ✦ Big tables
- ✦ Alteration of tables
- ✦ Connections
- ✦ Creation of tables

✦ Inserts

✦ Selects

✦ Query optimization and other aspects of the server

The final test in the suite is called the Wisconsin test. (And no, this isn't something I'm just making up because I'm from the state of Wisconsin.) The Wisconsin test is a comprehensive set of tests to look at query optimization and performance of other aspects of the server.

The `sql-bench` directory contains a number of scripts, as shown in Figure 11-3.

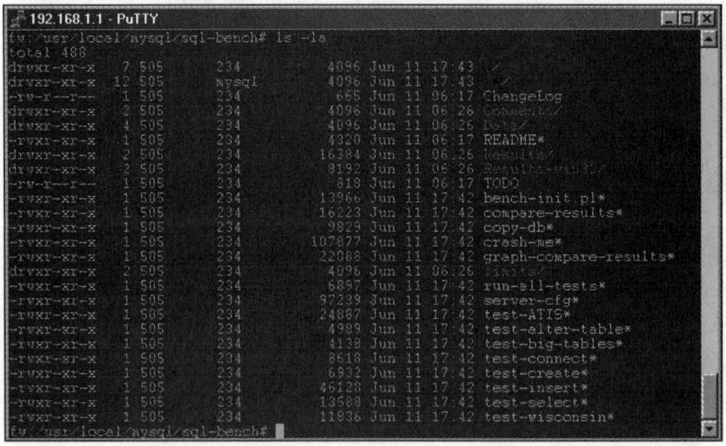

Figure 11-3: A directory listing for the sql-bench directory in MySQL

You can run the tests individually or all at once. Regardless of the whether you run them one at a time or all at once, you must specify at least a password to enable the programs to run. Other command-line switches are available to specify user and host. For example, to run the `test-select` application, the following command line would be used:

```
./test-select --password=password
```

As you can see, you have to specify the actual password on the command line for the application to run. If you specify the user, do so with the `--user=`*`username`* syntax. To specify the host, use `--host=`*`host`* syntax.

The script that calls all the other testing applications (and runs them all in sequence) is called `run-all-tests`. This script also requires that the password be given as an argument. Running this script on a slower server — say, a Pentium 200MMX with 96MB RAM — can increase the server load (not to mention that the tests themselves take hours). Therefore I would not recommend running these tests in a production environment.

Caution Running the testing suite can cause performance problems on the MySQL server. I recommend against running the testing suite during peak usage or in a production environment.

Currently the tests are not multithreaded; they open one connection at a time to the MySQL server. This does limit the ability of the tests to truly simulate a real-world environment where multiple users or threads frequently use the database simultaneously. In future versions, MySQL AB will add to the testing suite to run multiple threads.

If the tests are taking an incredibly long time and you think something may have gone wrong, you can check the progress of the tests with a couple commands on the MySQL server. Running the `SHOW PROCESSLIST` statement or `mysqladmin processlist` command will a single thread running for the tests, as shown in Figure 11-4. Note the different values in the `'Info'` field as the testing suite runs `INSERT` statements.

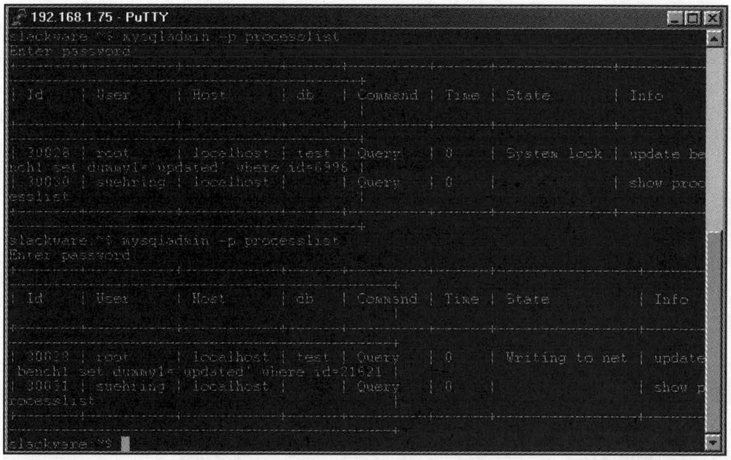
192.168.1.75 - PuTTY
slackware:~$ mysqladmin -p processlist
Enter password:
| Id | User | Host | db | Command | Time | State | Info
| 30028 | root | localhost | test | Query | 0 | System lock | update bench1 set dummy1='updated' where id=6996 |
| 30030 | suehring | localhost | | Query | 0 | | show processlist
slackware:~$ mysqladmin -p processlist
Enter password:
| Id | User | Host | db | Command | Time | State | Info
| 30028 | root | localhost | test | Query | 0 | Writing to net | update bench1 set dummy1='updated' where id=21621 |
| 30031 | suehring | localhost | | Query | 0 | | show processlist
slackware:~$

Figure 11-4: The mysqladmin processlist shows the progress of the testing suite, in this instance the INSERT tests.

Because the tests simulate so many different applications and implementations, if you know you're going to have an `INSERT`-heavy application, you can limit the testing to just the `INSERT` test. Then, by tweaking variables to improve `INSERT` performance and rerunning the test, you can see whether you get a noticeable performance improvement from the new settings.

Sample Configuration Files

Four sample configuration files come with MySQL. These files provide defaults based on the hardware that MySQL server will be run on. The sample configuration files can provide a good starting point for defaults. For most applications, the default settings will work just fine.

Examination of the sample configuration files

The sample configuration files can be found in the `'support-files'` directory of your MySQL installation. The four files range in recommended use from machines with less than 64MB RAM to machines with 1G to 2G RAM. For each of the files, I'm going to examine the main server portion underneath the `[mysqld]` section, and also other changes that take place in the file to affect other applications such as `Mysqldump` and so on.

The first file, for machines with less than 64MB RAM, is called `my-small.cnf`. MySQL AB recommends this configuration file for use where MySQL is not the primary application, and is only used now and then for minor database functions.

The relevant section from `my-small.cnf` is shown in Figure 11-5.

```
192.168.1.75 - PuTTY
# The MySQL server
[mysqld]
port            = 3306
socket          = /tmp/mysql.sock
skip-locking
set-variable    = key_buffer=16K
set-variable    = max_allowed_packet=1M
set-variable    = thread_stack=64K
set-variable    = table_cache=4
set-variable    = sort_buffer=64K
set-variable    = net_buffer_length=2K
server-id       = 1

# Uncomment the following if you want to log updates
#log-bin

# Uncomment the following if you are NOT using BDB tables
#skip-bdb

# Uncomment the following if you are using Innobase tables
#innodb_data_file_path = ibdata1:100M
#innodb_data_home_dir = /usr/local/var/
#innodb_log_group_home_dir = /usr/local/var/
#innodb_log_arch_dir = /usr/local/var/
#set-variable = innodb_mirrored_log_groups=1
#set-variable = innodb_log_files_in_group=3
#set-variable = innodb_log_file_size=5M
#set-variable = innodb_log_buffer_size=8M
#innodb_flush_log_at_trx_commit=1
#innodb_log_archive=0
#set-variable = innodb_buffer_pool_size=16M
#set-variable = innodb_additional_mem_pool_size=2M
#set-variable = innodb_file_io_threads=4
#set-variable = innodb_lock_wait_timeout=50
my-small.cnf line 25/78 84%
```

Figure 11-5: The [mysqld] section from the my-small.cnf example defaults file for MySQL

The second file, `my-medium.cnf`, is for machines with smaller amounts of memory (under 128MB). If MySQL is the sole application (or one of a few primary applications) running on a machine like this, then the `medium` configuration file may be for you. In addition, if you have 128MB to 256MB and MySQL will be working with other applications (such as Apache or other services), the medium configuration would be a good starting point for a configuration file.

The example section of the configuration file for `[mysqld]` is shown in Figure 11-6.

The third configuration file, `my-large.cnf`, is meant for systems that have more than 512MB RAM, though less than 1GB RAM. The server is mainly responsible for database tasks with MySQL—therefore it isn't running many other services. Of course, running a Web server for an interface would probably be acceptable. However, a production Web server for public use would be better run on a separate server.

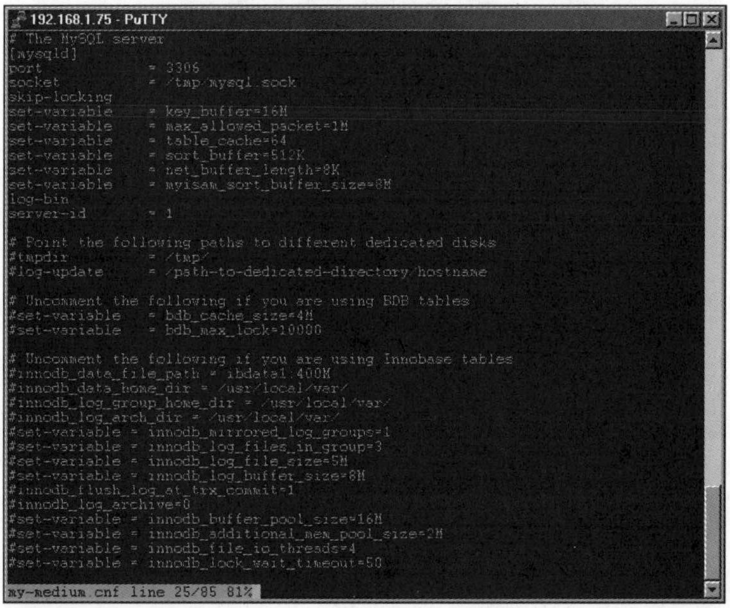

Figure 11-6: The [mysqld] section from the my-medium.cnf example defaults file for MySQL

The `[mysqld]` section for `my-large.cnf` is shown in Figure 11-7.

Finally, the example configuration file for the largest configurations is `my-huge.cnf`. This file is meant as an example file for systems with 1GB RAM or more, where MySQL is the *sole* application or service running on the server. If you intend to run any other applications or services, you should run them servers other than the MySQL server—and you can use this example file as a good starting point. If you are running a MySQL server in such an environment, you will probably have to set other variables specifically to match your application.

Figure 11-7: The [mysqld] section from the my-large.cnf example configuration file for MySQL.

The `[mysqld]` section from the example configuration file is shown in Figure 11-8.

Notice how the configuration file examples differ from each other. In the example configuration file for `Huge` database servers, the buffer sizes take advantage of the large amounts of RAM memory available for use. The configuration-file example for `Small` servers uses much less RAM for buffers and other parameters.

Developing your own configuration file

The first recommendation I have is to *use an example file that closely matches your configuration*—not only of your machine, but also of your planned application(s). For example, I use the `my-small.cnf` file for the example server that I'm using—a Pentium 200MMX with 96MB RAM.

After starting the database server, monitor the variables and performance through the use of the `mysqladmin extended-status` command. Of course, your users will tell you if the database is performing slowly.

Figure 11-8: The [mysqld] section from the my-huge.cnf example configuration file for MySQL.

When the performance of the MySQL server is degraded, it is time to analyze why it is happening. One item that can assist, though it does create performance degradation itself, is the `log` option in the configuration file. Using the `log` function, you can ensure that all queries to the server are logged (see Figure 11-9). Using this logfile, you can then determine whether queries can be optimized—or whether you have to fine-tune a server variable. To enable the `log` function, add the keyword `log` within the `[mysqld]` section of the MySQL configuration file.

Other logging options, as defined in Table 11-1, can assist in diagnosing what parameters and variables are working and which ones might not be. With some patience while tuning the server, you can use these logging options to help make MySQL's performance exceptional.

Tip Be sure to turn off logging when it's needed; it can degrade performance.

Caution Be careful not to increase too many values at once or make memory-based values too large. This can cause disk-swapping behavior as the server runs out of available RAM and has to use (slower) virtual memory.

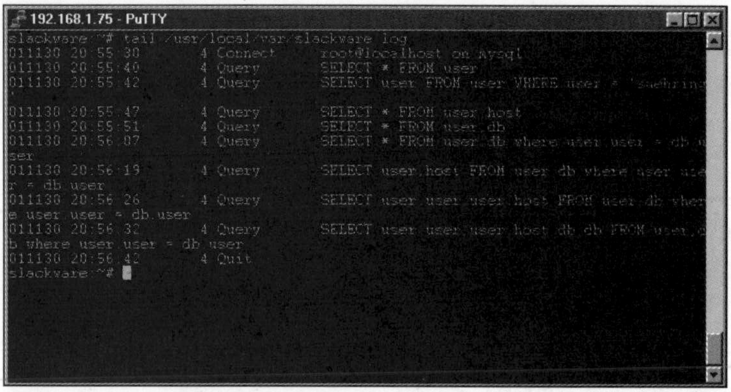

Figure 11-9: An example of the logfile for queries with the log option enabled in the configuration file

Figure 11-10, for example, shows sample output from a run of the `test-select` benchmark.

Figure 11-10: Sample output of the test-select benchmarking application running with the generic my-small.cnf configuration file

After getting the results, I take a look at the values from `mysqladmin extended-status`, as shown in Figure 11-11.

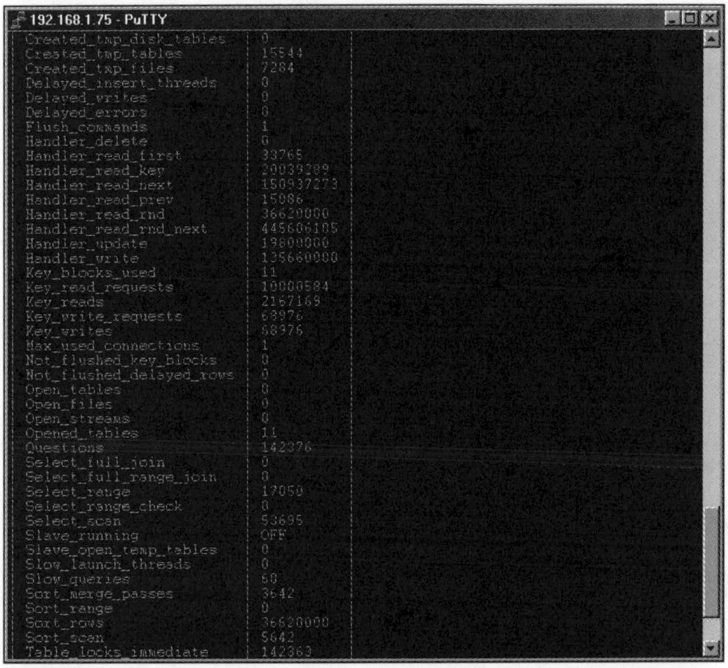

Figure 11-11: Examination of the values from the mysqladmin extended-status command after running the test-select benchmark

Notice the values for `key_read_requests` and `key_reads`. This indicates that there were a large number of requests for index use and that many of them couldn't be handled by the `key_buffer`. Therefore, I increase the `key_buffer_size` in the configuration file and re-run the tests to see whether I can get any improved results. The results of the new test are shown in Figure 11-12.

The increase in performance for the `test_select` application did not come without cost. To get the performance improvement, I increased the `key_buffer_size` value to 16M from 16K! On a server with only 96MB RAM to begin with, this might not be such a good idea—disk swapping can increase if other applications that are currently running require much memory.

Also, notice that the increase in `key_buffer_size` does not show up on the same order as the increase in performance. In effect, I increased the value from 16K to 16M. That's an increase of 1,000 times. If you compare the results from Figure 11-10 and Figure 11-12 you'll see that the times were cut by roughly 50%. Therefore increasing the `key_buffer_size` value to 16M is (to put it mildly) somewhat aggressive for this implementation.

The key_buffer_size example just given shows you how to diagnose the performance of your MySQL server. You should be able to use your knowledge of the commands to work with the server and improve performance where necessary.

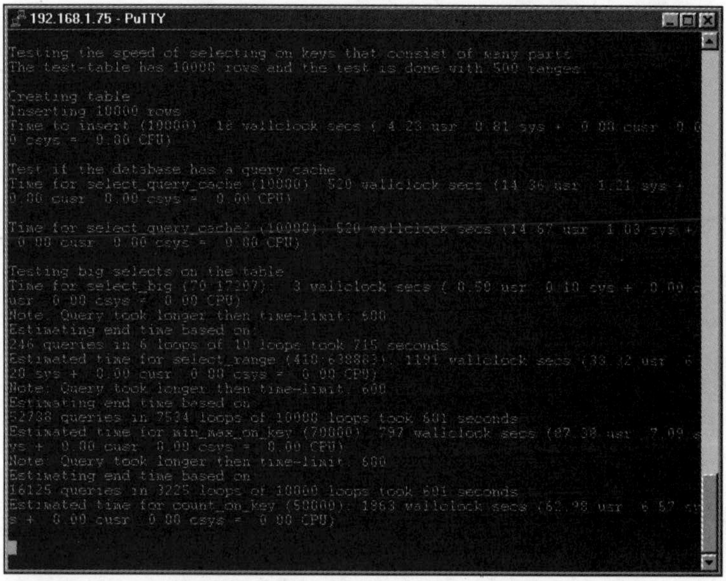

Figure 11-12: An increase in the key_buffer_size value greatly improved performance for the test-select benchmark.

Other variables that can assist in improving performance depend on the hardware and applications. For example, if you have an application that opens many threads and neglects to close them, you could lower the connect_timeout variable. Of course, the better solution would be to fix the faulty application and have a talk with the developer who designed it.

Another example: The error message "Too many open tables" indicates that you might consider increasing the table_cache size or changing the design of the databases on the server. Other variables (some of them relatively self-evident) can be set with little trouble—for example, the max_user_connections variable. If you need to make more connections available, you can increase this value and restart the server.

Bringing it all together

Applications change, data changes, and other parameters on the server have to change as well. Therefore tuning and monitoring of server variables is not a one-time task. You should check and monitor performance regularly through the extended-status and status commands, as well as by monitoring the logs.

If you notice a slowdown of MySQL during certain operations you may have to tweak a variable or two. Through proper diagnostics and testing, you can determine which variables to alter to improve performance. MySQL provides enough feedback and tools to help you get this job done.

Running More Than One MySQL Server on the Same Machine

A server configuration that some administrators find the need to implement is one where multiple instances of MySQL are running on the same physical machine. The MySQL server software uses completely separate databases that know nothing of the other MySQL server or servers running on that machine. This section looks at how to install multiple MySQL servers on the same computer.

Configuration of multiple MySQL servers

For more than one MySQL server to run successfully on the same machine, the servers must use different directories for the MySQL server files and databases. In addition, each server must use a unique socket file and port number. If you are installing from source, you can specify these parameters at compile time. This is the method recommended by MySQL AB; it looks like this:

```
./configure --with-tcp-port=<port_num>, with-unix-socket-
path=<socket_file>, --prefix=<directory>
```

If you want to use binary versions of MySQL you can specify the path and file options on the command-line or in a MySQL configuration file. Here's the syntax to use when you specify them on the command line:

```
./mysqld_safe --socket=<socket_file> --port=<port_num> --
datadir=<dir>
```

Note In older versions of MySQL, the command to start the server is `safe_mysqld`.

Connecting to multiple MySQL servers

When connecting to a MySQL server that is not listening on the default port of 3306 or is available through a non-default socket file you must specify this on the command-line. For example, to connect to a MySQL server running on port 6603 using the CLI, the additional switch `--port=<port>` or `-P <port>` is necessary:

```
mysql --port=6603
```

Other defaults may be read from the default MySQL configuration file. However, this file may refer to the wrong MySQL server. Using the `--defaults-file=<file-name>`, you can specify the file that is read for defaults.

If you don't specify a hostname, MySQL will assume that you are connecting to the server on localhost and will use the socket to connect to the server. In such an event you need to specify the location of the socket file. Do so with the `-S <socket_file>` or `--socket=<socket_file>` switch; the command looks like this:

```
mysql --socket=/directory/socketfile.sock
```

Summary

MySQL can be—and should be—tuned to the physical server hardware that it is running on, and configured for the main application or applications that it will be serving. When set correctly, the MySQL server variables can improve the performance of the server and thus the applications using the database.

- ✦ You can look at all the variables and settings for the server through the `SHOW VARIABLES` statement from within the MySQL CLI (or with the `mysqladmin` variables command).
- ✦ Though many settings are available for a MySQL server, most of them do need not be individually configured.
- ✦ MySQL comes with benchmarking and testing utilities for diagnosing server performance.
- ✦ MySQL AB has included sample configuration files for different sizes and applications.
- ✦ Among these configuration files, you can choose from small, medium, large, and huge implementations.
- ✦ Once an example configuration file has been chosen, it should be customized for the application and installation that the MySQL server will be used for.
- ✦ Customizing the server variables is a process that takes time. The administrator can change settings and then use one or all of the benchmarking utilities to test the performance of the MySQL server.
- ✦ Because data and applications change, the server should be monitored for performance issues. If you notice performance degradation, further testing should reveal where bottlenecks are.

✦ ✦ ✦

CHAPTER 12

Security

✦ ✦ ✦ ✦

In This Chapter

Implementing security for the MySQL host server

Setting up MySQL software security

Configuring MySQL authentication and privileges

Managing user accounts in MySQL

Coping with common security problems

✦ ✦ ✦ ✦

An oft-overlooked area of MySQL and computers in general is security. How many patches and security fixes have to come out for a Web server before an administrator updates it? How often does a server have to be broken into before an administrator turns off unnecessary services and changes unsecured default settings? These questions are not rhetorical; sooner or later, every administrator must face them.

This chapter introduces some simple security rules and suggestions to improve the security of your MySQL server and the integrity of the data you keep there.

Security of the MySQL Host Server

The *least-privilege system* is a high-security approach to the assigning of access privileges to users. It requires that no unnecessary services be enabled on the server, that the server software gets regular updates as soon as they are available, and that users are not given more privileges than their work requires.

If everyone subscribed to the least-privilege system, I believe there would be much less business for security consultants. Although I admit that it takes time to apply patches and keep up with security updates, the same arguments still apply: How much time does it take to repair a server damaged by unauthorized use? How valuable is your data if you "can't afford" to spend the time securing your systems?

A good starting point in any discussion of system security is to define *unauthorized use* and *attack* in consistent, practical terms. Although the words themselves may seem obvious, attacks and unauthorized uses actually incorporate several distinct concepts:

✦ Exploits, whether initiated from outside or inside, take advantage of a security hole for the attacker's own gain.

- Attacks (again, whether initiated from outside or inside) are often more aggressive and seek to disrupt, damage, or even bring down the target system.
- Unauthorized use is not limited to purposeful attacks or exploits on a server or network; it can also be unintended, as in these examples:
  - A user with too many privileges may not realize they are inappropriate, use them inefficiently or incorrectly, and waste system resources such as storage space and bandwidth.
  - A harried developer who means no harm can unleash faulty code that disrupts a server no less than does a hacker attack.
  - Sometimes an administrator's test of system security goes awry and interferes too much with its operation.

Knowing that your system is vulnerable to disruption, whether malicious or unintentional, should shape your security policy. The least-privilege concept provides a good starting point, as in these examples:

- Providing a well-thought-out set of limited privileges to a developer helps ensure that new applications for the server are realistically tested, but also limits the possible consequences of running faulty code.
- Limiting users to minimal necessary privileges can thwart some attacks before they even begin.

Note Although the usual assumption is that attacks always start outside and/or are always intentional, it's far from true. When I refer to attacks, attackers, or unauthorized uses, I have in mind a wider definition that includes both intentional and unintentional disruptions.

Locating security information

Many administrators and would-be administrators complain that they have trouble keeping up with updates. No central repository of information for updates and reports of exploits now exists (although that may be all to the good — why give hackers any more ideas than they already have?); in the world of network security, you're largely on your own. To give you a useful starting point as you grapple with issues of network security, I've included some online sites that can help, and interspersed this chapter with some essential security concepts to keep in mind, the first of which is as follows:

Note Maintain a proactive approach to keeping up with exploits and problems with software you are running.

Security does require a proactive approach; keeping servers and software secure is difficult enough. Companies that want to maintain a viable reputation for their products may want to suppress all knowledge of exploits or try to keep them secret, but by far the more ethical response to security vulnerability is to produce, document, and distribute an effective patch. The availability of such patches (and a good track record for producing them in a timely manner) is one telling criterion that helps define an above-average vendor.

Security focus

Even though information on security is scattered across the Internet at diffuse locations, one Web site stands out as a consistent repository for reliable information: Security Focus, `http://www.securityfocus.com/`. Using this site an administrator can keep up with exploits and security patches as soon as they are available.

The Security Focus Web site is also home to numerous mailing lists, security-related and otherwise. Figure 12-1 shows some of the mailing lists available for subscription on the Security Focus Web site. One of the most notable and famous is the Bugtraq mailing list, widely regarded as the most adept at keeping up with security issues across a wide variety of platforms. For people worried about being inundated with yet more e-mail, many high-volume lists at Security Focus offer digest-mode subscriptions as well.

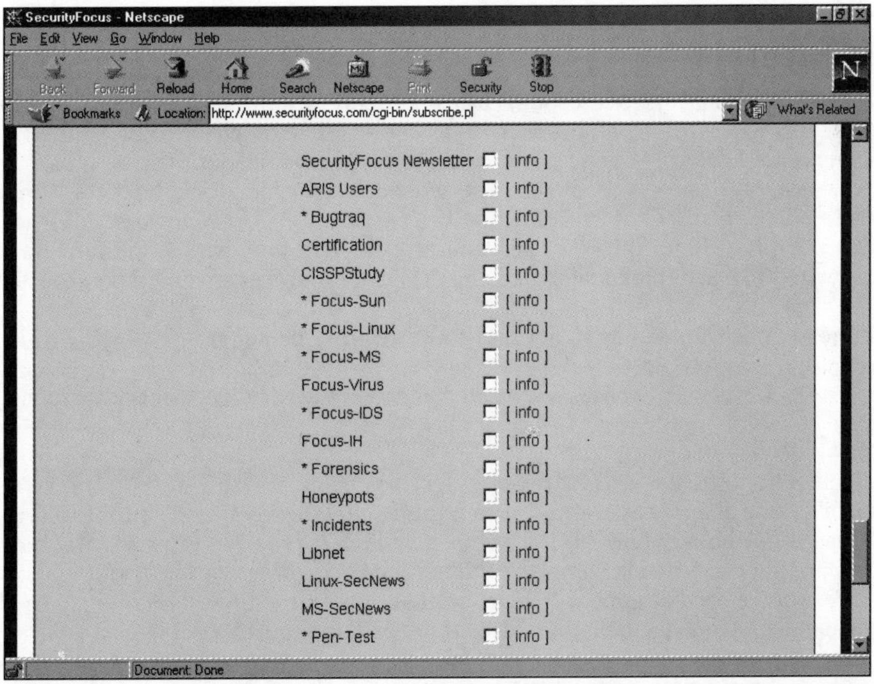

Figure 12-1: Some mailing lists, security-related and otherwise, available from the Security Focus Web site

Apply patches and fixes

Just keeping up with the exploits and holes that come to light in servers and software isn't enough. You must apply the patches and fixes as soon as they are released. This brings me to the simple second rule:

Note: Apply patches and fixes as soon as they are released.

If no patch is available, try to find a workaround that effectively thwarts attacks. For example, I've maintained a system that ran a public FTP server serving thousands of real users. Along with the real users, the FTP server also allowed anonymous access for non-paying people from all over the Internet to download files.

A certain exploit against that particular FTP server could only be done by anonymous access. No patch was immediately available from the vendor, so I chose to disable anonymous access until a patch could be released. Although this is not an optimal solution, sometimes you have to disable access for a relatively short time in order to avoid a much worse alternative—a non-trusted user getting administrative rights. As soon as a patch was available for the FTP server, I applied it and re-enabled anonymous access.

Disable unused programs and services

Every now and again, just for fun, I assist a friend with the security of his computer systems by performing a port scan of his servers. I never cease to be amazed at how many ports he leaves open for the world to take advantage of. He runs a basic Web server that also serves as an e-mail server. Such a server should have no more than three ports open: TCP port 80 for the Web server, TCP port 25 for the SMTP server and TCP port 110 for the POP3 server. Unfortunately, it doesn't stop there. He was surprised to learn that he also had an NNTP server and even an IRC server running!

The lesson is summed up in another basic security principle:

Note: Disable unused services and verify that only the services you specify are running.

Much of the problem with extraneous services being enabled stems from the default installations of many operating systems and software. My friend's problem arose because he chose default options while installing Microsoft's Internet Information Server. However, the problem isn't limited to Microsoft operating systems and software. Choosing what appear to be the default options with Red Hat Linux can also yield many invisibly enabled services that are also security problems.

With a program such as `nmap` you can effectively scan both TCP and UDP ports of an Internet server to find unexpected ports that may be running. The `nmap` program is available for Linux and Windows but can scan against any IP-based host. In Figure 12-2 I run a basic `nmap` scan against one of my local machines.

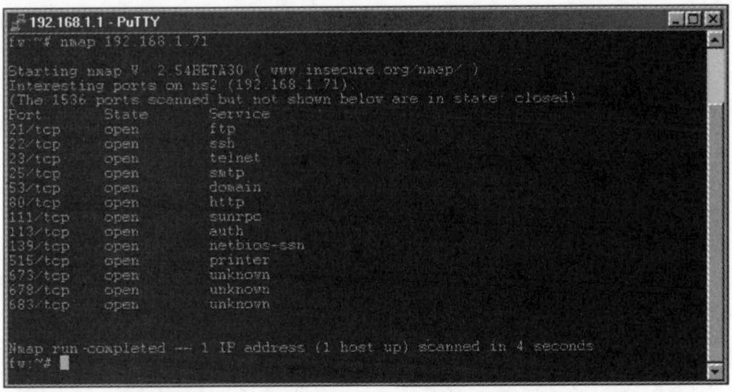

Figure 12-2: The nmap program can assist in determining open ports on one of your servers.

Caution Never perform port scans against any IP or server that you are not responsible for. Doing so can get you terminated by your ISP or worse!

Most versions of Linux and many other operating systems include a program called `netstat` that can help you determine which ports your sever is using to listen to online traffic. Although `netstat` is a powerful program that does much more than just showing which ports are listening, that listening function is a source of potential security headaches. In Figure 12-3, for example, I run the command `netstat -an` to produce basic output of the ports that this server is listening on. This server is listening for connections to TCP port 22 for `ssh` connections, UDP ports 67 and 68 to talk to a DHCP server, and TCP port 3306 for MySQL.

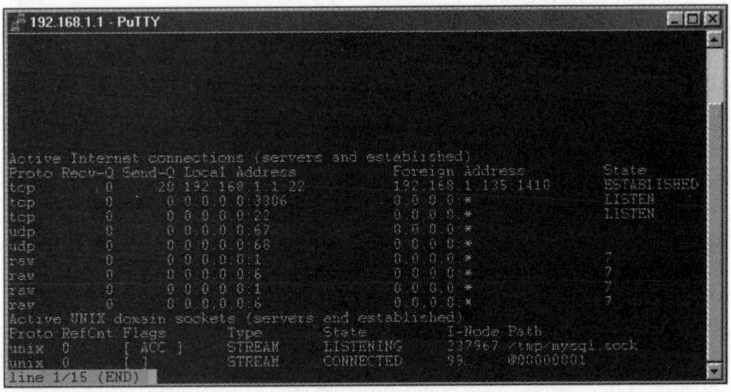

Figure 12-3: The netstat -an command shows the ports of this server that are available for connection.

After using a program such as `netstat` or `nmap`, you should have a clearer picture of what services are running on your server. The more services you have running, the more vulnerable the server is to attack. Thus turning off all unnecessary services can save you time and headaches.

MySQL Software Security

Up to this point, I've been looking at what you can do with the security of the host that runs the MySQL server. The security of the MySQL host server is an essential first step in enhancing the overall security of the database server (and thus the data). Without first securing the host server, no amount of MySQL security will keep your data safe.

In this section I'm going to examine what can be done with the MySQL server itself. This includes keeping the server up to date, securing communication channels, and monitoring the server status.

MySQL updates

Though only one piece of the security puzzle the MySQL software itself is (like any other software) susceptible to problems and security exploits. Though these have been very few and far between for MySQL, the problems can happen nonetheless. Developing a systematic approach for keeping up to date with MySQL software will assist in keeping the database safe from attack.

The best method for monitoring when a new version of MySQL is released is by subscribing to the MySQL Announce mailing list. Offered for free by MySQL AB, this mailing list will give you updates when new versions of MySQL are released. Don't worry about it overcrowding your inbox; the MySQL Announce list is low-volume.

Another mailing list available for MySQL is the main MySQL mailing list. This list is much higher volume as it contains questions from general users of MySQL and discussion of many MySQL-related topics. If you would like to learn more about the inner workings of MySQL, this mailing list can help.

On the CD-ROM

I've included a link to the mailing list section of the MySQL Web site on the Links document on the CD-ROM with this book.

When an update is released, you must make backups of your data prior to proceeding with the upgrade. This is necessary because of the inherent unknown in upgrades of any nature. I've usually found that if I take the time to make backups nothing will go wrong — but if I forego that step, inevitably something will fail.

Cross-Reference In Chapter 13 backup and recovery of MySQL databases is covered in detail.

Since the upgrade process is quite customized (depending on your installation), exhaustive coverage is neither possible nor desirable here. Often the solution is as simple as recompiling or overwriting an existing MySQL installation.

Run the server as a non-privileged user

In Linux/Unix, you can set the user account that runs the MySQL server process, `mysqld`. (This is as opposed to running the server process as the `root` superuser on the system.) Figure 12-4 shows a process listing from Linux, with the server running as a non-privileged regular user called `mysql`.

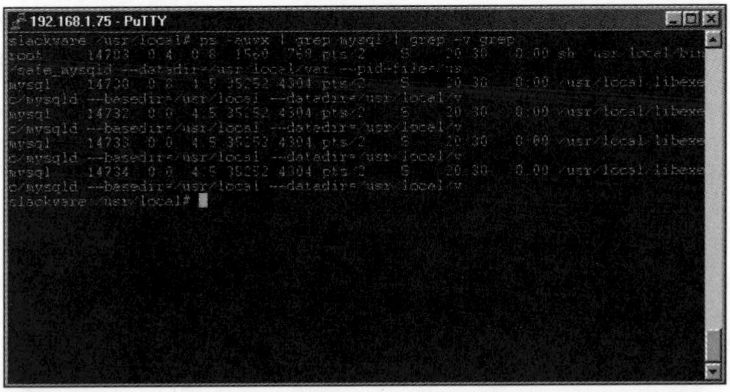

Figure 12-4: Running the MySQL server as a non-privileged user can prevent unauthorized access in the event of an exploit performed on the server.

By running the server as a normal user in Linux/Unix, the server only has the same privileges as that user. In other words, if the server is exploited the attacker cannot gain further access or perform other privileged processes on the server.

To enable MySQL to run as another user on the system, follow these steps:

1. Add the user, and if desired a group, to the server. This is normally accomplished via the `useradd` and `groupadd` commands.
2. Make sure the user has access to the data and server files for MySQL. This step is accomplished with a combination of `chown` and `chmod` in Linux.
3. Add the `--user=`*`username`* option to the `mysqld` command line, or add the line `user = `*`username`* to the `my.cnf` file under the `[mysqld]` section.

Cross-Reference

Full details of installation of the MySQL server, including details on configuring the server to run as a non-privileged user, are located in Chapter 3.

Firewalling the MySQL server

The most effective security to protect the MySQL server from outside attack is to prevent people from the outside from gaining access to the server. Installing a firewall to protect the server will help to prevent access from non-trusted hosts.

Using a passive firewalling solution to simply prevent attacks is a good solution. The use of a firewall stops outside or non-trusted locations from even knowing that a MySQL server is available at your location. An attacker can't gain access to your data if they can't find it.

Another option is to use an *active firewall* that listens on common (and even uncommon) ports for a non-trusted user sending a port-scan or probe to your machines. The active firewall then completely blocks access from that IP address to all ports.

If you must allow access to the MySQL server from outside the firewall, you need only allow access to the port on which MySQL listens for TCP connections. By default, this is port 3306. Further, you should only allow access to the MySQL port from specific trusted IP addresses. You could also create an SSH tunnel through a trusted host without having to open up any ports for MySQL on the firewall.

Even with a firewall in place, you must make sure that trusted hosts don't serve as a launching point for attackers. Monitor these machines to make sure they are up to date and have the latest security patches. Using the active firewalling solution, you can monitor these servers to make sure they aren't originating port scans or other common probes against the servers in your network or within your trusted domain.

Communicating securely with the MySQL server

As of version 4 of MySQL, communication over TCP via the Secure Sockets Layer (SSL) is possible. Prior to this all communication between server and client passed unencrypted. The ambitious attacker could therefore watch traffic as it passed and gather information on data as well as user and password information.

With SSL support enabled, the traffic between the MySQL server and the client is encrypted. Even if an attacker gains enough access to eavesdrop on an electronic conversation, he or she can't make sense of the resulting data.

Note

The SSL option is not enabled on a connection by default. However, you can enable it and even require it through the use of the additional user privilege system when SSL is compiled into MySQL.

Using socket-based connections

By default, MySQL listens for connections both through sockets for local connections and via TCP/IP for remote connections. If you will not be connecting to MySQL from any hosts other than the MySQL server itself, you should disable the TCP/IP option in MySQL.

Disabling networking prevents you from using the `-h` or `host` option, whether from the local machine or from other hosts on the network. Attempting to connect to a MySQL server that is not available (or not listening for connections) via TCP/IP will result in an error, as shown in Figure 12-5.

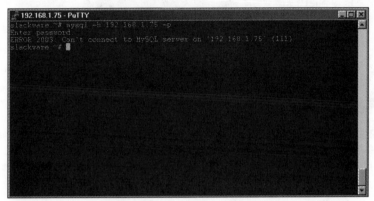

Figure 12-5: Attempting to connect to a MySQL server that is not listening for connections, using TCP/IP

You can disable TCP/IP-based connections by adding the `--skip-networking` option to the command line when starting the server. Another way to disable TCP/IP access is to add the `skip-networking` option to the `[mysqld]` section of the MySQL configuration file.

Note In the future, MySQL AB may alter the connection sequence, thus altering the fingerprint for MySQL. For older servers the fingerprint will remain the same.

Changing the MySQL default port

While certainly not a substitute for a firewall or for disabling TCP/IP networking, another method for slowing an attack is to change the port that MySQL listens on for connections. By default, MySQL listens on TCP port 3306 for connections. If you change the default port, a curious person who scans for port 3306 won't discover that you have a MySQL server unless he or she uses other methods for fingerprinting the server on another port.

Fingerprinting a MySQL server is possible. A curious person could open connections on random or sequential ports and see a familiar signature or fingerprint thus discovering your MySQL server. In Figure 12-6, I have the MySQL server set to listen on port 5150. Then, by simply telnetting to that port, I can see a repeatable pattern.

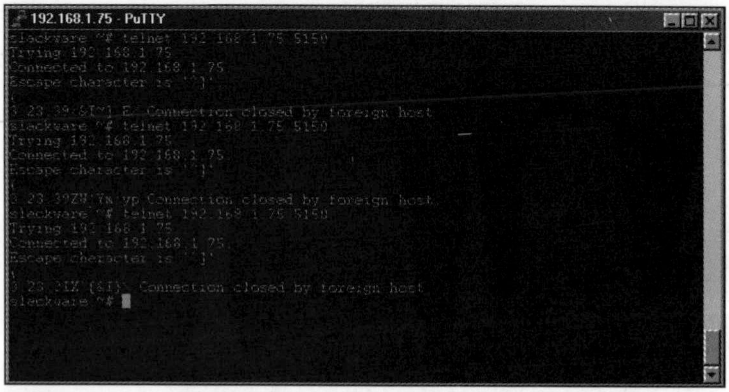

Figure 12-6: Telnetting to a port that MySQL listens on shows a definite fingerprint indicating that it is indeed a MySQL server.

Notice, in Figure 12-6, that the pattern is always the same. The beginning of the session opens with a left parentheses followed by a line-feed. Then a pattern of digits is shown followed by eight characters. Each time I telnet to the server, the pattern repeats. Now I know not only that there is a MySQL server on this host but also what version of the server is running, as indicated by the digits.

As you can see, simply changing the port will not stop an ambitious attacker. The speed and triviality with which an attacker could scan 65,000 ports for a MySQL server makes changing the default port somewhat of a moot point. However, I still believe that changing the default port can serve a purpose to discourage the casual onlooker or curious person.

To change the default port that MySQL listens for TCP/IP connections on, add the line `port = N` to the , section of the MySQL configuration file. For example, in Figure 12-7 the , section is shown from an example server configuration file. (Note that the port number has been changed for the server.)

Note For the sake of security, you must change any applications—including the MySQL CLI—so they connect via the alternative port number.

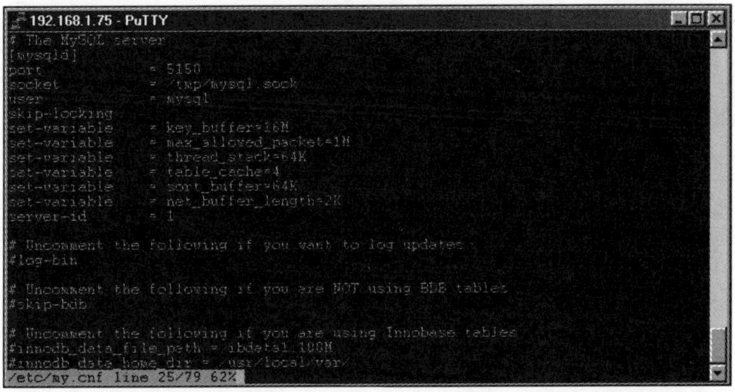

Figure 12-7: Changing the port that the MySQL server listens on can help to hide the server from a curious person.

Monitoring data sent to MySQL

When data is entered into a database from applications, especially those that allow users to type in their own values, you must check the data for errors and other anomalies. It is the responsibility of the developer to ensure that data sent to the MySQL server is clean and free from error. The errors occur from two sources:

- ✦ **A malicious attack:** With intentional attacks on the application and database, the attacker may attempt to escape DDL statements into the application. There are simple methods for preventing this type of attack including a least-privileged user and data cleansing.
- ✦ **Normal users:** Sometimes normal users of an application are more dangerous than a would-be attacker. Regardless of how many notes and documents you create for use of the application, inevitably someone will innocently enter an illegal value. The developer must account for these errors and provide some feedback to the user via error messages or regular beatings.

As an administrator, you should attempt to make sure that the developer understands what is needed from a database side to make sure the data is safe. This includes working with the developer on the design of the database and tables within the database so that the incoming data is of the proper length and type for the column.

Just as important is making sure the developer performs necessary cleansing of inputted data. These steps can be enumerated for items that the administrator and developer must work on together:

- ✦ Use a least-privileged user for connections from the application to the database or use more than one user; one user for inserts and updates, one for selects.
- ✦ Check all values to ensure that they are the expected format, string or number.

✦ Check all values for length.

✦ Check all values to make sure they contain no unexpected characters.

These tips may seem like common sense, but you might be surprised at how many applications don't check for errors in the data, or give incoming data only a glance.

Cross-Reference

Later in this chapter, I show how to add users to the database. Armed with this information, you can then add a least-privileged user account that you can use to connect to the database from applications. Thus, even if you miss a step in error checking (or someone finds a way around error checking), the damage is minimal.

Disabling DNS

One method of attacking a server or manipulating data is to masquerade as a trusted server or client in a MySQL client-server exchange. This type of attack is possible against all applications that utilize Domain Name System (DNS) data, not just MySQL. By posing as a trusted or known host, the attacker can potentially gain an inappropriate level of privileges.

For a DNS attack to occur, the attacker must be able to alter the DNS data on one of the resolvers for your MySQL server. For example, if you have 192.168.1.1 set as a DNS server for your MySQL server, the attacker must alter the DNS data on 192.168.1.1 and send back false information about hosts in your MySQL communication. An attacker could also spoof packets within the communication and pretend to be 192.168.1.1. If DNS data is altered or untrusted an attacker could also pretend to be a trusted host because the host is part of the MySQL authentication scheme.

DNS attacks are not limited solely to the server. A DNS attack could be performed against a client as well. In a client attack, false information is passed to the client and a fake MySQL server poses as the real server (thus getting authentication information as well as the data being passed from client to server).

Tip

To prevent a DNS attack from being successful, you can turn off hostname lookups in MySQL. All connections will be based on IP address, with the exception of localhost connections. To disable DNS use from MySQL, start `mysqld` with the command-line switch `--skip-name-resolve`. You can also add `skip-name-resolve` to the MySQL configuration file.

Dynamic MySQL monitoring of Web pages

Using the HTML function of the MySQL CLI you can create a Web page with server information. With a scheduler such as cron you could then create the Web page in regular intervals to monitor the performance of the MySQL server. The resulting Web pages won't win awards for design, but they will produce useful information for administration of the MySQL server.

Using these pages, the administrator can monitor the MySQL server's performance. This can save time and make it so other administrators can monitor the MySQL server without having to know the backend commands for MySQL administration.

Note You should protect these Web pages via effective passwords; unauthorized access to them is especially dangerous.

A requirement for viewing dynamic monitoring Web page on a network is to get a Web server running. This does not have to be the same physical machine as the one that houses the MySQL server. If the machines are separate you will need to automatically transfer the resulting output from the MySQL commands to the Web server.

The following example processes are performed in Linux, running an Apache Web server. (Your version of Linux may vary slightly from the one shown here.)

Creating the fake database

The steps involved to produce a MySQL monitoring Web page are as follows:

1. Make a publicly available directory to hold HTML output, using this command:

   ```
   mkdir mysqlmonitor
   ```

2. Create a password method to prevent unauthorized access to the directory; the `.htaccess` file is a useful example, and Figure 12-8 shows how to create one.

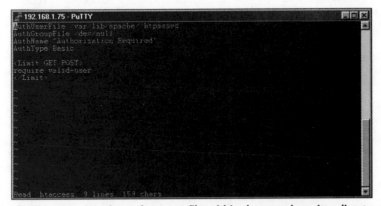

Figure 12-8: Creating a .htaccess file within the mysqlmonitor directory to prevent unauthorized access to the MySQL monitoring Web pages.

3. With the `.htaccess` file in place, you must create a password file to accompany the `.htaccess` file. The name of the file is specified in the `.htaccess` file.

The user that you add for htaccess does not need to be a system user or exist on the system in any way except in the password file for htaccess. The following command creates the password file (as specified in the .htaccess file) and adds a user called suehring to the access file (as shown in Figure 12-9):

```
htpasswd -c /var/lib/apache/.htpass suehring
```

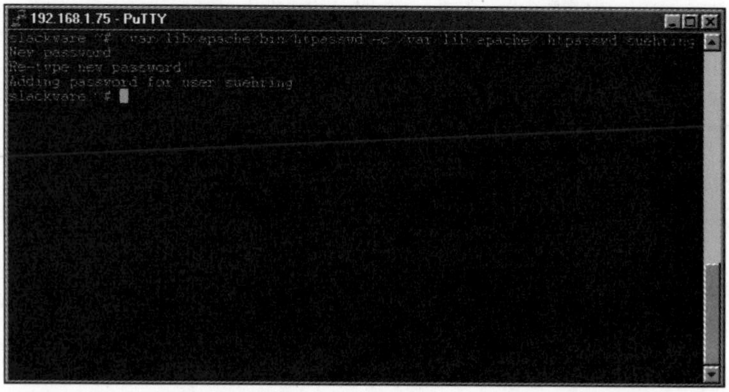

Figure 12-9: Using the htpasswd command to create the password file specified in the .htaccess file and adding a user called suehring to the password file

Note

The password file for .htaccess should not be in a publicly available directory. In addition, adding a user to the password file for htaccess does not affect the user's rights on the system, if any.

4. Now add a user to the MySQL database to retrieve the information for the Web pages. To accomplish this, create a fake database and give the user access to the database.

   Creating a fake database enables you to have a user on the database server with only a bare minimum of privileges—and then only on a database that holds no tables or data. You can use the mysqladmin command to create the fake database; do so from inside the CLI, or however you'd like. The command looks like this:

   ```
   mysqladmin -p create dummydb
   ```

5. With the fake database in place, you can add the user to the database server (normally done via the MySQL CLI, as shown in Figure 12-10).

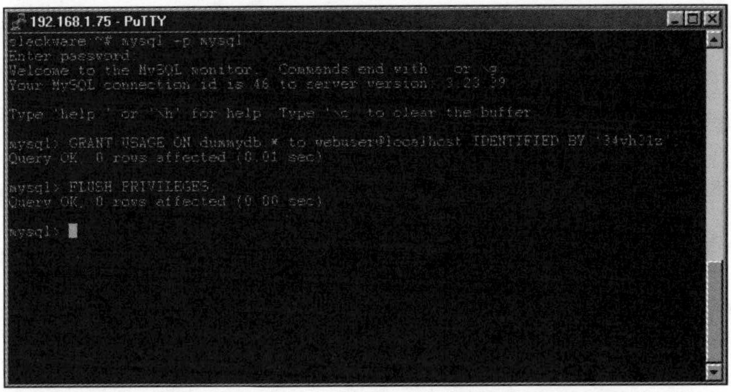

Figure 12-10: Adding a user to the MySQL database server

6. Since you're creating Web pages with status information, the user doesn't need any extra privileges. The following command simply creates the user on the database server (but does not give the user privileges such as `SELECT`, `INSERT`, `DELETE`, or the like):

```
GRANT USAGE ON dummydb.* to Webuser@localhost IDENTIFIED BY
'34vh21z';
```

Note: The `FLUSH PRIVILEGES` statement is not necessary when you're using the `GRANT` statement.

Creating the script that makes the Web pages

With the Web server and access method ready, you can create a script for producing the actual Web pages. The script itself can be a simple shell script (which Windows users know as a Windows script), or it can be done in another language such as Perl. The concept for the script is simple: Run the MySQL CLI command `mysql` in batch mode, use the `-H` switch to produce HTML output, and redirect that output to a file.

Figures 12-11 and 12-12 show examples of simple scripts to check the status of the server via the `SHOW STATUS` statement — and also to look at the processes running on the server via the `SHOW PROCESSLIST` statement. Figure 12-11 is a simple shell script; Figure 12-12 is a script written in Perl.

Note: You will probably need to change the paths to both the MySQL CLI and the directory in which you want to produce the HTML output from the script.

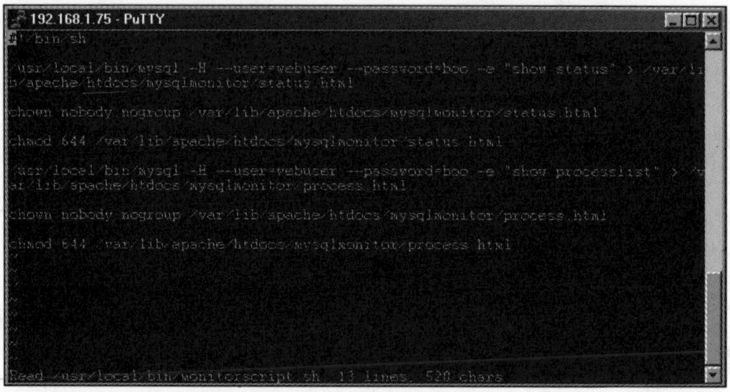

Figure 12-11: A shell script for creating two Web pages to monitor MySQL server information

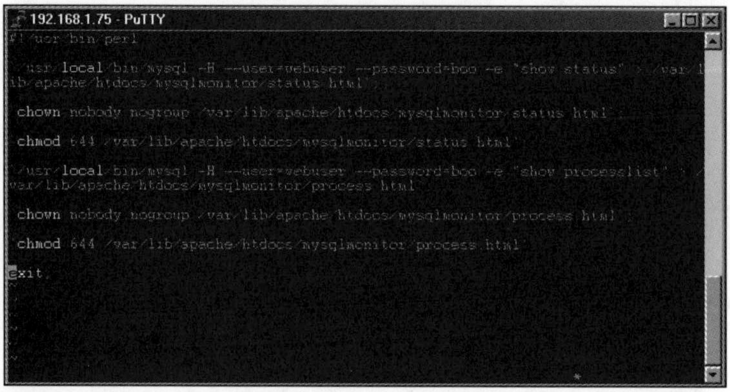

Figure 12-12: A Perl script for creating two Web pages to monitor MySQL server information. This script can be run on any system that has Perl, including Windows and Mac OS X systems, by changing the location of Perl at the top of the script.

On the CD-ROM Both these scripts are included on the CD-ROM.

Caution Be sure to control access to the script. It contains the password for one of the users on your MySQL server.

You could get fancy and use a concatenate redirect of the output to place both commands in one file. Adding the output into one file gives you one place to monitor. You could also create another script to produce output at opposite intervals; thus you could monitor changes in the variables over time.

The output from either script is shown (as viewed through a Web browser) in Figures 12-13 and 12-14.

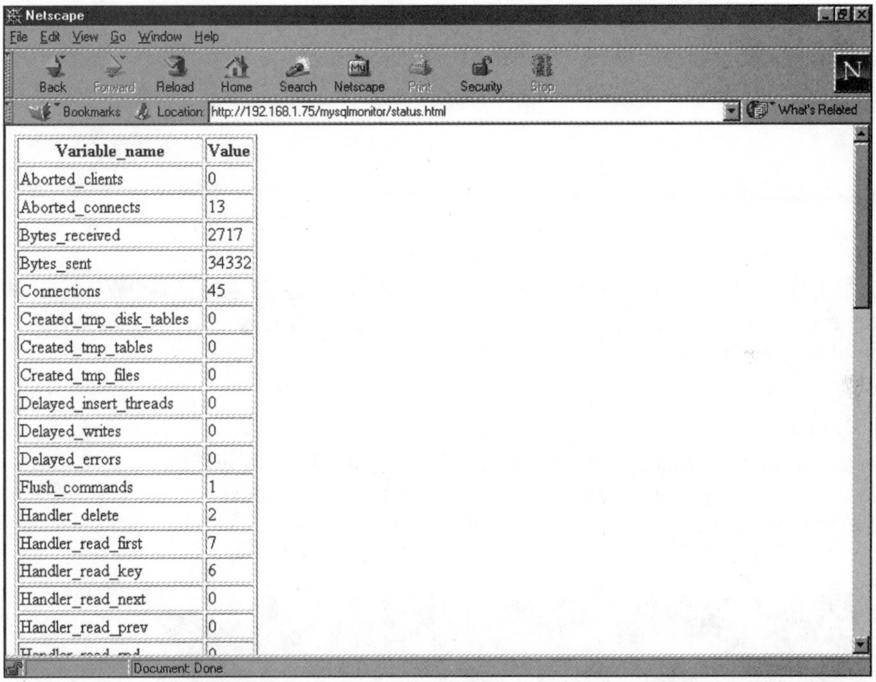

Figure 12-13: The output from the SHOW STATUS statement, as produced by the MySQL CLI HTML switch

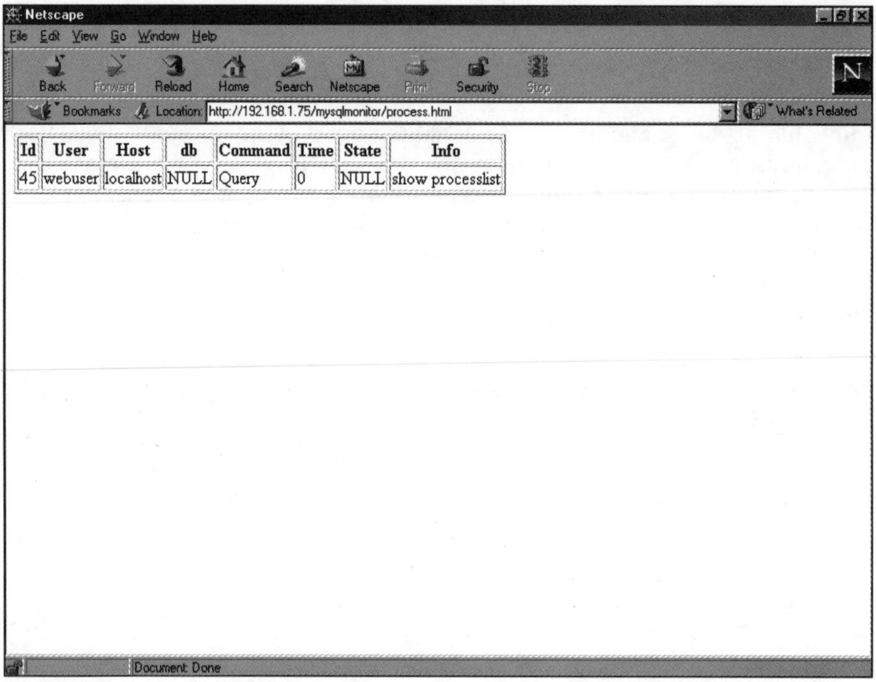

Figure 12-14: The remaining output from the SHOW PROCESSLIST statement as produced by the MySQL CLI HTML switch

The final step, though optional, is to schedule the script to run automatically. How often you would like to schedule the script depends on how busy your server is, and how often you want to schedule it. Using `cron` in Linux, I schedule the script to run every 15 minutes, as shown in Figure 12-15.

Figure 12-15: Scheduling the monitoring script to run every 15 minutes by using the cron command in Linux

MySQL Authentication and Privileges

Prior to getting down to the dirty business of working with users, I believe it is necessary to give an overview of the MySQL authentication system. This includes the stages of authentication as well as the privileges that can be granted and revoked. (This also gives me another chance to get on a soapbox about passwords.)

Overview of MySQL authentication

The MySQL privilege system works on a number of levels prior to allowing access to the server. Unlike systems where simply a username and password are examined to determine access, MySQL uses the username, password, and host to determine access level for the database.

MySQL uses a two-stage process for determination of your access level, the connection level and process level. Using these two levels, in two sequential steps, the MySQL server determines

✦ Whether you are allowed to connect at all.

✦ Whether you have privileges to perform the requested operation or statement.

During the first stage, which I will refer to as the Connection Stage, the MySQL server combines the user and host provided as credentials and determines if the given combination is allowed to connect with the given password.

1. The first phase of the Connection Stage combines the `host`, `user`, and `password` columns from the `users` table of the MySQL `grants` database.
   - If no database is included in the connection request, access is granted or denied at this point. The host column within the grants database can contain any valid hostname, IP address, or localhost. In addition, the wildcards `%` and _ are valid as are netmask values. For all hosts, the `%` wildcard can be used. For example, `username'192.168.1.%'` would grant access to username from any address within the 192.168.1.0/24 range. This is the same as username'192.168.1.0/255.255.255.0'. If given username'%' then username at any host would be allowed.
   - If a database is included within the connection request, the second phase begins.
2. The second phase of the Connection Stage of authentication is to verify credentials for the database.

   This phase is performed against the `db` table of the MySQL `grants` database. The `db` table is examined for host, database, and user. If access to all databases is granted to the user, this stage automatically passes; otherwise access is granted or denied, depending on the information in the `db` table.

3. The third phase of the Connection Stage is performed against the host table of the MySQL grants database. The host and db columns from the host table are included in this phase.

   If connections from a host are restricted in some way, this table determines appropriate access.

During the next (second) stage of MySQL authentication, the requested process is examined for specific privileges to determine access. For example, if the user attempts to issue a SELECT statement, the authentication process looks again at the user table of the MySQL grants database. If authentication passes the user table, it is again passed on to the db table and then to the host table. If the statement is run against a table, the tables_priv table is also consulted for authentication; if the statement runs against a column or columns, then the columns_priv table is consulted.

MySQL privileges

Each table of the MySQL grants database provides the privileges shown in Table 12-1 (with the exception of the RELOAD, SHUTDOWN, PROCESS, and FILE privileges, which are limited to the user table because they have no meaning in other contexts).

Table 12-1
MySQL Privileges and their functions

Privilege	*Function*
SELECT	Table–level privilege for selecting data or performing queries.
INSERT	Table-level privilege for adding data.
UPDATE	Table-level privilege for updating or changing data.
DELETE	Table-level privilege for deleting data from tables.
INDEX	Table-level privilege for creating and deleting indexes.
ALTER	Table-level privilege for changing table layout.
CREATE	Database-, table-, and index-level privilege for creation of databases, tables and indexes.
DROP	Database- and table-level privilege for deleting databases and tables.
GRANT	Database- and table-level privilege for enabling a user to alter privileges for other users including adding and deleting users.
REFERENCES	Database- and table-level privilege for using references.
RELOAD	Server-level privilege for reloading and flushing server parameters.
SHUTDOWN	Server-level privilege for stopping the MySQL database server.
PROCESS	Server- level privilege to enable process listing and killing.
FILE	Server- level privilege to work with files such as selecting into outfiles.

Note: If the `FILE` privilege is given to a user, that user will be able to read the contents of all other databases on the server.

The privileges are simple insofar as they mean what they are named. To issue a `SELECT` statement, you need the `SELECT` privilege, to insert data you need the `INSERT` privilege, and so on.

Security of passwords

Working with an Internet service provider, I can't count the number of times I've seen people choose bad passwords. I've seen all the mistakes in the book, from choosing the username as the password to using the worst old favorite possible (the word *password*). I believe these types of mistakes are, in the words of James R. Leu, "completely unacceptable." Regular users may have an excuse for choosing poor passwords, but System and Database Administrators don't. As the person who is in charge of a server or servers, it is your job to use passwords that cannot be easily guessed or cracked.

Password guidelines

I've put together some guidelines that should help you choose effective passwords, come up with stronger ones, and keeping the ones you have secure.

- ✦ Passwords should be six characters at an absolute minimum.
- ✦ Passwords should include a mix of alphanumeric characters such as letters and numbers and non-alphanumeric characters, such as "@#$^&*".
- ✦ When you create a password, never use words that you can find in a dictionary (or those same words spelled backwards).
- ✦ Passwords should include the use of both sides of the keyboard or both hands while typing. In other words, don't use passwords that require you to use only your left hand or the left side of the keyboard only.
- ✦ Passwords should be different across servers. Don't use the same password for all of your servers, routers, and other gear. Thus, if one machine is compromised, the attacker cannot automatically gain access to your other servers.
- ✦ Don't write your passwords down. If you feel you can't remember a password and must write something down, write down a word or phrase that will remind you of the password.

MySQL passwords

There is general confusion over whether the Unix encryption structure is compatible with MySQL because a UNIX encryption does look somewhat similar to a MySQL encryption. Even so, MySQL passwords are stored with an encryption algorithm different from that of the standard Unix encryption method. For this reason, you cannot simply transfer your password and its encryption key from a password file to the MySQL `grants` database.

MySQL includes a function to create a valid MySQL encryption: `PASSWORD()`. Using the `PASSWORD` function, a user with access to a MySQL CLI could create a valid encryption for use in MySQL. The user could then take the encryption and transfer it to the server administrator for addition to the MySQL `grants` database.

As stated previously there is some confusion over the use of crypts within the user table of the MySQL grants database. Part of this confusion comes because of the `ENCRYPT()` function. The `ENCRYPT()` function creates a Unix style encryption but it is not valid in the MySQL grants database. In Figure 12-16, for example, I use the `PASSWORD()` function to create a valid MySQL password. The resulting password could be transferred to the administrator for the server and he or she would never be able to see my unencrypted password. I also use the `ENCRYPT()` function as a reference to show the difference, given the same plaintext password.

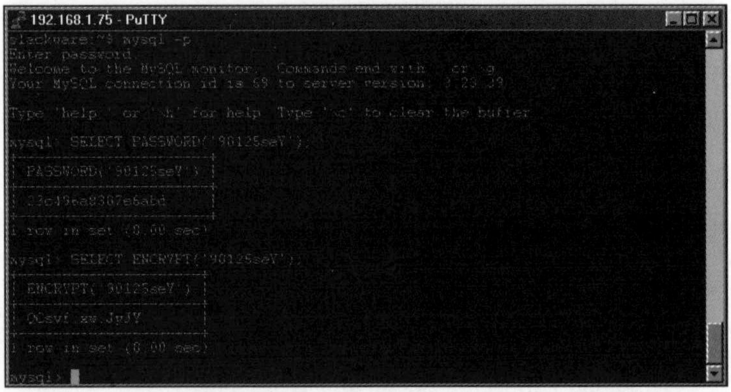

Figure 12-16: The PASSWORD() function creates a valid MySQL encryption while the ENCRYPT() function does not.

MySQL User Management

For maximum security, I recommend implementing the least-privilege concept of permissions. When issuing grants and privileges to users of a database, you should give them only the privileges they need to perform their jobs.

You can create user accounts in MySQL by one of two methods: Using the GRANT statement or using the INSERT statement. For the purposes of this chapter I will be concentrating solely on the GRANT statement and its opposite statement, REVOKE.

If you choose to use an INSERT or UPDATE statement for working with the grants database, you must use the FLUSH PRIVILEGES statement as well. If you use a GRANT or REVOKE statement, the database server sees the changes immediately.

If you change a user's access to a database while they are connected to that database, the change will not take effect immediately for that user. In addition, if you change a user's global privileges or change their password it will not take effect until the next time they connect. Therefore, you should kill the user's process in order for the changes to take effect for these instances.

Two macro-level grants are not listed in Table 12-1: the ALL PRIVILEGES and USAGE macros. The ALL PRIVILEGES macro can be substituted in a GRANT or REVOKE statement instead of having to enumerate each of the privileges. The USAGE macro simply creates the user account with no privileges. In other words, think of the USAGE macro as a placeholder. It allows the administrator to create the user account and come back to it later to set privileges.

Note — The ALL PRIVILEGES macro does not include (and so does not grant) the administrative privilege of granting and revoking privileges.

Adding users and granting privileges

In MySQL, adding a user and granting privileges can occur simultaneously. You can also add multiple users — with the same privileges — simultaneously. The basic statement for adding a user and setting privileges is the GRANT statement.

The syntax for the GRANT statement is as follows:

```
GRANT privilege [(<columnlist>)] [, privilege [(<columnlist>)]
...]
    ON {<tablename> | * | *.* | <databasename>.*}
    TO username(@<host>) [IDENTIFIED BY 'password']
        [, username(@<host>) [IDENTIFIED BY 'password'] ...]
    [REQUIRE
        [{SSL| X509}]
        [CIPHER cipher [AND]]
        [ISSUER issuer [AND]]
        [SUBJECT subject]]
    [WITH GRANT OPTION]
```

Note — To use the GRANT statement, you must have the GRANT privilege.

In my time as a database administrator, I've most frequently used the `USAGE` macro to initially create the user and then gone back and granted individual privileges for the user at a later time. With the `USAGE` macro the user will be added to the grants database as normal except no privileges will be given to the user. The `USAGE` macro can be helpful if the actual database hasn't been created yet (or tables haven't been created within the database).

As you can see by the syntax listing, the `GRANT` statement accepts wildcards for the database and also wildcards within the database context to indicate all tables. For example, to grant privileges on a specific table within a database, you can use *`databasename.tablename`* (or simply *`tablename`* if you are in the database at the time). Contrast this with granting privileges on all tables within a database (which you call with the `databasename.*` syntax, or simply with `*` from within the database). Also, granting privileges to all databases and tables is possible with the use of the `*.*` wildcard syntax. Examples of these grants are shown in Figure 12-17.

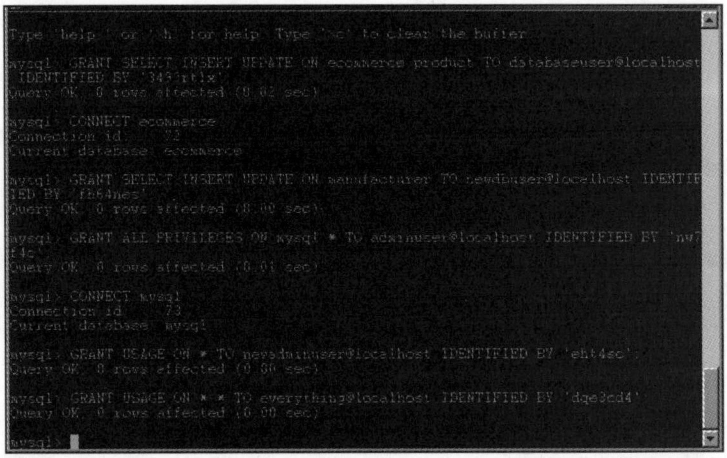

Figure 12-17: Examples of GRANT statements in differing scenarios

With the `GRANT` statement you can specify that the privilege will only apply to certain columns within a given table. You can also specify more than one privilege within a statement and apply that to the same or different columns within the same table or *`database.table`* structure. In addition, you can give the same privileges to multiple users at the same time if you separate the `users/host/password` portions with commas. Examples of these grants are shown in Figure 12-18.

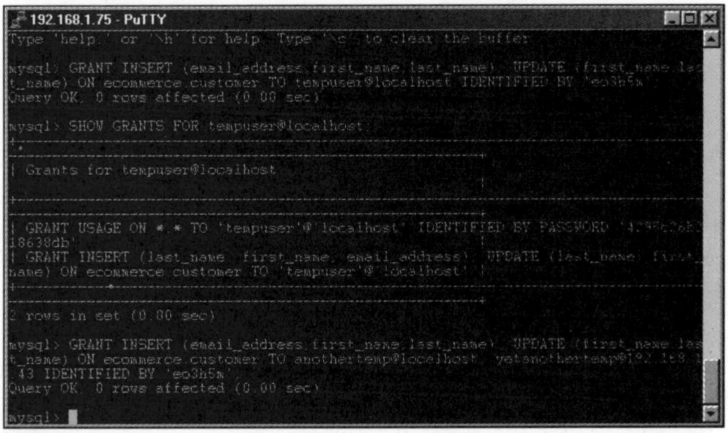

Figure 12-18: Some variations of the GRANT statement as useful syntax examples

The value for `<host>` can contain any valid hostname, IP address, or localhost. In addition, the wildcards `%` and _ are valid as are netmask values. For all hosts, the `%` wildcard can be used. When using a wildcard or netmask value, the `<host>` portion must be quoted. For example, `username'192.168.1.%'` would grant access to username from any address within the 192.168.1.0/24 range. This is the same as `username'192.168.1.0/255.255.255.0'`. If given username'%' then username at any host would be allowed.

You can require the user connect only via a secure connection such as Secure Sockets Layer (SSL) or with X509. This functionality is achieved by adding the `REQUIRE` modifier to the `GRANT` statement.

If you wish for the user to have the ability to add, delete, and alter privileges within the database you must add the `WITH GRANT OPTION` modifier to the end of the `GRANT` statement. This is true even if you use the `ALL PRIVILEGES` macro to enable all privileges for the user. The `GRANT` privilege is not included with the `ALL PRIVILEGES` macro.

Caution **Use care when issuing `GRANT` statements so as not to give too many privileges or give them to unintended users.**

As with all database administration, you should be careful when issuing GRANT statements. Since MySQL uses a user/host combination for authentication, there can be multiple users in the database with the same username. Ensuring that you are granting access to the correct user or users is very important.

If you are unsure of the grants that a given user has, you can issue the SHOW GRANTS FOR statement. For example, to find out the grants and privileges given to Webuser (from a previous example in this chapter), issue the following statement:

```
SHOW GRANTS FOR Webuser@localhost;
```

Deleting users and revoking privileges

The REVOKE statement is used to remove privileges from a user. The syntax for the REVOKE statement is as follows:

```
REVOKE privilege [(<columnlist>)] [, privilege [(<columnlist>)]
...]
    ON [<tablename> | * | *.* | <databasename>.*]
    FROM username [, username ...]
```

The syntax is quite similar to that of the GRANT statement. The REVOKE statement can apply to a column or columns, databases and tables can be specified and wildcarded and multiple users can be revoked simultaneously.

The ALL PRIVILEGES macro works with the REVOKE statement the same as with the GRANT statement. This is important to know because if you have granted the GRANT privilege to the user and use a REVOKE ALL PRIVILEGES statement, the GRANT option will still be there! Therefore, you must perform a separate statement of REVOKE GRANT OPTION ... for this occasion.

Issuing a REVOKE statement does not delete the user from the MySQL grants database. To delete a user from the grants database you must specifically issue a DELETE statement to remove them from the grants database.

Caution

Use caution when issuing any REVOKE or DELETE statements as you can easily revoke all privileges from all users or even delete all users from the database, including the root user!

The syntax for the DELETE statement is the same to remove user accounts as it is to delete rows from the tables of other databases. Remember that MySQL uses the user and host combined to identify a user. Therefore you can have as many users with the username robert in the database, but only one robert that connects *from a specific host.* Therefore you must be extremely careful when issuing the DELETE statement so as to not delete all those other Bobs from the database server! A misguided or careless DELETE statement can result in removal of all privileges for all users, not just for robert. After issuing the correct DELETE statement, don't forget to run the FLUSH PRIVILEGES statement so the deletion takes effect on the server.

Figure 12-19 shows all privileges being revoked from an example user, after which a deletion removes the user account entirely from the database.

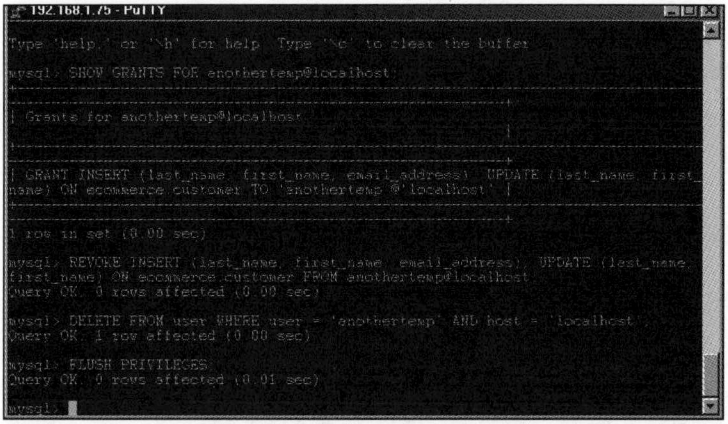

Figure 12-19: An example REVOKE statement, followed by an example DELETE statement. The FLUSH PRIVILEGES statement causes the delete to take effect immediately, preventing the (now-former) user from making a new connection.

Revoking all privileges from a user won't necessarily truly remove all of their privileges. Specific privileges need to be specifically revoked. The `SHOW GRANTS FOR` statement can be quite useful in this situation to determine what specific privileges a user has — for example, `SHOW GRANTS FOR Webuser@localhost`.

Changing passwords and other parameters

Sooner or later, you will have to change a user's password as you administer a database server. You may also have to change a username or alter the host parameters for a database user. MySQL provides a function specifically for changing passwords; for other changes, normal SQL statements are required.

There are two methods for changing a password in MySQL. The first is with the `SET PASSWORD` statement; the second is the `UPDATE` statement. Both statements make use of the `PASSWORD()` function to encrypt the password. Examples of both methods for changing a password are in Figure 12-20.

Use the `UPDATE` statement to change other parameters such as usernames and hosts. The syntax for the `UPDATE` statement is the same in this context as it is in other DML statements. In Figure 12-21, I issue various UPDATE statements to change usernames and hosts. Following the `UPDATE`, I issue the `FLUSH PRIVILEGES` statement to make the changes take effect immediately.

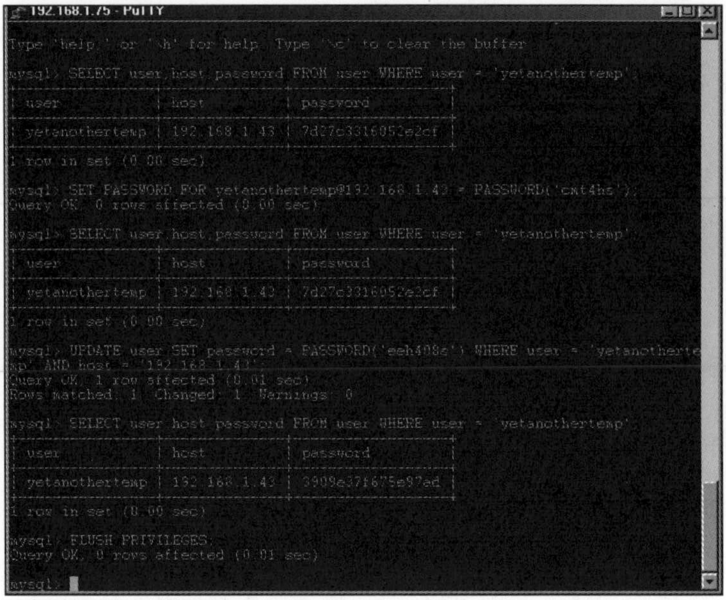

Figure 12-20: Using SET PASSWORD and UPDATE to change passwords for users in MySQL

Cross-Reference: The `UPDATE` statement is discussed In Chapter 9 and in Appendix A.

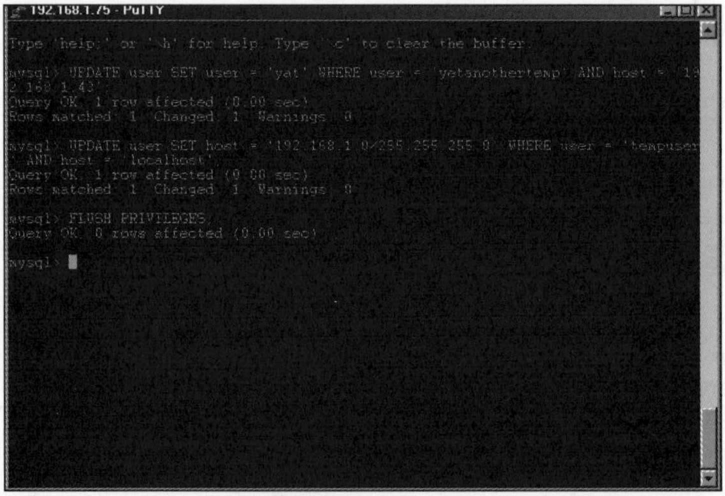

Figure 12-21: Examples of UPDATE statements to change usernames and hosts in the MySQL grants database

When using the `SET PASSWORD` statement, MySQL sees the change immediately. However, when using an `UPDATE` statement, whether for updating a password or changing another parameter, you must issue the `FLUSH PRIVILEGES` statement for the change to take effect.

Common Problems

Though there are many problems that on their face appear to be authentication problems, they are really related to server or other operating system issues. Those types of errors are hopefully covered elsewhere in this book. This section specifically examines some common error messages related to authentication. In addition, a recurring issue surfaces: Too often, people forget the `root` password for MySQL. I'd like to think that they forget because MySQL is so stable that they don't need to connect to it for administration tasks. Regardless, I'll look at how to change the `root` password if you do forget it.

Access denied

There are numerous reasons why you might receive an `Access Denied` error message when attempting to perform an operation. For that matter, you might get one simply by trying to connect to a MySQL server. This section examines the most common of these messages, which include the following:

- **Password:** Personally speaking, my most common cause of an `Access Denied` error is because I can't type my password straight. Therefore, this is the first thing that comes to mind when thinking of items to check when you receive an Access Denied error.
- **Username:** Is it allowed to connect?
- **Hostname or host:** MySQL might not be able to properly identify the user/host combination, in which case it refuses access.

The MySQL CLI is very good at remembering and telling you what was provided to it for credentials. I've provided some examples of error messages in Figure 12-22:

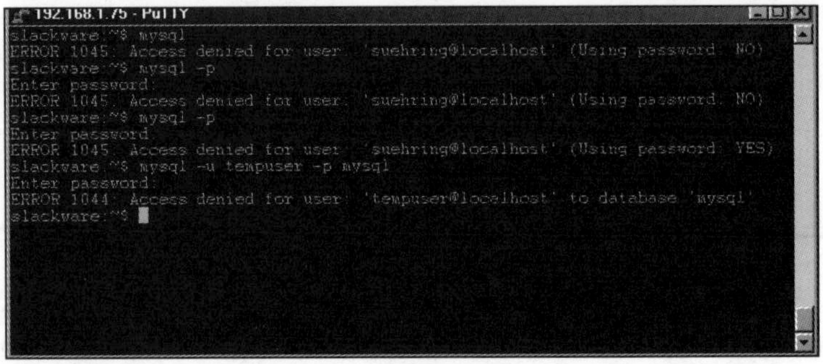

Figure 12-22: Various Access Denied errors

- ✦ In the first example, I simply forget to specify the `-p` switch to have MySQL prompt me for a password.
- ✦ In the second example, I remember the `-p` switch but only press Enter at the prompt.
- ✦ The third example is familiar to me (and to too many of us): a mistyped password.
- ✦ The final example is denied simply because the user does not have any privilege that allows connection to the `mysql` database.

The third example in Figure 12-22 is interesting because that same error can occur if the user exists but the password is different for that user/host combination. For example, if a database has two users called `suehring`, one user/host combination could be `suehring@localhost` and another could be `suehring@192.168.1.1`. If the passwords are different for each user/host combination and I typed the wrong password for either one, the same error would occur.

Note MySQL uses the user/host combination for authentication against a password.

Oops, I forgot the root password

Though you someday may be in a situation that requires you to perform these steps on your MySQL server, I sincerely hope you never have to. If you have forgotten the `root` password for MySQL and don't have any other users with `GRANT` privileges on the database server, you will need to reset the password in order to be able to perform `GRANTS` and possibly other functions. Here are the steps, and may you never need them:

1. Stop the database.

- If you have a user account in the database with the `SHUTDOWN` privilege, now would be the time to use that account. The first step in the process for emergency password recovery is to stop the MySQL server. In a perfect world, you could issue a `SHUTDOWN` command to the MySQL server.
- If you don't have a user with the `SHUTDOWN` privilege, you have to kill the server with an operating-system command (in Linux, this is the `kill` command; in Windows, it's the End Task box that appears after you use Ctrl+Alt+Del).

Caution MySQL AB specifically recommends that you *don't* use the `-9` signal when you issue the operating system's `kill` command.

2. Restart the server with the `--skip-grant-tables` command-line switch.
3. Set the password, using one of the following methods:
   - Set the password as you would for a new installation:

```
mysqladmin -h <hostname> -u root password '<password>'
```

Note The new password must be in single quotes. Substitute your host for *<hostname>* and the new password for *<password>*.

   - Alternatively, you can enter the MySQL CLI and change the password.
4. Issue the `FLUSH PRIVILEGES` statement so that MySQL reads the other grants and privileges and the new password takes effect.

Summary

MySQL security is a topic of many facets, but with three main areas of concern: the host server, the MySQL software, and the user accounts. No one facet is more important than another; securing all is necessary to protect the database. In pursuit of that goal, the least-privilege system is a security approach that gives users only the absolute minimum of access needed to perform their jobs.

✦ Implementing and preserving the security of the host server involves three basic rules:

- Maintain a proactive approach to keeping up with exploits and problems with software you are running.
- Apply patches and fixes as soon as they are released.
- Disable unused services and verify that only the services you specify are running.

- With MySQL software security there are a number of items you can do to improve security. These include keeping the software updated, firewalling the server, running the server as a non-privileged user, and additional steps to assist in security of the MySQL software.
- MySQL authentication and privileges determine what access a user will have for a database. Authentication is done with a user/host combination.
- There are many privileges that can be granted to a user. The privileges can be granted with granularity to the column level with a table.
- Privileges are normally given to a user through the use of the `GRANT` statement and taken away from a user with a `REVOKE` statement. The `DELETE` statement is necessary to remove a user completely from the database.
- It is common to receive `Access Denied` error messages when attempting to connect to a database. These errors can occur for a number of reasons, some as simple as typing the password incorrectly.

✦ ✦ ✦

CHAPTER 13

Debugging and Repairing Databases

✦ ✦ ✦ ✦

In This Chapter

Performing database backups

Troubleshooting and repairing database problems

Restoring a database

Devising a plan for regular backups

✦ ✦ ✦ ✦

In a perfect world, computers and computer software would work correctly the first time. In a perfect world, hard disks would never fail. In a perfect world, I would have a much better introduction for this chapter than a cliché about computer failures.

Part of administration of any computer system is a good routine of backups. In this chapter I'll look at methods for backing up the data in the MySQL server. MySQL AB includes several methods for producing backups of the data and datafiles.

Having backups is just one of the facets of managing a database server. If something goes awry with the data, know what can be done to correct the problems. I'll examine some tools included with MySQL for troubleshooting and repairing table problems.

If repairing can't fix a problem, you'll need to restore from a backup. The restore process and related commands are covered in this chapter as well.

After reading this chapter you should be able to successfully perform backups, restores, and troubleshooting for table problems. I recommend making a backup or two as soon as possible.

Performing Database Backups

As part of my consulting for business database systems, I once received an emergency call from a new client who had the unfortunate incident that everyone fears: A hard drive failure. The client and I tried desperately to recover the drive, even working with the manufacturer. It became evident that no amount of effort to recover the drive was going to bring it back to life. The obvious next step to get their business back online was to restore from backup. I'll never forget the pause when I said, "It appears we'll need to restore from backup." The client had no backup of the drive — thus no backup of the database.

The previous scenario is all too common. No backups are done to critical data and no extra copies are stored, even on the same disk. When something catastrophic happens, the hard drive and all the data on it can be lost. With the client, we eventually sent the hard drive back to the manufacturer and they were able to perform expensive data recovery. The client ended up with a week's worth of downtime and a large bill from the hard drive manufacturer for data recovery.

This section examines some tools for making backups of the data within MySQL. These tools include `mysqlhotcopy`, `mysqldump`, and the `BACKUP TABLE` statement.

mysqlhotcopy

The program `mysqlhotcopy` is the MySQL AB recommended method for backing up a database. With `mysqlhotcopy` you can make a backup of a live database and have the results copied to another directory. The `mysqlhotcopy` program is actually written in Perl — so be sure to have Perl and its related MySQL-Perl libraries installed.

As with all programs, `mysqlhotcopy` has its limitations:

- **It presently supports only `cp`.** Therefore `mysqlhotcopy` doesn't copy the resulting file to another server. However, this function can be added (along with other methods) for ensuring the storage of the backup in a different location.
- **It can run only on the actual database server.** An administrator must connect to the database server to run the command, or schedule it with a scheduling program such as `cron`.

Caution: Because `mysqlhotcopy` uses the `cp` command, it cannot run on Microsoft Windows platforms such as Windows 2000.

Should you want more information on the `mysqlhotcopy` command (and you don't have this book available), you can run the following command:

```
perldoc mysqlhotcopy
```

The result is a summary of the `mysqlhotcopy` command. As with many other MySQL commands and scripts, you can obtain a syntax description by simply typing the command, as shown in Figure 13-1.

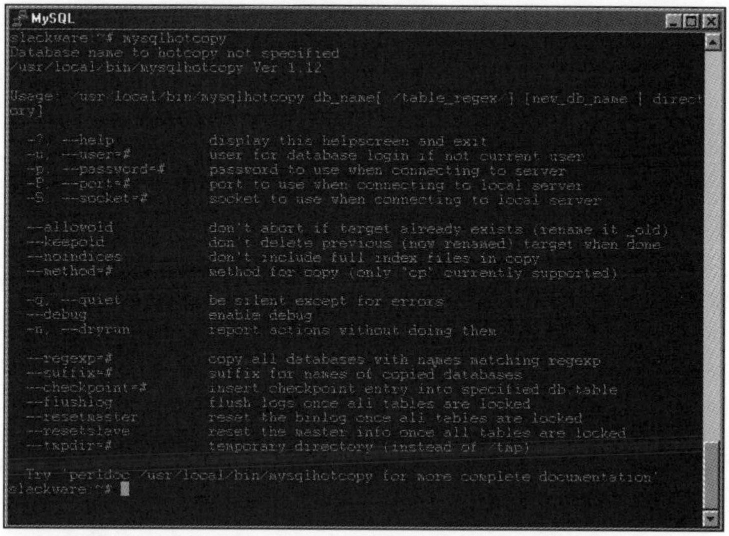

Figure 13-1: The syntax of the mysqlhotcopy command can be obtained by typing the command with no arguments.

As Figure 13-1 shows, the basic syntax for the `mysqlhotcopy` command is

```
mysqlhotcopy <databasename>[./<table_regexp>/]
[<newdatabasename> | <directory>]
```

Figure 13-1 also shows these other options and switches that you can use with the `mysqlhotcopy` command (note the case sensitivity):

`-u` or `--user`

`-S` or `--socket`

`-P` or `--port`

`--debug`

`-q` or `--quiet`

Cross-Reference Chapter 8 contains detailed discussion of switches (such as those for specifying username, port, and socket) to use with the `mysqlhotcopy` command.

One notable exception in the behavior of the switches is the `-p` or `--password` switch. Normally, programs such as the MySQL CLI and `mysqladmin` prompt for a password when you use the `-p` switch (as shown in Figure 13-2). You could also specify the password on the actual command line, also illustrated in Figure 13-2.

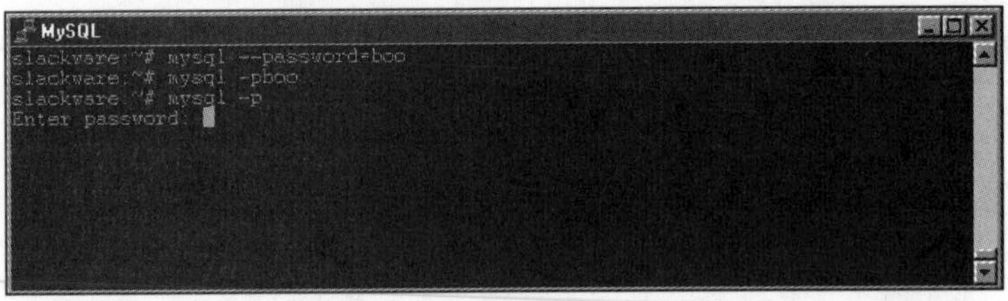

Figure 13-2: The variations of the types of password entry methods for most MySQL commands

Unlike most programs that come with MySQL, `mysqlhotcopy` doesn't prompt for a password. Rather, the password must be specified on the command line. In addition, if you use the -p switch `mysqlhotcopy` expects a space after the `-p`. Figure 13-3 shows an example of this behavior. If the space isn't given after the `-p` switch, an `Invalid Option` error message results.

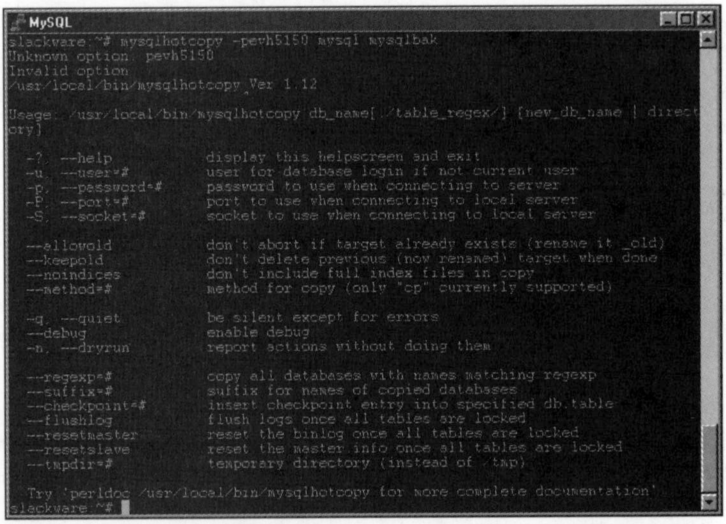

Figure 13-3: Attempting to give the password without a space after the -p switch results in an error.

At its most basic level, the `mysqlhotcopy` script performs the following three steps:

1. Locks the table or tables specified.
2. Flushes the tables to close any open tables.
3. Performs the actual copying of the data files.

- ✦ Because `mysqlhotcopy` performs a lock tables as the first step, no other clients can use the tables while `mysqlhotcopy` runs.
- ✦ The locking can take quite some time on large tables.
- ✦ The flushing of the tables will cause all open tables to close.
- ✦ The actual copy can be time-consuming if the tables are large as well.

The `mysqlhotcopy` script makes an actual electronic copy of the datafiles for the database. Therefore any user account that runs `mysqlhotcopy` must have sufficient privileges to read the directory in which the datafiles reside. For example, Figure 13-4 shows an attempt to run `mysqlhotcopy` as a normal user in Linux. Normal users don't have the requisite privileges on the database directory; the command fails.

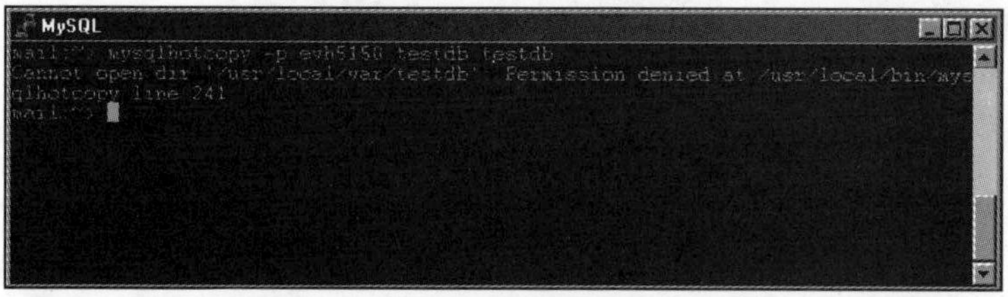

Figure 13-4: mysqlhotcopy requires that the user running the script have sufficient privileges to read the database directory.

A simple summary (a common usage of the `mysqlhotcopy` program) is shown in Figure 13-5. In the figure, the MySQL `grants` database `(mysql)` is copied or backed up to a new database called `mysqlbak`.

Figure 13-5: A common usage of the mysqlhotcopy program to make a copy of the MySQL grants database

mysqlhotcopy also copies any other files within the directory housing the database as well. For example, if you have files such as those produced with mysqldump, performing a mysqlhotcopy of the database copies those to the new location. Figure 13-6 shows an example of this behavior. A listing of the ecommerce database directory is done, then a mysqlhotcopy to make a backup of the database into ecommercebak, followed by a listing of the new ecommercebak directory.

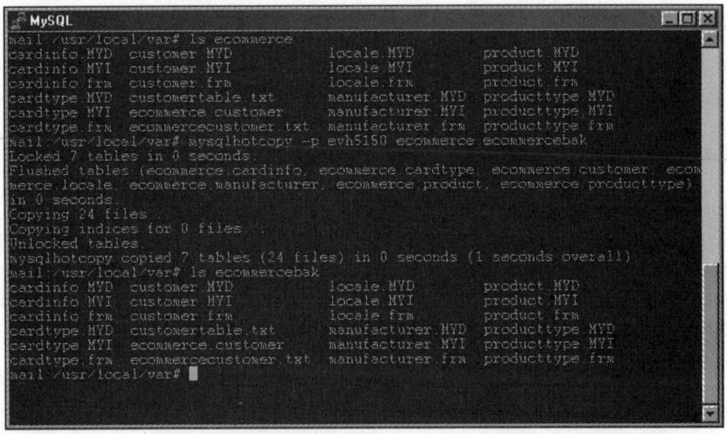

Figure 13-6: The mysqlhotcopy script copies all files located in the database's directory on the server.

Recall the basic syntax for the mysqlhotcopy program:

```
mysqlhotcopy <databasename>[./<table_regexp>/]
[<newdatabasename> | <directory>]
```

You have two possible destinations for the backup:

✦ A new database

✦ A directory in a different location

The examples in Figures 13-5 and 13-6 each made new databases. However, attempting to use either database can result in an error message, as shown in Figure 13-7.

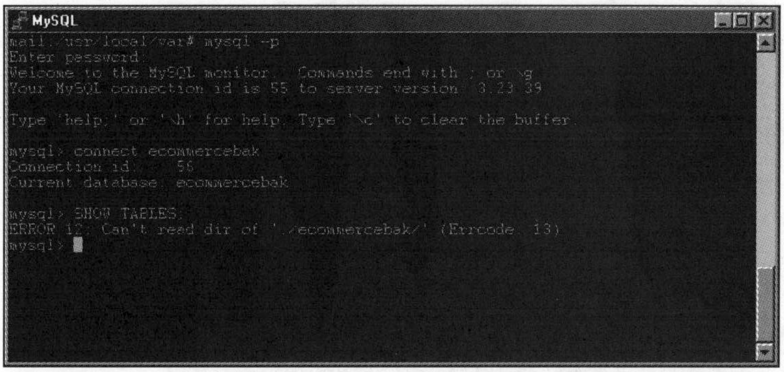

Figure 13-7: The MySQL server does not have sufficient privileges to read the database of a recently backed up database with mysqlhotcopy.

The error in Figure 13-7 occurs because the `mysqlhotcopy` script was run as the `root` or superuser. Therefore the new database directory was created by and is owned by `root`. Because the database server files are owned by the username `mysql` — and the server runs as that user — it cannot read the contents of the new database directory. You can fix this with a command such as `chown`. For example, Figure 13-8 shows the directory ownership and permissions before and after the `chown` command in Linux. Figure 13-8 also shows a successful connection to the backup copy created by `mysqlhotcopy`.

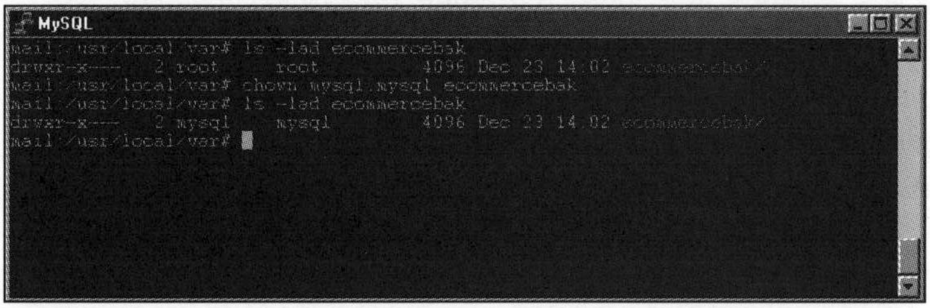

Figure 13-8: Changing ownership of the new database created by mysqlhotcopy

The other method for backing up a database is to another directory. For added precaution, the directory could be on a separate physical disk. Instead of providing a database name for `mysqlhotcopy` to back up to, you specify a directory name. You must make sure that the directory exists. Figure 13-9 shows an example of using `mysqlhotcopy` to make a backup of a database to a directory. In the first attempt, the directory does not exist. The second attempt is successful. A directory listing is provided for convenience.

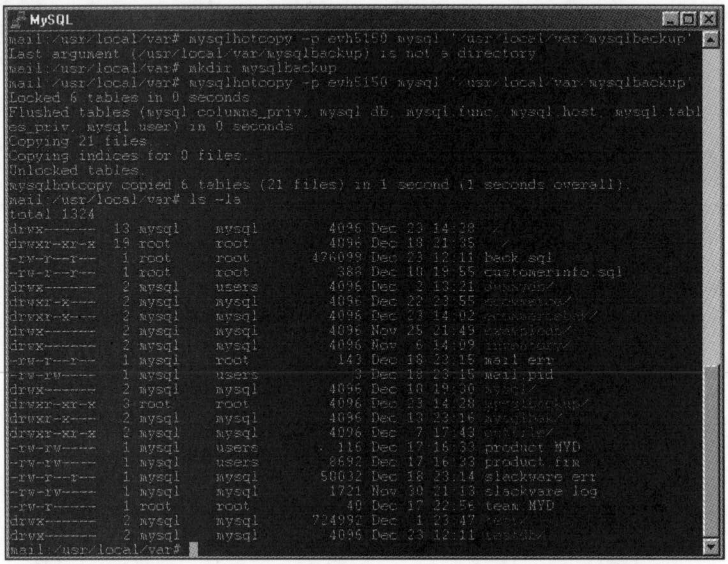

Figure 13-9: Using mysqlhotcopy to make a backup of a MySQL database to a directory

`mysqlhotcopy` isn't limited to simply making backups of the entire database—or even to one database. I'll look at how to back up more than one database within this section as well. For now, I'm going to examine how to make a backup of only certain tables within a database.

Again, recalling the syntax of the `mysqlhotcopy` program, you can specify tables within the format of a regular expression. In effect, you specify the tables that match a certain *pattern* that you want to back up. For example, to back up all tables in the `ecommerce` database that contain the word *product*, the command in Figure 13-10 is issued.

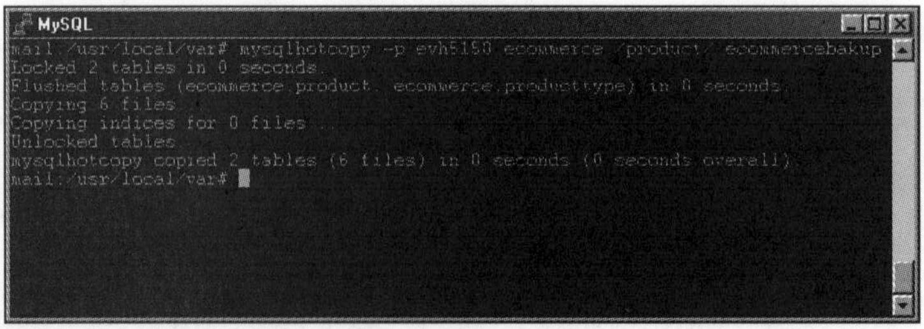

Figure 13-10: Backing up only certain tables with the mysqlhotcopy command

At first, you might not think this method convenient or powerful enough for backing up tables (more than one table cannot be specified). However, by using the regular expression character for logical "OR", you can back up more than one table name with `mysqlhotcopy`. In Figure 13-11, I re-run the command from Figure 13-10 and add the logical `OR` (or the pipe character) to the command because I want to back up the tables that contain the word `card`. Notice that the pipe character must be allowed to "escape" by using a backslash.

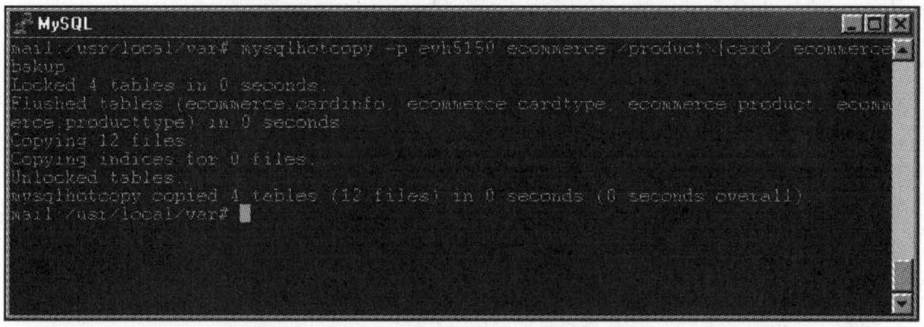

Figure 13-11: Using the regular expression syntax for a logical OR you can back up more than one table with mysqlhotcopy.

Up to this point I've only been looking at the basic syntax of `mysqlhotcopy`. `mysqlhotcopy` includes a number of switches that directly affect the operation of the program. These switches can change which databases are copied, how they are copied, and any extra functions that `mysqlhotcopy` should perform.

When `mysqlhotcopy` makes a backup copy of a database the process fails if there is already a database of the same name. This has the obvious advantage of preventing an accidental overwrite of a vital database. Figure 13-12 shows an example of the error message when the destination database already exists.

Note `mysqlhotcopy` **indicates an error if the destination exists regardless of whether the destination is a database or a directory.**

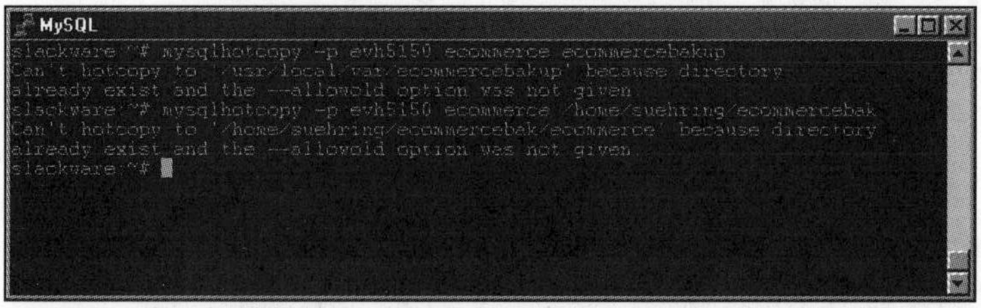

Figure 13-12: If the destination exists, whether it is a database or directory, the mysqlhotcopy script fails and generates the error message shown.

To allow mysqlhotcopy to overwrite the destination database or directory, you use the --allowold switch. The --allowold switch changes the existing destination and appends _old to the name of the existing destination. When the copy is successfully completed, the old directory and files therein are deleted. Figure 13-13 shows an example of this behavior.

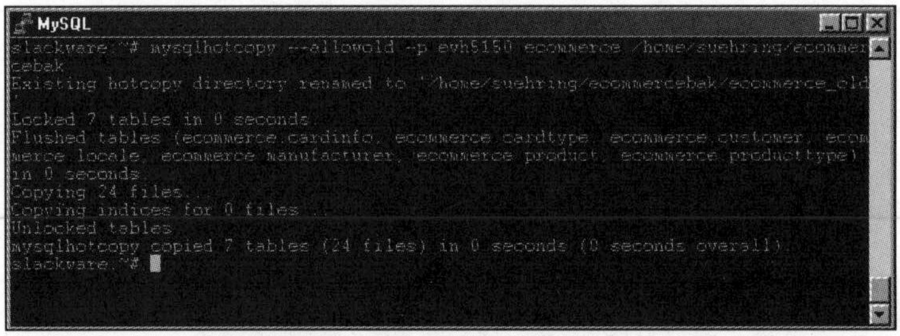

Figure 13-13: The --allowold switch moves the existing destination and appends the extension _old to the name. After the copy is complete, the old directory is deleted.

Although the --allowold switch enables you to perform a backup even if the stated destination already exists, mysqlhotcopy deletes the old copy as its final step in the backup process. If you want to keep the old copy after the command is complete, use the --keepold switch. Figure 13-14 shows mysqlhotcopy with the --keepold switch added as well as a listing of the MySQL data directory after the mysqlhot-copy command runs to keep the old copy of the data using the --keepold switch.

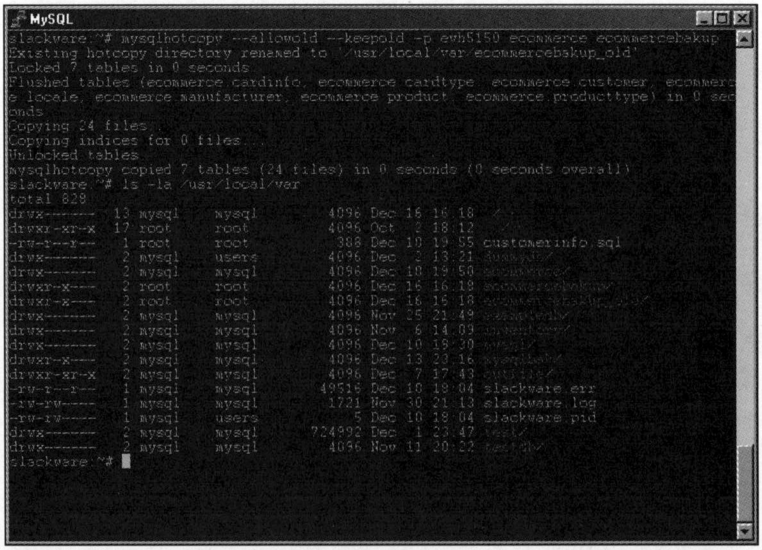

Figure 13-14: Adding the --keepold switch tells mysqlhotcopy to keep the old destination after performing a copy where the destination already exists.

To copy more than one database at a time, you can use the `--regexp` switch to create a regular expression of matching databases. This switch uses a syntax similar to the one that tells `mysqlhotcopy` which tables to copy. Figure 13-15 shows an example of the `--regexp` switch in action.

Caution The `--regexp` option does not run well currently; it may be fixed in a future version of `mysqlhotcopy`.

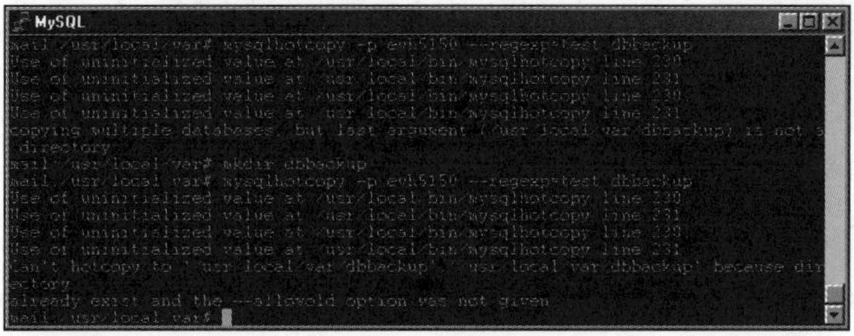

Figure 13-15: The --regexp switch serves to copy more than one database at a time but is currently quite buggy.

You can also specify a suffix for copied databases with the `--suffix` switch. Doing so can help to keep a standard suffix for all backed-up databases. In Figure 13-16, for example, I use the `--suffix` switch to create a backup with an extension of `_bak`.

Figure 13-16: Using the --suffix switch to create a backup with a special extension

To see an example of what `mysqlhotcopy` would do given a set of arguments, use the `-n` or `--dryrun` switch. The `-n` or `--dryrun` switch provides a listing of what would happen without actually performing the operation. An example of the `--dryrun` switch is shown in Figure 13-17.

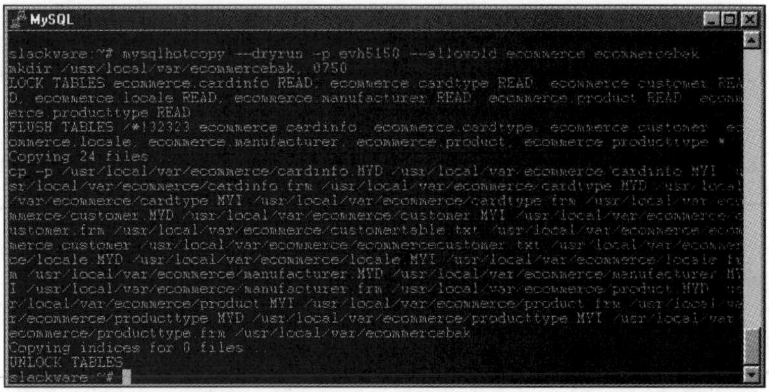

Figure 13-17: Using the --dryrun or -n switch you can see what would happen with mysqlhotcopy without actually performing the backup.

Other options for `mysqlhotcopy` include the following:

Option	*Description*
`--noindices`	Excludes any index files from the backup.
`--flushlog`	Performs the same functions as the `flush-logs` function with `mysqladmin` to reset any logging. Related to replication,
`--resetmaster`	Restarts the replication process.
`--resetslave`	Restarts the replication process.
`--tmpdir`	Changes the location of the temporary directory used by `mysqlhotcopy` (which is `/tmp` by default).

Later this chapter provides an example of a script that automates the process of making backups with `mysqlhotcopy`.

On the CD-ROM

The script for automating backups with `mysqlhotcopy` is also located on the CD ROM included with this book.

mysqldump

With `mysqldump`, you can obtain a copy of the database structure, as well as the actual data for all databases on the server. The `mysqldump` command is flexible enough that you can specify structural units as small as tables and export them. Taking the output from `mysqldump` and importing it back into MySQL, you can quickly reproduce an entire database server, along with all its data.

Cross-Reference For further details of the `mysqldump` program, see Chapter 10.

For example, in Figure 13-18 the `mysqldump` command runs to create a backup of all databases on the server and place the contents in a file called `serverbackup.sql`. The contents of the file include the DDL to create the databases and internal structure for the databases. The file also includes the DML and data contained in the databases.

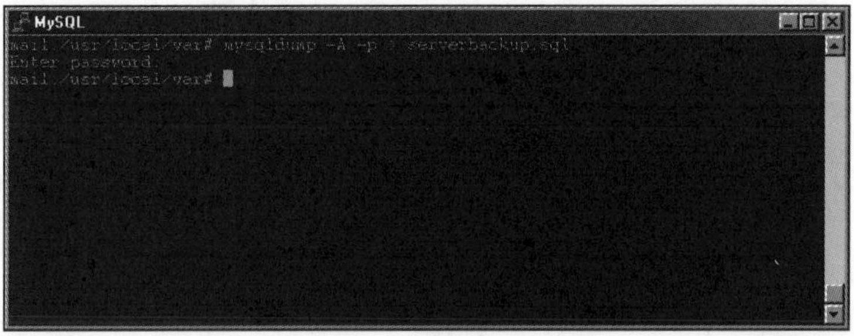

Figure 13-18: Using mysqldump to export the entire contents of a database server including DDL and DML

The file created by `mysqldump` could then be saved or archived to a remote location or tape drive. Because `mysqldump` can be run from a remote machine, the file would automatically be a redundant backup in case of hardware failure on the MySQL server. If the hard drive fails on the MySQL server, the file produced by `mysqldump` on the remote machine would still be intact.

The file produced by `mysqldump` can then be imported into a new MySQL server by simply reading it in through the CLI. Figure 13-19 shows an example of reading the output of a `mysqldump` into the CLI. No output or success message prints to the screen upon completion.

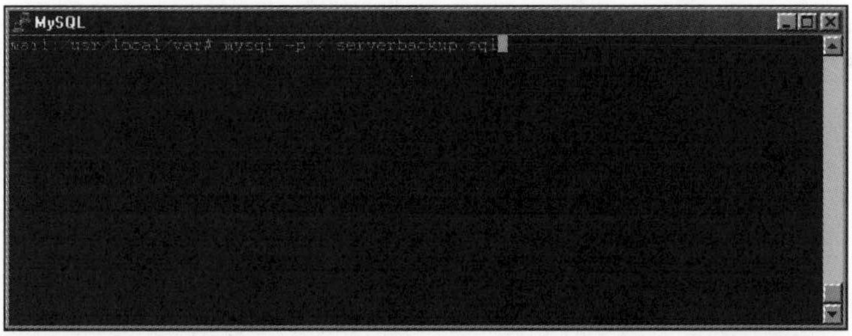

Figure 13-19: Importing the output of a mysqldump file is as easy as reading it into the CLI.

BACKUP TABLE

Another method for backing up an individual table is via the BACKUP TABLE statement. This statement runs from within (or using) the MySQL CLI. The syntax is as follows:

```
BACKUP TABLE <tablename>(, <tablename>) TO '<directory>'
```

The BACKUP TABLE statement expects a path and directory as the argument for backup location. The statement currently only works with MyISAM tables as well. The BACKUP TABLE statement makes a copy of the .frm and .MYD files for the given table. If you're backing up more than one table at a time, you should issue a LOCK TABLES statement before the BACKUP TABLE statement to ensure consistency amongst the tables. Don't forget to issue a FLUSH TABLES statement upon completion.

Upon completion, the BACKUP TABLE statement prints a status message. If an error occurs, its message is also printed as part of the BACKUP TABLE output. For example, if the target directory does not exist, you receive a message similar to that in Figure 13-20.

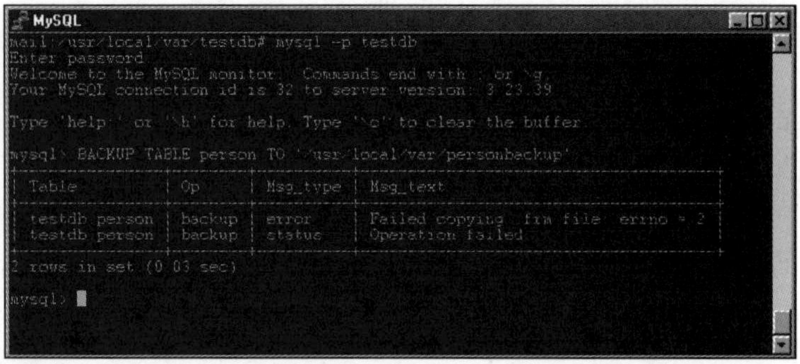

Figure 13-20: The BACKUP TABLE statement produces a status message upon completion, as well as an error message if needed.

In Figure 13-21, a successful example of the BACKUP TABLE statement is shown—along with the resulting status message.

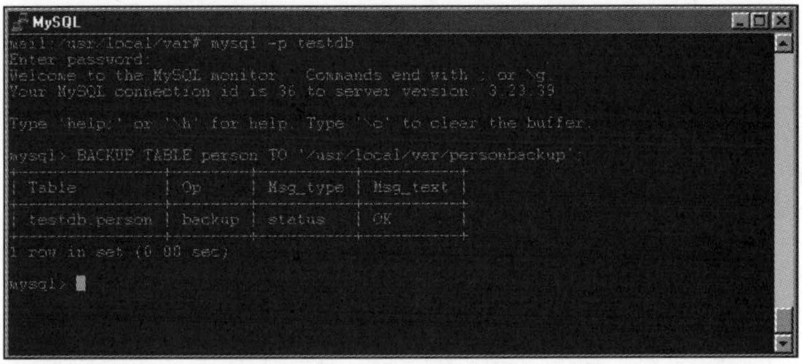

Figure 13-21: A successful run of the BACKUP TABLE statement

Troubleshooting and Repairing Table Problems

I once had a client who, instead of logging in to a machine and typing *reboot*, would simply turn the machine off and then back on. He couldn't figure out why the files on the system were corrupt and some tables in the database would often give errors and need repair. He blamed the corruption and errors on just about everything else, and didn't even think that turning the machine off *without shutting down the applications* could affect the integrity of anything on the computer. MySQL is a stable and robust database server, but even MySQL would have a hard time maintaining data integrity in such a situation.

Although I can't say that table corruption never results from an error in the database itself, normally the server maintains the integrity of its data at all times. Instances of table errors and corruption usually point to a dirty shutdown of MySQL or the server, a hardware failure, or some other catastrophe not directly related to the MySQL server.

When a failure does occur, make sure you have backups of both the data *and* the table structure that keeps your data organized. Having current and quality backups is the first line of defense in administration of the MySQL server. Aside from catastrophe, tables can sometimes suffer from fragmentation. This can occur because of deletes and updates to a table. Knowing how to optimize tables is another aspect of administration of a MySQL server.

This section examines the commands and statements you use for troubleshooting and repairing tables in MySQL. Most of the section concentrates on the `MyISAM` table type (the default in MySQL), although some tools can be used with the `BerkeleyDB` (BDB) transactional table type.

mysqlcheck

`mysqlcheck` is a relatively new command for working with `MyISAM` tables.

Note: The `myisamchk` program requires you to stop the server before running checks or repairs. However, the `mysqlcheck` command allows the server to be running while performing the checks and repairs.

Caution: If a client is working with the table at the same time that `mysqlcheck` attempts the requested operation, the operation fails.

The `mysqlcheck` command serves as the basis for most other troubleshooting functions with MySQL.

Cross-Reference: Like other commands with MySQL, `mysqlcheck` has many command-line switches and options the same. Refer to Chapter 8 on the MySQL CLI for full explanation of the common options, such as `-#` or `--debug`, `--character-sets-dir`, `--default-character-set`, `--compress`, `-?` or `--help`, `-h` or `--host`, `-p` or `--password`, `-P` or `--port`, `-S` or `--socket`, `-u` or `--user`, and `-V` or `--version`.

Tip: As with many other commands with MySQL, you can obtain a syntax reference simply by typing the command, as shown in Figure 13-22.

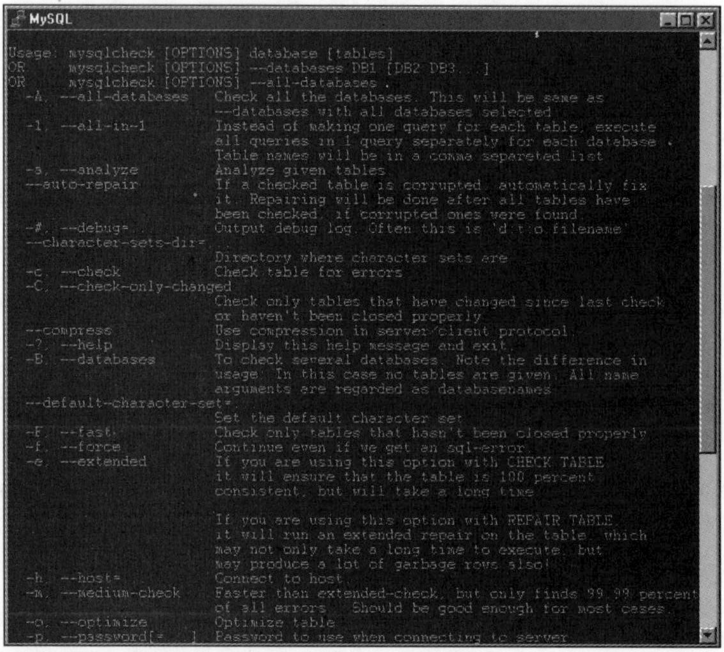

Figure 13-22: Typing mysqlcheck with no options yields a syntax and options reference for the command.

The basic syntax for the `mysqlcheck` command is as follows:

```
mysqlcheck [OPTIONS] database [tables]
```

When called with no options, `mysqlcheck` examines the tables within the given database for errors. If no errors are found, a status message of `OK` is printed for each table, as shown in Figure 13-23.

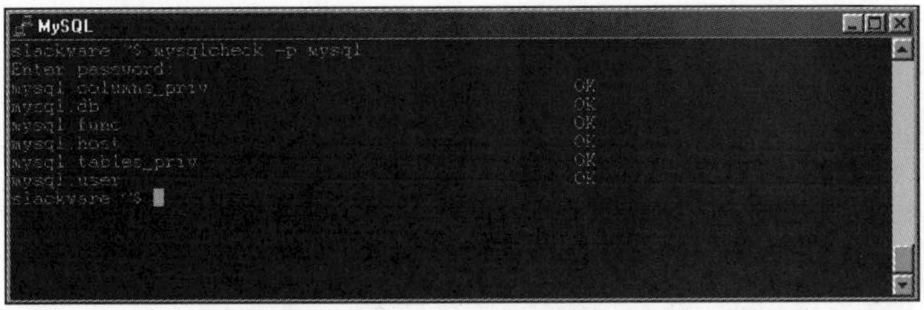

Figure 13-23: Mysqlcheck prints an OK status message for each table free from errors during the default check operation.

Mysqlcheck also includes a function to analyze the key distribution for a table. This function is called with the `-a` or `--analyze` switch on the command line. The output when using this function is the same as with the default use of mysqlcheck when called with no options; the command outputs an `OK` status message. If the table does not need further analysis the status message is `Table is already up to date`. For example, if no changes have taken place, `mysqlcheck` recognizes this fact and does not perform additional analysis, as shown in Figure 13-24.

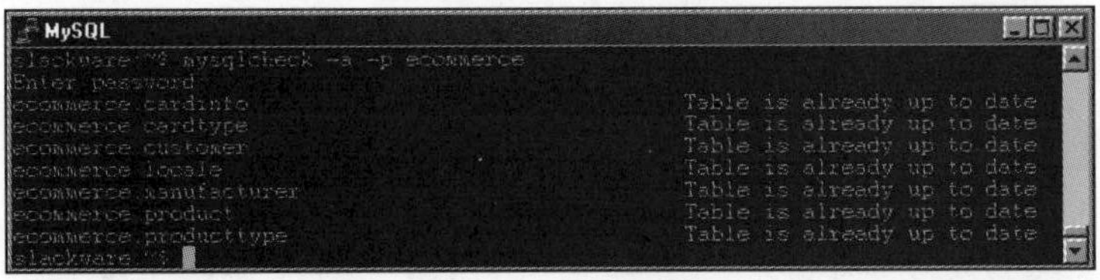

Figure 13-24: Mysqlcheck -a outputs a different status message if the table does not need analysis.

If you perform a large number of deletes or other changes to a table, you can improve performance by using the `-o` or `--optimize` switch with mysqlcheck. Optimizing the table will defragment the table. Like the process for analyzing a table, the optimization process will provide a status message for tables within the database.

The final main function with mysqlcheck is to repair the table. This function is called with the `-r` or `--repair` option. The repair function can fix most any problem with a table. However, the repair function can sometimes lose data; therefore I'll stress again to make sure you have backups. If `mysqlcheck` reports an error and you're going to repair it, it is always a good idea to check the integrity of your backups before proceeding. Figure 13-25 shows an example of `mysqlcheck` repairing a table. (Note that I purposely corrupted the table for this example.)

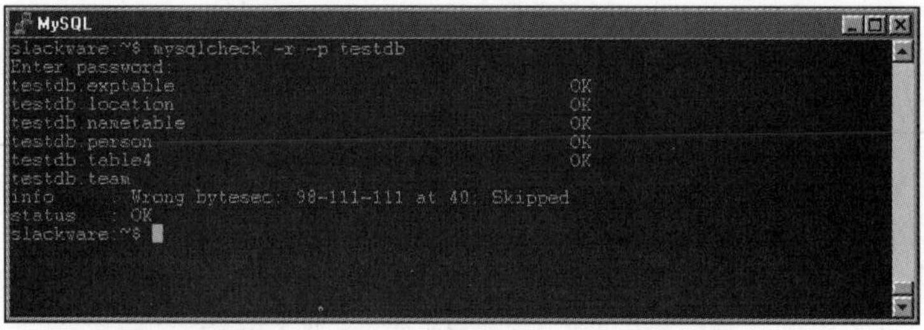

Figure 13-25: Using mysqlcheck to repair a corrupt table

When you use the main (default) option to check databases and tables with which `mysqlcheck`, you have several levels or degrees at which to examine the table(s) for errors:

Command	*Function*
`-c` or `--check`	The default option; checks all tables.
`-C` or `--check-only-changed`	Checks only tables that have changed since the last check.
`-F` or `--fast`	Looks for and examines tables that weren't closed properly.
`-q` or `--quick`	Does not check row-level objects.
`-m` or `--medium-check`	
`-e` or `--extended`	

If you want for `mysqlcheck` to automatically repair any errors it finds, add the `--auto-repair` switch. Figure 13-26 shows an example of using the `auto-repair` switch with `mysqlcheck` to repair a broken table.

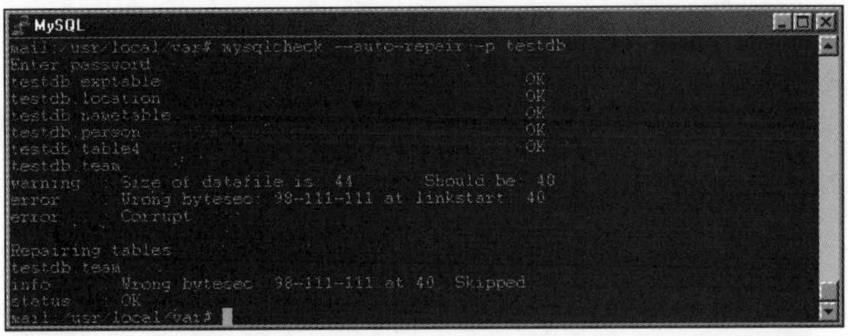

Figure 13-26: Use the --auto-repair switch to automatically repair a table when a problem is found.

Two functions defined with `mysqlcheck` examine all databases or more than one specified database.

Command	*Function*
`--all-databases`	Runs the specified operation on all databases within the MySQL server.
`-B` or `--databases`	Checks more than one, but not all, databases; used with the names of the databases separated by whitespace. Figure 13-27 shows an example of the `--databases` switch in use, examining three databases on the server.

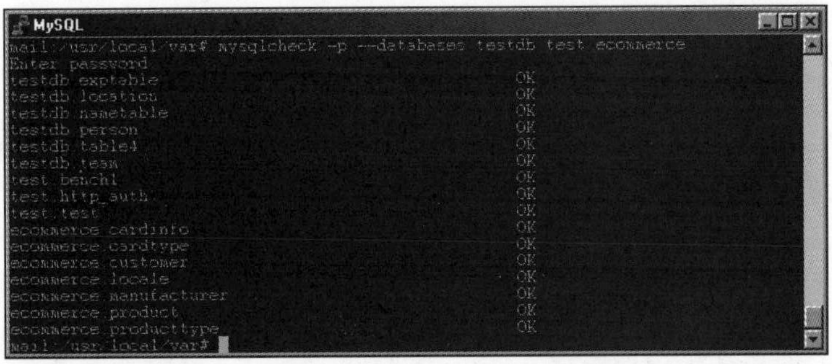

Figure 13-27: The --databases switch examines one or more databases with mysqlcheck.

If you want to only examine certain tables within a database, use the `--tables` switch. Because delete operations can cause fragmentation, you can speed up your examination by adding a `--tables` *<tablename>* clause so the `mysqlcheck` command examines only the specified table(s). To specify more than one table, separate the tablenames with whitespace. Figure 13-28 shows an example of `mysqlcheck` examining certain tables with the `--tables` switch.

Note The --tables switch cannot be used with the --databases or -B switch.

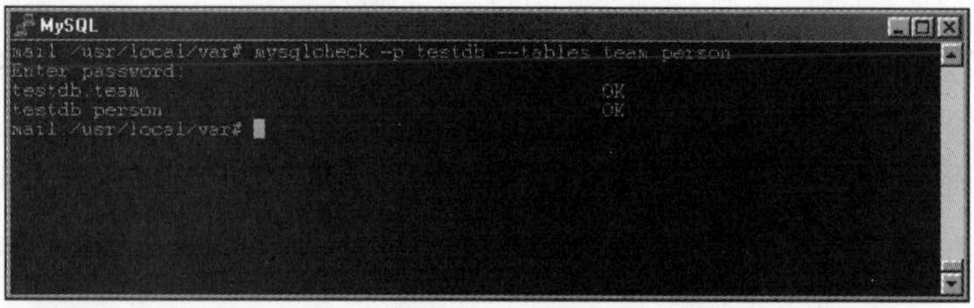

Figure 13-28: The --tables switch causes mysqlcheck to examine only the specified table or tables.

To change the performance of `mysqlcheck` the `-1` or `--all-in-one` switch can be used. This switch causes `mysqlcheck` to use a single query for all operations within a given database. This is as opposed to the normal behavior of one query per table.

The `-F` or `--force` option causes `mysqlcheck` to continue its operation even if an error is encountered. Using this option can sometimes cause corruption or other problems.

myisamchk

The `myisamchk` utility serves to check and repair `MyISAM` tables while the MySQL server is offline. Much of the syntax and many of the switches for `myisamchk` are the same as those for `mysqlcheck`.

The switches that `mysqlcheck` shares in common with other MySQL utilities include those for obtaining help and setting default character sets. As with the other utilities, I'll forego coverage of the following basic switches in this section:

-# or –debug

`--character-sets-dir`

`--default-character-set`

`--compress`

`-O` or `--set-variable`

-? **or** --help

-V **or** --version

The basic syntax for myisamchk is as follows:

```
myisamchk [OPTIONS] <tablename>[.MYI] (<tablename>[.MYI])
```

myisamchk has global options aside from those previously described. The --wait switch informs myisamchk to pause if the table is already locked. Using the -s switch causes myisamchk to be quieter as it goes about its business. Multiple -s switches can make the command even more silent. The -v switch causes myisamchk to print more information as it works. As with the -s switch, you can use more than one -v switch to increase the verbosity of myisamchk.

myisamchk has two basic modes of operation: Check and Repair. The default action for myisamchk is to check the tables specified. Figure 13-29 shows a basic usage of myisamchk.

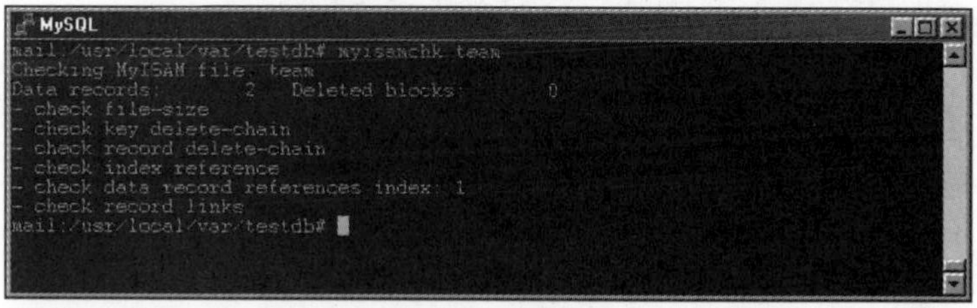

Figure 13-29: An example of basic usage of myisamchk

Options for checking tables with myisamchk

The options relating to checking tables with myisamchk are as follows:

-c **or** --check

-e **or** --extended-check

-F **or** --fast

-C **or** --check-only-changed

-f **or** --force

-i **or** --information

-m **or** --medium-check

-U **or** --update-state

-T **or** --read-only

The `-c` switch (which instructs the utility to check) is the default with `myisamchk`. The `--extended-check`, `--fast`, `--check-only-changed`, `--force`, and `--medium-check` options were discussed in the preceding section on `mysqlcheck`.

The `--information` switch prints more information on the table(s) examined. Figure 13-30 shows an example of the `myisamchk` command run with the `-i` switch. Compare the results to Figure 13-29 to see the extra information printed.

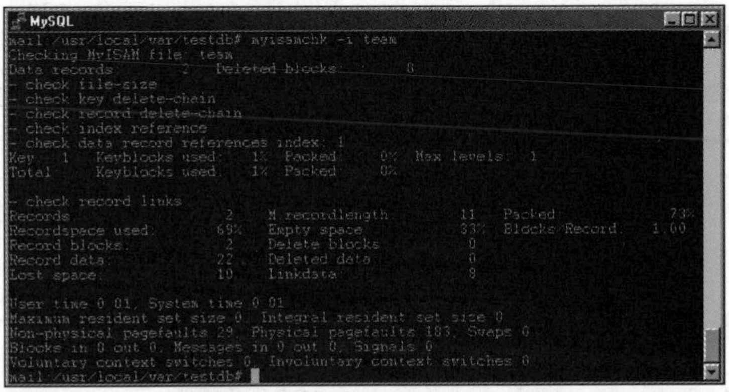

Figure 13-30: Using the -i or --information switch tells myisamchk to print more information about the table or tables that it examines.

The `-T` or `--read-only` switch tells `myisamchk` not to update the `Check_time` table variable. (Information about tables can be obtained with the `SHOW TABLE STATUS` statement using the CLI.) Normally, when `myisamchk` operates on a table, it updates the `Check_time` variable. Examples of the `-T` or `--read-only` switch appear in Figures 13-31 through 13-33.

Figure 13-31, the `SHOW TABLE STATUS` statement displays a table that hasn't been checked recently. Figure 13-32 shows a run of the `myisamchk` command with the `-T` switch. (Notice that the command operates the same as it would without the `-T` switch.) Figure 13-33 shows the `SHOW TABLE STATUS` command run again; notice that `Check_time` still hasn't changed.

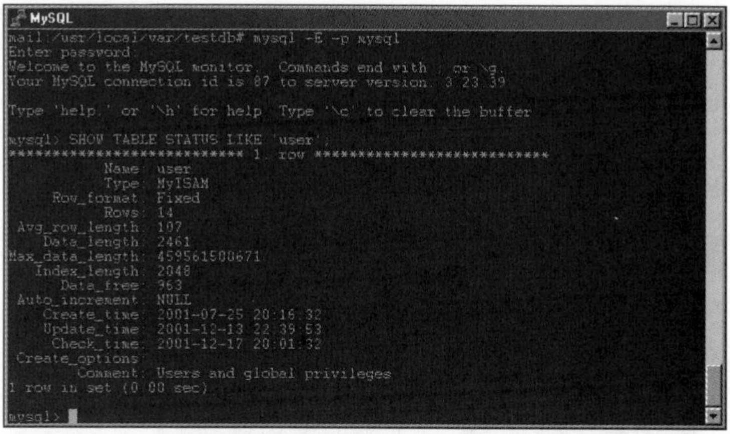

Figure 13-31: The SHOW TABLE STATUS statement shows that the table hasn't been checked recently.

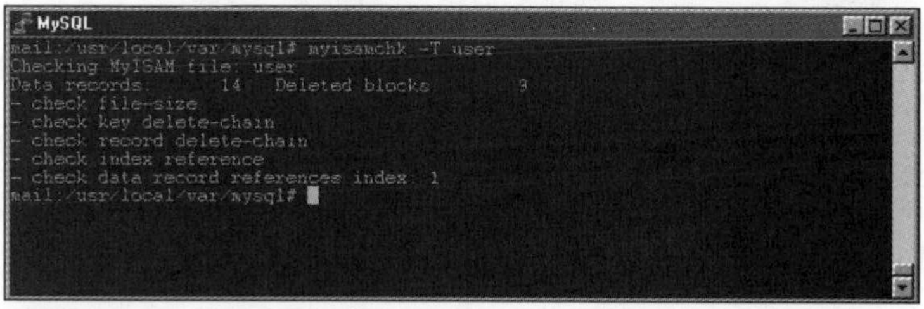

Figure 13-32: Performing a myisamchk with the -T switch that causes the Check_time to not be updated.

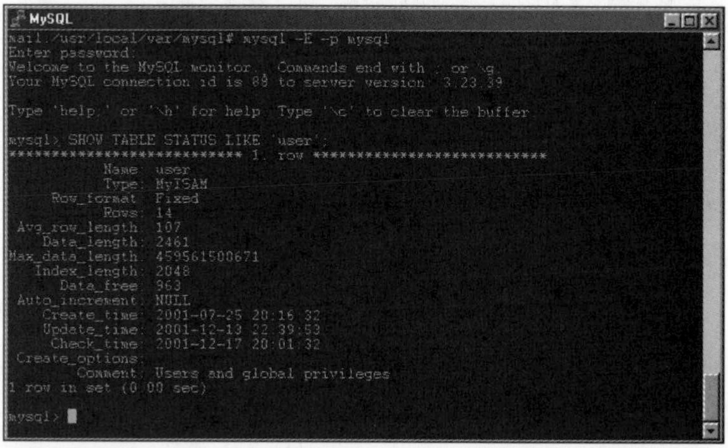

Figure 13-33: Looking at the output from SHOW TABLE STATUS again, the value for Check_time has indeed remained the same even though I checked the table with myisamchk.

If you suspect a table contains errors or corruption and want to prevent further use of the table, the `-U` or `--update-state` switch with `myisamchk` marks any table where an error is found as a *crashed table*—which effectively prevents any further use of the table, even with a `SELECT` statement, until the table is repaired. Clients attempting to work with the table receive an error message. Figure 13-34 shows an example of a simple `SELECT` statement performed on a table, using the MySQL CLI.

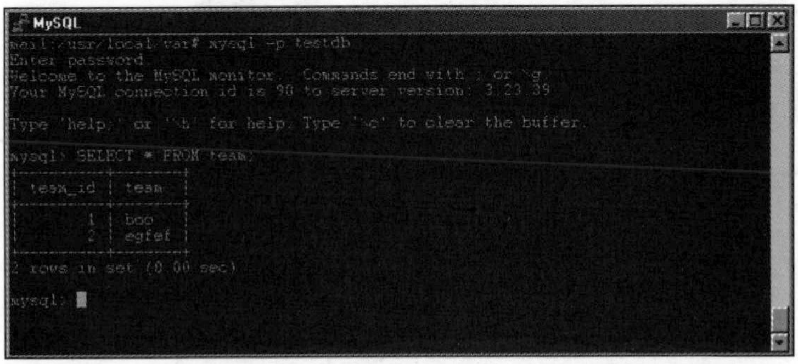

Figure 13-34: A simple SELECT statement, performed through the CLI on a table that I suspect to be corrupt

Although there's no way to tell from the `SELECT` statement, I suspect that this table might be corrupt. Therefore I perform a `myisamchk` on the table and use the `-U` switch, as shown in Figure 13-35.

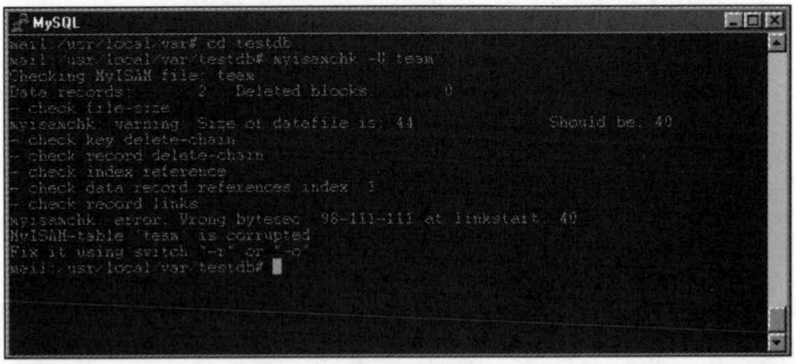

Figure 13-35: Running myisamchk with the -U switch to mark the table as crashed and prevent further use

Figure 13-36 shows what happens when I attempt to run the previously successful `SELECT` statement on the table again. The `SELECT` statement fails because the table is marked as crashed—which (even if it seems inconvenient at the moment) actually helps by preventing further corruption or invalid results.

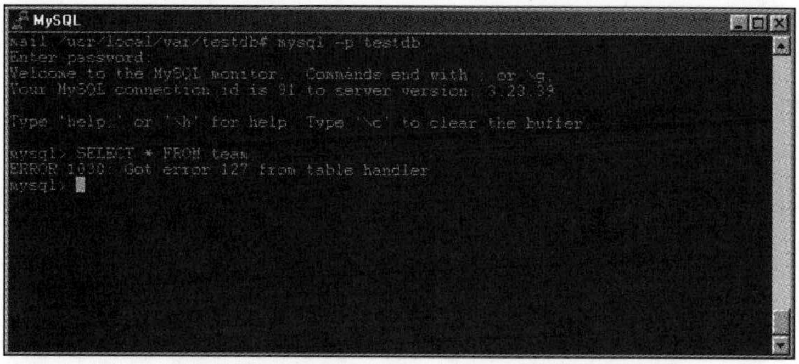
MySQL
mail /usr/local/var/testdb# mysql -p testdb
Enter password:
Welcome to the MySQL monitor. Commands end with ; or \g.
Your MySQL connection id is 91 to server version: 3.23.39
Type 'help;' or '\h' for help. Type '\c' to clear the buffer.
mysql> SELECT * FROM team
ERROR 1030: Got error 127 from table handler
mysql>

Figure 13-36: The same SELECT statement that was previously successful now fails because the table is marked as crashed.

Options for repairing tables with myisamchk

Because checking is the default option with `myisamchk`, you can only use the repair or recover function by specifying the `-r` or `--recover` switch on the `myisamchk` command line.

> **Tip:** If the normal `-r` switch fails, the options that repair or recover tables with `myisamchk` can also be used with the `-o` or `--safe-recover` switch

The repair or recover switches are as follows:

- `-B` or `--backup`
- `-D` or `--data-file-length`
- `-e` or `--extend-check`
- `-f` or `--force`
- `-k` or `--keys-used`
- `-l` or `--no-symlinks`
- `-n` or `--sort-recover`
- `-t` or `--tmpdir`
- `-q` or `--quick`
- `-u` or `--unpack`

A basic repair or recovery with `myisamchk` can be run with the following command syntax:

```
myisamchk -r -q <tablename>
```

Figure 13-37 shows the results of this command.

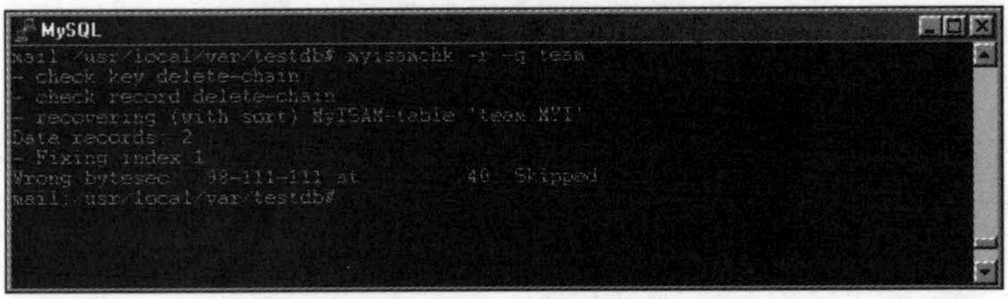

Figure 13-37: A basic quick repair with myisamchk

`myisamchk` does not necessarily use memory efficiently for repairs. Therefore you should set variables on the myisamchk command line using the `-O` or `--set-variable` switch. Doing so will make the repair process faster. Ideally, the key_buffer and sort_buffer values would be about a quarter of the total system memory to maximize efficiency of the myisamchk repair.

The following variables affect the performance of `myisamchk`:

```
key_buffer_size
read_buffer_size
write_buffer_size
sort_buffer_size
sort_key_blocks
decode_bits
```

To determine the current setting for the variables, simply type the `myisamchk` command with no arguments (as shown in Figure 13-38).

Tip: You can type the command shown in Figure 13-38 safely while the server runs.

As stated previously, the variables can be set on the command line using the `-O` or `--set-variable` switch (as shown in Figure 13-39). The variables can also be set inside the configuration file such as `my.cnf` in Linux. To set the variables in the configuration file, place them underneath the `[myisamchk]` section.

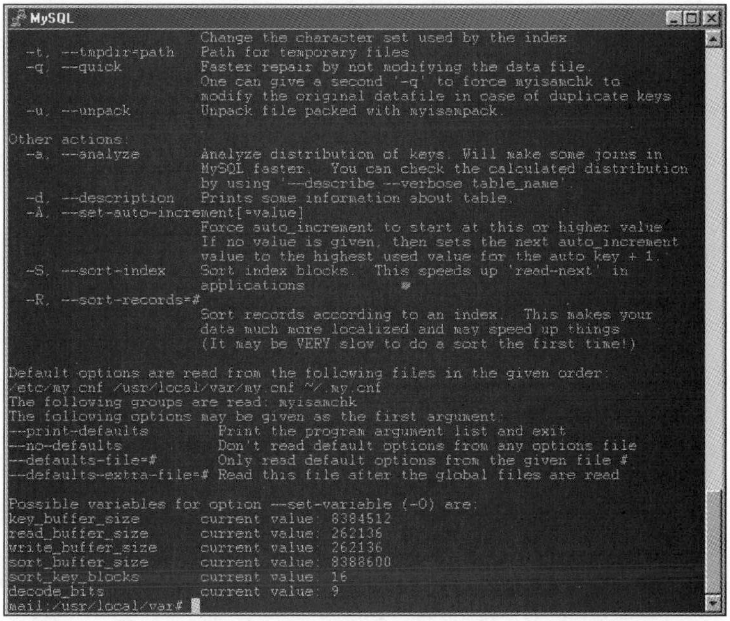

Figure 13-38: Determining the current values for myisamchk variables is done by simply typing the myisamchk command without switches or arguments.

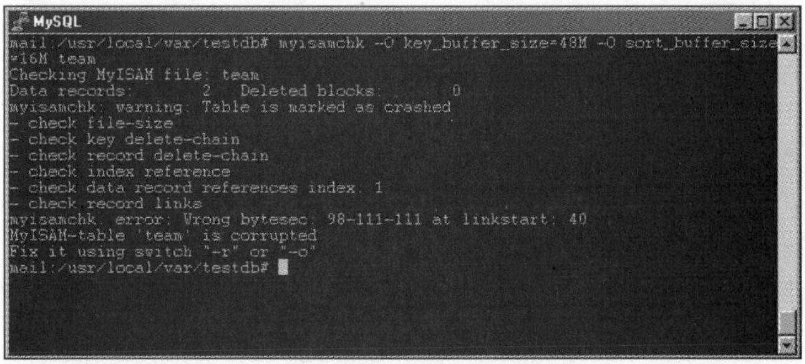

Figure 13-39: Setting variables on the myisamchk command line by using the -O switch.

One of the more important options to use when repairing a table is the `-B` or `--backup` switch. Using the `--backup` switch will cause `myisamchk` to make a backup copy of the data file before you attempt to repair or optimize it. Doing so can be extremely helpful if you want to safeguard the table contents where a repair or optimize function might cause a problem.

If you have a problem with a table that the normal repair process cannot fix, you may want to attempt the `-e` or `--extend-check` option. This switch tries to recover every row from a table. If you'd like to get a faster repair, the `-q` or `--quick` option performs the recovery without modifying the data file. The use of two `-q` switches on the command line fixes duplicate index values.

Three file-system options that affect the performance of `myisamchk` are

Command	*Function*
`-t` or `-tmpdir`	Changes the location that `myisamchk` uses for the temporary directory.
`-l` or `--no-symlinks`	Tells `myisamchk` not to follow symbolic links in the file system when examining tables.
`-u` or `-unpack`	Causes `myisamchk` to unarchive a file packed with `myisampack`.

ANALYZE TABLE

The `ANALYZE TABLE` statement runs through (or using) the MySQL CLI. It is the equivalent of running `mysqlcheck` with the `--analyze` switch.

Cross-Reference

For more information on optimizing tables, see the section on `mysqlcheck` in this chapter.

OPTIMIZE TABLE

The `OPTIMIZE TABLE` statement runs through (or using) the MySQL CLI. It is the equivalent of running `mysqlcheck` with the `--optimize` switch. Optimizing a table is useful if you have changed variable length rows or deleted many rows from a table. It reduces fragmentation within the tables that it checks. The syntax for the `OPTIMIZE TABLE` statement is as follows:

```
OPTIMIZE TABLE <tablename>(, <tablename>)
```

Cross-Reference

For more information on optimizing tables, see the section on `mysqlcheck` in this chapter.

CHECK TABLE

The CHECK TABLE statement runs through (or using) the MySQL CLI. It is the equivalent of running `mysqlcheck` with the `--check` switch or with no arguments at all, as it is the default for `mysqlcheck`.

Cross-Reference

For more information on optimizing tables, see the section on `mysqlcheck` in this chapter.

REPAIR TABLE

The `REPAIR TABLE` statement runs through (or using) the MySQL CLI. It is the equivalent of running `mysqlcheck` with the `--repair` switch.

Cross-Reference

For more information on optimizing tables, see the section on `mysqlcheck` in this chapter.

Restoring a MySQL Database

Restoring a database can be a stressful process — the database or server may have crashed, causing problems that need to be corrected; the repair process may not have worked on a corrupt table; a user may have inadvertently deleted all the data. Whatever the reason, a good backup can save the day. A previous section in this chapter discussed the process of creating the backups. This section looks at how to restore them.

There is no universally right or wrong way to restore from a backup, but there is a universally practical principle to use: *How you restore from a backup is determined by how the backup was created.* Consider these examples:

- ✦ If you used `mysqlhotcopy` to make the backup, you can use `mysqlhotcopy` to restore the database — or simply copy the database directory to the proper location and recreate the privileges for the individual accounts.
- ✦ If you created the backup by using the `BACKUP TABLE` statement, the `RESTORE TABLE` statement would be the natural complement.
- ✦ If you created the backup by using the `mysqldump` utility, then you can restore using the MySQL CLI.

mysqlhotcopy

The `mysqlhotcopy` program is for making backups of entire database directories. However, you can also use `mysqlhotcopy` to restore from a previously backed-up copy of a database directory. For example, suppose you've used `mysqlhotcopy` to create a backup of the `ecommerce` database called `ecommercebak`. If something happens to the `ecommerce` database and you have to restore it, the `mysqlhotcopy` program can do so.

The following command would restore the `ecommercebak` database to the `ecommerce` directory and make a backup of the broken `ecommerce` database at the same time:

```
mysqlhotcopy -p <password> --allowold --keepold ecommercebak
ecommerce
```

> **Note**
>
> Often, when `mysqlhotcopy` creates a backup, it doesn't update the permissions properly for your database server. Therefore using this utility to restore from a backup may generate a `No tables to copy` error. If you receive this error message, check the ownership of the directory holding the backup.

The results of this command are shown in Figure 13-40.

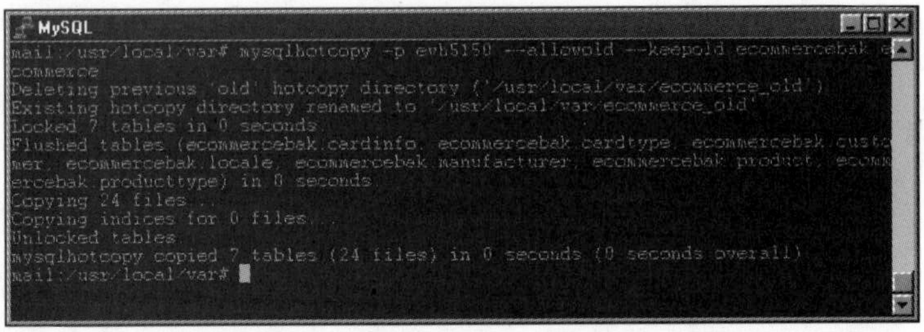

Figure 13-40: Restoring a previously backed-up database with the mysqlhotcopy program

RESTORE TABLE

The `RESTORE TABLE` statement is the complement to the `BACKUP TABLE` statement. If you used the `BACKUP TABLE` statement to back up your tables, you can easily restore them to your MySQL server by using the `RESTORE TABLE` statement with the MySQL CLI. The syntax for the `RESTORE TABLE` statement is as follows:

```
RESTORE TABLE <tablename> (, <tablename>) FROM '<directory>'
```

Like the BACKUP TABLE statement, the RESTORE TABLE statement produces a status message as the output for the command. Even an error message can serve as a kind of status message in this context. For example, earlier in the chapter (refer to Figure 13-21), I created a backup of the table testdb.person and put it in the directory /usr/local/var/personbackup. Suppose I try to restore that table through the CLI, using the following command:

```
RESTORE TABLE person FROM '/usr/local/var/personbackup'
```

The table already exists — so MySQL doesn't restore the table, producing (instead) the error message shown in Figure 13-41.

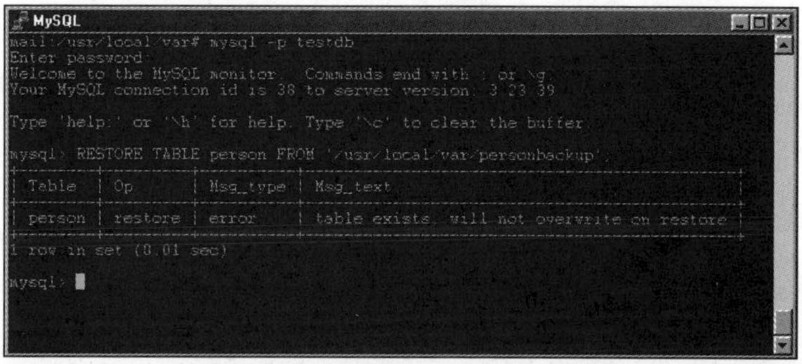

Figure 13-41: Attempting to overwrite an existing table causes a failure.

Before restoring from a backup with the RESTORE TABLE statement, you must drop the table. Figure 13-42 shows the DROP TABLE statement along with the successful results from the RESTORE TABLE statement.

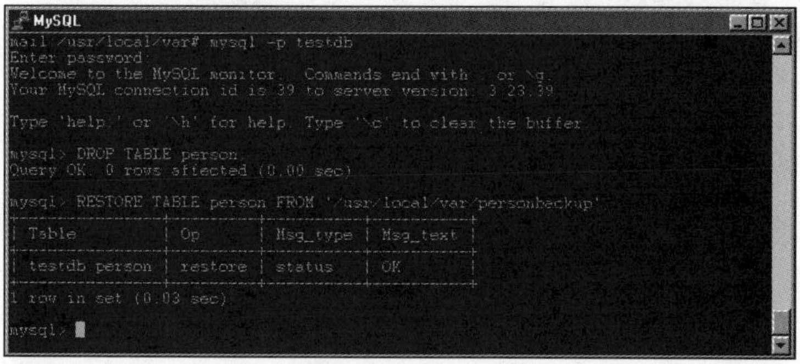

Figure 13-42: Using the RESTORE TABLE statement to restore a table backed up earlier with the BACKUP TABLE statement.

Caution Be extremely careful running the `DROP TABLE` statement; it deletes the entire contents – every last shred of data – in the directory!

The MySQL CLI

For backups or dumps created with the `mysqldump` utility, you can import or restore those into MySQL through the MySQL CLI. Because the `mysqldump` utility creates output as SQL statements, the files containing the output can then be imported or replayed simply by executing the statements.

Obviously for anything more than a few statements it becomes burdensome to copy and paste these into the CLI by hand. The use of the less-than sign (<) for redirecting the contents of a file into the CLI can alleviate the work of copying and pasting SQL into the CLI. Taking the contents of a file produced with `mysqldump` and redirecting it into MySQL is a simple process.

Recall that `mysqldump` produces output (as shown in Figure 13-43).

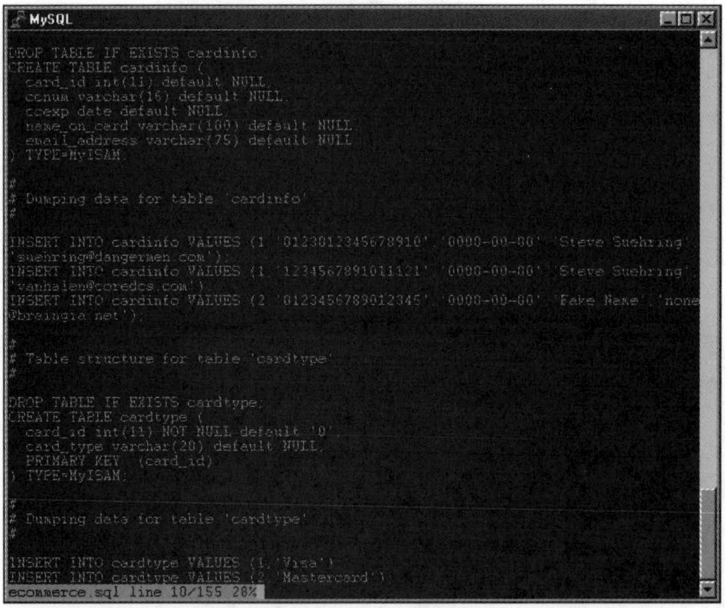

Figure 13-43: Example output from mysqldump

If you've made a complete backup of a database with `mysqldump` and need to recreate the database and data, you can import it through the MySQL CLI with a command line that looks like this:

```
mysql [OPTIONS] < <filetoinput>
```

As you can see from this command, importing into MySQL through the CLI is easy. The `[OPTIONS]` section can include things like username, password, host, and so forth. Another option that you may need to include is the name of the database. The output from `mysqldump` can include the DDL to create the database. If you do not have DDL to create the database included with the `mysqldump` output, then you will need to include the name of the database in your MySQL CLI command line. For example, the following command imports the contents of the file from Figure 13-43:

```
mysql -p <password> ecommerce < ecommerce.sql
```

The execution of this command is shown in Figure 13-44.

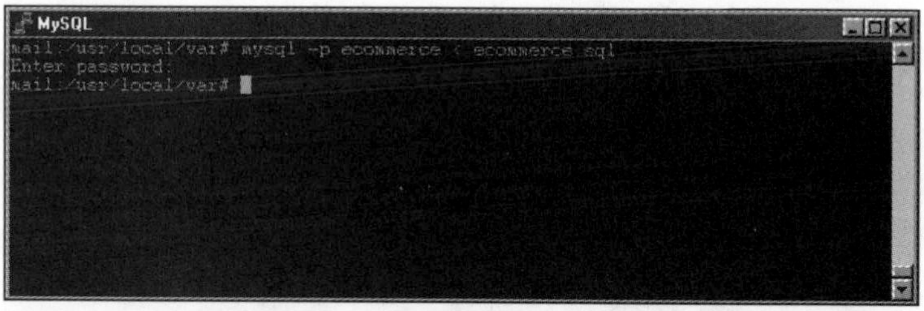

Figure 13-44: Importing an actual file produced with mysqldump into the CLI with the use of the redirect character

Devising a Plan for Database Backups

The programs and tools discussed in this chapter are only useful if you actually take the time to actually use them. Making backups and optimizing tables is an important part of database administration. In this section I'll give an example of a simple script and method for regularly backing up the data in your MySQL server.

Cross-Reference

Chapter 14 discusses methods for optimizing tables and suggests a regimen of table maintenance.

I'll be using the mysqldump command to create backups of the database server. The resulting output can be huge if you're backing up a large database or databases. However the advantage of mysqldump is that the output is in plaintext—you can edit the file so it only imports the data you want restored. The resulting output file can also be compressed, which saves space.

The command to back up all databases with mysqldump is as follows:

```
mysqldump -A [OPTIONS] > <outputfile>
```

For example, to create a backup of all databases on my example server, I run this command:

```
mysqldump -A -p > backup.sql
```

Ideally, I wouldn't need to be present to watch the command run—so I make a simple script to produce—and then compress—a backup. The script is shown in Figure 13-45.

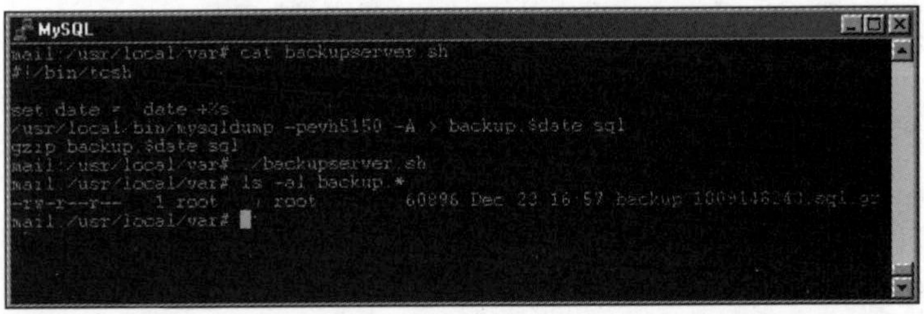

Figure 13-45: A simple shell script to make a backup of all databases using mysqldump

The script first gets the date so I can keep more than one day's worth of backup files. Next the script runs mysqldump and sends the output to a file containing the date variable set earlier. Finally, the script compresses the resulting file with the gzip utility.

Using a scheduler such as cron, you can schedule this script to run as often as you'd like.

Note Store this file in a secure location and make sure that it is archived to another medium (such as tape) or otherwise copied to another physical medium regularly.

Another method for creating a backup is with mysqlhotcopy. The same methods used for creating a script with mysqldump can also be used with mysqlhotcopy.

Cross-Reference The limitations and methods of mysqlhotcopy are covered earlier in this chapter.

Summary

MySQL has three basic methods for making backups: `mysqlhotcopy`, `mysqldump`, and `BACKUP TABLE`. Each has its own way of performing backups, an operation indispensable to data integrity and database security.

- The `mysqlhotcopy` utility works by making a copy of the actual directory containing the database files. It must be run from the actual database server.
- The `mysqldump` utility produces the DDL and DML to recreate the databases and tables as new. If can be run from a machine other than the database server and can back up one, more than one, or all databases at once.
- The `BACKUP TABLE` statement runs with the MySQL CLI. It can create backups of one or more than one table within a database.
- The two commands for checking most table types in MySQL are `mysqlcheck` and `myisamchk`.
- Four statements are used with the MySQL CLI for working with tables: `ANALYZE TABLE`, `CHECK TABLE`, `OPTIMIZE TABLE`, and `REPAIR TABLE`. The statements are similar in function to their `mysqlcheck` counterparts.
- The `mysqlcheck` utility can work with databases while the server is online whereas `myisamchk` should not be used in this manner.
- The `myisamchk` utility can repair most problems with tables and can create backups of tables before working with them for additional data safety.
- To restore databases and tables the `mysqlhotcopy` command can be used along with the MySQL CLI and the `RESTORE TABLE` statement.
- The MySQL CLI can be used to import files created with `mysqldump` such as a backup file of a database or table.
- Create a regular routine for backing up the database on your server. Without backups, you can lose all the data on your server in the event of a catastrophic event.

✦ ✦ ✦

CHAPTER 14

Performance Tuning

✦ ✦ ✦ ✦

In This Chapter

Troubleshooting the Server

Optimizing Databases and Tables

Optimizing Queries

✦ ✦ ✦ ✦

MySQL AB has gone to great lengths to see that MySQL performs well. However, the developers can't foresee every implementation of MySQL. It's impossible to set every variable appropriately by default. For this reason, many variables can be set by the database administrator to improve performance for the specific application.

Though tips and hints for enhancing and improving the performance of the MySQL server are dispersed throughout the book, this chapter provides additional information for setting variables and improving MySQL performance

Troubleshooting Servers

As with the first portion of Chapter 11 (which treats enhancing the performance of the MySQL server), this first part of Chapter 14 examines troubleshooting and improving the server itself. One of the most important methods for troubleshooting server problems is to examine logfiles. I'll look at the different logfiles that are available with MySQL as the first portion of this chapter.

Knowing how to determine what needs improvement is indispensable to improving server performance. Therefore I'll begin with basic troubleshooting techniques and commands, and then recap some server variables and performance-related options.

MySQL AB has included some good suggestions for performance-related variables within their sample configuration files. I recommend using those files for examples to match your server configuration and resource availability.

Cross-Reference: Chapter 11 examines the MySQL configuration files in detail.

MySQL logfiles

A feature I use frequently for troubleshooting is the MySQL logfiles. The four common logfile types are listed in Table 14-1.

Table 14-1
Types of Logfiles with MySQL

Log Type	*Use*
Binary log	Stores all updates or changes to data, used in replication
Error log	Records errors encountered by the server.
Query log	Stores all connections and queries.
Slow query log	Stores queries that take longer than `long_query_time` or don't use indexes.

Note: Two logfile types, the isam and the update logs, are outside the scope of this book.

One logfile of particular importance is the MySQL error log. If the server won't start, many operating systems will record a trace that can indicate why the server won't start or why it crashed. Starts and stops of the server are recorded in the error logfile. An example error log is shown in Figure 14-1.

By default, the *error log* is stored in the data directory for MySQL with a name of `<hostname>.err` (`<hostname>` is the hostname of the server). To change the location of the error log, set it with the `err-log` option underneath the `[safe_mysqld]` section of the MySQL configuration file.

```
err-log = /var/log/mysql.err
```

To store all inserts and updates to data, use the *binary log*. The `log-bin` option under the `[mysqld]` section of the configuration file enables the binary log, which is stored in the data directory. The binary log is also useful during replication on the replication master, as the logfile that records updates for the slaves. This file contains binary data; the contents of a binary update log are shown in Figure 14-2.

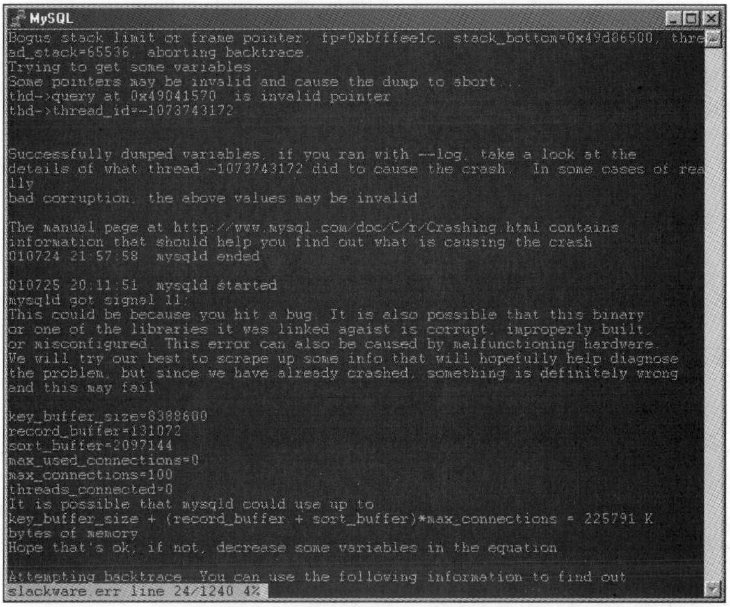

Figure 14-1: A sample error log where the server crashed

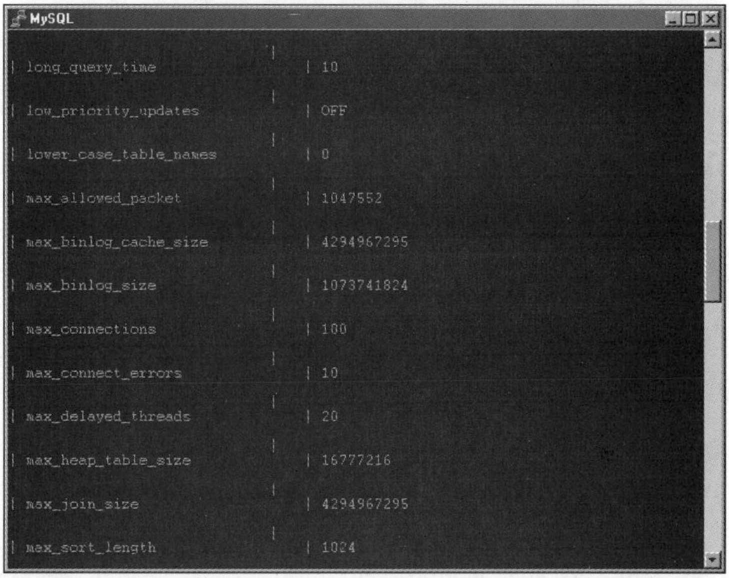

Figure 14-2: An example of the binary log recorded with MySQL

The *query log* records connections and queries made to the MySQL server. Using the query log, you can debug connection problems or query issues with the server. The query log is enabled by adding the `log` option below the `[mysqld]` section in the MySQL configuration file. By default, the query log is recorded in the data directory of your MySQL server and is named `<hostname>.log`. This can be changed by adding a `= <path/filename>` to the `log` option in the configuration file, like this:

```
log = /var/log/mysqlquery.log
```

An example of the data stored in the query log is shown in Figure 14-3.

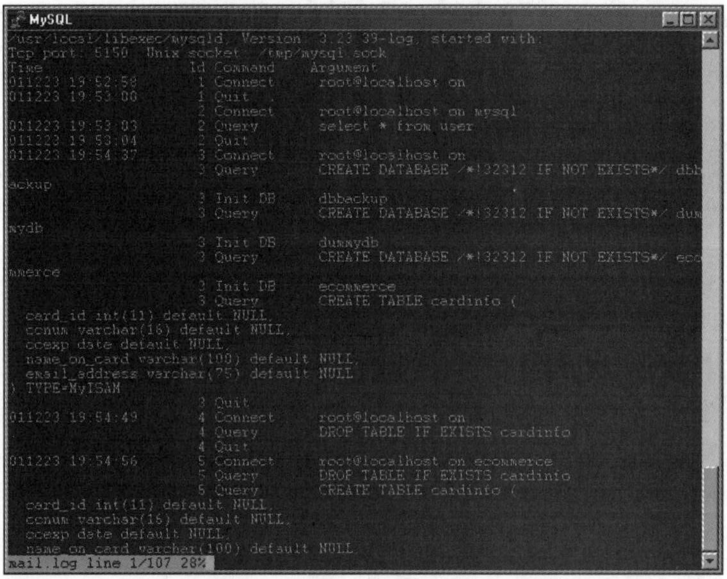

Figure 14-3: An example of the query log in MySQL

I've used the query log to watch poorly written applications perform poorly written queries and then leave their connections open. Another log that can be used for this purpose is the *slow query log*, which records two types of slow queries:

✦ Queries that take longer than the value of the `long_query_time` variable

✦ Queries that don't use an index with the `log-long-format` option

To enable the slow query log, add the `log_slow_queries` option underneath the `[mysqld]` section of the MySQL configuration file. You can also change the target for the logfile from the default of `<hostname>-slow.log` to another name by adding `=<filename>` when using the `log_slow_queries` option, as in the following example:

```
log_slow_queries = slowquery.log
```

To determine the value of the `long_query_time` variable, use the `mysqladmin variables` command. The results are shown in Figure 14-4.

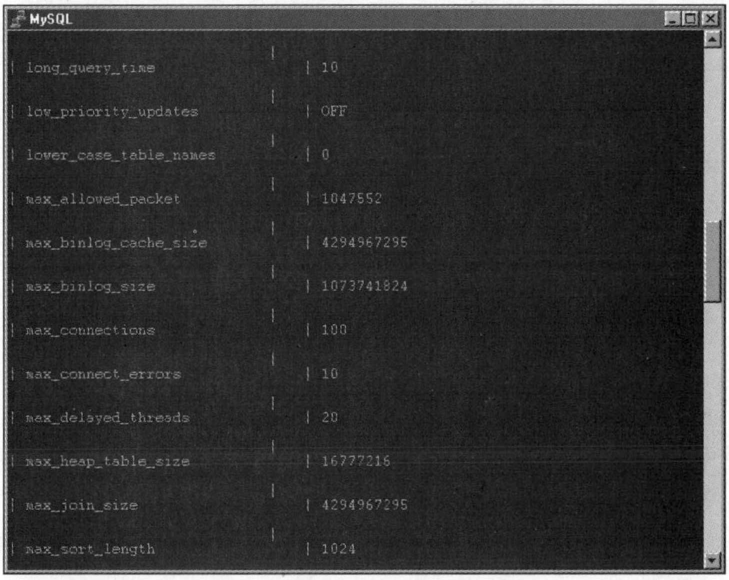
MySQL
| long_query_time | 10
| low_priority_updates | OFF
| lower_case_table_names | 0
| max_allowed_packet | 1047552
| max_binlog_cache_size | 4294967295
| max_binlog_size | 1073741824
| max_connections | 100
| max_connect_errors | 10
| max_delayed_threads | 20
| max_heap_table_size | 16777216
| max_join_size | 4294967295
| max_sort_length | 1024

Figure 14-4: The long_query_time variable controls how long a query has to take before it is recorded in the Slow Query Log.

You can change the value for `long_query_time` by adding the following to the MySQL configuration file under the `[mysqld]` section:

```
set-variable = long_query_time=<value>
```

The value is given in seconds. For example, to shorten the `long_query_time` value to 3 seconds, you would add the following line to the `[mysqld]` section to the MySQL configuration file, like this:

```
set-variable = long_query_time=3
```

Troubleshooting and performance functions with mysqladmin

The `mysqladmin` command has numerous functions that assist with server administration.

Cross-Reference Chapter 10 covers these functions in detail.

Functions to clear logfiles

Logfiles can be reset or rotated to the next logfile through the `flush-logs` function. For example, Figure 14-5 shows a directory listing of the numerous logfiles running on this server. Figure 14-6 shows the `mysqladmin flush-logs` function being run, followed by another directory listing. In that case, the binary log has been rotated to number `004` in the sequence and the server has also accessed other logs.

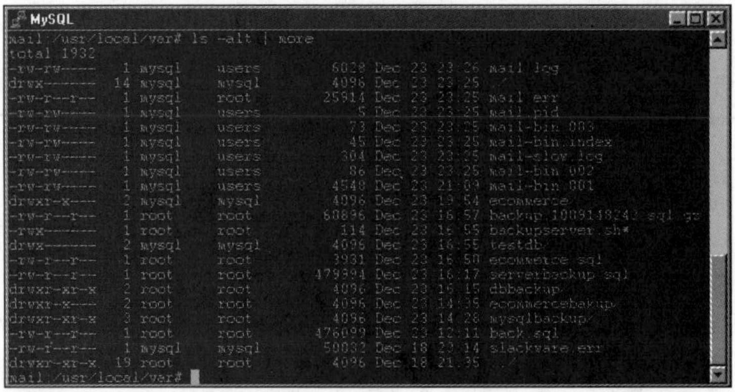

Figure 14-5: A directory listing showing the logfiles and timestamps before the flush-logs function is run

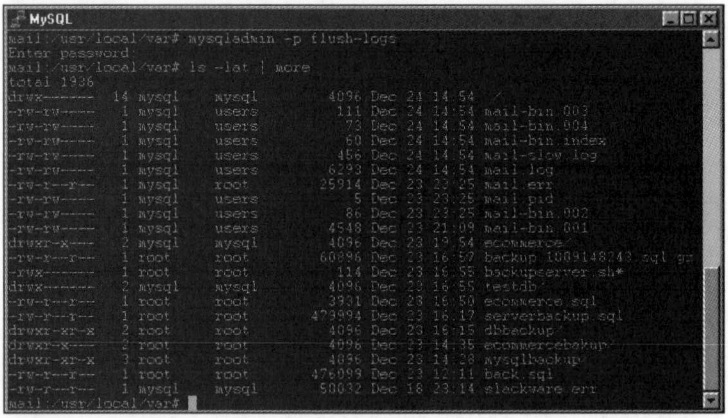

Figure 14-6: The mysqladmin flush-logs function is run along with another directory listing.

Other flush functions with mysqladmin

`mysqladmin` has five other functions for flushing objects. These are shown in Table 14-2.

Table 14-2
Flush functions with mysqladmin

Function name	*Purpose*
`flush-hosts`	Clears the DNS cache of MySQL. Can assist if a host gets blocked due to errors.
`flush-logs`	Clears and cycles MySQL logfiles.
`flush-privileges`	Reloads the MySQL grants database so privilege changes take effect.
`flush-status`	Clears server counters found with the `status` and `extended-status` functions.
`flush-tables`	Closes all open tables.
`flush-threads`	Closes all open threads.

Cross-Reference

The `flush` functions are discussed in detail in Chapter 10.

Two `flush` functions have *synonyms* or *aliases*.

- ✦ The `reload` function is an alias for the `flush-privileges` function. Both reload the grant tables.
- ✦ The `refresh` function is an alias that performs both the duties of the `flush-tables` function and the `flush-logs` function. Running a `mysqladmin refresh` will close all open tables and restart logging (or cycle the logfiles).

Status and variable functions

In addition to the functions that flush or reset values and objects with `mysqladmin`, other functions examine server status and variables.

Cross-Reference

The flush functions are discussed in detail in Chapter 10.

The functions and their purposes are shown in Table 14-3.

Table 14-3
Status and Variable functions with mysqladmin

Function	Purpose
`extended-status`	Prints the current value for many server counters and status-related objects.
`ping`	Checks to see if the mysqld process is still alive.
`processlist`	Lists the currently open processes, along with their status and action.
`status`	Prints a short status message on the server with some status-related objects.
`variables`	Outputs the current values for the variables set for the MySQL server.

The status and `extended-status` functions are related because they both output the current status of various counters within the server. The `status` message shows relatively few important objects; the output of `extended-status` shows many objects.

Tip

Unless you have an insanely small resolution on a huge monitor, you'll probably need to pipe or redirect the output from the `extended-status` function so it doesn't scroll by too fast on-screen.

Figure 14-7 shows an example of the status function. The full output from the `extended-status` function follows as well.

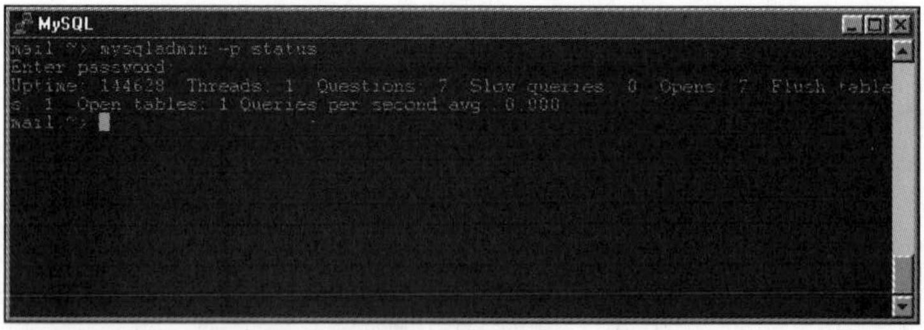

Figure 14-7: Output from the mysqladmin status function shows the current values for important counters.

Compare the output from the `status` function in Figure 14-7 to the following output from the `extended-status` function.

```
+--------------------------+--------+
| Variable_name            | Value  |
+--------------------------+--------+
| Aborted_clients          | 0      |
```

```
| Aborted_connects         | 0      |
| Bytes_received           | 280    |
| Bytes_sent               | 5745   |
| Connections              | 7      |
| Created_tmp_disk_tables  | 0      |
| Created_tmp_tables       | 0      |
| Created_tmp_files        | 0      |
| Delayed_insert_threads   | 0      |
| Delayed_writes           | 0      |
| Delayed_errors           | 0      |
| Flush_commands           | 1      |
| Handler_delete           | 0      |
| Handler_read_first       | 1      |
| Handler_read_key         | 2      |
| Handler_read_next        | 8      |
| Handler_read_prev        | 0      |
| Handler_read_rnd         | 0      |
| Handler_read_rnd_next    | 60     |
| Handler_update           | 0      |
| Handler_write            | 0      |
| Key_blocks_used          | 3      |
| Key_read_requests        | 8      |
| Key_reads                | 3      |
| Key_write_requests       | 0      |
| Key_writes               | 0      |
| Max_used_connections     | 0      |
| Not_flushed_key_blocks   | 0      |
| Not_flushed_delayed_rows | 0      |
| Open_tables              | 1      |
| Open_files               | 6      |
| Open_streams             | 0      |
| Opened_tables            | 7      |
| Questions                | 10     |
| Select_full_join         | 0      |
| Select_full_range_join   | 0      |
| Select_range             | 0      |
| Select_range_check       | 0      |
| Select_scan              | 1      |
| Slave_running            | OFF    |
| Slave_open_temp_tables   | 0      |
| Slow_launch_threads      | 0      |
| Slow_queries             | 0      |
| Sort_merge_passes        | 0      |
| Sort_range               | 0      |
| Sort_rows                | 0      |
| Sort_scan                | 0      |
| Table_locks_immediate    | 6      |
| Table_locks_waited       | 0      |
| Threads_cached           | 0      |
| Threads_created          | 6      |
| Threads_connected        | 1      |
| Threads_running          | 1      |
| Uptime                   | 145212 |
+--------------------------+--------+
```

Some of the same counters are included in the `status` and `extended-status` forms. (Chapter 10 has more information on the specific values.)

MySQL CLI troubleshooting and performance functions

The MySQL CLI includes many of the same functions as the `mysqladmin` command . For example, the `mysqladmin flush-logs` function is replaced with the `FLUSH LOGS` statement when executed with the CLI. The `mysqladmin status` command is replaced with the `SHOW STATUS` statement when used with the CLI. Table 14-4 shows `mysqladmin` functions with their CLI equivalents.

Table 14-4
Functions with mysqladmin and the MySQL CLI

Mysqladmin function	*MySQL CLI equivalent*
`Variables`	`SHOW VARIABLES`
`Status`	`SHOW STATUS`
`Processlist`	`SHOW PROCESSLIST`
`Flush-hosts`	`FLUSH HOSTS`
`Flush-privileges`	`FLUSH PRIVILEGES`
`Flush-logs`	`FLUSH LOGS`
`Flush-tables`	`FLUSH TABLES`
`Flush-status`	`FLUSH STATUS`

When run from within the CLI, the `FLUSH TABLES` statement has three variations. The first is the normal `FLUSH TABLES` statement that closes all open tables. The second variation closes only specified tables and can be called in singular or plural form:

```
FLUSH [TABLE | TABLES] <tablename> (, <tablename>)
```

Two examples of the `FLUSH TABLES` statement with specific tables are shown in Figure 14-8.

Figure 14-8: The FLUSH TABLES statement using specific tables

The third variation of the `FLUSH TABLES` statement is as follows:

```
FLUSH TABLES WITH READ LOCK <tablename>
```

The `FLUSH TABLES WITH READ LOCK` statement closes all open or in-use tables, just like the `FLUSH TABLES` statement. However, the `FLUSH TABLES WITH READ LOCK` statement also places a lock on the tables that must be manually unlocked with the `UNLOCK TABLES` statement.

Figure 14-9 shows an example of the `FLUSH TABLES WITH READ LOCK` statement, an attempt to read from one of the locked tables, and then the `UNLOCK TABLES` statement to allow access again.

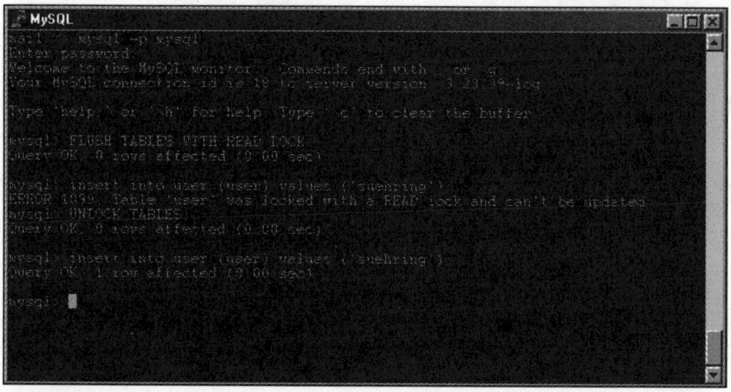

Figure 14-9: An example of the FLUSH TABLES WITH READ LOCK statement.

mysqlshow

Though complemented by SHOW statements in the CLI, the mysqlshow command can find the structure of databases, tables, and columns. The mysqlshow statement is unlike other commands in MySQL. You can't simply type the command to get a syntax printing. To see a syntax reference for the mysqlshow command, you should add the --help switch, as shown in Figure 14-10.

Caution The -? switch is listed as a synonym for the --help switch, but it doesn't work.

Figure 14-10: A syntax reference for the mysqlshow command is obtained by adding the --help switch.

Using the mysqlshow command is quite similar to using other commands with MySQL: The -u switch defines the user, the -p switch can define the password, the -h switch defines the host, and so on. The output from the mysqlshow command is similar to the output from the equivalent CLI command (such as SHOW TABLES or SHOW COLUMNS). Examples of the output from the mysqlshow command appear in Figures 14-11 and 14-12.

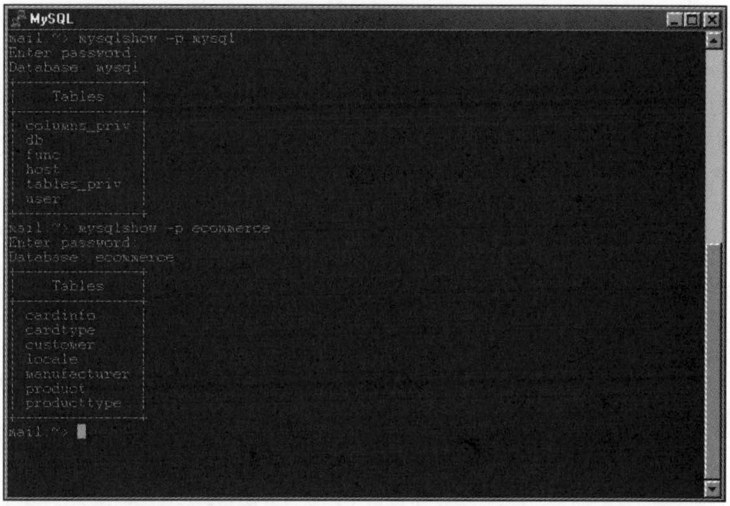

Figure 14-11: Using the mysqlshow command to show the tables within a database

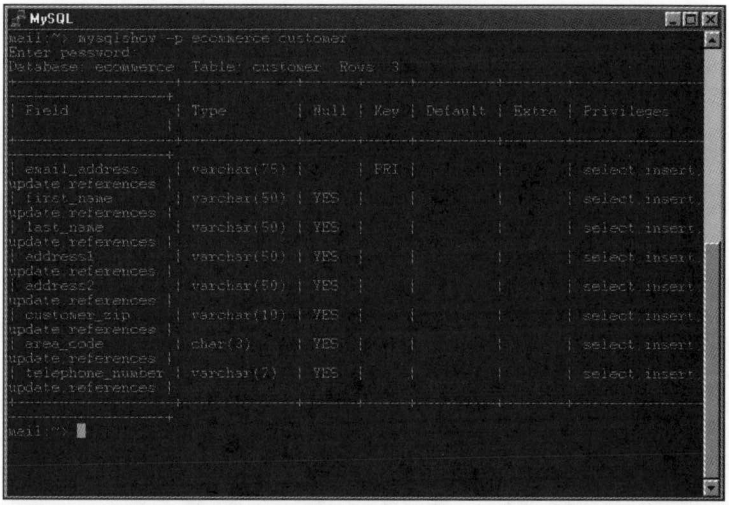

Figure 14-12: Using the mysqlshow command to list the columns within a table of the ecommerce database

Optimizing Databases and Tables

Certain optimizing techniques can change the structure of databases and tables to make them operate more efficiently. In addition, certain statements can optimize tables with performance enhancements such as defragmentation.

The use of indexes will help performance immensely on large datasets. MySQL stores indexes and data in separate files to maximize efficiency. Adding an index (or creating one with a table) will help when performing operations on the data; that way MySQL need only look at a subset of the data for the correct result.

If there is a `PRIMARY KEY` index on the table, it should be a short task to maximize speed. If you frequently search on multiple columns, index the columns with the most used column being the first in the list. However, don't make unnecessary indexes.

The `EXPLAIN` statement can assist in determining when an index might be useful. The `EXPLAIN` statement is used with a `SELECT` statement. For example, Figure 14-13 uses the `EXPLAIN` statement to show indexes used by a `SELECT` statement.

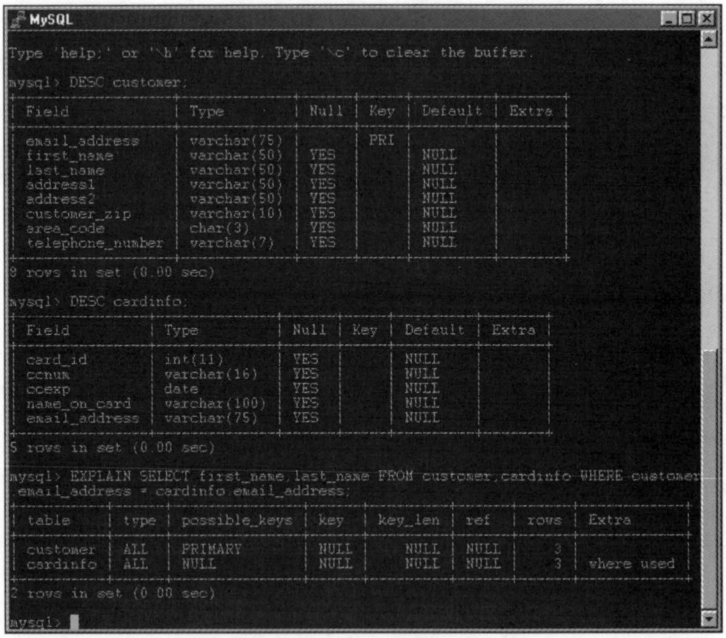

Figure 14-13: A description of two tables in the ecommerce database along with an EXPLAIN statement to examine the SELECT statement being used to find the first and last names of customers

The Possible_keys and Keys columns in the output of the EXPLAIN statement show possible keys that MySQL could use for the SELECT—and the actual key (if any) that MySQL used for the query.

All index types in MySQL are stored in B-Tree format. They can improve performance with a WHERE clause. Since most SELECT statements will use a WHERE clause, an index can be the single most important improvement you make for better performance. Indexes can also quickly sort, locate the maximum and minimum values for a column, and assist with a join of two or more tables.

The syntax for creating an index during a CREATE TABLE statement is

```
CREATE TABLE <tablename> (<columnname>, ...,
index <indexname> (column(s) to include in index)
);
```

Note: **Creating a column as a PRIMARY KEY also enables MySQL to optimize queries.**

You can also create an index after the table has been created through the create index or alter table commands. The create index command is actually an alias for an alter table statement. The syntax for a create index statement is as follows:

```
CREATE INDEX <indexname> on <tablename> (column(s) to include);
```

Save disk space by choosing the correct column types and making the data as small as possible. Choosing the *smallest* or *most appropriate* column type helps MySQL work efficiently with the data. Choosing fixed-length columns can also increase speed.

Note: **Fixed length columns may end up wasting space since MySQL will always allocate the defined amount of bytes for the column regardless of the actual data length.**

The OPTIMIZE TABLE statement run with the MySQL CLI is used to defragment a table or tables. The statement only works with MyISAM and BDB tables. OPTIMIZE TABLE repairs any deleted or split rows and also sorts indexes. Two examples of the OPTIMIZE TABLE statement are shown in Figure 14-14.

Caution: **While the OPTMIZE TABLE statement is running, the table is locked. Be aware that this can take a fair amount of time, depending on the size of the table.**

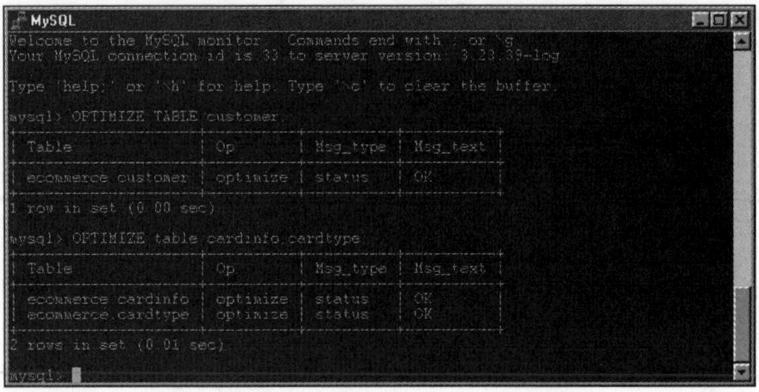

Figure 14-14: The OPTIMIZE TABLE statement in action

Optimizing Queries

MySQL performs many optimizations for queries and statements without the user having to be involved. These include processes like examination of clauses and statements to determine how they could be phrased in a more efficient manner, and rejection of some statements without running them if they are invalid. MySQL also performs background optimization of `DISTINCT` statements and `JOIN` statements.

If this process is automated, what's your role? In the previous section I examined the `EXPLAIN` statement. The `EXPLAIN` statement can help you determine the indexes to use with a `SELECT` statement. Useful indexes are the key to improving server performance when your database applications perform many reads.

After the database has been populated, sorting the indexes within the database may be helpful. You can do this with the `myisamchk` statement. For example, to sort on the first index, issue the following command:

```
myisamchk --sort-index --sort-records=1
```

Figure 14-15 shows the previous command when run against a few tables within the `ecommerce` database. The second attempt in the example fails because no indexes exist in the `cardinfo` table.

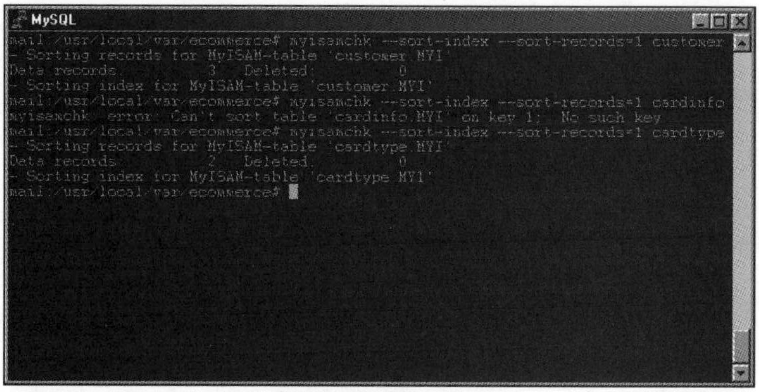

Figure 14-15: Examples of the myisamchk command to sort indexes on tables within the ecommerce database

Summary

The use of various MySQL logfiles is a major asset when troubleshooting the server or dealing with other database problems.

- ✦ The error log is an important tool for helping to determine why the server crashes or won't start.
- ✦ The binary update log and the query log can help you watch for updates that cause problems; they can also help you look for any `SELECT` statements that create performance problems.
- ✦ The slow query log shows queries that take longer than the specified time or don't use an index.
- ✦ The `mysqladmin` command contains useful functions for troubleshooting the server including flush functions and status and variable functions.
- ✦ The flush functions with `mysqladmin` reset or clear counters, logfiles, and even the MySQL privilege system.
- ✦ The MySQL CLI also includes `flush` functions along with functions to show variables and monitor server performance.

- ✦ Indexes can help speed up operations with databases.
- ✦ The `EXPLAIN` statement is used to look at the indexes that a `SELECT` statement can use or might benefit from.
- ✦ You can create indexes during the table creation statement or through the use of a separate `CREATE INDEX` statement.
- ✦ The `OPTIMIZE TABLE` statement is used to repair and defragment `MyISAM` and `BDB` tables.
- ✦ MySQL performs many optimizations in the background without any user intervention. Statements are analyzed before they are run to determine validity and how to phrase them better for improved performance.

✦ ✦ ✦

Development

PART

IV

✦ ✦ ✦ ✦

In This Part

✦ ✦ ✦ ✦

CHAPTER 15

Perl Development

◆ ◆ ◆ ◆

In This Chapter

Installing the Perl DBI and the MySQL DBD

Introducing the DBI

Using functions with the DBI

Building basic applications

Building Web applications

Producing a Web site for e-commerce

◆ ◆ ◆ ◆

I've been using Perl for many years. I've found the language extremely useful in server and network administration. Without Perl, my job would've been impossible to do.

MySQL has an application-programming interface (API) for Perl. It's called the Perl Database Interface (DBI), and programmers can use it to create powerful applications that perform every function imaginable — from administration tasks to reporting to Web applications — with a MySQL server. The Perl-DBI combines full access to the power of MySQL with the ease of Perl.

> **Note** The DBI allows access to many different database types. To enable access to MySQL, however, a MySQL-specific database driver (DBD) must be used. This chapter refers to the combination of DBI-and-DBD as either "the DBI" or "Perl-DBI."

This chapter builds a few applications that take advantage of the Perl-DBI. Before building the applications, I show you the Perl API itself — and the many functions included with it.

The example applications stick to the fundamentals of using the Perl DBI and the MySQL DBD. For the time being, you can forego building a guestbook application (a common exercise in books devoted to Perl). If you want to build a guestbook later, the examples in this chapter provide a good foundation for doing so.

Installing the Perl DBI And MySQL DBD

A prerequisite for installing the DBI and the MySQL DBD is having Perl itself installed. Installation of Perl is beyond the scope of this book; this section assumes that you already have Perl installed. The steps given here simply install the Perl-DBI and the MySQL DBD on a Linux system.

Where to get the DBI and DBD

The latest copies of the Perl DBI and MySQL DBD can be obtained at your local CPAN mirror, `http://www.cpan.org`. The MySQL DBD is actually a combination of the DBD for the `mSQL` database as well as the DBD for MySQL.

Installing the DBI

Once you've obtained the DBI and DBD for MySQL, you unpack the archive by using the `tar` command in Linux. The command syntax is

```
tar -zxvf <filename>
```

and here's an example:

```
tar -zxvf DBI-1.20.tar.gz
```

Unpacking the DBI results in a `DBI-<version>` directory that contains the files necessary to create the DBI, as shown in Figure 15-1.

Before unpacking and installing the DBD, you need to compile the DBI software. Change into the newly created DBI directory; the command syntax is

```
cd DBI-<version>
```

and here's an example:

```
cd DBI-1.20
```

The first step towards installation is executing the Makefile for the software. This is accomplished with the command:

```
perl Makefile.PL
```

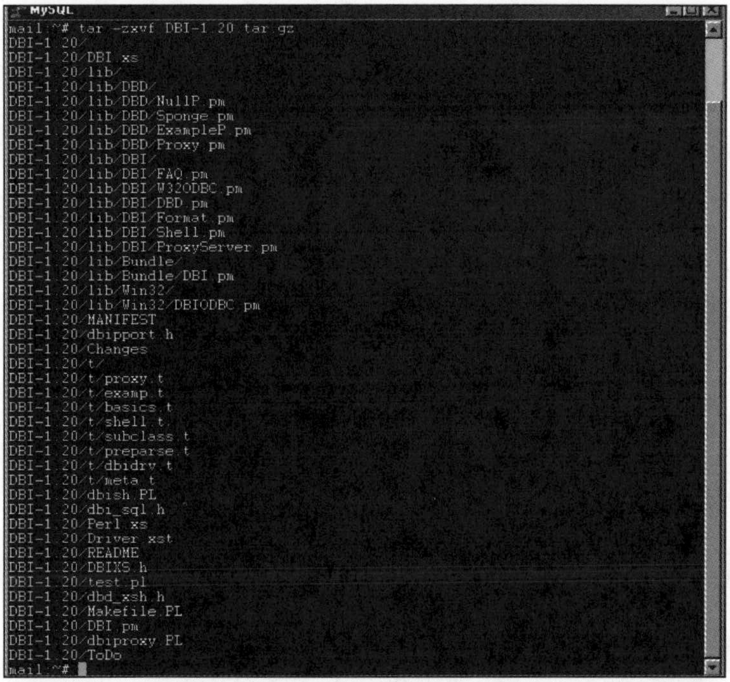

Figure 15-1: Unpacking the DBI results in a directory containing the files necessary to create the actual DBI software

Note

Because the `Makefile.PL` filename is case-sensitive, entering `makefile.pl` doesn't work.

Executing the command just described yields results similar to Figure 15-2.

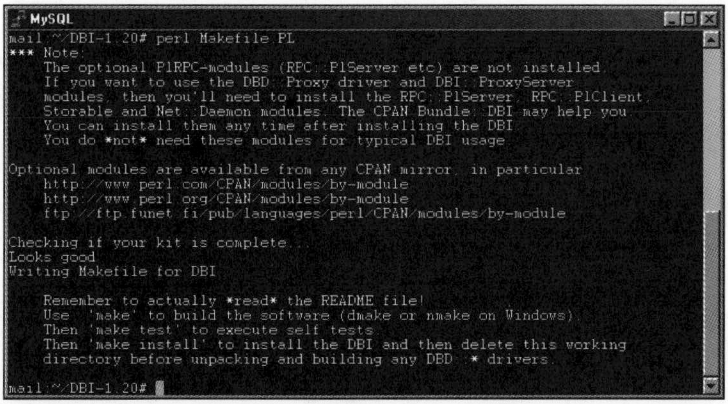

Figure 15-2: Executing the Makefile for the DBI

The next step for installation of the DBI is to compile the software. This is accomplished with the `make` command. Executing the `make` command results in a fair amount of output scrolling on the screen; this is normal (see Figure 15-3).

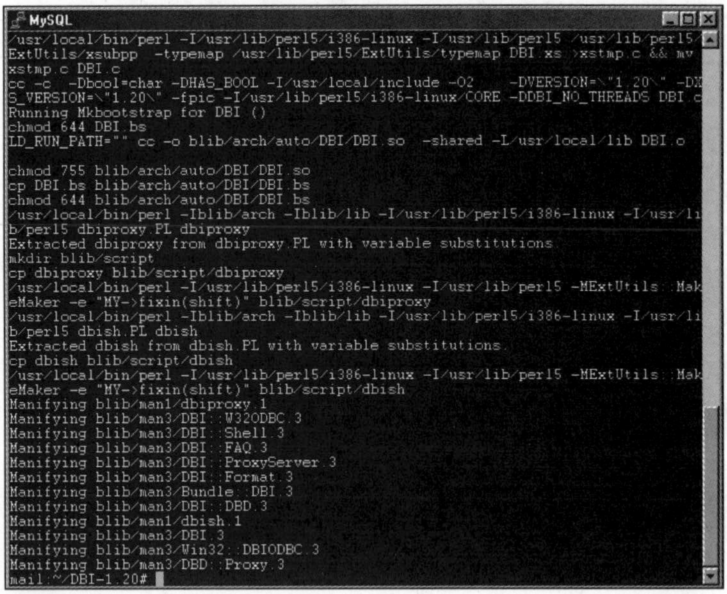
MySQL
/usr/local/bin/perl -I/usr/lib/perl5/i386-linux -I/usr/lib/perl5 /usr/lib/perl5/
ExtUtils/xsubpp -typemap /usr/lib/perl5/ExtUtils/typemap DBI.xs >xstmp.c && mv
xstmp.c DBI.c
cc -c -Dbool=char -DHAS_BOOL -I/usr/local/include -O2 -DVERSION=\"1.20\" -DX
S_VERSION=\"1.20\" -fpic -I/usr/lib/perl5/i386-linux/CORE -DDBI_NO_THREADS DBI.c
Running Mkbootstrap for DBI ()
chmod 644 DBI.bs
LD_RUN_PATH="" cc -o blib/arch/auto/DBI/DBI.so -shared -L/usr/local/lib DBI.o
chmod 755 blib/arch/auto/DBI/DBI.so
cp DBI.bs blib/arch/auto/DBI/DBI.bs
chmod 644 blib/arch/auto/DBI/DBI.bs
/usr/local/bin/perl -Iblib/arch -Iblib/lib -I/usr/lib/perl5/i386-linux -I/usr/li
b/perl5 dbiproxy.PL dbiproxy
Extracted dbiproxy from dbiproxy.PL with variable substitutions.
mkdir blib/script
cp dbiproxy blib/script/dbiproxy
/usr/local/bin/perl -I/usr/lib/perl5/i386-linux -I/usr/lib/perl5 -MExtUtils::Mak
eMaker -e "MY->fixin(shift)" blib/script/dbiproxy
/usr/local/bin/perl -Iblib/arch -Iblib/lib -I/usr/lib/perl5/i386-linux -I/usr/li
b/perl5 dbish.PL dbish
Extracted dbish from dbish.PL with variable substitutions.
cp dbish blib/script/dbish
/usr/local/bin/perl -I/usr/lib/perl5/i386-linux -I/usr/lib/perl5 -MExtUtils::Mak
eMaker -e "MY->fixin(shift)" blib/script/dbish
Manifying blib/man1/dbiproxy.1
Manifying blib/man3/DBI::W32ODBC.3
Manifying blib/man3/DBI::Shell.3
Manifying blib/man3/DBI::FAQ.3
Manifying blib/man3/DBI::ProxyServer.3
Manifying blib/man3/DBI::Format.3
Manifying blib/man3/Bundle::DBI.3
Manifying blib/man3/DBI::DBD.3
Manifying blib/man1/dbish.1
Manifying blib/man3/DBI.3
Manifying blib/man3/Win32::DBIODBC.3
Manifying blib/man3/DBD::Proxy.3
mail:~/DBI-1.20#

Figure 15-3: Compiling the DBI

There are two steps remaining for installation of the DBI. The next portion of the installation is to test the software before actually installing it on the system. This is accomplished with the `make test` command. The `make test` command tests the DBI to make sure that the upcoming installation works as planned. The output from the `make test` command for installation of the DBI should look much like Figure 15-4.

The final stage of the DBI installation is to run the `make install` command to actually install the software, as shown in Figure 15-5.

Note Systems and configurations differ; your output may look slightly different.

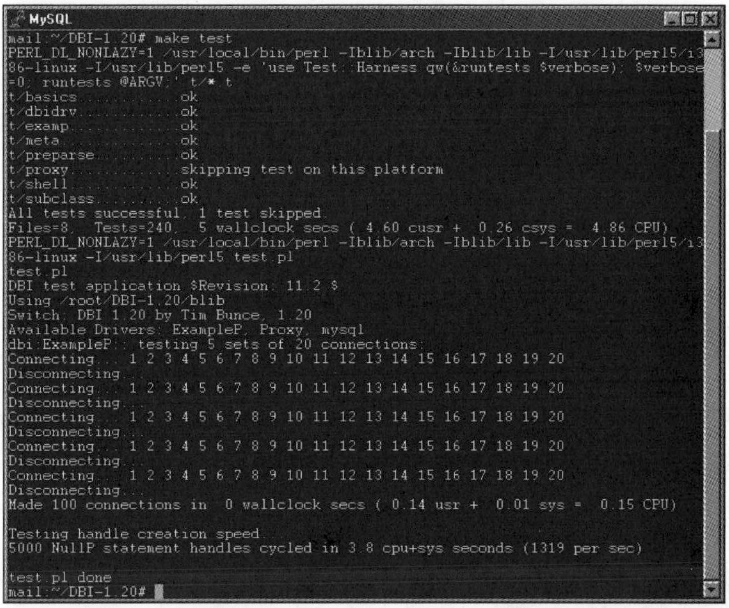

Figure 15-4: Output from your `make test` command (to test the DBI software before installation) is similar to that shown here.

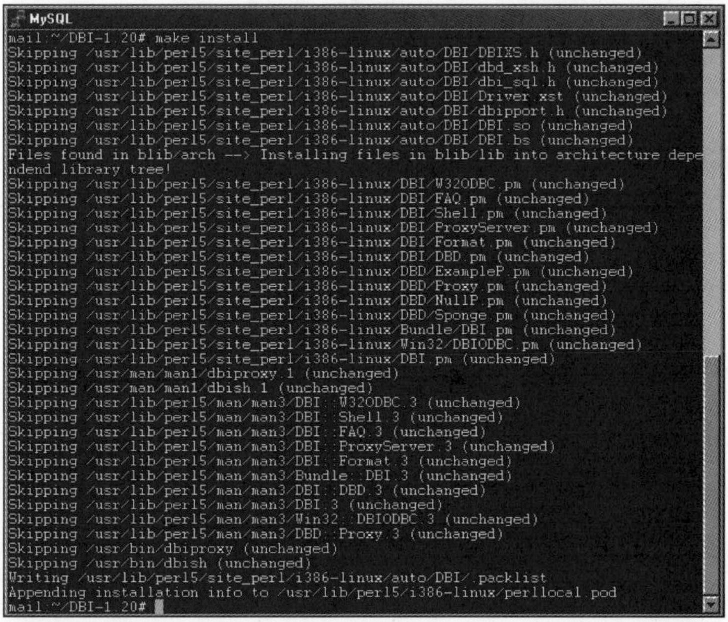

Figure 15-5: The final stage to actually install the DBI is accomplished with the `make install` command.

Installing the MySQL DBD

The MySQL Database Driver or DBD is a combined with the driver for the mSQL database system. As stated previously, the DBD can be obtained at your local CPAN mirror or at http://www.cpan.org. The installation process for the DBD is somewhat similar to the DBI however there are some questions that must be answered during the installation.

Use the tar command to unpack the MySQL DBD archive, typically called Msql-Mysql-modules-<version>.tar.gz. For example:

```
tar -zxvf Msql-Mysql-modules-1.2219.tar.gz
```

Change into the newly created Msql-Mysql-modules directory with the cd command and type **perl Makefile.PL** to begin the installation process for the MySQL DBD. You'll be asked a series of questions, the first of which determines whether you'd like to install the driver for MySQL, mSQL versions 1 and 2, or all drivers, as shown in Figure 15-6.

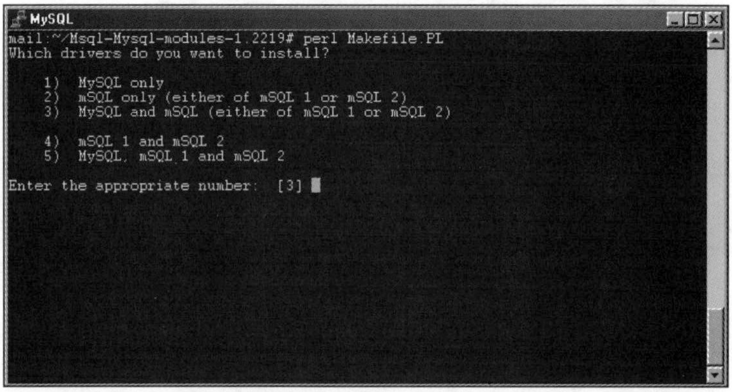

Figure 15-6: The first question for the Makefile command used to build the database drivers

For the purposes of this installation, I choose only the MySQL option, number 1.

The second question during the installation of the DBD is whether to install Mysqlperl emulation. (Mysqlperl is the old version of the DBD for MySQL and Perl.) If you have old applications that may have been created using the syntax of the Mysqlperl driver, then you should say yes to this option. For this installation, I don't need Mysqlperl emulation, so I answer N for *no*.

The third question asks for the location of the MySQL server files. For my test server, the default of /usr/local is correct. However, your installation of MySQL may be (and probably is) in a different location. As stated in the prompt in Figure 15-7, the location should be where the `Makefile` can find the `'include'` directory of the MySQL installation.

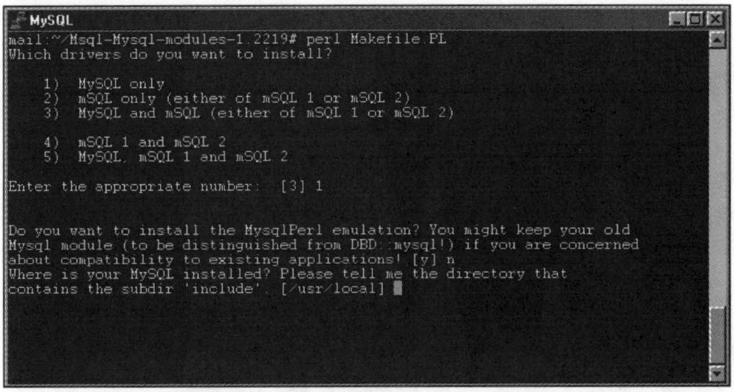

Figure 15-7: The location of the MySQL server files is necessary. The default (/usr/local) is correct for my example server.

The next series of questions sets the parameters for testing of the driver. The first question is the name of the database that the installation process should use for testing. The MySQL server usually includes a database called `'test'`; therefore this is an easy choice to leave at the default of `'test'` at the prompt. The second question in this series asks for the name of the server to use for testing. (The test server shown in Figure 15-8 runs on the local machine; the default of `localhost` is acceptable.)

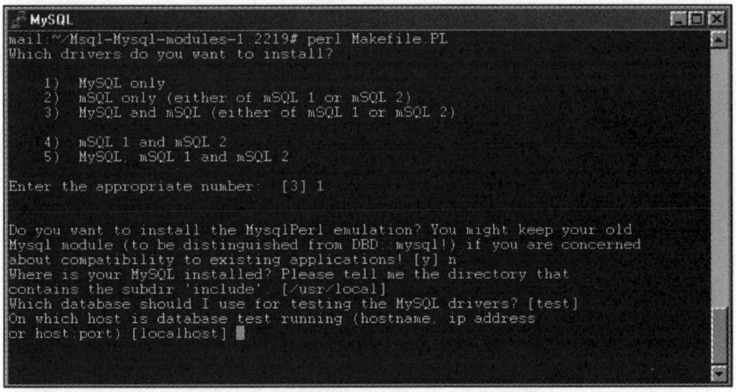

Figure 15-8: Using the test database for testing, with the server running on the local machine. Both defaults are accepted if you press Return or Enter.

The next two questions have no defaults. The first asks for the username to use for testing the driver; the second asks for the password for that user. I'll be using the `root` user account for testing and giving that password as well, as in Figure 15-9.

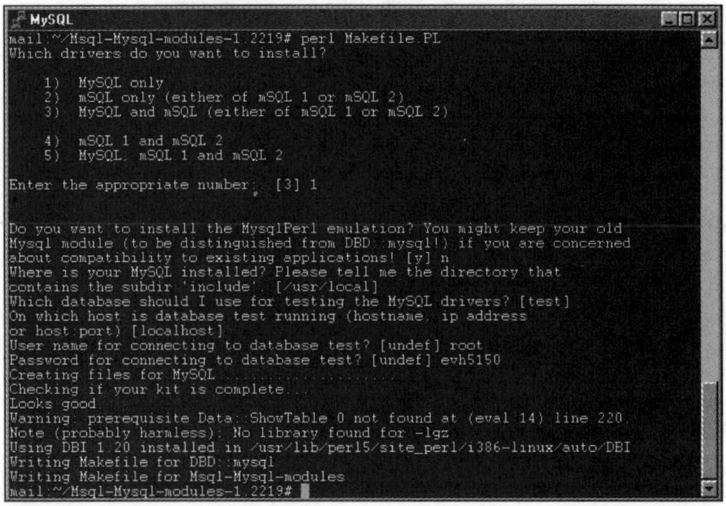

Figure 15-9: Using the root user account for testing of the MySQL DBD

The questions you just answered create files that serve as the basis for the next step in the process: the actual creation of the DBD. Warnings about a missing library and `Data-Showtable` can be ignored. Begin this next phase by typing **make**.

You begin the testing phase by typing the following command:

```
make test
```

If you happen to mistype (or specify a user, password, or test database that doesn't exist) during the initial stage of the installation, this testing phase fails miserably and shows errors that resemble Figure 15-10.

However, if you provided correct information for the testing portion of the initial phase the tests should complete successfully, as shown in Figure 15-11.

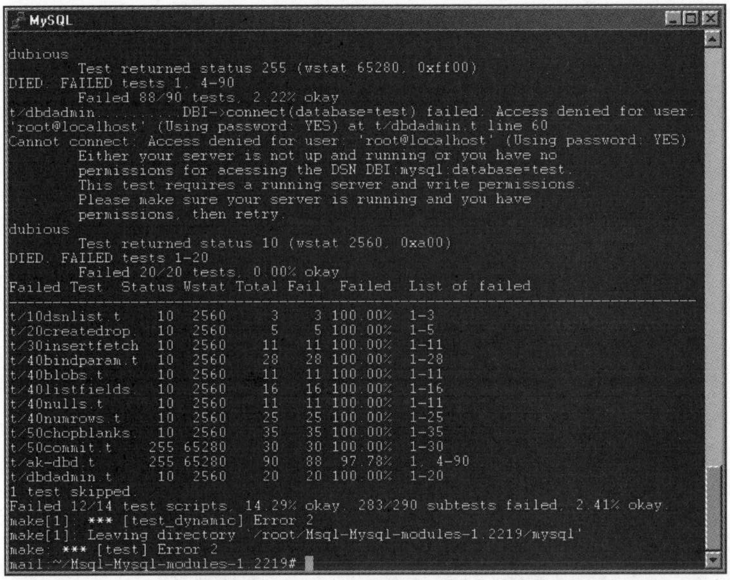

Figure 15-10: The testing phase of the DBD installation fails if you provided incorrect information during the initial stage of the installation.

Figure 15-11: Successful testing of the DBD

Finally, install the MySQL Perl DBD by typing the following command:

```
make install
```

The Normal installation dialog box should appear while the DBD is installed in the proper locations (see Figure 15-12).

Figure 15-12: Normal installation output when you run the make install command to install the MySQL DBD

Other specific drivers and tools can be installed to work with MySQL and Perl; their installation process looks much the same as this one.

Introducing the DBI

The Perl DBI is the name for a database-independent set of software programs that a programmer can use with many different databases — using the same functions in every case. The DBI saves having to account for the multitude of access methods used for different databases. For example, the DBI enables the programmer to use different database drivers (DBDs) for databases such as Oracle, mSQL, Sybase, and others — without having to learn an entirely new syntax to program each one.

The upcoming portion of the chapter introduces the DBI itself — in particular, the basics of DBI use (such as connecting to a database and disconnecting), as well as the DBI's error-handling capability.

Basic DBI Usage

The DBI is built around an object-oriented programming style. Within that context, the database driver is initialized, connections to the database are created, commands and statements are run, and the connections are destroyed. Whenever you create an object, the DBI identifies it—as a driver, a database, or a statement—by associating it with one of three logical markers (known as *handles*) that correspond to those three types of objects: (drivers, databases, or statements). The handles are actually pointers to specific *instances* of objects.

From a programming standpoint, you declare that you'd like to use the DBI in your program by adding the following line near the beginning of your program:

```
use DBI;
```

Driver handles

DBI driver handles are available for many database types. For the purposes of this book, you need be concerned only with the MySQL driver handle.

Tip You can use more than one driver handle within the same program to connect to different database types. You can only use one driver handle per database. (Then again, why would you need more than one handle to the same driver?)

You initialize the driver handle (or more properly, the DBI does so) behind the scenes. For example, the driver handle for MySQL is created when you call the `connect` method for the DBI.

Database handles

Database handles are the controls you use to manipulate database-related programs. When a database handle is created, you connect to the MySQL database and provide credentials such as username, password, and database name. These credentials are the same as those you would supply to connect with the MySQL CLI (or the `mysqladmin` command and so forth).

The standard naming scheme for a database handle is the `$dbh` variable (which I use throughout this chapter). A database handle is created automatically whenever you call the `connect` method; the syntax looks like this:

```
$dbh = DBI->connect($datasource, $credentials)
```

The parent driver handle is also created—automatically—when the database handle is created. (Connection and disconnection get a closer look in an upcoming section of this chapter.)

MySQL allows multiple simultaneous connections when using methods such as the CLI; connections using the DBI have the same capability. Therefore, multiple database handles can be created that attach to the same database. Further, each database handle is a completely separate object; you need not worry about commands or results colliding with each other.

Statement handles

Statement handles are the means by which actual SQL and related statements are executed against the MySQL server. The statement handle is the child of the database handle; can issue multiple statements using the same database handle.

Each statement you issue gets its own statement handle, usually referred to by the `$sth` variable name. Think of this process as issuing multiple statements from within the CLI. You don't have to reconnect to the CLI for each `SELECT` statement (for example); you can issue multiple statements.

Connecting to and disconnecting from the database with the DBI

Interaction with the database can only be done after a connection is made. The connection is known as a database handle and usually referred to by the `$dbh` variable name. The driver handle is created in the background when a connection is made.

Use the `connect` method to create a database handle and connect to the database. When using the `connect` method, you must supply credentials as you would if you were connecting through the CLI. For example, if you have to specify a password (and you should), then connecting through the CLI means you have to specify that same password when you connect through the DBI. Figure 15-13 shows some failed connections attempted with a DBI-based Perl program; they fail when proper credentials aren't supplied.

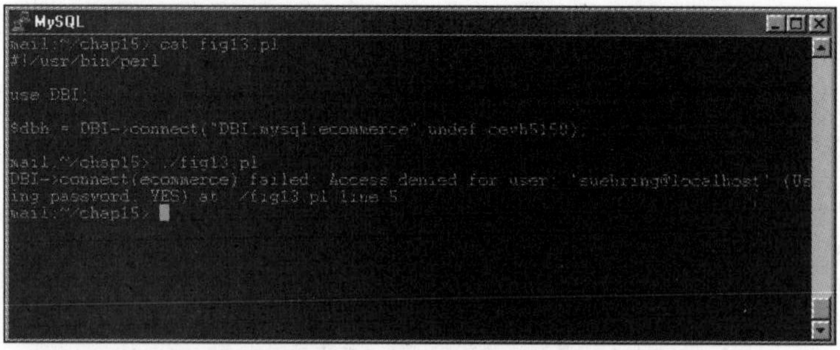

Figure 15-13: Errors when a DBI-based application doesn't have proper credentials to connect to the database requested

The authentication scheme is the same for a DBI-based Perl application as it is for any other connection to the database. The username supplied must be allowed access from the host where the program is running; the username must be allowed to access the database; the password supplied with the username must match; and other credentials must be correctly supplied, as is the case with any other connection to the database server.

Recall that the basic syntax for a connection is

```
$dbh = DBI->connect ($datasource, $credentials);
```

The `$datasource` for MySQL contains a reference to the MySQL DBD followed by the optional name of the database you want to connect to, followed by the optional hostname of the database server that houses the database. Here's an example:

```
$dbh = DBI->connect ("DBI:mysql:ecommerce", $credentials);
```

would connect to the `ecommerce` database on the local host and create a database handle (`$dbh`), assuming the credentials supplied in `$credentials` are correct.

For example, Figure 15-14 shows a small example application that, when executed, issues a simple `"Connection successful"` output message.

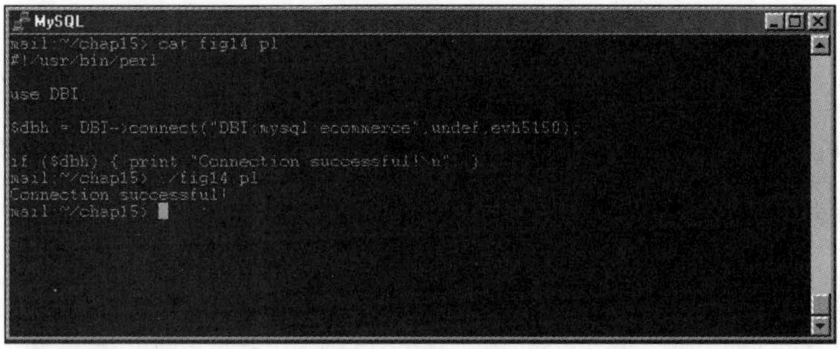

Figure 15-14: A small application for connecting to the ecommerce database

As stated previously, the database itself is optional within the `Datasource` portion of the DBI `connect` operation that creates the object. The following command (which creates a database handle) is valid as well:

```
$dbh = DBI->connect ("DBI:mysql:", $credentials);
```

Other portions of the `Datasource` include the optional host and port. If no host or port is supplied, the host is assumed to be `localhost` and the port is assumed to be the default port, 3306. For example, Figure 15-15 shows different methods for supplying the host and/or port for connecting to the database.

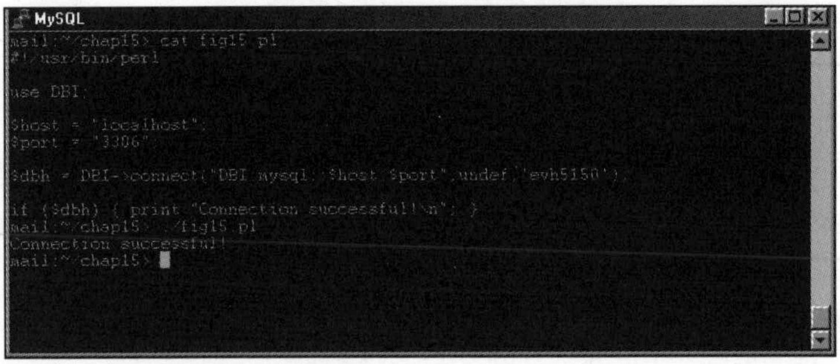

Figure 15-15: Methods for specifying host and port for the `Datasource` portion of the database handle

Notice the word `undef` within the program in Figure 15-14. The `undef` is a placeholder where the username would normally go. In this instance, `undef` is there; the DBI takes the value of the `user` environment variable and puts it in the place of the `username` credential.

If you want to supply the username, you should enclose the username in single or double quotation marks. However, if you supply the username as a variable, the DBI interpolates the variable without requiring you to use quotes. Figure 15-16 shows a few examples of correct methods for specifying the `username` credential as part of the `$dbh` creation.

If you supply `undef` as the password or don't use a password at all, it is assumed that no password is used. This is as opposed to specifying a blank password. Figure 15-17 shows examples of two scripts and the errors that result from running them with the different password methods. Notice the error from the first script (where MySQL believes no password is specified) and from the second script (where a blank password is specified).

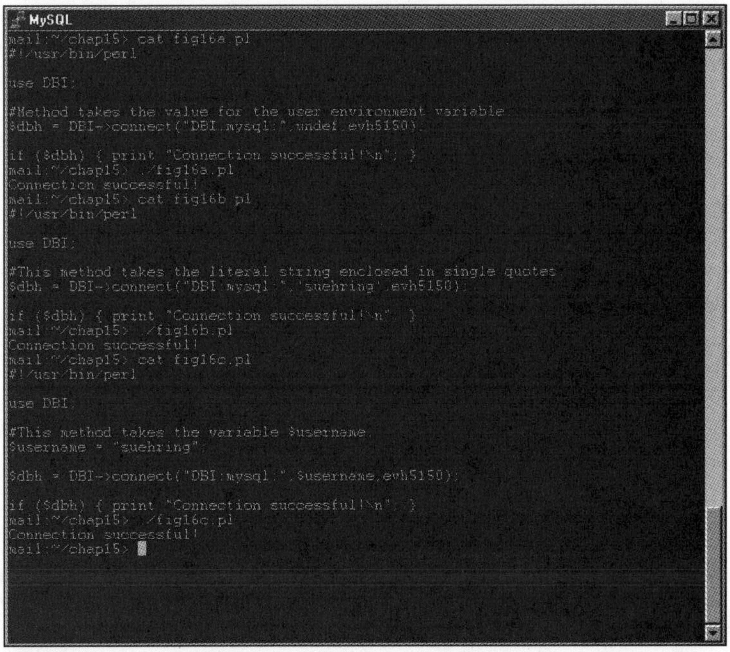

Figure 15-16: Various methods for specifying the username portion of the credentials when creating a connection

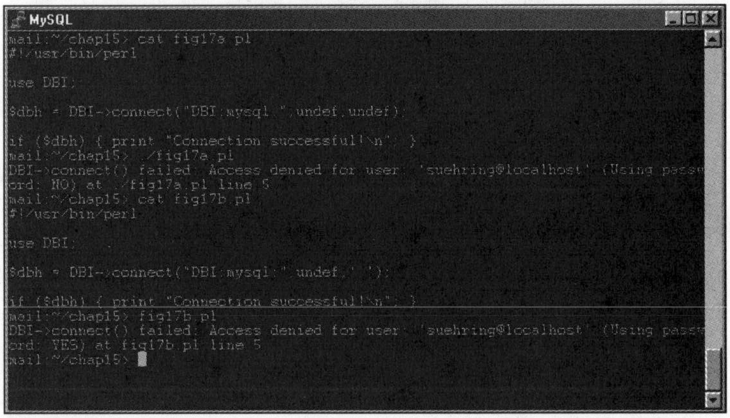

Figure 15-17: Different methods for specifying a password, one using the `undef` placeholder and one specifying a blank password

Of course, you could supply the credentials inside one variable as well (see Figure 15-18).

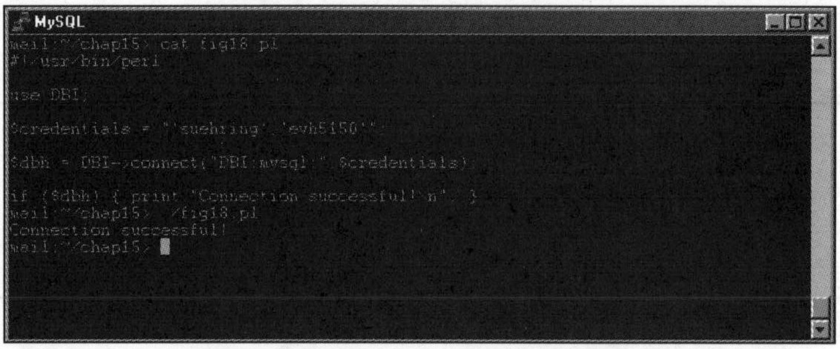

Figure 15-18: Creating the proper credentials inside a variable. `$credentials` is also a valid way to connect.

Also as the credentials portion of the connection can be supplied in a variable, the `Datasource` could also be supplied in whole or in part by variable interpolation. For example, you could define the host as `$host`, the database name as `$database`, and so forth: You could even supply the entire `Datasource` as a variable, `$datasource` (or the name of your choosing.) Figure 15-19 illustrates some of these points.

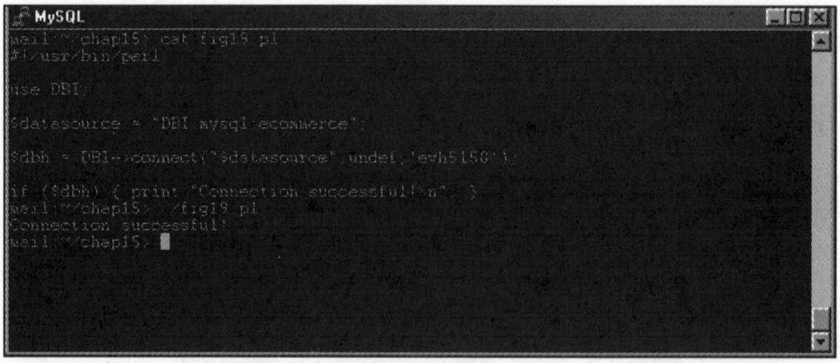

Figure 15-19: Specifying portions of the `Datasource` through the use of variables can help to make the program more readable.

Examining what I have defined so far:

```
$dbh = DBI->connect($datasource, $credentials);
```

I'd like to introduce the final portion of database handle creation with the DBI and MySQL DBD. The final portion is optional and consists of attributes or elements that affect the behavior of the handle itself. Therefore, adding this onto the `$dbh` definition I've been using:

```
$dbh = DBI->connect($datasource, $credentials, \%elements);
```

A number of elements are available here, most notably those that define how errors are handled and what to do with extra blank spaces for `CHAR` column types. I'll examine error handling in the next section; therefore I'll save further discussion of the optional elements until then.

Up until now, I've looked at methods for connecting to the database. By now, you have more than enough information to connect to a database. However, disconnecting from a database is important as well.

Normally, when your program exits, the disconnection is automatic thus saving the programmer the work of having to explicitly issue a `disconnect` command. In practice, however, always explicitly disconnect your database handles. This is because there are times when using multiple handles in a program that you may need to disconnect old handles to preserve resources.

If you do not issue an explicit disconnect, Perl disconnects the handle as part of the `DESTROY` process when a program terminates. You may see an error or warning like:

```
Database handle destroyed without explicit disconnect
```

This should remind you to go back and issue a `disconnect` statement within your program. The syntax for the `disconnect` method is:

```
$dbh->disconnect;
```

Therefore, you can see that it is possible to disconnect only certain database handles. For example, if your program has three database handles, `$dbh0`, `$dbh1`, `$dbh2`, you could simply issue a `disconnect()` to the specific handle or handles that you no longer need.

You may want to check the return status of the disconnection to make sure that it was successful. You can do this by checking the return value from the `disconnect` call, using the following command:

```
$dis = $dbh->disconnect;
```

If the value of `$dis` evaluates `true`, then the disconnection was successful; otherwise the disconnection failed.

Handling errors with the DBI

In most instances, error handling is automatic with the DBI. This was evidenced by earlier Figures and examples in this chapter. The error messages look quite similar to those you would see with other MySQL tools such as the CLI or `mysqladmin`. Sometimes you may want to disable this automatic error-checking in favor of manual error checking (or a combination of automatic and manual).

Error handling is configured using the attributes or elements discussed in a previous section. There are two attributes of DBI error-checking: `PrintError` and `RaiseError`. By default, `PrintError` is enabled. `PrintError` simply prints the error message to the screen and continues execution of the program as if nothing had happened. This is bad if your program is relying on information from the database and a statement or command fails to execute.

To illustrate this behavior, take a look at the program in Figure 15-20. In this program, I query a database for a number and then perform a computation based on that number. I allow `PrintError` to perform the error checking in the program, but do no further error handling myself. You can see the results of the program in action in Figure 15-20 as well. The program happily continues, even though the query execution failed. If these results were to be automatically e-mailed to me using a scheduling program such as `cron`, I wouldn't see these error messages.

Figure 15-20: A program continues execution in the event of an error when using the default `PrintError` for error-checking.

Though disabled by default, the `RaiseError` attribute causes the program to terminate immediately upon encountering an error with the DBI. By creating an attribute hash, `%attr`, and setting `RaiseError` to 1, the `RaiseError` attribute becomes operational and thus terminates the program if an error is encountered. Figure 15-21 shows an example of the same program from Figure 15-20 with the `%attr` hash created and then appended to the database handle initialization.

Tip: Note the use of the backslash to escape the `%` in the database handle creation.

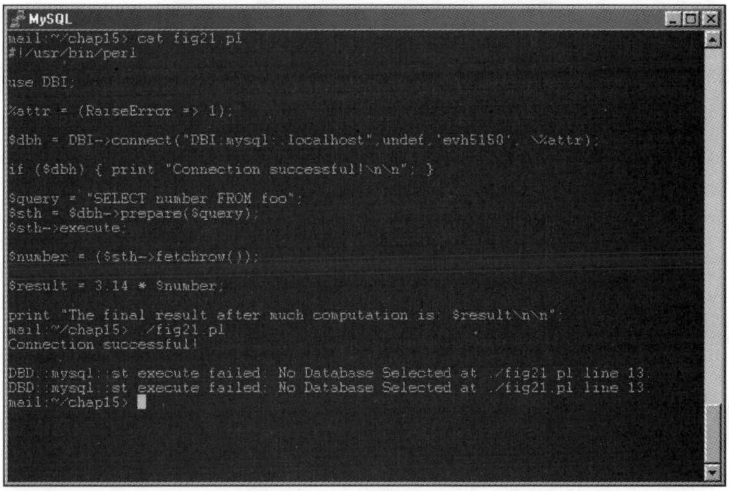

Figure 15-21: Using RaiseError to terminate a program immediately if an error occurs

Notice in Figure 15-21 that the same error message is printed twice. This is expected behavior. Remember that `PrintError` is enabled by default. Therefore, when an error occurs, `PrintError` sees it and prints the error. Only when `RaiseError` handles the error does the program terminate. If you want to disable `PrintError`, set its value to 0, as shown in Figure 15-22.

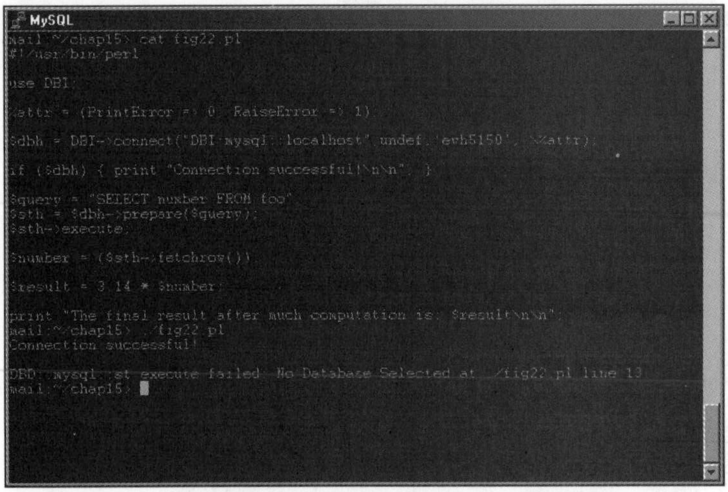

Figure 15-22: Setting PrintError to 0 in the %attr attribute hash to prevent duplicate printing of the error message

You can also toggle the behavior of the `PrintError` and `RaiseError` attributes within the program. For example, if you want to disable all error checking for a certain statement you can set the values of `PrintError` and `RaiseError` to 0 and then re-enable one or both after the statement executes. Figure 15-23 shows an example that disables all error checking by the DBI, performs a statement, and then re-enables the default `PrintError` error-checking method.

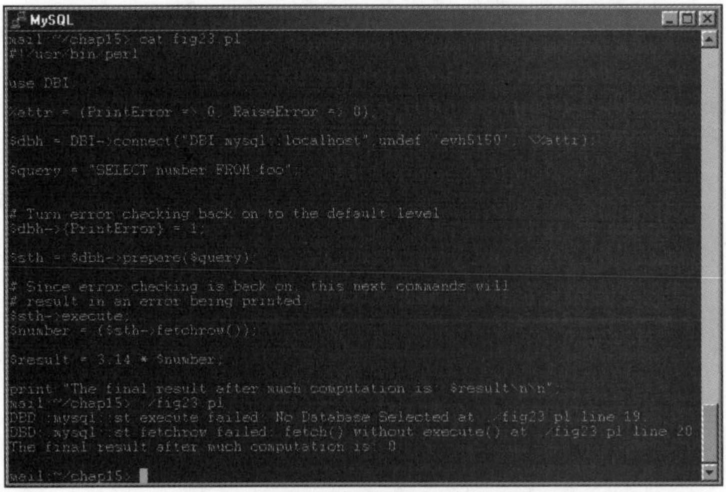

Figure 15-23: Selective error checking within the same program

If you choose to disable the error-checking feature, you must perform error checking and handling manually. This can be achieved in numerous ways including the die or warn functions. Another method for manual error checking is the use of an `IF` test. Because most operations with the DBI return a value of `undef` for a failure, if the value from the operation does not exist, then you can assume that the execution failed. If it evaluates `true`, then you can be assured that the database handle was created. Figure 15-24 shows some examples of manual error checking.

Tip

I've been using an `IF` test in the examples throughout this chapter to test whether the `$dbh` database-handle variable evaluated to `true` or `false`.

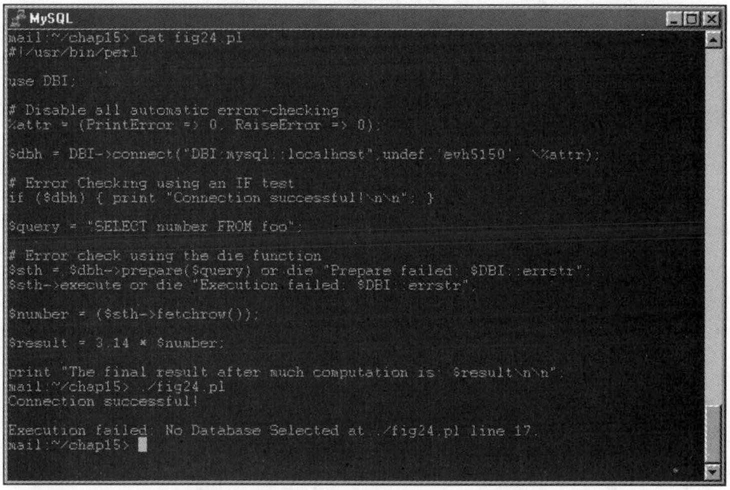

Figure 15-24: Using manual error-checking methods

Built-in error status methods

There are built-in methods for working with error status messages. The example program in Figure 15-24 showed one of these, `errstr`. Another method that I'll highlight is the `err()` method. The `errstr()` method contains the string text message of the error. The `err()` method contains the error number corresponding to the error.

The `errstr()` and `err()` methods exist both at the DBI level and at the handle level. At the DBI level, as used in Figure 15-24, the methods contain the information for the last-used handle. The handle-level methods are called as shown:

```
$dbh->errstr();
$dbh->err();
```

Modifying the program from Figure 15-24 to use the handle methods is quite simple, as shown in Figure 15-25.

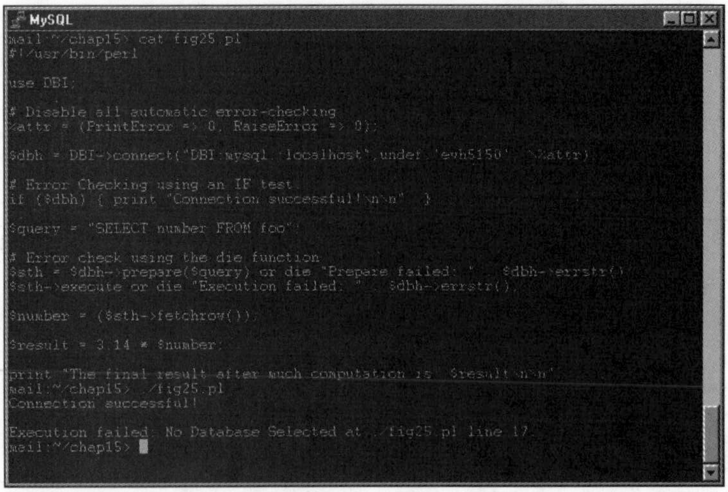

Figure 15-25: Using manual error checking and the handle-level error methods

Using handle-level error methods you could assign the `err` results to variables for later testing. An example of a program using this type of test is shown in Figure 15-26.

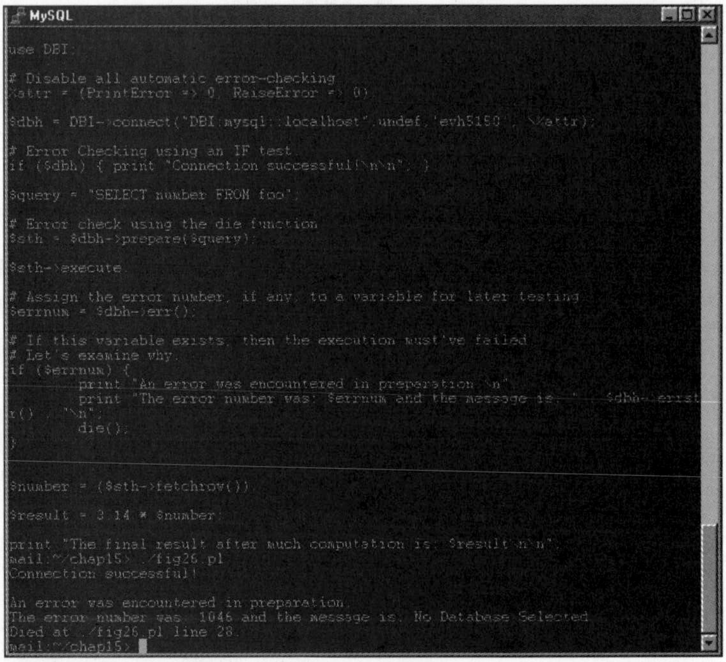

Figure 15-26: Using handle-level error methods and assigning one to a variable for later use

Functions with the DBI

So far, I've discussed four functions as an introduction to the DBI:

```
connect()
disconnect()
err()
errstr()
```

I've used some other functions in examples. This section examines those functions, along with others for use with the DBI and MySQL DBD.

Going back to examples shown in previous figures in this chapter you'll see the creation of a statement handle, `$sth`, and the use of the `prepare()` method along with the `execute()` method. The `prepare()` method takes an SQL statement and stores or parses it for later execution by the DBI. The `execute()` method then takes that prepared statement and runs it against the database engine. The `execute()` method returns the number of rows affected for non-`SELECT` statements. With a `SELECT` statement a `True` value is returned upon successful execution.

The examples of the `prepare()` and `execute()` methods shown previously were done in such a manner as to produce an error. Therefore, I'll leave those examples alone and show a new example program with a successful `prepare()` and `execute()` method call, as shown in Figure 15-27.

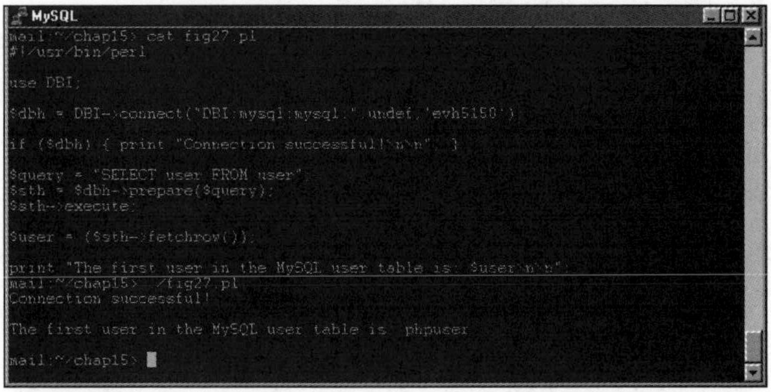

Figure 15-27: A successful execution of a MySQL statement using the Perl DBI

The `prepare()` and `execute()` methods both take optional arguments or placeholders that are substituted into the actual statement at execution time, much like a variable would be. The placeholder is the question mark (?). The `bind_param()` method substitutes the actual values for the question-mark placeholder when using prepare(). Alternatively, the substitution can take place at execution time by supplying an argument to the execute() call. Figure 15-28 shows an example of this behavior.

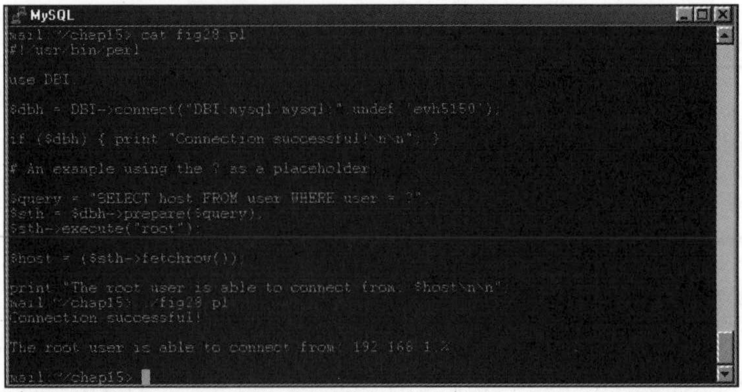

Figure 15-28: Using a placeholder to substitute a value at execution time for a SELECT statement

An example of the bind_param function is shown in Figure 15-29.

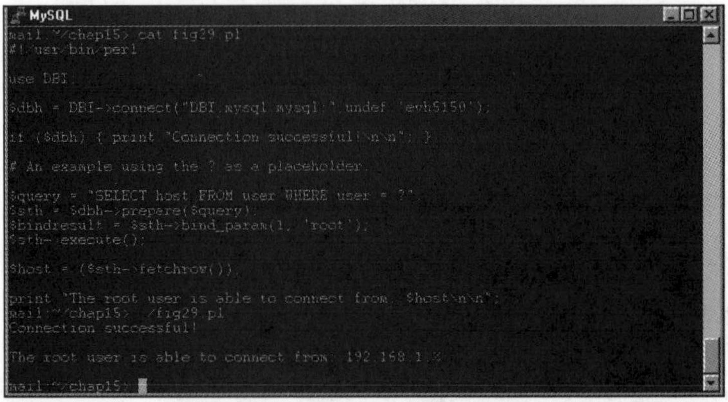

Figure 15-29: Using the bind_param function to substitute values in a prepare() call

Naturally, you could substitute variables for the values in the bind_param argument list. The bind_param argument list also takes an optional third argument for the type of data (such as CHAR, NUMERIC, and so on).

Another function in Figures 15-27 through 15-29 is of particular interest: `fetchrow()`. This and several related functions retrieve results from executed MySQL statements by using the DBI. The `fetch` functions are listed in Table 15-1.

Table 15-1
Fetch functions to retrieve statement results

Function name	*Description*
`fetchall_arrayref`	Retrieves all data as a reference to an array.
`fetchrow()`	Retrieves one value. Useful where one value is selected as a result.
`fetchrow_array()`	Retrieves results and places them in an array.
`fetchrow_arrayref()`	Retrieves data as a referenced array.
`fetchrow_hashref()`	Retrieves data as a hash. Operates similarly to `fetchrow_arrayref`.

I believe that examples of the different `fetch` functions serve better than a written explanation. For the examples in Figures 15-27 through 15-29, I retrieved only the first row of results. If you want to retrieve more than one row using the `fetchrow()` method, you have to loop through the results with a function such as `while`, as shown in Figure 15-30.

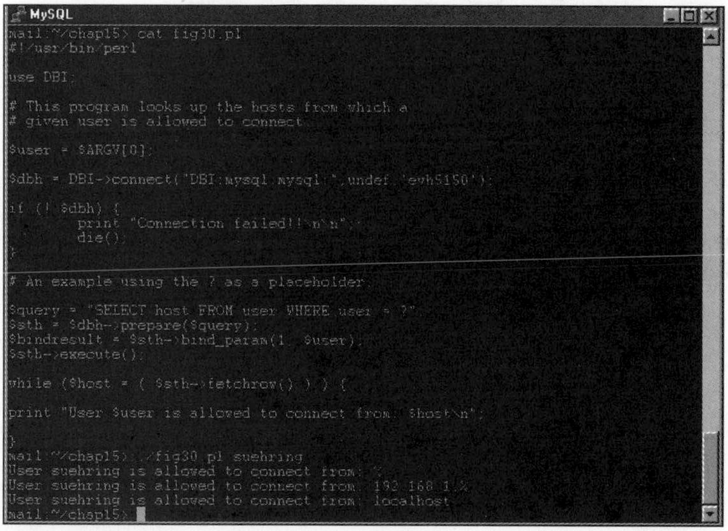

Figure 15-30: Retrieving all the results for the query, using a `while` loop and `fetchrow`

Figure 15-30 is a small useful program for determining the hosts that a user is allowed to connect from. The program takes the username to search for as an argument and returns the names of the hosts for which the user has an entry in the `user` table of the MySQL `grants` database.

Note If the `host` field of the `user` table is blank, the program from Figure 15-30 may return incomplete or incorrect results.

Figure 15-31 shows an example of the `fetchall_arrayref()` method for retrieving query results. The method gets all the results at once and places them in an array with each row contained as part of the array. As this is a multi-dimensional array, the results need to be accessed as such.

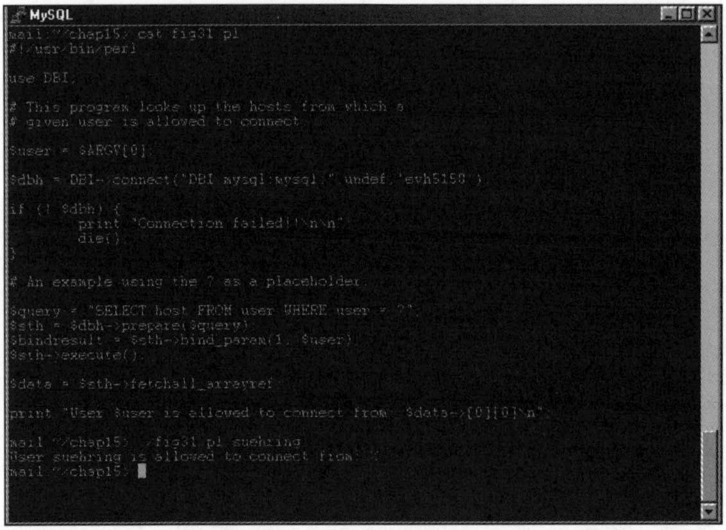

Figure 15-31: The `fetchall_arrayref()` method in action

Figure 15-32 modifies the same program from the previous two figure illustrations to use the `fetchrow_array()` method. This method is frequently used for retrieving results where the `SELECT` statement queries for more than one column.

The final two methods, `fetchrow_arrayref()` and `fetchrow_hashref()`, both retrieve results as references to arrays or hashes, respectively. With `fetchrow_hashref()` the first row of results contain the field names for the values with the actual values being stored thereafter. An example of the `fetchrow_arrayref()` method is shown in Figure 15-33.

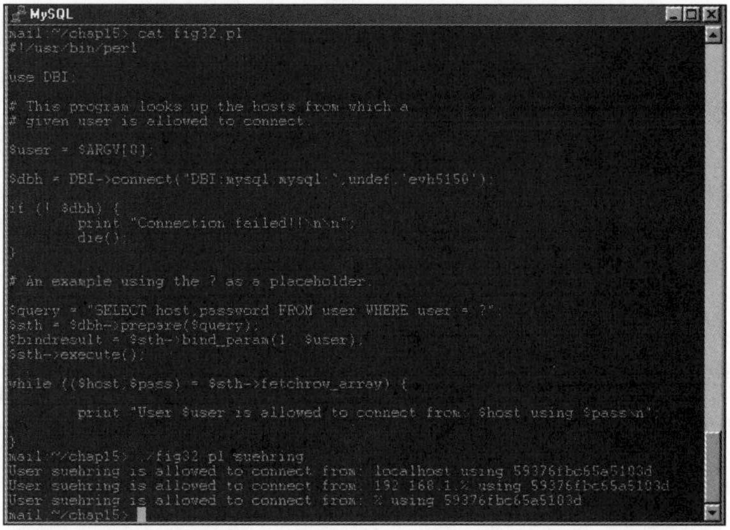

Figure 15-32: The `fetchrow_array()` method is frequently used as a means to retrieve results from a query.

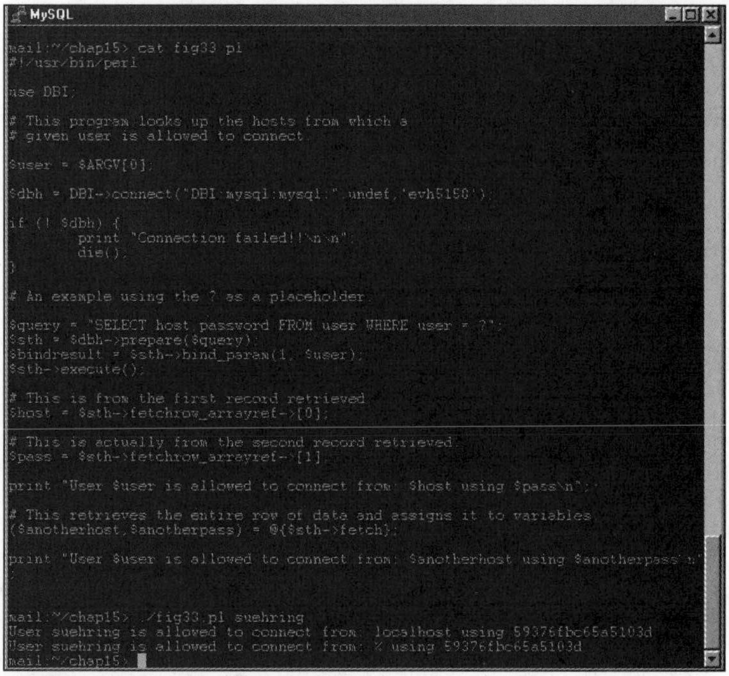

Figure 15-33: An example of the `fetchrow_arrayref` method for retrieving results from a query

Figure 15-33 illustrates the `fetchrow_arrayref()` method. Notice that the first call retrieves the host from the query, and the second call actually retrieves the password corresponding to the second entry or second row of results. The third method call retrieves an entire row of results from the query at once.

Not all interactions with the database require both a `prepare()` and `execute()` method call. The `do()` method enables you to execute statements without having to make two separate calls as with `prepare()` and `execute()`. Like the `prepare()` and `execute()` methods, `do()` can accept placeholders. The placeholders are question marks and should be included as the last argument of the `do()` method call. Figure 15-34 shows an example of `do()`.

Note: You cannot retrieve results using a `do()` method call, so it is not appropriate for `SELECT` statements. The `do()` method does return the number of rows affected by the statement. Therefore, it can be helpful to store this value for sanity checking. In other words, you can compare the number of returned rows to ensure that the value makes sense for the given query.

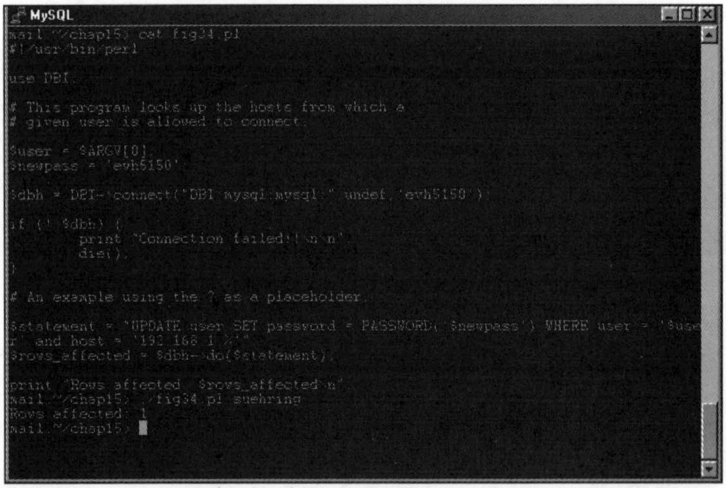

Figure 15-34: Using the `do()` method call to execute a statement without having to prepare it in a separate statement

Another method, `dump_results()`, can assist to print results for testing purposes while you are programming. `dump_results()` calls another method, `neat_string()`, to format the results and make them look nicer as output. The `dump_results()` method can take up to five arguments. The syntax is as follows:

```
$result = DBI::dump_results($sth, $length, $line_break,
$field_break, $filedes);
```

The first argument, `$sth` or the statement handle, is required. The second argument, represented by `$length` in the example, is the maximum length for the results to print. The third and fourth arguments specify how you want to separate the lines and fields respectively. The default for a line break is the newline (`\n`), and the default for a field separator is a comma. The final argument, represented by `$filedes`, is a pointer to a file handle to indicate a file to which the results should be dumped (instead of to the screen) on `STDOUT`. You don't save the results of the `dump_results()` method; rather, you use Perl's `print` function to print them.

More than one figure is necessary to fully illustrate the syntax and use of the `dump_results()` method. Figure 15-35 shows a basic instance; Figure 15-36 shows a basic usage. Figure 15-36 demonstrates setting a maximum length for the second argument.

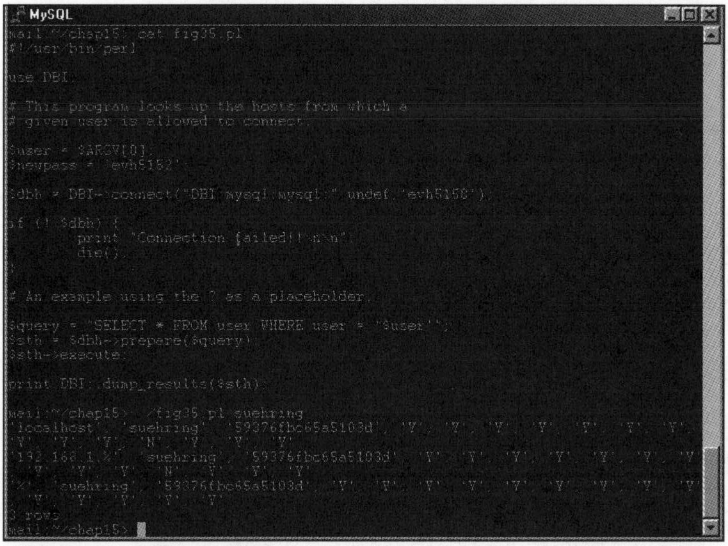

Figure 15-35: A basic use of the `dump_results()` method

Figure 15-37 shows a usage of field separators and the manual setting of line breaks; Figure 15-38 demonstrates the use of a file handle to dump results into a file instead of to the screen.

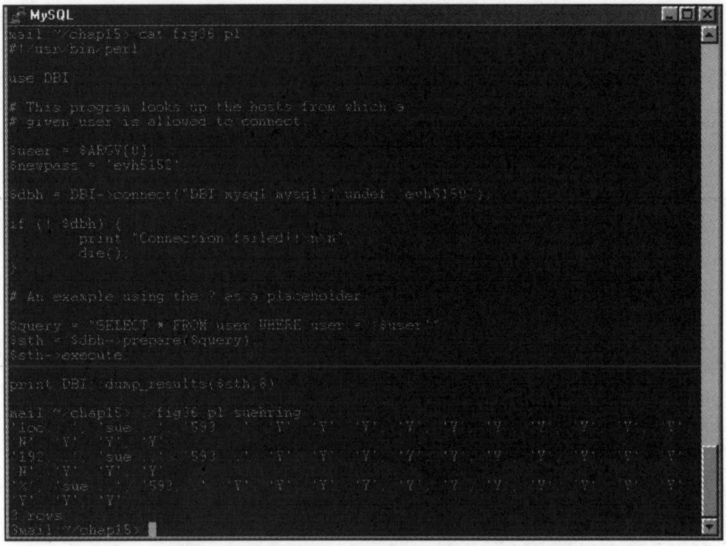

Figure 15-36: Setting the maximum length to 8 with the second argument of the `dump_results()` method

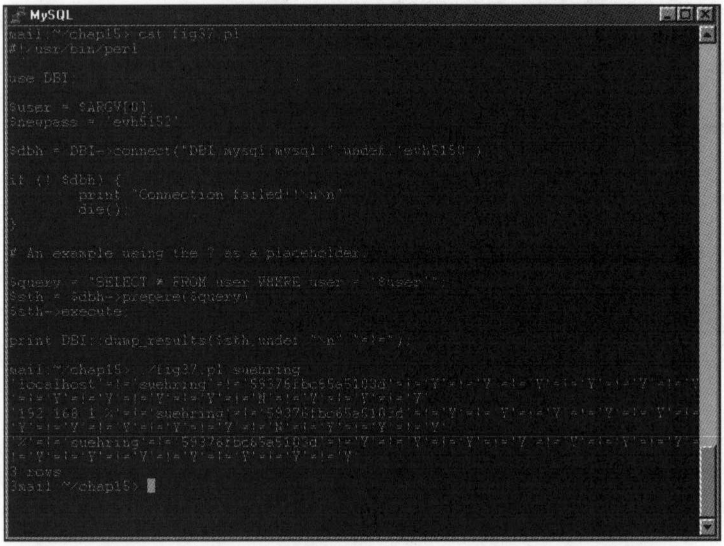

Figure 15-37: Using an odd combination of characters as a field separator and manually setting the line break to a newline

Figure 15-38: Using a file handle to dump the results to a file instead of to `STDOUT`

Though not technically necessary for the MySQL DBD, the `finish()` method can be used to recycle statement handles and improve the readability of your code. The `finish()` method releases the remaining results from a statement handle and frees it for another use. The MySQL DBD does not require you to finish before issuing another prepare statement, but doing so can greatly assist in tracing code if you need to go back and examine the code at a later date.

Finally, if you have to clean up input received from a user or through a Web form, you should know about the `quote()` method that makes strings safe for use inside an SQL statement. It takes a sole argument — the string to work with — and results in an SQL-safe string. Figure 15-39 shows an example of the `quote()` method.

> **Note** When using the `quote()` method, you do not need to include quotes around the strings inside queries. Notice, for example, the change in the way the variable `$safeuser` is called in Figure 15-39.

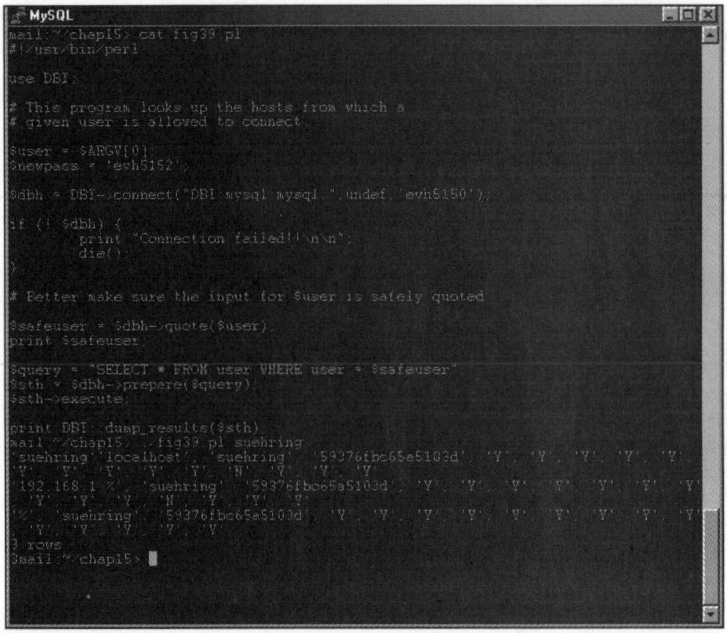

Figure 15-39: The `quote()` method serves to make strings SQL safe.

Building Basic Applications

I've been making basic applications throughout this chapter — inside examples of error messages, queries, and updates. This section expands on some of those examples to show a basic Perl-based DBI application that uses functions and methods discussed in the previous section. The goal is to prepare you for building the applications needed to manage an e-commerce Web site in a later section.

MySQL User Manager

An earlier example created a small application to look at the hosts from which a given user is allowed to connect. I'll expand on that example here, making a more powerful user manager to examine the privileges that a given user/host combination has. As a starting point, Figure 15-40 illustrates the earlier program.

This program, though fine for the examples, is woefully inadequate when it comes to error checking. For example, if the `host` field is blank, the program evaluates the `while` loop as `false` and stops iterating through it. Further, no input validation is done. I've made changes to the program to make it check for errors and continue through the `while` loop even if the `host` is blank. I'm doing some shenanigans on the actual query to make sure that it always returns something regardless of whether the `host` is blank. I added the user to the query results so as to make it always evaluate `true` for the `while` loop. The program is shown in Figure 15-41.

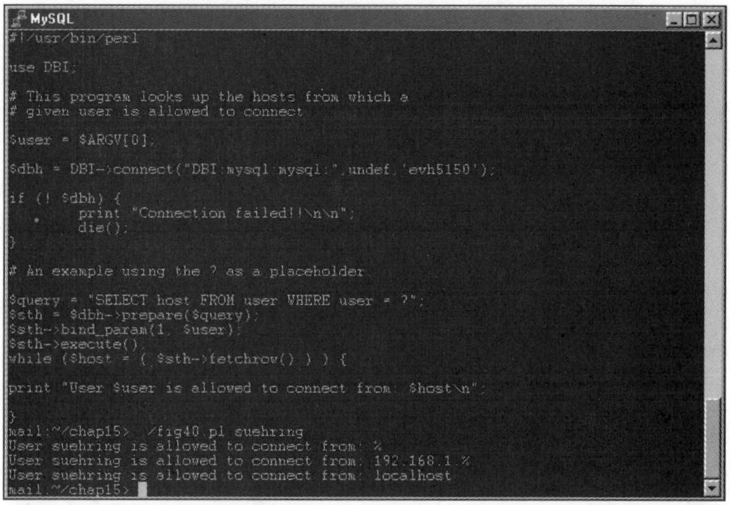

```
MySQL
#!/usr/bin/perl

use DBI;

# This program looks up the hosts from which a
# given user is allowed to connect

$user = $ARGV[0];

$dbh = DBI->connect("DBI:mysql:mysql:",undef,'evh5150');

if (! $dbh) {
        print "Connection failed!!\n\n";
        die();
}

# An example using the ? as a placeholder

$query = "SELECT host FROM user WHERE user = ?";
$sth = $dbh->prepare($query);
$sth->bind_param(1, $user);
$sth->execute();
while ($host = ( $sth->fetchrow() ) ) {

print "User $user is allowed to connect from: $host\n";

}
mail:~/chap15> ./fig40.pl suehring
User suehring is allowed to connect from: %
User suehring is allowed to connect from: 192.168.1.%
User suehring is allowed to connect from: localhost
mail:~/chap15>
```

Figure 15-40: A small program to query the hosts for a given user in the MySQL grants database

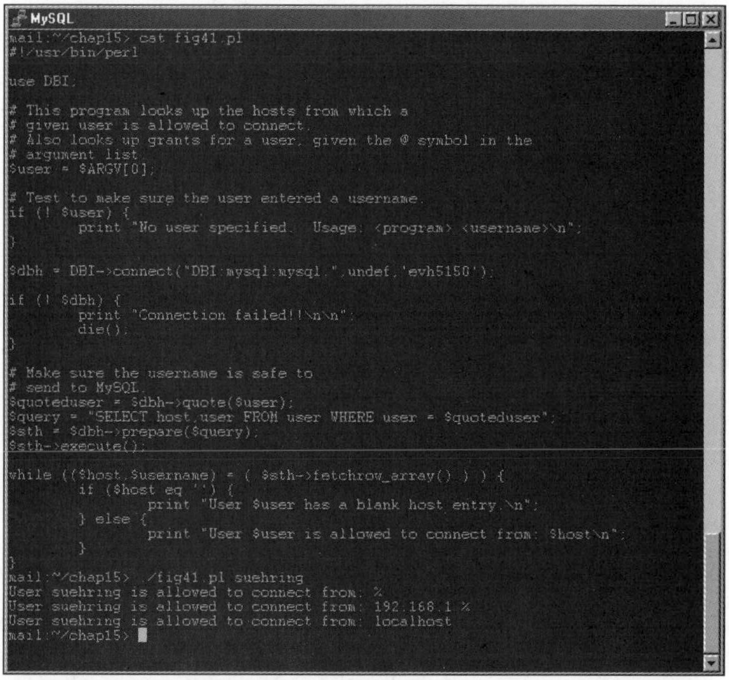

```
MySQL
mail:~/chap15> cat fig41.pl
#!/usr/bin/perl

use DBI;

# This program looks up the hosts from which a
# given user is allowed to connect.
# Also looks up grants for a user, given the @ symbol in the
# argument list.
$user = $ARGV[0];

# Test to make sure the user entered a username.
if (! $user) {
        print "No user specified.  Usage: <program> <username>\n";
}

$dbh = DBI->connect("DBI:mysql:mysql:",undef,'evh5150');

if (! $dbh) {
        print "Connection failed!!\n\n";
        die();
}

# Make sure the username is safe to
# send to MySQL.
$quoteduser = $dbh->quote($user);
$query = "SELECT host,user FROM user WHERE user = $quoteduser";
$sth = $dbh->prepare($query);
$sth->execute();

while (($host,$username) = ( $sth->fetchrow_array() ) ) {
        if ($host eq '') {
                print "User $user has a blank host entry.\n";
        } else {
                print "User $user is allowed to connect from: $host\n";
        }
}
mail:~/chap15> ./fig41.pl suehring
User suehring is allowed to connect from: %
User suehring is allowed to connect from: 192.168.1.%
User suehring is allowed to connect from: localhost
mail:~/chap15>
```

Figure 15-41: Adding error checking and other improvements to a small user management program with the Perl DBI

To make the program even more useful I've added the ability to look up the privileges that a given user/host pair has. This shows an example of another type of statement being performed on the MySQL database other than a SELECT. The program is too large to fit into a figure illustration but I've included the program here and also some sample output in Figure 15-42.

```
#!/usr/bin/perl

use DBI;

# This program looks up the hosts from which a
# given user is allowed to connect.
# Also looks up grants for a user, given the @ symbol
# in the argument list.

$user = $ARGV[0];

# Test to make sure the user entered a username.
if (! $user) {
        print "No user specified.  Usage: <program> \
<username>\n";
}

$dbh = DBI->connect("DBI:mysql:mysql:",undef,'evh5150');

if (! $dbh) {
        print "Connection failed!!\n\n";
        die();
}

# If there's an @ symbol then the user wants to look up
# grants.
if ($user =~ m/\@/) {
        ($user,$inhost) = split(/\@/, $user);

        # Make sure the username and host are safe to
        # send to MySQL.
        $quoteduser = $dbh->quote($user);
        $quotedhost = $dbh->quote($inhost);
        &priv($user,$inhost);
}
else {
        # User wants to simply lookup the hosts allowed
        # for given username.

        # Make sure the username is safe to
        # send to MySQL.
        $quoteduser = $dbh->quote($user);
```

```
        $query = "SELECT host,user FROM user WHERE \
        user = $quoteduser";
        $sth = $dbh->prepare($query);
        $sth->execute();

        while (($host,$username) = ( \
        $sth->fetchrow_array() ) ) {
                if ($host eq '') {
                        print "User $user has a \
                        blank host entry.\n";
                }
                else {
                        print "User $user is allowed \
                        to connect from: $host\n";
                }
        }
}

sub priv
{

# This subroutine looks up the grants for the given
# user/host pair.

($user,$host) = @_;

$query = "SHOW GRANTS FOR $user\@$host";
$sth = $dbh->prepare($query);
$sth->execute();

while ($grant = ( $sth->fetchrow() ) ) {
        print "$grant\n";
}

}
```

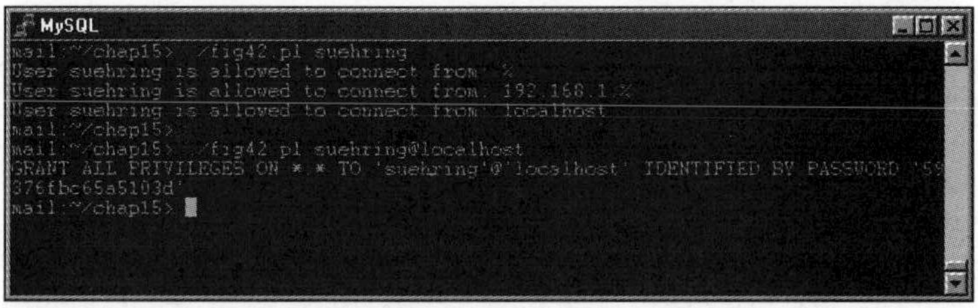

Figure 15-42: Usage examples of the MySQL User Management program I've built with the DBI

Other additions and modifications can be made to the simple user manager program that I've started. I'd still like to see better error checking in it as well as more features. Another modification that would be useful would be enabling the program to add users to MySQL. If a user isn't found, the program could ask whether to add the user and then ask for the password.

Cross-Reference Chapter 19 examines the integration of Linux and MySQL and offers some additional programs for management and administration.

On the CD-ROM The user-management program given in this section is included on the CD-ROM with this book.

Building Web Pages with the DBI

The e-commerce Web site that I'm building is mainly managed with Web-based tools. This offers the advantage of enabling employees to update the Web site from anywhere and with minimal training. Further, the use of Web-based tools for management lessens the risk of a user error accidentally ruining the data. This section examines how to build Web pages with data from a MySQL database. This is in preparation for the final section of this chapter, which entails the building of the e-commerce Web site.

Programs written to interact with a Web server are sometimes referred to as Common Gateway Interface or CGI programs, sometimes even as CGI scripts. Perl programs written for the Web are also sometimes called CGIs and are typically executed by the Web server. A better term would probably be Web applications. For this section I'll be referring to CGI programs or CGI scripts interchangeably with Web applications.

This section assumes that you have a Web server running and the ability to execute CGI programs with the Perl module `CGI.pm`. In the background, programs written for the Web operate the same as non-Web based programs; the same Perl routines that work in other programs work with a CGI script. It should be noted that because CGIs typically are executed by non-privileged Web servers that not all routines may work the same.

For the purposes of this book, a *static page* is one contained entirely in a file, typically with a `.html` or `.htm` extension. The page rarely changes; when it does, it is edited by hand. A *dynamic page* is a page built automatically (or by a process other than writing the HTML each time), and it contains data that changes often.

A simple Web application to query MySQL

One of the basic building blocks of a CGI program is the Web form called with the `<form>` HTML tag. The Web form calls an action or program to execute. This program is the CGI. As a simple example, consider the Web page in Figure 15-43 — a simple button created on a static Web page, using the HTML shown later. When clicked, that button calls a CGI (contained in Figure 15-44) and outputs the results to another Web page (as shown in Figure 15-45).

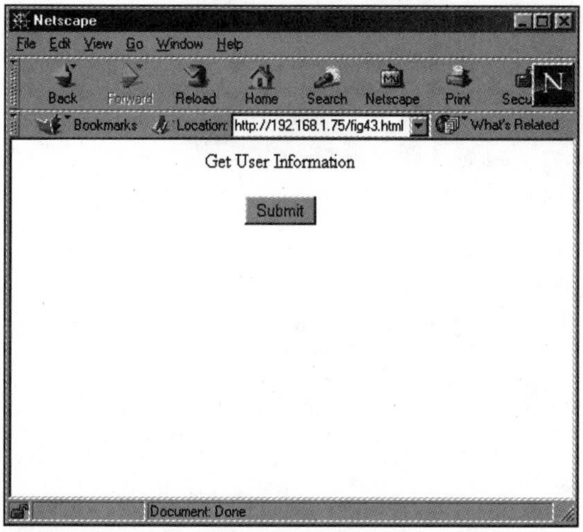

Figure 15-43: A static Web page with a form button to call a CGI

The HTML to produce the static Web page from Figure 15-43:

```
<html>
<center>
Get User Information
<form action="/cgi-bin/fig44.cgi">
<input type=button name=fig44 value="Submit">
</form>
</center>
</html>
```

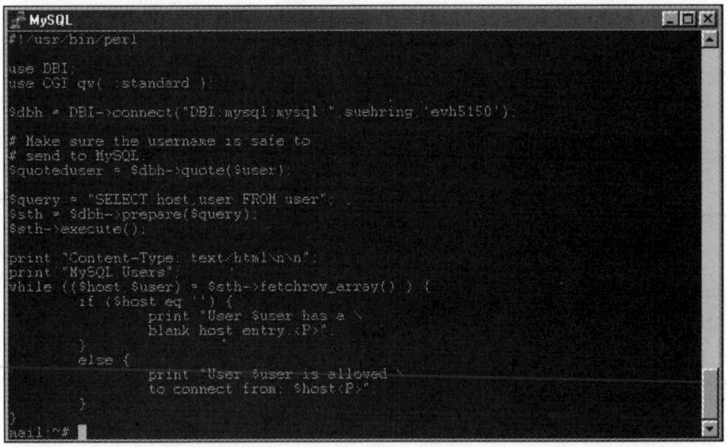

Figure 15-44: The CGI that is executed when the form button is selected

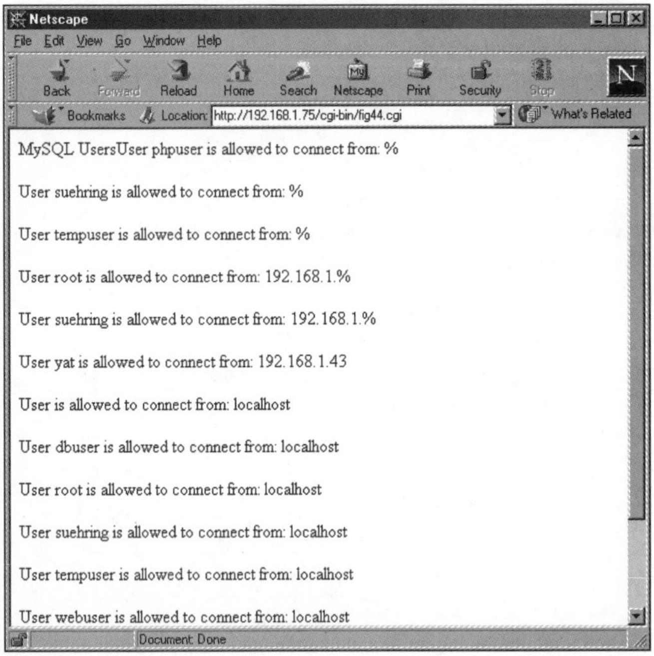

Figure 15-45: The results from the CGI automatically build a dynamic Web page.

Looking at the code in Figure 15-44, notice the addition of the `use CGI` directive. This addition takes advantage of the `CGI.pm` module and all its features to ease the burden on CGI programmers. Also note the addition of the following line:

```
print "Content-Type: text/html\n\n";
```

The previous line of code prints an HTML header to the Web browser so it knows to read the output as a Web page. Finally, notice that the newline characters (\n) in the print statements have been replaced with the HTML tag for a paragraph, <P>.

Accepting input from a form

The program shown in the previous section isn't powerful. I can enhance the program by allowing for user input, much like the User Management program shown in previous examples in this chapter. I'll add a text input box to enable the user to input a username to query against the MySQL database.

Much of the error checking that I added in the previous section is still applicable. The HTML for the new version of the Web page is shown with the resulting page in Figure 15-46.

```
<html>
<center>
Enter a user to retrieve User Information
<form method=post action="/cgi-bin/fig47.cgi">
<input type=text length=30 name=user><P>
<input type=submit name=fig44 value="Submit">
</form>
</center>
</html>
```

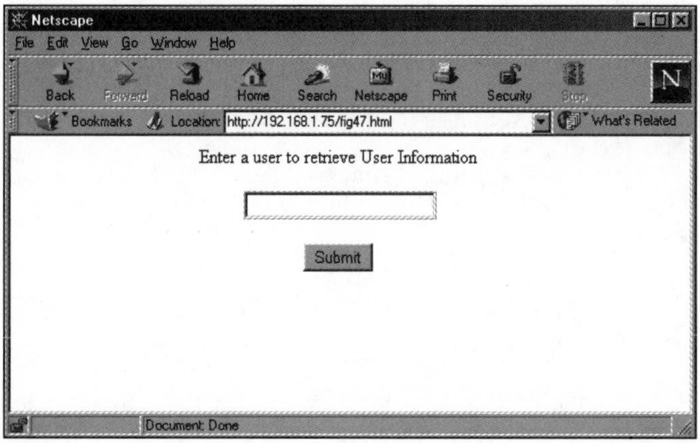

Figure 15-46: An input form for a Web-based version of the user manager program

The code for the Web version of the user manager is as follows:

```
#!/usr/bin/perl

use DBI;
```

```
use CGI qw( :standard );

# This program looks up the hosts from which a
# given user is allowed to connect.
# Also looks up grants for a user, given the @ symbol in the
# argument list.

# Get the input from the form.
$user = param("user");

# Test to make sure the user entered a username.
if (! $user) {
        print "No user specified.  Usage: <program>
<username><P>";
}

# Print an HTML header
print "Content-Type: text/html\n\n";

# Connect to the database
$dbh = DBI->connect("DBI:mysql:mysql:",suehring,'evh5150');

if (! $dbh) {
        print "Connection failed!!<P>";
        die();
}

# If there's an @ symbol then the user wants to look up
# grants.
if ($user =~ m/\@/) {
        ($user,$inhost) = split(/\@/, $user);

        # Make sure the username and host are safe to
        # send to MySQL.
        $quoteduser = $dbh->quote($user);
        $quotedhost = $dbh->quote($inhost);
        &priv($user,$inhost);
}
else {
        # User wants to simply lookup the hosts allowed
        # for given username.

        # Make sure the username is safe to
        # send to MySQL.
        $quoteduser = $dbh->quote($user);
```

```
        $query = "SELECT host,user FROM user WHERE \
        user = $quoteduser";
        $sth = $dbh->prepare($query);
        $sth->execute();

        while (($host,$username) = ( $sth->fetchrow_array() ) )
{
                if ($host eq '') {
                        print "User $user has a \
                        blank host entry.<P>";
                }
                else {
                        print "User $user is allowed \
                        to connect from: $host<P>";
                }
        }
}

sub priv
{

# This subroutine looks up the grants for the given
# user/host pair.

($user,$host) = (@_);

$query = "SHOW GRANTS FOR $user\@$host";
$sth = $dbh->prepare($query);
$sth->execute();

while ($grant = ( $sth->fetchrow() ) ) {
        print "$grant<P>";
}
}
```

The code is basically the same as the code used to produce Figure 15-42. The notable addition or change is the following line:

```
$user = param("user");
```

Instead of getting the user for input from the command line in `$ARGV[0]`, the input comes from the Web form. The `param()` function is contained the `CGI.pm` module. Some output examples from this program are shown in Figures 15-47 and 15-48.

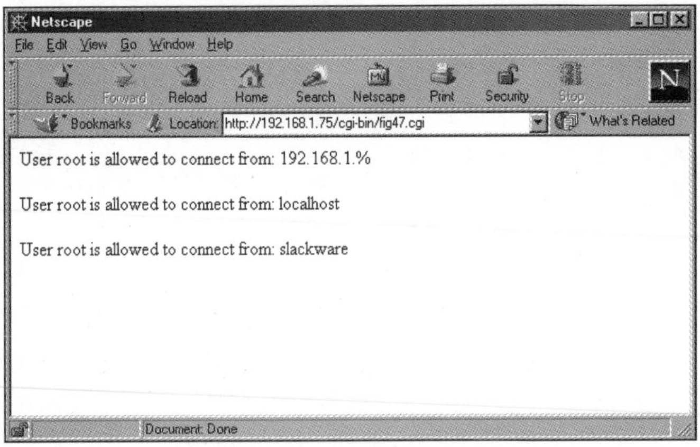

Figure 15-47: The Web version of the MySQL user-manager program

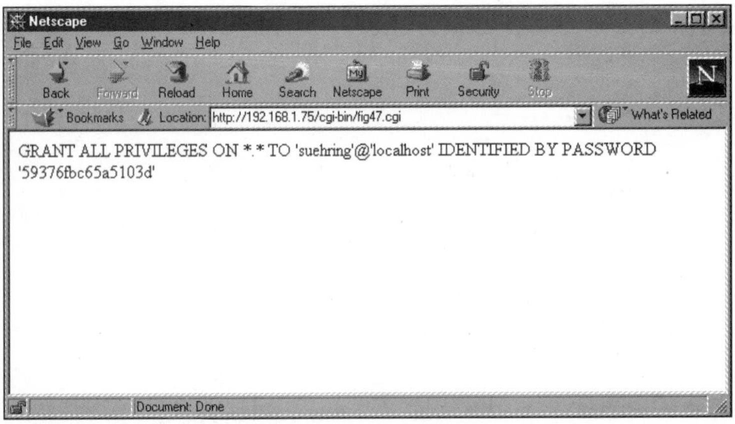

Figure 15-48: Another example of the Web version of the user-manager program, calling the program with the @ syntax

The examples in this section show how easy it is to write MySQL enabled applications for the Web in Perl. Knowledge of Perl is the key and beyond that implementing and modifying the programs for MySQL is a simple task.

Producing an E-Commerce Web site

The goal of this section is to produce a successful e-commerce Web site (built using the Perl DBI) that includes behind-the-scenes tools that aren't on the Web, as well as the engine that runs the Web site itself. The previous two sections have shown examples of building basic applications using the Perl DBI, as well as how to use the Perl DBI to build dynamic Web pages based on data in the MySQL database. This section combines those two components to produce a fully functional, albeit simple, e-commerce Web site.

Database layout

The initial database design and layout has already been done in previous chapters. I've modified it somewhat, altering it as I develop the Web site. The database layout now is as follows:

```
CREATE TABLE customer (
     email_address varchar(75) NOT NULL PRIMARY KEY,
     first_name varchar(50),
     last_name varchar(50),
     address1 varchar(50),
     address2 varchar(50),
     customer_zip varchar(10),
     area_code char(3),
     telephone_number char(7)
);
CREATE TABLE cardinfo (
     card_id int NOT NULL PRIMARY KEY,
     ccnum varchar(16),
     ccexp date,
     name_on_card varchar(100),
     email_address varchar(75)
);
CREATE TABLE cardtype (
     card_id int NOT NULL PRIMARY KEY,
     card_type varchar(20)
);
CREATE TABLE locale (
     zip varchar(10) NOT NULL PRIMARY KEY,
     city varchar(50),
     state char(2)
);
CREATE TABLE manufacturer (
     id int NOT NULL PRIMARY KEY,
     name varchar(50),
     address varchar(50),
     zip varchar(10),
     area_code char(3),
     telephone_number char(7),
     contact_name varchar(50)
);
CREATE TABLE product (
     id int NOT NULL PRIMARY KEY auto_increment,
     name varchar(50),
     artist varchar(50),
```

```
        price decimal(9,2),
        quantity integer,
        manu_id int,
        description varchar(255),
        category_id int
);
CREATE TABLE producttype (
        id int NOT NULL PRIMARY KEY,
        category varchar(50)
);
```

Note If you have the ecommerce database on your server now, it would be a good time to drop the database and start over with a fresh version, using the layout listed in this section.

One table, cardtype, needs to have a couple of credit card types entered into it. I could build a Web page and CGI for this purpose, but this data doesn't change frequently. Manual entry is quicker if all you need put in the database is the two card types that the site accepts.

```
INSERT INTO cardtype VALUES (1,'Visa');
INSERT INTO cardtype VALUES (2,'Mastercard');
```

Related to the cardtype input, the producttype table also needs to be populated with some initial data. I'll be selling music, movies, books, and video games at the site so I'll use three product types or categories.

```
INSERT INTO producttype VALUES (1, 'CD');
INSERT INTO producttype VALUES (2, 'DVD');
INSERT INTO producttype VALUES (3, 'Book');
INSERT INTO producttype VALUES (4, 'PC CD-ROM Video Game');
```

Building an inventory-input program

The first step to getting the site online is to get products listed in the database so people can locate them and buy them. To accomplish this task, I build a CGI that enables easy input of inventory items.

A static Web page can be used as the initial form for input. To input any of the four product types I'll need to enter the name of the product, the artist or author, the price, quantity on hand, the manufacturer if applicable, and a short description of the product. The simple static page is shown in Figure 15-49; the HTML to produce that page is as follows:

```
<html>
<form action="/cgi-bin/inventory.cgi">
Name of product:
<input type=text name=name length=30><P>
Artist/Author/Actor/Producer
```

```
<input type=text name=artist length=30><P>
Price: $
<input type=text name=price length=9><P>
Quantity on hand:
<input type=text name=quantity length=5><P>
Manufacturer:
<input type=text name=manu_id length=9><P>
Category:
<input type=text name=category_id length=4><P>
Short Description:
<input type=text name=description length=250><P>
<input type=submit name=submit value="Add to Database"><P>
</form>
</html>
```

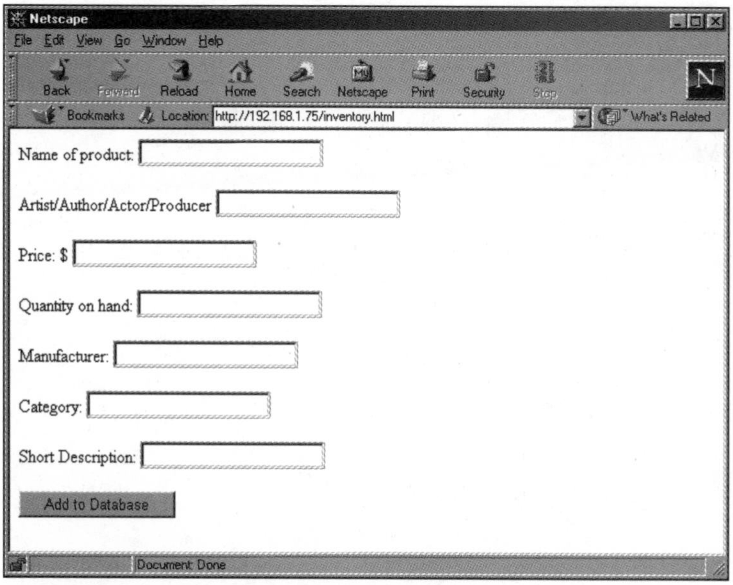

Figure 15-49: A static page for entering inventory

The CGI to add the products to the database is as follows:

```
#!/usr/bin/perl

use DBI;
use CGI qw( :standard );

# Get the input from the form.
$name = param("name");
$artist = param("artist");
$price = param("price");
```

```
$quantity = param("quantity");
$manu_id = param("manu_id");
$description = param("description");
$submit = param("submit");
$category_id = param("category_id");
$confirmed = param("confirmed");

$price =~ s/\s//g;
$quantity =~ s/\s//g;
$manu_id =~ s/\s//g;

# Print an HTML header
print "Content-Type: text/html\n\n";

# Test to make sure the user entered enough information.
if ((! $name) || (! $price) || (! $quantity)){
        print "Not enough info specified.<P>";
        exit;
}
elsif ($price =~ /\D\.?\D$/) {
        print "Please enter only digits and decimal point for
price.<P>\n";
        exit;
}
elsif ($quantity =~ /\D/) {
        print "Please enter only digits for quantity.<P>\n";
        exit;
}


# Connect to the database
$dbh = DBI->connect("DBI:mysql:ecommerce:",suehring,'evh5150');

if (! $dbh) {
        print "Connection failed!!<P>";
        die();
}

if ($submit) {
  # Look for a similar product to make sure we're not
  # adding a duplicate.
  $wcname = "%" . $name . "%";
  $wcartist = "%" . $artist . "%";
  $wcdescription = "%" . $description . "%";
  $quotedname = $dbh->quote($wcname);
  $quotedartist = $dbh->quote($wcartist);
  $quoteddescription = $dbh->quote($wcdescription);
  $query1 = "SELECT name,artist,description FROM product WHERE
name like $quotedname and artist like $quotedartist";
  $sth1 = $dbh->prepare($query1);
  $sth1->execute;
    while (($ename,$eartist,$edesc) = $sth1->fetchrow_array())
{
```

```
                print "Found a similar product:<P>\n";
                print "$ename - $eartist - $edesc<P>\n";
                exit;
    }

  #No existing product found, so print a confirm page.
  print "Confirm product addition<P>\n";
  print "<form action=\"/cgi-bin/inventory.cgi\"><P>\n";
  print "<input type=hidden name=name value=\"$name\"><P>\n";
  print "<input type=hidden name=artist
value=\"$artist\"><P>\n";
  print "<input type=hidden name=price value=\"$price\"><P>\n";
  print "<input type=hidden name=quantity
value=\"$quantity\"><P>\n";
  print "<input type=hidden name=manu_id
value=\"$manu_id\"><P>\n";
  print "<input type=hidden name=category_id
value=\"$category_id\"><P>\n";
  print "<input type=hidden name=description
value=\"$description\"><P>\n";
  print "Name: $name<P>Artist: $artist<P>Price: \$$price<P>\n";
  print "Quantity: $quantity<P>Manufacturer ID:
$manu_id<P>Category: $category_id<P>\n";
  print "Description: $description<P>\n";
  print "<input type=submit name=confirmed value=\"Add to
DB\"><P>\n";
  print "</form>";
  print "</html>";
}
#If user confirmed that it's ok, then add it.
elsif ($confirmed) {
  $quotedname = $dbh->quote($name);
  $quotedartist = $dbh->quote($artist);
  $quoteddescription = $dbh->quote($description);
  $ins_statement = "INSERT INTO product
(name,artist,price,quantity,manu_id,description,category_id)
VALUES
($quotedname,$quotedartist,'$price','$quantity','$manu_id',$quo
teddescription,'$category_id')";
  $sth = $dbh->do($ins_statement);
  if  (! $sth) {
        print "Apparently an error occured with the
statement<P>\n";
        print "$ins_statement<P>\n";
        exit;
  }
  else {
        print "$name added<P>\n";
  }
}
exit;
```

The program doesn't introduce any new concepts, so I'll just highlight some of its inner workings. The program makes use of the percent sign (%) as a wildcard in the SQL queries. The program accepts input from a form and does some simple error checking on the incoming data. If the first Submit button was clicked, the program then queries the product database for a similar product. If a similar product is found, a page is sent to the user, with information about the existing product (see Figure 15-50).

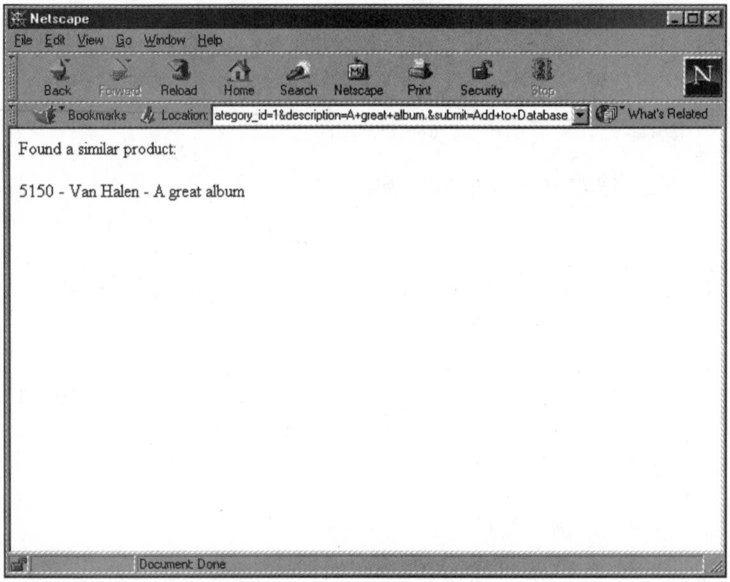

Figure 15-50: A similar product was found in the database, therefore this page is produced with results from the database query.

If no similar product is found, a confirmation page is produced as shown in Figure 15-51. Notice on that page that the existing values are included as hidden `form` tags; you don't see them in Figure 15-51 but, they exist if you view the page source. When the confirm button is clicked, those hidden `form` tags are passed back to the server the same as with any other form.

Finally, if the Confirmed button were clicked, the program adds the product to the database.

To develop this further, ideally you would add a method by which more than one item could be added at once. In addition, a method to search for `Manufacturer` or `Category ID` is needed. Many additional database tables and columns could be added with items such as warehousing, date of release, other formats, multiple categories, and so on. Look back at the example in the previous section for a simple search function with the DBI. The next section develops a product search engine.

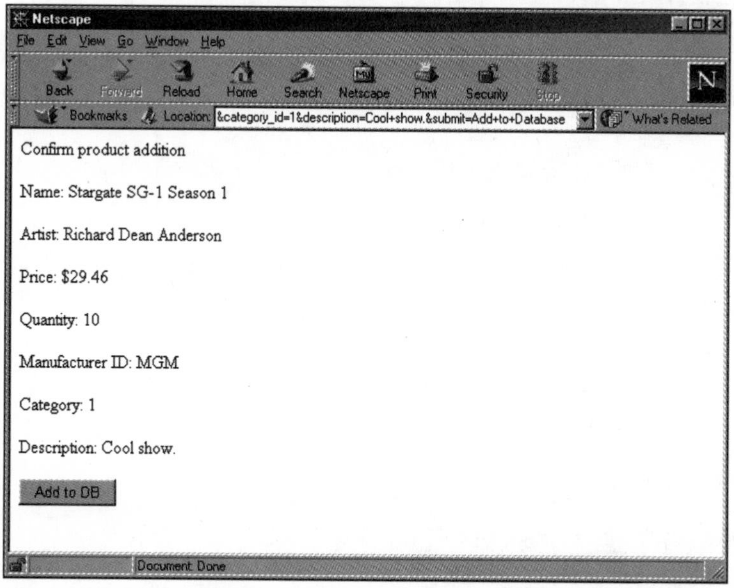

Figure 15-51: The confirm page produced by the inventory program

Note Please add some inventory to your sample database, using the inventory program or any other method. You'll need it for the next section.

Building a simple product search engine

To get the full benefit of this section, make sure you've added a few (or more) products to your database. This section builds a search engine to look for products in the database. The basis for the search engine is (again) a static page, which then links to a CGI to produce dynamic pages with the results.

I'll be making a simple search box that would probably go on the main page of the site — and a more complicated search page with more options (probably a separate page). Here is the HTML that produces the simple search page or box:

```
<html>
<center>
<form action="/cgi-bin/search.cgi" method="post">
<input type=text name=search size=20><P>
<input type=submit name=simple value=Search>
</center>
</html>
```

The simple search page is shown in Figure 15-52.

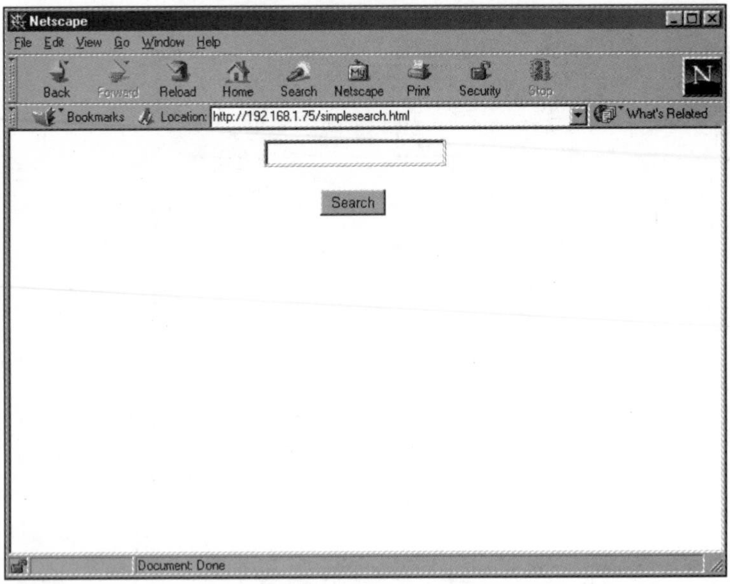

Figure 15-52: The simple search page

The HTML for producing the full search page looks like this:

```
<html>
<center>
<form action="/cgi-bin/search.cgi" method="post">
Product Name:<input type=text name=name size=20><P>
Artist/Author/Actor: <input type=text name=artist size=20><P>
Search item description?
<input type=radio name=description>Yes</input>
<input type=radio name=description checked>No</input><P>
<input type=submit name=full value=Search>
</center>
</html>
```

The full search page is shown in Figure 15-53.

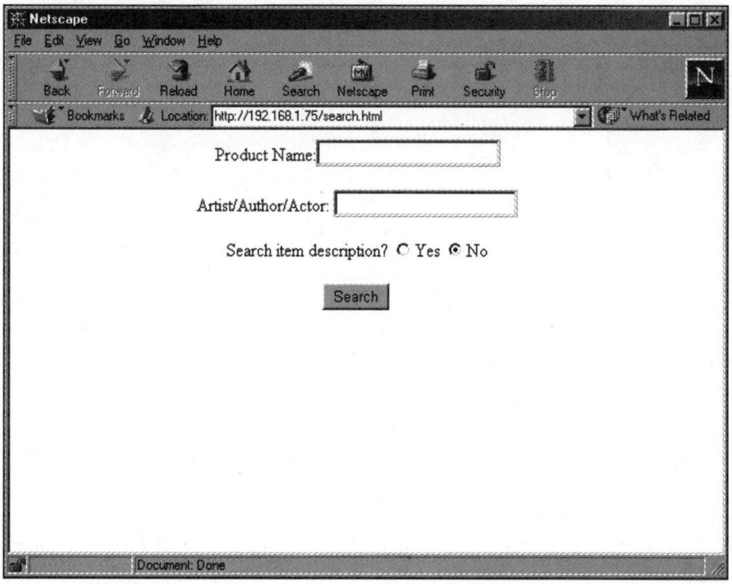

Figure 15-53: The full search page

The code to make the search functions work is as follows:

```
#!/usr/bin/perl

use DBI;
use CGI qw( :standard );

# Get the input from the form.
$name = param("name");
$artist = param("artist");
$search = param("search");
$description = param("description");
$simple = param("simple");
$full = param("full");

# Print an HTML header
print "Content-Type: text/html\n\n";

# Connect to the database
$dbh = DBI->connect("DBI:mysql:ecommerce:",suehring,'evh5150');
```

```
if (! $dbh) {
        print "Connection failed!!<P>";
        die();
}

if ($simple) {
  # Look for a product
  if (! $search) {
        print "Please go back and enter at least one search
term<P>\n";
        exit;
  }
  $wcsearch = "%" . $search . "%";
  $quotedsearch = $dbh->quote($wcsearch);
  $query1 = "SELECT name,artist,description,price,quantity FROM
product WHERE (name like $quotedsearch or artist like
$quotedsearch)";
  $sth1 = $dbh->prepare($query1);
  $sth1->execute;
  print "Search results for <B>$search</B><P>\n";
    while (($ename,$eartist,$edesc,$eprice,$equantity) = $sth1-
>fetchrow_array()) {
                $found = 1;
                print "<B>$ename:</B> $eartist - $edesc<P>\n";
                if ($equantity > 100) {
                        print " - Price: \$$eprice.  Usually
ships in 24 hours.<P>\n";
                } elsif ($equantity < 51) {
                        print " - Price: \$$eprice.  Usually
ships in 2 to 3 days.<P>\n";
                } elsif ($equantity > 50) {
                        print " - Price: \$$eprice.  Usually
ships in 2 to 3 days.<P>\n";
                }
    }
    if (! $found) {
        print "No products found like $search<P>\n";
    }
  exit;
}
#If using full search page
elsif ($full) {
  if ($name ne "") {
        $searchterm = 1;
        $wcname = "%" . $name . "%";
        $quotedname = $dbh->quote($wcname);
        $query = "name like $quotedname";
        $search = "$name";
  }
  if ($artist ne "") {
        $searchterm = 1;
```

```
        $wcartist = "%" . $artist . "%";
        $quotedartist = $dbh->quote($wcartist);
        if ($query) {
          $query = $query . " and artist like $quotedartist";
          $search = $search . " and $artist";
        } else {
          $query = "artist like $quotedartist";
          $search = "$artist";
        }
  }
  if ($description eq "Yes") {
        $wcdesc = "%" . $description . "%";
        $quoteddescription = $dbh->quote($wcdesc);
        $additional_search = " or description like
$quoteddescription";
  } else {
        $additional_search = "";
  }
  if (! $searchterm) {
        print "Please go back and enter at least one search
term<P>\n";
        exit;
  }
  $query1 = "SELECT name,artist,description,price,quantity FROM
product WHERE ($query $additional_search)";
  print "$query1<P>\n";
  $sth1 = $dbh->prepare($query1);
  $sth1->execute;
  print "Search results for $search<P>\n";
    while (($ename,$eartist,$edesc,$eprice,$equantity) = $sth1-
>fetchrow_array()) {
                $found = 1;
                print "<B>$ename:</B> $eartist - $edesc<P>\n";
                if ($equantity > 50) {
                        print " - Price: \$$eprice.  Usually
ships in 24 hours.<P>\n";
                } elsif ($equantity < 50) {
                        print " - Price: \$$eprice.  Usually
ships in 2 to 3 days.<P>\n";
                }
    }
    if (! $found) {
        print "No products found matching $name $artist <P>\n";
    }
  exit;
}
print "Error";
exit;
```

As with other programs shown as examples, this one could always be improved — say, with better error checking and handling, as well as with more robust searching capabilities. But you get the idea.

The program works in much the same way as the inventory program; it gets parameters from the incoming form and places them into variables. From there, it makes a decision based on which button was selected (simple search or more complicated search). Notice that during the `while` loop to retrieve results a decision is made based upon the quantity on hand of the given product. Aside from that (and a bit of Perl here and there to make things work correctly), you have a fully functional search engine. An example of the simple search result is shown in Figure 15-54.

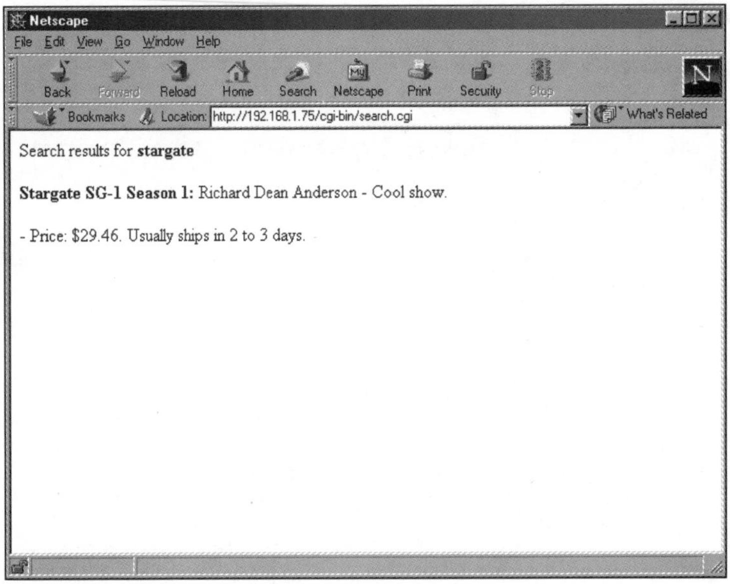

Figure 15-54: Results from the simple search

The more complicated search uses an `AND` if both the product name and artist are filled in. A sample result is shown in Figure 15-55.

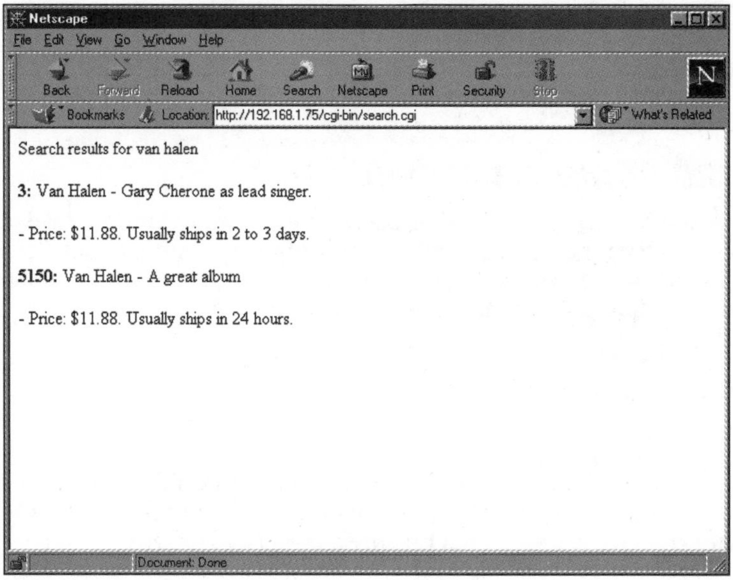

Figure 15-55: The full search page in action

Finally, if no results are found, that notification is sent to the visitor as well, as shown in Figure 15-56.

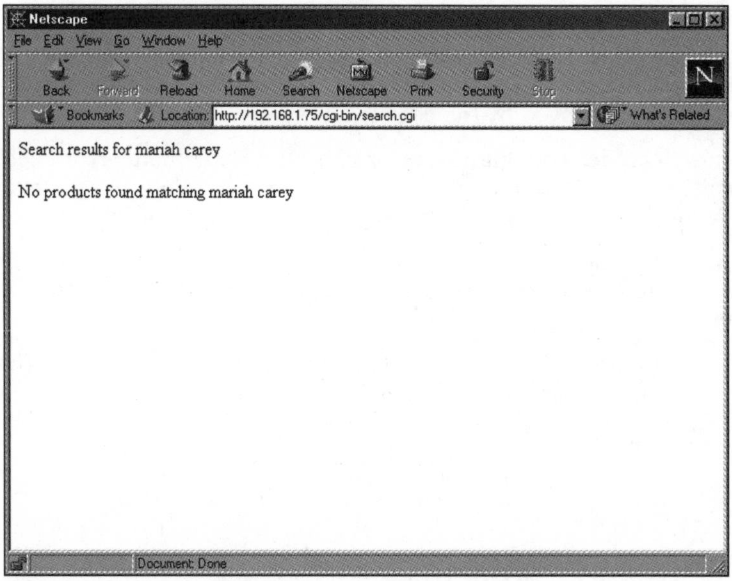

Figure 15-56: The page when no results are found

On the CD-ROM: The programs contained in this section are available on the CD-ROM.

Present and future expansion

The `ecommerce` site has a start. It's nowhere near ready to go online and take orders. A shopping-cart CGI must be built, as well as more robust inventory capabilities. Using a combination of cookies, knowledge of Perl, and the ideas in this chapter, it shouldn't be too much of a stretch to take the `ecommerce` site to the next step.

Summary

The Perl DBI is a generic interface used by many types of RDBMS to enable Perl programs to work with databases. MySQL has a database driver (DBD) to work with the DBI and enable the programmer to write powerful MySQL-enabled Perl programs.

- ✦ Both the DBI and the DBD for MySQL can be obtained at your nearest CPAN mirror or at `http://www.cpan.org`.
- ✦ The DBI takes advantage of handles to enable the developer to communicate with a database server. There are driver handles such as MySQL, database handles for connecting to the database server, and statement handles for working with SQL statements.
- ✦ The developer using the DBI communicates with the database using an object-oriented approach. Database handles are created manually by the user and can be destroyed by the user or automatically by Perl.
- ✦ The DBI also includes configurable error checking. By default, error checking is automatic. The programmer can control whether error checking is manual, automatic, or a combination of both even within the same program.
- ✦ The DBI includes many functions for working with databases, not just MySQL. These include functions to retrieve data such as `fetchrow`, `fetchrow_array`, and others.
- ✦ The DBI enables the Perl programmer to combine the power of Perl with the features of MySQL to make applications that run from the command line or in a CGI for the Web.

✦ ✦ ✦

CHAPTER 16

PHP Development

✦ ✦ ✦ ✦

In This Chapter

Installing PHP

Getting down to brass tacks with PHP

Configuring PHP MySQL

Listing PHP MySQL functions

Building MySQL-enabled applications with PHP

✦ ✦ ✦ ✦

A few years back, I devoted weeks to learning the Perl-DBI interface to MySQL so I could create MySQL-Perl applications for use in places other than the Web. When I did start writing Web-based applications, I was so immersed in the DBI that I neglected to look at other MySQL development languages for the Web; I had confidence in Perl as a powerful, stable development language.

Then one of my good friends told me I should be using yet another language — PHP. Even though I had spent a long time learning the DBI, I dove into PHP — an easy and powerful development language in its own right.

Why learn PHP? This is a valid question. If you don't need to write Web-based applications for MySQL, then PHP may be of limited usefulness for you. If, however, you do write Web-based applications and need them to interact with MySQL, PHP could be just what you're looking for. PHP is extremely useful for interacting with a MySQL database, is somewhat similar to Perl, and (dare I say) is somewhat intuitive.

This chapter examines how to install PHP and make it work with MySQL. I also cover some basic PHP concepts, as well as PHP-MySQL functions. The chapter concludes with a few example applications. (They're a little off the beaten track — no Guestbook application examples!)

PHP Installation

Unfortunately, installing PHP is not nearly as easy as installing the Perl DBI and MySQL DBD. However, the developers of PHP have taken great pains with their documentation; it's some of the best I've ever seen. This includes documentation of the installation software, as well as further coverage on their Web site, `http://www.php.net`.

This section concentrates on installing PHP on a Linux system, using the standard process based on `configure` and `make` commands. Your distribution of Linux may have a package-management tool, in which case you may already have a compiled version of PHP and Apache to work with. In addition, you may already have PHP installed, but it may not be MySQL-enabled. If such is the case, you'll need to reinstall a MySQL-enabled version of PHP. Finally, you'll probably have to reconfigure your Web server to work with PHP, so the chapter covers configuring Apache (the standard Linux Web-server software) with PHP.

What you need for installation

To install a MySQL-enabled version of PHP, you need three essential ingredients on hand:

- the PHP software itself
- the source code for Apache (or whatever Web server you're running)
- the MySQL client libraries

First, find out whether you already have PHP installed for use with Apache (and whether it's enabled for MySQL). On the Web server, type the following command:

```
httpd -l
```

Look for a line similar to this one:

```
mod_php4.c
```

If you see that line, congratulations — PHP is probably already installed and enabled on your Web server. Alternatively, look for lines like these:

```
Compiled-in modules:
  http_core.c
  mod_so.c
```

If you see those lines, then your server is configured to load dynamic modules — and you may have PHP support available.

Even if you have PHP installed, it may not be MySQL-enabled. To test an existing installation of PHP — and simultaneously check it for MySQL support — you should build a test PHP page. Simply create a regular file, save it with the filename `test.php`, and place it in the public `html` or `htdocs` folder, just as you would any page. The file itself needs no more than the following contents:

```
<?php
phpinfo()
?>
```

If everything is configured correctly, you should see a page similar to the one in Figure 16-1.

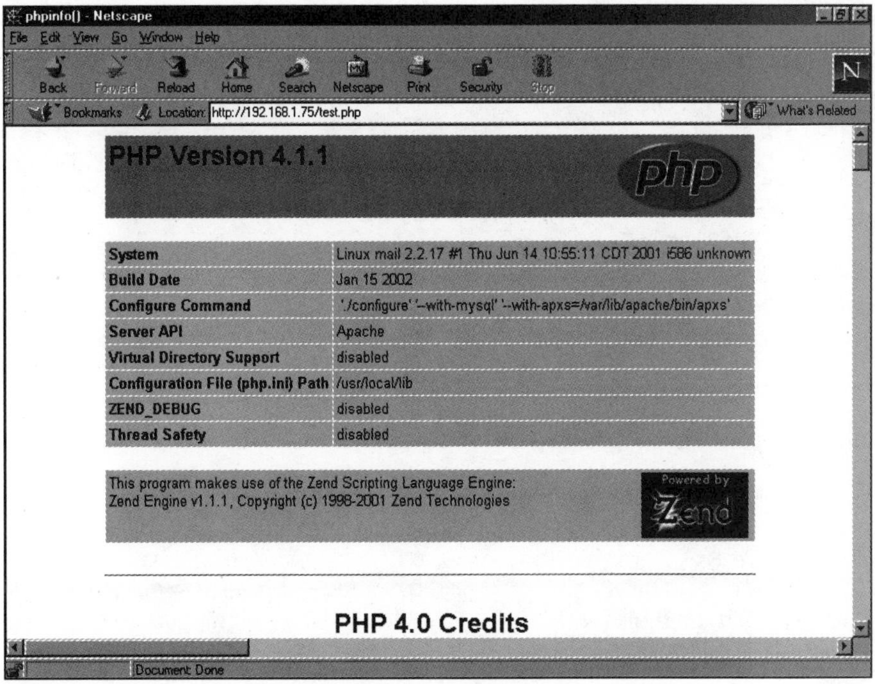

Figure 16-1: A server with PHP enabled and configured correctly

If, for whatever reason, the page does not come up, there is probably something wrong with your PHP configuration. Don't worry! I walk through the installation of PHP in this chapter; you can reconfigure as part of the installation process.

Scroll down in the PHP information page and look for the section on MySQL, as shown in Figure 16-2.

In the example in Figure 16-2, MySQL is enabled with PHP. If your page looks similar, you can skip the sections of this chapter concerned with installing and configuring PHP for use with MySQL.

If PHP is installed on your system but MySQL is not enabled, you'll want to reinstall PHP to enable MySQL.

Where to get the software

The main distribution site for PHP is `http://www.php.net`. I've also included PHP on the CD-ROM with this book (the PHP Web site probably has a newer version).

On the CD-ROM

The CD-ROM with this book includes the latest version of PHP available as of press time. This version works with the examples given in the book.

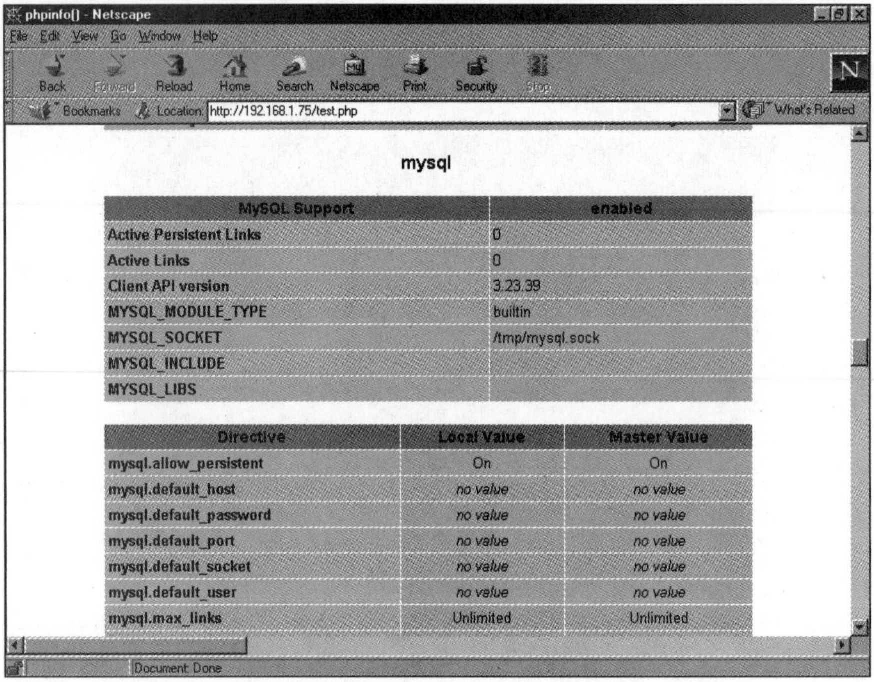

Figure 16-2: The MySQL section of the PHP information page

Installing PHP on a Linux system

Whether this is your first time installing PHP or a reinstallation (to enable MySQL on a system that already has PHP installed), this section can help. As a prerequisite, you should already have MySQL installed — including the libraries for MySQL. In addition, you should have a Web server running.

Note

This section examines the installation of PHP with Apache as the Web server software. If your Web server is not Apache, refer to the documentation included with your Web server – and with PHP itself – for help with installation.

Installing and configuring PHP

The steps for installing and configuring PHP on a Linux system (with Apache as the Web server) are as follows:

1. Unpack the PHP archive by issuing the following command:

   ```
   tar -zxvf php-<version>.tgz
   ```

   For example, Figure 16-3 shows PHP unpacked to its default directory.

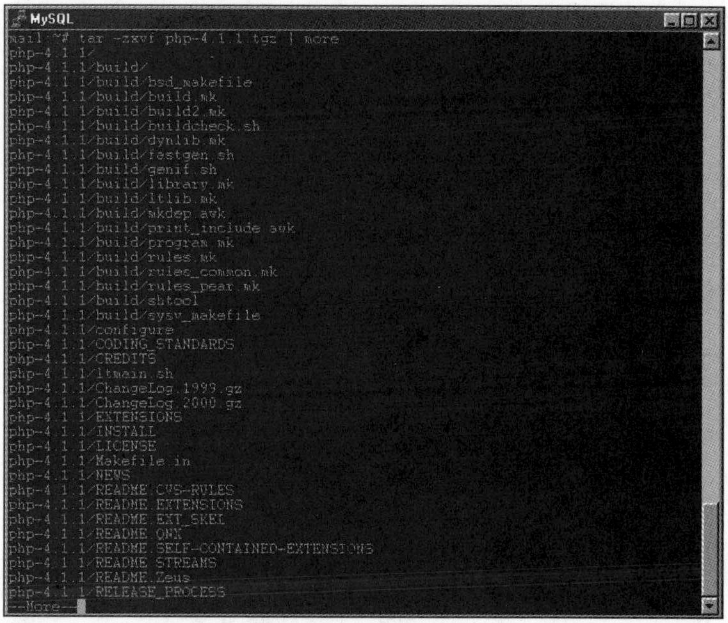

Figure 16-3: Unpacking the PHP archive

2. Change into the newly created PHP directory.

Note

If you have an existing PHP source directory that you've previously configured from, be sure to either remove the directory or at remove the `config.cache` file contained therein.

It is at this point where decisions must be made regarding your existing Apache installation as well as other options, you may want to enable with PHP. I'll show an example configuration that enables MySQL on an Apache server that uses Dynamic Shared Objects.

3. To configure PHP in the environment described in Step 2, type

```
./configure --with-mysql --with-apxs
```

You may receive an error message similar to that in Figure 16-4.

4. If you receive the error message shown in Figure 16-4, note what the message points out and respond accordingly. In this installation, I needed to add the path to the `apxs` module for Apache. First I needed to find it:

```
find / -name apxs
```

For the example, `apxs` is located in a couple of places; I chose the one in `/usr/local/apache/bin/` (your location may be different).

Figure 16-4: An error that occurs during PHP configuration

5. To tell the PHP `configure` script where it can find `apxs`, be sure to remove the existing `config.cache` file with the following code:

   ```
   rm config.cache ; ./configure --with-mysql --with-
   apxs=/usr/local/apache/bin/apxs
   ```

   An error similar to the previous one can occur if the `configure` script can't find the necessary MySQL libraries. If that happens, you have two possible fixes:

   * Add the path as part of the `--with-mysql` option.
   * Add the path to `/etc/ld.so.conf` and run `ldconfig`. (I've had better success with this option.)

   If the `configure` script runs successfully, congratulations! Although there's more to come, you now have a basic configuration in place to accommodate PHP. You may, however, receive one or more warnings when the `configure` script completes its run; a couple of these are shown in Figure 16-5.

6. Continue the installation process by building the software; type the following command:

   ```
   make
   ```

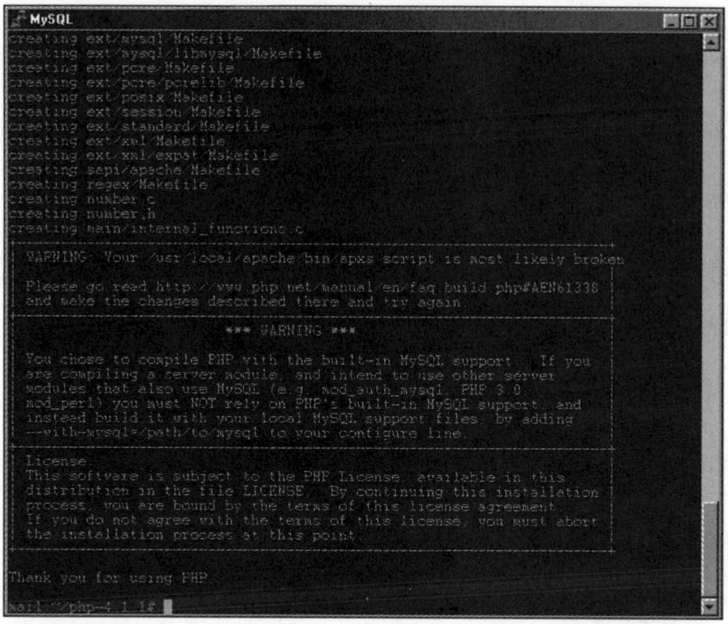

Figure 16-5: Some warnings produced by the PHP configure script

When you press Enter, the `make` process begins. How long it takes depends on the speed and resources available on your machine.

Tip

If the `make` process fails this time, don't worry. PHP installation can sometimes be difficult; often the build fails because a library is not found. Normally you can get good clues to what went wrong by closely examining the last few lines of code just before the point at which the build process died. For additional help, try the PHP Web site's section of search functions and FAQs. If you're getting error messages like those in Figure 16-5, chances are someone else has too—and there could be a simple fix.

If the `make` process is successful, congratulations!

7. Install the software, using the following command:

```
make install
```

Normally this is the final basic step in the build process. You're not done yet though. In particular, check inside your Apache Web server configuration file (usually called `httpd.conf`) for some lines like those shown in Figure 16-6.

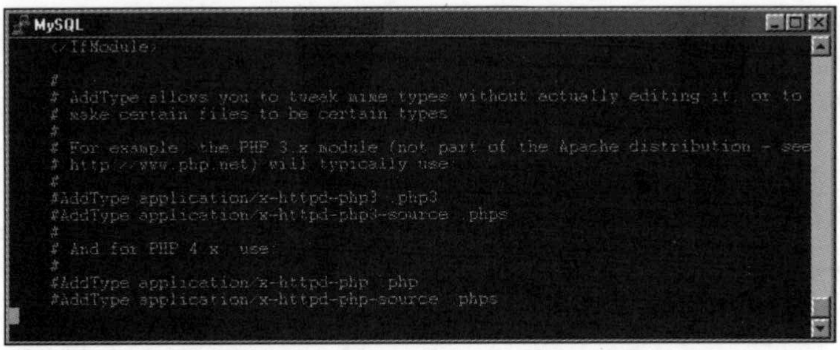

Figure 16-6: Lines relating to PHP 4.*x*, as they appear in the Apache Web server configuration file (httpd.conf)

8. Uncomment the lines that relate to PHP 4.*x* by removing the pound sign (#) from in front of those lines.
9. Save the uncommented configuration file and then restart the Web server software.

Tip: Truthfully, you could get by with just uncommenting the first line that mentions the `.php` extension.

The newly uncommented lines (which enable PHP when the Web server restarts) are shown in Figure 16-7.

Note: Don't forget to save the file and then restart the Web server for the changes to take effect. Simply restarting Apache will work, no need to reboot the entire machine; this is Linux!

10. Prepare to test your new configuration by creating a PHP file within the `htdocs` (or within a publicly available HTML directory) on your Web server.

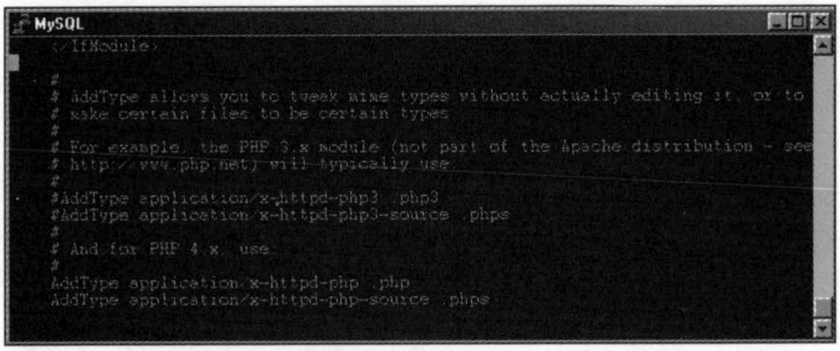

Figure 16-7: Uncommenting the PHP-related lines in httpd.conf enables PHP in the Apache Web server.

For example, you could create a file called `test.php` with the following contents:

```
<?php
phpinfo()
?>
```

11. Point your Web browser to your test page (which should resemble Figure 16-8) and scroll down to the MySQL section to verify that MySQL is enabled.

If the MySQL section in your test page indicates a successful PHP installation, congratulations! You can now skip ahead and start building MySQL-enabled PHP applications.

Even after a hassle-free installation process, however, two common errors can crop up:

- The page shows up on-screen as source code (as shown in Figure 16-9).
- The browser prompts you to Save or Open the file (it shouldn't).

If either of these errors happens to you, follow the troubleshooting steps given here (which use Figure 16-9 as an example).

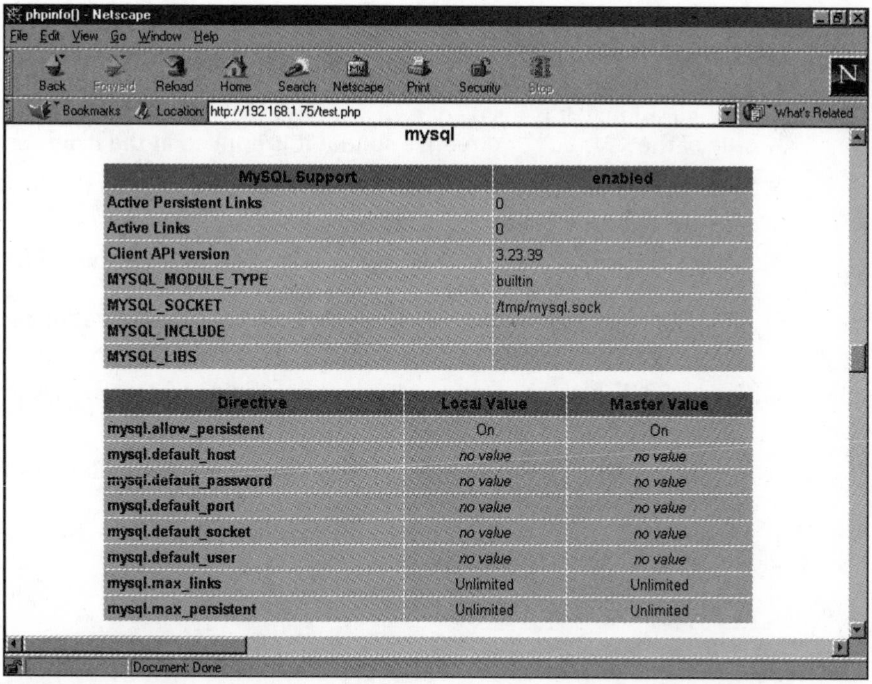

Figure 16-8: A successful PHP installation as shown by the MySQL section of the phpinfo() function

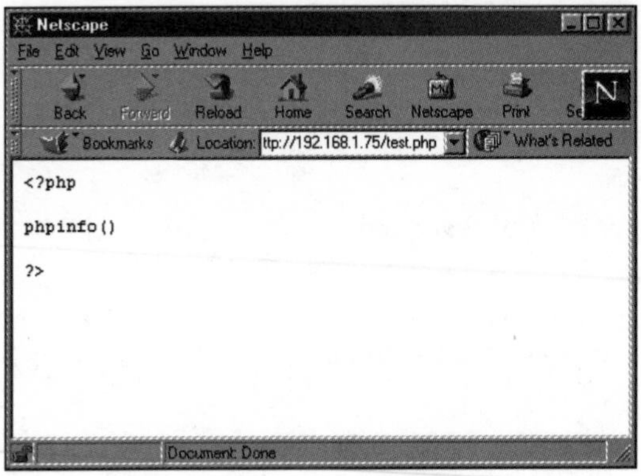

Figure 16-9: A common error that can occur after the installation process itself went smoothly

Troubleshooting a page that shows up as source code

Follow these steps to correct the error depicted in Figure 16-9:

1. Check that you actually enabled PHP in the `httpd.conf` configuration file for Apache (by uncommenting the PHP-related lines in the configuration file).
2. Check the line that normally enables PHP to determine whether it's enclosed in a `<Virtual>` directive. If it is, then it's effectively hidden from the main configuration. If it is inside of a virtual directive, you should move the line outside of the `<Virtual>` directive so that it is applied at the main server level.
3. Make sure you restarted the Web server software; examine any logfiles created when it restarted.
4. Another possibility is that the configuration file isn't the one being read. Search the computer for other configuration files (`find / -name "httpd.conf"`). One those files may be the actual configuration file for Apache on your server and you'll need to edit that file.
5. Check the Web server software itself to determine whether it has PHP enabled.

   I built the example as a dynamic module; if you are working with a dynamic module, make sure that when you run

   ```
   httpd -l
   ```

   you see lines similar to these:

   ```
   Compiled-in modules:
     http_core.c
     mod_so.c
   ```

Note

If a number of other modules are compiled in the dynamic module, chances are you'll have recompile Apache. Although Apache installation is outside the scope of this book, Apache does include a document with its installation files that can help: `README.configure`. This document contains detailed instructions for PHP installation. Also, don't forget to check the PHP and Apache Web sites; if you've encountered a problem, someone may have already tackled it.

6. Copy the file `<php-source-dir>/php.ini-dist` to the PHP install directory and name it `php.ini`.

   The `phpinfo()` function tells you where to put the configuration file within your server's file system. Usually `/usr/local/lib` is the correct place, but your installation may demand a different location (such as the `/etc` directory).

7. If you already have a `php.ini` installed, avoid overwriting it; use the `-i` option with the `cp` command, as follows:

```
cp -i php.ini-dist /usr/local/lib/php.ini
```

   The configuration of this file is now complete; your PHP capability should be ready to use.

Brass Tacks: PHP Essentials

On the assumption that it's wise to learn to walk before running or jumping (at least where the use of PHP with MySQL is concerned) this section presents some basics of PHP. Though powerful, PHP is relatively simple to learn, regardless of previous programming experience. (Naturally such experience is helpful, especially if you've programmed with a language such as Perl).

This section demonstrates essential PHP concepts by creating a simple Web page or two. Though by no means meant as a complete examination of PHP (or an exhaustive catalog of its basics), the section lays the groundwork for working with the language.

Tip

For quick access to more detailed information on PHP, refer to `http://www.php.net`.

A PHP Web page

PHP can be used to build complicated applications that do complex calculations, work with the file system, obtain and work with data from forms, and manipulate data inside many database systems. PHP can also be an especially powerful tool for creating and operating Web pages; a PHP-enabled Web page can perform functions and calculations dispersed throughout the HTML code that makes up the page.

PHP code can be enclosed within an HTML page, or PHP can produce the HTML itself. Regardless of the method, PHP sections within a file are enclosed like this:

```
<?php
  php code
?>
```

These tags, along with the code between them, indicate to the Web server that it must parse the indicated statements specifically as PHP. For example, the following code snippet creates a basic page (Figure 16-10 shows the result):

```
<?php
print "<html>\n";
print "This is a basic page<P>\n";
print "</html>";
?>
```

In Figure 16-11, you can see an example of interwoven PHP and HTML. The following code snippet produces the results depicted in the figure:

```
<?php

print "<html>";
print "This portion is printed within the PHP section.<P>\n";

?>

<P>
And this line is printed from outside the PHP section, back in
HTML.<P>

<?php

print "</html>";

?>
```

Here a PHP section begins the code, concludes its own operation, and makes way for regular HTML. The entire code snippet ends with another section of PHP. Figure 16-11 shows the result.

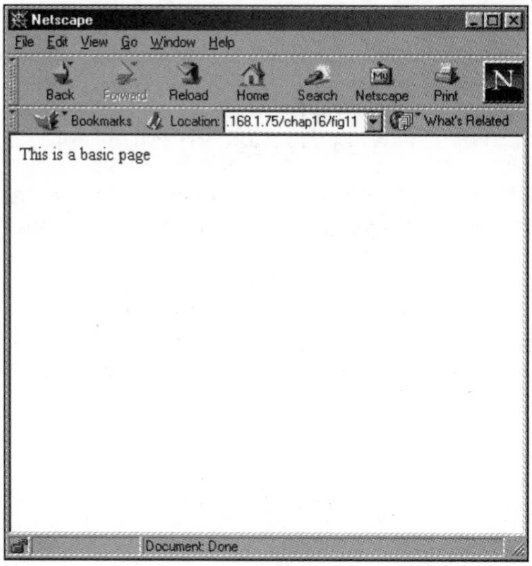

Figure 16-10: The results of the code shown to create HTML within PHP code

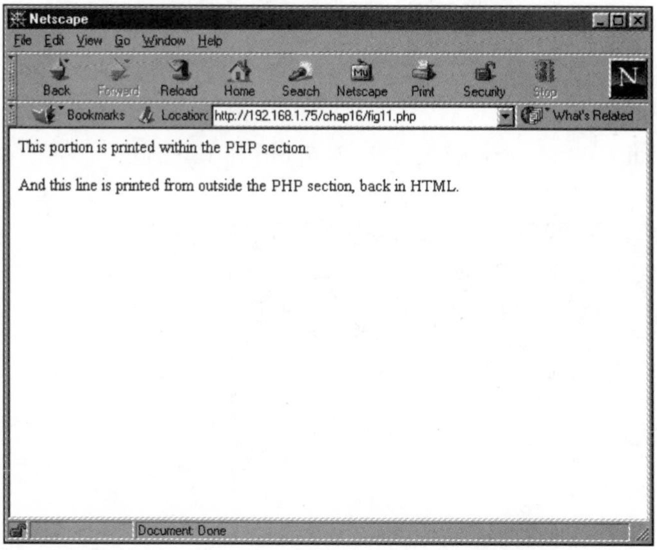

Figure 16-11: An example of PHP and HTML interwoven

PHP and forms

As stated previously, PHP is great for working with data gathered from Web forms. Because you can combine HTML and PHP easily, the form data can be manipulated and then a result page served without ever leaving the same PHP program.

Variables in PHP do not have to be explicitly declared and are called for the most part with the dollar sign ($). This includes arrays and marks a noticeable difference from Perl where arrays are indicated with the *at* symbol (@).

Web forms are easily handled with PHP. Simply create the form as you would any HTML Web form, calling a PHP page as the action. Often the same page that produces the form is also the action of the form. For example, consider the following code:

```
<?php
if (isset($name_submit) && ($name))
{
        print "Hello $name, how are you<P>\n";
}
else {
?>
        <form action=formtest.php method=post>
        <input type=text name=name length=20>
        <input type=submit name=name_submit>
        </form>
<?php
}
?>
```

The form and the results are shown in Figures 16-12 and 16-13.

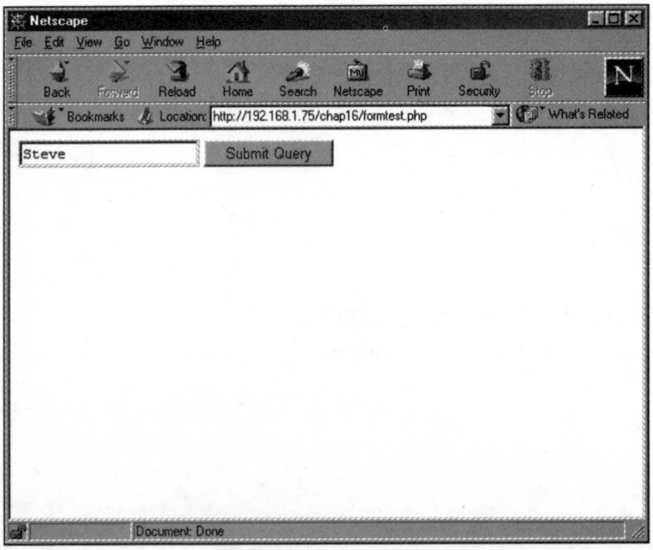

Figure 16-12: The simple form created with the code example in PHP

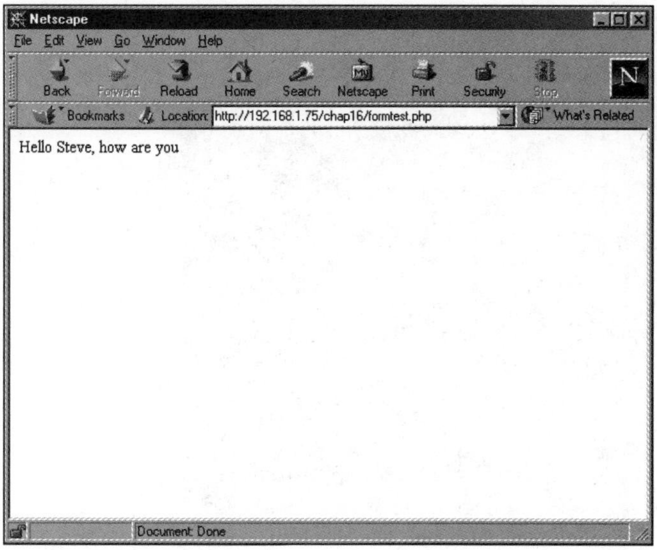

Figure 16-13: The results when a name is entered into the form

If no name is entered into the form, the code simply regenerates the form.

The simplicity with which this scenario is handled is just the tip of the iceberg when it comes to building dynamic pages with PHP. I am a Perl diehard, but producing the same result in Perl simply would not be as easy or elegant.

The rest of this chapter looks at functions and examples in PHP that are especially relevant to MySQL — starting with PHP configuration.

PHP MySQL Configuration

PHP doesn't require much configuration for it to work great with MySQL. The relevant configuration is contained in the `php.ini` file usually located in `/usr/local/lib` or `/etc`. This section examines those configuration options.

Configuration settings

The configuration file for PHP (`php.ini`) is usually located in the `/usr/local/lib` directory, but it may be in `/etc` or another location on your file system. The `phpinfo()` function will tell you where the file is located. See the previous section for information on how to use the `phpinfo()` function in a simple page.

The PHP configuration file has a section devoted to MySQL, as Figure 16-14 illustrates.

Figure 16-14: The MySQL section of the php.ini configuration file

The functions and their definitions are listed in Table 16-1.

Table 16-1
MySQL Configuration Options for PHP

Option	***Definition***
`mysql.allow_persistent`	Enables connections to stay active. Default `On`.
`mysql.max_persistent`	Maximum number of default connections. Default `unlimited` (-1).
`mysql.max_links`	Maximum number of total connections. Default `unlimited` (-1).
`mysql.default_port`	Port to connect to the server on. Default blank, read from config.
`mysql.default_socket`	Socket to connect to server on. Default blank, read from config.
`mysql.default_host`	Sets the host to connect to. Default blank.
mysql.default_user	Sets the user to connect as. Default blank.
`mysql.default_password`	Set a global password to authenticate as. Default blank.

The settings contained in the php.ini do not need to be set for PHP to work with MySQL.

Caution For security reasons, I strongly recommend against setting the user or password *inside* the php.ini. Anyone with read access to the file (or who can write a PHP script and get at the server variables) can determine the settings.

PHP MySQL Functions

PHP includes a large number of built-in functions — some of which can take the place of existing MySQL functions or statements to enhance or streamline operations. This section examines some functions that accomplish these goals with MySQL and PHP, and provides examples.

The functions

The best way to handle this abundance of MySQL-related functions in PHP is to list them in a table. Table 16-2 does so.

Table 16-2
PHP MySQL Functions

Function	Definition
mysql_affected_rows	Returns number of rows affected by a non-SELECT statement.
mysql_change_user	Changes the user currently logged in to the program.
mysql_close	Closes the connection to the MySQL server.
mysql_connect	Connects to the MySQL server.
mysql_create_db	Creates a MySQL database.
mysql_data_seek	Moves the internal pointer one row.
mysql_db_name	Returns the name of the current database.
mysql_db_query	Issues a query to the database.
mysql_drop_db	Drops or deletes a database.
mysql_errno	Returns the error number of the current error message.
mysql_error	Returns the text for the current error message.
.mysql_escape_string	Takes a string and returns a MySQL-safe quoted string.

Continued

Table 16-2 *(Continued)*

Function	*Definition*
mysql_fetch_array	Returns an array that can be numerical and/or associative.
mysql_fetch_assoc	Returns an associative array (similar to the fetchrow_array command in Perl).
mysql_fetch_field	Returns an object associated with a column.
mysql_fetch_lengths	Returns the length of the result set.
mysql_fetch_object	Returns an entire row as an object.
mysql_fetch_row	Returns a row of the result set.
mysql_field_flags	Returns the flags from a result set.
mysql_field_name	Returns the field name of a result set.
mysql_field_len	Returns length of the field.
mysql_field_seek	Moves the pointer of the result set.
mysql_field_table	Returns the name of the table associated with the field.
mysql_field_type	Returns column type.
mysql_free_result	Clears the results, empties the memory associated with them.
mysql_get_client_info	Returns information on the client connection.
mysql_get_host_info	Returns information on the MySQL host.
mysql_get_proto_info	Returns information on the MySQL protocol version.
mysql_get_server_info	Returns information on the MySQL server itself.
mysql_insert_id	Returns the ID of a column associated with the last INSERT statement.
mysql_list_dbs	Returns a list of available databases.
mysql_list_fields	Returns a list of available fields.
mysql_list_tables	Returns a list of tables available within a database.
mysql_num_fields	Returns the number of fields in a given table.
mysql_num_rows	Returns the number of rows in a result set.
mysql_pconnect	Creates a persistent connection to the server.
mysql_query	Issues a query.
mysql_result	Returns the result set.
mysql_select_db	Connects to a given database within a server.
mysql_tablename	Returns the table name.
mysql_unbuffered_query	Sends a query without regard for return values.

As I stated, quite a few of the numerous functions are substitutes for MySQL statements — for example, `mysql_list_dbs` replaces `SHOW DATABASES`. I'll use many of these functions in the code examples in upcoming sections.

Connecting to MySQL with PHP

It's finally time to build the first PHP MySQL program of the chapter — though I suppose the small example page you built with the `phpinfo()` function counts a little. So this will be the second PHP MySQL program but the first one where you will actively connect to MySQL.

You can connect to MySQL by using the `mysql_connect()` function; you terminate the connection with the `mysql_close()` function. Like the Perl DBI, the `mysql_connect` function requires some parameters for connecting.

Note You can specify some connection parameters within the `php.ini` configuration file.

The syntax for the `mysql_connect()` function is as follows:

```
mysql_connect (host, username, password)
```

Consider this example:

```
$dbconn = mysql_connect("localhost","suehring","evh5150");
```

As you would expect, you can set the values of `host`, `username`, and `password` to variables:

```
$host = "localhost";
$username = "suehring";
$password = "evh5150";
$dbconn = mysql_connect($host, $username, $password);
```

Once the connection is made, statements are issued or another function is used. Unlike Perl, PHP does not use the concept of handles for working with MySQL. Therefore, statements can be sent simply through the `mysql_query()` function and retrieved through one of the `fetch` functions.

Protecting PHP authentication information

A significant security issue with PHP is storage of the authentication information for MySQL. PHP puts authentication information in the PHP file — where it's readable by anyone on the Web server. One way around this potential security hole is to place authentication information inside a *function,* in a file separate from the PHP program being called by the Web server. The file containing the function must be readable by the user running the Web server, but should not be world-readable.

For example, suppose I create a simple PHP file called dbconnect.php, place it in a directory that the Web server can access, and use it for executing PHP files. The file's entire contents look like this:

```
<?php

$host = "localhost";
$username = "suehring";
$password = "evh5150";

?>
```

The file is owned by the user account that the Web server runs as (username nobody), and only that user has read-write (rw) access. The Web server can read the contents of the file but no other users can (not even if they're on the same server).

Altering the small connection commands I have given here, I use the PHP include() function. The contents of the file included will be available for the PHP script to execute. The code that uses the function looks like this:

```
include("/usr/local/apache/htdocs/chap16/dbconnect.php");


$dbconn = mysql_connect($host,$username,$password) or die
("Cannot connect to database server");
```

Examination of the code reveals the include() function followed by the mysql_connect() function. I've also used the die() function to add some error checking. If the connection cannot be made, an error message is returned and execution of the script terminates. The mysql_connect() function is related to two other functions with complementary capabilities:

- **mysql_close()** is the opposite of mysql_connect(). You can use mysql_close() to close or terminate a connection to a MySQL server. When a script completes its execution, however, its session terminates automatically; normally you don't have to use mysql_close().
- **mysql_pconnect()** opens a persistent connection to a MySQL server. This type of connection remains active even after the PHP script terminates.

Selecting data from a MySQL database

The functions in Table 16-2 include a number of functions for issuing statements or performing various tasks on the MySQL server. Some of the functions replace MySQL functions such as those for creation of a database and listing databases and tables.

mysql_select_db and mysql_query_db

Once a connection is made to the MySQL server, you can interact with a specific database by using the mysql_select_db() function, which takes the name of that database as an argument. The `mysql_query_db()` function is a bit more direct; it sends a query to a specified database without using the `mysql_select_db()` function. The syntax for both statements is as follows:

```
mysql_select_db(<databasename>)
mysql_query_db(<databasename>, query)
```

mysql_query

The `mysql_query()` function sends queries and other statements to the MySQL server. To retrieve the results of such a query or statement, use a `fetch` function such as `mysql_fetch_array` or `mysql_fetch_row`. The resulting value(s) can then be parsed and worked with, like any other variables. Examples of `mysql_query` are shown throughout the rest of the chapter.

mysql_fetch_assoc

The `mysql_fetch_assoc()` function is one method for retrieving the results of a MySQL query. Examine the following code:

```
<?php

include("/usr/local/apache/htdocs/chap16/dbconnect.php");

$dbconn = mysql_connect($host,$username,$password) or die
("Cannot connect to database server");

$db = mysql_select_db("mysql") or die ("Could not connect to
database\n");

$result = mysql_query("select user,host from user");

print "<table border=1><P>\n";

while ($row = mysql_fetch_assoc($result)) {
        print "<tr><P>\n";
        while (list ($key,$value) = each($row)) {
                print "<td><P>\n";
                print "$value\n";
                print "</td><P>\n";
        }
        print "</tr><P>\n";
}
print "</table><P>\n";

?>
```

This code example connects to the MySQL server, selects the MySQL grants database, and then issues a `SELECT` statement. The results from the `SELECT` statement are printed in table form; Figure 16-15 shows the resulting output.

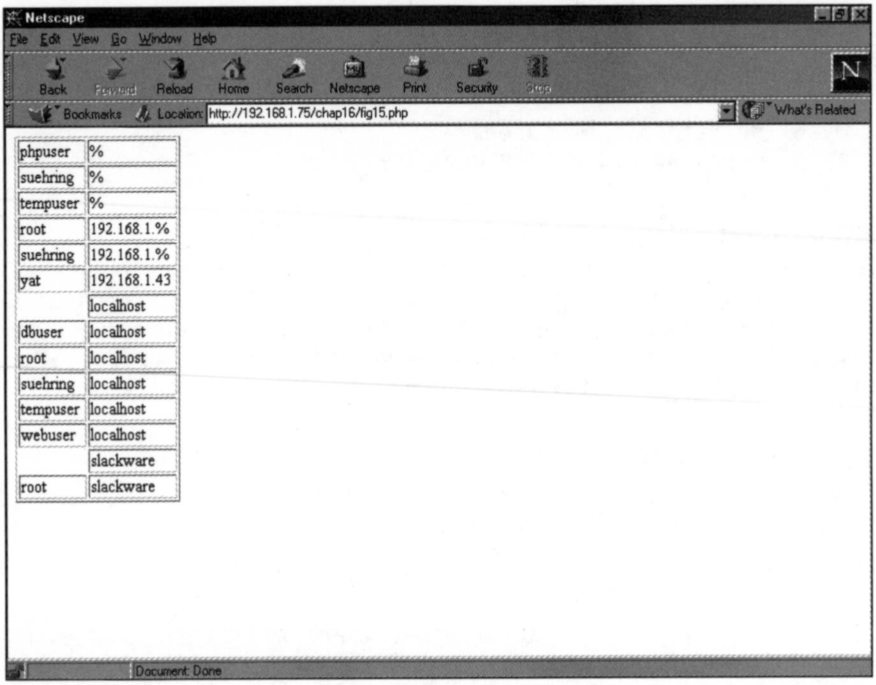

Figure 16-15: Results from the PHP code example

The code sample shown in this section uses `mysql_fetch_assoc` to get the results from the query in an associative array. Then, by using the PHP functions `list()` and `each()`, I can walk through the results row by row — and place them in a simple HTML table.

Tip **Using `mysql_fetch_assoc` is the same as using `mysql_fetch_array` with `MYSQL_ASSOC` as the second argument.**

mysql_fetch_row

I could use the `mysql_fetch_row` function for this query, but the results wouldn't go as nicely into a table format. The following code shows the program using `mysql_fetch_row`; Figure 16-16 shows the results.

```
<?php

include("/usr/local/apache/htdocs/chap16/dbconnect.php");
```

```
$dbconn = mysql_connect($host,$username,$password) or die
("Cannot connect to database server");

$db = mysql_select_db("mysql") or die ("Could not connect to
database\n");
$result = mysql_query("select user,host from user");

print "<table border=1><P>\n";

while ($row = mysql_fetch_row($result)) {
        print "<tr><P>\n";
        print "<td>$row[0]</td><P>\n";
        print "<td>$row[1]</td><P>\n";
        print "</tr><P>\n";
}

print "</table><P>\n";

?>
```

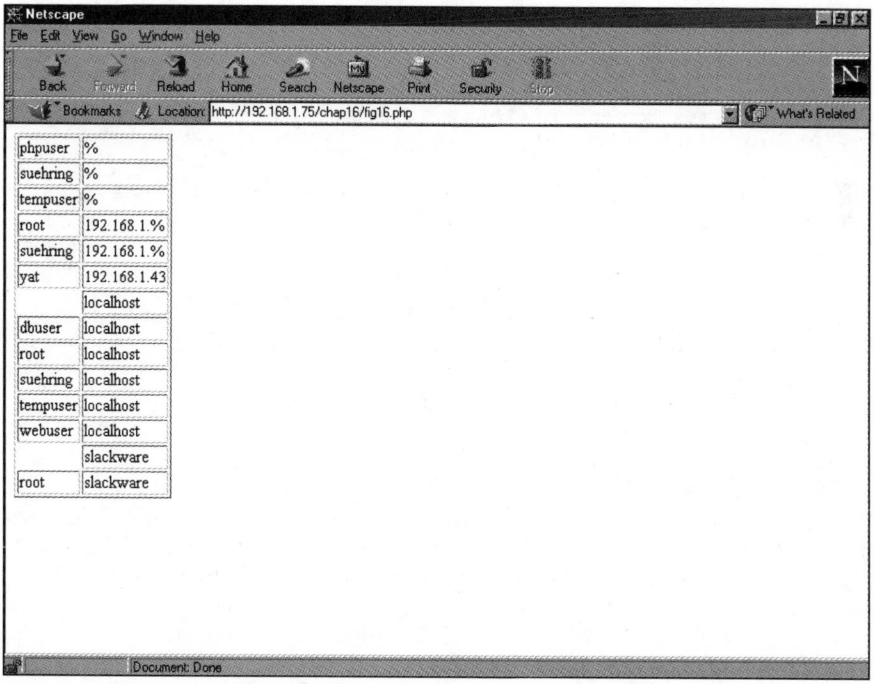

Figure 16-16: Using mysql_fetch_row to retrieve the results from a query

mysql_num_rows

It is sometimes useful to find out the number of rows returned by a MySQL query. The `mysql_num_rows` function is simply called with the result set as the argument. `mysql_num_rows()` only works with `SELECT` statements. The function doesn't work with other SQL statements such as `INSERT`, `UPDATE`, `DELETE` and so forth, as in the following example:

```
$num = mysql_num_rows($dbconn);
```

Note

The argument for `mysql_num_rows()` is the database connection identifier. In the examples I've shown, I've used the variable name `$dbconn` for the function call for `mysql_connect()`.

Inserting and updating data in MySQL

Inserts and other statements are performed just like `SELECT` statements, using the `mysql_query()` function. For example, to add a row, the syntax is simple:

```
<?php

include("/usr/local/apache/htdocs/chap16/dbconnect.php");

$dbconn = mysql_connect($host,$username,$password) or die
("Cannot connect to database server");

$db = mysql_select_db("ecommerce") or die ("Could not connect
to database\n");

$result = mysql_query("INSERT INTO customer VALUES
('suehring↓ngermen.com','Steve','Suehring','4 Main
St.','','54481','715','555-1212')") or die ("Could not execute
insert\n");

?>
```

mysql_affected_rows

The `mysql_affected_rows()` function serves to determine the number of rows affected by a non-`SELECT` operation such as an `INSERT` or a `DELETE`. Adding `mysql_affected_rows` to the previous application yields the following code example:

```
<?php

include("/usr/local/apache/htdocs/chap16/dbconnect.php");
```

```
$dbconn = mysql_connect($host,$username,$password) or die
("Cannot connect to database server");

$db = mysql_select_db("ecommerce") or die ("Could not connect
to database\n");

$result = mysql_query("INSERT INTO customer VALUES
('suehring↓ngermen.com','Steve','Suehring','4 Main
St.','','54481','715','555-1212')") or die ("Could not execute
insert\n");

# Determine the number of inserted rows.
$rows_inserted = mysql_affected_rows($dbconn);

print "Inserted $rows_inserted rows\n";

?>
```

The results from this modified code are shown in Figure 16-17.

Note

You run the `mysql_affected_rows()` function with the database connection name from `mysql_connect()` — instead of the result set — serving as the argument. This necessary substitution is a common source of confusion among first-time PHP programmers.

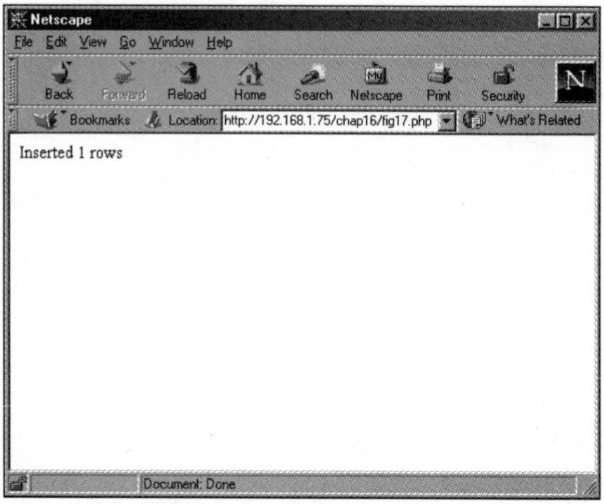

Figure 16-17: Using mysql_affected_rows to see how many rows were affected by the operation

Building MySQL-Enabled Applications With PHP

The previous sections of this chapter provided examples of connecting to MySQL through PHP, along with some functions used to work with data and databases. This section builds on those examples to produce some PHP applications.

A PHP version of the user manager

Chapter 15 builds a simple user-manager program in Perl; it queries the `users` table of the MySQL grants database. This section ports that same Perl application over to PHP. (I include the Perl code for reference here so you can easily see the changes needed to port it to PHP.) The Perl version of the code looks like this:

```
#!/usr/bin/perl

use DBI;
use CGI qw( :standard );

# This program looks up the hosts from which a
# given user is allowed to connect.
# Also looks up grants for a user, given the @ symbol in the
# argument list.

# Get the input from the form.
$user = param("user");

# Test to make sure the user entered a username.
if (! $user) {
        print "No user specified.  Usage: <program>
<username><P>";
}

# Print an HTML header
print "Content-Type: text/html\n\n";

# Connect to the database
$dbh = DBI->connect("DBI:mysql:mysql:",suehring,'evh5150');

if (! $dbh) {
        print "Connection failed!!<P>";
        die();
}

# If there's an @ symbol then the user wants to look up
# grants.
if ($user =~ m/\@/) {
```

```
        ($user,$inhost) = split(/\@/, $user);

        # Make sure the username and host are safe to
        # send to MySQL.
        $quoteduser = $dbh->quote($user);
        $quotedhost = $dbh->quote($inhost);
        &priv($user,$inhost);
}
else {
        # User wants to simply lookup the hosts allowed
        # for given username.

        # Make sure the username is safe to
        # send to MySQL.
        $quoteduser = $dbh->quote($user);

        $query = "SELECT host,user FROM user WHERE \
        user = $quoteduser";
        $sth = $dbh->prepare($query);
        $sth->execute();

        while (($host,$username) = ( $sth->fetchrow_array() ) )
{
                if ($host eq '') {
                        print "User $user has a \
                        blank host entry.<P>";
                }
                else {
                        print "User $user is allowed \
                        to connect from: $host<P>";
                }
        }
}

sub priv
{

# This subroutine looks up the grants for the given
# user/host pair.

($user,$host) = (@_);

$query = "SHOW GRANTS FOR $user\@$host";
$sth = $dbh->prepare($query);
$sth->execute();

while ($grant = ( $sth->fetchrow() ) ) {
        print "$grant<P>";
}

}
```

Porting the code to PHP is relatively easy because of some key similarities between Perl and PHP. The PHP version of the user-manager program code looks like this:

```
<?php

# This program looks up the hosts from which a
# given user is allowed to connect.
# Also looks up grants for a user, given the @ symbol in the
# argument list.

include("/usr/local/apache/htdocs/chap16/dbconnect.php");

if (! $submit) {
  echo "<form action=\"/chap16/fig18.php\" method=post>";
  echo "Enter Username: <input type=text name=user
length=20><P>\n";
  echo "<input type=submit name=submit><P>\n";
  echo "</form><P>\n";
  exit;
}

# Connect to the database
$dbconn = mysql_connect($host,$username,$password) or die
("Couldn't connect to database server");

$db = mysql_select_db("mysql");


# If there's an @ symbol then the user wants to look up
# grants.
if (ereg("@", $user)) {
        list ($user,$inhost) = split("\@", $user);

        # Make sure the username and host are safe to
        # send to MySQL.
        $quoteduser = mysql_escape_string($user);
        $quotedhost = mysql_escape_string($inhost);
        priv($user,$inhost);
}
else {
        # User wants to simply lookup the hosts allowed
        # for given username.

        # Make sure the username is safe to
        # send to MySQL.
        $quoteduser = mysql_escape_string($user);

        $query = "SELECT host,user FROM user WHERE user =
'$quoteduser'";
        $result = mysql_query($query) or die ("Cannot execute
query 1");

        while ( $row = mysql_fetch_array($result) ) {
```

```
                echo "User ". $row["user"] . " is allowed to
connect from: " . $row["host"] . "<P>";
        }
}

function priv($user,$inhost)
{

# This subroutine looks up the grants for the given
# user/host pair.

$query = "SHOW GRANTS FOR '$user''$inhost'";
$result = mysql_query($query);

$i = 0;

if (! $result) {
  print "No such grant<P>\n";
}
else {
  while ($grant = mysql_fetch_array($result) ) {
    print "$grant[$i]<P>";
    $i++;
  }
}
}

?>
```

Figures 16-18 through 16-21 show snippets of the PHP version, along with example runs of the program.

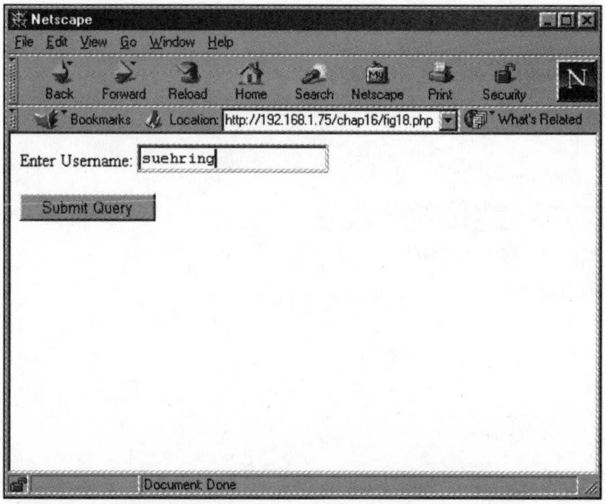

Figure 16-18: The form built by the PHP version of the user manager

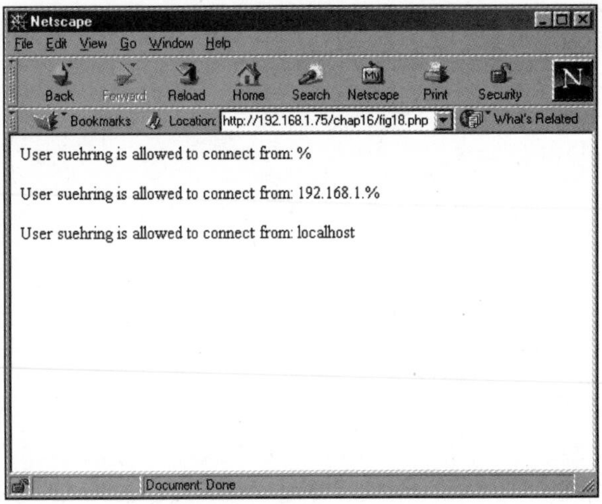

Figure 16-19: The results with the PHP version of the user manager look the same as those from the Perl CGI version.

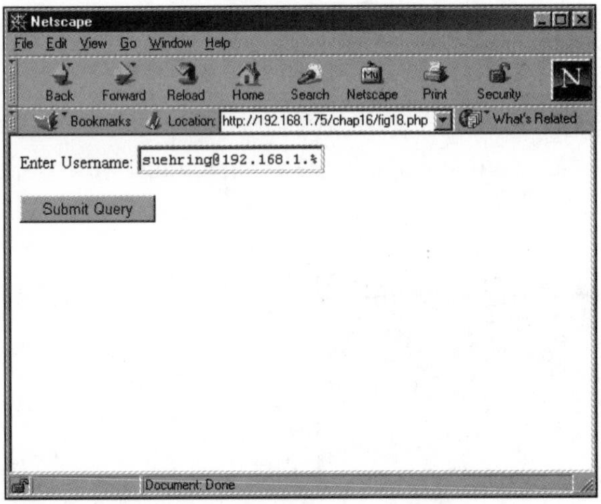

Figure 16-20: The privilege lookup with the PHP version of the user manager

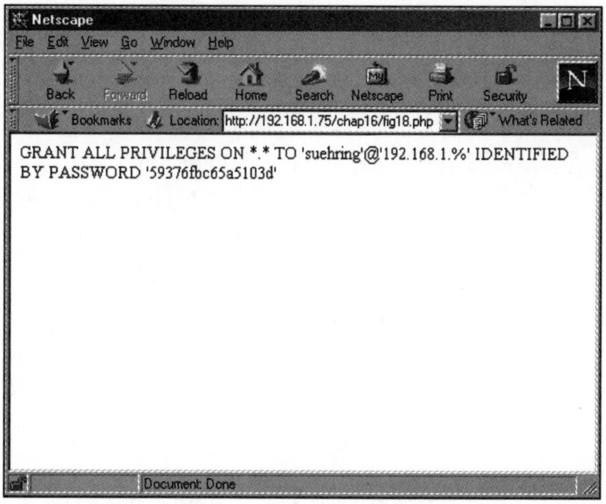

Figure 16-21: Querying for privileges works the same with the PHP version as with the Perl CGI version.

Examination of the PHP version of the user manager

Many of the user manager's basic functions are the same in both the Perl and PHP versions — in particular, functions such as `while` and `if`. Looking at the first bits of the PHP code, notice that the program no longer starts with `#!/usr/bin/perl` (which makes sense, since this PHP version isn't a Perl program). An `include` statement in the PHP code includes the database credentials; it's the last line of the following code snippet:

```
<?php

# This program looks up the hosts from which a
# given user is allowed to connect.
# Also looks up grants for a user, given the @ symbol in the
# argument list.

include("/usr/local/apache/htdocs/chap16/dbconnect.php");
```

The next portion is a new addition to the PHP version that's unnecessary in the Perl CGI version. Because the initial page in the Perl version is a static HTML page, the CGI doesn't create any HTML. Although the same could be done with the PHP version (and technically with the Perl version as well), it's easier to handle creating the

HTML directly in the PHP program. In this instance, if the Submit button isn't clicked (as it would be when you initially visit the page, or if the user field were blank), the page is simply served again.

```
if ((! $submit) || (! $user)) {
  echo "<form action=\"/chap16/fig18.php\" method=post>";
  echo "Enter Username: <input type=text name=user
length=20><P>\n";
  echo "<input type=submit name=submit><P>\n";
  echo "</form><P>\n";
  exit;
}
```

The PHP method for connecting to the database server and database is next in the script:

```
# Connect to the database
$dbconn = mysql_connect($host,$username,$password) or die
("Couldn't connect to database server");

$db = mysql_select_db("mysql");
```

The next bit of code examines the value that was input, looking for an @ symbol (which would indicate that the query is looking for the grants — privileges — afforded a given user). Notice the use of the PHP ereg function to examine the $user string variable. A PHP MySQL function introduced in this section — mysql_escape_string() — works somewhat like the mysql_quote() function in Perl.

The mysql_escape_string() function takes a string that was already input and makes it safe for use in a MySQL statement. The mysql_quote() function in Perl does the same thing, but it puts quotation marks around the string — which the mysql_escape_string() function in PHP does not. Therefore, to use mysql_escape_string(), put quotes around the string in your PHP MySQL statements. The following snippet is an example:

```
# If there's an @ symbol then the user wants to look up
# grants.
if (ereg("@", $user)) {
        list ($user,$inhost) = split("\@", $user);

        # Make sure the username and host are safe to
        # send to MySQL.
        $quoteduser = mysql_escape_string($user);
        $quotedhost = mysql_escape_string($inhost);
        priv($user,$inhost);
}
```

The next section is executed when no @ symbol is included from the form (hence, in effect, no grants are sought). The program queries for the already-input username and returns the result.

In addition to the functions used in this section, another method is possible for processing the returned results. It looks like this:

```
else {
        # User wants to simply lookup the hosts allowed
        # for given username.

        # Make sure the username is safe to
        # send to MySQL.
        $quoteduser = mysql_escape_string($user);

        $query = "SELECT host,user FROM user WHERE user =
'$quoteduser'";
        $result = mysql_query($query) or die ("Cannot execute
query 1");

        while ( $row = mysql_fetch_array($result) ) {
                echo "User ". $row["user"] . " is allowed to
connect from: " . $row["host"] . "<P>";
        }
}
```

The final section of the program is called when an @ symbol *is* included in the input that comes from the form:

```
function priv($user,$inhost)
{

# This subroutine looks up the grants for the given
# user/host pair.

$query = "SHOW GRANTS FOR '$user''$inhost'";
$result = mysql_query($query);

$i = 0;

if (! $result) {
  print "No such grant<P>\n";
}
else {
  while ($grant = mysql_fetch_array($result) ) {
    print "$grant[$i]<P>";
    $i++;
  }
}
}

?>
```

In the code snippet just given, notice that PHP calls the function with the name `function` (whereas Perl uses `sub` to designate a user-defined function). The function also uses a different method for receiving the variables that are called with it.

Throughout the program, the persistent challenge is to keep track of both the similarities and the significant differences between Perl and PHP to avoid losing functionality.

Cookies with no milk

Cookies are value-plus-parameter pairs stored in the HTTP header and sent to a Web agent (such as a browser) when retrieving an object—usually a Web page—from the Internet. They are commonly used to store user-related data (such as session identifiers) and can be set to expire at a point in the future determined by the site that sets and uses the cookie.

Although PHP includes functions for setting and easily retrieving cookies, it also includes other functions for setting and retrieving session identifiers; some of these don't use cookies. A developer can use either a cookie function or a session function in PHP to maintain state or authenticate users for Web pages.

There are probably endless methods for creating authentication mechanisms for Web sites and Web pages. This section examines one method for authenticating users that also sets a cookie with a session identifier. The approach that is specifically relevant to this book is to integrate the authentication mechanism with a MySQL database.

Once that integration is complete, visitors can enter a username and password. The credentials will be authenticated against data in a MySQL database. If the login is successful, a session ID and timestamp are recorded in the MySQL database. A cookie is sent to the user upon success, containing that same session ID and username (in encrypted form). When the user attempts to access another resource within the site, the user's cookie is examined and compared to the one in the database. If it's valid, the user is allowed to access the resource. In addition, the database includes a `group` function so resources can be limited by group (should the need arise).

Note: No need to undertake full normalization of the database for this site. Since the site is intended for low usage, normalization would have little or no effect on performance.

The first step toward the authentication system is to create the database—in effect, a big table with some special features. The table for the authentication system has the following structure:

```
CREATE TABLE `user_table` (
  `user` varchar(20) NOT NULL default '',
  `pass` varchar(20) default NULL,
  `session` varchar(50) default NULL,
  `auth_group` varchar(20) default NULL,
  `timestamp` varchar(32) default NULL,
  PRIMARY KEY  (`user`)
```

Two main PHP scripts make up the authentication system: a sign-in program and a cookie-validation program. The sign-in program prints a form for username and password, and then sets the cookie. It looks like this:

```
<?php

# This program creates an authentication system
# using MySQL and cookies.

include("/usr/local/apache/htdocs/chap16/dbconnect.php");

if (!isset($submit)) {
  echo "<form action=\"/chap16/signin.php\" method=post>";
  echo "Enter Username: <input type=text name=user
length=20><P>\n";
  echo "Enter Password: <input type=password name=pass
length=20><P>\n";
  echo "<input type=submit name=submit><P>\n";
  echo "</form><P>\n";
  exit;
}
elseif (!isset($user)) {
  echo "Please enter username<P>\n";
  echo "<form action=\"/chap16/signin.php\" method=post>";
  echo "Enter Username: <input type=text name=user
length=20><P>\n";
  echo "Enter Password: <input type=password name=pass
length=20><P>\n";
  echo "<input type=submit name=submit><P>\n";
  echo "</form><P>\n";
  exit;
}
elseif (!isset($pass)) {
  echo "Please enter password<P>\n";
  echo "<form action=\"/chap16/signin.php\" method=post>";
  echo "Enter Username: <input type=text name=user
length=20><P>\n";
  echo "Enter Password: <input type=password name=pass
length=20><P>\n";
  echo "<input type=submit name=submit><P>\n";
  echo "</form><P>\n";
  exit;
}
else {
# Connect to the database
  $dbconn = mysql_connect($host,$username,$password) or die
("Couldn't connect to database server");

  $db = mysql_select_db("auth");

  $quoteduser = mysql_escape_string($user);
  $quotedpass = mysql_escape_string($pass);
  authenticate($user,$pass);
```

```
}

function authenticate($user,$pass)
{

# This subroutine looks up the grants for the given
# user/host pair.

$query = "SELECT session FROM user_table WHERE user = '$user'
AND pass = password('$pass')";
$result = mysql_query($query) or die ("Query failed");
$num = mysql_num_rows($result);

if ($num == 0) {
  print "Username and/or password incorrect<P>\n";
  exit;
} else {
  $row = mysql_fetch_array($result);

  # Create a pseudo-random session id.
  srand((double)microtime()*99999999);
  $id = md5(rand(0,9999999));

  # Encrypt the username
  $encuser = md5($user);

  # Get rid of the result, so I can send another query
  mysql_free_result($result) or die ("An error was
encountered");

  $time = time();

  $query = "UPDATE user_table SET session = '$id',timestamp =
'$time' WHERE user  = '$user'";
  $result = mysql_query($query) or die ("UPDATE failed!");

  setcookie("cookie_session","$id",time()+60,"/","",0);
  setcookie("cookie_user","$encuser",time()+60,"/","",0);

  print "You have been successfully logged in<P>";

}
}  # End function authenticate

?>
```

Examination of the code reveals that many of the functions (and some of the logic) previously discussed in this chapter are incorporated into the program. A couple of snippets call for a closer look: One encrypts an otherwise-plaintext username before returning it to the browser; the other clears the memory associated with a result.

Encrypting a username before returning it

In this section, after the username and password have been validated, I create a couple of seemingly random strings for values to store in cookies later. The PHP function `md5()` is used twice. Because both the session ID and the username should be validated (I'll tell you why later), I'd like to send a username. However, sending a plaintext username back to the browser is not such a good idea (from the standpoint of security and privacy). The `md5()` function to the rescue! The relevant code looks like this:

```
# Create a pseudo-random session id.
srand((double)microtime()*99999999);
$id = md5(rand(0,9999999));

# Encrypt the username
$encuser = md5($user);
```

Clearing the memory associated with a result

The next PHP MySQL function hasn't been used before in this chapter's examples: `mysql_free_result()`, which clears the memory associated with a result. Although technically it doesn't *have* to be used here, it does ensure that the value in `$result` will be clean and fresh—and that's one less source of potential error.

Caution **Because the use of `mysql_free_result()` wipes the old result set out of memory, you can't glean any further information from the old result set! Make sure you have the information you need before you trash the old result set.**

Using `mysql_free_result()` can be a lifesaver if your system is operating near the limit of its resources and you have a huge result set that takes up too much memory. Here's what the code looks like:

```
  # Get rid of the result, so I can send another query
  mysql_free_result($result) or die ("An error was
encountered");
```

Note the comment that lets the programmer know what's intended here (and consider it a reminder to cultivate good documentation habits). Next, a call to the PHP `time()` function gives me a current Unix/Linux `timestamp` value (given as the number of seconds since the Epoch), and running the `UPDATE` statement sets the session ID in the `user_table` along with the `timestamp`. Here's the code:

```
  $time = time();

  $query = "UPDATE user_table SET session = '$id',timestamp =
'$time' WHERE user  = '$user'";
  $result = mysql_query($query) or die ("UPDATE failed!");
```

Using a `timestamp` together with the session ID helps ensure that the session is relatively recent (which is important to establish, as I'll show you in the program to validate cookies).

Setting and validating the cookie

The following code contains two examples of the `setcookie()` function:

```
setcookie("cookie_session","$id",time()+60,"/","",0);
setcookie("cookie_user","$encuser",time()+60,"/","",0);

print "You have been successfully logged in<P>";
```

The `print` statement at the end of this code snippet would be a good place to send a redirect to the client, sending it to another page or calling another function.

Note: In the first code snippet just given, normally you'd put the valid URL for the cookie between the final double quotes to the left of the 0—in both instances. As it happens, some crazy redirection on my network prevents me from placing that value correctly (within that final set of quotes) for the example.

The program to validate cookies is as follows:

```
<?php

function check_session($cookie_session,$cookie_user) {

include("/usr/local/apache/htdocs/chap16/dbconnect.php");

# Connect to the database
  $dbconn = mysql_connect($host,$username,$password) or die
("Couldn't connect to database server");

  $db = mysql_select_db("auth");

  $quoteduser = mysql_escape_string($cookie_session);

$query = "SELECT auth_group FROM user_table WHERE session =
'$cookie_session' AND timestamp > (unix_timestamp() - 600) AND
md5(user) = '$cookie_user'";

$result = mysql_query($query) or die ("Query failed");
$num = mysql_num_rows($result);

if ($num == 0) {
  print "Session has expired<P>\n";
  exit;
} else {
  $row = mysql_fetch_array($result);
  return $row["auth_group"];

}
}  # End function check_session

?>
```

The check_session function would normally be called from within another page. For example, I have a page called userpage.php that I do not want anyone to gain access to unless they are valid. Including a call to this function at the beginning of that page helps me ensure that the user has a valid cookie and is authorized to view the page.

Validating the user and the cookie

The query in the upcoming code snippet is the same one sent to actually validate the user and the cookie.

```
$query = "SELECT auth_group FROM user_table WHERE session =
'$cookie_session' AND timestamp > (unix_timestamp() - 600) AND
md5(user) = '$cookie_user'";
```

Here I'm using the WHERE clause to look for three matches:

- ✦ The session ID should match the one sent in the user cookie.
- ✦ The timestamp in the user_table is compared to the current time. If the timestamp is less than 10 minutes ago (600 seconds), then it's valid.
- ✦ The user in the table (sent through md5) should match the md5ed user from the cookie.

If all three of these values match appropriately, the cookie is valid.

Using three values in the database to validate cookies makes it more difficult for a malicious user to fake a session ID to try to gain access to protected resources. Even if a user can fake a session ID, he or she must tie in that session ID with the encrypted username within the time specified in the query (in this case, 10 minutes).

The function ends with a call to the PHP return() function. The function sends the value back to the calling program.

```
return $row["auth_group"];
```

As an example, here's the code that creates a page called userpage.php. That page calls the check_session function to validate the user before continuing. The code for the page is as follows:

```
<?php

$cookie_session = $HTTP_COOKIE_VARS["cookie_session"];
$cookie_user = $HTTP_COOKIE_VARS["cookie_user"];

if (!isset($cookie_session)) {
  print "Session expired\n";
  exit;
} elseif (! isset($cookie_user)) {

  # Probably should make a function to
```

```
    # inform an admin here since no user
    # cookie might mean someone is
    # doing something naughty.

    print "Invalid request\n";
    exit;
  } else {
    require ("/usr/local/apache/htdocs/chap16/cookie_auth.php");
    $group = check_session($cookie_session,$cookie_user);
    print "Cookie retrieval validated, you are a member of $group
  group\n";
  }

  ?>
```

In this instance, the resource I want to protect doesn't amount to much more than an example page. But that resource *could* be any page in which you can use a PHP function.

In the example page, first I get the values of the cookies. If they're not set, then something is wrong and the user can't continue. Otherwise (if both cookies are set) call the `check_session` function. Notice that the `check_session` function is called with `$group` as a target for the result. Doing so grabs the `return()` value from the function called. The checking of cookies that I get this page to do could also be done inside the `check_session` function as part of the cookie-checking function.

Figure 16-22 shows an example of the sign-in page; Figure 16-23 shows what happens when I type my password wrong.

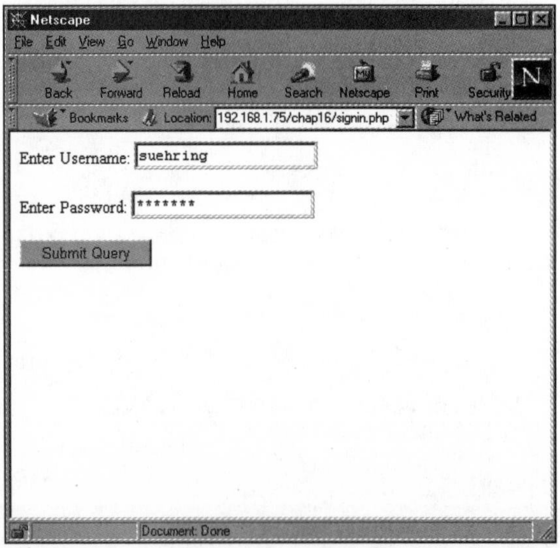

Figure 16-22: The sign-in page for the authentication system

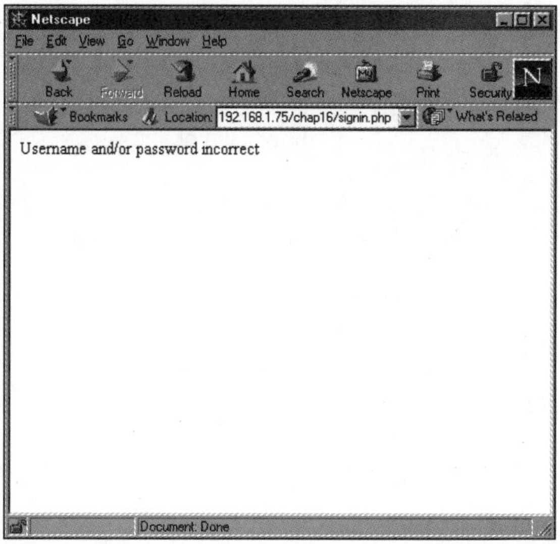

Figure 16-23: Password incorrect when attempting to sign in

When I manage to type my password correctly, the cookies are sent, as shown in Figures 16-24 through 16-26.

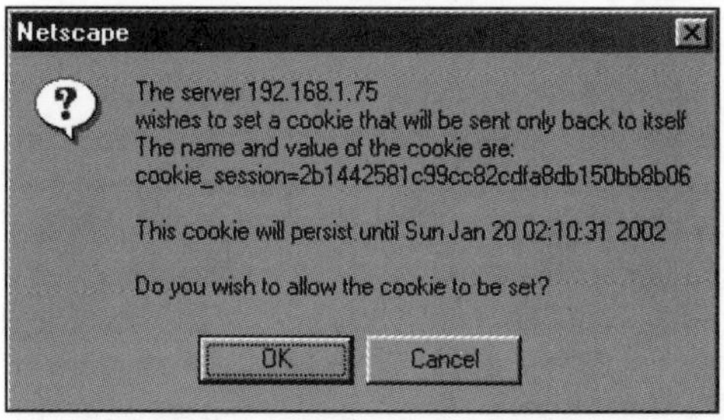

Figure 16-24: When authenticated, a session cookie is sent first.

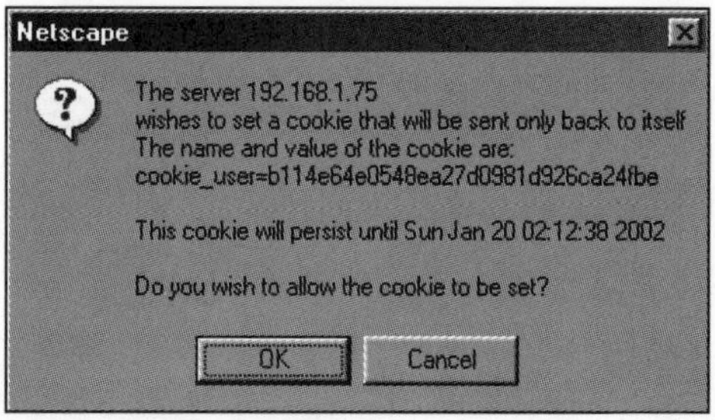

Figure 16-25: After the session-ID cookie is sent, an md5 version of my username is sent in a cookie.

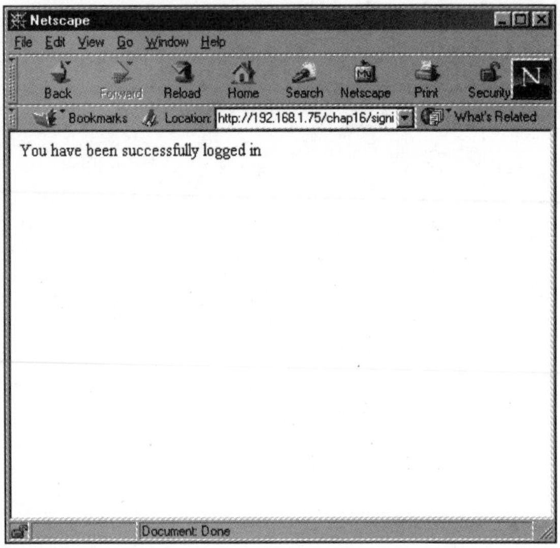

Figure 16-26: The resulting page when validated. This page could also be another resource, a redirect, or any other valid object.

When attempting to go to the protected resource, `userpage.php`, the cookies are validated against the database (as shown in Figure 16-27). In fact, the function call returns the group for my user, `admin`. Using this information, I could grant or deny further access by group within `userpage.php`.

Finally, if the session has expired (I allowed only a 60-second cookie life), the `userpage.php` script notices this and returns the appropriate result, as illustrated in Figure 16-28.

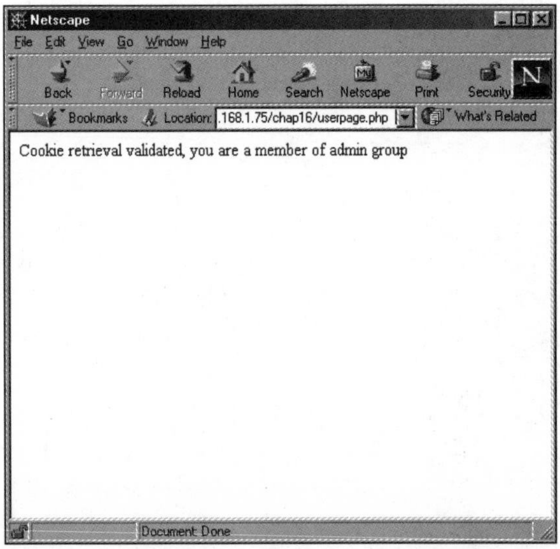

Figure 16-27: The cookies are validated when calling userpage.php.

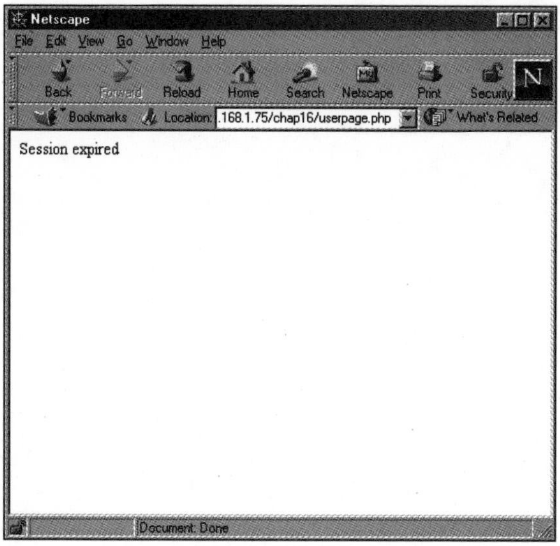

Figure 16-28: If I try to go to the page after the cookie has expired, I get a Session Expired message.

Summary

PHP, a development language that can be installed on a number of platforms and with many Web servers, includes many functions for interacting with a MySQL server. Some of these functions replace MySQL functions. PHP has some notable similarities to Perl. Using PHP and its MySQL functions, you can develop complex applications with relative ease.

- ✦ PHP can be interwoven within HTML to make complex programs while preserving the page design.
- ✦ PHP variables need not be declared explicitly. Most variables, including arrays, are called using a dollar-sign character (`$`).
- ✦ You connect to a MySQL server by using the `mysql_connect()` function. You disconnect using the `mysql_close()` function. Databases are selected with `mysql_select_db()`.
- ✦ Queries are sent to the database server with the `mysql_query()` function. The `mysql_unbuffered_query()` function can be used if you do not need to look at the results.
- ✦ There are numerous functions for retrieving the results of a query including `mysql_fetch_row, mysql_fetch_array`, and `mysql_fetch_assoc`.
- ✦ The `mysql_num_rows()` function is good for quickly determining the success or failure of an operation or statement.
- ✦ Keep `http://www.php.net` bookmarked for answers to most, if not all, your PHP-related questions.

✦ ✦ ✦

CHAPTER 17

ODBC/JDBC

✦ ✦ ✦ ✦

In This Chapter

Introducing MyODBC

Using MyODBC

Getting to know the MySQL JDBC API

Using the MySQL JDBC API

✦ ✦ ✦ ✦

Open Database Connectivity (ODBC) is the means by which third-party applications can connect to and work with data sources. Using ODBC, you can take data stored in a MySQL (or other) database and link it to ODBC-enabled applications. Such applications can include widely available products such as Microsoft Word and Access.

Note Check the documentation of your applications to make sure they are ODBC-enabled before you use ODBC to connect your documents to data sources.

In addition, an object called Java Database Connectivity (JDBC) defines the methods by which Java programs and applets connect to and work with data sources. In fact, MySQL offers a JDBC-enabled interface (JDBC API) used to connect Java programs and applets to MySQL. The JDBC API is available for download from MySQL AB's Web site.

This chapter examines ODBC with MySQL. The MySQL driver for ODBC is distributed by MySQL AB and is called MyODBC. MyODBC is available for a number of platforms including Linux and Windows. This chapter concentrates on the Windows installation and use of MyODBC.

I'll also examine the MySQL JDBC, concentrating on the Linux installation and use of the JDBC API. The MySQL JDBC driver is third-party software, not developed directly by MySQL AB.

Note

Throughout this chapter, I show examples of installing MyODBC and working with ODBC in Windows; the version of Windows that I use for these examples may be different from the version you're using—the ODBC Control Panel applet may not be located in Control Panel in your version. Though I've noted such differences throughout the chapter, I also believe that the locations for such features as the ODBC applet may change in future versions of Windows.

An Introduction to MyODBC

MyODBC is the MySQL AB driver for making an ODBC connection to MySQL. This section examines where to get the software as well as how to install and use MyODBC.

Where to get MyODBC

MyODBC can be downloaded directly from MySQL AB's Web site at `http://www.mysql.com/`. MyODBC comes packed in a zip archive for Windows, so you need some form of unzipping program to unpack the software.

Installing MyODBC

The first step in the installation of MyODBC is to unpack the zipped archive. Because the software comes with its own setup program, unpack it to a temporary location; the setup program installs it from there. For the example, I unpack the archive to `c:\temp\myodbc`, as in Figure 17-1.

Once unpacked, open Windows Explorer and point to the directory you just unpacked to, in this case `c:\temp\myodbc`. Double-click `setup.exe` to begin the setup of MyODBC, as in Figure 17-2.

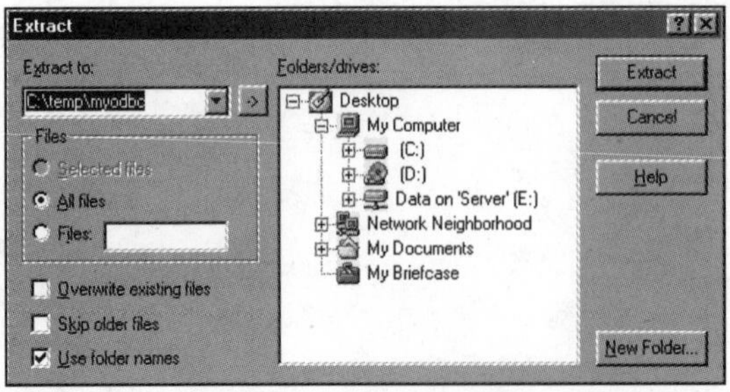

Figure 17-1: Unpacking the MyODBC archive

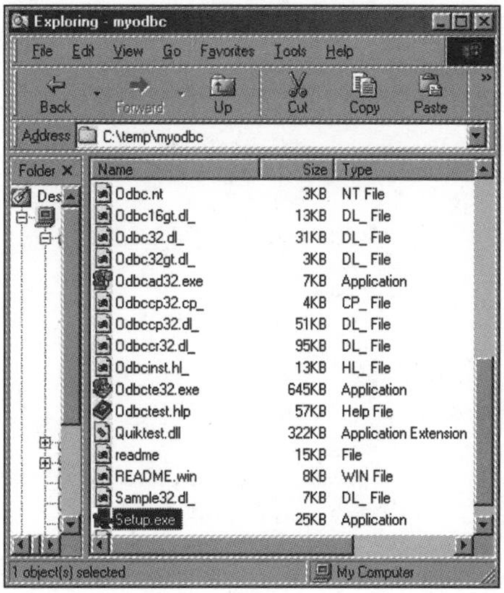

Figure 17-2: Locating the setup program in Windows Explorer

Setup of MyODBC begins with a Welcome screen (see Figure 17-3). What you're being welcomed to is actually the installation process, not MyODBC itself.

Click Continue to move to the next screen, which prompts you to choose a driver to install. MySQL is the only choice; click once to highlight it, and then click OK to continue, as shown in Figure 17-4.

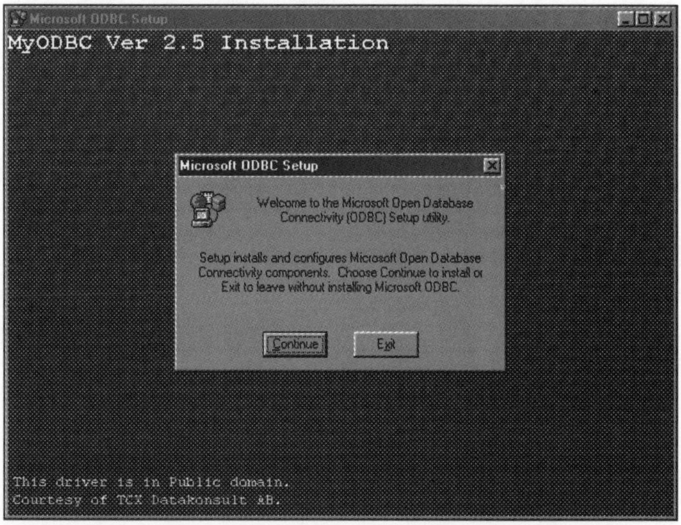

Figure 17-3: Don't be fooled; you're still installing MyODBC.

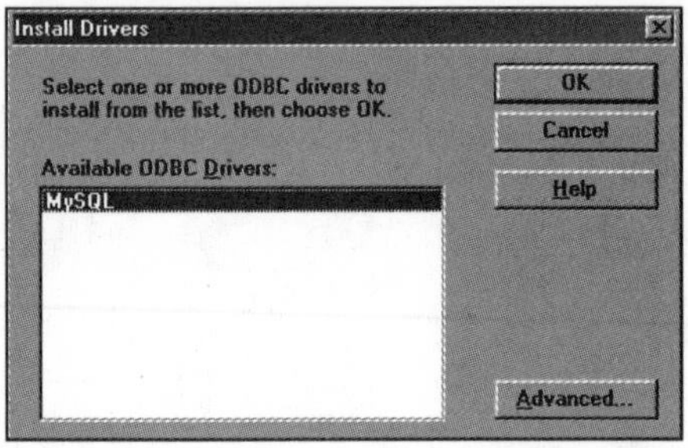

Figure 17-4: Click the MySQL driver to select it for installation.

Next you configure the MySQL data source. When presented with the list of Data Sources, click once to highlight `sample-MySQL (MySQL)`, as in Figure 17-5.

With `sample-MySQL (MySQL)` highlighted, click the Setup button to bring up the MySQL default configuration box. Set whichever options you need (for example, MySQL Host, User, Password, and so on), as illustrated in Figure 17-6. When finished, click OK. You can change the options later via the ODBC applet, located in Control Panel on Windows 95 and 98 and Administrative Tools on Windows 2000 and XP.

Once you have configured MyODBC, click Close. You should see a success message like that in Figure 17-7.

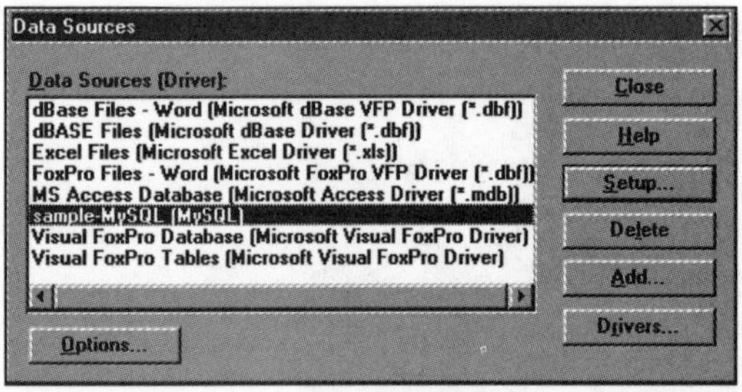

Figure 17-5: Click sample-MySQL (MySQL) in the list of available data sources.

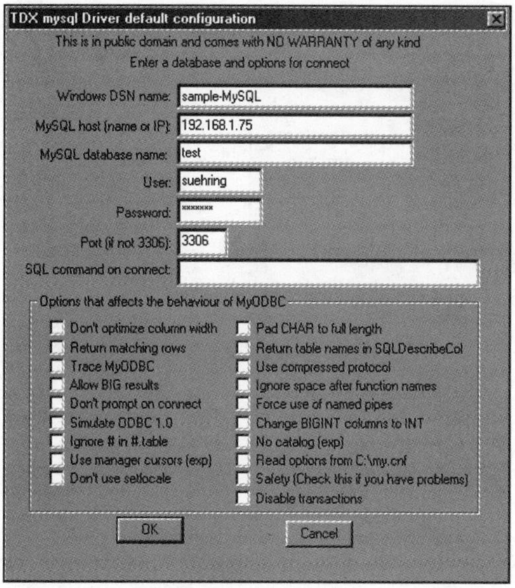

Figure 17-6: Setting the default configuration for MyODBC

Changing MyODBC Options

Should you want to change options for MyODBC at a later date, you do so through Control Panel on Windows 95 or 98 and through Administrative Tools on Windows 2000 and XP. Follow these steps:

1. Click Start ➪ Settings ➪ Control Panel.

   Control Panel opens.

2. Double-click ODBC Data Sources, as shown in Figure 17-8.

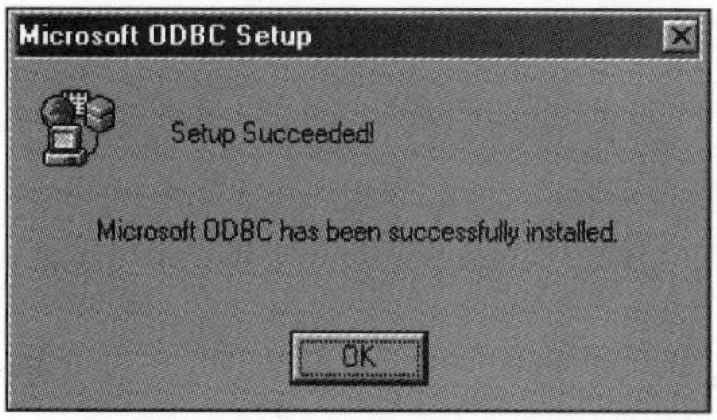

Figure 17-7: A successful installation of MyODBC

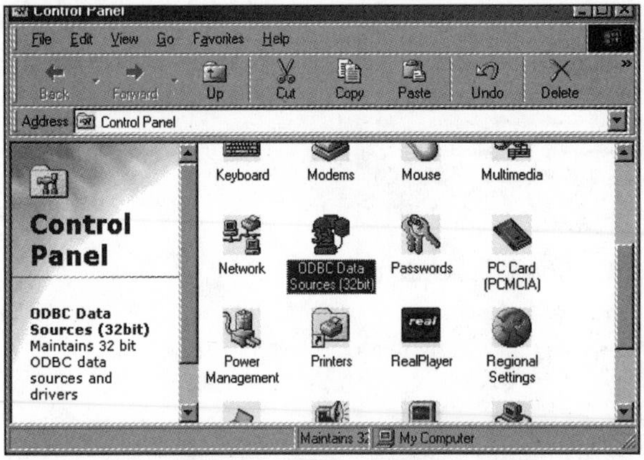

Figure 17-8: ODBC Data Sources (32 bit) contains the information about the MySQL ODBC connection.

The ODBC Data Source Administrator dialog box opens, showing the User DSN tab (as depicted in Figure 17-9).

3. Click `sample-MySQL` and then click Configure, as shown in Figure 17-10.

Tip

Each ODBC connection connects to an individual database. Therefore, if you want to connect to more than one database, you must add a new data source by clicking the Add button.

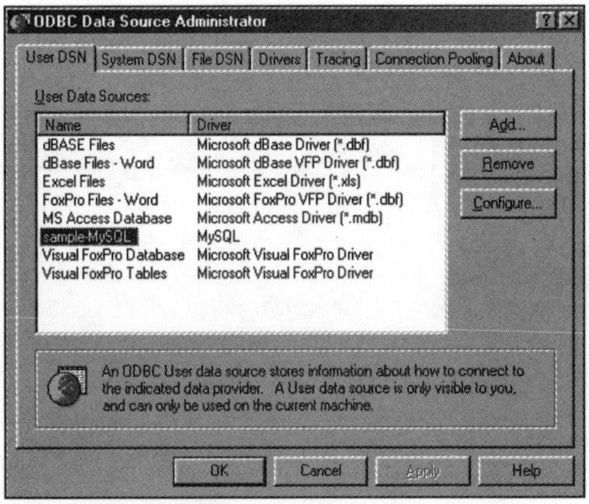

Figure 17-9: The default page in the ODBC Data Source Administrator

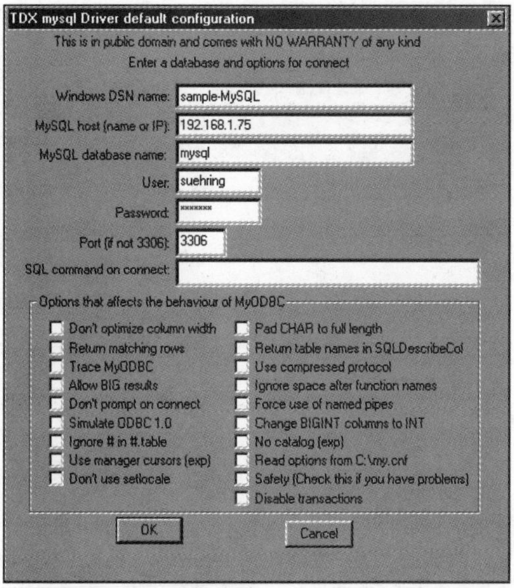

Figure 17-10: The Configuration page within the ODBC Data Sources Administrator

Using MyODBC

Once MyODBC is installed, you can start sharing data between MySQL and your ODBC-enabled applications (such as Word and Access). Understandably, a frequent practical question that crops up at this point is how to get data from a MySQL database into Microsoft Access, so it makes a good first example. The process is a little different for importing into Word. I look at both in the upcoming section.

Importing MySQL data into Microsoft Access

With MyODBC installed, importing data into Microsoft Access is quite easy. This section examines the process for importing tables into Access.

Caution

Microsoft seems to change the location and processes for import often, so the steps given here may change by the time you read this (or by the time I finish writing this section). Problems can arise working with Microsoft Access if you have an old version of the Microsoft Data Access Components (MDAC). Download a new version of these drivers from Microsoft. The current location of Microsoft's data-related software on the Web is `http://www.microsoft.com/data/`.

Currently the steps for importing tables into Access are as follows:

1. From within Access with a database open, click File ➪ Get External Data ➪ and ➪ Import, as shown in Figure 17-11.

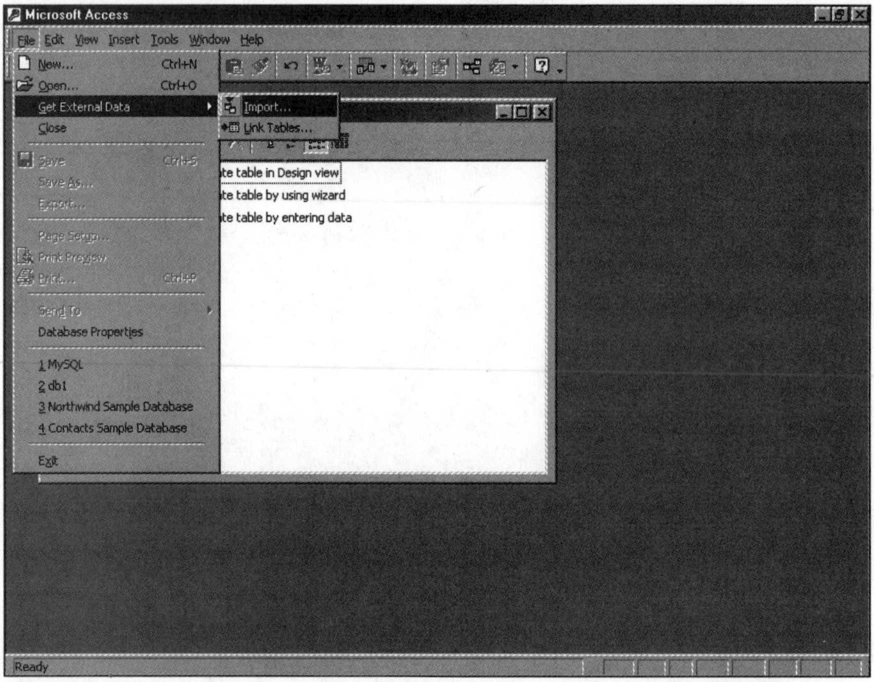

Figure 17-11: The current location where you can find the Import dialog box in Microsoft Access

The Import dialog box opens, as shown in Figure 17-12.

2. Within the Import dialog box, drop down the *Files of type* box and select ODBC Databases (), as shown in Figure 17-13.

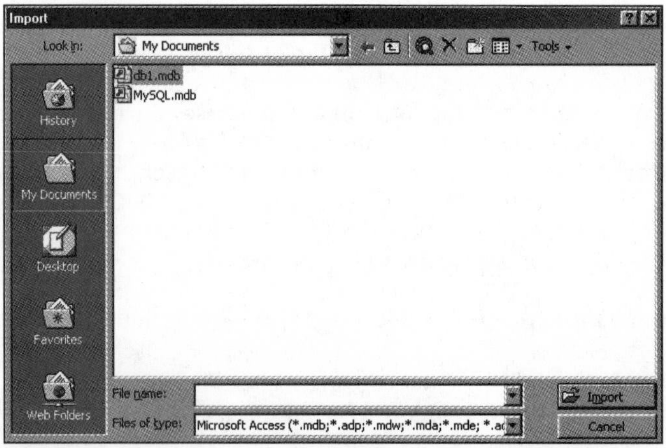

Figure 17-12: The Import dialog box in Microsoft Access

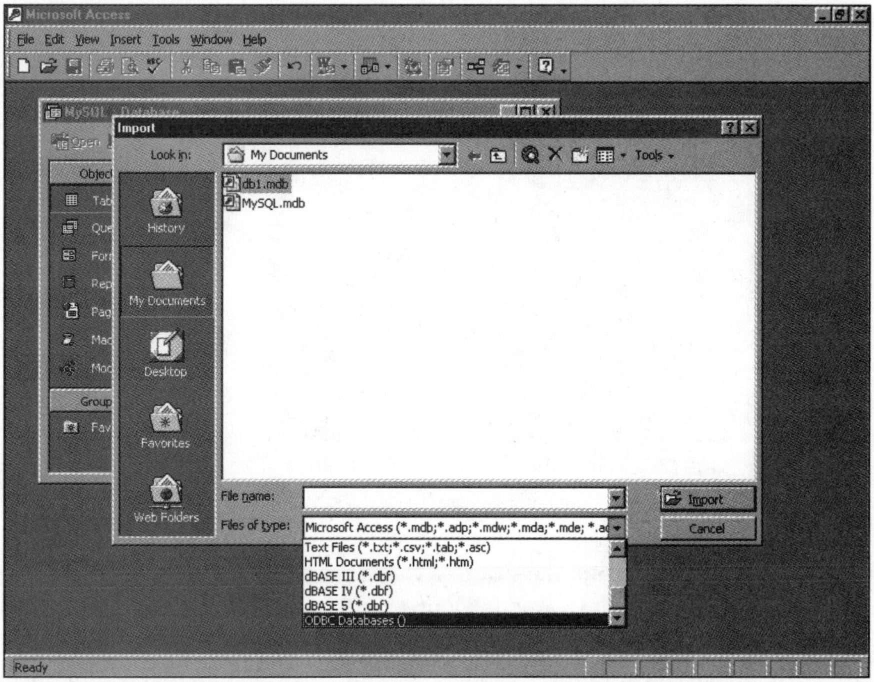

Figure 17-13: Selecting ODBC Databases () in the Files of type box

The Select Data Source box opens, as shown in Figure 17-14.

3. Click the Machine Data Source tab at the top of the Select Data Source dialog box, and then select the MySQL data source that you want to use (as shown in Figure 17-15).

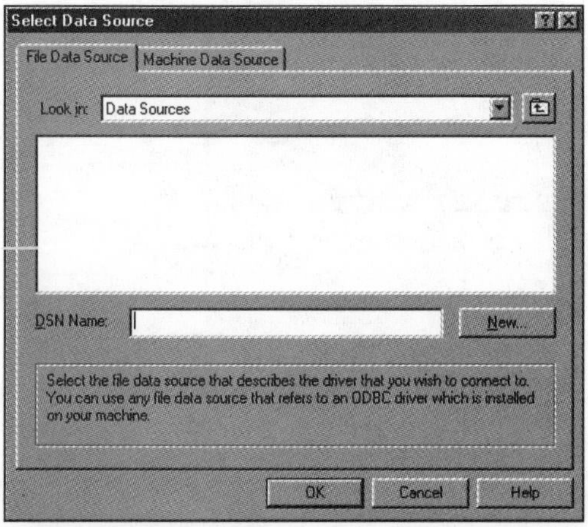

Figure 17-14: The Select Data Source dialog box as it appears when it opens

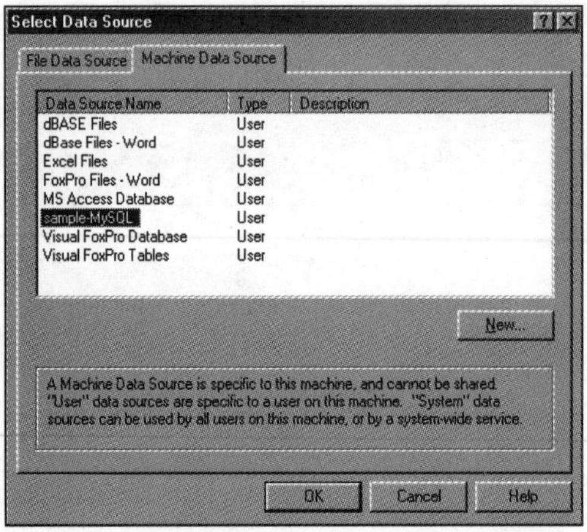

Figure 17-15: The Machine Data Source tab is where you select the MySQL ODBC data source.

Once your ODBC data source is selected and authenticated, a list of tables appears, as illustrated in Figure 17-16 (which shows and example from the `ecommerce` database).

4. Select the appropriate table that contains the data you are importing.

   In the example, I've selected the product table from the Import Objects dialog box. Doing so creates the `Products` table (see Figures 17-17).

Figure 17-16: The Import Objects dialog box, showing a list of tables

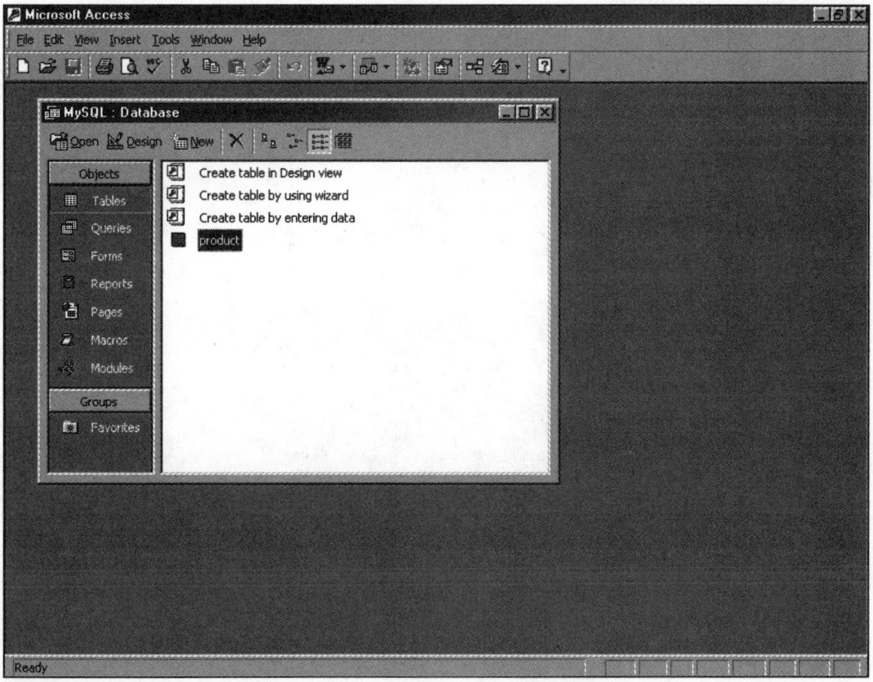

Figure 17-17: The Products table is created as a regular table.

With the creation of the new object (in this example, the `Products` table), the import process is complete. Figure 17-18 shows the completed `Products` table.

Note

If you update the data in the MySQL database directly, the data is not normally updated in the Access version of the table. Likewise, any operations performed on the Access version of the data are not performed on the MySQL copy of the data. You can use the Link Tables function in Microsoft Access to tie the Access version of the data back into MySQL.

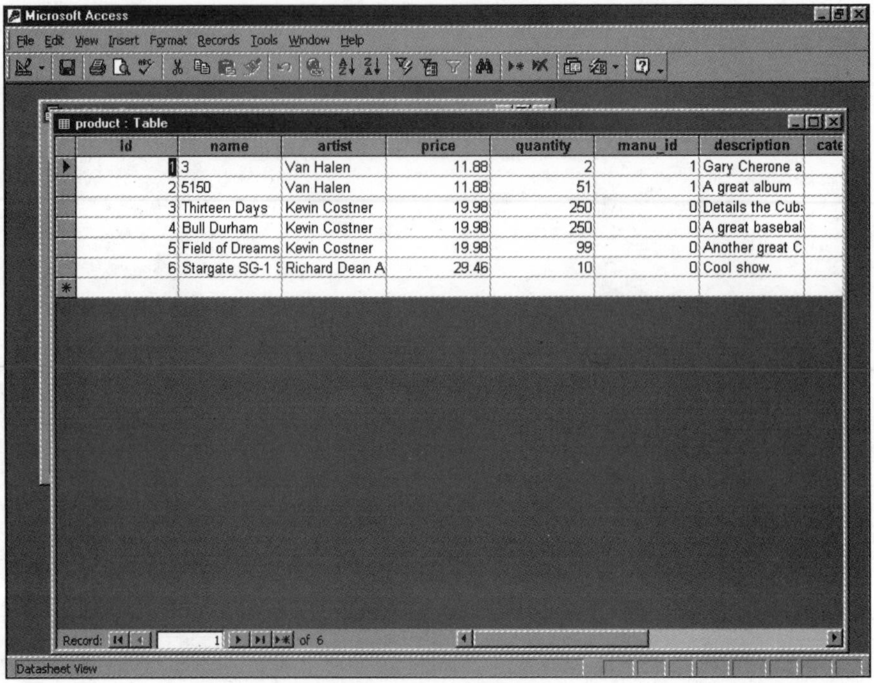

Figure 17-18: The Products table contains the data from MySQL, as you would expect.

Importing data into Microsoft Word

Importing data into a Microsoft Word document is not as simple as working with Microsoft Access. To import data into Microsoft Word, you must use Microsoft Query. Microsoft Query may or may not be installed with your version of Microsoft Word or Microsoft Office. If it is not installed, re-run the Microsoft Office Setup Wizard.

Assuming you have Microsoft Query installed, the steps for importing data into Word look like this:

1. Open the Word document into which you want to import the data (it can be a new document).
2. On the Database toolbar, click the icon that inserts a database (see Figure 17-19).

Tip If you don't have the Database toolbar available, select View ➪ Toolbars ➪ Database. Doing so adds a Database toolbar to the toolbars visible in Word.

3. Click the Insert Database button.

   The Database dialog box appears, showing two options: Get Data and Cancel.

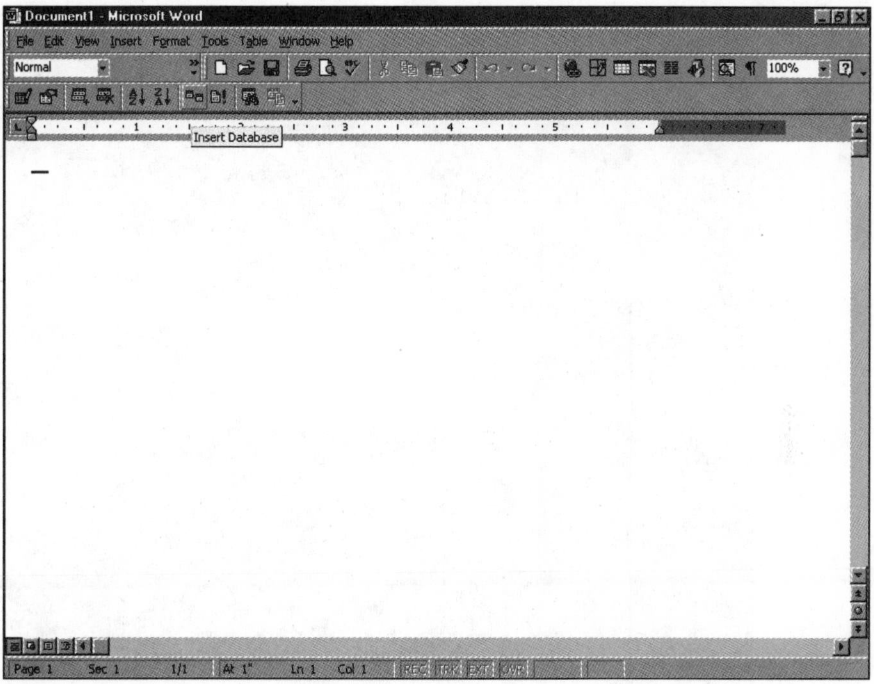

Figure 17-19: The Insert Database button on the database toolbar

4. Click Get Data.

   The Open Data Source box appears, as shown in Figure 17-20.

5. From within the Open Data Source dialog box, click MS Query.

   If Microsoft Query is installed, it opens as a new program with the Choose Data Source box open, as illustrated in Figure 17-21. Go directly to Step 6.

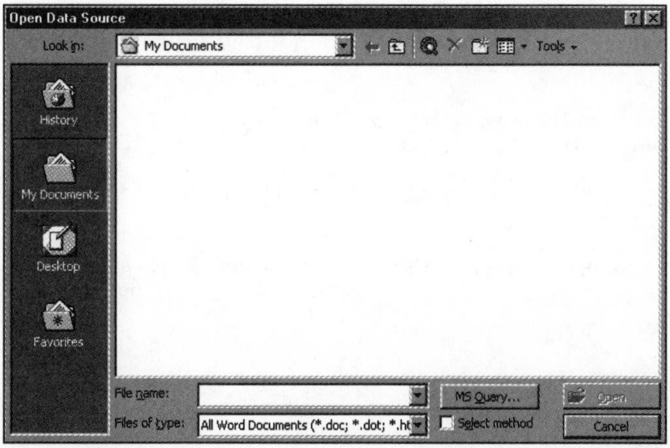

Figure 17-20: The Open Data Source dialog box

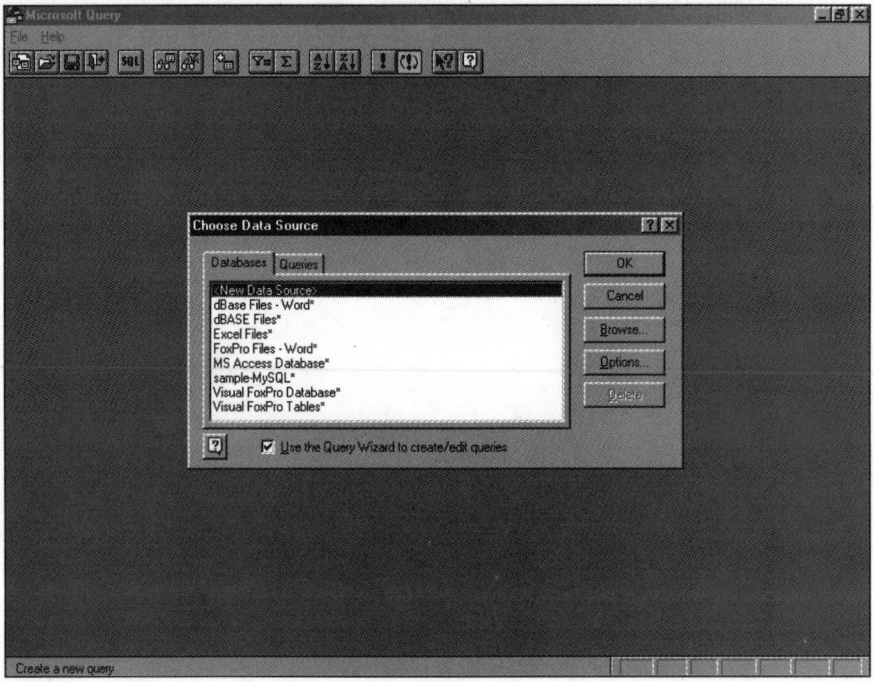

Figure 17-21: Microsoft Query opens with the Choose Data Source box.

If Microsoft Query is not installed, then (depending on the options you have enabled) you are prompted to install it. If you agree to install Query, a wizard guides you through the process. Follow the on-screen steps it presents, and then resume importing your data into Word, starting with Step 6 here (which uses the Query Wizard to complete the data transfer).

6. Select the MySQL ODBC connection that you'd like to begin working with and click OK (in this example, it's called `sample-MySQL`).

   The Query Wizard - Choose Columns dialog box opens; you should see all tables listed in the database configured in the ODBC connection, as in Figure 17-22.

7. From within the Choose Columns portion of the Query Wizard, choose the columns you want to include in the query.

   If there's a plus sign next the table name you can click it to expand the columns within the table.

8. Highlight a column name and then click the right arrow to move it into the Columns in your Query area, as illustrated in Figure 17-23 (where I select three columns for a query).

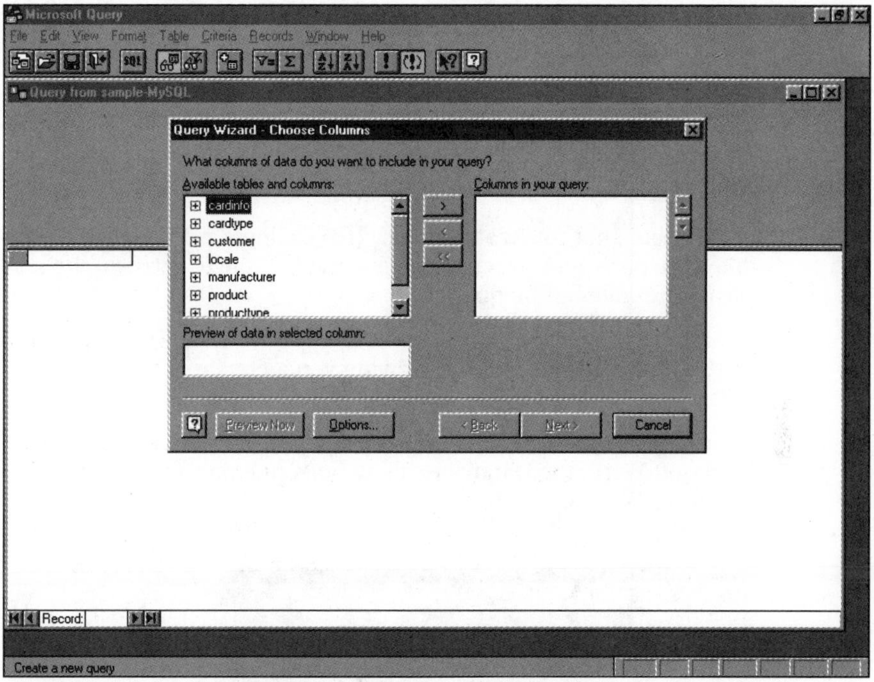

Figure 17-22: Query Wizard - Choose Columns opens with the tables from the database (as defined in the ODBC connection you chose).

9. Click Next to continue, which brings up a Filter Data dialog box (as shown in Figure 17-24).
10. The Filter Data dialog box assists you in determining if you want to select only certain records or rows. If you do not want to filter your data, click Next.

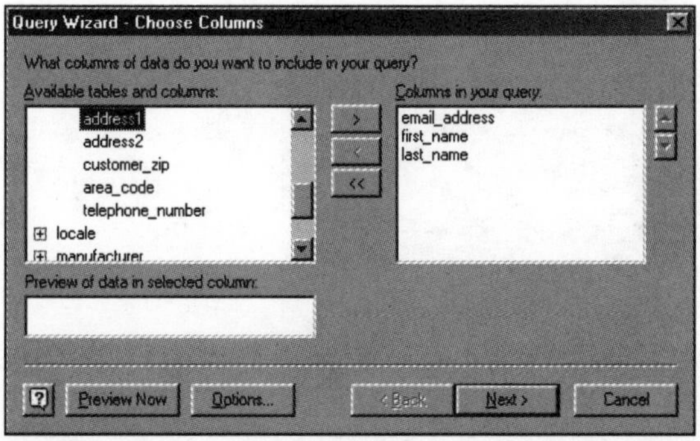

Figure 17-23: Selecting columns for a query in the Query Wizard

The Sort Order dialog box appears, as shown in Figure 17-25. If you want to sort your results, you can do so by selecting the appropriate columns and choosing a sort order.

11. When you've completed the Sort Order dialog box (or decided not to use it), click Next.

    A Finish box appears, as in Figure 17-26.

12. If you decide not to save the query (for example, when you follow the steps in this book purely for practice), you won't be able to retrieve the results later without rebuilding the query.

    To save your query for later retrieval, click the Save Query button, which starts the saving procedure by giving you a choice of locations for the saved query (see Figure 17-27).

13. Once you complete the Query Wizard, if you elect to send the data back to Microsoft Word, the Database dialog box appears again in Word, as illustrated in Figure 17-28.

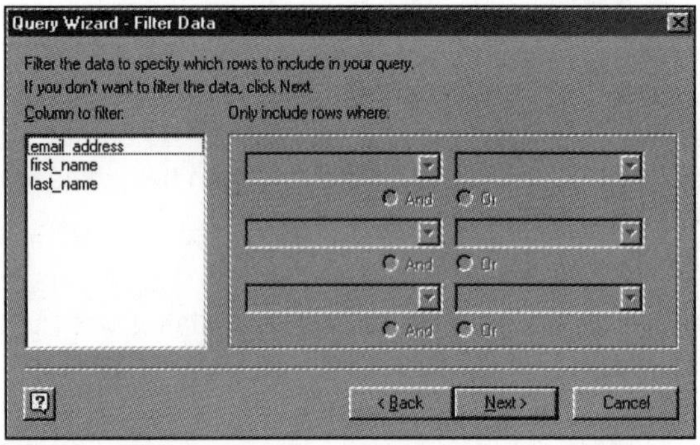

Figure 17-24: The Filter Data dialog box, as seen in the Query Wizard

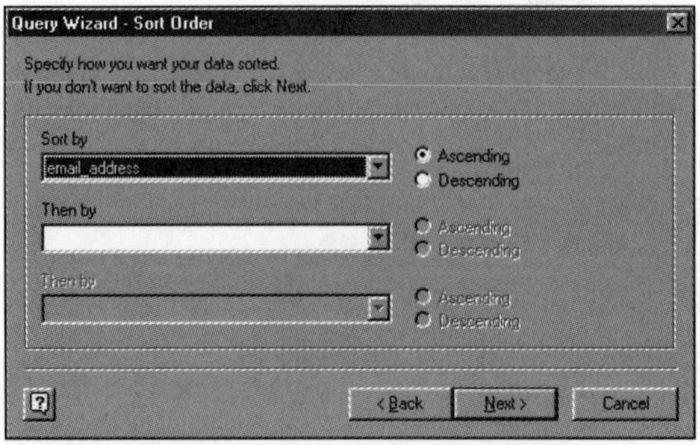

Figure 17-25: Sorting results by using the Sort Order dialog box

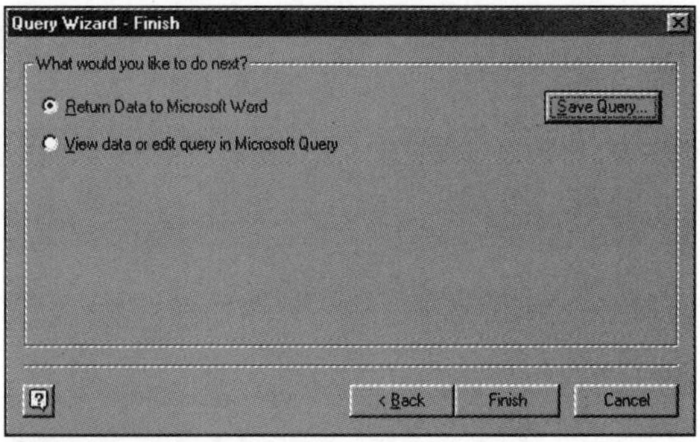

Figure 17-26: The Finish dialog box for the Query Wizard

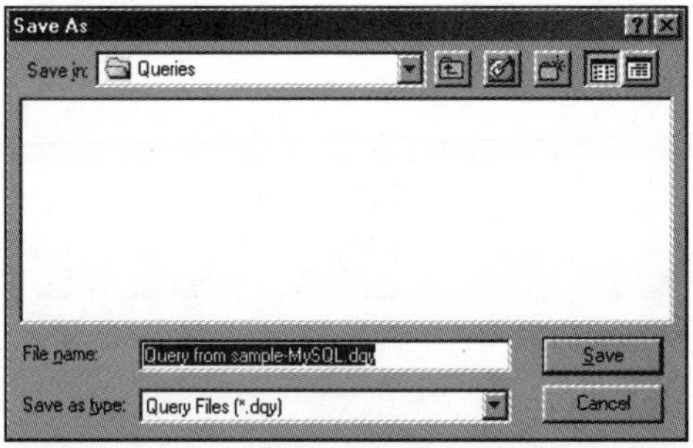

Figure 17-27: Choosing a location to which to save the query for later retrieval

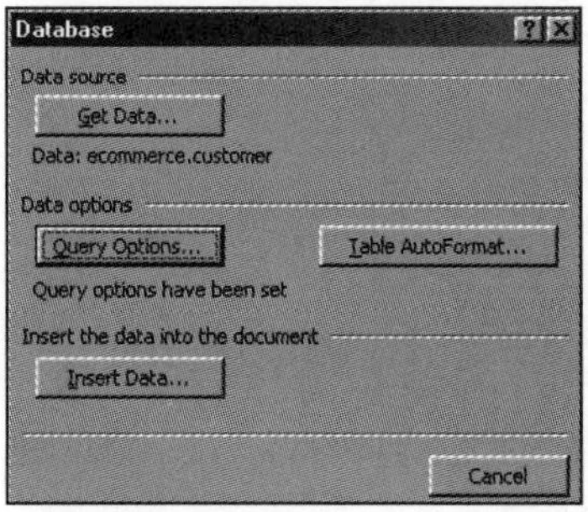

Figure 17-28: The Database dialog box in Microsoft Word after successful completion of the Microsoft Query Wizard

14. Click Insert Data.

The data appears in your Word document, as illustrated in Figure 17-29. Congratulations! You've imported the data into a Word document.

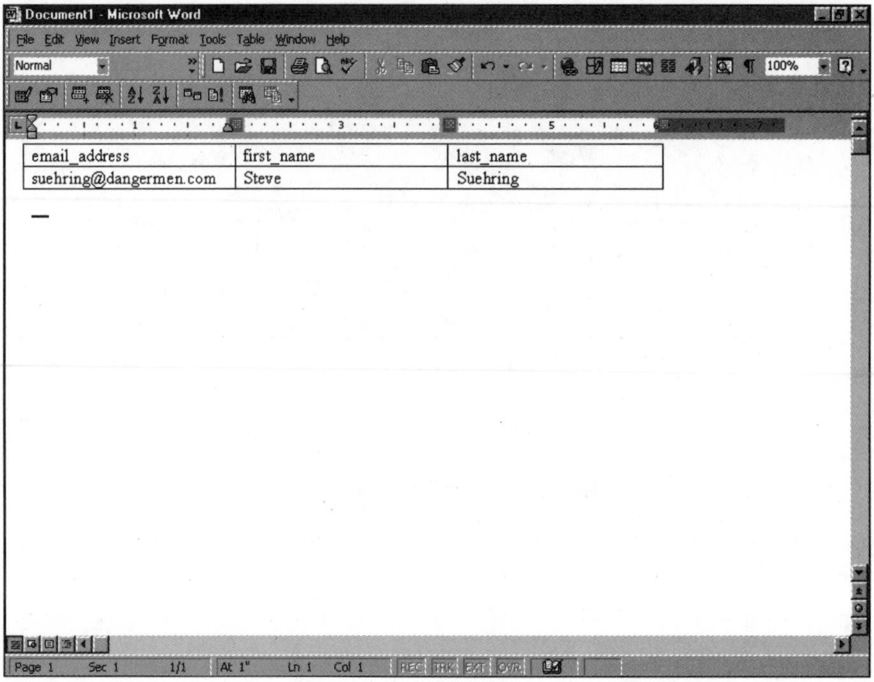

Figure 17-29: The data from MySQL imported through Microsoft Query

Tip

Should you encounter problems with the import process, check to make sure that your ODBC connection is working properly. The quickest fix is to get MySQL and Microsoft Access talking to each other. Try to connect with ODBC in Microsoft Access. If this works, then you may have a problem other than the import process itself (for example, an incompatibility in driver versions).

An Introduction to JDBC

Java Database Connectivity (JDBC) is the Java version of the interface used for connection to more than one relational database management system (RDBMS). A JDBC API exists for MySQL, in several versions. Presently only one version is available under the Lesser GNU Public License (LGPL).

Using the JDBC for MySQL, you can connect Java programs and applets to a MySQL database. This section examines the installation of the MySQL JDBC in Linux as well as how to connect to MySQL in a Java program.

The JDBC interface

JDBC *for MySQL* is a slight misnomer; Java database connectivity is, in fact, available for various RDBMS programs. In effect, JDBC functions like the Perl DBI—it enables a range of database drivers to connect to various RDBMS products. For the purposes of this book, when I refer to "the" JDBC interface, I refer to a particular API—the MySQL driver that works with the JDBC.

The JDBC API itself is included with the core Java Software Development Kit (abbreviated as SDK or JDK—I use *JDK* throughout this chapter). In particular, the `java.sql` package contains the classes needed for using MySQL to work with data.

Where to get the JDBC and MySQL JDBC Driver

The MySQL JDBC API is not an official MySQL AB product. However, the MySQL JDBC driver is linked from the MySQL AB Web site. I found the versions of the MySQL JDBC driver linked directly from MySQL AB's Web site to be relatively old. A newer version of the MySQL JDBC driver can usually be obtained directly from the following Web site: `http://mmmysql.sourceforge.net/`.

The file format for the MySQL JDBC driver is a Java archive; you need the `jar` program to unpack it. You can obtain `jar` at the following Web site:

```
http://mmmysql.sourceforge.net/
```

Getting the driver shouldn't be a problem; the Java Software Development Kit (JDK) is another a prerequisite to installing the JDBC MySQL driver. If you don't have the JDK, download it from the following Web site:

```
http://java.sun.com/products/
```

Although I'm hesitant to offer this link as the definitive Sun Java Web site (its location may change in the future), that's where you can download the latest JDK for Linux.

Installing the MySQL JDBC Driver

Before installing the MySQL JDBC driver, make sure you have the Java JDK installed. The JDK comes in a binary format, with a file extension of `.bin`. When you run the binary program, it creates a directory (below your current directory) and installs the Java JDK automatically.

After you download the Java JDK, you may have to change the mode of the file before you can execute it. The command for doing so is as follows:

```
chmod 700 j2sdk-<version>.bin
```

Execute the file as you would any other program located in a directory not in your path, as follows:

```
./j2sdk-<version>.bin
```

Again, be sure to run the JDK installer binary from the location where you want it installed. If you want the JDK in `/usr/local/j2sdk-<version>/` (for example), you should execute the installer from within `/usr/local`.

When you execute the installer, a License Agreement appears. Read the agreement; if you agree to its terms, type **yes** (see Figure 17-30).

The JDK installation then creates the necessary directories and files, as illustrated in Figure 17-31. No compilation is necessary with the Java JDK.

The current version of the MySQL JDBC driver comes packed in a `jar` archive and need not be compiled. For my installation, I unpacked the `jar` archive to the `jdk` directory.

```
cp mm.mysql-2.0.9-you-must-unjarme.jar /usr/local/ jdk1.3.1_02
cd /usr/local/jdk1.3.1_02
./bin/jar xvf mm.mysql-2.0.9-you-must-unjarme.jar
```

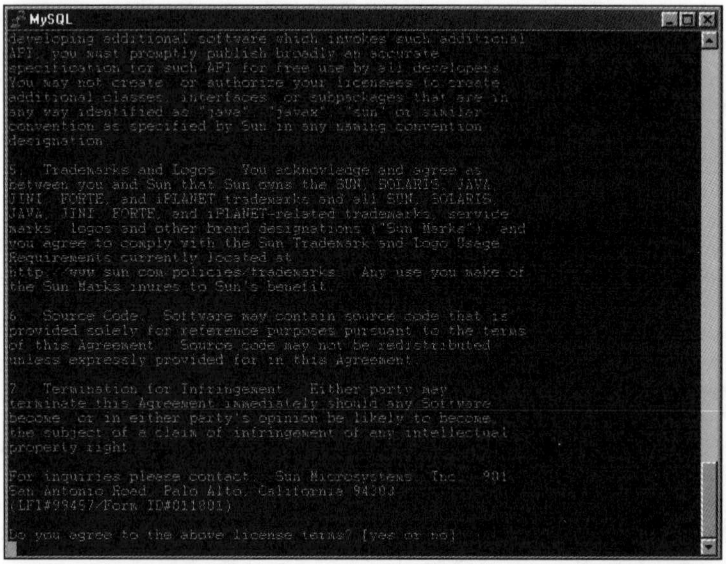

Figure 17-30: The license agreement is the first step in JDK installation.

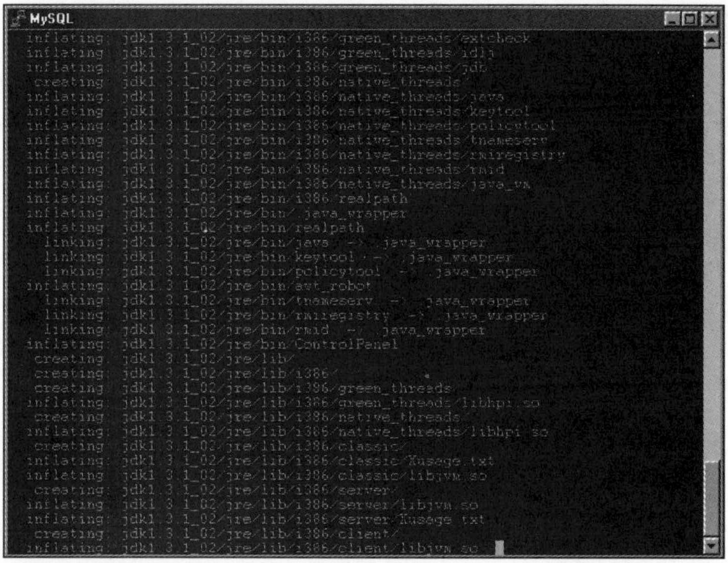

Figure 17-31: The Java JDK installer requires no compilation to install the software.

Running this command yields a directory called mm-2.0.9 in /usr/local/jdk1.3.1_02.

Inside of the mm-2.0.9 directory there is a file called mm.mysql-2.0.9-bin.jar. Copying that file to /usr/local/jdk1.3.1_02/jre/lib/ext copies the class files for the MySQL JDBC API. If your installation is in a different location, copy the file to <java_sdk_directory>/jre/lib/ext/.

Note Version numbers of both the Java JDK and the MySQL JDBC driver will probably change by the time you read this.

For my installation, I also added the JDK's binary directory to my path. In addition, you may want to add the MySQL JDBC driver location to your CLASSPATH. Using csh or tcsh, the command that does so looks like this:

```
setenv CLASSPATH /path/to/mysql-jdbc-class:.:$CLASSPATH
```

Should you receive an error such as that shown in Figure 17-32, then no CLASSPATH is defined at all. In this instance, I recommend setting it to include the JDK directory as well, using the following command line:

```
setenv CLASSPATH /path/to/jdk:/path/to/mysql-jdbc-class:
```

Figure 17-32: The error message given when the CLASSPATH variable hasn't been set

For more information on installing and using the Java Software Development Kit, see the Sun Web site, `http://java.sun.com`.

Using the JDBC and the MySQL Driver

The JDBC itself defines the methods by which you connect to a database. This section looks at how to create a connection to a MySQL database and issue statements with the JDBC. Before doing so, I'd like to go over some basic terminology and concepts.

The concepts and terms of JDBC

The first step involved in making the JDBC work with a database is loading a driver. The JDBC `java.sql.DriverManager` class performs this task. The `DriverManager` class also works with the `Driver` so you don't need to. The `forName()` method loads the `Driver` class.

> **Note:** Although you can also load the `Driver` class by using `jdbc.drivers`, I recommend using the `forName()` method for the sake of consistency.

The `Class.forname()` method takes a string as an argument. In the case of the MySQL JDBC driver, this string is:

```
org.gjt.mm.mysql.Driver
```

For example:

```
Class.forName("org.gjt.mm.mysql.Driver");
```

The `getConnection` method is called to make the actual connection to the database server. The `DriverManager` creates a `Connection` object when you call the getConnection method. GetConnection takes a string URL as an argument. In the case of MySQL, you provide the URL and credentials for the connection:

```
Connection con;
con = DriverManager.getConnection(url, "username", "password");
```

Alternatively:

```
Connection con = DriverManager.getConnection(url, "username",
"password");
```

The basics of handling statements and results

The Statement interface with the JDBC is not an object, but rather, an interface for *creating* an object that executes statements. You create a Statement object as follows:

```
Statement stmt = connection.CreateStatement();
```

With the Statement object created, you use an execute method on the object. There are four execute methods for use with the JDBC: executeQuery(), executeUpdate(), executeBatch(), and execute().

The executeQuery() method is for statements such as SELECT that retrieve values from a database. The executeUpdate() method is used commonly with DDL statements that don't return values but may return a number of rows affected by the operation. Finally, the execute() method is for statements that return greater than one result or count.

The executeUpdate() method returns an integer value that contains the number of rows affected by the operation.

The results from queries are retrieved using ResultSet. For example:

```
ResultSet result = statement.executeQuery("SELECT * FROM
user");
```

To access the results, use a get method. The basic methods for accessing data are as follows:

```
getBoolean()
getByte()
getDate()
getDouble()
getFloat()
getInt()
getLong()
getShort()
getString()
getTime()
getTimestamp()
```

The `getDate()`, `getTime()`, and `getTimestamp()` methods all return date or time values. When using a `get` method, you provide the column name in quotes. For example,

```
getString("columnname");
```

If you do not know the column name, you can identify the result with by its numerical column-position reference. If you don't know the number of columns, you can find that value in the realm of the upcoming section; it's a type of metadata.

Database metadata

To manipulate data, you need information about it — *metadata*. Database metadata, for example, is information *about* the database and the data it contains — for example, the number of columns returned from a query. There are two sets of metadata for JDBC objects — *connection* and *result*. Both are retrieved with the `getMetaData()` method. When called in reference to a `ResultSet`, the `ResultSetMetaData` object type is returned.

In answer to the question posed about the number of columns, the following code snippet shows how to determine the number of columns from a given result set.

```
ResultSetMetaData databaseinfo = result.getMetaData();
int columns = databaseinfo.getColumnCount();
System.out.println(columns);
```

Other useful methods within `ResultSetMetaData` are `getColumnName()`, and `getColumnType()`.

Metadata about the database and server is available through the `DatabaseMetaData` object, as follows:

```
import java.sql.*;

public class DBMeta {

  public static void main(String args[]) {

    String url = "jdbc:mysql://localhost/ecommerce";
    Connection con;

    try {
        Class.forName("org.gjt.mm.mysql.Driver");

    } catch(java.lang.ClassNotFoundException e) {
        System.err.print("ClassNotFoundException: ");
        System.err.println(e.getMessage());
    }

    try {
        con = DriverManager.getConnection(url, "suehring",
"evh5150");
```

```
        System.out.println("Connection established!");

        DatabaseMetaData dbmdata = con.getMetaData();
        System.out.println("Database Information");
        System.out.println("Database name: " +
dbmdata.getDatabaseProductName())
;
        System.out.println("Version: " +
dbmdata.getDatabaseProductVersion());
        System.out.println("Driver: " +
dbmdata.getDriverName());
        System.out.println("Version: " +
dbmdata.getDriverVersion());

        con.close();

    } catch(SQLException ex) {
        System.err.println("SQLException: " + ex.getMessage());
      }
  }
}
```

Working with JDBC errors

The main handler for errors with JDBC is `SQLException` class. `SQLException`, when invoked, sends a string with a description of the exception. This error message is retrieved with the `getMessage()` method. `SQLException` actually sends three pieces of information; in general terms, these are as follows:

- **Message string** — the message itself.
- **SQL state** — a five-character string retrieved with the `getSQLState()` method.
- **Vendor error code** — a code defined by the software vendor and retrieved with the `getErrorCode()` method.

Testing for NULL values

The `wasNull()` method serves to determine if a value returned from the database was `NULL`. The `wasNull()` method is called as part of the result set for a statement, as in the following example:

```
Statement stmt = con.createStatement();
result = stmt.executeQuery(sql);
while (result.next()) {
   if (result.wasNull()) {
      System.out.println("Null found.");
   }
}
```

Cached connections

Up to this point, I've been showing examples using the ResultSet object. The ResultSet object remains connected to the data source for result retrieval. Because the connection must remain intact and active, the ResultSet object is not useful for working with data over a networked connection. The JDBC API defines a RowSet interface that includes a CachedRowSet class that can be used to retrieve results and place them into a cache for later use.

Connecting to MySQL with the JDBC API and MySQL Driver

Connecting to MySQL with JDBC for the first time can be a humbling experience. After lurking on Java mailing lists for a long time (as well as watching the Usenet newsgroups), I've seen numerous questions by first-time developers who struggle with this initial JDBC connection.

The following code demonstrates a typical connection to a MySQL server, made with Java.

```
import java.sql.*;

public class FirstConnection {

  public static void main(String args[]) {

    String url = "jdbc:mysql://localhost/ecommerce";
    Connection con;

    try {
        Class.forName("org.gjt.mm.mysql.Driver");

    } catch(java.lang.ClassNotFoundException e) {
        System.err.print("ClassNotFoundException: ");
        System.err.println(e.getMessage());
    }

    try {
        con = DriverManager.getConnection(url, "suehring",
"evh5150");
        System.out.println("Connection established!");
        con.close();

    } catch(SQLException ex) {
        System.err.println("SQLException: " + ex.getMessage());
      }
  }
}
```

You can save this connection as a program named FirstConnection.java — and compile it — by typing

```
javac FirstConnection.java
```

Once the program is compiled, you can run it by typing

```
java FirstConnection
```

When your first connection is successful, a Connection Successful message appears.

Examining some of the code snippets reveals that a string variable, url, is initialized and contains the connection information for the server (localhost) that I want to connect to, along with the database (ecommerce) that I want to use. If I want to specify a port other than the default 3306, I can use localhost:port. For example, I could use localhost:5150 like this:

```
String url = "jdbc:mysql://localhost/ecommerce";
```

A connection object, con, is created next:

```
Connection con;
```

The MySQL JDBC driver is now loaded, according to the syntax discussed in the previous section. If the loading of the driver is unsuccessful, an error message is printed; the following code displays the error message:

```
try {
    Class.forName("org.gjt.mm.mysql.Driver");

} catch(java.lang.ClassNotFoundException e) {
    System.err.print("ClassNotFoundException: ");
    System.err.println(e.getMessage());
}
```

The connection is attempted next; if it does not succeed, use SQLException to retrieve the error message. That operation looks like this:

```
    try {
        con = DriverManager.getConnection(url, "suehring","evh5150");
        System.out.println("Connection established!");
        con.close();

    } catch(SQLException ex) {
        System.err.println("SQLException: " + ex.getMessage());
      }
}
```

Creating a basic MySQL JDBC Program

Building on the simple connection program from the last section, I'll retrieve some results from a query by using the following code:

```
import java.sql.*;

public class SimpleSelect {

  public static void main(String args[]) {

    String url = "jdbc:mysql://localhost/ecommerce";
    Connection con;

    try {
        Class.forName("org.gjt.mm.mysql.Driver");

    } catch(java.lang.ClassNotFoundException e) {
        System.err.print("ClassNotFoundException: ");
        System.err.println(e.getMessage());
    }

    try {
        con = DriverManager.getConnection(url, "suehring",
"evh5150");
        System.out.println("Connection established!");

        Statement stmt = con.createStatement();
        ResultSet productinfo =
          stmt.executeQuery("SELECT name,artist FROM product");

        while (productinfo.next()) {
          System.out.println(productinfo.getString("name") + "
"

                + productinfo.getString("artist"));
        }

        con.close();


    } catch(SQLException ex) {
        System.err.println("SQLException: " + ex.getMessage());
      }
  }
}
```

The code just given has a new section added to execute the statement and retrieve the results. A `Statement` object, `stmt`, is created. Then the query is issued. The results are then retrieved by using the `getString` method with the column name in quotes:

```
        Statement stmt = con.createStatement();
        ResultSet productinfo =
          stmt.executeQuery("SELECT name,artist FROM product");

        while (productinfo.next()) {
          System.out.println(productinfo.getString("name") + "
" + productinfo.getString("artist"));
        }
```

You can save the program as `SimpleSelect.java` and compile it by typing the following command:

```
javac SimpleSelect.java
```

Summary

MyODBC is MySQL AB's version of an ODBC driver for MySQL, available for Windows and for some versions of Unix and Linux.

- ✦ MyODBC can be obtained directly from MySQL AB's Web site.
- ✦ MyODBC installation in Windows is straightforward using a standard Windows-type setup program.
- ✦ During setup you enter in basic information about the MySQL ODBC Data Source including the name or IP of the server, username, password, and database to connect to.
- ✦ You can change the information or add Data Sources for MySQL at a later time through the ODBC Control Panel in Windows.
- ✦ Connecting MySQL to Microsoft Access is relatively simple and is done through the Get External Data process.
- ✦ Connecting MySQL to Microsoft Word is done through the use of Microsoft Query to build a `SELECT` query for the data you'd like to integrate.
- ✦ JDBC is the Java equivalent of ODBC. JDBC is distributed with the Java Software Development Kit from Sun.
- ✦ MySQL has a driver to integrate with the JDBC so you can connect MySQL to Java programs and applets.

✦ ✦ ✦

Advanced Performance

PART

V

✦ ✦ ✦ ✦

In This Part

✦ ✦ ✦ ✦

CHAPTER 18

Replication

✦ ✦ ✦ ✦

In This Chapter

Getting ready for replication

Setting your configurations for replication

Keeping an eye on replication

Using replication shortcuts

✦ ✦ ✦ ✦

An area that has received a lot of attention from the MySQL development team has been replication. Replication refers to the automated copying of changes made to databases and data between two or more MySQL servers. The MySQL development team has made replication in MySQL a robust and stable feature.

As part of my daily routine, I manage a fairly large-scale database that is replicated across five states in real time using MySQL replication. The system has been operational for two years with very little difficulty. Even two years ago, replication in MySQL was stable. The stability and added features of today's MySQL replication make it a good choice for redundancy and mission-critical applications alike.

This chapter looks at MySQL replication, including how to install and configure replication between two or more MySQL servers. MySQL AB has gone to great lengths to make replication configuration easy as you'll see in the following pages.

Planning and Preparing for Replication

Before undertaking the tasks involved in actually setting up replication, take some time to plan and prepare for those tasks. The planning includes making sure replication is right for your implementation, deciding what databases or tables will be replicated, how many servers will participate in the replication, and how you will monitor replication. Preparing for replication includes ensuring that all participating servers are running on the same MySQL version.

Considerations for replication

A couple of common terms that will be used throughout this chapter are master and slave. The *master server* receives updates to the data from applications and through other means and is considered the primary MySQL server in the replication set. The *slave server* receives updates only from the master server. The master server knows nothing about any slave servers that read the updates and replication information. The slave server is responsible for contacting the master server and reading the replication updates.

Replication does not require a constant or high-speed connection between the master and slave. If a slave loses its connection to the master, it will try to reconnect according to values set by the administrator. Further, if a slave server stops replicating, it will remember where it left off and catch up later. Replication does require that both the master and slave have the same data to begin with. Therefore, if you are beginning with a 6GB database, you need that data transferred to the slave. (There are a couple of methods for performing this task, which I discuss later.)

Replication uses a log, called the binary log, for tracking updates to data. This file is kept on the master in a replication set or on slave servers that have log-slave-updates enabled. On some file systems, notably `ext2` in Linux, the maximum default file size is 2GB. Therefore, you must monitor replication and perform a replication-and-restart operation before the binary log grows to 2GB.

Replication can be configured in a number of forms. The simplest and most widely used form of replication is with one master and one or more slaves. Replication can also be configured with more than one master though only one is active at any time. Finally, replication can be configured in a two-way format where updates are logged back to the master. Two-way replication can create problems such as when there is an update for the same record received at the same time.

MySQL enables the administrator to choose the data to replicate. The data can be selected with granularity down to the table level. Therefore, you can replicate all databases on the server, only certain databases, or simply a table. Additionally, you can select tables with wildcard-like matching and even select a table or tables not to include while including all others.

The values for `auto_increment` columns are automatically updated as part of the replication process. No need to worry about the values becoming skewed between replication participants.

MySQL server versions

For replication to work successfully, you must be running the same version of MySQL on all servers participating in the replication. There are exceptions to this rule, but for the most part it's a good idea to get the latest version of MySQL running on all participating replication servers so that the features and back-end code operate as expected.

The file format for replication changed in MySQL version 3.23.26 — and again in version 4. If you are running an older version and cannot update, you're required to run old versions of MySQL on *all* servers that participate in the replication.

Version 4 of MySQL can participate in a 3.23.26 (or greater) version of replication. The server will check the version running on the master, and if it is a 3.*x* version, the appropriate format is used.

Security

By default, replication traffic is sent via unencrypted packets — an unacceptable arrangement for secure databases and updates. This is especially true of updates that traverse untrusted networks.

Beginning with version 4 of MySQL you can configure replication to use Secure Sockets Layer (SSL) for replication traffic. Using SSL, traffic is encrypted and thus safer as it travels across an untrusted network. Using SSL with MySQL replication assumes that you have OpenSSL installed and working. If you do not have OpenSSL installed, you can't use SSL for MySQL replication.

Configuring Replication

This section gets down to the business of configuring replication. I'll begin by examining the variables and settings for replication and then continue by looking at a simple replication configuration between one master server and two slaves. Additional replication configurations are also examined in this section.

Replication variables and settings

Some options for replication are only available within a particular *context;* they apply only to a master server or only to a slave server. The options are set within the MySQL configuration file such as `my.cnf` or `my.ini`. Table 18-1 lists the settings applicable for a master server.

Table 18-1
Options For Master Server In MySQL Replication

Option	Description
`binlog-do-db`	Replication will be performed only on updates to database specified.
`binlog-ignore-db`	Replication will be done on all databases except database specified.
`log-bin`	Sends replication updates to logfile in binary format.
`log-bin-index`	Sets the filename of the file to track which log number is current.
`PURGE MASTER LOGS TO`	Deletes replication logs.
`RESET MASTER`	Purges replication-related logfiles and restarts replication.
`server-id`	Unique integer value of server within a replication set.
`SET SQL_LOG_BIN=0`	Stops replication or updating of the binary log.
`SET SQL_LOG_BIN=1`	Starts replication or updating of the binary log.
`SHOW BINLOG EVENTS`	Used for debugging, this statement shows items in the binary log.
`SHOW MASTER LOGS`	Gives information on the binary logs residing on the master.
`SHOW MASTER STATUS`	Gives information on the master replication process.

The options and settings applicable for a slave server are shown in Figure 18-2. As in Table 18-1, SQL statements are shown in all uppercase.

Table 18-2
Options For Slave Server In MySQL Replication

Option	Description
`CHANGE MASTER TO`	Changes the master that a slave replicates with.
`LOAD DATA FROM MASTER`	Transfers a snapshot copy of the data from master to begin replication.
`LOAD TABLE FROM MASTER`	Transfers a specific table from a master server.
`log-slave-updates`	Enables logging of updates on slave server.
`master-host`	The IP or hostname of the master server.
`master-user`	Username to use for replication.

Option	*Description*
master-password	Password to use for replication.
master-port	Port to use for replication, default 3306 or the MYSQL_PORT variable.
master-connect-retry	Value in seconds to wait before attempting to reconnect in the event of a non-fatal error.
master-ssl	Enables replication over SSL.
master-ssl-key	Name of keyfile to use for SSL-enabled replication.
master-ssl-cert	Name of certificate to use for SSL-enabled replication.
master-info-file	Location and name of file that contains replication information.
report-host	Special IP to report as when performing replication.
report-port	Port number to report to master for replication.
replicate-do-table	Name of table to replicate.
replicate-ignore-table	Name of table to ignore for replication.
replicate-wild-do-table	Wildcard matching for tables to replicate.
replicate-wild-ignore=table	Wildcard matching for tables to exclude from replication.
replicate-do-db	Name of database to include in replication.
replicate-ignore-db	Name of database to exclude from replication.
replicate-rewrite-db	Name of database to replicate and then rename on slave.
RESET SLAVE	Causes slave to restart replication from beginning of logfile.
server-id	Unique integer to identify the server in a replication set.
slave-skip-errors	Ignore errors that would normally be fatal. Use with care.
SHOW NEW MASTER	Used to assist in changing the master server for a replication. This statement is rarely used and requires additional syntax.
SHOW SLAVE STATUS	Gives information on the slave replication process.
SLAVE START	Starts the slave process, if it hasn't been started.
SLAVE STOP	Stops the slave process.
skip-slave-start	Prevents the replication slave process from starting with the MySQL server.
slave-read-timeout	Seconds before timing out the slave process if no activity is received.

A basic replication configuration

Only a few options are necessary to configure a basic replication set between a master and slave in MySQL. This section examines those configuration settings. I am assuming that you've read the section on planning and preparing for replication and have MySQL running with the same version on the participating hosts.

First, you must add a user to the master server. This user serves to communicate from the slaves to the master for replication. I strongly recommend that you create a separate user for replication and grant that user only the minimum privilege necessary, the `FILE` privilege. Consider this example:

```
GRANT FILE ON *.* TO replicateuser@replicatehost IDENTIFIED BY
'<password>';
```

Figure 18-1 illustrates this statement being executed on the server to be the master in the replication system. Remember, no need to issue a `FLUSH PRIVILEGES` statement when using a GRANT statement.

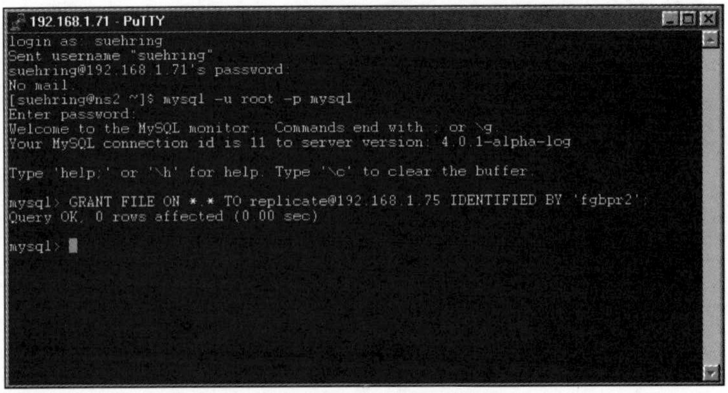

Figure 18-1: Adding the replication user account

On the master inside the MySQL configuration file, usually `my.cnf` or `my.ini`, add the following two lines to the `[mysqld]` section:

```
log-bin
server-id=1
```

The `log-bin` option turns on the binary log that tracks updates, the `server-id` option is a unique value for the replication partner in this set. The `server-id` value that you set must be unique across all partners in the replication set. For example, you cannot have two server IDs of `1` taking part in the same replication.

If you have existing data in a database, you should take a snapshot of that data prior to starting replication. Create a `.tar` or `.zip` file with the database or databases that you want to replicate. From a shell within the database directory, issue the following command:

```
tar -cvpf database.tar <databasename>
```

Transfer the resulting file to the slave server(s); unarchive (unzip) that file within the database directory. Your servers will now start with the same data. (This is an important step, as I show later in this chapter.)

Once you've taken the snapshot, stop the MySQL server on the master and restart it. Congratulations, you now have a master server in a replication set configured for MySQL.

On the slave, the process involves adding the following lines to the MySQL configuration file, again to the `[mysqld]` section:

```
master-host=192.168.1.71
master-user=replicate
master-password=fgbpr2
server-id=2
```

Substitute the host, user, and password values appropriate for your installation.

Stop the restart the MySQL server on the slave. You should now have a simple replication set running between two MySQL servers.

To test the configuration, issue the following command from within the MySQL CLI on the slave:

```
SHOW SLAVE STATUS;
```

You should see output similar to that in Figure 18-2.

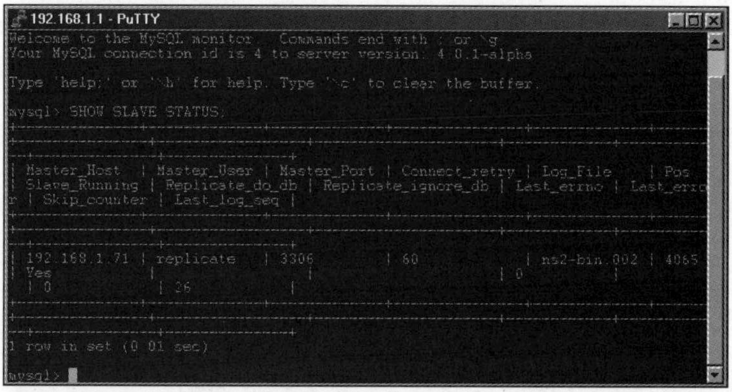

Figure 18-2: Issuing the SHOW SLAVE STATUS command on a slave server should result in output similar to this if the slave is running.

Note The values for many of the columns in Figure 18-2 will be different in your output. The important column is the `Slave_running` column. This column should be `Yes`.

If the `Slave_running` column in your output is `No` or if all values are zero or 0, then the slave didn't start. Examine the error log for MySQL on the slave—usually `<hostname>.err`—for clues. For instance, when I added a third server to the replication set (for another example), I neglected to add a privilege for that user from the new host. I received the error message shown in Figure 18-3. Once I added the user to the master, all was well. Replication on the slave automatically started itself when it retried in 60 seconds.

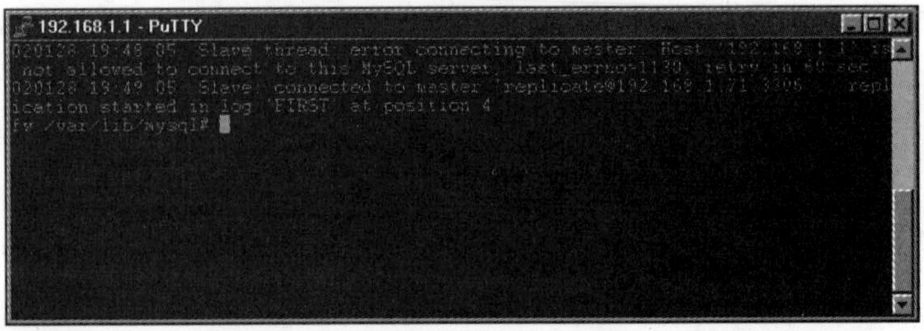

Figure 18-3: An error on the slave server shows I forgot to add the replication user account on the master.

Once replication is configured, MySQL automatically transfers a copy of the databases for replication. If these are large databases, you may want to transfer the databases manually via utility commands such as `ftp` or `scp`, which allows compression of the datafiles for quicker transfer.

When the initial database transfer is complete, any changes made on the master will be automatically and instantly replicated to a connected slave—including inserts, updates, and deletions. For example (in Figure 18-4), I issue a simple `SELECT` statement on a slave server—which puts seven products into the table.

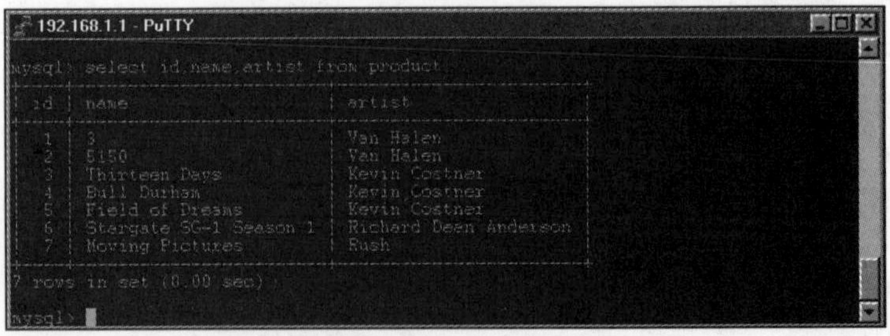

Figure 18-4: A listing of items in the product table on a slave server

In Figure 18-5, I send the following SQL statement to put a new product on the master server:

```
INSERT INTO product values ('','Next Friday','Ice
Cube','19.99','34','2','Follow up to Friday. Another great Ice
Cube movie.','2');
```

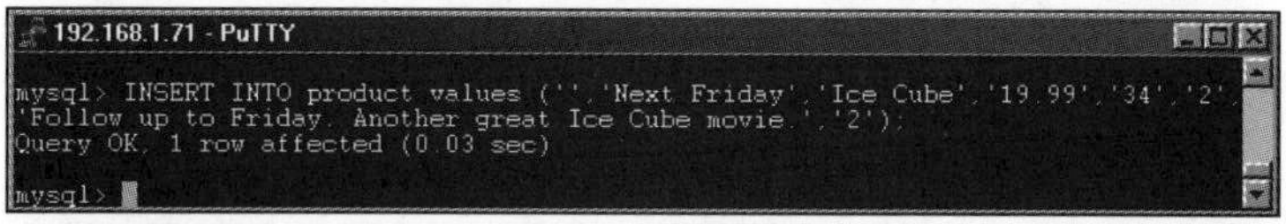

Figure 18-5: The INSERT statement, performed on the master server

Figure 18-6 shows the same query from Figure 18-4 on the slave server. Note that the new insert that was performed on the master is propagated to the slave.

Figure 18-6: The INSERT statement on the slave that propagated automatically from the master as part of the slave's replication update

If a slave becomes disconnected for a normal reason, such as a `SLAVE STOP` command, the slave remembers its position and can catch up with any updates once it restarts. If the slave stops for an abnormal reason such as a system crash, the slave may not be able to correctly re-initialize and find its position to catch up with updates. I've seen either outcome from situations in which the MySQL server was killed abruptly on the slave — upon restart, sometimes the slave process caught up successfully, and sometimes it could not find its place.

Multiple slave replication

Configuring replication for multiple slaves is as simple as repeating the steps for configuring a basic replication. On the master, make sure that the replication user is granted the `FILE` privilege from the new slave host. Add the lines to the configuration file of the new slave host, just as you did for the first slave.

Note Be sure to use a different value for each `server-id`. The value for every host's `server-id` must be unique!

Multiple master replication

To achieve additional peace of mind that comes from redundancy, you can configure multiple masters in a single replication set. In the background, you are really still using one master — but enabling the logging of updates on one or more slaves. Should the master server fail, any of the slave(s) can act as master.

To enable multiple masters in a replication set, edit the MySQL configuration file on one of the slave servers. Add the following lines to the `[mysqld]` section:

```
log-bin
log-slave-updates
```

The previous lines should be in addition to the others for slave replication, including (but not necessarily limiting `yourself` to) these settings:

```
master-host=<host>
master-user=<username>
master-password=<password>
server-id=<id#>
```

Stop and restart the MySQL server on the slave. It should remember its position within the slave replication and also add the files you specified so it can act as a master (including the binary update log and the index log).

Also, add users and privileges for the replication user on the candidate master server. For example, I'm going to grant access for a user named replicate with a password of `fgbpr2` to access from `192.168.1.1`.

```
GRANT FILE ON *.* TO replicate@192.168.1.1 IDENTIFIED BY
'fgbpr2';
```

The current status of replication on the slave `192.168.1.1` is shown in Figure 18-7. Note that it is using master `192.168.1.71`.

Assume that, for whatever reason, I have to change the master server to the candidate master. I simply issue the following statement on the slave:

```
CHANGE MASTER TO MASTER_HOST='192.168.1.136';
```

Alter the host from `192.168.1.136` for your implementation. It is important to note that when you change master servers, you may need to issue privileges so that the slave server has permission to connect to the new master. Also, you may need to make firewall or other connectivity changes to reflect the new replication master.

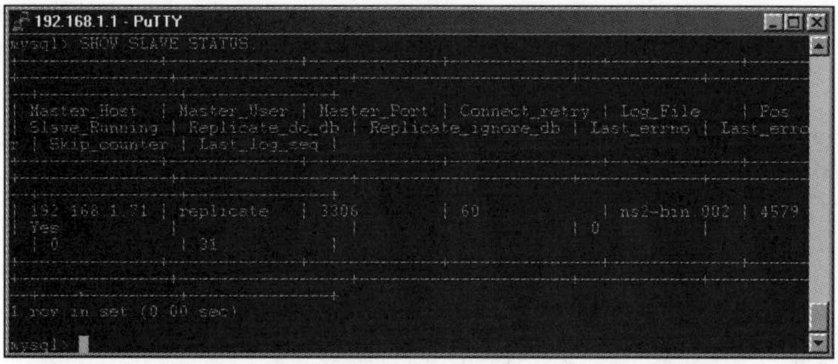

Figure 18-7: The current status of replication on a slave in my replication set

Re-examining the status of the slave with the SHOW SLAVE STATUS statement reveals that the change took effect as expected. The results are shown in Figure 18-8.

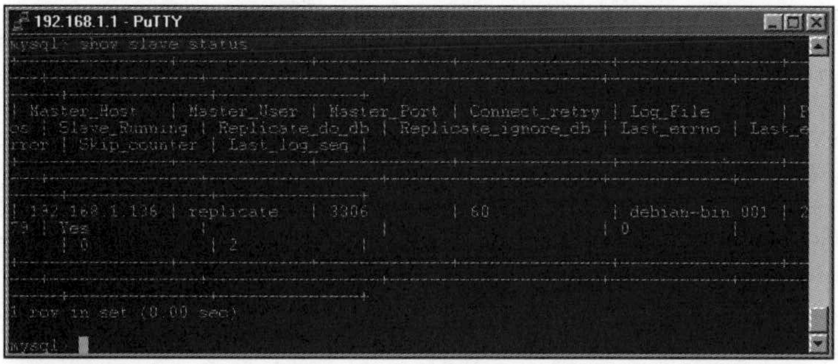

Figure 18-8: The results from the SHOW SLAVE STATUS statement reveal that the CHANGE MASTER TO statement worked as planned.

In Figure 18-8, notice the values of the Log_file and Pos columns. Compare those to the SHOW MASTER STATUS statement run on the new master server, as illustrated in Figure 18-9.

Figure 18-9: The SHOW MASTER STATUS statement on the new master matches the values for the slave server.

Recall the current table contents for the `ecommerce` example database (shown in Figure 18-10 for convenience). These values are taken from the slave server.

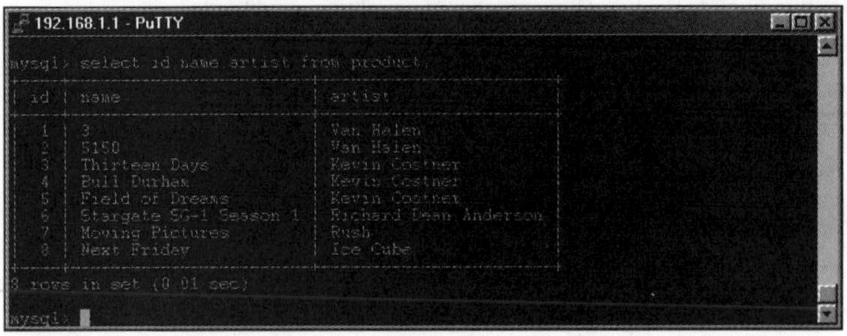

Figure 18-10: The current contents of the products table

I now insert a value on the new master server as shown:

```
INSERT INTO product values ('','Clear and Present
Danger','Harrison Ford','19.99','3','2','Harrison Ford in one
of the Clancy Jack Ryan series.','2');
```

It is important to note that I updated this value on the new master server. If I inserted or performed any changes on the old master server, the slave or slaves would not see them. Keep this in mind for any applications that update or work with data. If you change replication master servers, those applications must be informed of the update so they send their information to the correct master server.

Examining the table contents of the product table on the slave server again reveals the new product in the database, as shown in Figure 8-11. Ignore the missing ninth value in the `id` column. This was expected and correct behavior. I made a slight mistake behind the scenes and had to delete a row. Therefore even the `auto_increment` carried over correctly. Maybe it wasn't a mistake after all, I wanted to show that `auto_increment` columns even worked when changing master servers.

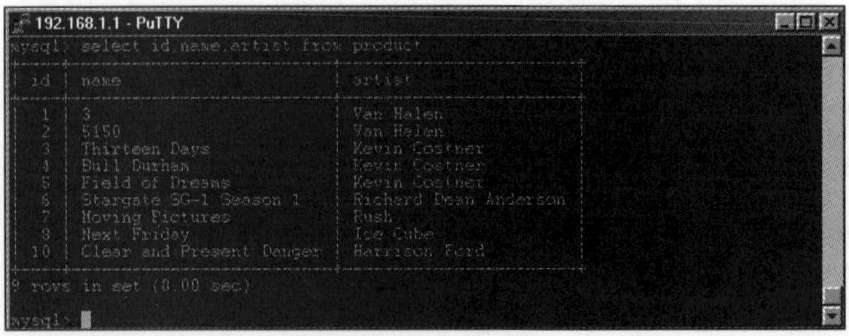

Figure 18-11: The new values in the product table show that replication is working from the new master.

Note You must update your applications and any other processes so that they use the new master server. If you don't do this, updates made to the old master won't be propagated to the replication partners!

Unfortunately, there is no elegant solution for switching to original master server. Changing back so that the original server is again the master in the replication set involves making the original master a slave server and then following the steps in this section to change master servers on the slaves. The applications will also need to be updated to point back to the original master.

Pass-through slave replication

Pass-through or daisy-chain replication is a term to describe replication from a single master to a slave that then acts as a master for one or more slaves. Configuration of this type of replication is simple and similar to configuration of multiple master servers.

On the slave that you want to act as a master add the following lines to the MySQL configuration file under the `[mysqld]` section:

```
log-bin
log-slave-updates
```

Stop and restart the MySQL server. Add users and grants for the replication user or users that will be connecting as slaves.

On each slave server configure the master as you would any other master, pointing it to the appropriate master server. Those steps are all necessary for pass-through replication.

Monitoring Replication

Even though replication is stable and constantly being improved, it is still another level of complication to a database. In addition, it creates yet another item that can fail and cause the administrator to lose time and sleep. Therefore, it is necessary to monitor the replication cluster to ensure that it is behaving as expected.

This section examines some methods for monitoring replication including manual and semi-automated monitoring.

Monitoring replication with Perl

The simplest way to monitor replication is simply by typing `SHOW SLAVE STATUS`— although this approach can quickly become a burden for a replication set of any size. Even the smallest replication set must have its status monitored—fortunately, a relatively efficient method for doing so exists.

Using Perl you can quickly build a custom monitoring solution for your replication implementation. At the most basic level, an administrator has to know when a slave server stops replicating. What methods you use to notify the administrator upon failure are dependent on your needs.

Examine the following code:

```
#!/usr/bin/perl

use DBI;

$thishost = `ifconfig | grep -1 eth | grep inet | cut -d':' -f2
| cut -d' ' -f1`;

$dbh = DBI->connect("DBI:mysql::localhost",undef,'boo');

# Error Checking using an IF test.
if (! $dbh) { print "Connection unsuccessful!\n\n"; }

$query = "SHOW SLAVE STATUS";
$sth = $dbh->prepare($query);
$sth->execute();

while ((@status) = ( $sth->fetchrow_array() ) ) {
  $host = $status[0];
  $file = $status[4];
  $position = $status[5];
  $run = $status[6];
}
if ($run ne "Yes") {
  open MAIL, "|mail -s 'Replication Problem: $thishost'
suehring\@braingia.org";
  print MAIL "REPLICATION PROBLEM on $thishost\n";
  print MAIL "Replicating from: $host\n";
  print MAIL "Replication file: $file.  Position: $position\n";
  print MAIL "Replication running: $run\n";
  close (MAIL);
}
```

The code shows a small but useful monitoring script for watching slave replication. If something goes wrong and the slave reports a running status other than "Yes", an e-mail will be sent to an administrator.

Examining code snippets for some interesting (and not-so-interesting) areas:

```
$thishost = `ifconfig | grep -1 eth | grep inet | cut -d':' -f2
| cut -d' ' -f1`;
```

The previous code runs the system command `ifconfig` and does some minor massaging to get the IP address of this host.

```
$dbh = DBI->connect("DBI:mysql::localhost",undef,'boo');

# Error Checking using an IF test.
if (! $dbh) { print "Connection unsuccessful!\n\n"; }

$query = "SHOW SLAVE STATUS";
$sth = $dbh->prepare($query);
$sth->execute();
```

Nothing new for this section of the script. Standard Perl-DBI.

Cross-Reference For more information on the Perl-DBI and MySQL DBD, see Chapter 15.

The next snippet, however, shows some essential differences:

```
while ((@status) = ( $sth->fetchrow_array() ) ) {
  $host = $status[0];
  $file = $status[4];
  $position = $status[5];
  $run = $status[6];
}
```

The previous section takes the output from the `SHOW SLAVE STATUS` statement and parses it into variables that make sense for the various columns in the statement.

```
if ($run ne "Yes") {
  open MAIL, "|mail -s 'Replication Problem: $thishost'
suehring\@braingia.org";
  print MAIL "REPLICATION PROBLEM on $thishost\n";
  print MAIL "Replicating from: $host\n";
  print MAIL "Replication file: $file.  Position: $position\n";
  print MAIL "Replication running: $run\n";
  close (MAIL);
}
```

The final section of the script evaluates the `Slave_running` column. Under normal operations the `Slave_running` column is Yes if replication is running. However, if the result is anything other than `Yes`, an e-mail will be sent to an administrator. The e-mail contents from the script are shown in Figure 18-12:

This script could be run on a schedule with `cron` so that the system is automatically monitored.

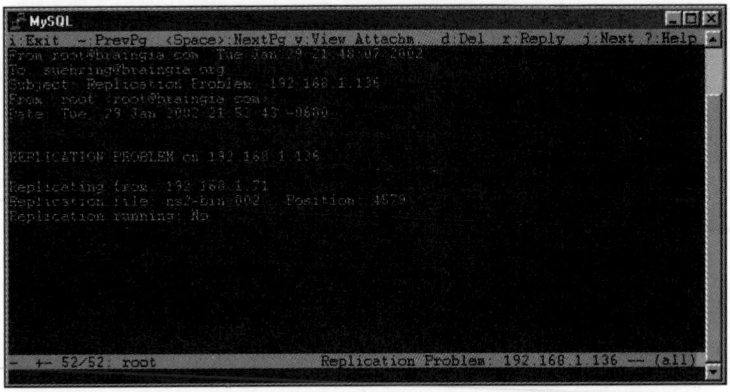

Figure 18-12: The e-mail that results when there is a replication problem.

Monitoring replication through the Web

The script from the previous section can easily be enhanced to monitor a number of servers. In addition, that monitoring data can then be used to create a dynamic Web page with the results. This type of monitoring can be useful for proactively watching a group of servers.

This section shows an example of replication monitoring through the Web. If, however, I use PHP to make a dynamic Web page, I have to convert the script to PHP.

Note For this section, I assume you have PHP with MySQL enabled, as well as a working Web server.

PHP offers an advantage over Perl for this application. Ideally, the monitoring page would include an auto-refresh so that the administrator can monitor the replication in pseudo–real time. It can be done in Perl; however the solution is much more elegant in PHP.

It can be done with a CGI; however, PHP makes it much easier. Using PHP as the development language, I can add an auto-refresh easily; and when the page updates, it will automatically re-run the statements to gather the performance data from the members of the replication set.

The basis for the program will be a central monitoring host that sends the `SHOW SLAVE STATUS` statement to the replication slaves at regular intervals and also sends the `SHOW MASTER STATUS` statement to the replication master. The program then outputs a Web page in table format with some pretty colors.

To enable the program on the monitor host to query the slaves adding a user on the slaves' MySQL server is necessary. The user must have the `process` privilege to issue the `SHOW` statement. Consider this example:

```
grant process on *.* to rmonitor@192.168.1.75 identified by
'maddog31';
```

This statement is issued on all MySQL servers in the replication set. The monitoring host will be `192.168.1.75` and will be monitored by user `rmonitor`.

The code for the monitoring program is as follows:

```
<?php

$slave = array(0=> "192.168.1.136", 1=> "192.168.1.1");
$master = array(0=> "192.168.1.71");
```

The previous code snippet builds arrays for master and slave servers. In my replication setup, there are only two slave servers and one master server. For an enhancement of this script, you could store the replication servers within a database and query for those servers.

```
$username = "rmonitor";
$password = "maddog31";

print "<table border=1><P>\n";
print "<tr><td>Last
Update</td><td>Type</td><td>IP</td><td>Replication
File</td><td>Position</td><td>Run?</td><P>\n";
```

The previous snippet sets the values for connecting to the MySQL servers in the replication set as well as some basic HTML.

```
foreach ($slave as $server) {
  print "<tr><P>\n";
  slavestatus($server,$username,$password);
  print "</tr><P>\n";
}
foreach ($master as $server) {
  print "<tr><P>\n";
  masterstatus($server,$username,$password);
  print "</tr><P>\n";
}
```

The previous snippet calls the functions for querying the various replication servers. Again, by adding a feature to gather this data from a MySQL database, you could use one function and call the server based on what type it is as stored in your database.

```
function slavestatus ($host,$username,$password) {
  $dbconn = mysql_connect($host,$username,$password) or die
("Cannot connect to database server");
  $result = mysql_query("SHOW SLAVE STATUS");
  $timeresult = mysql_query("SELECT NOW()");
  $time = mysql_result($timeresult, 0, 0);
```

The next step is to make a connection to the database and issue statements, including one that queries for the current time from the replication server.

```
  while ($status = mysql_fetch_array($result)) {
    $mysqlserver = $host;
    $file = $status[4];
    $position = $status[5];
    $run = $status[6];
    $errnum = $status[9];
    $errmsg = $status[10];
  }
```

Taking the results from `SHOW SLAVE SERVER`, I parse them into variables that make some sense for the application context. The code looks like this:

```
  if ($run != "Yes") {
    $color = "<td bgcolor=\"#CC3333\">";
    $additional = "<td>$errnum - $errmsg</td>";
  } else {
    $color = "<td bgcolor=\"#33FF33\">";
  }
print "<td>$time</td>$color Slave</td>$color
$host</td><td>$file</td><td>$position</td><td>$run</td>$additio
nal<P>\n";
}
```

The contents of the `$run` variable are examined. If it is anything other than `Yes` is found, the background color of the table cell changes to red (otherwise it's green).

Pointing a Web browser to the page results in the listing illustrated in Figure 18-13.

The replication status from Figure 18-13 is taken directly from output of the appropriate `SHOW` statement. Notice that there is no `Yes` or `No` applicable for the master server. This is because the master server doesn't know anything about replication or the slaves that replicate from it. It simply goes about its business of recording updates and changes to the binary replication log.

Examination of the output in Figure 18-13 shows that I have a problem with a slave in the replication set. It just so happens that the error leads directly into the next section of the chapter. Before you do so, however, you may have to make another improvement on the monitoring PHP script — adding a refresh to the page so that it automatically runs every *N* seconds or minutes.

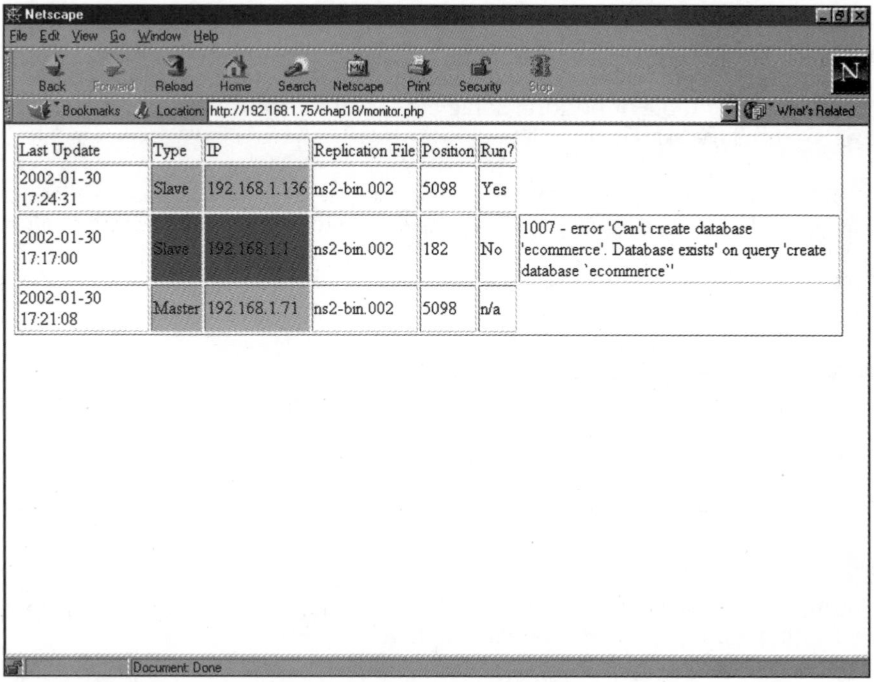

Figure 18-13: The monitoring application built into PHP

Kick-starting Replication

Replication has become quite a robust addition to MySQL. As part of my work with MySQL, I administer a large MySQL replication cluster. Unfortunately, the cluster is built on an older version of MySQL — and it's too vital to update in place. Accordingly (though the actual replication is acceptably stable), I've had to get by without the benefit of some of the better — and more recent — replication commands shown in this chapter.

This section examines what can be done if replication goes wrong — including commands and statements that can kick-start replication.

When good replication goes bad

Monitoring replication regularly, you may encounter errors. For example, an error occurred within in my replication set (as shown in Figure 18-13). I attempted to restart the replication by using the `RESET SLAVE` command—but because the `ecommerce` database already exists, the replication failed.

Behind the scenes, the `RESET SLAVE` statement tells the slave server to forget its position in the replication logs and start over. For updates and changes, this can cause replication to fail on that slave server. The slave server attempts to re-create the database or table or perform some other statement. However; a conflict exists—thus the statement will fail.

In an instance such as this, you must restart replication across your replication set. The procedure to use follows some of the same steps you took to start replication:

1. Stop the MySQL server on the master.
2. Take a snapshot of the data.
3. Start the MySQL server on the master.
4. Copy the snapshot of the data to the slaves.
5. Stop the slave server.
6. Move the snapshot data into the data directory on the slave.
7. Start the slave server.

The master and slave(s) now have the same starting point for data and can begin replicating from that known good set of data.

Kick-starting replication revealed

As a replication best practice, I make one snapshot of data on the master and copy that to a separate location on the master server. Then, when I have to restart replication on one or more slave servers, I can simply take that snapshot from the beginning of the replication and copy it to the slave server.

Restarting replication on the slave server with that known data—and issuing a `RESET SLAVE` statement—causes the slave to play back the entire replication log from the beginning, thus catching up with the master server.

1. Copy the snapshot of the data to the slaves.
2. Stop the slave server.

3. Move the snapshot data into the data directory on the slave.

4. Start the slave server.

Since you don't have to get a snapshot from the master, you don't have to stop MySQL on the master. This is a key feature for systems where uptime of the master server is crucial.

Examining this type of method a little closer might be helpful. I set up an example that starts from the beginning — creating a snapshot on the master. This step has to be performed just this one time; afterward, it won't be necessary unless the master server must be stopped for some unforeseen reason.

I am replicating only the `ecommerce` database. To do that, I add the following line to the `[mysqld]` section of the MySQL configuration file on the master:

```
replicate-do-db = ecommerce
```

I stop the MySQL server on the master and make a backup of the `ecommerce` database.

```
cd /var/lib/mysql
mkdir snapshot
tar -zcvpf ecommerce.tgz ecommerce
mv ecommerce.tgz snapshot
```

On the master server, I now have a snapshot of the `ecommerce` database as it exists at this point in time. That snapshot is safely stored in the `snapshot` directory on the master server. I can restart the master server's MySQL process.

I now copy that snapshot to the slave servers. Personally, I prefer to use `scp` for this task; you may want to use `ftp` or some other method for transferring the file to the slave server.

On each slave server, I stop the MySQL server and then change to the data directory. Next I unarchive the snapshot file that I transferred from the master, and use that file to overwrite the existing `ecommerce` database folder and files — after which I can start the MySQL server on the slave servers. The replication set is up and running, as evidenced by Figure 18-14.

If one of the slave servers goes down for any reason, I can simply copy the snapshot that I already created from the master, stop the slave server, overwrite the database, and start the slave server again.

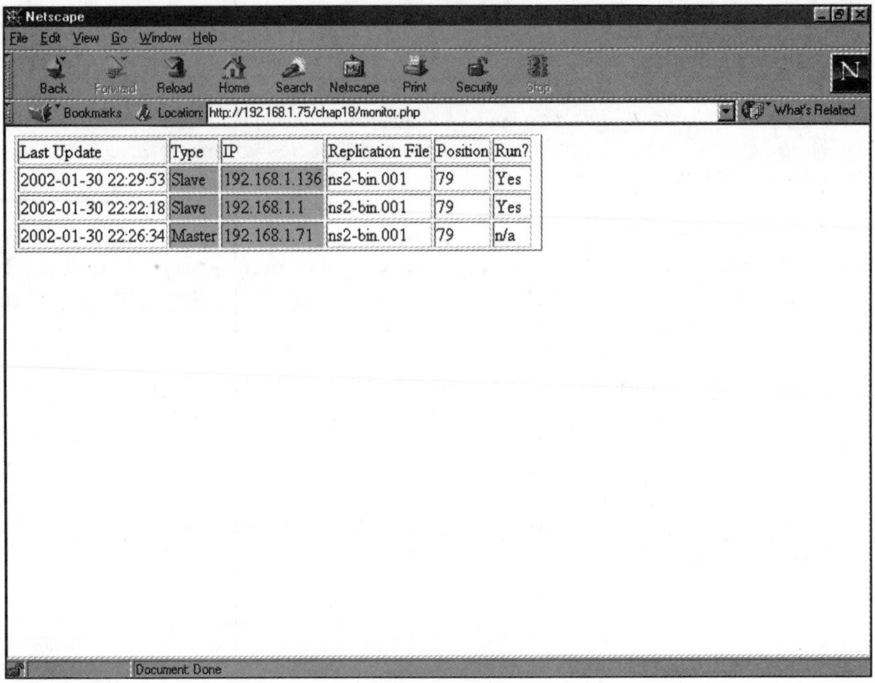

Figure 18-14: The replication set after kick-starting

Summary

Replication does not require a constant connection between the master and slave servers in a replication set. The administrator can fine-tune the databases or tables that he or she wants to replicate. This is done during the original configuration process for replication.

✦ All servers in a replication set should be running the same version of MySQL because the format and options can change from version to version.

✦ The `server-id` value set in the configuration file must be different for all servers in the replication set, regardless of their status as master or slave server.

✦ The most common replication type is one master and multiple slaves. MySQL currently does not support multiple master replication, but there is some minor trickery that you can do to add redundancy.

✦ A snapshot should be taken of the data to be replicated prior to starting the replication set. That snapshot must be distributed to all replication partners prior to starting replication.

- Regardless of the type chosen for the replication set, monitoring replication is important. The size of the binary log can grow to no more than 2 gigabytes on some file systems; other issues can also arise that cause replication to fail.
- Perl with the DBI/DBD can be used to produce a simple replication monitoring program for replication.
- Using PHP, a more sophisticated monitoring program can be built that is accessible from the Web.
- If an error or other unexpected event occurs, one or more servers in the replication set may break out of the set. If this happens, you will have to kick-start the replication by issuing commands or manually restarting replication.
- One way to kick-start replication is to keep the original snapshot on the master and distribute that to the slave server. The slave server then replays the replication log to catch up.

✦ ✦ ✦

CHAPTER 19

Integration of Internet Services

In This Chapter

- Authenticating users with PAM and NSS via MySQL
- Managing DNS with MySQL
- Integrating RADIUS with MySQL
- Using MySQL to integrate and manage e-mail
- Building a full-scale virtual-services interface

In many ways, MySQL makes a great database and backend for many Internet and e-commerce services. MySQL offers a no-cost/low-cost licensing system, MySQL is versatile, and MySQL is both stable and fast. When combined with a low-cost/no-cost operating system such as Linux, MySQL can be the perfect backend for Internet services such as e-mail, customer tracking, virtual services, DNS, and authentication.

> **Note** Some privately funded studies claim that the Total Cost of Ownership (TCO) is at least as high with Linux as it is with Microsoft Windows—although (given the fierce competition among vendors of operating systems), such studies may be less than objective. On the other hand, if you implement Linux on an Internet server, the low initial cost of acquiring the OS (as basic freeware) may not be the only outlay required. Other potential costs may crop up in such areas as technical support, overall network security, and compatibility with legacy systems—though these are not unique to Linux. In my experience, running Linux often costs less—but evaluate the needs of your own system carefully before you commit to a major change of operating systems.

Linux can be downloaded for free or purchased for a relatively low cost with no additional licensing costs for 5 or 500,000 users. Powerful server software such as Sendmail and Apache do not require additional licenses and virtually no maintenance once installed. Linux is secure. When an update is released for almost any service running on Linux, the server does not need to be rebooted to apply the update. Finally, Linux has low overhead and can be installed on machines with lower hardware requirements.

For these and other reasons, this chapter concentrates on integrating MySQL with Linux services for the Internet. These services include PAM (Pluggable Authentication Modules,) virtual services, e-mail, and more. I also show an example of a Web-based management application for virtual services.

PAM and NSS User Authentication in MySQL

Pluggable Authentication Module (PAM) technology is the basis for the integration of MySQL with many services in Linux. Using PAM, the administrator can configure PAM-aware applications to use complex (or simple) methods for authenticating users and allowing access to resources.

As the name suggests, PAM uses modules for authentication. There are different modules used for different types of authentication. For a given program, the administrator can configure the use of one or more modules to use for authentication. Such modules can be the `passwd/shadow` files or other methods including a module that rejects all authentication requests.

Of special relevance to a book on MySQL is a module that enables PAM-aware applications to use a MySQL database for authentication. This section looks at the PAM-MySQL module including installation and use as it relates to MySQL.

Note This section is not meant to be a comprehensive guide to PAM. Later sections of this chapter examine integration of PAM-MySQL with other applications.

Figure 19-1 shows an example of a PAM configuration file for the `ftp` service. The file is located in `/etc/pam.d`.

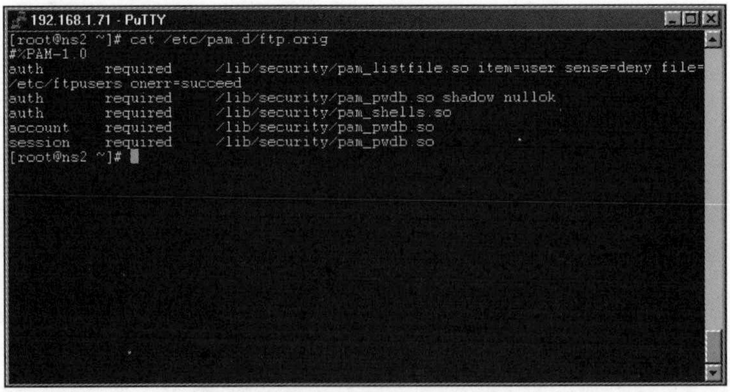
192.168.1.71 - PuTTY
[root@ns2 ~]# cat /etc/pam.d/ftp.orig
#%PAM-1.0
auth required /lib/security/pam_listfile.so item=user sense=deny file=
/etc/ftpusers onerr=succeed
auth required /lib/security/pam_pwdb.so shadow nullok
auth required /lib/security/pam_shells.so
account required /lib/security/pam_pwdb.so
session required /lib/security/pam_pwdb.so
[root@ns2 ~]#

Figure 19-1: An example PAM configuration file

NSS (Name Service Switch) refers to the organization of services queried for information on an account. The NSS configuration is stored in a file called `nsswitch.conf` and is usually located in `/etc`. A sample `/etc/nsswitch.conf` file is shown in Figure 19-2. Using `nsswitch.conf`, the administrator can configure the sequence of locations that the system checks when it tries to determine identifying data such as a user's home directory or group.

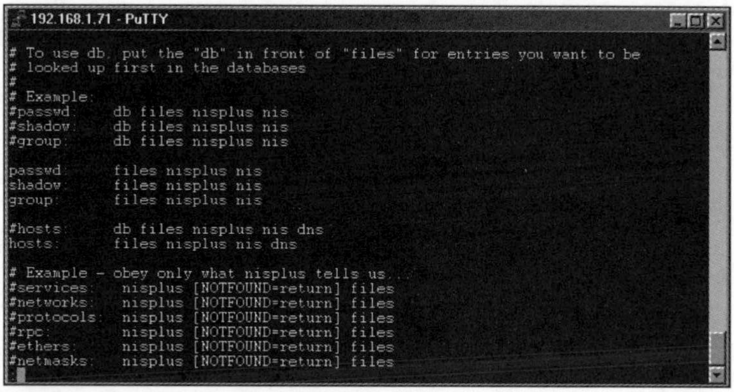

Figure 19-2: The /etc/nsswitch.conf file

As with PAM, a version of NSS exists that is specifically for MySQL. I'll examine installation and use of NSS within this chapter.

Installing PAM-MySQL

You may already have PAM installed on your computer or server. You can determine whether PAM is installed by looking at the contents of the `/etc/pam.d/` directory or `/etc/pam.conf`.

Because PAM comes installed on many distributions, I won't include specific coverage of PAM installation. Before continuing with the demonstrations in this section, however, make sure you have PAM installed and configured on your system.

Downloading and configuring PAM

If you don't have either `/etc/pam.d/` directory or `/etc/pam.conf`, on your system, then PAM is not currently installed. You can download the PAM-MySQL module from `https://sourceforge.net/projects/pam-mysql/`. Once the download is complete, unpack the archive and simply type make at the command line within the `pam-mysql` directory. Copy the resulting `pam_mysql.so` file to the `/lib/security` directory, using the following command:

```
cp pam_mysql.so /lib/security
```

If you encounter problems compiling, it might be because you don't have the development headers for MySQL installed. The computer on which you're installing PAM-MySQL need not be the same as the MySQL server — but PAM-MySQL requires that the development headers (and thus the client) for MySQL be installed on the host.

PAM-MySQL syntax

Recall the syntax of the example PAM configuration file shown in Figure 19-1. Configuring an application to use PAM-MySQL requires the editing of the file. There are options that can be set to configure how PAM-MySQL connects to and queries for valid users when processing a request. The options and their defaults are shown in Table 19-1.

Table 19-1
PAM-MySQL Configuration Options

Option	*Default*	*Description*
`Host`	`localhost`	The MySQL server to connect to for authentication.
`User`	`nobody`	The user to use for connecting to the MySQL server.
`Passwd`	none	The password to use for connecting to the MySQL server.
`Db`	`mysql`	The name of the database containing the user information.
`Table`	`user`	The name of the table containing the user information.
`Usercolumn`	`user`	The name of the column containing the username.
`Passwdcolumn`	`password`	The name of the column containing passwords.
`Crypt`	0	How passwords are encrypted. 0=none, 1=crypt, 2=mysql.
`where=`	none	Additional `WHERE` clause to add to the select.

For example, a configuration file for PAM-MySQL to use with FTP might look like the one shown in Figure 19-3.

In the example shown in Figure 19-3, the user account that connects to the MySQL server on host `192-168.1.75` is `root` and passwords sent to MySQL were encrypted with MySQL's internal `PASSWORD` function. The rest of the settings were left at their defaults; thus the MySQL `grants` database will be used for authentication. I'll be building a customized user database later in this chapter for use with PAM-MySQL and NSS-MySQL.

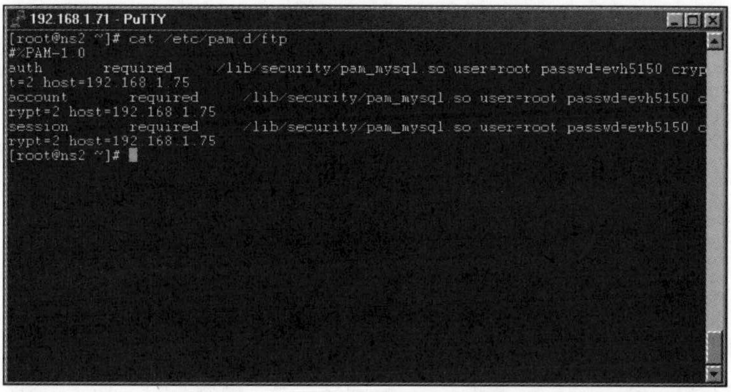

Figure 19-3: An example configuration file for ftp on a system with PAM-MySQL

Caution I recommend that you create a user with only the privileges needed to connect using PAM. *Never use the* `root` *user as shown in the example!*

Testing PAM-MySQL

Prior to attempting to test PAM-MySQL you should test the service to make sure that it is currently working. It doesn't pay to attempt to get PAM-MySQL working with a service if the service isn't working to begin with. In this section I'll be testing PAM-MySQL with FTP using Wu-ftpd.

I've shown examples of the original PAM configuration file for ftp, as well as an example of a PAM-MySQL configuration file for ftp. Using the configuration file shown in Figure 19-3, I attempt to connect via ftp to the server. The attempt fails. Examining the `messages` logfile on the server, I notice that a number of errors refer to a faulty module, as shown in Figure 19-4.

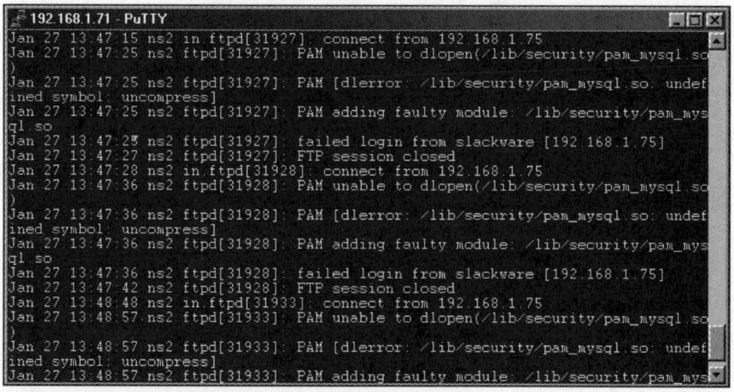

Figure 19-4: Errors from a test of PAM-MySQL

Apparently the module is missing something; it can't figure out a call to `uncompress` (which is part of the `zlib` library). I already have `zlib` installed. An examination of the `Makefile` for PAM-MySQL reveals that there is no reference to `zlib`. Therefore I need to add a reference (`-lz`) to the `Makefile` and recompile. Figure 19-5 illustrates the section of the `Makefile` where I placed `-lz`.

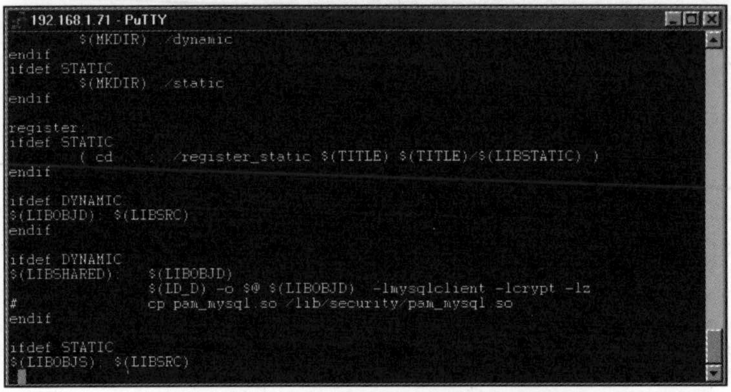

Figure 19-5: Adding -lz to the Makefile for PAM-MySQL

I then recompile the software by typing `make`, and copy the new `pam_mysql.so` file to `/lib/`security. Another attempt to log in still fails. Examination of the logfile now reveals that the failed connection has a MySQL error message like the one in Figure 19-6.

Figure 19-6: Another examination of the logfile to look for errors relating to the failed ftp login

The error shown in Figure 19-6 is due to the fact that the user I defined in the PAM configuration file for ftp simply does not have access from this host. To correct this problem, I had to grant access and ensure the password was correct for the user within the MySQL server's grants database.

Finally, with all the problems corrected I'm able to test the connection again via ftp. The test is successful.

However, even though the test is successful, it could still fail for no apparent reason. If more than one user with the same password is defined in the database, the authentication fails.

Tip Checking for duplicate passwords can be a good place to start troubleshooting if your authentication is failing for what appears to be no reason.

Installing NSS-MySQL

With PAM-MySQL installed, you can perform authentication. However, some needed information about users (such as user ID or home directory) is not available. Enter NSS-MySQL. NSS-MySQL provides an interface into NSS for MySQL.

Installation of NSS-MySQL begins with obtaining the software. The current location for the NSS-MySQL project is `http://savannah.gnu.org/projects/nss-mysql/`. Download and unpack the NSS-MySQL archive. The installation process is standard:

```
./configure
make
make install
```

Configuration of NSS-MySQL

NSS-MySQL's configuration file is called `nss-mysql.conf` and is located in `/etc`. The options contained in the NSS-MySQL configuration file are highly specialized and dependent on your installation and desired functionality. When you've configured `nss-mysql.conf` you need to add the ability for NSS to utilize NSS-MySQL. This is accomplished by adding the word `mysql` to the appropriate lines of `/etc/nsswitch.conf`. Figure 19-7 shows an example of an `nsswitch.conf` file where NSS-MySQL has been installed.

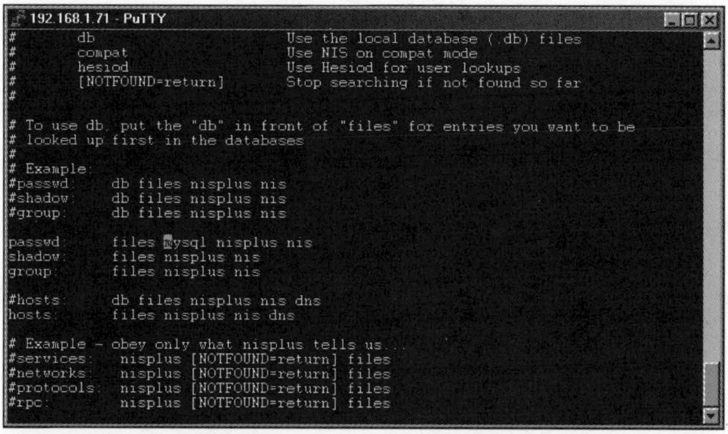

Figure 19-7: Enabling NSS-MySQL in the /etc/nsswitch.conf configuration file for NSS

DNS Management with MySQL

DNS, which I've seen defined as Domain Name System and Domain Name Service, is the term for the service or protocol that translates names such as `www.braingia.org` into IP addresses and vice versa. Though MySQL isn't directly tied into any DNS software (yet), MySQL can be used as a backend for a DNS management interface. This section examines how you can use MySQL to assist with DNS management. I'll be utilizing BIND as the DNS server software — though the application built here should be relatively easy to port to other software.

Creating a DNS management interface

The BIND DNS server software uses configuration files for reading about domain configuration and name service. There is no direct interface between BIND and MySQL. Therefore, to enable MySQL and BIND to work together, data must be converted from the MySQL database to the configuration files that BIND reads.

A DNS configuration file for a generic domain can look like this:

```
$ttl 38400
@        IN      SOA     ns1.braingia.com. root.braingia.com. (
                         2001112702
                         10810
                         3600
                         432000
                         38400  )

         IN      NS      ns1.braingia.com.
         IN      NS      ns2.braingia.com.
         MX      0       mail.braingia.com.

$ORIGIN braingia.com.
ns1      IN      A       192.168.1.75
mail     IN      CNAME   mail.braingia.com.
www      IN      CNAME   mail.braingia.com.
ns2      IN      A       192.168.1.71
fw0      IN      A       192.168.1.1
```

Taking this domain as an example, I can quickly create a database schema to match it. I am going to do without some specialty things and assume that all `$ORIGIN` values will be within the domain. In my experience, there are few instances where the origin will be different. If your implementation calls for the `$ORIGIN` to be changed frequently, you should alter the database schema accordingly. I'll also assume that `TTL` values will be the same across all domains. Again, if these are values you need to change frequently for your domains, you can add to the schema as needed.

The database schema is as follows:

```
CREATE TABLE domain (
        id int NOT NULL PRIMARY KEY AUTO_INCREMENT,
        domain_name varchar(255)
);

CREATE TABLE record (
        id int NOT NULL PRIMARY KEY AUTO_INCREMENT,
        domain_id int,
        name varchar(255),
        type varchar(10),
        address varchar(255)
);

CREATE TABLE nameservers (
        id int NOT NULL PRIMARY KEY AUTO_INCREMENT,
        domain_id int,
        address varchar(255)
);

CREATE TABLE mx (
        id int NOT NULL PRIMARY KEY AUTO_INCREMENT,
        domain_id int,
        cost int,
        address varchar(255)
);

CREATE TABLE serial (
        domain_id int,
        serial varchar(50)
);
```

With that schema, I can convert the basic domain info to DDL—like this:

```
insert into domain values ('','braingia.com');
insert into record values ('','1','ns1','A','192.168.1.75');
insert into record values
('','1','mail','CNAME','ns1.braingia.com');
insert into record values
('','1','www','CNAME','ns1.braingia.com');
insert into record values ('','1','ns2','A','192.168.1.71');
insert into record values ('','1','fw0','A','192.168.1.1');
insert into nameservers values ('','1','ns1.braingia.com');
insert into nameservers values ('','1','ns2.braingia.com');
insert into serial values ('1','2001112702');
insert into mx values ('','1',0,'mail.braingia.com.');
```

Selecting the records results in some familiar-looking data, as illustrated in Figure 19-8.

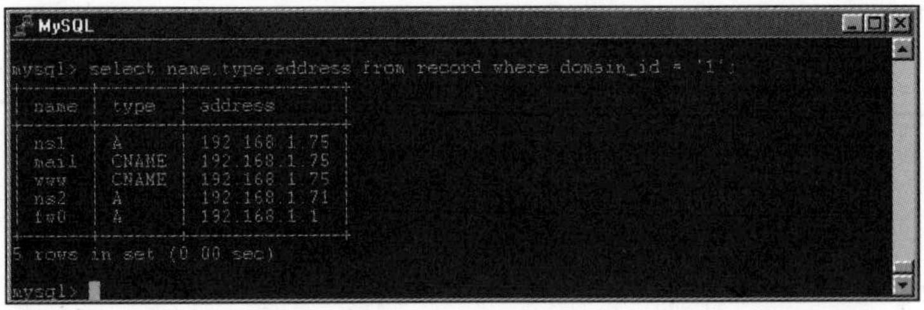

Figure 19-8: The record data for the domain, as entered into the database

Based on the work already done, a program could be written in the language of your choice to convert the data into the flat file record that BIND prefers. However, I'd rather build a management system for the Web. Therefore, I'll be using PHP.

The DNS Web interface is meant to be used by an administrator but could be modified to be used by a customer to modify their domain or domains as well. Providers such as Fibernet, `http://www.fibernetcc.com/` allow their customers to edit DNS entries for accounts using a similar interface. (The front page of the interface is shown in Figure 19-9.)

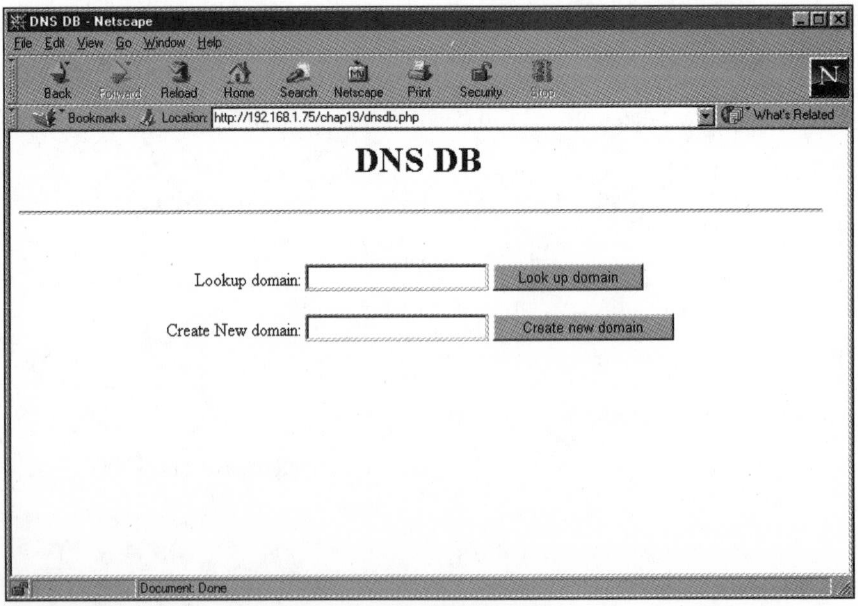

Figure 19-9: The front page for the DNS Web interface

The two input boxes shown in Figure 19-9 could easily be combined into one with a little coding in the backend program. Entering an existing domain yields a page where the address records can be edited, as illustrated in Figure 19-10. The data for the page is built from data within the database.

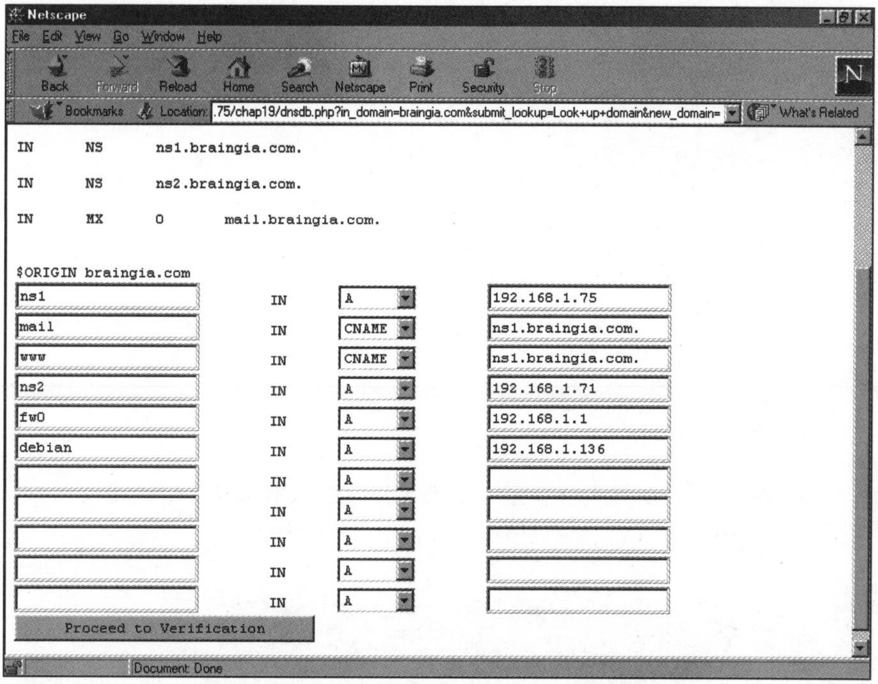

Figure 19-10: Records can be edited easily within an existing domain.

Adding a new server is as simple as entering the values in a blank space and clicking Proceed to Verification. Figure 19-11 shows a new server (which I unimaginatively call `newserver`) being added.

The output shows what the zone file will look like in BIND format. Clicking the "Implement Change" button adds the new record to the database. Looking at the data through the MySQL CLI reveals that the new record was added, as shown in Figure 19-12.

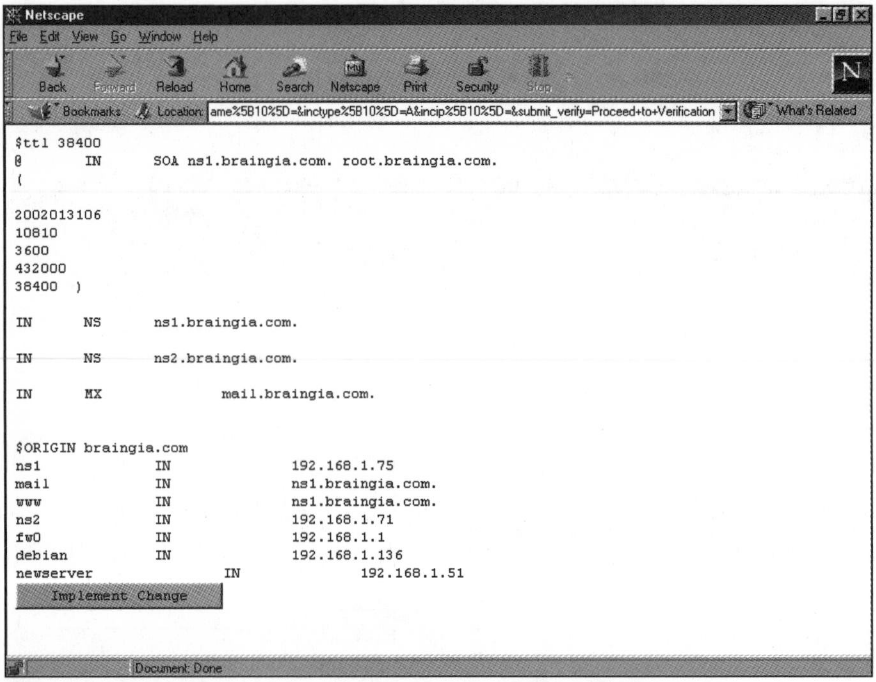

Figure 19-11: Adding a new server with the DNS Web interface

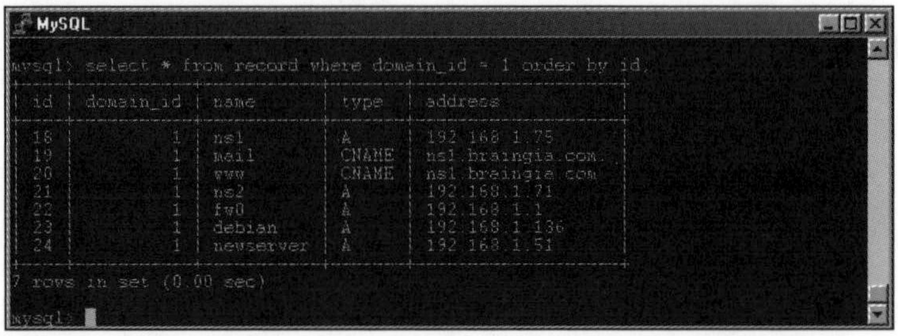

Figure 19-12: The new data, as shown through the MySQL CLI

Behind the scenes, the DNS interface program must convert the zone record to the BIND file format.

Cross-Reference

The MySQL-related functions used for building the Web interface for DNS are discussed in the chapter on PHP.

MySQL and RADIUS Integration

RADIUS (Remote Authentication Dial-In User Service) is the protocol that enables a server to allow access to resources. In general, a user request includes a username and password. If these match the corresponding values on the server, then the user is granted access. There is also RADIUS accounting data that can be sent for the session as well. This includes a time for the start of the session along with other pertinent data and can include the number of bytes sent in the transfer at the end of the session.

Many vendors have versions of RADIUS. One that I would like to highlight is Radiator RADIUS. Though not free software, Radiator includes features necessary for large-scale implementations, good documentations, stability, and simple configuration file syntax. Radiator also features good integration with MySQL, which is why I'm highlighting in this book. More information on Radiator can be obtained at `http://www.open.com/au/radiator/`.

A closer look at Radiator

Radiator is written in Perl. Though I was initially skeptical of the scalability of the software, I now have no such reservations. I've used Radiator for large-scale authentication implementations of over a half-million users, and the software has had no problem handling authentication requests. Since Radiator is robust, I suffered none of the growing pains that other software might when handling thousands of requests per second. These growing pains could include memory or CPU utilization problems or simply refusing connections. Even when a misconfigured access server sends thousands of invalid requests to the Radiator software, it keeps right on handling other requests.

Since Radiator is written in Perl, it uses the Perl DBI to access MySQL. Although Radiator installation is well outside the scope of this book, I'd like to examine a couple of examples of Radiator configuration file syntax to show the ease with which MySQL can be integrated into Radiator.

For example, the Client list can be stored in a MySQL table. The database is easily called with the `DBSource` function.

```
<ClientListSQL>
        DBSource        dbi:mysql:radius
        DBUsername      username
        DBAuth          password
        GetClientQuery select NASIDENTIFIER,SECRET from
CLIENTLIST
</ClientListSQL>
```

Other portions of the Radiator configuration file are simple to configure as well. The `DBSource` is used throughout the configuration file as a means by which the administrator can specify the database and driver to use.

Tip Auxiliary `SELECT` statements can be based on the criteria in the User-Request packet and added later.

Radiator also handles accounting requests with the same ease as authentication. The server for accounting can be different from the authentication MySQL server. Column definitions can be customized within the configuration file so that you can track only the items that you need.

E-Mail Integration and Management with MySQL

MySQL can be used as a backend to store e-mail address information. As with DNS, data stored in a MySQL database must be converted to native format for the mail application to work with. With the use of PAM-MySQL, MySQL can be integrated into POP3 for authentication. This section looks at integration of MySQL with Sendmail, the popular e-mail software.

Building a virtual users table for Sendmail

The virtual-users table in Sendmail is where the mappings are stored for virtual domains on a server. This is where an administrator tells the mail-server software (in this case, Sendmail) where to send mail for @<*domain*>.com and so on. This section tackles the building of a virtual users table from data contained in a MySQL database. A sample virtual users table might look like this:

```
suehring@onlyplanet.com     suehring@braingia.org
no_one@onlyplanet.com       error:nouser User Not Found
@onlyplanet.com             all@braingia.org
steve@linuxgamehq.com       suehring@braingia.org
bob@nightmaresquad.com      bob_s↓ngermen.com
ernie@nightmaresquad.com    ernie_t↓ngermen.com
mike@nightmaresquad.com     mike_f↓ngermen.com
@nightmaresquad.com         %1@braingia.com
```

Any mail received for `suehring@onlyplanet.com` is sent to `suehring@braingia.org`. Any other mail received for the `onlyplanet.com` domain, regardless of address, goes to `all@braingia.org`. The user `no_one@onlyplanet.com` gets returned with an error. For the `nightmaresquad.com` domain, three users are defined that have different addresses. The final entry sends any mail destined for the nightmaresquad.com to the same user@braingia.com. For example, if mail comes in to user001@nightmaresquad.com, it will be automatically sent to user001@braingia.com and so on.

The virtual users table is stored in a nontext format in the sendmail directory; my server, for example, stores that file as hashed data. Therefore, whenever I make a change to the virtual users table, I need to update (actually rebuild) that hash by using the makemap command. The file on my server is called virtusertable. Therefore the command that I must run after a change to the file is

```
makemap hash virtusertable < virtusertable
```

This command reads the file virtusertable into the makemap command. The result is a hashed file called virtusertable.db.

A virtual e-mail database

A simple database layout for the virtual users database might look like this:

```
CREATE TABLE domain (
  id int NOT NULL PRIMARY KEY AUTO_INCREMENT,
  name varchar(255) NOT NULL UNIQUE
);

CREATE TABLE mapping (
  id int NOT NULL PRIMARY KEY AUTO_INCREMENT,
  domain_id int,
  username varchar(255),
  target varchar(255)
);
```

The database layout could be enhanced with a column that indicates whether the mapping is active. Additionally, a column or table tying the domain into a customer ID might be helpful.

Recall a sample entry from the virtusertable file for Sendmail:

```
bob@nightmaresquad.com     bob_s↓ngermen.com
```

The virtual e-mail address recipient is bob@nightmaresquad.com and the target for any e-mail sent to bob@nightmaresquad.com is bob_s↓ngermen.com. With that in mind, the database layout for virtual e-mail operates in much the same way. However, it doesn't make much sense to store the recipient domain over and over; it's a safe bet that there will be more than one virtual user recipient. Therefore an ID is assigned and the domain is stored only once in the domain table. The username in the mapping is the username for the recipient. The entire target address is then stored in the target column of the mapping table.

Importing existing virtual e-mail entries

As with the interface built for DNS, I will be using PHP as the backend language of choice to build the virtual uses interface to MySQL. Because I only have a few virtual e-mail entries currently, I don't need to perform a mass-import of the data. However, I would probably use Perl to build an import program should the need arise. A simple program for importing small virtual user tables might look like this:

```
#!/usr/bin/perl

use DBI;

# Connect to the database
$dbh = DBI-
>connect("DBI:mysql:mman:",'USERHERE','PASSWORDHERE!') or die
"No database\n";

open (FILE, "virtusertable");
while (<FILE>) {
chomp;
@mapping = split(/\t+/, $_);
@fullrecipient = split(/\@/, $mapping[0]);
$domain = $fullrecipient[1];
$query1 = "INSERT IGNORE INTO domain values ('','$domain')";
$sth1 = $dbh->prepare($query1);
$sth1->execute;
}
close (FILE);


open (FILE, "virtusertable");
while (<FILE>) {
chomp;
@mapping = split(/\t+/, $_);
@fullrecipient = split(/\@/, $mapping[0]);
$username = $fullrecipient[0];
$domain = $fullrecipient[1];
$target = $mapping[1];
if ($username eq "") {
  $username = "CATCHALL";
}
$query1 = "SELECT id FROM domain WHERE name = '$domain'";
print "$query1\n";
$sth1 = $dbh->prepare($query1);
$sth1->execute or die "Can't run $query1";
$domainid = $sth1->fetchrow_array();

$insmap = "insert into mapping values
('','$domainid','$username','$target')";
$sth = $dbh->prepare($insmap);
$sth->execute or die "Can't insert\n";
```

```
print "Inserted $username to $target for domain $domainid\n";
}
close(FILE);
```

The program passes through the file twice. Therefore if you have a large `virtusertable` file, it may be in your best interest to rewrite the program to be a little less resource-intensive. Executing the program with the `virtusertable` shown in this section yields the results shown in Figure 19-13.

Figure 19-13: Importing the existing virtual users table

Wherever a catchall entry exists in the virtual users table, I use the phrase `CATCHALL`. When the data from MySQL is converted back to `virtusertable` format, all `CATCHALL` entries must be converted back to blank entries.

The data as it now resides in the database is illustrated in Figure 19-14.

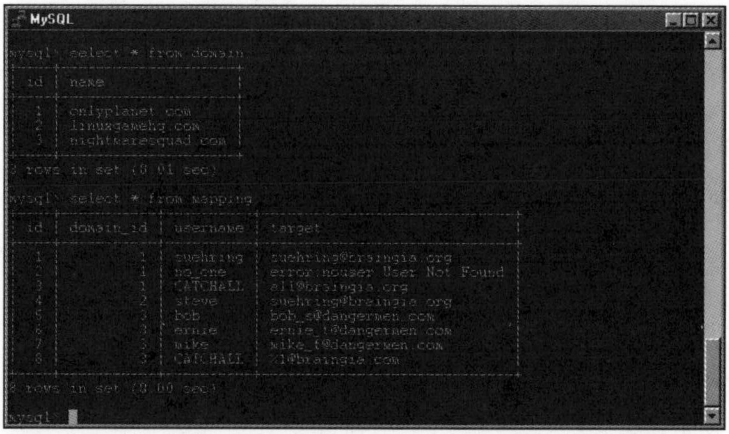

Figure 19-14: The virtusertable data inside the MySQL database

On the CD-ROM

The Perl program for importing virtual user tables is also available on the CD-ROM with this book. You'll need to modify it for your implementation but it provides a good starting point.

A Web interface for virtual e-mail management

Taking the virtual e-mail database onto the Web is a good job for PHP. Using a PHP-based management system the administration of domains and virtual e-mail becomes easy. The administrator can manage virtual e-mail for a customer or provide the ability for the customer to do it themselves without worry of the underlying data being compromised.

For example, Figure 19-15 shows an administration front page for the e-mail management system. You can search for (or add) an entry by typing the search term into the box and clicking the button.

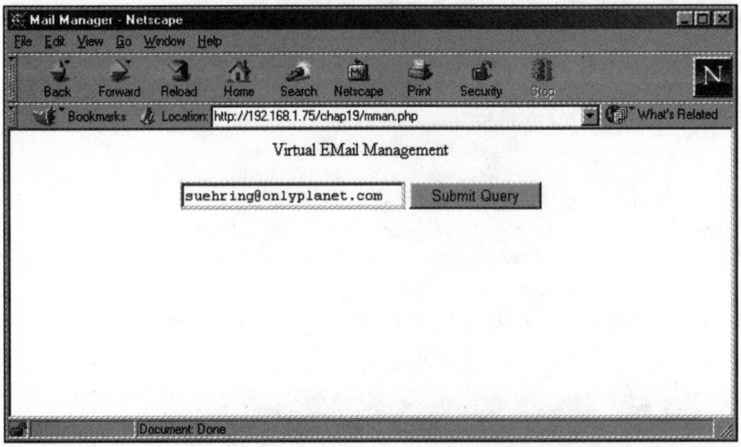

Figure 19-15: The administrator's front page for the virtual e-mail management Web interface

If found, the resulting page is shown; the administrator can delete the entry if necessary (see Figure 19-16).

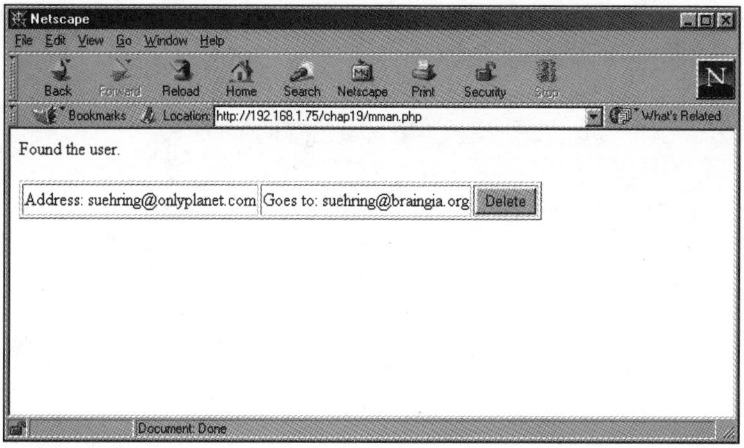

Figure 19-16: An entry that is found shows the results to the administrator.

If an entry is not found, the administrator is informed — and given the opportunity to add the entry, as illustrated in Figure 19-17.

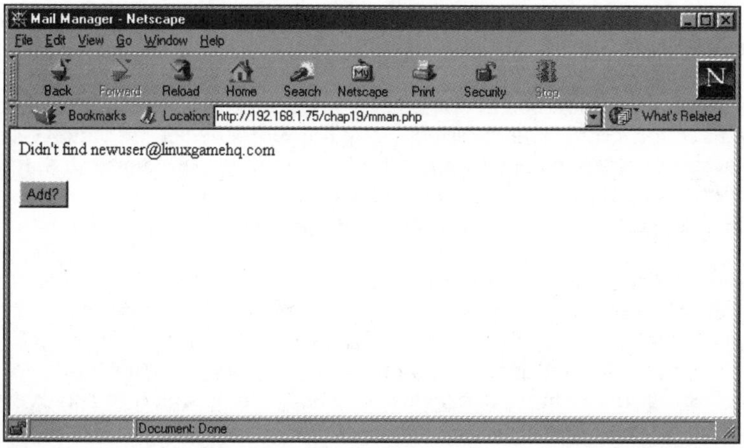

Figure 19-17: An entry that is not found gives the administrator a chance to add the entry.

Clicking the Add button shown in Figure 19-17 yields a page where the administrator can input the pertinent details (see Figure 19-18).

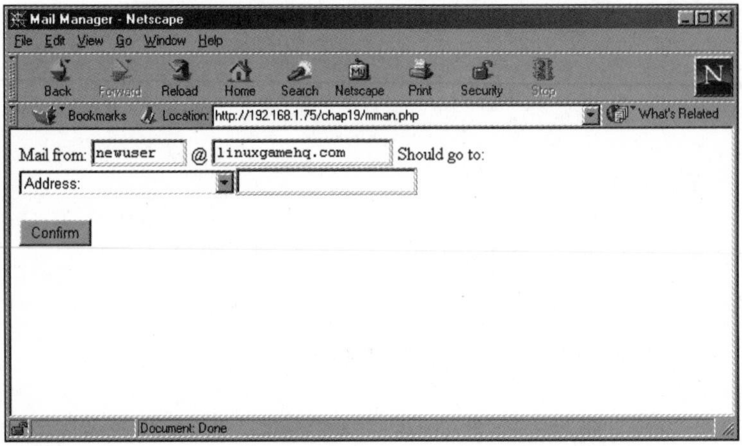

Figure 19-18: The page shown to add an entry for virtual e-mail

Figure 19-18 shows a Select box for the target of the virtual e-mail. The administrator has a choice: Send the e-mail to another address (the default,) make it a straight mapping (`%1`), or return an error.

Once the relevant information has been entered, an error-checking function is called in the backend PHP program. The error-checking function checks the validity of the e-mail addresses entered to make sure they don't contain invalid characters. In addition, the error-checking function looks one more time at the database to make sure the entry doesn't already exist (just in case the administrator changed it).

Once confirmed, the entry is added to the virtual e-mail database. However, at this point, Sendmail still knows nothing of the new address. A program must be written to extract the data from the MySQL database and put it back into the `virtusertable` format for Sendmail. This program could be another function within this PHP program or (more likely) a Perl program scheduled to run every *N* minutes on the system.

Building a Full-Scale Virtual-Services Interface

Taking the interfaces used throughout this chapter for things such as DNS and e-mail, the developer could build an interface for management of these services by clients. The clients could control their own DNS and e-mail configurations while stored virtually on a server owned by their provider.

The provider could implement the interface worry-free knowing that the customer can only affect their own entries for DNS and e-mail. With a little error checking, the client could be saved from making many common errors as well. Both aspects save the provider money by cutting down on support calls — whether for DNS, e-mail changes, or to correct a change that was implemented incorrectly.

Some providers have such an interface in place. One such provider is Fibernet, `http://www.fibernetcc.com/`. Using the Fibernet interface, customers can manage their own DNS and e-mail entries (as well as other tools for running Web sites and virtual services). Another provider is Communitech, `http//www.communitech.net/` who provide a virtual-services interface for their customers as well.

Summary

The numerous and powerful APIs available for MySQL make services relatively easy to integrate in an operating system such as Linux.

- ✦ PAM-MySQL is a module for performing authentication with MySQL and PAM-aware applications.
- ✦ NSS-MySQL provides an interface into Name Service Switch to give account information through MySQL.
- ✦ MySQL makes for a great backend management system for applications such as DNS and e-mail.
- ✦ Using a MySQL database and Web interface in PHP, an administrator can manage domains or enable customers to manage their own DNS information.
- ✦ E-mail can also be tied into MySQL through Pam-MySQL for POP3 and by using MySQL as a management system for virtual users.

✦ ✦ ✦

CHAPTER 20

NuSphere Enhanced MySQL

✦ ✦ ✦ ✦

In This Chapter

Taking a detailed look at NuSphere MySQL Advantage

Installing NuSphere Pro Advantage on a Linux system

Installing NuSphere Pro Advantage on a Windows 2000 system

✦ ✦ ✦ ✦

NuSphere — a company not affiliated with MySQL AB — has its own version of MySQL, based on the same MySQL code released by MySQL AB. However, the NuSphere version of MySQL (called Enhanced MySQL) comes within a suite of products collectively titled MySQL Advantage. NuSphere MySQL Advantage includes integrated versions of Enhanced MySQL, Perl, PHP, and Apache. NuSphere also makes an enhanced version of PHP called NuSphere PHPed Advantage, as well as NuSphere Pro Advantage — a product that combines MySQL and PHPed Advantage.

MySQL Advantage offers many enhancements to the MySQL versions released by MySQL AB. One such enhancement is another table type called Gemini, which is a transactional table.

NuSphere MySQL Advantage is not free software. However, for the enhancements it provides for larger implementations, the cost is minimal. The software purchase even includes technical support directly from NuSphere included in the price.

This chapter examines NuSphere Pro Advantage, including its enhancements and installation.

NuSphere MySQL Advantage: A Closer Look

Since NuSphere's MySQL is based on the main MySQL code base, many options (as well as the command syntax) are the same as for non-enhanced MySQL from MySQL AB. Accordingly, this chapter skips any discussion of how to use MySQL or MySQL-related tools; instead, it looks at the additions that NuSphere MySQL Advantage adds to a MySQL installation. For more information on NuSphere Enhanced MySQL see the NuSphere Web site at `http//www.nusphere.com/`.

Gemini: A new table type

Gemini is a transactional table type available with NuSphere MySQL. Gemini includes full ACID support, row-level locking, and excellent crash recovery. Recall that ACID is an abbreviation referring to Atomicity, Consistency, Isolation, and Durability. ACID support in NuSphere Enhanced MySQL means that `Gemini` tables can update records in an isolated environment. If a part of a transaction fails, the entire transaction is rolled back so as to prevent possible inconsistencies in the data. Even when there is a catastrophic system crash, `Gemini` tables will perform automatic crash recovery to restore data to a known good state.

NuSphere integration with popular software

NuSphere MySQL Advantage is integrated with Apache, Perl, and PHP to make development easy. With normal MySQL you have to install MySQL-aware PHP, install various Perl libraries for MySQL, and install Apache with PHP enabled. NuSphere Enhanced MySQL takes care of these for you. In addition, the Apache installed with NuSphere MySQL Advantage also includes SSL support for serving secure Web sites.

NuSphere management tools

NuSphere MySQL Advantage also includes Web-based tools for management of MySQL and Apache. The management tools enable easy administration of Web sites and security. Further, a security console is included to provide utilities for network security.

Installing NuSphere Pro Advantage on Linux

In both the Linux and Windows versions of NuSphere, installation uses a Web interface. This makes configuration easy (though unfortunately somewhat less configurable than some Linux users may prefer). For example, many Linux users are familiar with installing software through the `configure ; make ; make install` commands. Those offer flexibility to the installer so that they can edit the source files prior to installation. This section describes the installation process for NuSphere Pro Advantage in Linux.

The NuSphere installation process

NuSphere Pro Advantage is distributed on CD-ROM; to begin installation, insert the CD-ROM into the drive. Because this installation is for a server, I assume that you aren't running a GUI such as KDE or GNOME. Therefore, from a command-line prompt, you mount the CD-ROM drive with the following command as shown in Figure 20-1:

```
mount -t iso9660 /dev/cdrom /mnt/cdrom
```

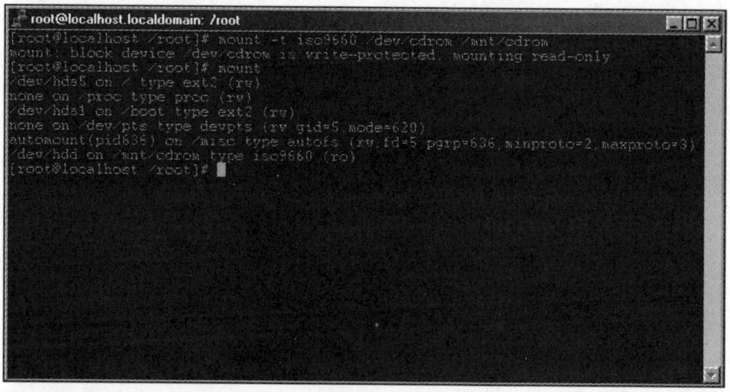

Figure 20-1: Mounting the NuSphere installation CD in Linux

Change (**cd**) into the newly mounted CD-ROM directory:

```
cd /mnt/cdrom
```

Run the setup script from within that directory (as shown in Figure 20-2):

```
./setup
```

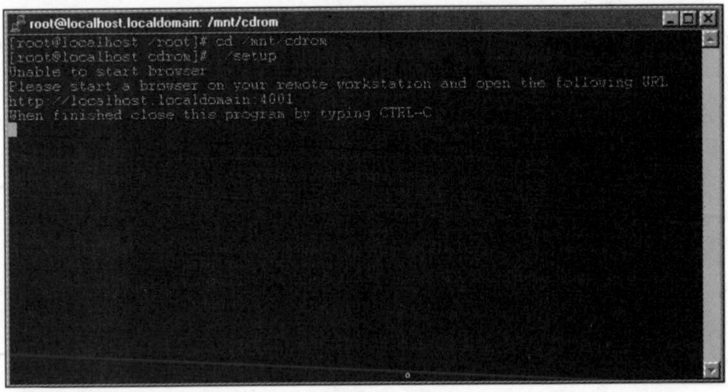

Figure 20-2: Executing the setup script from within the CD-ROM directory

The instructions in Figure 20-2 tell the user to point a Web browser to that machine, port 4001. Figure 20-3 shows what happens when I do so.

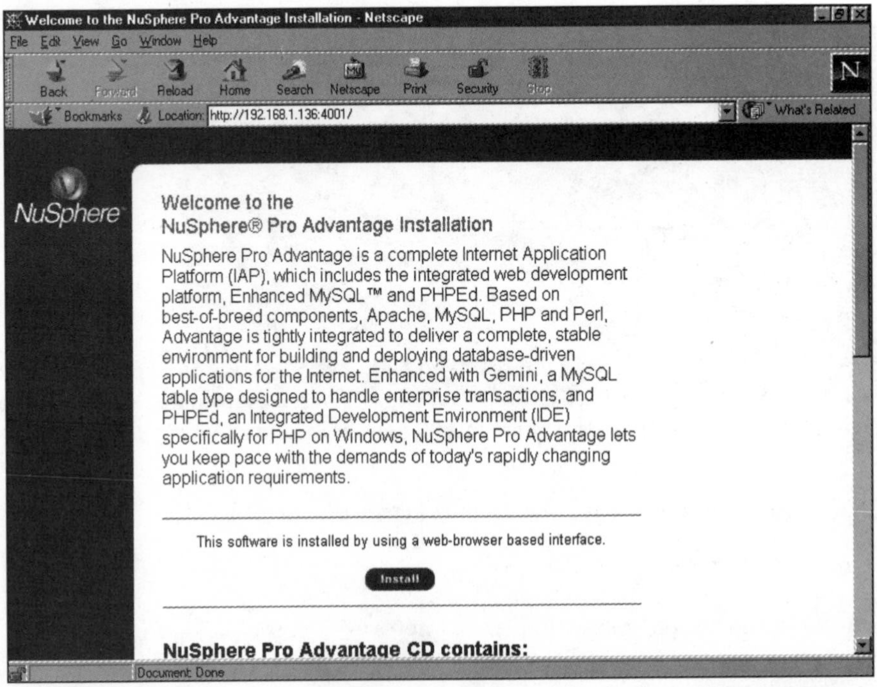

Figure 20-3: Pointing a Web browser to port 4001 on the server with the NuSphere CD-ROM mounted

You should see a similar welcome screen when you go to port 4001 on your server. Begin the installation by clicking the Install button.

You are now presented with three types of installation to choose from: Quick, Custom, and RPM installation (see Figure 20-4).

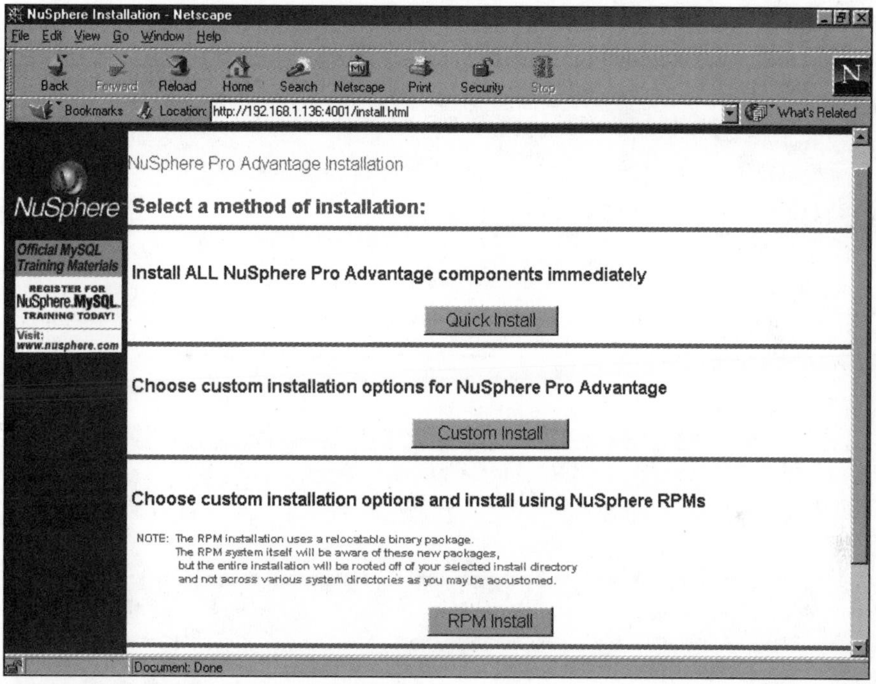

Figure 20-4: The three types of installation

The RPM installation method enables Red Hat Linux systems to update the RPM database with the new package information. This can be useful for administrators who frequently use RPM as a management tool for new software.

Both Custom and RPM installation enable the administrator to choose other options for installation — for example, default ports for software and installation paths. Some of these options are shown in Figure 20-5.

In this case, I use the Quick Installation method (which chooses the defaults shown in Figure 20-5). The installation program takes over; the Web page tracks its progress (as illustrated in Figure 20-6).

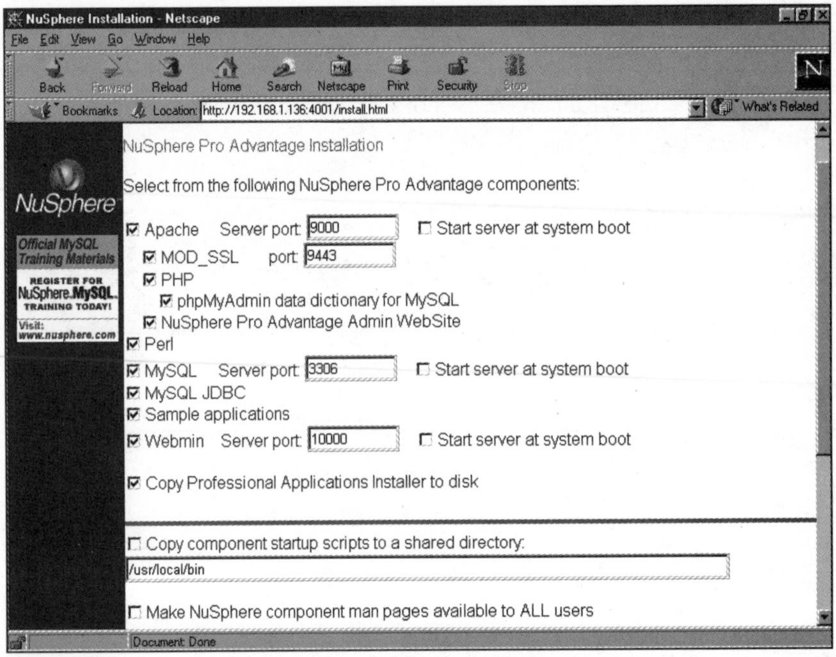

Figure 20-5: The Custom and RPM installation methods enable the administrator to choose ports and locations for software.

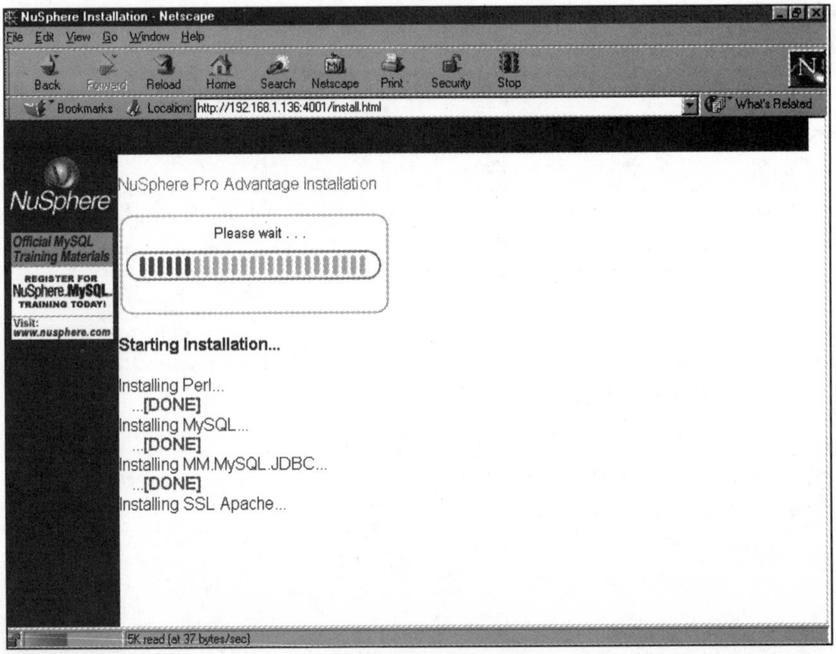

Figure 20-6: The progress of the NuSphere installation is tracked via the Web page.

When the installation is complete, a new link appears so I can continue, as in Figure 20-7.

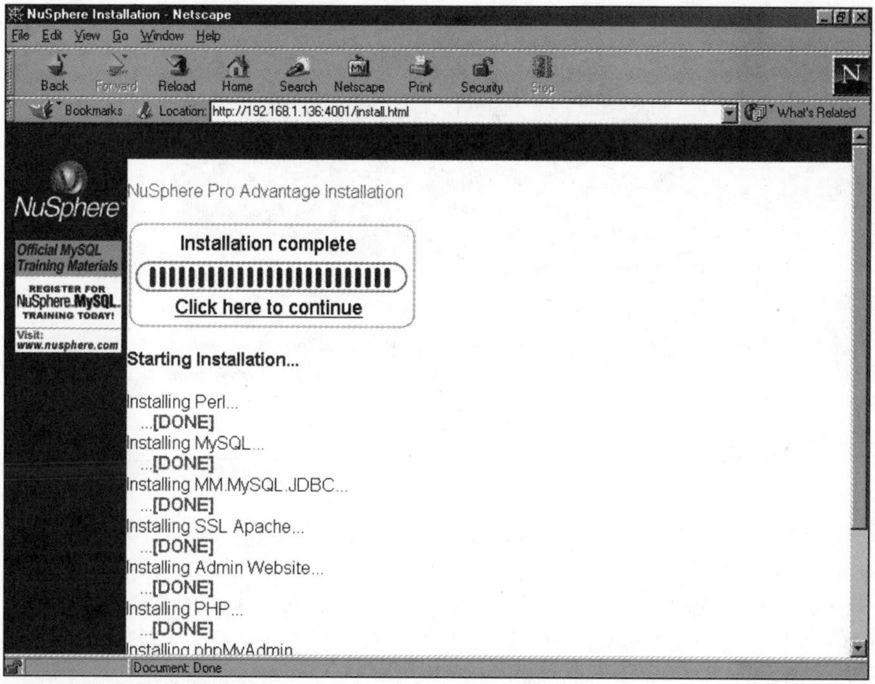

Figure 20-7: The Click Here To Continue link appears when the NuSphere installer is done installing the software.

When you click to continue you'll be presented with a link to remind you to register with NuSphere as well as instructions to start some of the services just installed.

Clicking the Quick Start link starts the services just installed.

Many NuSphere products install software that you might not want to run on a publicly available Web server (such as Webmin) for security reasons. Refer to the documentation on Webmin and Apache to configure those services so that outside users cannot gain access to them.

Going back to the console or terminal window from Figure 20-2, you can press Ctrl+C to stop the setup script, as shown in Figure 20-8.

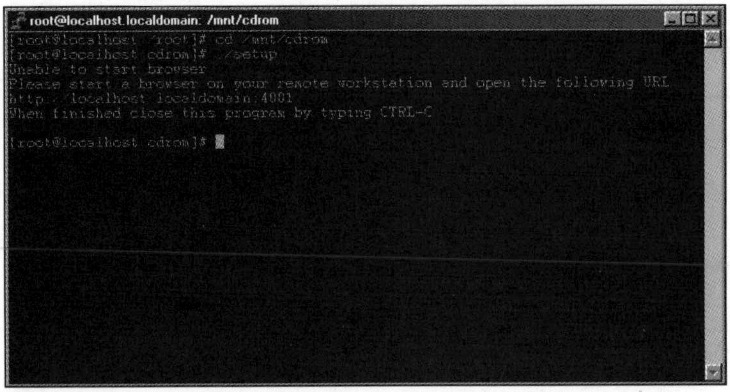

Figure 20-8: Press Ctrl+C to stop the setup script for NuSphere installation.

NuSphere administration

NuSphere includes a Web site for administration of your server. This is located at port 9000 on your Web server. For example, if your Web server IP address is `192.168.1.1`, you would point the Web browser to `http://192.168.1.1:9000/` (as illustrated in Figure 20-9, where the server is located at `192.168.1.136`).

From within the administration Web site, you can run tests of the PHP environment—as well as utilize Webmin and the Apache Access Manager. `PHPmyAdmin` is also included within this administration Web site. However, you will need to use the MySQL CLI to create Gemini table types unless you set the default table type to `Gemini`. (The next section explains creating Gemini tables, as well as setting `Gemini` as your default table type.)

The location of many of the MySQL programs such as the CLI will be dependent on where you chose to install them. If you chose the Quick Installation method, the programs will be located in `/usr/local/nusphere/mysql`. I strongly recommend that you set a password for the MySQL `root` user.

Cross-Reference: See Chapter 3 for more information on setting a password with the `mysqladmin` program.

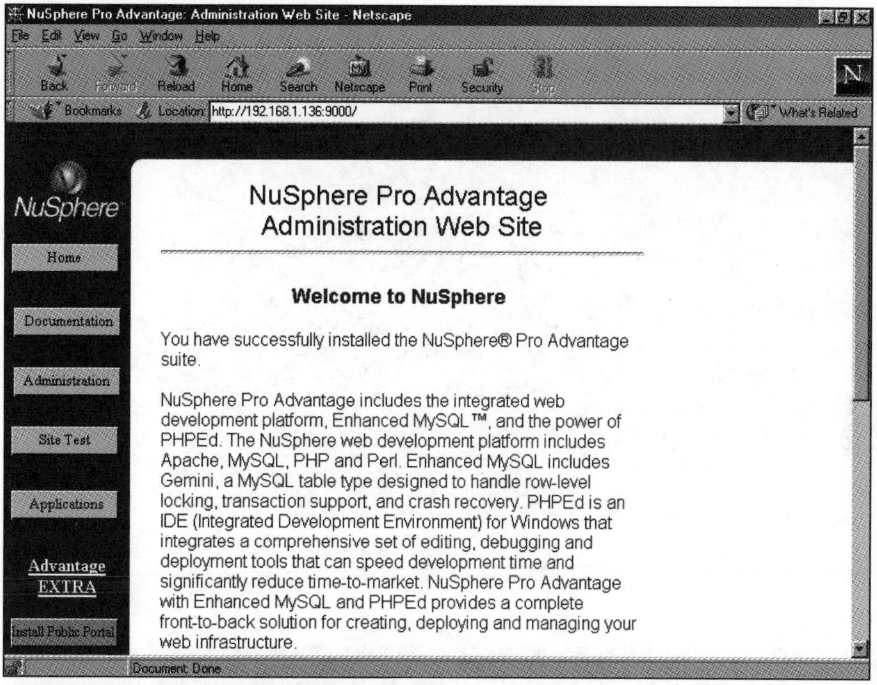

Figure 20-9: The NuSphere administration Web site for this server

Creating Gemini tables

Tables within NuSphere Enhanced MySQL can be the normal `MyISAM` or the `Gemini` table type. By default, tables are created as `MyISAM` (for example, the table created in Figure 20-10).

To create a `Gemini` table and take advantage of its specific enhancements, you simply tell MySQL to create the table as a `Gemini` type while you are creating the table. To do so, add the following line to the `CREATE TABLE` definition.

```
TYPE = Gemini
```

Figure 20-11 shows an example of creating a `Gemini` table through the MySQL CLI.

To enable MySQL to use `Gemini` as the default table type, you need to add the following line when starting MySQL:

```
--default-table-type=gemini
```

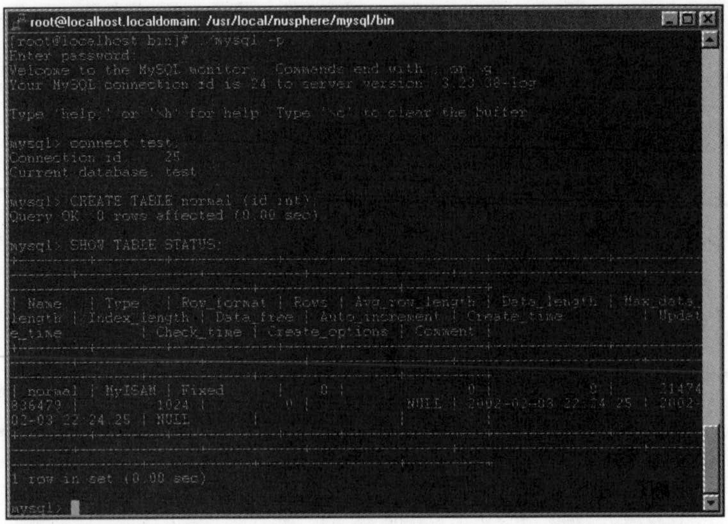

Figure 20-10: NuSphere Enhanced MySQL still uses MyISAM as the default table type.

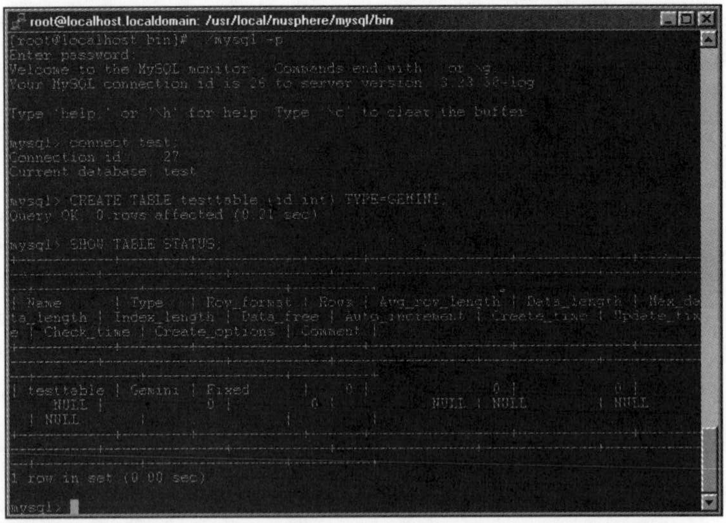

Figure 20-11: Creating a Gemini table through the MySQL CLI

After adding the line to enable `Gemini` as the default table type and restarting the server I create a table without a `TYPE` clause. The result is a `Gemini` table, as illustrated in Figure 20-12.

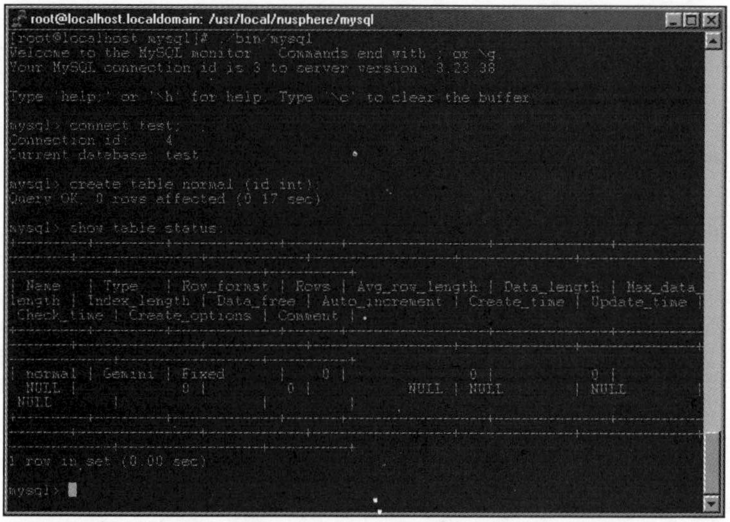

Figure 20-12: After enabling Gemini as the default table type, creation of Gemini tables does not require the extra TYPE clause.

If you want to create a `MyISAM` table after enabling `Gemini` as the default, add a `TYPE=MyISAM` clause to the `CREATE TABLE` statement.

Once the server is configured to use `Gemini` as the default table type you can use `PHPmyAdmin` or other tools for creating `Gemini` tables. In effect, you do not have to solely use the MySQL CLI for creating `Gemini` tables since you don't have to specify the `TYPE` clause as part of the `CREATE TABLE` statement.

Gemini configuration options

You can set other options for `Gemini` tables at the command line or in the MySQL configuration file `my.cnf`. The options to use are listed in Table 20-1.

Table 20-1
Gemini Table Options And Variables

Option	*Description*
`gemini_buffer_cache=`	Variable set with `set-`*`variable`* syntax to control the size of the memory pool available for buffers.
`gemini_connection_limit=`	Variable set with the `set-`*`variable`* syntax to control the maximum number of allowed connections.

Continued

Table 20-1 (continued)

Option	*Description*
`gemini_io_threads=`	Variable to set the number of threads to open at once.
`gemini_lock_table_size=`	Variable to set the maximum number of locks.
`gemini_lock_wait_timeout=`	Variable set in seconds to control the amount of time MySQL will wait before releasing an apparently dead lock.
`--gemini-flush-log-at-commit`	Tells the server to flush the buffers of the flush log after every `commit` operation. This enhances safety but can significantly decrease performance.
`--gemini-recovery=`	Options include `FULL`, `NONE`, or `FORCE` and they determine how the server performs recovery.
`--gemini-unbuffered-io`	Prevents write operations to the table from using the Linux cache.
`--skip-gemini`	Option that tells MySQL to skip `Gemini` support entirely.
`--transaction-isolation=`	Sets the transaction level as `READ-UNCOMMITTED`, `READ-COMMITTED`, `REPEATABLE-READ`, or `SERIALIZABLE`. Can be overridden with the `SET ISOLATION LEVEL` statement.

Installing NuSphere Pro Advantage on Windows 2000

As with the installation of NuSphere products in Linux, installing NuSphere Pro Advantage on Windows uses a Web-based program. The installation process simply involves clicking a series of buttons (the usual process for installing software in Windows). NuSphere products run on later versions of Windows, including Windows 95, 98, and 2000. In all likelihood, the products run on other Windows platforms, check with `http://www.nusphere.com/` for more information. For this installation, I use Windows 2000 Server.

The NuSphere installation process

NuSphere Pro Advantage is distributed on CD-ROM. Therefore, to begin the installation insert the CD-ROM into the drive. The CD should run automatically. If the CD does not start automatically, simply go into Windows Explorer, point to the CD-ROM drive containing the NuSphere CD, and click `Setup.exe`. Either method will open a Web browser pointing to port 4001 on the `nusphere-cd` URL, as shown in Figure 20-13.

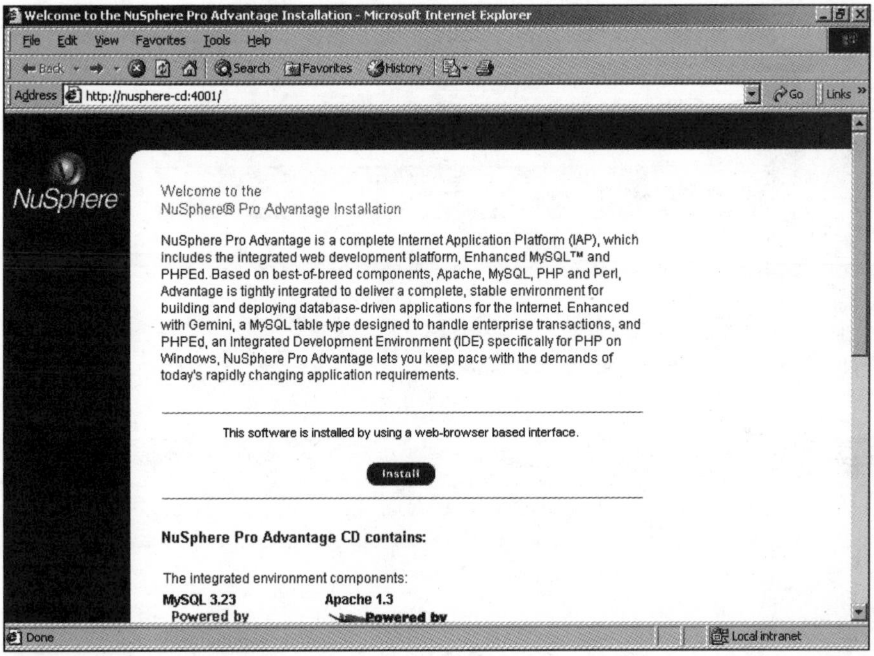

Figure 20-13: Pointing a Web browser to port 4001 on the nusphere-cd URL with the NuSphere CD-ROM inserted

You should see a similar welcome screen though it may vary slightly depending on which version of the NuSphere product you are installing. Begin the installation by clicking the Install button.

You are presented with two options for the type of installation to proceed with, Quick or Custom, as illustrated in Figure 20-14.

The Custom installation option enables the administrator to choose other options (such as default ports for software and installation paths), some of which are shown in Figure 20-15.

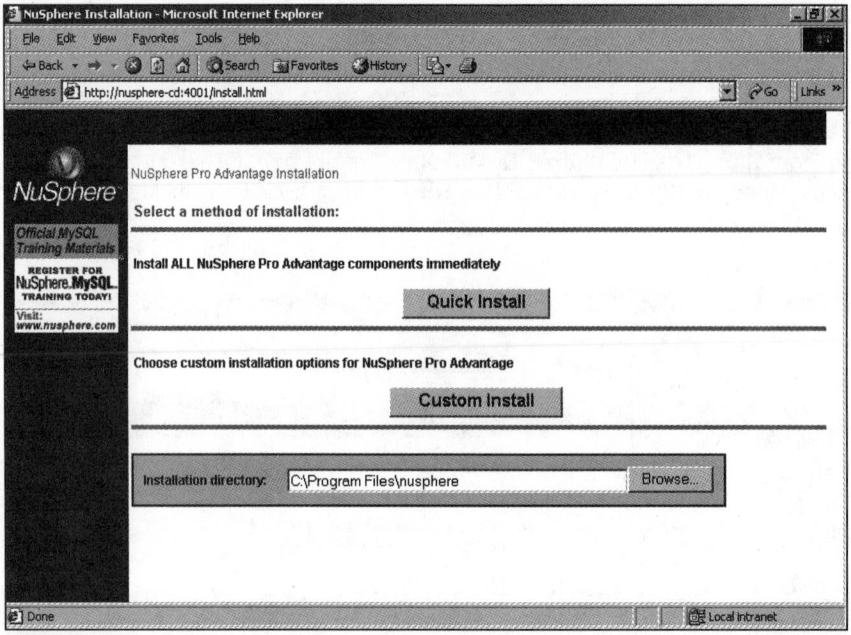

Figure 20-14: The two types of installation

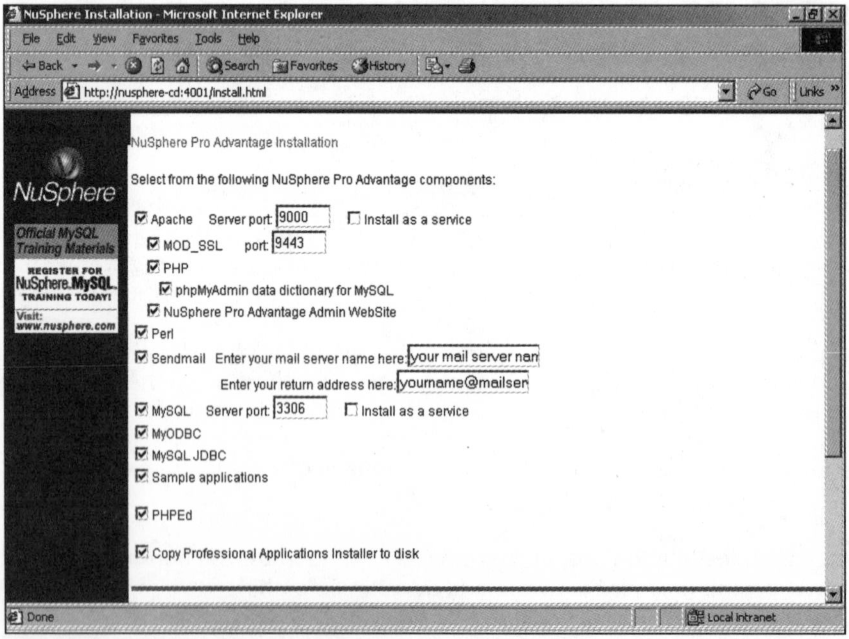

Figure 20-15: The Custom installation method enables the administrator to choose ports and locations for software.

For this installation, I use the Quick Installation method that chooses the defaults shown in Figure 20-15. The installation program takes over; the Web page tracks its progress, as illustrated in Figure 20-16.

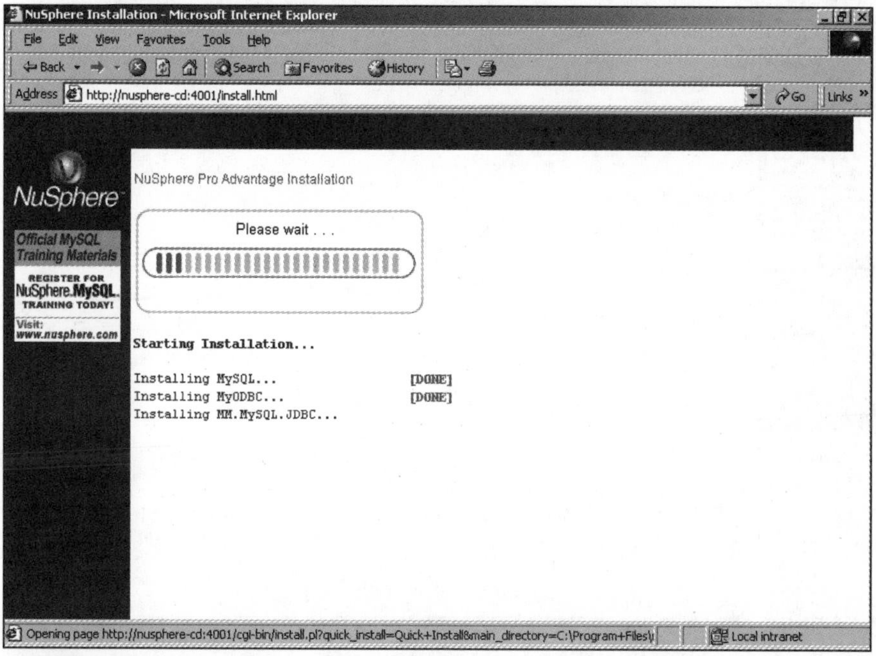

Figure 20-16: The progress of the NuSphere installation is tracked via the Web page.

When the installation is complete a new link is presented; click it to continue, as shown in Figure 20-17.

When you click to continue, you get a link that reminds you to register with NuSphere — as well as instructions to start some of the services just installed (see Figure 20-18).

The Programs menu shows a new program group for NuSphere. Inside this group are shortcuts for starting and stopping services such as Apache and MySQL, as well as for configuring some of the programs as Services in Windows.

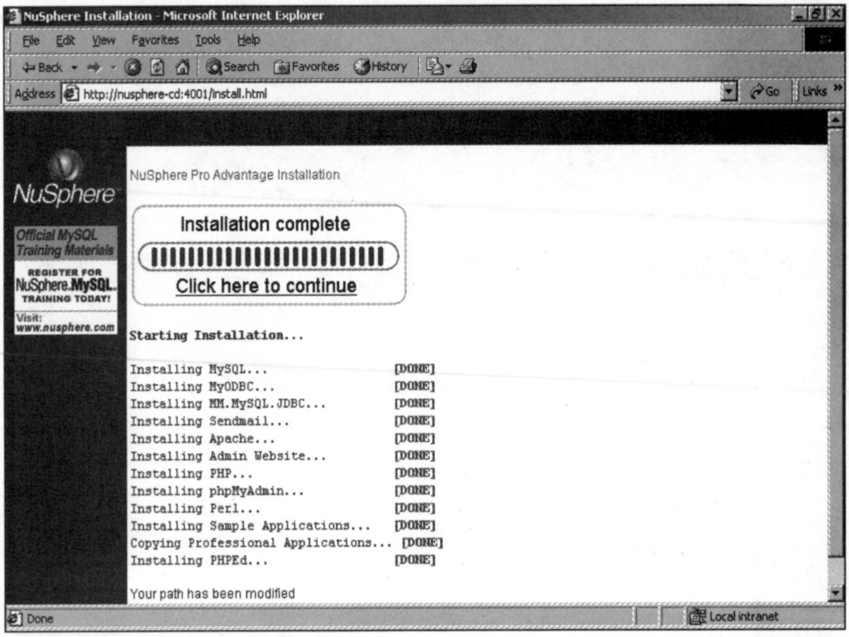

Figure 20-17: The Click Here To Continue link is presented when the NuSphere installer is done installing the software.

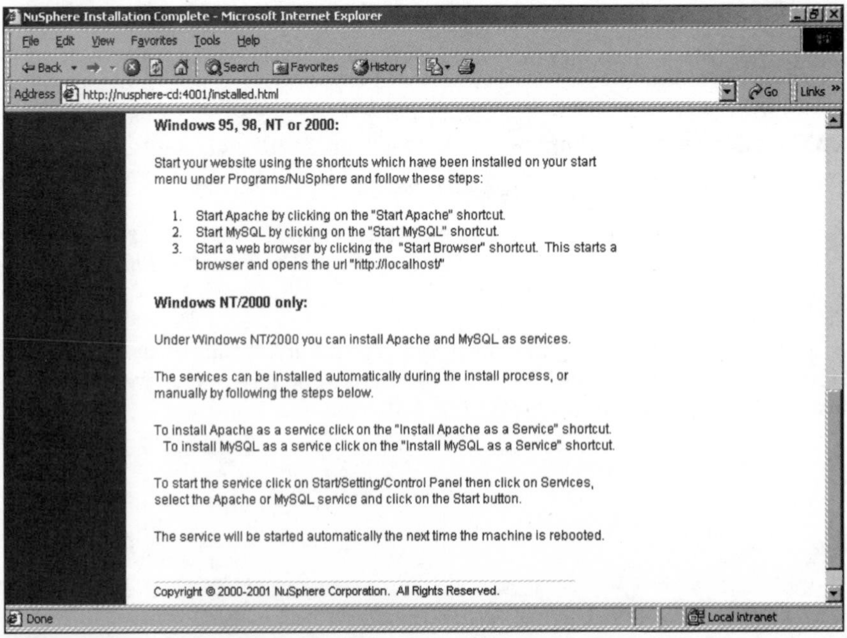

Figure 20-18: Instructions for starting services related to NuSphere as provided by the installation program

NuSphere administration

NuSphere includes a Web site for administration of your server. This is located at port 9000 on your Web server. For example, if your Web server IP address is `192.168.1.1`, you would point the Web browser to `http://192.168.1.1:9000/` (as illustrated in Figure 20-19, where the server is located at `192.168.1.136`).

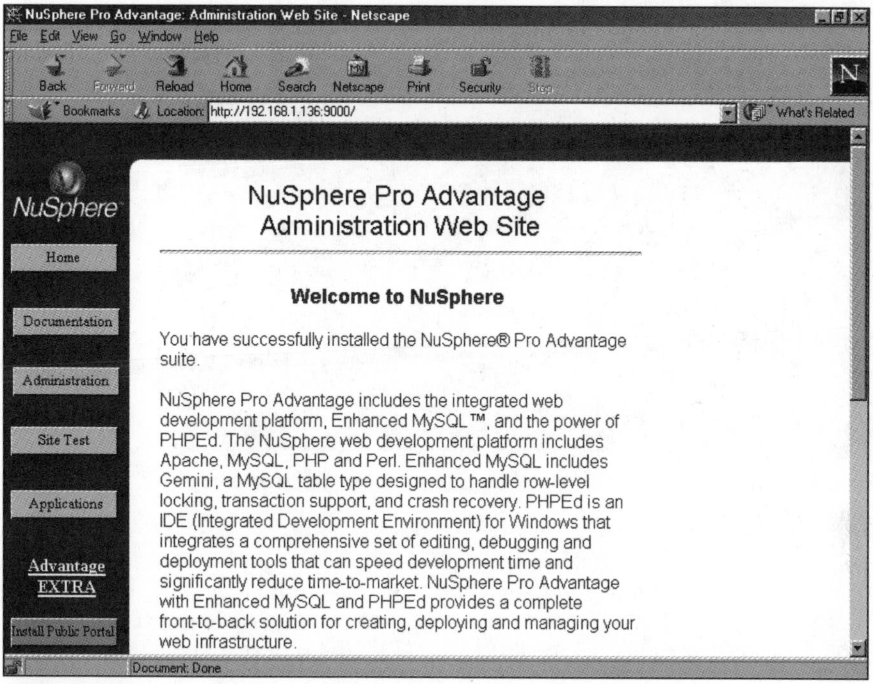

Figure 20-19: The NuSphere administration Web site for this server

From within the administration Web site you can run tests of the PHP environment as well as Perl script and perform administration for Apache. `PHPmyAdmin` is also included within this administration Web site. However, you will need to use the MySQL CLI to create `Gemini` table types unless you set the default table type to Gemini. The next section describes creating `Gemini` tables, as well as setting `Gemini` as your default table type.

The location of many MySQL programs — for example, the CLI — depends on where you chose to install them. Before you continue, however, I strongly recommend that you set a password for the MySQL `root` user.

Cross-Reference

See Chapter 3 for more information on setting a password with the `mysqladmin` program.

Creating Gemini tables

Tables within NuSphere Enhanced MySQL can be the normal `MyISAM` or the `Gemini` table type. By default, tables are created as `MyISAM` (as illustrated in Figure 20-20).

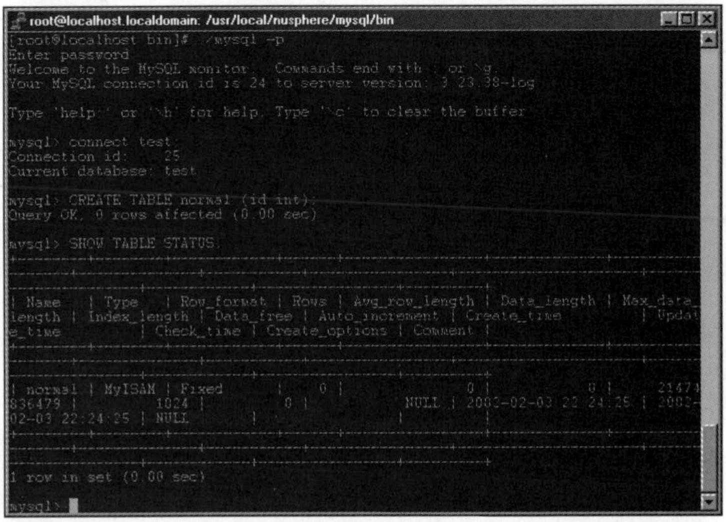

Figure 20-20: NuSphere Enhanced MySQL still uses MyISAM as the default table type.

To create a `Gemini` table and take advantage of its enhancements, you simply tell MySQL to create a table as the `Gemini` type when you create the table; do so by adding the following line to the `CREATE TABLE` definition.

```
TYPE = Gemini
```

Figure 20-21 shows an example of creating a `Gemini` table through the MySQL CLI.

To enable MySQL to use `Gemini` as the default table type, add the following line when you start MySQL:

```
--default-table-type=gemini
```

After adding the line to enable `Gemini` as the default table type and restarting the server I create a table without a `TYPE` clause. The result is a `Gemini` table, as illustrated in Figure 20-22.

If you want to create a `MyISAM` table after enabling `Gemini` as the default, add a `TYPE=MyISAM` clause to the `CREATE TABLE` statement.

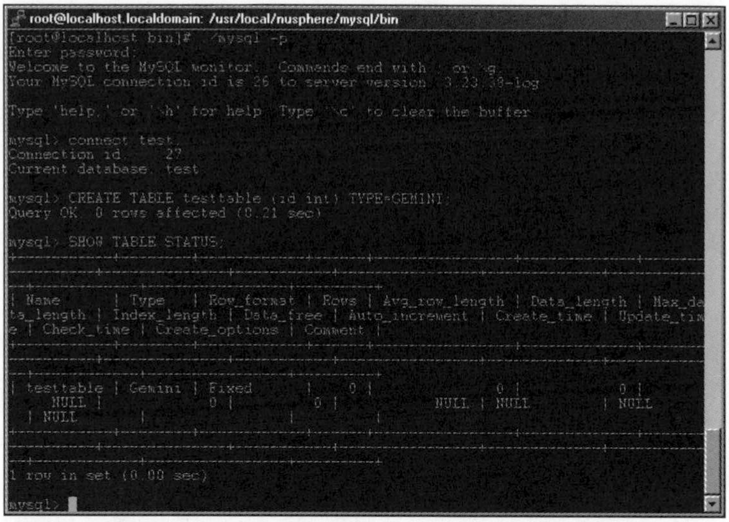

Figure 20-21: Creating a Gemini table through the MySQL CLI

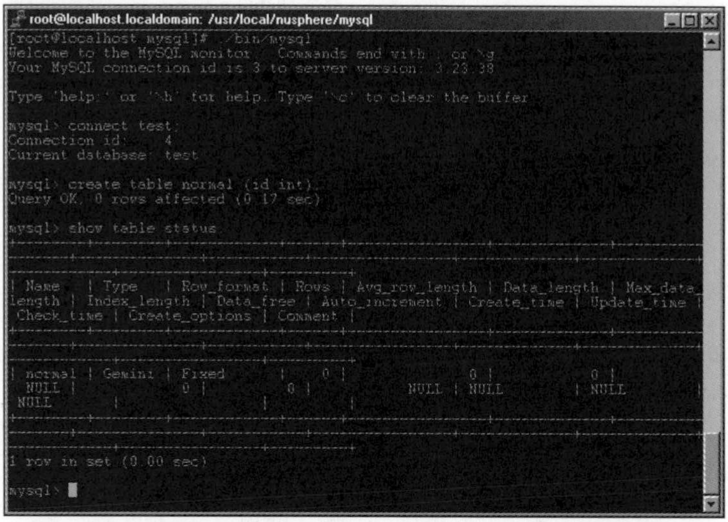

Figure 20-22: After enabling Gemini as the default table type, creation of Gemini tables does not require the extra TYPE clause.

Once the server is configured to use `Gemini` as the default table type, the MySQL CLI is no longer the only way to create a `Gemini` table. You can use `PHPmyAdmin` or other tools for that purpose because you don't have to specify the `TYPE` clause as part of a `CREATE TABLE` statement.

Gemini configuration options

Other for Gemini tables can be set on the command line or in the MySQL configuration file my.ini. These options are listed in Table 20-2.

Table 20-2
Gemini Table Options And Variables

Option	*Description*
gemini_buffer_cache=	Variable set by using the set-*variable* syntax to control the size of the memory pool available for buffers.
gemini_connection_limit=	Variable set by using the set-*variable* syntax to control the maximum number of allowed connections.
gemini_io_threads=	Variable that sets the number of threads to open at once.
gemini_lock_table_size=	Variable that sets the maximum number of locks.
gemini_lock_wait_timeout=	Variable (specified in number of seconds) that controls how long MySQL waits before releasing an apparently dead lock.
--gemini-flush-log-at-commit	Tells the server to flush the buffers of the flush log after every commit operation. This enhances safety but can significantly decrease performance.
--gemini-recovery=	Options include FULL, NONE, or FORCE (which determine how the server performs a recovery operation).
--gemini-unbuffered-io	Prevents write operations to the table from using the Linux cache.
--skip-gemini	Option that tells MySQL to skip Gemini support entirely.
--transaction-isolation=	Sets the transaction level as READ-UNCOMMITTED, READ-COMMITTED, REPEATABLE-READ, or SERIALIZABLE. Can be overridden with the SET ISOLATION LEVEL statement.

Summary

NuSphere produces enhanced and integrated versions of popular software such as MySQL and PHP. The products from NuSphere come bundled as a suite, which installs more smoothly than each product would separately.

- The version of MySQL included with NuSphere products comes with a new transactional table type called `Gemini`.
- NuSphere MySQL Advantage integrates enhanced MySQL with PHP, Perl, the JDBC and Apache.
- NuSphere Pro Advantage has integrated an enhanced PHP development environment with the products in MySQL Advantage.
- NuSphere products also come with Web-based administration tools to make management of the products easier. These tools include Access Manager for Apache and `PHPmyAdmin`. For Linux, Webmin is also included.

✦ ✦ ✦

Appendixes

PART

VI

In This Part

APPENDIX A

MySQL Application Reference

A.1 Data-Access Applications

The following applications are used to access the data stored within the MySQL database.

mysql

The `mysql` application provides basic access to the Command-Line Interface (CLI). Additionally, it can be used to import and export data.

Argument	*Description*
`-?, --help`	Displays basic help information and descriptions of command-line arguments.
`-A, --no-auto-rehash`	This flag prevents the automatic hashing of tables and fields. Removing table hashing results in faster load times for the `mysql` client.
`-B, --batch`	Returns a tab-delimited list for returned data from the result set.
`--character-sets-dir=`	Uses the following directory for specific character sets.
`-C, --compress`	Forces the connection to use compression for data delivery.
`-D, --database=`	Specifies a database to connect with. If no database is supplied, the connection will start without a specific database connection.
`--default-character-set=`	Specifies an alternate character set.
`-e, --execute`	Executes the given command and exit.
`-E, --vertical`	Displays data output vertically from the result sets.
`-f, --force`	Forces the execution of the command even if an error is returned from the server.
`-g, --no-named-commands`	Disables the use of named commands. This option is set by default.
`-G, --enable-named-commands`	Enables the use of named commands.
`-h, --host=`	Connects to specified host. If none is given, localhost is assumed. The value given can be either an IP address, domain name or server alias.
`-H, -html`	Displays the query return output in HTML format.
`-i, --ignore-space`	Disregards spaces after function name calls.
`-L, --skip-line-numbers`	If an error is returned, does not return the line number associated with what caused the error.
`--no-pager`	Disables the use of a system pager file located by determining the value of its `ENV` variable.
`--no-tee`	Disables use of outfiles.
`-n, --unbuffered`	Flushes the buffer after each query is performed.
`-N, --skip-column-names`	Omits the column names from the output on query return sets.

Argument	***Description***
`-O, --set-variable var=option`	Assigns the given option value to the `ENV` variable given as `var`.
`-o, --one-database`	Skips the execution of any updates except those that affect the default database.
`--pager=`	Designates an alternate pager file to the default `ENV` value.
`-p, --password=`	Uses a password to connect to a server. If no password is given, a prompt requests that the user enter the password.
`-P, --port=`	Designates a specific port that the connection to the MySQL database should use.
`-q, --quick`	Returns data rows without caching the return values. By including this option you will also disregard the use of the history file.
`-r, --raw`	When used in conjunction with the `-B` or `--batch` flags, returns fields without converting to the normal display format.
`-s, --silent`	Does not return any standard output messages (error messages are still returned).
`-S, --socket=`	Uses the given socket file for connection to the server.
`-t, --table`	Returns the data in standard table formatting.
`-T, --debug-info`	At termination of the application, delivers any debugging information that is available.
`--tee=`	Outputs all returned data to a file with a specified filename.
`-u, --user=`	Designates the username passed when connecting to the MySQL database. If no username is given, the current system username is assumed for the connection.
`-U, --safe-updates`	Prevents use of `DELETE` for queries that do not designate a key for the row to be deleted.
`-v, --verbose`	Displays more verbose system error messages.
`-V, --version`	Displays the MySQL version number and then exits.
`-w, --wait`	Retries a connection if an attempted connection is not initially successful.

mysqldump

The mysqldump application provides export, statements for database creation, and file-creation support.

Argument	Description
-A, --all-databases	Returns data from all databases contained on the MySQL server.
-a, --all	Returns table data with complete create syntax.
--add-drop-table	Returns table data that includes a "DROP TABLE" command before each table create syntax.
	This option is useful when the formats of existing tables differ from the formats of data being imported into the server.
--add-locks	Specifies that the data returned from the server include locking syntax to prevent tables from being altered during the dump process.
--allow-keywords	This flag allows the return of column names that are also MySQL internal keywords.
-B, --databases	Returns data from the following databases.
-c, --complete-insert	Returns data with complete insert statements.
-C, --compress	Forces connection to use compression for data delivery.
-d, --no-data	Skips row insert syntax for the data contained in the table data being exported.
--default-character-set=	Specifies an alternate character set for the data.
--delayed-insert	Includes "INSERT DELAYED" syntax with data insert syntax.
-e, --extended-insert	Returns insert data with a faster syntax.
	This option may remove any backward compatibility with older MySQL versions.
-F, --flush-logs	Executes a flush of the MySQL log file prior to the execution of the dump process.
-f, --force	Forces execution even if the server returns an error.
-h, --host=	Connects to a specified host. If none is given, localhost is assumed. The value given can be either an IP address, domain name or server alias.
-l, --lock-tables	Locks the designated tables prior to reading the data to be returned for the dump.

Argument	*Description*
`-n, --no-create-db`	Skips create syntax for all or specified databases. This can be used in conjunction with `-all-databases` to force exclusion of the `create` syntax for each individual database.
`-O, --set-variable var=option`	Assign the given option value to the `ENV` variable given as `var`.
`-t, --no-create-info`	Omits table-creation syntax from the returned data.

`--opt`	Activates all of the following options:
	`--add-drop-table`
	`--add-locks`
	`--all`
	`--extended-insert`
	`--quick`
	`--lock-tables`

`-p, --password`	Uses password to connect to database. If no password is given, a prompt requests that the password be entered.
`-P, --port=`	Designates a specific port that the connection to the MySQL database should use.
`-q, --quick`	Skips buffering of returned output. This forces the return or the data directly to `STDOUT`.
`-Q, --quote-names`	Appends single quotes (`''`) to all table and column names returned.
`-r, --result-file=`	Returns data to specified file.
`-S, --socket`	Uses the given socket file for connection to the server.
`--tables`	Overrides the `-B, --databases` flag.
`-T, --tab=`	Returns data to individual files for each table in a database, using the given path. This option can only be executed on the same machine that the MySQL server is operating.
`--fields-terminated-by=`	Designates a delimiter for the data output files created by `-T`. Defaults to tab.
`--fields-enclosed-by=`	Designates surrounding character(s) in returned fields for the data output files created by `-T`.

Continued

Argument	Description
`--fields-optionally-enclosed-by=`	Designates surrounding character(s) in returned fields which consist of a non-numeric data type for the data output files created by `-T`.
`--fields-escaped-by=`	Designates escape character(s) in returned fields for the data output files created by `-T`.
`--lines-terminated-by=`	Designates character(s) for end of line datatype for the data output files created by `-T`. Defaults to newline (`\n`).
`-w, --where=`	Uses the following `WHERE` clause on all data to be returned.

mysqlshow

The `mysqlshow` application delivers table or database listings for a designated server.

Argument	Description
`-c, --character-sets-dir=`	Uses the following directory for specific character sets.
`-C, --compress`	Forces connection to use compression for data delivery.
`-h, --host=`	Connects to specified host. If none is given, localhost is assumed. The value given can be either an IP address, domain name or server alias.
`-i, --status`	Returns specific status information regarding each table in the designated db. If no db is passed, flag is ignored.
`-k, --keys`	Returns keys for designated tables.
`-p, --password=`	Uses a password to connect to the server. If no password is given, a prompt will be displayed requesting for the password to be entered.
`-P, --port=`	Designates a specific port that the connection to the MySQL database should use.
`-S, --socket=`	Uses the given socket file for connection to the server.
`-u, --user=`	Designates the username to connect to the MySQL database as. If none is given, current username is assumed.
`-v, --verbose`	Displays more verbose system error messages.
`-V, --version`	Displays the MySQL version number and exit.

A.2 Server-Administration Applications

The following applications control the function of the MySQL database. Many of them have been covered in more detail throughout the book.

mysqladmin

The `mysqladmin` application performs management functions on the server.

Argument	*Description*
`-?, --help`	Displays basic help information and description of command line arguments.
`-C, --compress`	Force connection to use compression for data delivery.
`--character-sets-dir`	Uses the given directory for all character sets.
`-E, --vertical`	Returns the requested output vertically.
`-f, --force`	Forces execution of the command regardless of errors returned. DROP DATABASE commands will be performed without a warning prompt.
`-h, --host`	Connects to specified host. If none is given, localhost is assumed. The value given can be either an IP address, domain name or server alias.
`-i, --sleep=`	Sleeps for the given number of seconds before repeating the given command. The option will continue to loop until the process is terminated.
`-p, --password=`	Uses a password to connect to the server. If no password is given, a prompt will be displayed requesting for the password to be entered.
`-P, --port=`	Designates a specific port that the connection to the MySQL database should use.
`-r, --relative`	In combination with `-i, --sleep=`, shows the difference between the current data returned and the previous set.
`-s, --silent`	Prevents the return of any standard output messages, though error messages are still returned.
`-S, --socket`	Uses the given socket file for connection to the server.
`-u, --user=`	Designates the username to connect to the MySQL database as. If none is given, current username is assumed.

Continued

Argument	***Description***
`-v, --verbose`	Displays more verbose system error messages.
`-V, --version`	Displays the MySQL version number and exit.
`-w, --wait=`	Retries the command the given number of times if the server connection is unavailable.

Command	***Description***
`create [db]`	Creates new database named `[db]`.
`drop [db]`	Drops database named `[db]`.
`extended-status`	Delivers an extended status message from the daemon.
`flush-hosts`	Deletes all hosts that the system has cached.
`flush-logs`	Deletes all logs.
`flush-status`	Deletes all status variables on the server.
`flush-tables`	Flushes all tables in designated database.
`flush-threads`	Deletes the current thread cache.
`flush-privileges`	Reloads internal user privilege tables.
`kill [id]`	Stops a particular MySQL process.
`password [new password]`	Changes the current password to the given password.
`ping`	Checks to be sure the MySQL process is up and running.
`processlist`	Returns a listing of all current threads active on the server.
`reload`	Reloads all internal MySQL tables.
`refresh`	Flushes all internal tables and restart logging.
`shutdown`	Shuts down the MySQL server.
`status`	Returns the current system status for the server.
`start-slave`	Starts the slave.
`stop-slave`	Stops the slave.
`variables`	Returns all of the available variables.
`version`	Returns MySQL version for selected server.

mysqlcheck

The mysqlcheck application performs verification, repair, analysis, and optimization of MySQL databases, tables, and data.

Argument	*Description*
-?, --help	Displays basic help information and description of command line arguments.
-#, --debug=	Creates debugging log file to given file name.
-1, --all-in-1	Combines all table queries into one query upon the database.
-a, --analyze	Analyzes the given tables.
-A, --all-databases	Returns data from all databases contained on the MySQL server.
--auto-repair	Automatically repair any damaged tables found.
-B, --databases	Returns data from the following databases.
--character-sets-dir=	Uses the following directory for specific character sets.
-c, --check	Checks the given table for errors, this flag does not designate the process to repair errors it finds.
-C, --check-only-changed	Checks only the tables that have changed since the last check on the table was performed. Additionally check all tables that return to be improperly closed.
--compress	Forces connection to use compression for data delivery.
-F, --fast	Checks only tables that return to be improperly closed.
-f, --force	Forces execution of the command regardless of errors returned.
-e, --extended	Performs exhaustive checks upon the table structures. Use this flag with caution.
-h, --host=	Connects to specified host. If none is given, localhost is assumed. The value given can be either an IP address, domain name or server alias.
-m, --medium-check	Checks for most common errors. This process is not as thorough, however will catch nearly all errors.
-o, --optimize	Optimizes tables during action.

Continued

Argument	*Description*
`-p, --password`	Uses a password to connect to the server. If no password is given, a prompt will be displayed requesting for the password to be entered.
`-P, --port=`	Designates a specific port that the connection to the MySQL database should use.
`-q, --quick`	Skips less important checks.
`-r, --repair`	Repairs any problems found during process of databases and tables.
`-s, --silent`	Prevents the return of any standard output messages, though error messages are still returned.
`-S, --socket=`	Uses the given socket file for connection to the server.
`--tables`	Overrides the `-B, --databases` flag.
`-u, --user=`	Designates the username to connect to the MySQL database as. If none is given, current username is assumed.
`-v, --verbose`	Displays more verbose system error messages.
`-V, --version`	Displays the MySQL version number and exit.

mysqlimport

The `mysqlimport` application provides a command-line mechanism for importing data to the MySQL database directly from a preformatted text file.

Argument	*Description*
`-?, --help`	Displays basic help information and description of command line arguments.
`-#, --debug=`	Creates debugging log file to given file name.
`-c, --columns=`	Uses the given list of columns for creation of the LOAD DATA INFILE declaration. List format should be comma separated with no spaces.
`-C, --compress`	Forces connection to use compression for data delivery.
`-d, --delete`	Removes all data from affected tables prior to processing the import.
`-f, --force`	Forces execution of the command regardless of errors returned.
`--fields-terminated-by=`	Designates a delimiter for the data received from the import file. Defaults to tab.

Argument	*Description*
`--fields-enclosed-by=`	Designates surrounding character(s) in returned fields for the data received from the import file.
`--fields-optionally-enclosed-by=`	Checks the data received from the import file; designates those surrounding character(s) in returned fields which are of a non-numeric datatype.
`--fields-escaped-by=`	Designates escape character(s) in returned fields for the data received from the import file.
`-h, --host=`	Connects to specified host. If none is given, localhost is assumed. The value given can be either an IP address, domain name or server alias.
`-i, --ignore`	If importing data into a table with preexisting rows, skips importing data from rows that have matching keys.
`-l, --lock-tables`	Locks all affected tables prior to data import. This function prevents other processes from modifying data during import.
`-L, --local`	Takes datafile to use for import from localhost.
`--lines-terminated-by=`	Designates character(s) for the end-of-line data type for the data received from the import file. Defaults to newline (\n).
`--low-priority`	Utilizes `LOW_PRIORITY` syntax for query string used for `INSERT`.
`-p, --password`	Uses password to connect to database. If no password is given, a prompt will be displayed requesting for the password to be entered.
`-P, --port=`	Designates a specific port that the connection to the MySQL database should use.
`-r, --replace`	If importing data into a table with preexisting rows, forces replacement of existing data in rows that have matching keys.
`-s, --silent`	Prevents the return of any standard output messages, though error messages are still returned.
`-S, --socket=`	Uses the given socket file for connection to the server.
`-u, --user=`	Designates the username to connect to the MySQL database as. If none is given, current username is assumed.
`-v, --verbose`	Displays more verbose system error messages.
`-V, --version`	Displays the MySQL version number and exit.

mysqltest

The `mysqltest` application provides command-line access to the MySQL database testing scripts that are provided with non-package distributions.

Argument	Description
`-?, --help`	Displays basic help information and description of command line arguments.
`-D, --database=`	Uses the given database for testing with the test script.
`-h, --host=`	Connects to specified host. If none is given, localhost is assumed. The value given can be either an IP address, domain name or server alias.
`-p, --password=`	Uses password to connect to server. If no password is given, a prompt will be displayed requesting for the password to be entered.
`-P, --port=`	Designates a specific port that the connection to the MySQL database should use.
`-q, --quiet, --silent`	Prevents the return of any standard output, though error messages are still returned.
`-r, --record`	Record output from testing script into the designated result-file.
`-R, --result-file=`	Uses the given file for recording results from the testing script. Must be used with `-r, --record`.
`-S, --socket=`	Uses the given socket file for connection to the server.
`-t, --tmpdir=`	Uses the given directory for storage of the socket file.
`-T, --sleep=`	Sleeps for the number of seconds given when the testing script calls a `sleep` request.
`-u, --user=`	Designates the username to connect to the MySQL database as. If none is given, current username is assumed.
`-v, --verbose`	Displays more verbose system error messages.
`-V, --version`	Displays the MySQL version number and then exits.

A.3 The mysqld Server Daemon

The `mysqld` application — usually considered the server for MySQL — controls the process of the MySQL database.

Argument	*Description*
-?, --help	Displays basic help information and descriptions of command-line arguments.
--ansi	Forces any ALTER syntax to use the ANSI SQL standard.
-b, --basedir=	Identifies the given path as the path to the MySQL installation directory.
--bdb-home=	Identifies the given path as leading to the directory for the Berkeley DB.
--bdb-lock-detect=	Defines the Berkeley DB lock to detect as one of the following: DEFAULT OLDEST RANDOM YOUNGEST Additionally the number of seconds for the lock detect can be given.
--bdb-logdir=	Identifies the given path as the one leading to the Berkeley DB log files.
--bdb-no-sync	Disables synchronous flushing of the system logs.
--bdb-no-recover	Disables recovery of Berkeley DB table upon start.
--bdb-shared-data	Upon startup, allows the Berkeley DB to maintain multiple processes.
--bdb-tmpdir=	Identifies the given path as that leading to the system temp file.
--big-tables	Saves all temporary result sets to a temp file.
--bind-address=	Identifies the given address as the IP that the server is bound to.
--bootstrap	This option is utilized for the MySQL installation.
--character-sets-dir=	Identifies the given path as leading to the directory that houses character sets.
--chroot=	Identifies the given path as leading to the directory in which MySQL will be chroot jailed.
--core-file	Produces a core-dump file on SIGSEGV signal.
--default-character-set=	Identifies the given id as the default character set.

Continued

Argument	Description
--default-table-type=	Identifies the given table name as the default table type.
--delay-key-write-for-all-tables	Disables key buffer flushing between writes for MyISAM tables.
--enable-locking	Enables the server to perform system locking.
--flush	Writes the contents of tables to disk after SQL commands.
-h, --datadir=	Identifies the given path as that of the database root.
--init-file=	Upon startup, executes the following SQL commands from the given file path.
-l, --log=	Enables system logging to given file name.
-L, --language=	Returns error messages to the client in the given language. Can be given as a path.
--log-bin=	Identifies the given path to the file as the one to used for binary logging.
--log-bin-index=	Identifies the given path as the one to the file holding the index of binary log files.
--log-update=	Identifies the given path as the one to the file descriptor used for incrementally updated log files that will be sequentially rotated.
--log-isam=	Identifies the given path as the one to the file used to log all MyISAM changes.
--log-long-format	Utilizes more verbose logging.
--low-priority-updates	Gives SELECT queries higher priority than INSERT, UPDATE, and DELETE queries.
--log-slow-queries=	Keeps the given path to the log file for slow queries on the DB.
--memlock	Locks mysqld into system memory.
--myisam-recover=	Executes the given MyISAM recovery command. Options are DEFAULT, BACKUP or FORCE.
-n, --new	Utilizes any new, potentially unstable functionality included with the distribution.
-o, --old-protocol	Utilizes the older 3.20.x MySQL protocol.
-O, --set-variable var=option	Assigns the given option value to the ENV variable given as var.
-P, --port=	Designates a specific port that the client connection to the MySQL database should use.

Argument	Description
-Sg, --skip-grant-tables	Starts the server without using GRANT tables. This will give all users access to all tables, including the mysql system db tables.
--safe-mode	During startup, disables certain optimizations for the system. This option should only be used for system testing.
--safe-show-database	In the MySQL CLI, disallows viewing of databases to which the user does not have access.
--safe-user-create	Disallows any user attempt to create new system accounts by using the `GRANT` command.
--skip-concurrent-insert	Disables concurrent inserts using MyISAM.
--skip-delay-key-write	Ignores the action if the DELAY_KEY_WRITE option is defined in table create syntax.
--skip-host-cache	Prevents the caching of host domain names.
--skip-locking	Disable system locking.
--skip-name-resolve	Disables IP name resolution to full domain names.
--skip-networking	Disables TCP/IP connections to the server.
--skip-new	Disables any new, potentially unstable functionality included with the distribution.
--skip-stack-trace	Disables the display of a stack trace upon server failure.
--skip-show-database	Disables usage of the SHOW DATABASE command.
--skip-thread-priority	All threads will have the same priority to the system process.
--socket=	Uses the given socket file for connection to the server.
-t, --tmpdir=	Given path is the directory used for temporary system files.
--sql-mode=	Activates the following mode options, multiples must be comma separated with no spaces. REAL_AS_FLOAT PIPES_AS_CONCAT ANSI_QUOTES IGNORE_SPACE SERIALIZE ONLY_FULL_GROUP_BY

Continued

Argument	*Description*
`--skip-bdb`	Skips the system usage of the Berkeley DB.
`--transaction-isolation`	Utilizes the transaction isolation level at default.
`--temp-pool`	Utilizes multiple temp files.
`-u, --user=`	Given username will be the user account as which the process is run.
`-v, --version`	Displays the MySQL version number and exit.
`-W, --warnings`	Returns verbose messages to the system log file.

✦ ✦ ✦

APPENDIX B

Language Reference

This Appendix examines the Data Definition Language (DDL) and Data Markup Language (DML) SQL statements for MySQL. (Appendix C examines the numerous functions used in `SELECT` statements.)

B.1 Data Definition Language and Data Markup Language

This section lists and describes various DDL and DML statements.

ALTER TABLE

```
ALTER [IGNORE] TABLE table_name
alter_definition
```

The `ALTER TABLE` command changes the state of a preexisting table. Including the `IGNORE` option allows changes that affect primary keys to be overwritten or deleted. Without the `IGNORE` option, the operation indicates an error and rolls back to the prior status of the table.

alter_definition	**Description**
ADD *create_definition* [FIRST or AFTER *column_name*]	The first version of the ADD syntax allows specific placement of an appended column. If no modifier is specified, the appended column will become last. The FIRST modifier will append before all columns. The AFTER modifier will insert after the given *column_name*.
ADD (*create_definition*, *create_definition*, ...)	The second version of the ADD syntax allows the passing of multiple *create_definition* to append multiple columns (in sequence) to the current table structure.
ADD INDEX [*index_name*] *index_column_name* (, *index_column_name*, ...)	The ADD INDEX alter type allows creation of a new table index given by the name *index_name*. The index can be made up of one or multiple column entities.
ADD PRIMARY KEY *index_column_name* (, *index_column_name*, ...)	The ADD PRIMARY KEY type will create a new primary key for the designated table. If there is currently a primary key on the table, it will be overridden.
ADD UNIQUE [*index_name*] *index_column_name* (, *index_column_name*, ...)	The ADD UNIQUE type will add a new unique index to the table.
ADD FULLTEXT [*index_name*] *index_column_name* (, *index_column name*, ...)	The ADD FULLTEXT option will add a new FULLTEXT index to the table. This allows use of MATCH ... AGAINST syntax in the definition of where clauses.
ADD [CONSTRAINT *const_symbol*] FOREIGN KEY *index_name* *index_column_name* (, *index_column_name*, ...) [*reference_definition*]	The ADD FOREIGN KEY type is included purely for ANSI SQL92 compatibility. This call performs no action.
ALTER *column_name* { DROP DEFAULT or SET DEFAULT *literal*}	The ALTER type allows modification of an existing column in a table. The command takes on either the DROP or SET options for removing or changing the given column_name to the new literal type.
CHANGE *old_column_name* *create_syntax* [FIRST or AFTER *column_name*]	The CHANGE type allows complete modification of a column given by *old_column_name*. The new column position can be created with the FIRST or AFTER options.
MODIFY *create_syntax* [FIRST or AFTER *column_name*]	The MODIFY type will change the definition of a given column but will keep the name for the column. The new column position can be designated by including either the FIRST or AFTER options.

alter_definition	*Description*
DROP *column_name*	The DROP option will remove the entered *column_name* from the designated table.
DROP PRIMARY KEY	Removes (drops) the PRIMARY KEY for the designated table. If no PRIMARY KEY exists, the first UNIQUE index for the table is dropped.
DROP INDEX *index_name*	Removes (drops) the given *index_name* from the table.
DISABLE KEYS	The DISABLE KEYS type forces MySQL to omit updating any indices that are not unique in the MyISAM table.
ENABLE KEYS	The ENABLE KEYS type recreates missing keys upon a table.
RENAME *new_table_name*	The RENAME option renames the table to a given *new_table_name*.
ORDER BY *column_name*	The ORDER BY option re-sorts the given table by the designated column_name.

CREATE DATABASE

```
CREATE DATABASE [IF NOT EXISTS] database_name
```

The CREATE DATABASE command adds a database to the MySQL server. If the If NOT EXISTS condition is specified, and a database with the same name is present the command will return an error, and no changes to the server will occur.

CREATE TABLE

```
CREATE [TEMPORARY] TABLE [IF NOT EXISTS] table_name
[table_definition]
[select_statement]
```

The CREATE TABLE command creates a new table in the database to which you are presently connected. If you are not connected to a database, the process indicates an error and no table is created.

DESCRIBE

```
DESCRIBE table_name [column_name]
```

The DESCRIBE command returns the create syntax for the table given in table_name. Additionally a specific column given as *column_name* can be entered to limit the CREATE listing.

DELETE FROM

```
DELETE [LOW PRIORITY or QUICK] FROM table_name
[WHERE where_definition]
[ORDER BY order_definition]
[LIMIT row_value]
```

The `DELETE FROM` command removes data from *`table_name`*. If the `LOW PRIORITY` argument is specified, the delete process waits until there is no client access to the table. If the `QUICK` argument is specified, there will be no merging of table leaves during the process. `DELETE` commands with no `WHERE` arguments delete all data housed in the given table. The `ORDER BY` clause can be issued in conjunction with the `LIMIT` clause to remove a certain number of records according to their order within the table.

EXPLAIN SELECT

```
EXPLAIN SELECT select_definition
```

The `EXPLAIN SELECT` command returns information on how MySQL will process the given *`select_definition`*. The `EXPLAIN` command determines the need for optimizations in a table's `CREATE` syntax.

HANDLER

```
HANDLER table_name handler_option
```

The `HANDLER` command is utilized as a fast mechanism for returning table data. The `HANDLER` command returns results much faster than the `SELECT` command due to the SQL Optimizer being excluded. During the execution of the command no table locking occurs, thus allowing other connections to perform updates to table data during the process.

handler_option	**Description**
`OPEN [AS alias]`	The `OPEN` option is the first step in preparing the `HANDLER` command. Opening the table, the option prepares all commands for the `READ` members listed in this table.
`READ index { = or >= or <= or < } ( value, value, ... ) [WHERE where_definition] [LIMIT row_limit]`	This `READ` option allows a comparison of the index to a list of values. You can also designate a comparison by using the *`where_definition`* to limit the rows returned. The `READ` command returns 1 row by default (unless the `LIMIT` option designates otherwise).

handler_option	**Description**
READ *index* { FIRST or LAST or NEXT or PREV } [WHERE *where_definition*] [LIMIT *row_limit*]	This READ option reads data in the order of the index. The return can be limited by a WHERE clause. The READ command returns 1 row by default (unless the LIMIT option designates otherwise).
READ { FIRST or NEXT } [WHERE *where_definition*] [LIMIT *row_limit*]	This READ option is used to read the raw table data in natural order as stored in the table. An optional *where_definition* can also be applied to this option to limit the data returned. The READ command returns 1 row by default (unless the LIMIT option designates otherwise).
CLOSE	The CLOSE command terminates the current thread. Issue this closing command at the conclusion of the HANDLER subsets.

INSERT INTO

```
INSERT [LOW_PRIORITY or DELAYED] [IGNORE] INTO table_name
(column_list) VALUES (value_list)
```

The INSERT INTO command is the basic mechanism for inserting data into a table. If the LOW PRIORITY argument is specified, the insert will be delayed until there is no client access to the designated table. If the DELAYED argument is specified, clients are allowed to continue as the inserts are bundled for one mass insert. The DELAYED option may improve speed for large inserts. If the IGNORE argument is specified, inserts that would duplicate the insertion of a primary key are ignored. Without the IGNORE option (given a duplicate primary key), the insert terminates.

SELECT

```
SELECT [SQL_SMALL_RESULT]
[SQL_BIG_RESULT]
[SQL_BUFFER_RESULT]
[SQL_CACHE or SQL_NO_CACHE]
[SQL_CALC_FOUND_ROWS]
[STRAIGHT_JOIN]
[HIGH_PRIORITY]
[DISTINCT or DISTINCTROW or ALL] select_definition
   [INTO {OUTFILE or DUMPFILE} file_name export_options]
   [FROM table_definition
      [WHERE where_definition]
      [GROUP BY {unsigned_integer or column_name or formula}]
      [HAVING where_definition]
      [ORDER BY {unsigned_integer or column_name or formula}]
      [LIMIT {offset_value,} row_value]
      [PROCEDURE procedure_name]
      [FOR UPDATE or LOCK IN SHARE MODE]
```

The SELECT command allows access to the data in a given table, and can also select data in several different tables by using the syntax of the JOIN command.

SELECT arguments

The arguments of the SELECT command perform specialized tasks:

- The SQL_SMALL_RESULT argument will optimize the data returned for a small query set.
- SQL_BIG_RESULT optimizes the data for a large query set, tending toward large data returns. Additionally, MySQL will write out temporary tables to disk to minimize memory usage.
- SQL_BUFFER_RESULT causes MySQL to place the results in a temporary table.

Tip Locked tables may be released faster by using the SQL_BUFFER_RESULT option.

- SQL_CACHE and SQL_NO_CACHE modifiers regulate the usage of the MySQL query cache. Using the cache speeds up queries for identical data.
- SQL_CALC_FOUND_ROWS instructs MySQL to calculate the number of rows returned from the given query. This data can by retrieved by using the FoundRows() definition of SELECT.
- STRAIGHT_JOIN is a clause that instructs the MySQL optimizer to join the tables in the order listed in the WHERE definition.
- HIGH_PRIORITY is a clause that forces the SELECT operation to precede any otherwise-simultaneous updates to the table.
- DISTINCT, DISTINCTROW, and ALL are clauses that (respectively) either limit the data to unique sets or show all data in a given query.

Using SELECT with JOIN syntax

The SELECT command offers the following options to control table joins. The JOIN syntax can be created by the use of 3 elements. The *table_definition*, *table_reference*, and *join_condition* make up all options to control table joins. The standard sequence looks like this:

1. *table_definition* allows the use of JOIN syntax in the SELECT statement.

   Valid JOIN clauses are as follows:

   table_reference, table_reference

   table_reference [CROSS] JOIN *table_reference*

   table_reference INNER JOIN *table_reference join_condition*

   table_reference STRAIGHT_JOIN *table_reference*

   table_reference LEFT [OUTER] JOIN *table_reference*
       join_condition

```
table_reference LEFT [OUTER] JOIN table_reference
```

```
table_reference NATURAL [LEFT [OUTER]] JOIN table_reference
```

```
{ oj table_reference LEFT OUTER JOIN table_reference ON
    conditional_expr }
```

```
table_reference RIGHT [OUTER] JOIN table_reference
    join_condition
```

```
table_reference RIGHT [OUTER] JOIN table_reference
```

```
table_reference NATURAL [RIGHT [OUTER]] JOIN table_reference
```

2. The *table_reference* syntax is then formed as follows:

```
table_name [[AS] alias]
[USE INDEX (key_list)]
[IGNORE INDEX (key_list)]
```

3. The *join_condition* syntax is then formed as follows:

```
ON conditional_expr | USING (column_list)
```

SHOW TABLES

```
SHOW [OPEN] TABLES [FROM database_name] [LIKE
database_wildcard]
```

The `SHOW TABLES` command is a member of the `SHOW` command group. This command is used to generate a listing of all tables in the database given as *database_name*; this will also default to the currently connected database if none is specified. Including `LIKE`—along with a string containing a wildcard—limits the returned listing to specified tables.

UNION

```
SELECT select_clause UNION [ALL] SELECT select_clause
[UNION SELECT select_clause ...]
```

The `UNION` command allows combinations of multiple `SELECT` statements into a single return. In the *select_clause* syntax, only the last statement may contain a declared `ORDER BY` or `INTO OUTFILE` modifier. Identical row data can be returned unless the `ALL` option is specified.

UPDATE

```
UPDATE [LOW_PRIORITY] [IGNORE] table_name
SET column1=value1 [, column2=value2, ...]
[WHERE where_definition]
[LIMIT row_value]
```

The UPDATE command allows modification of data currently housed in a table. Including the LOW_PRIORITY option will force the UPDATE to be delayed until there is no further client access to the affected table. The IGNORE option overrides errors if multiple primary keys are generated by the UPDATE command. UPDATE commands with no WHERE clause will modify all columns that are given a value. The LIMIT clause can also be used to restrict the UPDATE to a specified number of rows given by *row_value*.

B.2. Administrative Commands

The administrative commands in MySQL allow access to control and configure the internals of the MySQL database.

ANALYZE TABLE

```
ANALYZE TABLE table_name [, table_name]
```

The ANALYZE TABLE command creates a key distribution listing for the designated table(s), which is utilized when performing a join on the table. During the process of the command, the affected tables are read locked. The process of analyzing a table provides information to MySQL used in determining the order in which tables should be joined based on the key distribution.

FLUSH

```
FLUSH flush_option [, flush_option, ...]
```

The FLUSH command is used to force a reload of internal MySQL data. The option given determines what portions of the internal cache are reloaded within the server.

flush_option	**Description**
HOSTS	Reloads the domain to IP translations created when a user from a particular host given by a domain name connects to the database. This function should be used if a connection is denied due to a particular hostname changing its cached IP address to domain record.
DES_KEY_FILE	Reloads the DES file specified during the startup of the MySQL server.

flush_option	**Description**
LOGS	Closes all system log files and then reopens them. If log has been specified for an update, the command increments the filename(s) for the existing logs, and then starts a new log file for the current process. This option is equivalent to giving the SIGHUP signal to the daemon.
PRIVILEGES	Reloads the grant tables that define access rights within the server.
TABLE *table_name*	Flushes only the specified table given by *table_name*.
TABLES [*table_name*, *table_name*]	Flushes only the specified tables given by *table_name*.
TABLES WITH READ LOCK	Closes all open tables and places a read lock on all tables. The database stays in that state until an UNLOCK TABLES command is issued to the server.
STATUS	Resets all status variables to zero.

KILL

```
KILL thread_id
```

The KILL command stops a connection to the database, identifying the prospective connection by its *thread_id*. Every client that accesses the database has a socket identified by a unique *thread_id* (which can be seen by issuing the SHOW PROCESSLIST command). Additionally, the mysqladmin PROCESSLIST command delivers a list of all threads, as covered in Appendix A (heading A.2).

The KILL command does not immediately kill a given process; instead, it issues a *kill flag* (an instruction to terminate at a specified time). The client's connection will only be terminated when the client checks for the issued kill flag.

To prevent processes from being killed in a state that could adversely affect the database, client checks are performed at different times that depend on the type of action occurring:

- ALTER TABLE commands check for the kill flag before the reading of a new block of data from the originating table.
- UPDATE, DELETE, SELECT, ORDER BY and GROUP BY check for the kill flag immediately after reading a block of data.
- UPDATE and DELETE threads check for the kill flag after a row modification.

OPTIMIZE TABLE

```
OPTIMIZE TABLE table_name [, table_name, ...]
```

The OPTIMIZE TABLE command is used when a table's data has been significantly changed. If significant quantities of data are either updated or deleted from the given table(s), many records may become unusable. Issuing this command defragments the datafiles used, reclaiming the space still allocated to the removed records.

When the command is issued upon the designated tables, the process checks for deleted or split rows, repairs them if they exist, re-sorts all index pages, and updates all statistics.

RESET

```
RESET reset_option [, reset_option, ...]
```

The RESET command clears the logs and queries the caches used in the MySQL database. The options in the RESET command can additionally be performed by the various FLUSH commands.

Reset_option	**Description**
MASTER	Deletes all binary logs in the index file and then resets the binlog file to its empty state.
SLAVE	Forces the slave to forget the current replication position being used in the master log file.
QUERY_CACHE	Removes all current queries from the query cache.

SHOW

```
SHOW show_option
```

The SHOW command returns data specific to a particular system, database, or table.

Show_option	**Description**
CREATE TABLE *table_name*	Returns the full CREATE syntax for the designated table.
COLUMNS FROM *table_name*	Returns a listing of all columns and their CREATE values. This option is equivalent to the DESCRIBE command.

Show_option	**Description**
DATABASES	Returns a listing of all databases available to the connected user.
GRANTS FOR *username@hostname*	Returns the syntax of the GRANT command to recreate the permissions currently assigned to the given *username* by the designated *hostname*.
INDEX FROM *table_name*	Returns a listing of all index data from the given table.
LOGS	Returns the filename, file type, and status of the logfiles currently active in the system.
MASTER LOGS	Returns system status for the binlog files.
MASTER STATUS	Returns the filename, position, and status of the active binlog files.
PROCESSLIST	Returns a listing of all current system processes—including the command issued, the host doing the accessing, the database connected to, the time, and the system state.
SLAVE STATUS	Returns system information on all connected slave servers.
STATUS	Returns a complete listing of current internal system status.
TABLE STATUS	Returns internal status information on all tables in the database to which you are currently and actively connected.
TABLES	Returns an exclusive list of all tables contained in the active database.
VARIABLES	Returns a listing of all system variables currently present.

B.3 Backup / Recovery Commands

The following sections describe the backup and disaster-recovery commands used in MySQL.

BACKUP TABLE

```
BACKUP TABLE table_name [, table_name, ...] TO file_path
```

The BACKUP TABLE command allows current state of the designated tablename(s) to be written to file. This file can then be used (in conjunction with the RESTORE TABLE command) to return a table to its initial state at the time the file was created.

CHECK TABLE

```
CHECK TABLE table_name [, table_name, ...]
[check_option [, check_option, ...]]
```

The CHECK TABLE command is used to verify the condition of given tablename(s) for inconsistencies. The *check_option* types determine how thorough the checks to be performed will be. The last piece of data returned on the verified table will be Msg_type *value*. The returned *value* should be 'OK' or 'Not Checked' (depending on the state of the table). For any other value, use a REPAIR TABLE command.

Check_option	**Description**
CHANGED	Checks only the tables modified since the last check, and all tables not closed properly in the last session.
EXTENDED	Performs a complete check on designated tables, including a complete key lookup for all keys in every row of the given *table_name*.
FAST	Limits its checks to the tables not properly closed.
MEDIUM	Checks all rows to ensure that deleted links are actually and correctly deleted. Additionally, generates a key checksum and checks it against current values.
QUICK	Performs a minimal verification of the table, without verifying row data.

REPAIR TABLE

```
REPAIR TABLE table_name [, table_name, ...] [QUICK] [EXTENDED]
```

The REPAIR TABLE command fixes a damaged or corrupted table, generally after a CHECK TABLE command returns a bad status for the table. If the QUICK option is specified the repair will only affect the index tree. With the EXTENDED option, the index will be recreated row by row. The last piece of data returned on the repaired table will be Msg_type *value*. The returned *value* should be 'OK'. Any other value indicates that the REPAIR TABLE command has failed.

RESTORE TABLE

```
RESTORE TABLE table_name [, table_name, ...] FROM file_path
```

The `RESTORE TABLE` command is used to recreate tables from a file generated by the `BACKUP TABLE` command—and only from such a file. If executed upon existing tables, the `RESTORE TABLE` command returns an error message.

B.4. User-Account Commands

This section lists and describes the MySQL user-account commands. Both the `GRANT` and `REVOKE` commands use the same *priv_type* to designate specific access rights within the database. Updated user data doesn't take effect on the system until a `FLUSH PRIVILEGES` command is issued.

GRANT

```
GRANT priv_type [column_list] [, priv_type [column_list] ...]
ON {table_name or * or database_name.* or *.*}
TO user_name [IDENTIFIED BY [PASSWORD] password]
[REQUIRE
   [{SSL or X509}]
   [CIPHER cipher_type [AND]]
   [ISSUER issuer_type [AND]]
   [SUBJECT subject_type]]
[WITH GRANT OPTION]
```

The `GRANT` command is used to designate a specific access level for a given username. The `GRANT` command can designate privileges to a designated *column_list*, *table_name*, or *database_name*, or grant privileges globally.

Tip

Using a `GRANT` command for a currently nonexistent user account creates that user on the server. The syntax for the username can be either *name* or *name@host*.

REVOKE

```
REVOKE priv_type [column_list] [, priv_type [column_list] ...]
ON ON {table_name or * or database_name.* or *.*}
FROM username [, user_name, ...]
```

The REVOKE command performs the opposite action to that of the GRANT command, removing access rights on the server for the designated user. The REVOKE command can also designate *colunn_list*, *table_name*, or *database_name* — or be used globally.

priv_type	**Description**
ALL PRIVILEGES	Affects all access types.
ALTER	Gives the user access to alter tables within the access of the user.
CREATE	Allows the creation of tables.
DELETE	Allows removal of row data in tables that can be accessed.
DROP	Allows the removal of existing tables.
FILE	Allows access to external files for system backup and restoration.
INDEX	Allows the creation of table indexes.
INSERT	Places data within tables a user may access.
PROCESS	Gives access to the internal listing of current server processes.
RELOAD	Gives the user access to the FLUSH command.
SELECT	Gives the user access to read data from accessible tables.
SHUTDOWN	Terminates the MySQL service.
UPDATE	Allows the user to modify current table data.
USAGE	Gives the user access to system-usage statistics.

✦ ✦ ✦

APPENDIX C

Function and Operator Reference

C.1. MySQL Operators

Comparing the elements in the `where_clause` for MySQL commands requires operators to determine what comparison to make between objects. Operators provide the mechanism for case-based testing between objects.

Comparison operators

The *comparison operators* perform the base logic needed to compare arguments. The following operators function on both strings and numbers. All comparison operators return a True (1), False (0) or `NULL` value. If a string is compared to a number, the string is converted to a floating-point number.

Operator	Description
=	Equal-to operator.
!=, <>	Not-equal-to operator.
>	Greater-than operator.
>=	Greater-than-or-equal-to operator.
<	Less-than operator.
<=	Less-than-or-equal-to operator.
<=>	Equal-to operator for NULL-safe equations. This operator returns True (1) for operations based on NULL <=> NULL.

Flow-control operators

The *flow-control operators* allow sequential, comparison-based conditional clauses.

Operator	Description
CASE *base* WHEN [*value1*] THEN *return1* [WHEN [*value2*] THEN *return2* ...] [ELSE *alt_return*] END	This iteration of the CASE operator performs a series of checks between the base value and the return series, the returned value being the first to match values. If no values match the base and the ELSE option is included, the *alt_return* value is returned by the function. The END syntax must be included in all CASE operations.
CASE WHEN *conditional* THEN *result1* [WHEN [*conditional*] THEN *return1* ...] [ELSE *return2*] END	The second iteration of the CASE operator allows conditional equations to determine the result to be returned by the function. If none of the given values match the base and the ELSE option is included, the *alt_return* value is returned. The END syntax must be included in all CASE operations.
IF(*conditional*, *value1*, *value2*)	The IF operator returns either *value1* if *conditional* is True or *value2* if *conditional* is False.
IFNULL(*value1*, *value2*)	The IFNULL operator returns *value1* if it is not NULL; if *value1* is NULL, then *value2* is returned.
NULLIF(*value1*, *value2*)	The NULLIF operator returns NULL if *value1* = *value2*, otherwise *value1* is returned.

Logical operators

The *logical operators* perform base binary comparisons. For all comparison operations, the return value is one of three values: True (1), False (0), or NULL.

Operator	Description
NOT, !	The NOT operator is for base-logical negation. The return value is always 0 unless the base value is 0 (in which case the return value is 1). The only exception is the case of NOT NULL: The negation of the NULL value returns NULL.
OR, ||	The OR operator produces the inclusive -OR logical function. The return value is 1 if either comparator of the statement is 1.
AND, &&	The AND operator produces the basic AND logical function. The return value for the operation is 1 only if both comparators are 1. In all other cases, the operation returns 0.

Statement operators

The *statement operators* expand the options for comparative operations. The NOT operator can be applied to negate the expression formed by the Statement operators. All String operators that are compared perform case-insensitive pattern-matching. Using the BINARY keyword allows case-sensitive operation.

Operator	Description
expression BETWEEN *min_value* AND *max_value*	The BETWEEN operator returns True (1) if the given expression has a value greater than or equal to the *min_value* and less than or equal to the *max_value*. Otherwise the operator returns False (0).
COALESCE(*value*, ...)	The COALESCE operator returns the first non-NULL value from the given list of values. If all given values in the list are NULL, then a NULL value is returned.
expression IN (*value*, ...)	The IN operator returns True (1) if the given expression is equal to any item that is given in the value list. If no value matches, the operator returns False (0).
INTERVAL(*base*, *value1*, *value2*, ...)	The INTERVAL operator returns the index of the first value that is greater than the base. The index of the series starts with a value of 0 being returned for a base greater than *value1*.
expression IS NULL	The IS NULL operator returns True (1) if the given *expression* is NULL. If the expression is not NULL, False (0) is returned.

String operators

The *string operators* are used on strings or on numbers to perform string-based comparisons. The NOT operator can be applied to negate the expression formed by the String operators. All String operators perform case-insensitive pattern matching. Using the BINARY keyword allows case-sensitive operation.

Operator	***Description***
LIKE '*wildcarded_string*'	The LIKE operator is for comparison operations based on the given *wildcarded_string*. The operation can be done upon both string and numeric datatypes. The *wildcarded_string* uses two characters to denote random character space. The '%' character denotes a variable length string consisting of any characters. The '_' character represents any single character.
REGEXP '*regular_expression*'	The REGEXP operator provides matching capacity for regular expressions. Unlike standard regular expressions, the REGEXP operator performs case-insensitive matches unless used in conjunction with the BINARY keyword.

C.2. MySQL Functions

Functions within MySQL allow the conversion of data from one form to another. These transformations expand the scope of information that can be obtained from the database.

Binary math functions

Binary math functions allow binary calculations upon decimal values. The calculations are done with 64 bits; any numeric value created larger than a BIGINT incurs rounding errors. Binary math functions cannot be performed on floating-point numbers. If a floating-point number is given to the function, an error is returned.

Function	***Description***
value1 & *value2*	The & function performs a bitwise AND between the binary equivalents of *value1* and *value2*.
value1 | *value2*	The | function performs a bitwise OR between the binary equivalents of *value1* and *value2*.

Function	***Description***
value1 << *value2*	The << function performs a bitwise shift to the left of all bits given as the 64-bit binary representation of *value1*. The shift moves the number of places designated by *value2*. A padding of 0 is applied to all places that are shifted out from the 64-bit binary value.
value1 >> *value2*	The >> function performs a bitwise shift to the right of all bits given as the 64-bit binary representation of *value1*. The shift moves the number of places designated by *value2*. A padding of 0 is applied to all places that are shifted out from the 64-bit binary value.
BIT_COUNT(*value*)	The BIT_COUNT function returns the number of digits required to represent a given integer in binary format.

Date functions

The *date functions* allow operations on the various types of date or time values.

Function	***Description***
CURDATE()	The CURDATE function returns the current date from the server on which MySQL is running. If used as a string CURDATE returns values in the 'YYYY-MM-DD' format. If used as a number, the date is returned in the YYYYMMMDD format.
CURTIME()	The CURTIME function returns the current time from the server on which MySQL is running. If used as a string, CURTIME returns values in the 'HH:MM:SS' format. If used as a number, the time is returned in the HHMMSS format.
DATE_ADD(*date*, INTERVAL *value date_type*)	The DATE_ADD function returns the given date incremented by the given value. The value may be any *date_type* value listed in the table below, and must follow its format.
DATE_FORMAT(*date*, *date_string_format*)	The DATE_FORMAT function returns the given date formatted to fit a particular date style. Valid *date_string_format* structures are listed in the table below.

Continued

Function	***Description***
DATE_SUB(*date*, INTERVAL *value date_type*)	The DATE_SUB function returns the given *date*, decremented by the given *value*. The given value may be *date_type* listed in the table below, and must follow its format.
DAYNAME(*date*)	The DAYNAME function returns the full day of the week string name for the given *date* value.
DAYOFMONTH(*date*)	The DAYOFMONTH function returns the day of the month as an integer for the given *date* value. The values returned range from 1 to 31.
DAYOFWEEK(*date*)	The DAYOFWEEK function returns a numeric representation of the weekday given by *date*. The values returned are 1 for Sunday through 7 for Saturday.
DAYOFYEAR(*date*)	The DAYOFYEAR function returns a numeric representation (an integer) of the current day in the calendar year. Values returned range from 1 to 366, depending on whether the current year is a leap year.
EXTRACT(*date_type* FROM date)	The EXTRACT function returns the portion of the given date specified by the date_type. The values for the *date_type* can be found in the table below.
FROM_DAYS(*value*)	The FROM_DAYS function returns the date, counting up from 0 B.C. The FROM_DAYS function should not be used with dates preceding the year 1582, due to the loss of calendar days caused by the advent of the Gregorian Calendar.
FROM_UNIXTIME(*stamp*), FROM_UNIXTIME(*stamp*, *date_string_format*)	The FROM_UNIXTIME function returns a date string based upon the given UNIX time stamp. If a *date_string_format* option is given the string is formatted by the given parameter. With no format option, the data returned is given as "YYYY-MM-DD HH:MM:SS" if referenced as a string. If used as a number, the return is formatted as YYYYMMDDHHMMSS.
HOUR(*time*)	The HOUR function returns the hour value in integer format from the given time string. Values returned range from 1 to 12.
MINUTE(*time*)	The MINUTE function returns the minute value in integer format from the given time string. The function returns values between 0 and 59.

Function	Description
MONTH(*date*)	The MONTH function returns the month value in integer format from the given time string. Values returned range from 1 to 12.
MONTHNAME(*date*)	The MONTHNAME function returns the full text-string representation of the month for the given date (January, February, March, . . .).
NOW()	The NOW function returns the current date and time. The data returned is given as "YYYY-MM-DD HH:MM:SS" if referenced as a string. If used as a number, the return format follows YYYYMMDDHHMMSS.
PERIOD_ADD(*date*, *months*)	The PERIOD_ADD function allows the addition of months to a given date. The date can be formatted either as YYMM or YYYYMM. Data is returned as YYYYMM.
PERIOD_DIFF (*date1*, *date2*)	The PERIOD_DIFF function calculates the number of months between two dates. The dates can be given in either the YYMM or YYYYMM formats. Data returned is in the YYYYMM format.
QUARTER(*date*)	The QUARTER function returns the quarter of the year given by the specified date. The function returns values between 1 and 4.
SECOND(*time*)	The SECOND function returns the second value from the given time string. Return values range from 0 to 59.
SEC_TO_TIME(*seconds*)	The SEC_TO_TIME function returns the time in the HH:MM:SS format from the given number of seconds.
SYSDATE()	The SYSDATE function returns the current date and time. The data returned is given as "YYYY-MM-DD HH:MM:SS" if referenced as a string. If used as a number, the return is formatted as YYYYMMDDHHMMSS.
TIME_FORMAT(*time*, *date_string_format*)	The TIME_FORMAT function returns the given time formatted to fit a particular date style. The function may only use the date format options used for time display. Use of the other options returns 0 or NULL. The *date_string_format* structures are listed in the table below.
TIME_TO_SEC(*time*)	The TIME_TO_SEC function returns the given time, converted to seconds.
TO_DAYS(*date*)	The TO_DAYS function returns the number of days associated with a given date, counting up from 0 A.D. The TO_DAYS function should not be used with dates preceding the year 1582, due to the loss of calendar days caused by the advent of the Gregorian Calendar.

Continued

Function	*Description*
UNIX_TIMESTAMP([*date*])	The UNIX_TIMESTAMP function is used to return the UNIX timestamp for Epoch time. (Epoch time is the number of seconds since 1970-01-01 00:00:00.) If the optional *date* is given, the stamp returned is for the particular date given. The date can be in the format of DATE, DATETIME, YYMMDD, or YYYYMMDD. With no date, the stamp returned shows the current system time.
WEEK(*date* [,*day_indicator*])	The WEEK function returns the integer value for the week of the given *date*. If the *day_indicator* option is included, the first day of the week can be specified as either Sunday (0) or Monday (1).
WEEKDAY(*date*)	The WEEKDAY function returns a numeric representation of the day for the week given by date. The values returned are 0 for Monday through 6 for Sunday.
YEAR(*date*)	The YEAR function returns the year portion of the given date. Return value is formatted as YYYY.
YEARWEEK(*date* [,*day_indicator*])	The YEARWEEK function returns the year and week for the given date. The data returned is in the format YYYYWW. If the *day_indicator* option includes the first day of the week, either Sunday (0) or Monday (1) can be specified.

date_type	*Value*
SECOND, MINUTE, HOUR, DAY, MONTH, YEAR	The listed *date_type* values can take any integer value as their internal representation.
MINUTE_SECOND	The MINUTE_SECOND value must be formatted as "MINUTES:SECONDS".
HOUR_MINUTE	The HOUR_MINUTE value must be formatted as "HOURS:MINUTES".
DAY_HOUR	The DAY_HOUR value must be formatted as "DAYS HOURS".
YEAR_MONTH	The YEAR_MONTH value must be formatted as "YEARS-MONTHS".
HOUR_SECOND	The HOUR_SECOND value must be formatted as "HOURS:MINUTES:SECONDS".
DAY_MINUTE	The DAY_MINUTE value must be formatted as "DAYS HOURS:MINUTES".
DAY_SECOND	The DAY_SECOND value must be formatted as "DAYS HOURS:MINUTES:SECONDS".

date_string_format	***Description***
%a	Displays the day of the week abbreviated as a three-letter string. (Sun, Mon, Tue, . . .)
%b	Displays the month abbreviated as a three-character string. (Jan, Feb, Mar, . . .)
%c	Displays the month as an integer with no zero padding. (1 . . . 12)
%D	Displays the day of the month with the English suffix. (1st, 2nd, 3rd, ...)
%d	Displays the day of the month as a two-digit integer. (1 . . . 12)
%e	Displays the day of month as an integer with no zero padding. (1 . . . 31)
%H	Displays the hour as a two-digit integer in military time format. (00 . . . 23)
%h	Displays the hour as a two-digit integer in the standard clock format. (01 . . . 12)
%I	Displays the hour as a two-digit integer in the standard clock format. (01 . . . 12)
%i	Displays the minutes as a two-digit integer. (00 . . . 59)
%j	Displays the day of year as a three-digit integer. (001 . . . 366)
%k	Displays the hour as an integer with no zero padding, in military time format. (0 . . . 23)
%l	Displays the hour as an integer with no zero padding, in the standard clock format. (1 . . . 12)
%M	Displays the month as its full text string. (January, February, March, . . .)
%m	Displays the month as a two-digit integer. (01 . . . 12)
%p	Displays either AM or PM, depending on the time of day.
%r	Displays the time in standard clock format (including AM or PM). All integer values are zero-padded.
%S	Displays the seconds as a two-digit integer (00 . . . 59).
%s	Displays the seconds as a two digit integer (00 . . . 59).
%T	Displays the time in standard military format. (00:00:00 . . . 23:59:59)
%U	Displays the week of the year in integer format, with no zero padding, where Sunday is the first day of the week (0 . . . 53).
%u	Displays the week of the year in integer format, with no zero padding, where Monday is the first day of the week (0 . . . 53).

Continued

date_string_format	*Description*
%V	Displays the week of the year in integer format, with no zero padding, where Sunday is the first day of the week. This is used in conjunction with %X.
%v	Displays the week of the year in integer format, with no zero padding, where Monday is the first day of the week. This is used in conjunction with %x.
%W	Displays the day of the week as its full text string (Monday, Tuesday, Wednesday, . . .).
%X	Displays the year designated by the first Sunday of the calendar year. This is used in conjunction with %V.
%x	Displays the year designated by the first Monday of the calendar year. This is used in conjunction with %v.
%Y	Displays the year as a four-digit integer.
%y	Displays the year as a two-digit integer.
%%	Displays a %.

Decimal math functions

The *decimal math* functions allow basic decimal procedures. If a string is given as either operand, most decimal math functions attempt to treat it as a decimal. A good example of this conversion is the expression (1apple + 2orange). The value returned from the Addition function would be 3.

Function	*Description*
+	Addition function operator.
-	Subtraction function operator.
*	Multiplication function operator.
/	Division function operator.
CEILING(*value*)	The CEILING function is used to round values to the nearest whole number above the given value.
DEGREES(*value*)	The DEGREES function returns the conversion of the given value from radians to degrees.
EXP(*value*)	The EXP function returns the value of e raised to the given value. The base of natural logs is represented by e in its notation.
FLOOR(*value*)	The FLOOR function is used to round values to the nearest whole number less than the given value.

Function	*Description*
GREATEST(*value1*, *value2*, ...)	The GREATEST function determines the largest entity in a list of values. In addition to comparing numbers, stings can be compared with the GREATEST function. The value for the largest item in the list is returned.
LEAST(*value1*, *value2*, ...)	The LEAST function being the inverse of the GREATEST function returns the value for the lowest value. The LEAST function can additionally take on string values.
LOG(*value*)	The LOG function returns the natural log of the given value.
LOG10(*value*)	The LOG10 function returns the base-10 logarithm of the given value.
MOD(*value1*, *value2*)	The MOD function returns the modulus of operation that divides the given *value1* by *value2*. The modulus is the remainder given after division.
PI()	The PI function takes on no values and returns the value for PI. Although the values are displayed with a precision of 5 digits, the system uses the precision of a double to perform its internal calculations.
POW(*value1*, *value2*)	The POW function is used for exponentiation. The data returned is given as *value1* raised to the power of *value2*.
RADIANS(*value*)	The RADIANS function converts a given value from degrees to radians.
RAND([*value*])	The RAND function returns a "random" number between 0 and 1. The function additionally can take a value as the seed for the number generation.
ROUND(*value1* [, *value2*])	The ROUND function is used to round the number given as *value1* to the nearest whole number. If the optional *value2* is given, the number is rounded to the specified number of decimal places.
SIGN(*value*)	The SIGN function is used to determine whether a given value is negative, positive, or zero. Values returned are –1, 1, or 0.
SQRT(*value*)	The SQRT function returns the square root of the given value. If a negative value is given, the function returns NULL.
TRUNCATE (*value1*, *value2*)	The TRUNCATE function is used to alter the precision of the given number *value1* that contains a decimal portion. The integer given for *value2* determines the number of places in the return value. If the given *value2* equals 0, the return value has no decimal, and no decimal point.

Select operators

The *select operators* are a specific subset used in addition to the GROUP BY syntax. Using these operators without a GROUP BY clause causes the system to return an error.

Operator	***Description***
AVG(*column_name*)	The AVG function returns the average value of the return set for the designated *column_name*.
BIT_OR(*column_name*)	The BIT_OR function performs a binary OR upon the designated *column_name* for all rows returned to the SELECT statement.
BIT_AND(*column_name*)	The BIT_AND function additionally performs a binary AND upon the designated *column_name*. The return value also encompasses all rows from the SELECT.
COUNT([DISTINCT] * or *column_name* [, *column_name*])	The COUNT function performs differently depending on the declaration. Purely the COUNT(*) and COUNT(*column_name*) versions return a count of all non-NULL values returned in a given column. The COUNT(*column_name*, ...) version returns a count of all non-NULL cells for the columns specified. The DISTINCT modifier can be applied to the function to force the data that is counted to be unique.
MAX(*column_name*)	The MAX function returns the largest value for a column based upon a given GROUP BY clause.
MIN(*column_name*)	The MIN function returns the smallest value for a column based upon a given GROUP BY clause.
STDDEV(*column_name*)	The STDDEV function produces the standard deviation for the given *column_name*.
SUM(*column_name*)	The SUM function returns the total of all values for a column, based on a given GROUP BY clause.

String functions

The *string functions* provide the capability to modify the format of text values.

Function	*Description*
`ASCII(string)`	The `ASCII` function returns the ASCII value for the first character in the given string. Any characters other than the leftmost is ignored.
`BIN(value)`	The `BIN` function returns the binary string representation of the integer given as value.
`BIT_LENGTH(string)`	The `BIT_LENGTH` function returns the number of bits required to represent the given string.
`CHAR(value1 [, value2 ...])`	The `CHAR` function returns a string made up of the ASCII representation of the decimal value list. Strings in numeric format are converted to a decimal value.
`CONCAT(string1, string2, ...)`	The `CONCAT` function returns a string created by appending all values in the string list.
`CONCAT_WS(separator, string1, string2, ...)`	The `CONCAT_WS` function much like the `CONCAT` function appends the given values. The string created has all elements of the list separated by the given `separator` value.
`CONV(value1, base1, base2)`	The `CONV` function converts a given value from one numeric base to another. The value given as `base1` is the current state; `base2` is the state the number is converted to. Values for the bases may be in a range from 2 to 32.
`ELT(value, string1, string2, ...)`	The `ELT` function returns the string represented by the index given as `value`. If the value given is negative, it returns `NULL`. If there are fewer elements than the given value, `NULL` is returned.
`EXPORT_SET(value, string1, string2 [, separator_string [, length_value]])`	The `EXPORT_SET` function is used to generate binary strings with custom atoms. The `on` bit is given as `string1` and the `off` bit by `string2`. The value given must be an integer; any floating-point values are rounded. If the optional `separator_string` is given, each atom is separated by the string. If a `length_value` is given, the returned string is right-padded with `string2` to the given length.
`FIELD(base_string, string1, string2, ...)`	The `FIELD` function returns the index value of the string that matches the given `base_string`. If none of the strings in the list is a match, the function returns 0.

Continued

Function	***Description***
FIND_IN_SET(*base_string*, *string1* [, *string2*, ...])	The FIND_IN_SET function returns the index value of the string that matches the base string. If none of the given strings match the function, it returns 0. If either the *base_string* or all values given in the list are NULL, the function returns NULL. The function has a similarity to the FIELD function, however: It uses bitwise arithmetic to optimize the operation time.
HEX(*value*)	The HEX function returns the hexadecimal value if *value* is given as an integer. If a string is given, the return is a 2-digit hexadecimal representation of the string.
INSTR(*string*, *substring*)	The INSTR function is used to determine the first character of a matching subset in the given string. If the substring value matches the value of the first character in the matching set is returned. If there are no matching subsets, 0 is returned.
INSERT(*string1*, *position_value*, *length_value*, *string2*)	The INSERT function is used to place one string into another, replacing the existing characters. The value of *string2* is placed upon *string1*. The position of the insertion places the first character of *string2* at the *position_value*. If *length_value* is larger than the length of *string2*, that many characters are removed from *string1*.
LEFT(*string*, *length_value*)	The LEFT function returns the leftmost number of characters given as *length_value* from the string.
LCASE(*string*)	The LCASE function returns the given string in all-lowercase letters.
LENGTH(*string*)	The LENGTH function returns the length of the given string. If *string* is given as a column name, the length of the text column or the number of digits is returned.
LOAD_FILE(*file_path*)	The LOAD_FILE function reads in the given *file_path* and returns the contents of the file. If the file cannot be read or does not exist, the function returns NULL.

Function	Description
LOCATE(*substring*, *string* [, *position_value*])	The LOCATE function attempts to match a substring in the given string. If an optional position value is given the search begins at that point. The function returns the position of the first character in the matching substring. If there are no matches found, 0 is returned.
LPAD(*string1*, *length_value*, *string2*)	The LPAD function applies *string2* as left-padding to the value given as *string1*. The *length_value* determines the length of the string returned. If the value is less than *string1*, if returns the string shortened to that length.
LTRIM(*string*)	The LTRIM function returns the given string with all of the left whitespace removed.
MAKE_SET(*value*, *string1*, *string2*, ...)	The MAKE_SET function creates a comma-delimited string based on the binary representation of *value*. All *on* bits (1s) in the binary value associate with their matching element positions in the string list.
OCT(*value*)	The OCT function converts the given integer value into its octal representation as a string.
ORD(*string*)	The ORD function returns the ASCII code for the leftmost character of the given string. If the leftmost character in the string is a multiple-byte character, the values returned are added (where all character values after the first are multiplied by 256). If the leftmost character does not take up multiple bytes, the function performs exactly like the ASCII function.
REPEAT(*string*, *value*)	The REPEAT function returns the given string repeated the number of times given as value. The function returns a NULL value if either the string or value is NULL.
REPLACE(*string1*, *string2*, *string3*)	The REPLACE function substitutes a specific subset of a string with another value. The value of *string1* is returned with all instances of *string2* being replaced by *string3*.
REVERSE(*string*)	The REVERSE function returns the given string with the order of the characters inverted.
RIGHT(*string*, *length_value*)	The RIGHT function returns the rightmost number of characters given as length_value from the string.

Continued

Function	Description
RPAD(*string1*, *length_value*, *string2*)	The RPAD function is used to apply *string2* as right-padding to the value given as *string1*. The *length_value* determines the length of the string returned. If the value is less than *string1*, the returned string is shortened to that length.
RTRIM(*string*)	The RTRIM function returns the given string with all of the right whitespace removed.
SOUNDEX(*string*)	The SOUNDEX function converts strings into their soundex notation. The conversion of any two strings that sound the same when pronounced should return the same soundex value. The value returned is an arbitrary length, although soundex format is traditionally 4 characters in length.
SPACE(*value*)	The SPACE function returns a string made up of the number of spaces designated by the given value.
STRCMP(*string1*, *string2*)	The STRCMP function is used to determine whether two given strings are larger, smaller, or equal to one another. The values returned are 1, -1, and 0 respectively.
SUBSTRING(*string*, *position_value* [, *length_value*])	The SUBSTRING function is used to remove all characters in a given string that come before the given *position_value*. Additionally an optional *length_value* can be given to designate the number of characters in the return value.
SUBSTRING_INDEX(*string*, *delimiter*, *value*)	The SUBSTRING_INDEX function is used to return a subset of a delimited list. If the given value is positive, the returned string consists of the number of segments given (starting from the left). If the value is negative, the function starts from the right, with the number of segments equaling a positive value.
TRIM([[BOTH or LEADING or TRAILING] [*remove_string*] FROM] *string*)	The TRIM function is used to remove extra characters from a given string. The characters to be removed are denoted by the *remove_string*. If an optional LEADING, TRAILING, or BOTH modifier is included, the function is applied only to the specified side. If no modifier is given, BOTH is assumed as default.
UCASE(*string*)	The UCASE function returns the given string in all-uppercase letters.

System functions

The System functions are used to gather system specific data.

Function	Description
BENCHMARK(*value*, *expression*)	The BENCHMARK function performs time testing upon a call to a database. The given value determines how many iterations of the expression to perform. In general, this function is used in the CLI because of the process time returned. The function always returns 0.
CONNECTION_ID()	The CONNECTION_ID function returns the identifier for the current thread. Every connection to the MySQL server has a different ID for its connection.
DATABASE()	The DATABASE function returns the name of the database to which the client is presently connected. If there is no current connection to a database, an empty string is returned.
DECODE(*crypt_string*, *string*)	The DECODE function deciphers a string encrypted with a key given as *crypt_string*.
ENCODE(*string*, *crypt_string*)	The ENCODE function performs the inverse operation of the DECODE function. The given string is encrypted with the key given as *crypt_string*.
ENCRYPT(*string* [, *salt_string*])	The ENCRYPT function encrypts a string using the UNIX crypt() system function. An optional, 2-character *salt_string* can also be used. Extra characters in strings with a length longer than 8 are ignored. If the crypt() function is not available on the system, NULL is returned.
FORMAT(*value*, *decimal_value*)	The FORMAT function creates a string representation of a number. The returned value has as many decimal places as the given *decimal_value*. Data returned has comma-separated sets for every 3 places in the whole portion of the number.
FOUND_ROWS()	The FOUND_ROWS function is used to return the number of rows in the preceding SELECT query.

Continued

Function	**Description**
GET_LOCK(*string, value*)	The GET_LOCK function determines whether a lock designated by the given string is in use. The value given is the number of seconds the request should wait before timing out on the request for the lock. The function returns 1 if the request for the lock was successful, 0 if it was denied or NULL if there was an error in the function. The GET_LOCK function is used in conjunction with the RELEASE_LOCK function to allow external representation of locking without actual locks being applied to tables. The GET_LOCK is also terminated if the system thread concludes.
INET_ATON(*ip_address*)	The INET_ATON function returns the numeric representation of an IP address. This value is created by adding each segment of the dotted quad, raised to the power of the index of its segment from the right (starting with 0). For example, 10.0.0.1 is calculated as (10*256^3) + (0*256^2) + (0*256^1) + (1*256^0).
INET_NTOA(*value*)	The INET_NTOA function performs the inverse of the INET_ATON function. The given numeric value is converted to an IP address and is returned.
LAST_INSERT_ID([*exp*])	The LAST_INSERT_ID function returns the key of the last insert done on a column with the AUTO INCREMENT property. This function operates only for the current connection, so an INSERT command from a different client does not affect the return value. If the last INSERT spanned multiple rows, the value for the first row inserted is returned.
MASTER_POS_WAIT(*log_path, log_position*)	The MASTER_POS_WAIT function is used during data replication to force a client to wait. The client does not resume until the position in the master log file is past the given *low_position* in its replication. If the master log has not been created, the function returns NULL. Otherwise the function returns the number of positions elapsed before the client resumed.
MD5(*string*)	The MD5 function returns a hexadecimal checksum for the given string. The return value for the function is 32 characters long.

Function	Description
PASSWORD(*string*)	The PASSWORD function creates a password string from a given cleartext string. (Unlike the ENCRYPT function, the PASSWORD function does not create passwords equal to UNIX passwords.)
RELEASE_LOCK(*string*)	The RELEASE_LOCK function designates that the lock given by *string* is no longer in use. The function returns 1 if the lock has been released, 0 if the given lock was not created by the current thread, or NULL if the lock does not exist.
USER()	The USER function returns the current user account as which the client is connected. The data is returned in the format *user@hostname*.
VERSION()	The VERSION function returns a string with the MySQL version for the current server.

Trigonometric math functions

The *trigonometric math* functions allow computations using the sides and angles of triangles.

Function	Description
ACOS(*value*)	The ACOS function represents the *arc cosine*, or the inverse of the COS function. The given value is assumed to be in radians.
ASIN(*value*)	The ASIN function represents the arc sine, or the inverse of the SIN function. The given value is assumed to be in radians.
ATAN(*value1* [, *value2*])	The ATAN function represents the *arc tangent*, or the inverse of the TAN function. If an optional value2 is given, the function is used to determine the quadrant that the values would exist in as (X,Y) in a graph. The given values are assumed to be in radians.
COS(*value*)	The COS function represents the cosine function. The given value is assumed to be in radians.
COT(*value*)	The COT function represents the cotangent function. The given value is assumed to be in radians.
SIN(*value*)	The SIN function represents the sine function. The given value is assumed to be in radians.
TAN(*value*)	The TAN function represents the tangent function. The given value is assumed to be in radians.

✦ ✦ ✦

APPENDIX D

Datatype Reference

D.1. Integer Datatypes

All Integer types can take on two additional modifiers, ZEROFILL and UNSIGNED. The ZEROFILL modifier will force column data to be stored left, padded with zeroes filling the maximum length of the column. For example an INT(6) ZEROFILL given a value of 8 will return 000008 for all queries on the column. The UNSIGNED modifier designates that no negative values for the column are allowed. If you use the ZEROFILL modifier, UNSIGNED is automatically assigned.

BIGINT

The BIGINT type is the largest of the Integer members. The range of this column covers –9223372036854775808 to +9223372036854775807 for the signed values and 0 to 18446744073709551615 for unsigned values.

Designated by BIGINT(*p*) where *p* equals the number of digits allowed, and the maximum length for the BIGINT type is 20 digits.

Due to the size of the unsigned BIGINT, it is possible to cause rounding errors in arithmetic when using values larger than 9223372036854775807. This can be avoided by using bitwise shift operators or by using external systems from MySQL for the math calculations.

INT

The INT datatype is generally considered the median of the Integer types; it also has the shortest designation. The range of the INT column covers –2147483648 to 2147483647 for the signed values and 0 to 4294967295 for unsigned values.

Designated by `INT(p)` where *p* equals the number of digits allowed, and the maximum length for the `INT` type is 10 digits.

MEDIUMINT

The `MEDIUMINT` type has a range of –8388608 to 8388607 for the signed values and 0 to 16777215 for unsigned values.

Designated by `MEDIUMINT(p)` where *p* equals the number of digits allowed, the maximum length for the `MEDIUMINT` type is 8 digits.

SMALLINT

The `SMALLINT` type has a range of –32768 to 32767 for the signed values and 0 to 65535 for unsigned values.

Designated by `SMALLINT(p)` where *p* equals the number of digits allowed, the maximum length for the `SMALLINT` type is 5 digits.

TINYINT

The `TINYINT` type has a range of –128 to 127 for the signed values and 0 to 256 for unsigned values.

Designated by `TINYINT(p)` where *p* equals the number of digits allowed, the maximum length for the `TINYINT` type is 3 digits.

D.2. Decimal Datatypes

Identical to the `Integer` datatype in the way they work, the `Decimal` datatypes can take on the `ZEROFILL` and `UNSIGNED` modifiers. A `Decimal` type with the `ZEROFILL` modifier will be left padded to the precision of the column with zeroes. The `UNSIGNED` modifier also behaves equivalently and disallows negative values on the column.

Tip: **Using the `ZEROFILL` modifier assigns the `UNSIGNED` modifier automatically.**

Each `Decimal` datatype encompasses a range of numbers it can represent. Due to a limit on how many bits can be allocated for any given column, eventually a number is too small to represent. Thus each `Decimal` type represents a range of numbers that each decimal type can represent both in the negative and positive. Additionally, each type can hold a value of zero.

FLOAT

The FLOAT datatype is the smallest of the 3 numeric datatypes used for fractional values. The ranges for the column are –3.402823466 * 10^{38} to –1.175494351 * 10^{-38} for negative values and 1.175494351 * 10^{-38} to 3.402823466 * 10^{38} for positive values.

Designated by FLOAT(*p*,*m*) where *m* is the number of digits in the mantissa or decimal portion of the number and *p* is the precision of the number, or number of places in the entire number.

DECIMAL

The DECIMAL datatype while having an identical range to the DOUBLE type is stored as a string much like the CHAR types. The ranges for the column are –1.7976931348623157 * 10^{308} to –2.2250738585072014 * 10^{-308} for negative values and 2.2250738585072014 * 10^{-308} to 1.7976931348623157 * 10^{308} for positive values. The storage of the value being a string, each digit in the number is written as a character.

Designated by DECIMAL(*p*,*m*) where *m* is the number of digits in the mantissa or decimal portion of the number and *p* is the precision of the number, or number of places in the entire number.

DOUBLE

The DOUBLE datatype is the largest fractional column type that is stored in a binary format. The ranges for the column are –1.7976931348623157 * 10^{308} to –2.2250738585072014 * 10^{-308} for negative values and 2.2250738585072014 * 10^{-308} to 1.7976931348623157 * 10^{308} for positive values.

Designated by DOUBLE(*p*,*m*) where *m* is the number of digits in the mantissa or decimal portion of the number and *p* is the precision of the number, or number of places in the entire number.

D.3 Date Datatypes

The DATE types encompass all of the time-based datatypes in MySQL. The major difference in behavior between the Date types and all other numeric types is in the zero value. All DATE types return the full date string with every digit zeroed. For example the DATE type would return 0000-00-00 and TIME would return 00:00:00.

DATE

The DATE type represents a full calendar date in the format YYYY-MM-DD. Legal values for the DATE column range between 1000-01-01 and 9999-12-31. Invalid values for the column will result in a value of 0000-00-00.

DATETIME

The DATETIME type is equivalent to the DATE column with the addition of a time constituent. The DATETIME column follows the format YYYY-MM-DD HH:MM:SS. Valid DATETIME values can range between 1000-01-01 00:00:00 to 9999-12-31 23:59:59. Invalid column values result in a value of 0000-00-00 00:00:00.

TIMESTAMP

The TIMESTAMP column is a string representation of the Unix timestamp. The Unix timestamp is derived from what is known as Epoch time. Valid TIMESTAMP values range from 1970-01-01 00:00:00 through 2038-01-19 03:14:07. An invalid value will return a zerofill to the designated size of the column.

Designated by TIMESTAMP(*p*) where *p* is the number of digits displayed and returned on queries to the column. The maximum length of the TIMESTAMP type is 14 places. If a TIMESTAMP is designated with 0 digits or greater than 14 it will default to 14. If an odd value is given for *p* it will be converted to *p*+1. NULL inserts into the first timestamp column in a table will result in the current date and time being returned.

p	***Maximum Size***
2	YY
4	YYMM
6	YYMMDD
8	YYYYMMDD
10	YYMMDDHHMM
12	YYMMDDHHMMSS
14	YYYYMMDDHHMMSS

TIME

The TIME type is a generic representation of time values in hours, minutes, and seconds. The column besides representing time in the standard from of a 24-hour clock also can represent time in both the past and future. The valid range for the TIME type is –838:59:59 to 838:59:59.

The TIME type can additionally take a day modifier upon inserts. The valid formats for inserts are D HH:MM:SS, HH:MM:SS, MM:SS, and SS. Where the day or time constituent can be preceeded by – to represent negative time. Return values will have left zero padding.

YEAR

The YEAR type represents the calendar year in either a 2-digit or 4-digit format.

In the 4-digit format, YEAR can range from 1901 to 2155 or 0000. In the 2-digit format, the YEAR range is 1970 through 2069, represented as 70 to 69. Invalid values inserted into the YEAR column will return 0000. With the 2-digit format, a single 0 is considered an invalid value; 00 must be used to represent the year 2000.

D.4. STRING Datatypes

The STRING datatypes encompass all column types used for textual data. In addition to the NULL value, all STRING types additionally have the empty string value (''). Inserts into STRING types that exceed the maximum allotted length will be truncated to fit the space allocated.

BLOB

TINYBLOB, BLOB, MEDIUMBLOB, LONGBLOB

BLOB is the STRING datatype used for binary data. Any queries on a BLOB type result in a case-sensitive return. For example a BLOB type with the value 'string' will not be matched by queries for 'STRING'. This is opposite to the behavior of the TEXT type.

Note: Data exceeding the maximum size of the column is forcibly truncated after insertion.

Column Type	*Maximum Size*
TINYBLOB	255
BLOB	65535
MEDIUMBLOB	16777215
LONGBLOB	4294967295

CHAR

The CHAR datatype is used for string storage.

Designated by CHAR(*p*) where *p* designates the field length, the maximum length for the CHAR type is 255. When stored the data in the column will pad to the full length (*p*) of the field with whitespace. Upon retrieval from the database, the appended whitespace is removed.

TEXT

```
TINYTEXT, TEXT, MEDIUMTEXT, LONGTEXT
```

TEXT is the STRING datatype used for character data. It works much like the BLOB datatype; queries upon the TEXT type will return case insensitive values. For example a TEXT type with the value 'string' will be matched by queries for 'STRING'. This is opposite to the behavior of the BLOB type.

Column Type	*Maximum Size*
TINYTEXT	255
TEXT	65535
MEDIUMTEXT	16777215
LONGTEXT	4294967295

VARCHAR

The VARCHAR datatype works like the CHAR type except for its data-storage method. The VARCHAR type removes all trailing whitespace from inserted data.

Designated by VARCHAR(*p*) where *p* designates the field length, the maximum length of the VARCHAR type is 255 characters.

In considering space requirements for some systems, the VARCHAR type should be used as opposed to the CHAR type. The addition of whitespace trailing all CHAR entities can dramatically increase the space used in a table containing even very few rows of data.

D.5. Grouping Datatypes

The `Grouping` datatypes are the only types that all valid values can be defined for a column. Declaring a `Grouping` type as `NULL` will force the first member in the group to be `NULL`.

ENUM

The `ENUM` type allows for the casting of particular values as valid within the column. When a value which not yet cast into the type is inserted into the column, an empty value ("") is assigned.

Designated by `ENUM('string1','string2','string3'...)` where the numbered strings are the casted members. The maximum number of constituents for the `ENUM` datatype is 65535.

SET

The `SET` type works much like the `ENUM` type except it can store multiple values in the column.

Designated by `SET('string1','string2','string3'...)` where the numbered strings are the casted members. The maximum number of constituents for the `SET` datatype is 64.

The `SET` type allows insertion of the strings given during the creation of the table; integer values can be used to assign members by their binary values. For example, a `SET` consisting of values `('mother','father','sister','brother','dog','cat')`, each member is assigned a numeric value of 2^n where *n* is the member's order alphabetically. Therefore `'brother'` = 1, `'cat'` = 2, `'dog'` = 4, `'father'` = 8, `'mother'` = 16 and `'sister'` = 32. By binary math the members that would be assigned can be determined. For example 7 = 1 + 2 + 4 returning `('brother', 'cat', 'dog')` additionally 12 = 8 + 4 would return `('dog', 'father')`.

✦ ✦ ✦

APPENDIX E

Glossary

ACID Acronym for Atomic, Consistent, Isolated, Durable, refers to an ideal environment within which database transactions can take place. For example, if a given database transaction fails, it does not affect other transactions currently running.

ANSI92 SQL Standard specifying how to implement SQL in your RDBMS according to a set of conventions developed by the American National Standards Institute (ANSI).

API Acronym for *Application Programming Interface*. The API defines which functions of a software program are available for modification via programming techniques.

BerkeleyDB A transaction-safe table type, supported by MySQL. BDB tables can be compiled in or installed with the Max versions of MySQL.

CGI Short for Common Gateway Interface. CGI provides a programming interface to enable programs operating on the backend to work with a Web server. CGI programs or CGI scripts are the names given to programs that produce or work with World Wide Web data.

character set In a particular language, the entire range of characters available for use with MySQL. The Default Character Set determines sorting order for columns.

CLI Acronym for *command-line interface*. The MySQL CLI is the program through which users frequently interact with MySQL databases. The MySQL CLI can be used interactively or in a non-interactive mode.

command recall In the MySQL CLI's interactive mode, use the up-arrow on the keyboard to display the most recently entered MySQL command(s) on-screen.

connection-level authentication The first step in the authentication process when a user or program attempts to connect to a MySQL database server. Authentication at the level of the connection checks the username, password, and host that the information is coming from.

constraints Restrictions placed on columns to determine what is and is not acceptable for that column. An example would be a UNIQUE constraint that requires that every value in the column be different from every other.

cookies Information that the server sets inside an HTTP header for later use, includes in the response it sends to the client via browser, and stores on the client machine. Cookies are frequently used to track and store customer information (or values referring to the information that a query requests from a database).

`datadir` (also `DATADIR)` The path or location within the file system where the MySQL databases are stored.

DBD Short for *DataBase Driver*, the software integrated with the Perl DBI that actually interacts with a database.

DBI Short for *DataBase Interface*, the software written in (and for) Perl to enable Perl to interact with a particular RDBMS.

DDL Short for *Data Definition Language*. DDL includes SQL statements to create, delete or alter databases, tables, columns, indices, and the like.

DML Short for Data Markup Language. DML includes SQL statements to modify actual data within databases.

foreign key A database constraint that refers to a column in another table for reference.

FTP Short for *File Transfer Protocol*. Protocol to transfer files over TCP.

`Gemini` A transaction-safe table type included with NuSphere Enhanced MySQL.

GPL Short for the *General Public License* that MySQL is released under. This is the most popular license for Open Source software.

GUI Short for *Graphical User Interface*—the environment, tools, pictures, buttons, menus, and the like that produce a non-text-based method for interacting with a computer. Examples include Microsoft Windows and XWindows.

HEAP A volatile-memory-based table in MySQL that is very useful for creation of temporary tables.

`InnoDB` A transaction-safe table type supported by MySQL. `InnoDB` tables can be compiled into MySQL or installed with the Max version.

ISAM Acronym for *Indexed Sequential Access Method*. ISAM is the original table type supported by MySQL. ISAM tables are not transaction-safe and are deprecated.

JDBC Short for Java Database Connectivity. JDBC is the API for connecting Java to a relational database. MySQL has a JDBC API to enable Java programs and applets to work with MySQL.

JDK (also SDK) Short for the *Java Software Development Kit*, is the software released by Sun as a development tool that uses the Java programming language.

LGPL Short for *Lesser General Public License*. Some MySQL software is released under the LGPL as is some Open Source software. It is the sister to the main GPL or General Public License and provides for the use of a software library to be used in proprietary software. More information is available at `http://www.gnu.org/`.

`libdir` (also `LIBDIR`) The directory or location on the file system where MySQL libraries are installed. Some software needs access to the MySQL libraries in order to function.

localhost The current host or machine that you are operating on. By default, MySQL CLI connections (and many other programs with MySQL) attempt to connect to the MySQL server on localhost, or the local machine.

lock A hold, placed at either the table or row level, that lasts until a process such as an update is complete. No other similar operation can take place when a lock is in place.

master replicator In a replication set, the host or other MySQL server that receives updates and other data changes and places them in a log for the slave replicators to use.

`Merge` A table type in MySQL that results from combining tables.

`my.cnf` Filename of the file that contains the configuration settings and variables settings for MySQL programs including the main server. The my.cnf file usually refers to the Linux or Unix variant of the configuration file.

`my.ini` Filename of the file (in this case, a Windows configuration file) that contains the settings that determine configuration and variables for MySQL programs, including the main server.

`MyISAM` The default table type in MySQL. It is not transaction-safe.

`mysqladmin` The main administration program for MySQL where the administrator can set passwords, look at server status, and shut down the server.

`mysqld` The name of the program that is the MySQL server.

MySQLGUI A graphical user interface for MySQL, usable for creating SQL statements and performing server administration.

NSS Short for *Name Service Switch*, configured through the `/etc/nsswitch.conf` configuration file. NSS defines the order for a given account's information queries. There is software called NSS-MySQL to enable MySQL integration with NSS.

`NULL` A logical value that is, literally, nothing (which differs from zero because zero can often be a mathematical placeholder). `NULL` can be thought of as an object that is nothing, holds nothing, and can be nothing. `NULL` is neither zero nor an empty string. You may commonly hear that a column or value is `NULL`. If a value is `NULL`, there is nothing in it.

ODBC Short for *Open Database Connectivity*—ODBC defines the API by which applications work with data. MySQL AB has a version of ODBC called MyODBC.

Open Source Software-development approach that keeps an application's source code *open* (available) for contributions from the programming community. Although not proprietary in the same sense (or to the same degree) as closed-source commercial software, Open Source software is not necessarily available free of charge, and is almost always covered by a license (such as the GNU GPL or LGPL). MySQL, for example, is covered by the GPL and/or LGPL, depending on the portion of the software you are using.

pager In programming terms, a program that splits output into virtual pages on the screen or terminal. Without the pager capabilities of the `more` and `less` commands in MySQL, output would scroll off the screen too quickly to read.

PAM Short for *Pluggable Authentication Modules*, standardized units of code that define methods for authentication and access to resources.

Perl Originally an acronym for *Practical Extraction and Reporting Language*, Perl is now the name of a powerful and versatile programming language used for system administration, as well as for creating CGIs for Web applications.

PHP Acronym meaning *Hypertext Preprocessor*, a powerful and somewhat intuitive programming language frequently used to create Web applications.

`phpinfo` A PHP function used to determine settings for the PHP environment, often given as `phpinfo()`.

PHPMyAdmin A program developed in PHP that handles administration and management of a MySQL server and databases.

process-level authentication The second tier of authentication that takes place for every MySQL operation, the first being *connection-level authentication*. During process-level authentication, the MySQL `grants` database is examined to determine whether the given user/password/host combination has the permissions or privileges it needs to perform the requested operation.

RDBMS Short for *Relational Database Management System*, software that stores data within tables, columns, and rows and supports relationships between tables. Examples include MySQL, Oracle, Informix, and Microsoft SQL Server.

replication The process that automatically copies the changes to data — exactly, and almost instantly — from one MySQL server to another.

RPM Acronym for *Red Hat Package Manager*, the format for many software packages in the Red Hat Linux operating system. Various Linux versions, both commercial and freeware, can support RPMs.

`root` In UNIX-based operating systems (including Linux), the "superuser" account that has all possible privileges; `root` should be used primarily for administration activities.

`scp` Short for *Secure Copy*, a program that uses encryption to transfer files between hosts.

slave replicator A host or other MySQL server in a replication set that receives updates from the master server.

SQL Short for *Structured Query Language*, a language created for working with relational databases (such as MySQL).

SQL-92 Another name for ANSI92 SQL, the industry standard by which an RDBMS implements SQL.

SSL Short for *Secure-Sockets Layer*. As of MySQL 4.0, many functions in MySQL can use this encrypted form of communication.

subselect A `SELECT` statement within a `SELECT` statement, normally used to obtain more specific information from the `SELECT` statement.

symbolic link An alias that points to a file on the file system. Symbolic links (also called *symlinks*) can point to system files (such as the MySQL socket file).

TCO Acronym for *Total Cost of Ownership*, the sum of all money spent on a system — including the cost of hardware, software, operating system, installation, configuration, maintenance, and the like.

transaction-safe Said of a table in MySQL that complies with and supports the ACID concept of database environment. For example, if a given SQL statement fails, it can be rolled back so as not to affect the consistency of other operations within the database.

WinMySQLAdmin A GUI-based program for administering and managing a MySQL server running on a Windows-based operating system. WinMySQLAdmin and can perform the same operations and tasks as the text-based `mysqladmin` program.

✦ ✦ ✦

APPENDIX F

About the CD-ROM

The CD at the back of the book contains programs discussed in the book as well as some other goodies.

System Requirements

You need this hardware and software to use the CD:

- A Pentium or greater PC or a Mac
- One of: Linux, Microsoft Windows 9x, Windows Me, Windows 2000, Windows XP, Mac OS X
- At least 16 MB of RAM installed, depending on OS
- A CD-ROM drive
- A VGA monitor
- An Internet connection (to use the links file)

What's on the CD

This section provides a summary of the software on the *MySQL Bible* CD-ROM.

- **Scripts and Programs** There are scripts and programs within chapters of the book. The scripts are written in Perl or they are plain shell scripts.
- **SQL** There are two plain text files that contain SQL used in some chapters.
- **Links page** The links in a file called Links.htm jump to useful internet sites.

- **Perl** The scripting language Perl is on the CD and in most Linux distributions.
- **Perl DBI** The Perl interface for databases connects Perl programs through Msql-Mysql-modules, included on the CD.
- **Acrobat Reader** The Adobe Acrobat Reader program opens the PDF version of the book from the CD.
- **Apache** The web server Apache is included on the CD so that you can use it with the other software such as Perl and PHP to build MySQL-enabled web applications.
- **PHP** PHP is popular scripting software frequently used to build web-based applications.
- **phpMyAdmin** phpMyAdmin controls MySQL databases through a web-based interface.
- **msql-mysql-modules** msql-mysql-modules enables Perl support with MySQL.
- **PDF copy of the book** A copy of the book in electronic PDF format is included on the CD.

If You Have Problems

If you have problems with programs on the CD, try these troubleshooting steps.

- Disable any antivirus software
- Close running programs
- Try loading/running the program through Windows Explorer

If you still have trouble, you can call at (800) 762-2974, or (317) 596-5430 outside the US or email at techsudum@wiley.com.

✦ ✦ ✦

Index

SYMBOLS AND NUMERICS

A

C

E

F

G

J

M

Continued

N

O

Continued

S

T

U

W

X

Y

Z

[More information available at `http://www.gnu.org/copyleft/gpl.html`]

GNU General Public License

Version 2, June 1991

Preamble

The licenses for most software are designed to take away your freedom to share and change it. By contrast, the GNU General Public License is intended to guarantee your freedom to share and change free software—to make sure the software is free for all its users. This General Public License applies to most of the Free Software Foundation's software and to any other program whose authors commit to using it. (Some other Free Software Foundation software is covered by the GNU Library General Public License instead.) You can apply it to your programs, too.

When we speak of free software, we are referring to freedom, not price. Our General Public Licenses are designed to make sure that you have the freedom to distribute copies of free software (and charge for this service if you wish), that you receive source code or can get it if you want it, that you can change the software or use pieces of it in new free programs; and that you know you can do these things.

To protect your rights, we need to make restrictions that forbid anyone to deny you these rights or to ask you to surrender the rights. These restrictions translate to certain responsibilities for you if you distribute copies of the software, or if you modify it.

For example, if you distribute copies of such a program, whether gratis or for a fee, you must give the recipients all the rights that you have. You must make sure that they, too, receive or can get the source code. And you must show them these terms so they know their rights.

We protect your rights with two steps: (1) copyright the software, and (2) offer you this license which gives you legal permission to copy, distribute and/or modify the software.

Also, for each author's protection and ours, we want to make certain that everyone understands that there is no warranty for this free software. If the software is modified by someone else and passed on, we want its recipients to know that what they have is not the original, so that any problems introduced by others will not reflect on the original authors' reputations.

Finally, any free program is threatened constantly by software patents. We wish to avoid the danger that redistributors of a free program will individually obtain patent licenses, in effect making the program proprietary. To prevent this, we have made it clear that any patent must be licensed for everyone's free use or not licensed at all.

The precise terms and conditions for copying, distribution and modification follow.

TERMS AND CONDITIONS FOR COPYING, DISTRIBUTION AND MODIFICATION

0. This License applies to any program or other work which contains a notice placed by the copyright holder saying it may be distributed under the terms of this General Public License. The "Program", below, refers to any such program or work, and a "work based on the Program" means either the Program or any derivative work under copyright law: that is to say, a work containing the Program or a portion of it, either verbatim or with modifications and/or translated into another language. (Hereinafter, translation is included without limitation in the term "modification".) Each licensee is addressed as "you".

Activities other than copying, distribution and modification are not covered by this License; they are outside its scope. The act of running the Program is not restricted, and the output from the Program is covered only if its contents constitute a work based on the Program (independent of having been made by running the Program). Whether that is true depends on what the Program does.

1. You may copy and distribute verbatim copies of the Program's source code as you receive it, in any medium, provided that you conspicuously and appropriately publish on each copy an appropriate copyright notice and disclaimer of warranty; keep intact all the notices that refer to this License and to the absence of any warranty; and give any other recipients of the Program a copy of this License along with the Program.

You may charge a fee for the physical act of transferring a copy, and you may at your option offer warranty protection in exchange for a fee.

2. You may modify your copy or copies of the Program or any portion of it, thus forming a work based on the Program, and copy and distribute such modifications or work under the terms of Section 1 above, provided that you also meet all of these conditions:

a) You must cause the modified files to carry prominent notices stating that you changed the files and the date of any change.

b) You must cause any work that you distribute or publish, that in whole or in part contains or is derived from the Program or any part thereof, to be licensed as a whole at no charge to all third parties under the terms of this License.

c) If the modified program normally reads commands interactively when run, you must cause it, when started running for such interactive use in the most ordinary way, to print or display an announcement including an appropriate copyright notice and a notice that there is no warranty (or else, saying that you provide a warranty) and that users may redistribute the program under these conditions, and telling the user how to view a copy of this License. (Exception: if the Program itself is interactive but does not normally print such an announcement, your work based on the Program is not required to print an announcement.)

These requirements apply to the modified work as a whole. If identifiable sections of that work are not derived from the Program, and can be reasonably considered independent and separate works in themselves, then this License, and its terms, do not apply to those sections when you distribute them as separate works. But when you distribute the same sections as part of a whole which is a work based on the Program, the distribution of the whole must be on the terms of this License, whose permissions for other licensees extend to the entire whole, and thus to each and every part regardless of who wrote it.

Thus, it is not the intent of this section to claim rights or contest your rights to work written entirely by you; rather, the intent is to exercise the right to control the distribution of derivative or collective works based on the Program. In addition, mere aggregation of another work not based on the Program with the Program (or with a work based on the Program) on a volume of a storage or distribution medium does not bring the other work under the scope of this License.

3. You may copy and distribute the Program (or a work based on it, under Section 2) in object code or executable form under the terms of Sections 1 and 2 above provided that you also do one of the following:

a) Accompany it with the complete corresponding machine-readable source code, which must be distributed under the terms of Sections 1 and 2 above on a medium customarily used for software interchange; or,

b) Accompany it with a written offer, valid for at least three years, to give any third party, for a charge no more than your cost of physically performing source distribution, a complete machine-readable copy of the corresponding source code, to be distributed under the terms of Sections 1 and 2 above on a medium customarily used for software interchange; or,

c) Accompany it with the information you received as to the offer to distribute corresponding source code. (This alternative is allowed only for noncommercial distribution and only if you received the program in object code or executable form with such an offer, in accord with Subsection b above.)

The source code for a work means the preferred form of the work for making modifications to it. For an executable work, complete source code means all the source code for all modules it contains, plus any associated interface definition files, plus the scripts used to control compilation and installation of the executable. However, as a special exception, the source code distributed need not include anything that is normally distributed (in either source or binary form) with the major components (compiler, kernel, and so on) of the operating system on which the executable runs, unless that component itself accompanies the executable.

If distribution of executable or object code is made by offering access to copy from a designated place, then offering equivalent access to copy the source code from the same place counts as distribution of the source code, even though third parties are not compelled to copy the source along with the object code.

4. You may not copy, modify, sublicense, or distribute the Program except as expressly provided under this License. Any attempt otherwise to copy, modify, sublicense or distribute the Program is void, and will automatically terminate your rights under this License. However, parties who have received copies, or rights, from you under this License will not have their licenses terminated so long as such parties remain in full compliance.

5. You are not required to accept this License, since you have not signed it. However, nothing else grants you permission to modify or distribute the Program or its derivative works. These actions are prohibited by law if you do not accept this License. Therefore, by modifying or distributing the Program (or any work based on the Program), you indicate your acceptance of this License to do so, and all its terms and conditions for copying, distributing or modifying the Program or works based on it.

6. Each time you redistribute the Program (or any work based on the Program), the recipient automatically receives a license from the original licensor to copy, distribute or modify the Program subject to these terms and conditions. You may not impose any further restrictions on the recipients' exercise of the rights granted herein. You are not responsible for enforcing compliance by third parties to this License.

7. If, as a consequence of a court judgment or allegation of patent infringement or for any other reason (not limited to patent issues), conditions are imposed on you (whether by court order, agreement or otherwise) that contradict the conditions of this License, they do not excuse you from the conditions of this License. If you cannot distribute so as to satisfy simultaneously your obligations under this License and any other pertinent obligations, then as a consequence you may not distribute the Program at all. For example, if a patent license would not permit royalty-free redistribution of the Program by all those who receive copies directly or indirectly through you, then the only way you could satisfy both it and this License would be to refrain entirely from distribution of the Program.

   If any portion of this section is held invalid or unenforceable under any particular circumstance, the balance of the section is intended to apply and the section as a whole is intended to apply in other circumstances.

   It is not the purpose of this section to induce you to infringe any patents or other property right claims or to contest validity of any such claims; this section has the sole purpose of protecting the integrity of the free software distribution system, which is implemented by public license practices. Many people have made generous contributions to the wide range of software distributed through that system in reliance on consistent application of that system; it is up to the author/donor to decide if he or she is willing to distribute software through any other system and a licensee cannot impose that choice.

   This section is intended to make thoroughly clear what is believed to be a consequence of the rest of this License.

8. If the distribution and/or use of the Program is restricted in certain countries either by patents or by copyrighted interfaces, the original copyright holder who places the Program under this License may add an explicit geographical distribution limitation excluding those countries, so that distribution is permitted only in or among countries not thus excluded. In such case, this License incorporates the limitation as if written in the body of this License.

9. The Free Software Foundation may publish revised and/or new versions of the General Public License from time to time. Such new versions will be similar in spirit to the present version, but may differ in detail to address new problems or concerns.

   Each version is given a distinguishing version number. If the Program specifies a version number of this License which applies to it and "any later version", you have the option of following the terms and conditions either of that version or of any later version published by the Free Software Foundation. If the Program does not specify a version number of this License, you may choose any version ever published by the Free Software Foundation.

10. If you wish to incorporate parts of the Program into other free programs whose distribution conditions are different, write to the author to ask for permission. For software which is copyrighted by the Free Software Foundation, write to the Free Software Foundation; we sometimes make exceptions for this. Our decision will be guided by the two goals of preserving the free status of all derivatives of our free software and of promoting the sharing and reuse of software generally.

No Warranty

11. BECAUSE THE PROGRAM IS LICENSED FREE OF CHARGE, THERE IS NO WARRANTY FOR THE PROGRAM, TO THE EXTENT PERMITTED BY APPLICABLE LAW. EXCEPT WHEN OTHERWISE STATED IN WRITING THE COPYRIGHT HOLDERS AND/OR OTHER PARTIES PROVIDE THE PROGRAM "AS IS" WITHOUT WARRANTY OF ANY KIND, EITHER EXPRESSED OR IMPLIED, INCLUDING, BUT NOT LIMITED TO, THE IMPLIED WARRANTIES OF MERCHANTABILITY AND FITNESS FOR A PARTICULAR PURPOSE. THE ENTIRE RISK AS TO THE QUALITY AND PERFORMANCE OF THE PROGRAM IS WITH YOU. SHOULD THE PROGRAM PROVE DEFECTIVE, YOU ASSUME THE COST OF ALL NECESSARY SERVICING, REPAIR OR CORRECTION.
12. IN NO EVENT UNLESS REQUIRED BY APPLICABLE LAW OR AGREED TO IN WRITING WILL ANY COPYRIGHT HOLDER, OR ANY OTHER PARTY WHO MAY MODIFY AND/OR REDISTRIBUTE THE PROGRAM AS PERMITTED ABOVE, BE LIABLE TO YOU FOR DAMAGES, INCLUDING ANY GENERAL, SPECIAL, INCIDENTAL OR CONSEQUENTIAL DAMAGES ARISING OUT OF THE USE OR INABILITY TO USE THE PROGRAM (INCLUDING BUT NOT LIMITED TO LOSS OF DATA OR DATA BEING RENDERED INACCURATE OR LOSSES SUSTAINED BY YOU OR THIRD PARTIES OR A FAILURE OF THE PROGRAM TO OPERATE WITH ANY OTHER PROGRAMS), EVEN IF SUCH HOLDER OR OTHER PARTY HAS BEEN ADVISED OF THE POSSIBILITY OF SUCH DAMAGES.

END OF TERMS AND CONDITIONS